Numerical Lir   T0179884

This self-contained introduction to Numerical Linear Algebra provides a
comprehensive, yet concise, overview of the subject. It includes standard material
such as direct methods for solving linear systems and least-squares problems, error,
stability and conditioning, basic iterative methods and the calculation of eigenvalues.
Later chapters cover more advanced material, such as Krylov subspace methods,
multigrid methods, domain decomposition methods, multipole expansions,
hierarchical matrices and compressed sensing.

   The book provides rigorous mathematical proofs throughout, and gives algorithms
in general-purpose language-independent form. Requiring only a solid knowledge in
linear algebra and basic analysis, this book will be useful for applied mathematicians,
engineers, computer scientists and all those interested in efficiently solving linear
problems.

HOLGER WENDLAND holds the Chair of Applied and Numerical Analysis at the
University of Bayreuth. He works in the area of Numerical Analysis and is the author
of two other books, *Scattered Data Approximation* (Cambridge, 2005) and
Numerische Mathematik (Springer 2004, with Robert Schaback).

Cambridge Texts in Applied Mathematics

All titles listed below can be obtained from good booksellers or from Cambridge University Press. For a complete series listing, visit www.cambridge.org/mathematics.

Numerical Linear Algebra

An Introduction

HOLGER WENDLAND

Universität Bayreuth, Germany

CAMBRIDGE
UNIVERSITY PRESS

CAMBRIDGE
UNIVERSITY PRESS

University Printing House, Cambridge CB2 8BS, United Kingdom

One Liberty Plaza, 20th Floor, New York, NY 10006, USA

477 Williamstown Road, Port Melbourne, VIC 3207, Australia

4843/24, 2nd Floor, Ansari Road, Daryaganj, Delhi – 110002, India

79 Anson Road, #06-04/06, Singapore 079906

Cambridge University Press is part of the University of Cambridge.

It furthers the University's mission by disseminating knowledge in the pursuit of
education, learning, and research at the highest international levels of excellence.

www.cambridge.org
Information on this title: www.cambridge.org/9781107147133
DOI: 10.1017/9781316544938

© Holger Wendland 2018

First published 2018

Printed in the United Kingdom by Clays, St Ives plc

A catalogue record for this publication is available from the British Library.

ISBN 978-1-107-14713-3 Hardback
ISBN 978-1-316-60117-4 Paperback

Contents

Preface

Numerical Linear Algebra (NLA) is a subarea of Applied Mathematics. It is mainly concerned with the development, implementation and analysis of numerical algorithms for solving linear problems. In general, such linear problems arise when discretising a continuous problem by restricting it to a finite-dimensional subspace of the original solution space. Hence, the development and analysis of numerical algorithms is almost always problem-dependent. The more is known about the underlying problem, the better a suitable algorithm can be developed.

Nonetheless, many of the so-derived methods are more general in the sense that they can be applied to larger classes of problems than initially intended. One of the challenges in Mathematics is deciding how to describe the necessary assumptions, under which a certain method works, in the most general way. In the context of NLA, this means finding for each method the most general description of matrices to which the method can be applied. It also means extracting the most general methods from the vast number of available algorithms. Particularly for users with new problems this is crucial, as it allows them to apply and test well-established algorithms first, before starting to develop new methods or to extend existing ones.

In this book, I have attempted to use this *matrix-driven* approach rather than the *problem-driven* one. Naturally, the selection of the material is biased by my own point of view. Also, a book on NLA without any examples would be rather dire, so there are typical examples and applications included to illustrate the methods, but I have tried to restrict myself to simple examples, which do not require much previous knowledge on specific problems and discretisation techniques.

During the past years, I have given courses on Numerical Linear Algebra at advanced BSc and early MSc level at the University of Sussex (UK), the University of Oxford (UK) and the University of Bayreuth (Germany). I have also given courses on Numerical Analysis which covered parts of the NLA material in Oxford, Göttingen (Germany) and Bayreuth.

This book on Numerical Linear Algebra is based on these courses and the material of these courses. It covers the standard material, as well as more recent and more specific techniques, which are usually not found in standard textbooks on NLA. Examples include the multigrid method, the domain decomposition method, multipole expansions, hierarchical matrices and applications to compressed or compressive sensing. The material on each of these topics fills entire books so that I can obviously present only a selection. However, this selection should allow the readers to grasp the underlying ideas of each topic and enable them to understand current research in these areas.

Each chapter of this book contains a small number of theoretical exercises. However, to really understand NLA one has to implement the algorithms by oneself and test them on some of the matrices from the examples. Hence, the most important exercises intrinsic to each chapter are to implement and test the proposed algorithms.

All algorithms are stated in a clean pseudo-code; no programming language is preferred. This, I hope, allows readers to use the programming language of their choice and hence yields the greatest flexibility.

Finally, NLA is obviously closely related to Linear Algebra. However, this is not a book on Linear Algebra, and I expect readers to have a solid knowledge of Linear Algebra. Though I will review some of the material, particularly to introduce the notation, terms like linear space, linear mapping, determinant etc. should be well-known.

PART ONE

PRELIMINARIES

1

Introduction

In this book, we are concerned with the basic problem of solving a linear system

$$A\mathbf{x} = \mathbf{b},$$

where $A \in \mathbb{R}^{n \times n}$ is a given invertible matrix, $\mathbf{b} \in \mathbb{R}^n$ is a given vector and $\mathbf{x} \in \mathbb{R}^n$ is the solution we seek. The solution is, of course, given by

$$\mathbf{x} = A^{-1}\mathbf{b},$$

but does this really help if we are interested in actually computing the solution vector $\mathbf{x} \in \mathbb{R}^n$? What are the problems we are facing? First of all, such linear systems have a certain background. They are the results of other mathematical steps. Usually, they are at the end of a long processing chain which starts with setting up a partial differential equation to model a real-world problem, continues with discretising this differential equation using an appropriate approximation space and method, and results in such a linear system. This is important because it often tells us something about the structure of the matrix. The matrix might be symmetric or *sparse*. It is also important since it tells us something about the size n of the matrix. With simulations becoming more and more complex, this number nowadays becomes easily larger than a million, even values of several hundreds of millions are not unusual. Hence, the first obstacle that we encounter is the size of the matrix. Obviously, for larger dimensions n it is not possible to solve a linear system by hand. This means we need an algorithmic description of the solution process and a computer to run our program.

Unfortunately, using a computer leads to our second obstacle. We cannot represent real numbers accurately on a computer because of the limited number system used by a computer. Even worse, each calculation that we do might lead to a number which is not representable in the computer's number system.

Hence, we have to address questions like: Is a matrix that is invertible in the real numbers also invertible in the number system used by a computer? What are the errors that we make when representing the matrix in the computer and when using our algorithm to compute the solution. Further questions that easily come up are as follows.

1. How expensive is the algorithm? How much time (and space) does it require to solve the problem? What is the best way of measuring the cost of an algorithm?
2. How stable is the algorithm? If we slightly change the input, i.e. the matrix A and/or the right-hand side $\mathbf{b}$, how does this affect the solution?
3. Can we exploit the structure of the matrix A, if it has a special structure?
4. What happens if we do not have a square system, i.e. a matrix $A \in \mathbb{R}^{m \times n}$ and a vector $\mathbf{b} \in \mathbb{R}^m$. If $m > n$ then we have an *over-determined* system and usually cannot find a (unique) solution but might still be interested in something which comes close to a solution. If $m < n$ we have an *under-determined* system and we need to choose from several possible solutions.

Besides solving a linear system, we will also be interested in a related topic, the computation of *eigenvalues* and *eigenvectors* of a matrix. This means we are interested in finding numbers $\lambda \in \mathbb{C}$ and vectors $\mathbf{x} \in \mathbb{C}^n \setminus \{\mathbf{0}\}$ such that

$$A\mathbf{x} = \lambda\mathbf{x}.$$

Finding such eigenvectors and eigenvalues is again motivated by applications. For example, in structural mechanics a vibrating system is represented by finite elements and the eigenvectors of the corresponding discretisation matrix reflect the shape modes and the roots of the eigenvalues reflect the frequencies with which the system is vibrating. But eigenvalues will also be helpful in better understanding some of the questions above. For example, they have a crucial influence on the stability of an algorithm.

In this book, we are mainly interested in systems of real numbers, simply because they arise naturally in most applications. However, as the problem of finding eigenvalues indicates, it is sometimes necessary to consider complex valued systems, as well. Fortunately, most of our algorithms and findings will carry over from the real to the complex case in a straightforward way.

We will look at *direct* and *iterative* methods to solve linear systems. Direct methods compute the solution in a finite number of steps, iterative methods construct a sequence of approximations to the solution.

We will look at how efficient and stable these methods are. The former means that we are interested in how much time and computer memory they require. Particular emphasis will be placed on the number of *floating point operations* required with respect to the dimension of the linear system. The latter means for example investigating whether these methods converge at all, under what conditions they converge and how they respond to small changes in the input data.

1.1 Examples Leading to Linear Systems

As mentioned above, linear systems arise naturally during the discretisation process of mathematical models of real-world problems. Here, we want to collect three examples leading to linear systems. These examples are our model problems, which we will refer to frequently in the rest of this book. They comprise the problem of interpolating an unknown function only known at discrete data sites, the solution of a one-dimensional boundary value problem with finite differences and the solution of a (one-dimensional) integral equation with a Galerkin method. We have chosen these three examples because they are simple and easily explained, yet they are significant enough and each of them represents a specific class of problems. In particular, the second problem leads to a linear system with a matrix A which has a very simple structure. This matrix will serve us as a role model for testing and investigating most of our methods since it is simple to analyse yet complicated enough to demonstrate the advantages and drawbacks of the method under consideration.

1.1.1 Interpolation

Suppose we are given data sites $X = \{\mathbf{x}_1, \ldots, \mathbf{x}_n\} \subseteq \mathbb{R}^d$ and observations $f_1, \ldots, f_n \in \mathbb{R}$. Suppose further that the observations follow an unknown generation process, i.e. there is a function f such that $f(\mathbf{x}_i) = f_i$, $1 \leq i \leq n$.

One possibility to approximately reconstruct the unknown function f is to choose *basis functions* $\phi_1, \ldots, \phi_n \in C(\mathbb{R}^d)$ and to approximate f by a function s of the form

$$s(\mathbf{x}) = \sum_{j=1}^{n} \alpha_j \phi_j(\mathbf{x}), \qquad \mathbf{x} \in \mathbb{R}^d,$$

where the coefficients are determined by the interpolation conditions

$$f_i = s(\mathbf{x}_i) = \sum_{j=1}^{n} \alpha_j \phi_j(\mathbf{x}_i), \qquad 1 \leq i \leq n.$$

This leads to a linear system, which can be written in matrix form as

$$
\begin{pmatrix}
\phi_1(\mathbf{x}_1) & \phi_2(\mathbf{x}_1) & \cdots & \phi_n(\mathbf{x}_1) \\
\phi_1(\mathbf{x}_2) & \phi_2(\mathbf{x}_2) & \cdots & \phi_n(\mathbf{x}_2) \\
\vdots & \vdots & \cdots & \vdots \\
\phi_1(\mathbf{x}_n) & \phi_2(\mathbf{x}_n) & \cdots & \phi_n(\mathbf{x}_n)
\end{pmatrix}
\begin{pmatrix}
\alpha_1 \\ \alpha_2 \\ \vdots \\ \alpha_n
\end{pmatrix}
=
\begin{pmatrix}
f_1 \\ f_2 \\ \vdots \\ f_n
\end{pmatrix}. \tag{1.1}
$$

From standard Numerical Analysis courses we know this topic usually in the setting that the dimension is $d = 1$, that the points are ordered $a \leq x_1 < x_2 < \cdots < x_n \leq b$ and that the basis is given as a basis for the space of polynomials of degree at most $n-1$. This basis could be the basis of monomials $\phi_i(x) = x^{i-1}$, $1 \leq i \leq n$, in which case the matrix in (1.1) becomes the transpose of a so-called *Vandermonde matrix*, i.e. a matrix of the form

$$
\begin{pmatrix}
1 & x_1 & x_1^2 & \cdots & x_1^{n-1} \\
1 & x_2 & x_2^2 & \cdots & x_2^{n-1} \\
\vdots & \vdots & \vdots & \cdots & \vdots \\
1 & x_n & x_n^2 & \cdots & x_n^{n-1}
\end{pmatrix}.
$$

This matrix is a *full matrix,* meaning that each entry is different from zero, so that the determination of the interpolant requires the solution of a linear system with a full matrix.

However, we also know, from basic Numerical Analysis, that we could alternatively choose the so-called *Lagrange functions* as a basis:

$$
\phi_j(x) = L_j(x) = \prod_{\substack{i=1 \\ i \neq j}}^{n} \frac{x - x_i}{x_j - x_i}, \qquad 1 \leq j \leq n.
$$

They obviously have the property $L_j(x_j) = 1$ and $L_j(x_i) = 0$ for $j \neq i$. Thus, with this basis, the matrix in (1.1) simply becomes the identity matrix and the interpolant can be derived without solving a linear system at all.

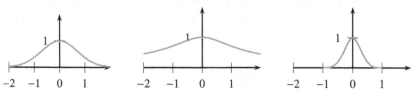

Figure 1.1 Typical radial basis functions: Gaussian, inverse multiquadric and a compactly supported one (from left to right).

In higher dimensions, i.e. $d \geq 2$, polynomial interpolation can become quite problematic and a more elegant way employs a basis of the form $\phi_i = \Phi(\cdot - \mathbf{x}_i)$, where $\Phi : \mathbb{R}^d \to \mathbb{R}$ is a fixed function. In most applications, this function is chosen to be *radial*, i.e. it is of the form $\Phi(\mathbf{x}) = \phi(\|\mathbf{x}\|_2)$, where $\phi : [0, \infty) \to \mathbb{R}$ is a univariate function and $\|\mathbf{x}\|_2 = \sqrt{x_1^2 + \cdots + x_d^2}$ denotes the Euclidean norm. Examples of possible univariate functions are

Gaussian:	$\phi(r) = \exp(-r^2),$
Multiquadric:	$\phi(r) = (r^2 + 1)^{1/2},$
Inverse Multiquadric:	$\phi(r) = (r^2 + 1)^{-1/2},$
Compactly Supported:	$\phi(r) = (1 - r)_+^4 (4r + 1),$

where $(x)_+$ is defined to be x if $x \geq 0$ and to be 0 if $x < 0$. The functions are visualised in Figure 1.1.

In all these cases, except for the multiquadric basis function, it is known that the resulting interpolation matrix is positive definite (with the restriction of $d \leq 3$ for the compactly supported function). Such functions are therefore called *positive definite*. More generally, a good choice of a basis is given by $\phi_j(\mathbf{x}) = K(\mathbf{x}, \mathbf{x}_j)$ with a *kernel* $K : \mathbb{R}^d \times \mathbb{R}^d \to \mathbb{R}$, which is *positive definite* in the sense that for all possible, pairwise distinct points $\mathbf{x}_1, \ldots, \mathbf{x}_n \in \mathbb{R}^d$, the matrix $(K(\mathbf{x}_i, \mathbf{x}_j))$ is symmetric and positive definite.

In the case of the multiquadric basis function, it is known that the interpolation matrix is invertible and has only real, non-vanishing eigenvalues and that all but one of these eigenvalues are negative.

Note that in the case of the inverse multiquadric and the Gaussian the matrices are dense while in the case of the compactly supported basis function the matrix can have a lot of zeros depending on the distribution of the data sites. Details on this topic can be found in Wendland [133].

1.1.2 Boundary Value Problem

Another application is to compute a stationary solution to the heat equation. In one dimension, we could imagine an infinitely thin rod of length one, which is heated in the interior of $(0, 1)$ with a heat source f and is kept at zero degrees at the boundary points $0, 1$. Mathematically, this means that we want to find a function $u : [0, 1] \to \mathbb{R}$ with

$$-u''(x) = f(x), \qquad x \in (0, 1),$$

with boundary conditions $u(0) = u(1) = 0$. If the function f is too complicated or even given only at discrete points then it is not possible to compute the solution u analytically. In this case a numerical scheme has to be used and the simplest idea is to approximate the derivative by differences:

$$u'(x) \approx \frac{u(x+h) - u(x)}{h}, \quad \text{or} \quad u'(x) \approx \frac{u(x) - u(x-h)}{h}.$$

The first rule could be referred to as a forward rule while the second is a backward rule. Using first a forward and then a backward rule for the second derivative leads to

$$u''(x) \approx \frac{u'(x+h) - u'(x)}{h} \approx \frac{1}{h} \left(\frac{u(x+h) - u(x)}{h} - \frac{u(x) - u(x-h)}{h} \right)$$

$$= \frac{u(x+h) - 2u(x) + u(x-h)}{h^2}.$$

For finding a numerical approximation using such finite differences we may divide the domain $[0, 1]$ into $n + 1$ pieces of equal length $h = 1/(n + 1)$ with nodes

$$x_i = ih = \frac{i}{n+1}, \quad 0 \leq i \leq n+1,$$

and set $u_i := u(x_i)$. We now define the finite difference approximation u^h to u, as follows: find u^h such that $u_0^h = u_{n+1}^h = 0$ and

$$-\left(\frac{u_{i+1}^h - 2u_i^h + u_{i-1}^h}{h^2} \right) = f_i, \quad 1 \leq i \leq n.$$

Alternatively this linear system of n equations may be written in the form

$$\frac{1}{h^2} \begin{pmatrix} 2 & -1 & & & & & 0 \\ -1 & 2 & -1 & & & & \\ & -1 & 2 & -1 & & & \\ & & \ddots & \ddots & \ddots & & \\ & & & -1 & 2 & -1 \\ 0 & & & & -1 & 2 \end{pmatrix} \begin{pmatrix} u_1^h \\ u_2^h \\ u_3^h \\ \vdots \\ u_{n-1}^h \\ u_n^h \end{pmatrix} = \begin{pmatrix} f_1 \\ f_2 \\ f_3 \\ \vdots \\ f_{n-1} \\ f_n \end{pmatrix}. \tag{1.2}$$

This system of equations is *sparse*, meaning that the number of non-zero entries is much smaller than n^2. This sparsity can be used to store the matrix and to implement matrix–vector and matrix–matrix multiplications efficiently.

To obtain an accurate approximation to u, we may have to choose h very small, thereby increasing the size of the linear system.

For a general boundary value problem in d-dimensions the size of the linear system can grow rapidly. For example, three-dimensional problems grow over eight times larger with each uniform refinement of the domain.

1.1.3 Integral Equations

In the last section we have introduced a way of solving a differential equation. A differential equation can also be recast as an integral equation but integral equations often also come up naturally during the modelling process. Hence, let us consider a typical integral equation as another example.

We now seek a function $u : [0, 1] \to \mathbb{R}$ satisfying

$$\int_0^1 \log(|x - y|)u(y)dy = f(x), \qquad x \in [0, 1],$$

where $f : [0, 1] \to \mathbb{R}$ is given. Note that the integral on the left-hand side contains the *kernel* $K(x, y) := \log(|x - y|)$, which is singular on the diagonal $x = y$.

To solve this integral equation numerically we will use a *Galerkin approximation*. The idea here is to choose an approximate solution u_n from a fixed, finite-dimensional subspace $V = \text{span}\{\phi_1, \ldots, \phi_n\}$ and to test the approximate solution via

$$\int_0^1 \int_0^1 \log(|x - y|)u_n(y)dy\,\phi_i(x)dx = \int_0^1 f(x)\phi_i(x)dx, \qquad 1 \le i \le n. \quad (1.3)$$

Since we choose $u_n \in V$ it must have a representation $u_n = \sum_{j=1}^n c_j\phi_j$ with certain coefficients c_j. Inserting this representation into (1.3) and changing the order of summation and integration yields

$$\sum_{j=1}^n c_j \int_0^1 \int_0^1 \log(|x - y|)\phi_j(y)\phi_i(x)dy\,dx = \int_0^1 f(x)\phi_i(x)dx, \qquad 1 \le i \le n,$$

which we easily identify as a linear system $A\mathbf{c} = \mathbf{f}$ with the matrix A having entries

$$a_{ij} = \int_0^1 \int_0^1 \log(|x - y|)\phi_j(y)\phi_i(x)dy\,dx, \qquad 1 \le i, j \le n.$$

A typical choice for the space V is the space of piece-wise constant functions. To be more precise, we can choose

$$\phi_i(x) = \begin{cases} 1 & \text{if } \frac{i-1}{n} \le x < \frac{i}{n}, \\ 0 & \text{else,} \end{cases}$$

but other basis functions and approximation spaces are possible. But we note that particularly in this case the matrix A is once again a full matrix as its entries are given by

$$a_{ij} = \int_{(i-1)/n}^{i/n} \int_{(j-1)/n}^{j/n} \log(|x - y|)dy\,dx.$$

An obvious generalisation of this problem to arbitrary domains $\Omega \subseteq \mathbb{R}^d$ leads to matrix entries of the form

$$a_{ij} = \int_\Omega \int_\Omega K(\mathbf{x}, \mathbf{y}) \phi_i(\mathbf{x}) \phi_j(\mathbf{y}) dy \, dx$$

with a given kernel $K : \Omega \times \Omega \to \mathbb{R}$.

1.2 Notation

Now, it is time to set up the notation which we will use throughout this book. However, we will specify only the most basic notation and definitions here and introduce further concepts whenever required.

1.2.1 Mathematics

We will denote the real, complex, natural and integer numbers as usual with $\mathbb{R}$, $\mathbb{C}$, $\mathbb{N}$ and $\mathbb{Z}$, respectively. The natural numbers will not include zero. We will use the notation $\mathbf{x} \in \mathbb{R}^n$ to denote vectors. The components of $\mathbf{x}$ will be denoted by $x_j \in \mathbb{R}$, i.e. $\mathbf{x} = (x_1, \ldots, x_n)^\mathsf{T}$. Thus vectors will always be column vectors. We will denote the unit standard basis of $\mathbb{R}^n$ by $\mathbf{e}_1, \ldots, \mathbf{e}_n$, where the ith unit vector $\mathbf{e}_i$ has only zero entries except for a one at position i. In general, we will suppress the dimension n when it comes to this basis and we might use the same notation to denote the ith unit vector for $\mathbb{R}^n$ and, say, $\mathbb{R}^m$. It should be clear from the context which one is meant. On $\mathbb{R}^n$ we will denote the inner product between two vectors $\mathbf{x}$ and $\mathbf{y}$ by either $\mathbf{x}^\mathsf{T}\mathbf{y}$ or $\langle \mathbf{x}, \mathbf{y} \rangle_2$, i.e.

$$\mathbf{x}^\mathsf{T}\mathbf{y} = \langle \mathbf{x}, \mathbf{y} \rangle_2 = \sum_{j=1}^n x_j y_j.$$

For a matrix A with m rows, n columns and real entries we will write $A \in \mathbb{R}^{m \times n}$ and $A = (a_{ij})$, where the index i refers to the rows and the index j refers to the columns:

$$A := (a_{ij}) := \begin{pmatrix} a_{11} & a_{12} & \cdots & a_{1n} \\ a_{21} & a_{22} & \cdots & a_{2n} \\ \vdots & & & \vdots \\ a_{m1} & a_{m2} & \cdots & a_{mn} \end{pmatrix}.$$

For a non-square matrix $A \in \mathbb{R}^{m \times n}$, we can write $a_{ij} = \mathbf{e}_i^\mathsf{T} A \mathbf{e}_j$, where the first unit vector is from $\mathbb{R}^m$ while the second unit vector is from $\mathbb{R}^n$.

We will use the *Kronecker δ-symbol* δ_{ij}, which is defined as

$$\delta_{ij} = \begin{cases} 1 & \text{if } i = j, \\ 0 & \text{if } i \neq j. \end{cases}$$

For the *identity matrix* in $\mathbb{R}^n$ we will use the symbol $I \in \mathbb{R}^{n \times n}$. We obviously have $I = (\delta_{ij})_{1 \leq i, j \leq n}$. Again, as in the case of the unit vectors, we will usually refrain from explicitly indicating the dimension n of the underlying space $\mathbb{R}^n$. We will also denote the columns of a matrix $A \in \mathbb{R}^{m \times n}$ by $\mathbf{a}_j := A\mathbf{e}_j \in \mathbb{R}^m$, $1 \leq j \leq n$. Hence, we have

$$A = (\mathbf{a}_1, \mathbf{a}_2, \ldots, \mathbf{a}_n).$$

For a matrix $A \in \mathbb{R}^{m \times n}$ and a vector $\mathbf{x} \in \mathbb{R}^n$, we can write $\mathbf{x} = \sum_j x_j \mathbf{e}_j$ and hence

$$A\mathbf{x} = \sum_{j=1}^{n} x_j \mathbf{a}_j.$$

We will encounter specific forms of matrices and want to use the following, well-known names.

Definition 1.1 A matrix $A = (a_{ij}) \in \mathbb{R}^{m \times n}$ is

- a *square matrix*, if $m = n$,
- a *diagonal matrix*, if $a_{ij} = 0$ for $i \neq j$,
- an *upper triangular matrix*, if $a_{ij} = 0$ for $i > j$,
- a *lower triangular matrix*, if $a_{ij} = 0$ for $i < j$,
- a *band-matrix*, if there are $k, \ell \in \mathbb{N}_0$ such that $a_{ij} = 0$ if $j < i - k$ or $j > i + \ell$,
- *sparse*, if more than half of the entries are zero,
- *dense* or *full*, if it is not sparse.

In the case of a diagonal matrix A with diagonal entries $a_{ii} = \lambda_i$, we will also use the notation

$$A = \text{diag}(\lambda_1, \ldots, \lambda_n).$$

In particular, we have for the identity matrix $I = \text{diag}(1, \ldots, 1) \in \mathbb{R}^{n \times n}$.

Most of these names are self-explanatory. In the case of a band matrix, we have all entries zero outside a diagonally bordered band. Only those entries a_{ij} with indices $i - k \leq j \leq i + \ell$ may be different from zero. This means we have at most k sub-diagonals and ℓ super-diagonals with non-zero entries. The most prominent example is given by $k = \ell = 1$, which has one super-diagonal and one sub-diagonal of non-zero entries and is hence called a *tridiagonal* matrix.

Schematically, upper triangular, lower triangular and tridiagonal matrices look as follows:

$$
\begin{pmatrix} * & * & * & \cdots & * \\ & * & * & & \vdots \\ & & \ddots & \ddots & * \\ & & & * & * \\ 0 & & & & * \end{pmatrix}, \quad
\begin{pmatrix} * & & & & 0 \\ * & * & & & \\ * & & \ddots & \ddots & \\ \vdots & & & * & * \\ * & \cdots & * & * & * \end{pmatrix}, \quad
\begin{pmatrix} * & * & 0 & \cdots & 0 \\ * & * & * & & \vdots \\ 0 & \ddots & \ddots & \ddots & 0 \\ \vdots & & * & * & * \\ 0 & \cdots & 0 & * & * \end{pmatrix},
$$

where a $*$ marks a possible non-zero entry.

For a matrix $A = (a_{ij}) \in \mathbb{R}^{m \times n}$ we denote the *transpose* of A by A^T. It is given by exchanging columns and rows from A, i.e. $A^T = (a_{ji}) \in \mathbb{R}^{n \times m}$. A square matrix $A \in \mathbb{R}^{n \times n}$ is said to be *symmetric* if $A^T = A$. If the matrix A is invertible, we have $(A^{-1})^T = (A^T)^{-1}$ which we will simply denote with A^{-T}. If A is symmetric and invertible then also the inverse A^{-1} is symmetric. Both the transpose and the inverse satisfy the rules

$$(AB)^T = B^T A^T, \qquad (AB)^{-1} = B^{-1} A^{-1},$$

as long as these operations are well-defined.

1.2.2 Algorithms

We will not use a specific computing language to describe the algorithms in this book. However, we will assume that the reader is familiar with basic programming techniques. In particular, we expect the reader to know what a **for** and a **while** loop are. We will use **if, then** and **else** in the usual way and, when assigning a new value to a variable x, this variable might appear also on the right-hand side of the assignment, i.e. such an assignment can, for example, be of the form $x := x + y$, which means that x and y are first evaluated and the sum of their values is then assigned to x. For each algorithm we will declare the essential input data and the output data. There will, however, be no explicit return statement. Each algorithm should also have a deterministic stopping criterion. To demonstrate this, a first example of an algorithm is given in Algorithm 1, which computes the inner product $s := \mathbf{x}^T \mathbf{y}$ of the two vectors $\mathbf{x}, \mathbf{y} \in \mathbb{R}^n$.

At the beginning, we will formulate algorithms very close to actual programs using only basic operations. An implementation within a modern computing language should be straightforward. Later on, when it comes to more sophisticated algorithms, we will use higher-level mathematical notation to compress the representation of the algorithm. For example, an inner product will then only appear as $s := \mathbf{x}^T \mathbf{y}$.

Algorithm 1: Inner product

Input : $x, y \in \mathbb{R}^n$.

Output: $s = x^T y$.

1   $s := 0$

2   **for** $j = 1$ **to** n **do**

3     $\lfloor \quad s := s + x_j y_j$

In this book, we will not discuss low-level data structures, i.e. ways of storing a vector or a matrix within a computer. We will assume that the reader is familiar with the concepts of arrays, which are usually used to store (full) matrices, and index lists, which can be used to store sparse matrices.

1.3 Landau Symbols and Computational Cost

Before developing algorithms to solve linear equations, we will introduce concepts to analyse the cost of such algorithms and their stability. Though, of course, it is possible to compare the actual run-times of two algorithms on a computer, the actual run-time is not a particularly good measure. It is more important to understand how the computational cost of an algorithm changes with the number of unknowns.

The multiplication of a matrix $A \in \mathbb{R}^{m \times n}$ with a vector $x \in \mathbb{R}^n$ results in a vector $b = Ax \in \mathbb{R}^m$ with components

$$b_i = (Ax)_i = \sum_{j=1}^{n} a_{ij} x_j, \qquad 1 \leq i \leq m.$$

The multiplication of a matrix $A \in \mathbb{R}^{m \times n}$ with a matrix $B \in \mathbb{R}^{n \times p}$ gives a matrix $C = AB \in \mathbb{R}^{m \times p}$, with entries

$$c_{ij} = \sum_{k=1}^{n} a_{ik} b_{kj}, \qquad 1 \leq i \leq m, \quad 1 \leq j \leq p.$$

So, how much does the computation of it cost? Usually, the cost is measured in *flops*, which stands for *floating point operations*. A floating point operation consists of one addition plus one multiplication. Sometimes, it is helpful to distinguish between additions and multiplications and count them separately. This was particularly true when a multiplication on a computer was substantially more expensive than an addition. However, as this is no longer the case on modern computers, where multiplications are realised as efficiently as additions, we will stick to the above definition of flops. It is nonetheless important to note that while subtractions are as efficient as additions and multiplications, this is not true for divisions, which are significantly slower.

Most of the time, we will not be interested in the actual number of floating point operations but rather in the asymptotic behaviour with respect to the dimension.

For example, if we look at a matrix–vector multiplication $\mathbf{b} = A\mathbf{x}$, then we must for every index i compute the sum

$$\sum_{j=1}^{n} a_{ij} x_j,$$

which means we have n multiplications and $n-1$ additions, i.e. n floating point operations. Hence, if we double the size of the matrix, we would require twice as many flops for each component. This, however, would also be true if the actual computing cost would be cn with a positive constant $c > 0$. The total cost of the matrix–vector multiplication becomes mn since we have m entries to compute.

If we are not interested in the constant $c > 0$ then we will use the following notation.

Definition 1.2 (Landau notation) For two functions $f, g : \mathbb{N}^d \to \mathbb{R}$, we will write

$$f(\mathbf{n}) = O(g(\mathbf{n}))$$

if there is a constant $c > 0$ such that

$$|f(\mathbf{n})| \leq c|g(\mathbf{n})|, \qquad \mathbf{n} \in \mathbb{N}^d.$$

It is important to see that the constant has to be independent of the argument $\mathbf{n} \in \mathbb{N}^d$. Moreover, though in most cases we will ignore the constant c in our considerations, a huge $c > 0$ can mean that we will never or only for very large $\mathbf{n}$ see the actual asymptotic behaviour.

With this definition, we can say that matrix–vector multiplication of a matrix $A \in \mathbb{R}^{m \times n}$ with a vector $\mathbf{x} \in \mathbb{R}^n$ costs

$$\text{time}(A\mathbf{x}) = O(mn).$$

In the case of a square matrix $m = n$, the cost is therefore $O(n^2)$, which means that doubling the input size of the matrix and the vector, i.e. replacing n by $2n$, will require four times the time of the original matrix–vector multiplication.

We can also use this notation to analyse the space required to store the information on a computer. We will have to store each matrix entry a_{ij} and each entry of $\mathbf{x}$ as well as the result $A\mathbf{x}$. This requires

$$O(mn + n + m) = O(mn)$$

space. When developing algorithms it is important to consider both resources, time and space, and it might sometimes be necessary to sacrifice something of one resource to gain in the other.

It is now easy to see that for the matrix–matrix multiplication $C = AB$, we would require $O(mnp)$ operations. Hence, for square systems with $m = n = p$ the time is $O(n^3)$ and doubling the input size results in computations that are eight times longer.

Let us summarise our findings so far, with some obvious additions.

Lemma 1.3 *Let $A \in \mathbb{R}^{m \times n}$, $B \in \mathbb{R}^{n \times p}$, $\mathbf{x} \in \mathbb{R}^n$ and $\alpha \in \mathbb{R}$.*

- *It costs $O(n)$ space to store the vector $\mathbf{x} \in \mathbb{R}^n$ and $O(mn)$ space to store the matrix A.*
- *It costs $O(n)$ time to compute the product $\alpha \mathbf{x}$.*
- *It costs $O(mn)$ time to compute the product $A\mathbf{x}$.*
- *It costs $O(mnp)$ time to compute the product AB.*

The cost is called *linear* if it is $O(n)$, *quadratic* if it is $O(n^2)$ and *cubic* if it is $O(n^3)$.

More sophisticated matrix–matrix products have been developed with the goal of reducing the computational cost by reducing the number of multiplications at the cost of a mild increase in the number of additions. The most famous one is a recursive algorithm by Strassen (see [120]) which can compute the product of two $n \times n$ matrices using at most $4.7 \cdot n^{\log_2 7} = O(n^{2.807355})$ flops. Since then, other such algorithms have been introduced, most notably one by Coppersmith and Winograd in [37] which reduces the cost to $O(n^{2.375477})$. The latter algorithm is, however, more complicated and the constant hidden in the O-notation substantially larger so that the algorithm is not used in practice. Though superior in this context, even the Strassen algorithm is not seriously used in practical applications, which is due to the fact that it is not as stable as the conventional scheme, see Higham [84].

Finally, let us see how additional information can be used to reduce the cost. If, for example, we have a *tridiagonal matrix*, i.e. a matrix which has only non-zero entries on the diagonal and the sub- and super-diagonal, i.e. which is of the form

$$A = \begin{pmatrix} a_{11} & a_{12} & 0 & \cdots & & 0 \\ a_{21} & a_{22} & a_{23} & & & \vdots \\ 0 & \ddots & \ddots & \ddots & & 0 \\ \vdots & & a_{n-1,n-2} & a_{n-1,n-1} & a_{n-1,n} \\ 0 & \cdots & & 0 & a_{n,n-1} & a_{nn} \end{pmatrix},$$

then a matrix–vector multiplication reduces to

$$(Ax)_i = \sum_{j=1}^{n} a_{ij}x_j = a_{i,i-1}x_{i-1} + a_{ii}x_i + a_{i,i+1}x_{i+1}.$$

Hence, the time for the full matrix–vector product is now only $O(n)$ instead of $O(n^2)$. Also the matrix can be stored by exploiting its special form in $O(n)$ space instead of $O(n^2)$.

We will sometimes encounter algorithms which have a recursive structure. This means, for example, that solving a problem with problem size n is reduced to solving problems with problem size n/b, where $b > 1$. The Strassen algorithm mentioned above is one such example. To analyse the cost of such an algorithm it is often helpful to assume that $n = b^k$ with some $k \in \mathbb{N}$. The following result will be helpful.

Lemma 1.4 *The recursion $T(1) = c$ and $T(n) = aT(n/b) + cn^\alpha$ with $c, a, \alpha > 0$ and $b > 1$ satisfies*

$$T(n) \leq \begin{cases} c\frac{b^\alpha}{b^\alpha-a}n^\alpha & \text{if } a < b^\alpha, \\ cn^\alpha(\log_b n + 1) & \text{if } a = b^\alpha, \\ c\frac{a}{a-b^\alpha}n^{\log_b a} & \text{if } a > b^\alpha. \end{cases}$$

Proof As mentioned above, we will prove this only for $n = b^k$. Though the results remain true for general n, the proof is more tedious in the general case. Using induction, it is easy to see that

$$T(b^k) = c\sum_{i=0}^{k} a^i(b^\alpha)^{k-i}.$$

Hence, if $a < b^\alpha$, we have

$$T(b^k) = cb^{k\alpha}\sum_{i=0}^{k}\left(\frac{a}{b^\alpha}\right)^i = cn^\alpha\frac{1-\left(\frac{a}{b^\alpha}\right)^{k+1}}{1-\frac{a}{b^\alpha}} < cn^\alpha\frac{b^\alpha}{b^\alpha-a}.$$

For $a = b^\alpha$ we have

$$T(b^k) = cn^\alpha(k + 1) = cn^\alpha(\log_b n + 1)$$

and for $a > b^\alpha$ we finally use

$$T(b^k) = ca^k \sum_{i=0}^{k} \left(\frac{b^\alpha}{a}\right)^i = ca^k \frac{1 - \left(\frac{b^\alpha}{a}\right)^{k+1}}{1 - \frac{b^\alpha}{a}} \le ca^k \frac{a}{a - b^\alpha} = c\frac{a}{a - b^\alpha} n^{\log_b a},$$

where we have used

$$a^k = e^{k \log a} = \exp\left[\frac{\log a}{\log b} \log b^k\right] = (b^k)^{\frac{\log a}{\log b}} = n^{\log_b a}. \qquad \square$$

Finally, let us mention that the definition of the Landau symbol O can even be further generalised in the following sense.

Definition 1.5 For two functions $f, g : \mathbb{R}^n \to \mathbb{R}$ and $\mathbf{x}_0 \in \mathbb{R}^n$, we will write

$$f(\mathbf{x}) = O(g(\mathbf{x})), \qquad \mathbf{x} \to \mathbf{x}_0,$$

if there is a constant $c > 0$ and a surrounding $U = U(\mathbf{x}_0) \subseteq \mathbb{R}^n$ of $\mathbf{x}_0$ such that

$$|f(x)| \le c|g(\mathbf{x})|, \qquad \mathbf{x} \in U.$$

1.4 Facts from Linear Algebra

In this section, we want to collect further material on matrices and vectors, which should be known from classical, basic linear algebra courses. The character of this section is more to remind the reader of the material and to introduce the notation. However, we will also prove some results which are less familiar.

In $\mathbb{R}^n$ we have the canonical inner product defined by $\langle \mathbf{x}, \mathbf{y} \rangle_2 := \mathbf{x}^T \mathbf{y}$ for all $\mathbf{x}, \mathbf{y} \in \mathbb{R}^n$. It particularly satisfies $\langle \mathbf{x}, \mathbf{x} \rangle_2 = x_1^2 + \cdots + x_n^2 > 0$ for all $\mathbf{x} \ne \mathbf{0}$. As mentioned above, we will use both notations $\langle \mathbf{x}, \mathbf{y} \rangle_2$ and $\mathbf{x}^T \mathbf{y}$ equally. The canonical inner product defines a canonical norm or length $\|\mathbf{x}\|_2 := \sqrt{\langle \mathbf{x}, \mathbf{x} \rangle_2}$, the *Euclidean norm*. This norm has the usual properties of a norm, which can more generally be defined for an arbitrary linear space. Of course, we assume the reader to be familiar with the concept of linear spaces, linear sub-spaces, linear independent vectors and the dimension of a linear space.

Definition 1.6 Let V be a real (or complex) linear space. A mapping $\| \cdot \| : V \to [0, \infty)$ is called a *norm* on V if it satisfies

1. homogeneity: $\|\lambda \mathbf{x}\| = |\lambda| \|\mathbf{x}\|$ for all $\mathbf{x} \in V$ and $\lambda \in \mathbb{R}$ (or $\lambda \in \mathbb{C}$),

2. definiteness: $\|\mathbf{x}\| = 0$ if and only if $\mathbf{x} = \mathbf{0}$,
3. triangle inequality: $\|\mathbf{x} + \mathbf{y}\| \le \|\mathbf{x}\| + \|\mathbf{y}\|$ for all $\mathbf{x}, \mathbf{y} \in V$.

The space V with norm $\| \cdot \|$ is called a *normed space*.

In the case of $V = \mathbb{R}^n$ and $\|\cdot\| = \|\cdot\|_2$, the first two properties follow immediately from the definition, while the triangle inequality follows from the *Cauchy–Schwarz inequality*

$$|\langle \mathbf{x}, \mathbf{y} \rangle_2| \le \|\mathbf{x}\|_2 \|\mathbf{y}\|_2$$

which holds for all $\mathbf{x}, \mathbf{y} \in \mathbb{R}^n$ and where equality occurs if and only if $\mathbf{y}$ is a scalar multiple of $\mathbf{x}$. This all remains true, in the more general situation when the norm is defined by an inner product.

Definition 1.7 Let V be a real linear space. A mapping $\langle \cdot, \cdot \rangle : V \times V \to \mathbb{R}$ is called an *inner product* if it is

1. symmetric: $\langle \mathbf{x}, \mathbf{y} \rangle = \langle \mathbf{y}, \mathbf{x} \rangle$ for all $\mathbf{x}, \mathbf{y} \in V$,
2. linear: $\langle \alpha \mathbf{x} + \beta \mathbf{y}, \mathbf{z} \rangle = \alpha \langle \mathbf{x}, \mathbf{z} \rangle + \beta \langle \mathbf{y}, \mathbf{z} \rangle$ for all $\mathbf{x}, \mathbf{y}, \mathbf{z} \in V$ and $\alpha, \beta \in \mathbb{R}$,
3. definite: $\langle \mathbf{x}, \mathbf{x} \rangle > 0$ for all $\mathbf{x} \in V \setminus \{\mathbf{0}\}$.

A space V with an inner product $\langle \cdot, \cdot \rangle : V \times V \to \mathbb{R}$ is called a *pre-Hilbert space*.

The second property together with the first property indeed guarantees that the mapping $\langle \cdot, \cdot \rangle$ is bilinear, i.e. it is also linear in the second argument. Each pre-Hilbert space becomes a normed space upon defining the canonical norm $\|\mathbf{x}\| := \sqrt{\langle \mathbf{x}, \mathbf{x} \rangle}$.

If V is a complex linear space then an inner product on V is again a mapping $\langle \cdot, \cdot \rangle : V \times V \to \mathbb{C}$ but the first two conditions above have to be modified appropriately. For example, the first condition becomes $\langle \mathbf{x}, \mathbf{y} \rangle = \overline{\langle \mathbf{y}, \mathbf{x} \rangle}$ for all $\mathbf{x}, \mathbf{y} \in V$, where $\overline{\alpha}$ is the complex conjugate of $\alpha \in \mathbb{C}$. The second property must now hold for all $\alpha, \beta \in \mathbb{C}$, which means that the inner product is linear in its first and anti-linear in its second component. The canonical norm is then defined as before.

Throughout this book, we will mainly be concerned with the space $V = \mathbb{R}^n$ and hence introduce most concepts only for this space. But it is worth noting that some of them immediately carry over to more general spaces.

As usual, for given $\mathbf{x}_1, \ldots, \mathbf{x}_n \in V$, we use the notation $\operatorname{span}\{\mathbf{x}_1, \ldots, \mathbf{x}_n\}$ to denote the linear sub-space of V spanned by these elements, i.e.

$$\operatorname{span}\{\mathbf{x}_1, \ldots, \mathbf{x}_n\} = \left\{ \sum_{j=1}^{n} \alpha_j \mathbf{x}_j : \alpha_1, \ldots, \alpha_n \in \mathbb{R} \right\}.$$

Definition 1.8 Let V be a finite-dimensional pre-Hilbert space with basis $x_1, \ldots, x_n$. A basis is called an *orthonormal basis* if all basis vectors have unit length, i.e. $\|x_i\| = \langle x_i, x_i \rangle^{1/2} = 1$ and two different vectors are *orthogonal*, i.e $\langle x_i, x_j \rangle = 0$ for $i \neq j$.

It is always possible to transform a given basis into an orthonormal basis.

Lemma 1.9 (Gram–Schmidt) *Let* $x_1, \ldots, x_n$ *be linearly independent vectors of a pre-Hilbert space V. Define* $u_1 = x_1 / \|x_1\|$ *and then for* $k = 1, 2, \ldots, n$,

$$\tilde{u}_{j+1} := u_{j+1} - \sum_{j=1}^{k} \langle u_{j+1}, u_j \rangle u_j,$$

$$u_{j+1} := \tilde{u}_{j+1} / \|\tilde{u}_{j+1}\|.$$

Then, the set $\{u_1, \ldots, u_k\}$ *forms an orthonormal basis of* $\operatorname{span}\{x_1, \ldots, x_k\}$ *for* $1 \leq k \leq n$.

The Gram–Schmidt orthonormalisation process should be well-known and we leave a proof of the above lemma to the reader. Though the Gram–Schmidt procedure is obviously easily implemented, it is numerically often problematic. We will later discuss better methods of finding orthonormal bases.

Definition 1.10 Let $A \in \mathbb{R}^{m \times n}$ be given. Its *null space* is defined to be the set

$$\ker(A) = \{x \in \mathbb{R}^n : Ax = 0\} \subseteq \mathbb{R}^n$$

and its *range* to be

$$\operatorname{range}(A) = \{Ax : x \in \mathbb{R}^n\} \subseteq \mathbb{R}^m.$$

The *rank* of $A \in \mathbb{R}^{m \times n}$ is defined as

$$\operatorname{rank}(A) = \dim\{Ax : x \in \mathbb{R}^n\} = \dim \operatorname{range}(A).$$

It is easy to see that the null space of a matrix $A \in \mathbb{R}^{m \times n}$ is a subspace of $\mathbb{R}^n$, while the range of A is a subspace of $\mathbb{R}^m$.

Definition 1.11 Let $A \in \mathbb{R}^{n \times n}$ be a square matrix.

1. The matrix is called *positive semi-definite* if, for all $x \in \mathbb{R}^n$, we have

$$x^T A x = \sum_{i=1}^{n} \sum_{j=1}^{n} x_i x_j a_{ij} \geq 0.$$

   It is called *positive definite* if the above expression is positive for all $x \neq 0$.
2. The matrix is called *orthogonal* if $A^T A = I$.

3. The matrix is called *diagonalisable* if there exist an invertible matrix $S \in \mathbb{R}^{n \times n}$ (or more generally $S \in \mathbb{C}^{n \times n}$) and a diagonal matrix $D \in \mathbb{R}^{n \times n}$ ($\in \mathbb{C}^{n \times n}$) such that $A = SDS^{-1}$.

If a matrix $A \in \mathbb{R}^{n \times n}$ is symmetric then there is an orthonormal basis of $\mathbb{R}^n$ consisting of eigenvectors of A. This means that there are real values $\lambda_1, \ldots, \lambda_n \in \mathbb{R}$ and vectors $\mathbf{w}_1, \ldots, \mathbf{w}_n \in \mathbb{R}^n \setminus \{\mathbf{0}\}$, which satisfy

$$A\mathbf{w}_j = \lambda_j \mathbf{w}_j, \qquad \langle \mathbf{w}_j, \mathbf{w}_k \rangle_2 = \delta_{jk}.$$

The eigenvectors form an orthogonal matrix $Q = (\mathbf{w}_1, \ldots, \mathbf{w}_n) \in \mathbb{R}^{n \times n}$ and hence we have the following result.

Proposition 1.12 *If $A \in \mathbb{R}^{n \times n}$ is symmetric then there is an orthogonal matrix $Q \in \mathbb{R}^{n \times n}$ such that $Q^T A Q = D$ is a diagonal matrix with the eigenvalues of A as diagonal entries.*
A symmetric matrix is positive definite (positive semi-definite) if and only if all its eigenvalues are positive (non-negative).

As a consequence, a symmetric and positive definite matrix possesses a *square root*.

Corollary 1.13 *If $A \in \mathbb{R}^{n \times n}$ is symmetric and positive (semi-)definite then there is a symmetric and positive (semi-)definite matrix $A^{1/2} \in \mathbb{R}^{n \times n}$ such that $A = A^{1/2} A^{1/2}$. The matrix $A^{1/2}$ is called a* square root *of A.*

Proof According to Proposition 1.12, we can write $A = QDQ^T$ with a diagonal matrix $D = \text{diag}(\lambda_1, \ldots, \lambda_n)$ and an orthogonal matrix Q. The diagonal entries of D are non-negative. Hence, we can define the diagonal matrix $D^{1/2} := \text{diag}(\sqrt{\lambda_1}, \ldots, \sqrt{\lambda_n})$ and then $A^{1/2} := QD^{1/2}Q^T$. This matrix is obviously symmetric and because of

$$\mathbf{x}^T A^{1/2} \mathbf{x} = \mathbf{x}^T Q D^{1/2} Q^T \mathbf{x} = \mathbf{y}^T D^{1/2} \mathbf{y} = \sum_{j=1}^{n} y_j^2 \sqrt{\lambda_j} \geq 0$$

also positive (semi-)definite, where we have set $\mathbf{y} := Q^T \mathbf{x}$. Finally, we have

$$A^{1/2} A^{1/2} = (QD^{1/2}Q^T)(QD^{1/2}Q^T) = QD^{1/2}D^{1/2}Q^T = QDQ^T = A. \qquad \square$$

We also remark that for a matrix $A \in \mathbb{R}^{m \times n}$, the matrix $A^T A \in \mathbb{R}^{n \times n}$ is obviously symmetric and positive semi-definite, simply because of

$$\mathbf{x}^T (A^T A) \mathbf{x} = (A\mathbf{x})^T (A\mathbf{x}) = \|A\mathbf{x}\|_2^2 \geq 0.$$

As a matter of fact, each symmetric and positive definite matrix can be written in this form, see Exercise 1.5. An orthogonal matrix is always invertible and its rows and columns, respectively, form an orthonormal basis of $\mathbb{R}^n$.

Sometimes it is necessary to consider a generalised eigenvalue problem. This occurs, for example, when discussing discretised systems coming from elasticity theory. Later on, it will also be important when we look at preconditioning.

Definition 1.14 Let $A, B \in \mathbb{R}^{n \times n}$ be matrices. Then, $\lambda \in \mathbb{C}$ is a *generalised eigenvalue* with respect to A, B if there is a non-zero vector $\mathbf{x} \in \mathbb{C}^n$ such that

$$A\mathbf{x} = \lambda B\mathbf{x}.$$

The vector $\mathbf{x}$ is called *generalised eigenvector*.

If the matrix B is invertible, finding a generalised eigenvalue and eigenvector is equivalent to finding a classical eigenvalue and eigenvector of the matrix $B^{-1}A$. However, even if A and B are symmetric, i.e. both have only real eigenvalues and a complete set of eigenvectors, then the matrix $B^{-1}A$ is in general not symmetric. Nonetheless, we have the following result.

Theorem 1.15 *Let $A, B \in \mathbb{R}^{n \times n}$ be symmetric and positive definite. Then, all eigenvalues of $B^{-1}A$ are real and positive. Moreover, there exist n pairs of generalised eigenvalues λ_j and eigenvectors $\mathbf{v}_j$, $1 \leq j \leq n$, satisfying $A\mathbf{v}_j = \lambda_j B\mathbf{v}_j$ and*

$$\mathbf{v}_i^{\mathrm{T}} B\mathbf{v}_j = \mathbf{v}_i^{\mathrm{T}} A\mathbf{v}_j = 0, \qquad i \neq j.$$

The matrix $V = (\mathbf{v}_1, \ldots, \mathbf{v}_n)$ diagonalises the matrices A and B simultaneously. If the eigenvectors are normalised such that $\mathbf{v}_i^{\mathrm{T}} B\mathbf{v}_i = 1$, $1 \leq i \leq n$, then

$$V^{\mathrm{T}} BV = I, \qquad V^{\mathrm{T}} AV = \mathrm{diag}(\lambda_1, \ldots, \lambda_n).$$

Proof As mentioned above, a generalised eigenvalue is simply an eigenvalue of $B^{-1}A$. Since B is symmetric and positive definite, it has a symmetric and positive definite root $B^{1/2}$ with inverse denoted by $B^{-1/2}$. The matrix $B^{-1/2}AB^{-1/2}$ is symmetric and positive definite since we have on the one hand

$$(B^{-1/2}AB^{-1/2})^{\mathrm{T}} = (B^{-1/2})^{\mathrm{T}} A^{\mathrm{T}} (B^{-1/2})^{\mathrm{T}} = B^{-1/2}AB^{-1/2}$$

and on the other hand for $\mathbf{x} \in \mathbb{R}^n$:

$$\mathbf{x}^{\mathrm{T}} B^{-1/2}AB^{-1/2}\mathbf{x} = (B^{-1/2}\mathbf{x})^{\mathrm{T}} A(B^{-1/2}\mathbf{x}) > 0,$$

unless $B^{-1/2}\mathbf{x} = \mathbf{0}$ which is equivalent to $\mathbf{x} = \mathbf{0}$. Thus, all eigenvalues of

$B^{-1/2}AB^{-1/2}$ are positive. Next, for $\lambda \in \mathbb{C}$ we have

$$
\begin{aligned}
\det(B^{-1/2}AB^{-1/2} - \lambda I) &= \det(B^{-1/2}A - \lambda B^{1/2})\det(B^{-1/2}) \\
&= \det(B^{-1/2})\det(B^{-1/2}A - \lambda B^{1/2}) \\
&= \det(B^{-1}A - \lambda I),
\end{aligned}
$$

meaning that $B^{-1/2}AB^{-1/2}$ and $B^{-1}A$ have exactly the same eigenvalues. Finally, let $\lambda_1, \ldots, \lambda_n$ be the eigenvalues of $B^{-1/2}AB^{-1/2}$ with corresponding, orthonormal eigenvectors $\mathbf{w}_1, \ldots, \mathbf{w}_n$. If we set $\mathbf{v}_j := B^{-1/2}\mathbf{w}_j$ then we have

$$
B^{-1/2}A\mathbf{v}_j = B^{-1/2}AB^{-1/2}\mathbf{w}_j = \lambda_j\mathbf{w}_j = \lambda_j B^{1/2}\mathbf{v}_j,
$$

or $A\mathbf{v}_j = \lambda_j B\mathbf{v}_j$. Moreover, we have

$$
\mathbf{v}_j^\mathsf{T} B\mathbf{v}_k = \mathbf{w}_j^\mathsf{T} B^{-1/2}BB^{-1/2}\mathbf{w}_k = \mathbf{w}_j^\mathsf{T}\mathbf{w}_k = \delta_{jk}
$$

and

$$
\mathbf{v}_j^\mathsf{T} A\mathbf{v}_k = \mathbf{w}_j^\mathsf{T} B^{-1/2}AB^{-1/2}\mathbf{w}_k = \lambda_k\delta_{jk}. \qquad \square
$$

In several places we will require the notion of orthogonal projection. Again, we define things immediately in a more general setting though we will mainly be interested in the case of $\mathbb{R}^n$.

Definition 1.16 Let V be a pre-Hilbert space. A linear mapping $P : V \to V$ is called a *projection* if $P^2 = P$. A linear mapping $P : V \to U \subseteq V$ is called *orthogonal projection onto* U, if

$$
\langle \mathbf{x} - P\mathbf{x}, \mathbf{u} \rangle = 0, \qquad \mathbf{x} \in V, \quad \mathbf{u} \in U. \tag{1.4}
$$

It is easy to see that a linear mapping $P : V \to V$ is a projection if and only if $P\mathbf{u} = \mathbf{u}$ for all $\mathbf{u} \in \mathrm{range}(P) = \{P\mathbf{x} : \mathbf{x} \in V\}$. Moreover, an orthogonal projection is indeed a projection since we have for $\mathbf{x} \in U$ also $\mathbf{x} - P\mathbf{x} \in U$ and hence by the orthogonality condition $\|\mathbf{x} - P\mathbf{x}\|^2 = \langle \mathbf{x} - P\mathbf{x}, \mathbf{x} - P\mathbf{x} \rangle = 0$, i.e. $P\mathbf{x} = \mathbf{x}$ for all $\mathbf{x} \in U$.

If $\mathbf{u}_1, \ldots, \mathbf{u}_k \in U$ form an orthonormal basis of the finite-dimensional subspace $U \subseteq V$, then the orthogonal projection onto U is given by

$$
P\mathbf{x} = \sum_{j=1}^{k} \langle \mathbf{x}, \mathbf{u}_j \rangle \mathbf{u}_j. \tag{1.5}
$$

Obviously, this so-defined P is linear and maps onto U. To see that it is also the orthogonal projection, let us assume that V is also finite-dimensional, as we are only concerned with finite-dimensional spaces in this book, though the result is also true for infinite-dimensional spaces. If V is finite-dimensional, we can extend $\mathbf{u}_1, \ldots, \mathbf{u}_k$ to an orthonormal basis $\mathbf{u}_1, \ldots, \mathbf{u}_k, \ldots, \mathbf{u}_n$ of V. Then, we have, for any $\mathbf{x} \in V$,

$$\mathbf{x} = \sum_{j=1}^{n} \langle \mathbf{x}, \mathbf{u}_j \rangle \mathbf{u}_j, \qquad \mathbf{x} - P\mathbf{x} = \sum_{j=k+1}^{n} \langle \mathbf{x}, \mathbf{u}_j \rangle \mathbf{u}_j,$$

so that the orthogonal condition (1.4) yields for P defined by (1.5) that

$$\langle \mathbf{x} - P\mathbf{x}, \mathbf{u}_i \rangle = \left\langle \sum_{j=k+1}^{n} \langle \mathbf{x}, \mathbf{u}_j \rangle \mathbf{u}_j, \mathbf{u}_i \right\rangle = \sum_{j=k+1}^{n} \langle \mathbf{x}, \mathbf{u}_j \rangle \langle \mathbf{u}_j, \mathbf{u}_i \rangle = 0$$

for all $1 \le i \le k$.

The orthogonal projection $P\mathbf{x}$ also describes the *best approximation* to $\mathbf{x}$ from U.

Proposition 1.17 *Let V be a pre-Hilbert space and let $U \subseteq V$ be a finite-dimensional subspace. Then, for $\mathbf{x} \in V$ and $\mathbf{u}^* \in U$ are equivalent:*

1. $\mathbf{u}^*$ *is the best approximation to $\mathbf{x}$ from U, i.e.*

$$\|\mathbf{x} - \mathbf{u}^*\| = \min_{\mathbf{u} \in U} \|\mathbf{x} - \mathbf{u}\|.$$

2. $\mathbf{u}^*$ *is the orthogonal projection of $\mathbf{x}$ onto U, i.e.*

$$\langle \mathbf{x} - \mathbf{u}^*, \mathbf{u} \rangle = 0, \qquad \mathbf{u} \in U.$$

Proof Let $\mathbf{u}_1, \ldots, \mathbf{u}_k$ be an orthonormal basis of U. Then, using the orthonormality we have with $P\mathbf{x}$ from (1.5) for arbitrary $\alpha_1, \ldots, \alpha_k \in \mathbb{R}$,

$$\|\mathbf{x} - P\mathbf{x}\|^2 = \left\| \mathbf{x} - \sum_{j=1}^{k} \langle \mathbf{x}, \mathbf{u}_j \rangle \mathbf{u}_j \right\|^2 = \left\langle \mathbf{x} - \sum_{i=1}^{k} \langle \mathbf{x}, \mathbf{u}_i \rangle \mathbf{u}_i, \mathbf{x} - \sum_{j=1}^{k} \langle \mathbf{x}, \mathbf{u}_j \rangle \mathbf{u}_j \right\rangle$$

$$= \|\mathbf{x}\|^2 - 2 \sum_{j=1}^{k} |\langle \mathbf{x}, \mathbf{u}_j \rangle|^2 + \sum_{i,j=1}^{k} \langle \mathbf{x}, \mathbf{u}_j \rangle \langle \mathbf{x}, \mathbf{u}_i \rangle_2 \langle \mathbf{u}_i, \mathbf{u}_j \rangle$$

$$= \|\mathbf{x}\|^2 - \sum_{j=1}^{k} |\langle \mathbf{x}, \mathbf{u}_j \rangle|^2 \le \|\mathbf{x}\|^2 - \sum_{j=1}^{k} |\langle \mathbf{x}, \mathbf{u}_j \rangle|^2 + \sum_{j=1}^{k} (\langle \mathbf{x}, \mathbf{u}_j \rangle - \alpha_j)^2$$

$$= \|\mathbf{x}\|^2 - 2 \sum_{j=1}^{k} \alpha_j \langle \mathbf{x}, \mathbf{u}_j \rangle + \sum_{j=1}^{k} \alpha_j^2 \langle \mathbf{u}_j, \mathbf{u}_j \rangle$$

$$= \left\| \mathbf{x} - \sum_{j=1}^{k} \alpha_j \mathbf{u}_j \right\|^2.$$

This shows that $P\mathbf{x}$ from (1.5) is the unique best approximation to $\mathbf{x}$ from U.

As we already know that $P\mathbf{x}$ is also the orthogonal projection of $\mathbf{x}$ onto U, the proof is finished.   □

1.5 Singular Value Decomposition

The geometric interpretation of Proposition 1.12 is simple. The linear mapping $A : \mathbb{R}^n \to \mathbb{R}^n$, which is given by the matrix A in the standard basis, has a much simpler representation when going over to the basis consisting of the eigenvectors of A. If this basis is used in both the domain and the range of the mapping then it can be represented by the diagonal matrix D. While the simplicity of this representation is indeed appealing, it is not possible to find such a simple representation for all matrices $A \in \mathbb{R}^{n \times n}$ let alone for non-square matrices $A \in \mathbb{R}^{m \times n}$. However, if we relax the requirement of using the same orthogonal basis in the domain and the range, i.e. in $\mathbb{R}^n$ and $\mathbb{R}^m$, to represent the mapping, we can find a similarly simple representation. This is the so-called *singular value decomposition*, which we want to discuss now.

To understand it, we need to recall a few more facts from linear algebra. We already introduced the rank and null space of a matrix. We also need the intrinsic, well-known relations

$$n = \dim \ker(A) + \mathrm{rank}(A), \qquad \mathrm{rank}(A) = \mathrm{rank}(A^\mathrm{T}). \qquad (1.6)$$

Note that an element $\mathbf{x} \in \ker(A)$ satisfies $A\mathbf{x} = \mathbf{0}$ and hence also $A^\mathrm{T}A\mathbf{x} = \mathbf{0}$, i.e. it belongs to $\ker(A^\mathrm{T}A)$. If, on the other hand $\mathbf{x} \in \ker(A^\mathrm{T}A)$ then $A^\mathrm{T}A\mathbf{x} = \mathbf{0}$, thus $0 = \mathbf{x}^\mathrm{T}(A^\mathrm{T}A\mathbf{x}) = \|A\mathbf{x}\|_2^2$ and hence $\mathbf{x} \in \ker(A)$. This means

$$\ker(A) = \ker(A^\mathrm{T}A).$$

Similarly, we can easily see that $\ker(A^\mathrm{T}) = \ker(AA^\mathrm{T})$. Hence, the dimension formula above immediately gives

$$\mathrm{rank}(A) = \mathrm{rank}(A^\mathrm{T}) = \mathrm{rank}(A^\mathrm{T}A) = \mathrm{rank}(AA^\mathrm{T}).$$

This means that the symmetric and positive semi-definite matrices $A^\mathrm{T}A \in \mathbb{R}^{n \times n}$ and $AA^\mathrm{T} \in \mathbb{R}^{m \times m}$ have the same rank.

As before, we choose for $A^\mathrm{T}A$ a system of eigenvalues $\lambda_1 \geq \lambda_2 \geq \cdots \geq \lambda_n \geq 0$ and associated eigenvectors $\mathbf{v}_1, \ldots, \mathbf{v}_n \in \mathbb{R}^n$ satisfying $A^\mathrm{T}A\mathbf{v}_j = \lambda_j\mathbf{v}_j$ and $\mathbf{v}_j^\mathrm{T}\mathbf{v}_k = \delta_{jk}$. Exactly the first $r = \mathrm{rank}(A)$ eigenvalues are positive and the remaining ones are zero.

According to the considerations we just made, also the matrix AA^T must have exactly r positive eigenvalues. We will now see that, interestingly, the positive eigenvalues of AA^T are exactly the positive eigenvalues of $A^\mathrm{T}A$ and that there is a very simple connection between the corresponding eigenvectors. To see this, let us define

$$\sigma_j := \sqrt{\lambda_j}, \qquad 1 \le j \le n,$$

$$\mathbf{u}_j := \frac{1}{\sigma_j} A \mathbf{v}_j, \qquad 1 \le j \le r.$$

Then, we have on the one hand that

$$AA^T \mathbf{u}_j = \frac{1}{\sigma_j} AA^T A \mathbf{v}_j = \frac{1}{\sigma_j} \lambda_j A \mathbf{v}_j = \lambda_j \mathbf{u}_j, \qquad 1 \le j \le r.$$

On the other hand, we have that

$$\mathbf{u}_j^T \mathbf{u}_k = \frac{1}{\sigma_j \sigma_k} \mathbf{v}_j^T A^T A \mathbf{v}_k = \frac{\lambda_k}{\sigma_j \sigma_k} \mathbf{v}_j^T \mathbf{v}_k = \delta_{jk}, \qquad 1 \le j, k \le r.$$

Thus, $\mathbf{u}_1, \ldots, \mathbf{u}_r \in \mathbb{R}^m$ form an orthonormal system of eigenvectors corresponding to the eigenvalues $\lambda_1 \ge \lambda_2 \ge \cdots \ge \lambda_r > 0$ of AA^T. Since this matrix also has rank r and is positive semi-definite, all other eigenvalues have to be zero. It is now possible to complete the system $\{\mathbf{u}_1, \ldots, \mathbf{u}_r\}$ to an orthonormal basis $\{\mathbf{u}_1, \ldots, \mathbf{u}_m\}$ consisting of eigenvectors. If we define the matrices $U := (\mathbf{u}_1, \ldots, \mathbf{u}_m) \in \mathbb{R}^{m \times m}$ and $V = (\mathbf{v}_1, \ldots, \mathbf{v}_n) \in \mathbb{R}^{n \times n}$ then we have

$$A \mathbf{v}_j = \sigma_j \mathbf{u}_j, \qquad 1 \le j \le r,$$

$$A \mathbf{v}_j = \mathbf{0}, \qquad r + 1 \le j \le n,$$

by definition and by the fact that $\ker(A) = \ker(A^T A)$. This can alternatively be written as

$$AV = U\Sigma,$$

where $\Sigma = (\sigma_j \delta_{ij}) \in \mathbb{R}^{m \times n}$ is a non-square diagonal matrix. This altogether proves the following result.

Theorem 1.18 (Singular Value Decomposition (SVD)) *A matrix* $A \in \mathbb{R}^{m \times n}$ *has a* singular value decomposition $A = U\Sigma V^T$ *with orthogonal matrices* $U \in \mathbb{R}^{m \times m}$ *and* $V \in \mathbb{R}^{n \times n}$ *and a diagonal matrix* $\Sigma = (\sigma_j \delta_{ij}) \in \mathbb{R}^{m \times n}$.

Note that some of the σ_j may be zero, depending on the rank of the matrix A. If r is the rank of A, then there are exactly r non-zero and hence positive σ_j. Furthermore, the singular value decomposition is not unique. To be more precise, the matrices U and V are not unique, since we can, for example, change the sign of the columns. Moreover, if some of the σ_j have the same value, then we can choose different bases for the corresponding eigenspaces. However, the values σ_j are uniquely determined by A and thus, if we order the σ_j, then the matrix Σ is unique.

Definition 1.19 Those σ_j in the singular value decomposition which are positive are called the *singular values* of the matrix A.

Taking $r = \text{rank}(A)$ into account, we can also rewrite the representation $A = U\Sigma V^{\mathrm{T}}$ from Theorem 1.18 in the form

$$A = \sum_{j=1}^{n} \sigma_j \mathbf{u}_j \mathbf{v}_j^{\mathrm{T}} = \sum_{j=1}^{r} \sigma_j \mathbf{u}_j \mathbf{v}_j^{\mathrm{T}}.$$

Hence, if we define the matrices $\hat{U} := (\mathbf{u}_1, \ldots, \mathbf{u}_r) \in \mathbb{R}^{m \times r}$, $\hat{V} := (\mathbf{v}_1, \ldots, \mathbf{v}_r) \in \mathbb{R}^{n \times r}$ and $\hat{\Sigma} := \text{diag}(\sigma_1, \ldots, \sigma_r) \in \mathbb{R}^{r \times r}$ then we have the alternative representation

$$A = \hat{U}\hat{\Sigma}\hat{V}^{\mathrm{T}},$$

which is also called *reduced singular value decomposition* of the matrix A. Since we can also write the reduced form as $A = \hat{U}(\hat{V}\hat{\Sigma})^{\mathrm{T}}$, we have the following result.

Corollary 1.20 *Every matrix $A \in \mathbb{R}^{m \times n}$ of $\text{rank}(A) = r$ can be written in the form $A = BC^{\mathrm{T}}$ with $B \in \mathbb{R}^{m \times r}$ and $C \in \mathbb{R}^{n \times r}$.*

In particular, we see that every rank 1 matrix is necessarily of the form $\mathbf{b}\mathbf{c}^{\mathrm{T}}$ with $\mathbf{b} \in \mathbb{R}^m$ and $\mathbf{c} \in \mathbb{R}^n$.

There are efficient methods available to compute the singular value decomposition and we will discuss some of them in Section 5.7.

1.6 Pseudo-inverse

We can use the singular value decomposition to define a kind of inverse to a singular and even non-square matrix.

Definition 1.21 Let $A \in \mathbb{R}^{m \times n}$ have rank $r = \text{rank}(A)$. Let $A = U\Sigma V^{\mathrm{T}}$ be the singular value decomposition of A with orthogonal matrices $U \in \mathbb{R}^{m \times m}$, $V \in \mathbb{R}^{n \times n}$ and with $\Sigma \in \mathbb{R}^{m \times n}$ being a diagonal matrix with non-zero diagonal entries $\sigma_1 \geq \sigma_2 \geq \cdots \geq \sigma_r > 0$. Let $\Sigma^+ \in \mathbb{R}^{n \times m}$ be the matrix

$$\Sigma^+ = \begin{pmatrix} 1/\sigma_1 & & & 0 & \cdots & 0 \\ & \ddots & & \vdots & & \vdots \\ & & 1/\sigma_r & 0 & & 0 \\ 0 & \cdots & 0 & 0 & \cdots & 0 \\ \vdots & & \vdots & \vdots & & \vdots \\ 0 & \cdots & & 0 & \cdots & 0 \end{pmatrix}.$$

Then, the *pseudo-inverse* of A is defined as

$$A^+ := V\Sigma^+ U^T \in \mathbb{R}^{n \times m}. \tag{1.7}$$

We know that the singular values of a matrix $A \in \mathbb{R}^{m \times n}$ are uniquely determined. However, the orthogonal matrices U and V are not unique and hence we have to make sure that the pseudo-inverse is well-defined before we investigate its properties.

Theorem 1.22 *Let $A \in \mathbb{R}^{m \times n}$ with $r = \text{rank}(A)$.*

1. Each pseudo-inverse $A^+ \in \mathbb{R}^{n \times m}$ of A satisfies

$$AA^+ = (AA^+)^T, \quad A^+A = (A^+A)^T, \quad AA^+A = A, \quad A^+AA^+ = A^+. \tag{1.8}$$

2. The properties

$$AB = (AB)^T, \quad BA = (BA)^T, \quad ABA = A, \quad BAB = B \tag{1.9}$$

determine a matrix $B \in \mathbb{R}^{n \times m}$ uniquely. This means in particular that the pseudo-inverse is well-defined.

Proof 1. By definition of a pseudo-inverse, we have

$$AA^+ = (U\Sigma V^T)(V\Sigma^+ U^T) = U\Sigma\Sigma^+ U^T.$$

Since $\Sigma\Sigma^+ \in \mathbb{R}^{m \times m}$ is a diagonal matrix with r diagonal entries equal to 1 and $m - r$ diagonal entries equal to 0 it is obviously symmetric and hence $AA^+ = (AA^+)^T$. The equality $A^+A = (A^+A)^T$ is shown in the same way. Moreover, we have

$$AA^+A = (U\Sigma V^T)(V\Sigma^+ U^T)(U\Sigma V^T) = U\Sigma\Sigma^+\Sigma V^T = U\Sigma V^T = A$$

and $A^+AA^+ = A^+$ follows in the same way.

2. Now assume that both B and C satisfy the stated equalities (1.9). Then, we can conclude that

$$\begin{aligned}
B &= BAB = B(AB)^T = (BB^T)A^T = BB^TA^TC^TA^T = B(AB)^T(AC)^T \\
&= (BAB)AC = BAC = (BA)^TC = (BA)^T(CAC) = (BA)^T(CA)^TC \\
&= A^TB^TA^TC^TC = A^TC^TC = (CA)^TC = CAC = C.
\end{aligned}$$ □

From this we have the uniqueness of the pseudo-inverse. Moreover, we see that the pseudo-inverse is uniquely determined by the so-called *Penrose conditions* (1.9), i.e. we could have also used these conditions to define the pseudo-inverse.

Moreover, if $A \in \mathbb{R}^{n \times n}$ is invertible then $B = A^{-1}$ obviously satisfies the conditions (1.9). This means that for an invertible matrix the pseudo-inverse and the classical inverse are the same.

Finally, if $m \geq n$ and rank$(A) = n$, the following representation of the pseudo-inverse will become important later on.

Lemma 1.23 *Let $A \in \mathbb{R}^{m \times n}$ satisfy* rank$(A) = n$. *Then, the pseudo-inverse of A is given by*

$$A^+ = (A^\mathrm{T} A)^{-1} A^\mathrm{T}. \tag{1.10}$$

Proof Since $A \in \mathbb{R}^{m \times n}$ with rank$(A) = n$, we find that $A^\mathrm{T} A \in \mathbb{R}^{n \times n}$ has also rank n and is hence invertible. Thus, the expression $B := (A^\mathrm{T} A)^{-1} A^\mathrm{T}$ is well-defined. Moreover, B satisfies (1.9), since, using the symmetry of $A^\mathrm{T} A$, we have

$$(AB)^\mathrm{T} = (A(A^\mathrm{T} A)^{-1} A^\mathrm{T})^\mathrm{T} = A(A^\mathrm{T} A)^{-1} A^\mathrm{T} = AB,$$
$$(BA)^\mathrm{T} = ((A^\mathrm{T} A)^{-1} A^\mathrm{T} A)^\mathrm{T} = I^\mathrm{T} = I = (A^\mathrm{T} A)^{-1} A^\mathrm{T} A = BA,$$
$$ABA = A(A^\mathrm{T} A)^{-1} A^\mathrm{T} A = A,$$
$$BAB = ((A^\mathrm{T} A)^{-1} A^\mathrm{T})A(A^\mathrm{T} A)^{-1} A^\mathrm{T} = (A^\mathrm{T} A)^{-1} A^\mathrm{T} = B. \qquad \square$$

The pseudo-inverse will play an important role when it comes to solving and analysing least-squares problems. The next result relates the pseudo-inverse to the orthogonal projections onto the ranges of A and A^T.

Lemma 1.24 *Let $A \in \mathbb{R}^{m \times n}$ with pseudo-inverse $A^+ \in \mathbb{R}^{n \times m}$. Then,*

1. *$P := AA^+ : \mathbb{R}^m \to \mathbb{R}^m$ is the orthogonal projection onto* range(A),
2. *$P := A^+A : \mathbb{R}^n \to \mathbb{R}^n$ is the orthogonal projection onto* range(A^T).

Proof We will only prove the first statement since the proof of the second statement is very similar, as range$(A^+) = $ range(A^T).

By definition $P\mathbf{x} = A(A^+\mathbf{x}) \in $ range(A). Moreover, using the properties (1.8) we find for each $\mathbf{x} \in \mathbb{R}^m$ and $\mathbf{u} = A\mathbf{v} \in $ range(A) that

$$\langle \mathbf{x} - P\mathbf{x}, \mathbf{u} \rangle_2 = \langle \mathbf{x} - P\mathbf{x}, A\mathbf{v} \rangle_2 = \mathbf{v}^\mathrm{T} A^\mathrm{T}(\mathbf{x} - AA^+\mathbf{x})$$
$$= \mathbf{v}^\mathrm{T}[A^\mathrm{T}\mathbf{x} - A^\mathrm{T}(AA^+)^\mathrm{T}\mathbf{x}] = \mathbf{v}^\mathrm{T}[A^\mathrm{T}\mathbf{x} - (AA^+A)^\mathrm{T}\mathbf{x}]$$
$$= \mathbf{v}^\mathrm{T}[A^\mathrm{T}\mathbf{x} - A^\mathrm{T}\mathbf{x}] = 0,$$

which shows that $P\mathbf{x} = AA^+\mathbf{x}$ is indeed the orthogonal projection of $\mathbf{x}$ onto range(A). $\qquad \square$

Exercises

1.1 Let V be a pre-Hilbert space. Use $0 \leq \langle \alpha \mathbf{x} + \beta \mathbf{y}, \alpha \mathbf{x} + \beta \mathbf{y} \rangle$ for $\alpha, \beta \in \mathbb{R}$ and $\mathbf{x}, \mathbf{y} \in V$ to prove the Cauchy–Schwarz inequality.

1.2 Let V be a normed space with norm $\| \cdot \| : V \to \mathbb{R}$. Show that V is a pre-Hilbert space and that the norm comes from an inner product $\langle \cdot, \cdot \rangle$: $V \times V \to \mathbb{R}$ if and only if the *parallelogram equality*

$$\|\mathbf{x} + \mathbf{y}\|^2 + \|\mathbf{x} - \mathbf{y}\|^2 = 2\|\mathbf{x}\|^2 + 2\|\mathbf{y}\|^2, \qquad \mathbf{x}, \mathbf{y} \in V$$

holds and that in this case the inner product satisfies

$$\langle \mathbf{x}, \mathbf{y} \rangle = \frac{1}{4} \left[\|\mathbf{x} + \mathbf{y}\|^2 - \|\mathbf{x} - \mathbf{y}\|^2 \right], \qquad \mathbf{x}, \mathbf{y} \in V.$$

1.3 Let V be a pre-Hilbert space. Show that the norm induced by the inner product satisfies $\|\mathbf{x} + \mathbf{y}\| < 2$ for all $\mathbf{x} \neq \mathbf{y} \in V$ with $\|\mathbf{x}\| = \|\mathbf{y}\| = 1$.

1.4 Let $A \in \mathbb{R}^{n \times n}$ be symmetric and positive definite and let $C \in \mathbb{R}^{n \times m}$. Show:

1. the matrix $C^T A C$ is positive semi-definite,
2. $\mathrm{rank}(C^T A C) = \mathrm{rank}(C)$,
3. the matrix $C^T A C$ is positive definite if and only if $\mathrm{rank}(C) = m$.

1.5 Show that a matrix $A \in \mathbb{R}^{n \times n}$ is symmetric and positive definite if and only if it is of the form $A = BB^T$ with an invertible matrix $B \in \mathbb{R}^{n \times n}$.

1.6 Let $A, B, C \in \mathbb{R}^{2 \times 2}$ with $C = AB$. Let

$$
\begin{aligned}
p &= (a_{11} + a_{22})(b_{11} + b_{22}), & q &= (a_{21} + a_{22})b_{11}, \\
r &= a_{11}(b_{12} - b_{22}), & s &= a_{22}(b_{21} - b_{11}), \\
t &= (a_{11} + a_{12})b_{22}, & u &= (a_{21} - a_{11})(b_{11} + b_{12}), \\
v &= (a_{12} - a_{22})(b_{21} + b_{22}). &
\end{aligned}
$$

Show that the elements of C can then be computed via

$$
\begin{aligned}
c_{11} &= p + s - t + v, & c_{12} &= r + t, \\
c_{21} &= q + s, & c_{22} &= p + r - q + u.
\end{aligned}
$$

Compare the number of multiplications and additions for this method with the number of multiplications and additions for the standard method of multiplying two 2×2 matrices.

Finally, show that if the above method is recursively applied to matrices $A, B \in \mathbb{R}^{n \times n}$ with $n = 2^k$ then the method requires 7^k multiplications and $6 \cdot 7^k - 6 \cdot 2^{2k}$ additions and subtractions.

2

Error, Stability and Conditioning

2.1 Floating Point Arithmetic

Since computers use a finite number of bits to represent a real number, they can only represent a finite subset of the real numbers. In general the range of numbers is sufficiently large but there are naturally gaps, which might lead to problems.

Hence, it is time to discuss the representation of a number in a computer. We are used to representing a number in digits, i.e.

$$105.67 = 1000 \cdot 0.10567 = +10^3(1 \cdot 10^{-1} + 0 \cdot 10^{-2} + 5 \cdot 10^{-3} + 6 \cdot 10^{-4} + 7 \cdot 10^{-5}).$$

However, there is no need to represent numbers with respect to base 10. A more general representation is the B-adic representation.

Definition 2.1 A *B-adic, normalised floating point number of precision m* is either $x = 0$ or

$$x = \pm B^e \sum_{k=-m}^{-1} x_k B^k, \qquad x_{-1} \neq 0, \quad x_k \in \{0, 1, 2, \ldots, B - 1\}.$$

Here, e denotes the *exponent* within a given range $e_{\min} \leq e \leq e_{\max}$, $B \geq 2$ is the *base* and $\sum x_k B_k$ denotes the *mantissa*.
The corresponding *floating point number system* consists of all of the numbers which can be represented in this form.

For a computer, the different ways of representing a number, like single and double precision, are defined by the IEEE 754 norm and we will also refer to them as *machine numbers*.
For example, the IEEE 754 norm states that for a double precision number we have $B = 2$ and $m = 52$. Hence, if one bit is used to store the sign and if 11 bits are reserved for representing the exponent, a double precision number

30

can be stored in 64 bits. In this case, the IEEE 754 norm defines the following additional values:

- $\pm Inf$ for $\pm\infty$ as the result of dividing positive or negative numbers by zero, for the evaluation of log(0) and for *overflow* errors, meaning results which would require an exponent outside the range $[e_{\min}, e_{\max}]$.
- *NaN* (not a number) for undefined numbers as they, for example, occur when dividing 0 by 0 or evaluating the logarithm for a negative number.

As a consequence, the distribution of floating point numbers is not uniform. Furthermore, every real number and the result of every operation has to be rounded. There are different rounding strategies, but the default one is rounding x to the nearest machine number rd(x).

Definition 2.2 The *machine precision*, eps, is the smallest number which satisfies

$$|x - \text{rd}(x)| \leq \text{eps}|x|$$

for all $x \in \mathbb{R}$ within the range of the floating point system.

Another way of expressing this is that for such x there is an $\epsilon \in \mathbb{R}$ with $|\epsilon| \leq$ eps and rd(x) = $(1 + \epsilon)x$.

It is easy to determine the machine precision for the default rounding strategy.

Theorem 2.3 *For a floating point number system with base B and precision m the machine precision is given by* eps = B^{1-m}, *i.e. we have*

$$|x - \text{rd}(x)| \leq |x|B^{1-m}.$$

Proof For every real number x in the range of the floating point system there exists an integer e between $e_{\min}$ and $e_{\max}$ such that

$$x = \pm B^e \sum_{k=-\infty}^{-1} x_k B^k = \pm B^e \sum_{k=-m}^{-1} x_k B^k \pm B^e \sum_{k=-\infty}^{-m-1} x_k B^k = \text{rd}(x) + (x - \text{rd}(x)).$$

Hence, we have

$$|x - \text{rd}(x)| \leq B^e \sum_{k=-\infty}^{-m-1} x_k B^k \leq B^e \sum_{k=-\infty}^{-m-1} (B-1)B^k = B^{e-m}.$$

However, as $x_{-1} \neq 0$, we also have $|x| \geq B^e B^{-1} = B^{e-1}$ such that

$$\frac{|x - \text{rd}(x)|}{|x|} \leq B^{e-m-e+1}. \qquad \square$$

Note that for $B = 2$ and $m = 52$ this means eps $= 2^{-51} \approx 4.4409 \cdot 10^{-16}$, giving the precision of real numbers stored in a 64-bit floating point system.

Since numbers are usually provided in decimal form, they must be converted to the B-adic form for their representation within the computer, which usually differs from the original number. Even if then all computations are done in exact arithmetic, this *input error* cannot be avoided.

However, the limitation of the floating point system also means that standard operations like adding, subtracting, multiplying and dividing two machine numbers will not result in a machine number and hence the results have to be rounded again. The best we can hope for is that the result of such an elementary operation is given by the rounded number of the exact result of such an operation, i.e., for example, $\mathrm{rd}(x + y)$ instead of $\mathrm{rd}(\mathrm{rd}(x) + \mathrm{rd}(y))$. The IEEE 754 norm guarantees that this is indeed the case and not only for adding, subtracting, multiplying and dividing but also in the case of evaluating standard functions like $\sqrt{x}$, $\sin(x)$, $\log(x)$ and $\exp(x)$. This can be reformulated as follows.

Theorem 2.4 *Let $*$ be one of the operations $+, -, \cdot, /$ and let $\circledast$ be the equivalent floating point operation, then for all x, y from the floating point system, there exists an $\epsilon \in \mathbb{R}$ with $|\epsilon| \le$ eps such that*

$$x \circledast y = (x * y)(1 + \epsilon).$$

2.2 Norms for Vectors and Matrices

In this section we will study norms for vectors and matrices in greater detail, as these norms are essential for analysing the stability and conditioning of a linear system and any method for solving it.

We start with the following example.

Example 2.5 (Matrix–vector multiplication)   Let us consider the goal of multiplying a matrix $A \in \mathbb{R}^{n \times n}$ with a vector $\mathbf{x} \in \mathbb{R}^n$. Let us assume, however, that the data given is inexact, for example, because it contains noise from measurements or because the representation of the real numbers on the computer causes rounding errors. For simplicity and for the time being, we will still assume that the matrix $A \in \mathbb{R}^{n \times n}$ is exactly given but that the vector $\mathbf{x}$ is given as something of the form $\mathbf{x} + \Delta \mathbf{x}$, where $\Delta \mathbf{x}$ is a vector with, one hopes, small entries representing the error. Hence, instead of computing $\mathbf{b} := A\mathbf{x}$ we are computing $(\mathbf{b} + \Delta \mathbf{b}) = A(\mathbf{x} + \Delta \mathbf{x})$ with $\Delta \mathbf{b} = A\Delta \mathbf{x}$ and we have to analyse the error $\Delta \mathbf{b}$ in the output.

To achieve the goal of this example, we have to introduce a few theoretical concepts. We need to know how to "measure". After that we will subsequently come back to this introductory example. Let us recall Definition 1.6, the definition of a norm on a linear space V as a mapping $\| \cdot \| : V \to [0, \infty)$ satisfying

1. homogeneity: $\|\lambda \mathbf{x}\| = |\lambda| \|\mathbf{x}\|$ for all $\mathbf{x} \in V$ and $\lambda \in \mathbb{R}$,
2. definiteness: $\|\mathbf{x}\| = 0$ if and only if $\mathbf{x} = \mathbf{0}$,
3. triangle inequality: $\|\mathbf{x} + \mathbf{y}\| \leq \|\mathbf{x}\| + \|\mathbf{y}\|$ for all $\mathbf{x}, \mathbf{y} \in V$.

The norm of a vector allows us to measure the length of it. In particular, a *unit vector* with respect to a norm $\| \cdot \|$ is a vector $\mathbf{x} \in V$ with $\|\mathbf{x}\| = 1$.
From basic courses on Analysis and Linear Algebra, the reader should know the following list of standard norms on $\mathbb{R}^n$.

Definition 2.6 For $1 \leq p \leq \infty$, the ℓ_p-norm on $\mathbb{R}^n$ is defined to be

- $\|\mathbf{x}\|_p := \left(\sum_{i=1}^n |x_i|^p \right)^{1/p}$ for $1 \leq p < \infty$,
- $\|\mathbf{x}\|_\infty := \max_{1 \leq i \leq n} |x_i|$.

Besides the ℓ_∞-norm, the ℓ_2-norm or Euclidean norm and the ℓ_1-norm are the most popular ones:

$$\|\mathbf{x}\|_1 := \sum_{i=1}^n |x_i|, \qquad \|\mathbf{x}\|_2 := \left(\sum_{i=1}^n |x_i|^2 \right)^{1/2}.$$

It is quite easy to verify that $\| \cdot \|_1$ and $\| \cdot \|_\infty$ are indeed norms. For $\| \cdot \|_2$ and more generally $\| \cdot \|_p$ the first and second properties of a norm are also easily verified. The triangle inequality, however, requires more work and needs the *Cauchy–Schwarz* or more generally the *Hölder inequality*

$$\sum_{j=1}^n |x_j y_j| \leq \|\mathbf{x}\|_p \|\mathbf{y}\|_q, \qquad \mathbf{x}, \mathbf{y} \in \mathbb{R}^n, \quad p, q \geq 1 \text{ with } \frac{1}{p} + \frac{1}{q} = 1. \qquad (2.1)$$

Here, the expression $1/p$ is interpreted as zero for $p = \infty$. Since this is done in basic courses on Linear Algebra and Analysis, we will assume that the reader is familiar with these facts.

Example 2.7 The unit ball with respect to the ℓ_p-norm is defined to be the set $B_p := \{\mathbf{x} \in \mathbb{R}^n : \|\mathbf{x}\|_p \leq 1\}$. For $\mathbb{R}^2$, Figure 2.1 shows B_1, B_2, B_∞.

Note that the "length" of a vector depends on the chosen norm. The choice of the norm might depend on the application one has in mind. For example, if a vector contains temperatures at a certain position at n different times, we can use the ℓ_∞-norm to determine the maximum temperature. If we are, however, interested in an average temperature, the ℓ_1- or ℓ_2-norm would be our choice.

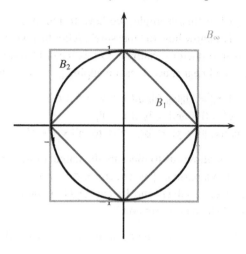

Figure 2.1 B_1, B_2 and B_∞ in $\mathbb{R}^2$.

Though we are given different norms on $\mathbb{R}^n$, the following theorem shows that these do not differ too much in a topological sense.

Theorem 2.8 *On $\mathbb{R}^n$, all norms are equivalent, i.e. for two norms $\|\cdot\|$ and $\|\cdot\|_*$ on $\mathbb{R}^n$, there are two constants $c_1, c_2 > 0$ such that*

$$c_1\|\mathbf{x}\| \leq \|\mathbf{x}\|_* \leq c_2\|\mathbf{x}\|, \qquad \mathbf{x} \in \mathbb{R}^n.$$

Proof First of all, we note that this indeed defines an equivalence relation. Hence, it suffices to show that all norms are equivalent to one specific norm, say the ℓ_1-norm.

Thus, let $\|\cdot\|$ be an arbitrary norm on $\mathbb{R}^n$. If $\mathbf{x} = (x_1, \ldots, x_n)^{\mathrm{T}}$ is a vector of $\mathbb{R}^n$, the triangle inequality yields

$$\|\mathbf{x}\| = \left\| \sum_{j=1}^{n} x_j \mathbf{e}_j \right\| \leq \sum_{j=1}^{n} |x_j| \|\mathbf{e}_j\| \leq \left(\max_{1 \leq j \leq n} \|\mathbf{e}_j\| \right) \|\mathbf{x}\|_1 =: M\|\mathbf{x}\|_1.$$

From this we can conclude that the norm $\|\cdot\|$, as a function on $\mathbb{R}^n$, is continuous with respect to the ℓ_1-norm, since we have

$$| \|\mathbf{x}\| - \|\mathbf{y}\| | \leq \|\mathbf{x} - \mathbf{y}\| \leq M\|\mathbf{x} - \mathbf{y}\|_1$$

for $\mathbf{x}, \mathbf{y} \in \mathbb{R}^n$. Since the unit sphere $K = \{\mathbf{x} \in \mathbb{R}^n : \|\mathbf{x}\|_1 = 1\}$ with respect to the ℓ_1-norm is a compact set, the continuous function $\|\cdot\|$ attains its minimum and maximum on it, i.e. there are positive constants $c \leq C$ such that

$$c \leq \|\mathbf{x}\| \leq C, \qquad \mathbf{x} \in K.$$

A simple scaling argument now shows the equivalence of the norms $\|\cdot\|$ and $\|\cdot\|_1$. □

It is sometimes good to know what the equivalence constants look like. In the case of the ℓ_p-norms, the optimal constants are well-known.

Example 2.9 For the standard ℓ_p-norms, it is not too difficult to compute the equivalence constants. For example,

$$\|\mathbf{x}\|_2 \le \|\mathbf{x}\|_1 \le \sqrt{n}\|\mathbf{x}\|_2,$$

$$\|\mathbf{x}\|_\infty \le \|\mathbf{x}\|_2 \le \sqrt{n}\|\mathbf{x}\|_\infty,$$

$$\|\mathbf{x}\|_\infty \le \|\mathbf{x}\|_1 \le n\|\mathbf{x}\|_\infty.$$

A general formula is given in the next proposition.

Proposition 2.10 *Let $\mathbf{x} \in \mathbb{R}^n$ be given. Let $1 \le p, q \le \infty$ with $\frac{1}{p} + \frac{1}{q} = 1$. If $q \ge p$ then*

$$\|\mathbf{x}\|_p \le n^{\frac{1}{p} - \frac{1}{q}}\|\mathbf{x}\|_q. \tag{2.2}$$

If $p \ge q$ then

$$\|\mathbf{x}\|_p \le \|\mathbf{x}\|_q. \tag{2.3}$$

In both cases, the constants are optimal in the sense that there is no smaller constant for which (2.2) or (2.3) holds for all $\mathbf{x} \in \mathbb{R}^n$.

Proof In the case $p = q = \infty$ both bounds are obviously true. We start with showing (2.2), i.e. we assume $q \ge p$. There is nothing to show if $\mathbf{x} = \mathbf{0}$ so we may assume $\mathbf{x} \ne \mathbf{0}$. Moreover, if $q = \infty$ and $1 \le p < \infty$ we have

$$\|\mathbf{x}\|_p^p = \sum_{j=1}^{n} |x_j|^p \le n\|\mathbf{x}\|_\infty^p,$$

which gives the result in this case. For $1 \le p \le q < \infty$, we can use Hölder's inequality with $r = q/p \ge 1$ and $s \ge 1$ with $\frac{1}{r} + \frac{1}{s} = 1$, i.e. with $s = q/(q - p)$, to derive

$$\|\mathbf{x}\|_p^p = \sum_{j=1}^{n} |x_j|^p \le \left(\sum_{j=1}^{n} 1^s\right)^{1/s} \left(\sum_{j=1}^{n} |x_j|^{pr}\right)^{1/r} = n^{1 - p/q}\|\mathbf{x}\|_q^{p/q}.$$

Taking the pth root yields the desired result. The constant is the best possible because we have equality in (2.2) for the vector $\mathbf{x} = (1, \dots, 1)^{\mathrm{T}}$.

Next, let us consider the case that $p \ge q \ge 1$. If $p = \infty$ and $q < \infty$ then we have

$$\|\mathbf{x}\|_\infty = \max_j |x_j| = \max_j (|x_j|^q)^{1/q} \le \left(\sum_{j=1}^n |x_j|^q \right)^{1/q} = \|\mathbf{x}\|_q.$$

If, however, $q \le p < \infty$, then

$$|x_j|^p = |x_j|^q |x_j|^{p-q} \le |x_j|^q \|\mathbf{x}\|_\infty^{p-q} \le |x_j|^q \|\mathbf{x}\|_q^{p-q},$$

such that

$$\|\mathbf{x}\|_p^p = \sum_{j=1}^n |x_j|^p \le \sum_{j=1}^n |x_j|^q \|\mathbf{x}\|_q^{p-q} = \|\mathbf{x}\|_q^q \|\mathbf{x}\|_q^{p-q} = \|\mathbf{x}\|_q^p,$$

which also gives the desired result. To see that this bound is also sharp, we can simply pick $\mathbf{x} = \mathbf{e}_1 = (1, 0, \ldots, 0)^T$. □

Next, we return to our initial motivational example, the analysis of a matrix–vector multiplication with a perturbed input vector, see Example 2.5.

Example 2.11 (Matrix–vector multiplication)   We are now looking again at the situation

$$\mathbf{b} := A\mathbf{x},$$
$$\mathbf{b} + \Delta\mathbf{b} := A(\mathbf{x} + \Delta\mathbf{x}).$$

We would like to have $\Delta\mathbf{b}$ be small if $\Delta\mathbf{x}$ is small. However, what does small mean? It will depend on the size of $\mathbf{x}$ and hence it makes more sense to look at the *relative errors*

$$\frac{\|\Delta\mathbf{x}\|}{\|\mathbf{x}\|}, \qquad \frac{\|\Delta\mathbf{b}\|}{\|\mathbf{b}\|},$$

provided $\mathbf{x}, \mathbf{b} \ne \mathbf{0}$.

Let us assume that we have fixed a norm on $\mathbb{R}^n$ and that there are two constants $c_1 > 0$ and $c_2 > 0$ such that

$$c_1 \|\mathbf{x}\| \le \|A\mathbf{x}\| \le c_2 \|\mathbf{x}\|, \qquad \mathbf{x} \in \mathbb{R}^n. \tag{2.4}$$

The left inequality guarantees that A is injective and hence, as a square matrix, bijective, i.e. invertible. Under these assumptions we have

$$\frac{\|\Delta\mathbf{b}\|}{\|\mathbf{b}\|} = \frac{\|A(\mathbf{x} + \Delta\mathbf{x}) - A\mathbf{x}\|}{\|A\mathbf{x}\|} = \frac{\|A\Delta\mathbf{x}\|}{\|A\mathbf{x}\|} \le \frac{c_2}{c_1} \frac{\|\Delta\mathbf{x}\|}{\|\mathbf{x}\|}. \tag{2.5}$$

This means that the relative input error $\frac{\|\Delta\mathbf{x}\|}{\|\mathbf{x}\|}$ is "magnified" by the factor c_2/c_1 in the relative output error. If this factor is large, we have to expect large relative output errors even for small relative input errors.

So far, the findings for our matrix–vector multiplication example have been for square matrices. However, a thorough inspection of what we have just outlined shows that particularly (2.5) remains true as long as (2.4) holds. We will see that the latter also holds for non-square matrices $A \in \mathbb{R}^{m \times n}$ as long as A is injective, which means that we need $m \geq n$ and $\text{rank}(A) = n$.

It is now time to describe a systematic way of handling the constants c_2 and c_1 from above by introducing matrix norms.

Since the space of all $m \times n$ matrices forms a vector space by adding two matrices component-wise and multiplying a matrix by a scalar also component-wise, we already know what a norm on the space of matrices is. However, in this context it is important how matrix norms interact with vector norms.

Definition 2.12 Given vector norms $\| \cdot \|_{(n)}$ and $\| \cdot \|_{(m)}$ on $\mathbb{R}^n$ and $\mathbb{R}^m$, respectively, we say that a matrix norm $\| \cdot \|_*$ is *compatible* with these vector norms if

$$\|A\mathbf{x}\|_{(m)} \leq \|A\|_* \|\mathbf{x}\|_{(n)}, \qquad \mathbf{x} \in \mathbb{R}^n.$$

A matrix norm will be called *compatible* if there are two vector norms so that the matrix norm is compatible with these vector norms.

We define the *subordinate or induced matrix norm* with respect to the above vector norms as

$$\|A\|_{(m,n)} := \sup_{\substack{\mathbf{x} \in \mathbb{R}^n \\ \mathbf{x} \neq 0}} \frac{\|A\mathbf{x}\|_{(m)}}{\|\mathbf{x}\|_{(n)}}.$$

Obviously, for any $\mathbf{x} \in \mathbb{R}^n, \mathbf{x} \neq \mathbf{0}$ we have by definition

$$\|A\|_{(m,n)} \geq \frac{\|A\mathbf{x}\|_{(m)}}{\|\mathbf{x}\|_{(n)}}$$

or

$$\|A\mathbf{x}\|_{(m)} \leq \|A\|_{(m,n)} \|\mathbf{x}\|_{(n)},$$

which shows that every induced matrix norm is compatible with the vector norms used in its definition.

Theorem 2.13 *The induced matrix norm is indeed a norm. It is the "smallest" compatible matrix norm.*

Proof First of all, we notice that using the third property of a norm and the linearity of A yields

$$\|A\|_{(m,n)} = \sup_{\substack{\mathbf{x} \in \mathbb{R}^n \\ \mathbf{x} \neq 0}} \frac{\|A\mathbf{x}\|_{(m)}}{\|\mathbf{x}\|_{(n)}} = \sup_{\substack{\mathbf{x} \in \mathbb{R}^n \\ \mathbf{x} \neq 0}} \left\| A \left(\frac{\mathbf{x}}{\|\mathbf{x}\|_{(n)}} \right) \right\|_{(m)} = \sup_{\|\mathbf{x}\|_{(n)} = 1} \|A\mathbf{x}\|_{(m)}.$$

Since $\mathbf{x} \mapsto \|A\mathbf{x}\|_{(m)}$ is a continuous function it attains its maximum on the compact set $\{\mathbf{x} : \|\mathbf{x}\|_{(n)} = 1\}$. This means that there is an $\mathbf{x}_0 \in \mathbb{R}^n$ with $\|\mathbf{x}_0\|_{(n)} = 1$ and

$$\|A\|_{(m,n)} = \|A\mathbf{x}_0\|_{(m)} \qquad (2.6)$$

such that the induced norm is well-defined. The three norm properties now easily follow from the fact that $\|\cdot\|_{(m)}$ is a norm and that A is linear.

Finally, we have already noticed that the induced matrix norm is compatible. It is the smallest compatible norm in the sense that there is a vector $\mathbf{x} \in \mathbb{R}^n$ with

$$\|A\mathbf{x}\|_{(m)} = \|A\|_{(m,n)}\|\mathbf{x}\|_{(n)},$$

which simply follows from (2.6).   □

In many cases, we will suppress index notation and simply write $\|A\|$, when the chosen norm is not relevant or obvious from the context.

In many situations, the following concept will turn out useful.

Definition 2.14 Let $\|\cdot\|_{m \times n}$, $\|\cdot\|_{n \times p}$ and $\|\cdot\|_{m \times p}$ denote norms on the matrix spaces $\mathbb{R}^{m \times n}$, $\mathbb{R}^{n \times p}$ and $\mathbb{R}^{m \times p}$, respectively. Such norms are called *multiplicative* if they satisfy

$$\|AB\|_{m \times p} \leq \|A\|_{m \times n}\|B\|_{n \times p}, \qquad A \in \mathbb{R}^{m \times n}, B \in \mathbb{R}^{n \times p}.$$

Lemma 2.15 *Let $\|\cdot\|_{(m)}$, $\|\cdot\|_{(n)}$ and $\|\cdot\|_{(p)}$ denote vector norms on $\mathbb{R}^n$, $\mathbb{R}^m$ and $\mathbb{R}^p$, respectively. Then, the induced matrix norms satisfy*

$$\|AB\|_{(m,p)} \leq \|A\|_{(m,n)}\|B\|_{(n,p)}$$

for all $A \in \mathbb{R}^{m \times n}$ and $B \in \mathbb{R}^{n \times p}$, i.e. induced matrix norms are always multiplicative. The same is true for compatible matrix norms.

Proof With $\mathbf{x} \in \mathbb{R}^p$ we have $B\mathbf{x} \in \mathbb{R}^n$ and $AB\mathbf{x} \in \mathbb{R}^m$ and hence

$$\|AB\mathbf{x}\|_{(m)} \leq \|A\|_{(m,n)}\|B\mathbf{x}\|_{(n)} \leq \|A\|_{(m,n)}\|B\|_{(n,p)}\|\mathbf{x}\|_{(p)},$$

which immediately gives the stated inequality. As the above inequality holds also for compatible matrix norms, such norms are also multiplicative.   □

Coming back to our example of matrix–vector multiplication, see Example 2.5 and Example 2.11, we can now give bounds for the constants c_1 and c_2 in (2.4).

Example 2.16 (Matrix–vector multiplication) The constant c_2 in (2.4) can obviously be chosen to be $c_2 = \|A\|$. For the constant c_1 we note that

$$\|\mathbf{x}\| = \|A^{-1}A\mathbf{x}\| \leq \|A^{-1}\|\|A\mathbf{x}\|.$$

Hence, c_1 can be chosen to be $c_1 = 1/\|A^{-1}\|$. Thus (2.5) becomes

$$\frac{\|\Delta \mathbf{b}\|}{\|\mathbf{b}\|} \leq \|A\| \|A^{-1}\| \frac{\|\Delta \mathbf{x}\|}{\|\mathbf{x}\|}. \tag{2.7}$$

The number $\|A\| \|A^{-1}\|$ which can be assigned to any square, invertible matrix $A \in \mathbb{R}^{n \times n}$ plays an important role in the upcoming analysis of algorithms and methods.

Definition 2.17 The number $\kappa(A) := \|A\| \|A^{-1}\|$ is called the *condition number* of the invertible matrix $A \in \mathbb{R}^{n \times n}$.

With this definition, (2.7) means that the condition number of the matrix gives the maximum factor by which the relative input error can be enlarged. Hence, we want to have a condition number as small as possible to ensure that the relative output error is of the same size as the relative input error. Note, however, that for every compatible matrix norm we have

$$\|\mathbf{x}\| = \|I\mathbf{x}\| \leq \|I\| \|\mathbf{x}\|,$$

meaning $\|I\| \geq 1$. If the norm is induced, we obviously even have $\|I\| = 1$. In any case, we can conclude that

$$1 \leq \|I\| = \|AA^{-1}\| \leq \|A\| \|A^{-1}\| = \kappa(A)$$

for every compatible matrix norm.

Proposition 2.18 *For every compatible matrix norm $\| \cdot \|$, the condition number satisfies $\kappa(A) \geq 1$ for every $A \in \mathbb{R}^{n \times n}$ invertible. If the matrix norm is induced, then we also have $\|I\| = 1$ if I is the identity matrix.*

The condition number obviously depends on the matrix norm used. But since we can identify the space of all $m \times n$ matrices with $\mathbb{R}^{m \cdot n}$, we see that also all matrix norms are equivalent and so are the different condition numbers.

Hence, our conclusion so far is that for matrix–vector multiplications a large condition number of the matrix is extremely problematic when it comes to propagating input or rounding errors. So far, we were only able to draw this conclusion for square, invertible matrices. Soon, we will return to our matrix–vector multiplication example for non-square matrices and generalise the concept of the condition number.

The induced norms, which are what we are mostly interested in, are given by the standard ℓ_p vector norms defined previously. Hence, for $1 \leq p \leq \infty$ we define the induced matrix p-norm by

$$\|A\|_p = \sup_{\mathbf{x} \neq 0} \frac{\|A\mathbf{x}\|_p}{\|\mathbf{x}\|_p}. \tag{2.8}$$

This expression is of course only of limited use if we cannot really compute the matrix norm explicitly. Fortunately, this is in the most important cases possible. The proof of the following theorem uses the fact that the induced matrix norm is the smallest compatible norm. If we want to show that the induced matrix norm $\|A\|$ equals a certain number C then we only have to show that $\|A\mathbf{x}\| \leq C\|\mathbf{x}\|$ for all $\mathbf{x} \in \mathbb{R}^n$ and that there is at least one $\mathbf{x} \in \mathbb{R}^n$ with $\|A\mathbf{x}\| = C\|\mathbf{x}\|$.

Theorem 2.19 *Let $A \in \mathbb{R}^{m \times n}$ and let $\lambda_1 \geq 0$ be the largest eigenvalue of $A^T A$. Then*

$$\|A\|_1 = \max_{1 \leq j \leq n} \sum_{i=1}^{m} |a_{ij}|, \tag{2.9}$$

$$\|A\|_2 = \sqrt{\lambda_1}, \tag{2.10}$$

$$\|A\|_\infty = \max_{1 \leq i \leq m} \sum_{j=1}^{n} |a_{ij}|. \tag{2.11}$$

Proof Let us first consider the 1-norm of a matrix $A \in \mathbb{R}^{m \times n}$. For every $\mathbf{x} \in \mathbb{R}^n$ we have

$$\|A\mathbf{x}\|_1 = \sum_{i=1}^{m} |(A\mathbf{x})_i| = \sum_{i=1}^{m} \left| \sum_{j=1}^{n} a_{ij} x_j \right| \leq \sum_{i=1}^{m} \sum_{j=1}^{n} |a_{ij}||x_j|$$

$$= \sum_{j=1}^{n} \left(\sum_{i=1}^{m} |a_{ij}| \right) |x_j| \leq \left(\max_{1 \leq j \leq n} \sum_{i=1}^{m} |a_{ij}| \right) \sum_{j=1}^{n} |x_j| =: C\|\mathbf{x}\|_1,$$

showing that $\|A\|_1 \leq C$. Next, let us pick an index k such that $C = \sum_{i=1}^{m} |a_{ik}|$ and $\mathbf{x} = \mathbf{e}_k$ the kth unit vector. Then, we have $\|\mathbf{x}\|_1 = 1$ and

$$\|A\mathbf{x}\|_1 = \|A\mathbf{e}_k\|_1 = \sum_{i=1}^{m} |(A\mathbf{e}_k)_i| = \sum_{i=1}^{m} |a_{ik}| = C,$$

which shows $\|A\|_1 = C$.

In the case of the 2-norm of a matrix $A \in \mathbb{R}^{m \times n}$, we have

$$\|A\mathbf{x}\|_2^2 = \mathbf{x}^T A^T A \mathbf{x}.$$

Since, $A^T A \in \mathbb{R}^{n \times n}$ is symmetric and positive semi-definite there are n orthonormal eigenvectors, $\{\mathbf{z}_i\}_{i=1}^n$ corresponding to the real, non-negative eigenvalues $\lambda_1 \geq \lambda_2 \geq \cdots \geq \lambda_n \geq 0$ of $A^T A$.

Let $\mathbf{x} = \alpha_1 \mathbf{z}_1 + \cdots + \alpha_n \mathbf{z}_n$ so that $\|\mathbf{x}\|_2^2 = \mathbf{x}^T \mathbf{x} = |\alpha_1|^2 + \cdots + |\alpha_n|^2$. Furthermore,

$$\mathbf{x}^T A^T A \mathbf{x} = \lambda_1 |\alpha_1|^2 + \cdots + \lambda_n |\alpha_n|^2 \leq \lambda_1 \mathbf{x}^T \mathbf{x}. \tag{2.12}$$

Hence we have $\|A\|_2^2 \leq \lambda_1$. Finally, choosing $\mathbf{x} = \mathbf{z}_1$ gives equality in (2.12), which shows $\|A\|_2^2 = \lambda_1$.

Finally, for the ∞-norm we have

$$\|A\|_\infty = \max_{\|\mathbf{x}\|_\infty = 1} \|A\mathbf{x}\|_\infty = \max_{\|\mathbf{x}\|_\infty = 1} \max_{1 \le i \le m} \left| \sum_{j=1}^{n} a_{ij} x_j \right|$$

$$\le \max_{1 \le i \le m} \sum_{j=1}^{n} |a_{ij}| = \sum_{j=1}^{n} |a_{kj}|,$$

for some k. To show that this upper bound is also attained we may choose $\mathbf{x} \in \mathbb{R}^n$ with

$$x_j = \begin{cases} \frac{a_{kj}}{|a_{kj}|} & \text{if } a_{kj} \ne 0, \\ 0 & \text{else} \end{cases}$$

to obtain it. $\qquad\qquad\square$

Another way of expressing the result for the Euclidean norm is to use the singular values of the matrix, see Definition 1.19. The singular values $\sigma_1 \ge \sigma_2 \ge \cdots \ge \sigma_r$ with $r = \text{rank}(A) \le \min(m, n)$ of a matrix $A \in \mathbb{R}^{m \times n}$ are the positive square roots of the positive eigenvalues of $A^T A$. Hence, we have $\|A\|_2 = \sigma_1$, i.e. $\|A\|_2$ is given by the largest singular value of A. This is the first half of the following corollary.

Corollary 2.20 *Let $A \in \mathbb{R}^{m \times n}$ have the singular values $\sigma_1 \ge \sigma_2 \ge \cdots \ge \sigma_r$ with $r = \text{rank}(A) \le \min(m, n)$. Then, we have $\|A\|_2 = \sigma_1$. Moreover, if $m \ge n$ and A has full rank $r = n$, then we have*

$$\|A\mathbf{x}\|_2 \ge \sigma_n \|\mathbf{x}\|_2, \qquad \mathbf{x} \in \mathbb{R}^n.$$

Proof The second statement follows immediately from the representation (2.12). $\qquad\qquad\square$

Another consequence is that for symmetric matrices, the norm can directly be computed from the eigenvalues of A rather than those of $A^T A$.

Corollary 2.21 *Let $A \in \mathbb{R}^{n \times n}$ be symmetric. Then we have $\|A\|_2 = |\lambda_1|$ if $\lambda_1, \ldots, \lambda_n$ are the eigenvalues of A ordered so that $|\lambda_1| \ge |\lambda_2| \ge \cdots \ge |\lambda_n|$. Moreover, if $A \in \mathbb{R}^{n \times n}$ is of the form $A = C^T C$ with $C \in \mathbb{R}^{n \times n}$ then $\|A\|_2 = \|C\|_2^2$.*

Proof Since $A \in \mathbb{R}^{n \times n}$ is symmetric, there is an orthogonal matrix $U \in \mathbb{R}^{n \times n}$ such that $A = UDU^T$ with D being a diagonal matrix with the eigenvalues of A as diagonal entries. From this we can conclude that $A^T A = UD^2 U^T$. Hence, the eigenvalues of $A^T A$ are the squares of the eigenvalues of A. Finally, if $A = C^T C$ then we have just proven that $\|A\|_2 = \|C^T C\|_2$ is given by the largest eigenvalue of $C^T C$. But Theorem 2.19 tells us that the square root of the largest eigenvalue of $C^T C$ is just $\|C\|_2$. Hence, we have $\|A\|_2 = \|C\|_2^2$. □

Yet another way of computing the 2-norm of a symmetric or normal matrix is the following one, which is based upon the so-called *Rayleigh quotient*.

Proposition 2.22 *Let $A \in \mathbb{R}^{n \times n}$ be symmetric. Then, the 2-norm is given by*

$$\|A\|_2 = \sup_{\|\mathbf{x}\|_2 = 1} |\langle A\mathbf{x}, \mathbf{x} \rangle_2|.$$

Proof As in the last corollary, we can pick an orthogonal matrix $U \in \mathbb{R}^{n \times n}$ such that $A = UDU^T$ with $D \in \mathbb{R}^{n \times n}$ containing the eigenvalues $\lambda_1, \ldots, \lambda_n \in \mathbb{R}$ of A, sorted such that $|\lambda_1| \geq \cdots \geq |\lambda_n|$. Then, as in the corollary, we have $\|A\|_2 = |\lambda_1|$. However, we also have $|\langle A\mathbf{x}, \mathbf{x} \rangle_2| \leq \|A\mathbf{x}\|_2 \|\mathbf{x}\|_2 \leq \|A\|_2$ for all $\mathbf{x} \in \mathbb{R}^n$ with $\|\mathbf{x}\|_2 = 1$ and if $\mathbf{v} \in \mathbb{R}^n$ denotes a normalised eigenvector of A to the eigenvalue λ_1 then $|\langle A\mathbf{v}, \mathbf{v} \rangle_2| = |\langle \lambda_1 \mathbf{v}, \mathbf{v} \rangle_2| = |\lambda_1|$, which shows

$$\|A\|_2 = |\langle A\mathbf{v}, \mathbf{v} \rangle_2| \leq \sup_{\|\mathbf{x}\|_2 = 1} |\langle A\mathbf{x}, \mathbf{x} \rangle_2| \leq \|A\|_2,$$

i.e. the stated result. □

The above result shows that if A is symmetric and positive semi-definite then its largest eigenvalue $\lambda_{\max}$ is given by

$$\lambda_{\max} = \sup_{\|\mathbf{x}\|_2 = 1} \langle A\mathbf{x}, \mathbf{x} \rangle_2.$$

However, the ideas used in Proposition 2.22 can also be used to show that the smallest eigenvalue $\lambda_{\min}$ of a symmetric and positive (semi-)definite matrix A is given by

$$\lambda_{\min} = \inf_{\|\mathbf{x}\|_2 = 1} \langle A\mathbf{x}, \mathbf{x} \rangle_2. \tag{2.13}$$

This follows directly with the notation of the proof by noting that

$$\langle A\mathbf{x}, \mathbf{x} \rangle_2 = \mathbf{x}^T A\mathbf{x} = \mathbf{x}^T UDU^T \mathbf{x} \geq \lambda_{\min} \|U^T \mathbf{x}\|_2^2 = \lambda_{\min} \mathbf{x}^T UU^T \mathbf{x} = \lambda_{\min} \|\mathbf{x}\|_2^2,$$

where equality holds if $\mathbf{x}$ is an eigenvector of A to the eigenvalue $\lambda_{\min}$. Later on, we will generalise these results when discussing more general localisation techniques for eigenvalues.

We will now briefly motivate how to generalise the concept of the condition number to non-square matrices. We will, however, restrict ourselves to the matrix norm induced by the ℓ_2 vector norm. Moreover, for our example, we will only look at injective matrices.

Example 2.23 (Matrix–vector multiplication) Let $A \in \mathbb{R}^{m \times n}$ be given with $m \geq n = \mathrm{rank}(A)$. If we compute once again $\mathbf{b} + \Delta \mathbf{b} = A(\mathbf{x} + \Delta \mathbf{x})$ for given $\mathbf{x}, \Delta \mathbf{x} \in \mathbb{R}^n$, then the relative output error can be bounded by

$$\frac{\|\Delta \mathbf{b}\|_2}{\|\mathbf{b}\|_2} \leq \frac{\sigma_1}{\sigma_n} \frac{\|\Delta \mathbf{x}\|_2}{\|\mathbf{x}\|_2},$$

where σ_1 is the largest and σ_n is the smallest singular value of A. This follows immediately from (2.5), our earlier findings $c_2 = \|A\|_2 = \sigma_1$ and

$$c_1^2 = \inf_{\|\mathbf{x}\|_2 = 1} \|A\mathbf{x}\|_2^2 = \inf_{\|\mathbf{x}\|_2 = 1} \langle A^T A \mathbf{x}, \mathbf{x} \rangle_2 = \lambda_{\min}(A^T A) = \sigma_n^2.$$

Hence, we can generalise the condition number for a non-square matrix as follows.

Definition 2.24 Let $A \in \mathbb{R}^{m \times n}$ have the singular values $\sigma_1 \geq \sigma_2 \geq \cdots \geq \sigma_r > 0$ with $r = \mathrm{rank}(A)$. Then, the condition number of A subordinate to the ℓ_2-norm is defined to be

$$\kappa_2(A) := \frac{\sigma_1}{\sigma_r}.$$

Obviously, this definition coincides with our earlier definition in the case of a square and invertible matrix.

We also note that we have $\|A\|_2 = \sigma_1$ and, using the pseudo-inverse A^+ from (1.7), we can easily see that $\|A^+\|_2 = 1/\sigma_r$. Hence, we can express the condition number also as

$$\kappa_2(A) = \|A\|_2 \|A^+\|_2.$$

Remark 2.25 When dealing with complex-valued matrices $A \in \mathbb{C}^{n \times n}$, we can proceed in exactly the same way and introduce an induced matrix norm via

$$\|A\| := \sup_{\substack{\mathbf{x} \in \mathbb{C}^n \\ \|\mathbf{x}\| = 1}} \|A\mathbf{x}\|,$$

with $\mathbf{x} \in \mathbb{C}^n$ now. Note that if $A \in \mathbb{R}^{n \times n}$ and $\| \cdot \| : \mathbb{C}^n \to \mathbb{R}$ is a norm, then we can define an induced matrix norm over $\mathbb{R}^n$ and over $\mathbb{C}^n$. Since $\mathbb{R}^n \subseteq \mathbb{C}^n$, we obviously have

$$\|A\|^{\mathbb{R}} := \sup_{\substack{\mathbf{x} \in \mathbb{R}^n \\ \|\mathbf{x}\| = 1}} \|A\mathbf{x}\| \leq \sup_{\substack{\mathbf{x} \in \mathbb{C}^n \\ \|\mathbf{x}\| = 1}} \|A\mathbf{x}\| =: \|A\|^{\mathbb{C}}.$$

Indeed, there exist vector norms for which $\|A\|^{\mathbb{R}} < \|A\|^{\mathbb{C}}$, which we will discuss later on. Fortunately, in the case of the matrix norms (2.8) induced by the ℓ_p-norms, the two norms coincide. In particular, the statements of Theorem 2.19 remain true for real-valued matrices no matter which definition we use, and even for complex-valued matrices. We only have to replace $A^T A$ by $\overline{A}^T A$ in the case of the 2-norm. Here, $\overline{A}$ is the complex-conjugate of the matrix A, i.e. each entry of $\overline{A}$ is the complex-conjugate of the corresponding entry of A.

However, instead of using the same ℓ_p-norm in the domain and range of our matrix A, we can also choose different ℓ_p-norms. Then, it is possible to show the following result. A proof can be found in [62, 93].

Theorem 2.26 *Let $1 \leq p,q \leq \infty$. For a matrix $A \in \mathbb{R}^{m\times n}$, the subordinate matrix norms*

$$\|A\|_{q,p}^{\mathrm{R}} := \sup_{x\in\mathbb{R}^n\setminus\{0\}} \frac{\|Ax\|_q}{\|x\|_p}, \qquad \|A\|_{q,p}^{\mathrm{C}} := \sup_{x\in\mathbb{C}^n\setminus\{0\}} \frac{\|Ax\|_q}{\|x\|_p}$$

satisfy for $p \leq q$

$$\|A\|_{q,p}^{\mathrm{R}} = \|A\|_{q,p}^{\mathrm{C}}.$$

For $p > q$ and $m, n \geq 3$ there exists a matrix A such that

$$\|A\|_{q,p}^{\mathrm{R}} < \|A\|_{q,p}^{\mathrm{C}}.$$

The following, simple example illustrates the situation for $p > q$.

Example 2.27 We want to compute the norm $\|A\|_{1,\infty}$ of the matrix $A \in \mathbb{R}^{2\times2}$ given by

$$A = \begin{pmatrix} 1 & -1 \\ 1 & 1 \end{pmatrix}$$

both in the complex setting and the real setting. To this end, we note that we can simplify the formula for computing the matrix norm to

$$\|A\|_{1,\infty} = \sup_{x\neq 0} \frac{\|Ax\|_1}{\|x\|_\infty} = \sup_{\|x\|_\infty=1} [|x_1 - x_2| + |x_1 + x_2|].$$

The supremum is taken either over all $x = (x_1, x_2)^{\mathrm{T}}$ from $\mathbb{R}^2$ or $\mathbb{C}^2$, respectively. In the first case, the possible candidates $x \in \mathbb{R}^2$ with $\|x\|_\infty = 1$ must have either $x_1 = \pm 1$ or $x_2 = \pm 1$. Since the norm is symmetric in x_1 and x_2 it suffices to look at $x_1 = \pm 1$. In the case of $x_1 = 1$ we must find the maximum of

$$f(x_2) = |1 - x_2| + |x_2 - 1|, \qquad x_2 \in [-1, 1].$$

However, on this domain the function obviously reduces to $f(x_2) = 1 - x_2 + x_2 - 1 = 2$. The other case of $x_1 = -1$ follows in the same fashion so that we have

$$\|A\|_{1,\infty}^{\mathrm{R}} = 2.$$

In the situation of complex $x \in \mathbb{C}^2$ with $\|x\|_\infty = 1$ it suffices to look at the case

$|x_1| = 1$ and $|x_2| = r \leq 1$. Hence, we can write $x_1 = e^{i\theta_1}$ and $x_2 = re^{i\theta_2}$ with $\theta_j \in \mathbb{R}$ for $j = 1, 2$ and $r \in [0, 1]$. We have to find the maximum of

$$|e^{i\theta_1} + re^{i\theta_2}| + |e^{i\theta_1} - re^{i\theta_2}| = |e^{i\theta_1}(1 + re^{i(\theta_2-\theta_1)})| + |e^{i\theta_1}(1 - re^{i(\theta_2-\theta_1)})|$$

$$= |1 + re^{i\theta}| + |1 - re^{i\theta}| \tag{2.14}$$

$$=: f(r, \theta)$$

with $\theta := \theta_2 - \theta_1$. Both expressions on the right-hand side of (2.14) denote the distance of a point in $\mathbb{C}$ from the origin, where, in the first summand, the point is on the circle about 1 with radius r and, in the second summand, the point is on the circle about -1 with radius r. The maximum of this expression is attained if both distances are the same. To see this let us further express

$$f(r, \theta) = (1 + r\cos\theta)^2 + r^2\sin^2\theta)^{1/2} + (1 - r\cos\theta)^2 + r^2\sin^2\theta)^{1/2}$$

$$= (1 + r^2 + 2r\cos\theta)^{1/2} + (1 + r^2 - 2r\cos\theta)^{1/2}.$$

For $r = 0$ the latter expression has value 2. For a fixed $r \in (0, 1]$, the latter expression is as a function of θ a periodic function with period π and attains its maximum for $\theta = \pi/2 + \pi\mathbb{Z}$, which gives $f(r, \pi/2) = 2(1 + r^2)^{1/2}$ which is largest when $r = 1$. This shows altogether

$$\|A\|_{1,\infty}^{\mathbb{C}} = |1 - i| + |1 + i| = 2\sqrt{2}.$$

After this example, we return to the more common situation of $p = q$ and in particular to $p = q = 2$, where Corollary 2.21 and Proposition 2.22 can be generalised as follows.

Corollary 2.28 *Let $A \in \mathbb{C}^{n\times n}$ be normal, i.e. $\overline{A}^{\mathrm{T}}A = A\overline{A}^{\mathrm{T}}$. Then, the 2-norm of A is given by*

$$\|A\|_2 = |\lambda_n| = \sup_{\|\mathbf{x}\|_2=1} |\langle\mathbf{x}, A\mathbf{x}\rangle_2|,$$

where $\langle\mathbf{x}, \mathbf{y}\rangle_2 = \overline{\mathbf{y}}^{\mathrm{T}}\mathbf{x}$ and where λ_n is the eigenvalue of A with the largest absolute value.

The following example shows how to compute the induced matrix norm if the vector norm is defined by $\|\mathbf{x}\|_A := \|A\mathbf{x}\|$ with an invertible matrix A and a vector norm $\|\cdot\|$. We will run into such norms frequently.

Example 2.29 Suppose $S \in \mathbb{R}^{n\times n}$ is an invertible matrix and $\|\cdot\|$ is a vector norm on $\mathbb{R}^n$. Then, it is easy to see that $\mathbf{x} \mapsto \|\mathbf{x}\|_{S^{-1}} := \|S^{-1}\mathbf{x}\|$ is also a vector norm on $\mathbb{R}^n$. The induced matrix norm is given by

$$\|A\|_{S^{-1}} := \sup_{\mathbf{x}\neq 0} \frac{\|A\mathbf{x}\|_{S^{-1}}}{\|\mathbf{x}\|_{S^{-1}}} = \sup_{\mathbf{x}\neq 0} \frac{\|S^{-1}ASS^{-1}\mathbf{x}\|}{\|S^{-1}\mathbf{x}\|} = \sup_{\mathbf{y}\neq 0} \frac{\|S^{-1}AS\mathbf{y}\|}{\|\mathbf{y}\|} = \|S^{-1}AS\|.$$

The above example remains true in the complex setting. Assume that $S \in \mathbb{C}^{n \times n}$ is invertible and that $\| \cdot \| : \mathbb{C}^n \to \mathbb{C}$ is a norm with induced matrix norm. Then, the above mapping $\| \cdot \|_{S^{-1}} : \mathbb{C}^n \to \mathbb{R}$, $\mathbf{x} \mapsto \| S^{-1}\mathbf{x} \|$ defines a norm on $\mathbb{C}^n$ with induced matrix norm $\| \cdot \|_{S^{-1}} : \mathbb{C}^{n \times n} \to \mathbb{R}$ given by $\|A\|_{S^{-1}} = \| S^{-1}AS \|$. We can restrict both norms to $\mathbb{R}^n$ and $\mathbb{R}^{n \times n}$ and, even though the resulting matrix norm on $\mathbb{R}^{n \times n}$ is in general not the induced matrix norm of the restricted vector norm, the two norms are still compatible in the real setting.

These considerations imply that not every matrix norm is an induced norm, not even every compatible norm has to be an induced norm. Another, simpler example is given by the so-called Frobenius norm.

Definition 2.30 The *Frobenius norm* of a matrix $A \in \mathbb{R}^{m \times n}$ is defined to be

$$\|A\|_F = \left(\sum_{i=1}^{m} \sum_{j=1}^{n} |a_{ij}|^2 \right)^{1/2}.$$

The Frobenius norm is indeed a norm. This follows immediately by realising that it is the Euclidean norm if we identify $\mathbb{R}^{m \times n}$ with $\mathbb{R}^{m \cdot n}$. Moreover, the Frobenius norm is compatible with the ℓ_2 vector norm, since we have

$$\|A\mathbf{x}\|_2^2 = \sum_{i=1}^{m} \left| \sum_{j=1}^{n} a_{ij}x_j \right|^2 \leq \sum_{i=1}^{m} \left(\sum_{j=1}^{n} |a_{ij}|^2 \sum_{j=1}^{n} |x_j|^2 \right) = \|A\|_F^2 \|\mathbf{x}\|_2^2.$$

Corollary 2.31 *The Frobenius norm is compatible with the Euclidean norm. Moreover, it can be expressed alternatively as*

$$\|A\|_F^2 = \mathrm{tr}(A^\mathsf{T}A) = \mathrm{tr}(AA^\mathsf{T}), \qquad A \in \mathbb{R}^{m \times n},$$

where $\mathrm{tr}(B) = \sum_i b_{ii}$ denotes the trace of the matrix B.

Proof The additional representation follows from the fact that all three terms give the sum over the squared entries of the matrix. □

The Frobenius norm cannot be induced since we have $\|I\|_F = \sqrt{\min(m,n)} \neq 1$. But as a compatible norm the Frobenius norm is multiplicative.

2.3 Conditioning

In the last section, while discussing the problem of multiplying a matrix with a vector, we encountered the idea of conditioning. We associated a *condition number* with a matrix, which gave some insight into whether small input errors are magnified or not.

We now want to discuss this more generally and in more detail.

Definition 2.32 Consider a problem $f : V \to W$ from a normed vector space V of data to a normed vector space W of solutions. For a particular point $\mathbf{x} \in V$ we say that the problem $f(\mathbf{x})$ is *well-conditioned* if all small perturbations of $\mathbf{x}$ lead only to small changes in $f(\mathbf{x})$. A problem is *ill-conditioned* if there exists a small perturbation that leads to a large change in $f(\mathbf{x})$.

To make this more precise, we want to introduce the concept of a condition number also in this context.

In general, one distinguishes between the *absolute condition number*, which is the smallest number $\tilde{\kappa}(\mathbf{x})$ which satisfies

$$\|f(\mathbf{x} + \Delta\mathbf{x}) - f(\mathbf{x})\| \le \tilde{\kappa}(\mathbf{x})\|\Delta\mathbf{x}\|,$$

for all $\mathbf{x}$ and all small $\Delta\mathbf{x}$, and the more useful *relative condition number*, $\kappa(\mathbf{x})$, given by the smallest number $\kappa(\mathbf{x})$ satisfying

$$\frac{\|f(\mathbf{x} + \Delta\mathbf{x}) - f(\mathbf{x})\|}{\|f(\mathbf{x})\|} \le \kappa(\mathbf{x})\frac{\|\Delta\mathbf{x}\|}{\|\mathbf{x}\|}, \tag{2.15}$$

for all $\mathbf{x} \ne \mathbf{0}$ with $f(\mathbf{x}) \ne \mathbf{0}$ and all small $\Delta\mathbf{x}$. We still need to make the notion of small errors $\Delta\mathbf{x}$ more precise. In the case of the relative condition number this is done as follows.

Definition 2.33 Let V, W be normed spaces and $f : V \to W$. The *(relative) condition number* of f at $\mathbf{x} \in V$ is defined to be

$$\kappa(\mathbf{x}) = \kappa(f, \mathbf{x}) := \lim_{\epsilon \to 0} \sup_{\|\Delta\mathbf{x}\| \le \epsilon} \left[\frac{\|f(\mathbf{x} + \Delta\mathbf{x}) - f(\mathbf{x})\|}{\|f(\mathbf{x})\|} \Big/ \frac{\|\Delta\mathbf{x}\|}{\|\mathbf{x}\|} \right].$$

We will soon derive a general formula for the condition number in the case of differentiable functions. But before that, let us discuss a few simple examples.

Example 2.34 (Matrix–vector multiplication) As a first example, let us review our previous example of matrix–vector multiplication. Here, we have $f(\mathbf{x}) = A\mathbf{x}$. Hence,

$$\frac{\|A(\mathbf{x} + \Delta\mathbf{x}) - A\mathbf{x}\|}{\|A\mathbf{x}\|} = \frac{\|A\,\Delta\mathbf{x}\|}{\|A\mathbf{x}\|} \le \frac{\|A\|\,\|\mathbf{x}\|}{\|A\mathbf{x}\|}\frac{\|\Delta\mathbf{x}\|}{\|\mathbf{x}\|} =: \kappa(\mathbf{x})\frac{\|\Delta\mathbf{x}\|}{\|\mathbf{x}\|}.$$

If A is invertible we have $\|\mathbf{x}\| = \|A^{-1}A\mathbf{x}\| \le \|A^{-1}\|\,\|A\mathbf{x}\|$ such that

$$\kappa(\mathbf{x}) \le \|A\|\,\|A^{-1}\| = \kappa(A).$$

The next two examples deal with the simple operation of adding and multiplying two numbers. Since subtraction and division can be recast as addition and multiplication, these operations are covered by these examples, as well. We leave it to the reader to determine the actual condition number and rather concentrate on the question of whether the operation is well-conditioned or not.

Example 2.35 (Addition of two numbers) Let $f : \mathbb{R}^2 \to \mathbb{R}$ be defined as $f(x, y) = x + y$. Then,

$$\frac{f(x + \Delta x, y + \Delta y) - f(x, y)}{f(x, y)} = \frac{x + \Delta x + y + \Delta y - (x + y)}{x + y}$$

$$= \frac{x}{x + y} \frac{\Delta x}{x} + \frac{y}{x + y} \frac{\Delta y}{y}.$$

Hence, the addition of two numbers is well-conditioned if they have the same sign and are sufficiently far away from zero. However, if the two numbers are of the same magnitude but with different signs, i.e. $x \approx -y$, then adding these numbers is highly ill-conditioned because of *cancellation*.

Example 2.36 (Multiplying two numbers) The procedure is similar to the one of the previous example. This time, we have $f(x, y) = x \cdot y$. Hence, we have

$$\frac{f(x + \Delta x, y + \Delta y) - f(x, y)}{f(x, y)} = \frac{(x + \Delta x)(y + \Delta y) - (xy)}{xy}$$

$$= \frac{\Delta y}{y} + \frac{\Delta x}{x} + \frac{\Delta x}{x} \frac{\Delta y}{y},$$

which shows that the multiplication of two numbers is well-conditioned.

Next, let us consider a more general approach. Recall that for a differentiable function $f : \mathbb{R}^n \to \mathbb{R}$, the *gradient* of f at $\mathbf{x}$ is defined to be the vector

$$\nabla f(\mathbf{x}) = \left(\frac{\partial f(\mathbf{x})}{\partial x_1}, \ldots, \frac{\partial f(\mathbf{x})}{\partial x_n} \right)^{\mathrm{T}}.$$

Theorem 2.37 *Let* $f : \mathbb{R}^n \to \mathbb{R}$ *be a continuously differentiable function. Then, for* $\mathbf{x} \in \mathbb{R}^n$, *the condition number of* f *with respect to the* ℓ_2-*norm in* $\mathbb{R}^n$ *satisfies*

$$\kappa(\mathbf{x}) = \frac{\|\nabla f(\mathbf{x})\|_2}{|f(\mathbf{x})|} \|\mathbf{x}\|_2. \tag{2.16}$$

Proof The Taylor expansion of f gives

$$f(\mathbf{x} + \Delta \mathbf{x}) - f(\mathbf{x}) = \nabla f(\boldsymbol{\xi})^{\mathrm{T}} \Delta \mathbf{x}$$

with a $\boldsymbol{\xi}$ on the straight line between $\mathbf{x}$ and $\mathbf{x} + \Delta \mathbf{x}$. Hence, we can bound the relative output error by

$$\frac{|f(\mathbf{x} + \Delta \mathbf{x}) - f(\mathbf{x})|}{|f(\mathbf{x})|} \frac{\|\mathbf{x}\|_2}{\|\Delta \mathbf{x}\|_2} = \frac{|\nabla f(\boldsymbol{\xi})^{\mathrm{T}} \Delta \mathbf{x}|}{|f(\mathbf{x})|} \frac{\|\mathbf{x}\|_2}{\|\Delta \mathbf{x}\|_2} \leq \frac{\|\nabla f(\boldsymbol{\xi})\|_2}{|f(\mathbf{x})|} \|\mathbf{x}\|_2,$$

where we have used the Cauchy–Schwarz inequality in the last step. The expression on the right-hand side depends only implicitly on Δx as ξ is on the line segment between x and $x + \Delta x$. If we now take the limit $\|\Delta x\|_2 \to 0$ as in Definition 2.33 we have that $\xi \to x$, which shows that $\kappa(x)$ is at most the expression on the right-hand side of (2.16). If Δx is parallel to $\nabla f(x)$ we even have equality in the above inequality, which shows that $\kappa(x)$ does indeed have the stated form. $\qquad\square$

Example 2.38 (Square root)   Let $f(x) = \sqrt{x}$, $x > 0$. Then, we have $f'(x) = \frac{1}{2}x^{-1/2}$ and hence

$$\kappa(x) = \frac{|f'(x)|}{|f(x)|}|x| = \frac{1}{2}\frac{x}{\sqrt{x}\sqrt{x}} = \frac{1}{2}.$$

Hence, taking the square root is a well-conditioned problem with condition number $1/2$.

The next example is another application of (2.16). This time we look at the exponential function.

Example 2.39 (Function evaluation)   Let $f(x) = e^{x^2}$, $x \in \mathbb{R}$. Since $f'(x) = 2xe^{x^2} = 2xf(x)$, we can use (2.16) to see that

$$\kappa(x) = \frac{|f'(x)|}{|f(x)|}|x| = 2x^2.$$

Hence, the problem is well-conditioned for small x and ill-conditioned for large x.

So far, we have dealt with the condition number of a problem. While there is not much choice in computing the sum of two real numbers, the situation is already different when it comes to computing the square root. Here, we did not consider a particular method to compute the square root but only the problem itself. However, it might happen that a problem is well-conditioned but the algorithm or method we use is not.

Definition 2.40   A method for solving a numerical problem is called *well-conditioned* if its condition number is comparable to the condition number of the problem.

Let us explain this with a simple example.

Example 2.41   We consider the quadratic equation $x^2 + 2px - q = 0$ with $p, q > 0$. Then, we know from elementary calculus that the positive solution to this problem is given by

$$x = -p + \sqrt{p^2 + q}. \tag{2.17}$$

We can expect that this formula is ill-conditioned if p is much larger than q since then we will have $x \approx -p + p$ and the last expression is prone to cancellation. We will make this more precise later but we first want to look at the condition number of the problem of finding the positive solution itself. To do this, let us introduce the notation $x(p, q)$ for the solution of the equation with coefficients p and q. Then, the relative output error is given by

$$\epsilon_x = \frac{\Delta x}{x} = \frac{x(p + \Delta p, q + \Delta q) - x(p, q)}{x(p, q)}.$$

If we also write $\epsilon_p = \frac{\Delta p}{p}$ and $\epsilon_q = \frac{\Delta q}{q}$ for the relative input error, we find $p + \Delta p = p(1 + \epsilon_p)$ and $q + \Delta q = q(1 + \epsilon_q)$. Using that $x(p + \Delta p, q + \Delta q)$ solves the quadratic equation with coefficients $p + \Delta p$ and $q + \Delta q$ yields

$$0 = (1 + \epsilon_x)^2 x^2 + 2px(1 + \epsilon_p)(1 + \epsilon_x) - q(1 + \epsilon_q)$$
$$= (1 + 2\epsilon_x + \epsilon_x^2)x^2 + 2px(1 + \epsilon_p + \epsilon_x + \epsilon_p\epsilon_x) - q - q\epsilon_q.$$

If we now ignore all quadratic ϵ terms in this equation (which we will denote with a dot above the equal sign), i.e. ϵ_x^2 and $\epsilon_p\epsilon_x$, and rearrange the terms, we derive

$$0 \doteq x^2 + 2px - q + 2\epsilon_x(x^2 + px) + 2\epsilon_p px - q\epsilon_q = 2\epsilon_x(x^2 + px) + 2\epsilon_p px - q\epsilon_q.$$

This resolves to

$$\epsilon_x \doteq \frac{1}{2}\frac{q\epsilon_q - 2\epsilon_p px}{x^2 + px} = \frac{1}{2}\frac{(q - px)\epsilon_q + px\epsilon_q - 2\epsilon_p px}{q - px} = \frac{1}{2}\left[\epsilon_q + \frac{px(\epsilon_q - 2\epsilon_p)}{x^2 + px}\right]$$

and this finally gives the bound

$$|\epsilon_x| \doteq \frac{1}{2}|\epsilon_q| + \frac{1}{2}\frac{px(|\epsilon_q| + 2|\epsilon_p|)}{px} = |\epsilon_q| + |\epsilon_p|.$$

This means that finding the positive solution to our quadratic equation is a well-conditioned problem.

As mentioned above, (2.17) is not a well-conditioned method to compute the solution. To see this, let us analyse the method in more detail. Using the same ϵ notation as above to denote the relative error, we can, first of all, summarise the findings of our previous examples as follows:

$$|\epsilon_{\sqrt{x}}| \leq \frac{1}{2}|\epsilon_x|,$$

$$|\epsilon_{x+y}| \leq \left|\frac{x}{x + y}\right||\epsilon_x| + \left|\frac{y}{x + y}\right||\epsilon_y|,$$

$$|\epsilon_{x\cdot y}| \doteq |\epsilon_x| + |\epsilon_y|.$$

Under the assumption $\epsilon_p, \epsilon_q \in [-\epsilon, \epsilon]$, this means for the solution formula (2.17) successively

$$|\epsilon_{p^2}| \dot{\leq} |\epsilon_p| + |\epsilon_p| \leq 2\epsilon,$$

$$|\epsilon_{p^2+q}| \dot{\leq} \frac{p^2}{p^2+q}|\epsilon_{p^2}| + \frac{q}{p^2+q}|\epsilon_q| \leq 2\epsilon,$$

$$|\epsilon_{\sqrt{p^2+q}}| \leq \frac{1}{2}|\epsilon_{p^2+q}| \dot{\leq} \epsilon$$

and finally, with $y = \sqrt{p^2+q}$,

$$|\epsilon_x| = |\epsilon_{-p+y}| \dot{\leq} \left|\frac{-p}{-p+y}\right||\epsilon_p| + \left|\frac{y}{-p+y}\right||\epsilon_y| \leq \frac{p+y}{y-p}\epsilon.$$

The term $y - p$ in the denominator becomes problematic in the situation that p is much larger than q due to cancellation. Thus, in this situation, the formula is ill-conditioned. However, in this situation we can rewrite it as

$$x = -p + \sqrt{p^2+q} = \left(-p + \sqrt{p^2+q}\right)\frac{p + \sqrt{p^2+q}}{p + \sqrt{p^2+q}}$$

$$= \frac{p^2 + q - p^2}{p + \sqrt{p^2+q}} = \frac{q}{p + \sqrt{p^2+q}}.$$

To show that this formula is well-conditioned we define $z = p + \sqrt{p^2+q}$ and find

$$|\epsilon_z| = |\epsilon_{p+y}| \leq \frac{p}{p+y}|\epsilon_p| + \frac{y}{y+p}|\epsilon_y| \leq \epsilon.$$

Using the easily verifiable

$$\epsilon_{x/y} \dot{=} \epsilon_x - \epsilon_y$$

then finally gives

$$|\epsilon_x| = |\epsilon_{q/z}| \dot{=} |\epsilon_q - \epsilon_z| \leq 2\epsilon,$$

i.e. the well-conditioning of the new formula.

Let us now return to linear algebra. We will finish this section by studying the problem of solving a linear system of the form $Ax = b$ with an invertible matrix $A \in \mathbb{R}^{n \times n}$ and given $b \in \mathbb{R}^n$.

Suppose our input data A and b have been perturbed such that we are actually given $A + \Delta A$ and $b + \Delta b$. We can try to model the error in the output by assuming that $x + \Delta x$ solves

$$(A + \Delta A)(x + \Delta x) = b + \Delta b.$$

Multiplying this out and using $Ax = \mathbf{b}$ yields

$$(A + \Delta A)\Delta x = \Delta \mathbf{b} - (\Delta A)x.$$

For the time being, let us assume that $A + \Delta A$ is invertible, which is, by continuity, true if A is invertible and ΔA only a small perturbation. Then,

$$\Delta x = (A + \Delta A)^{-1}(\Delta \mathbf{b} - (\Delta A)x),$$

i.e.

$$\|\Delta x\| \le \|(A + \Delta A)^{-1}\|(\|\Delta \mathbf{b}\| + \|\Delta A\|\|x\|),$$

which gives a first estimate on the absolute error. However, more relevant is the relative error

$$\frac{\|\Delta x\|}{\|x\|} \le \|(A + \Delta A)^{-1}\|\|A\|\left(\frac{\|\Delta \mathbf{b}\|}{\|A\|\|x\|} + \frac{\|\Delta A\|}{\|A\|}\right)$$

$$\le \|(A + \Delta A)^{-1}\|\|A\|\left(\frac{\|\Delta \mathbf{b}\|}{\|\mathbf{b}\|} + \frac{\|\Delta A\|}{\|A\|}\right).$$

The last estimate shows that the relative input error is magnified by a factor

$$\|(A + \Delta A)^{-1}\|\|A\| \tag{2.18}$$

for the relative output error. This demonstrates the problem of conditioning. The latter expression can further be modified to incorporate the condition number of a matrix.

It is now time to make our assumptions more rigorous, which ultimately also leads to a further bound on (2.18).

Lemma 2.42 *If $A \in \mathbb{R}^{n \times n}$ is a non-singular matrix and $\Delta A \in \mathbb{R}^{n \times n}$ a perturbation, which satisfies*

$$\|A^{-1}\|\|\Delta A\| < 1$$

in a compatible matrix norm, then, $A + \Delta A$ is non-singular and we have

$$\|(A + \Delta A)^{-1}\| \le \frac{\|A^{-1}\|}{1 - \|A^{-1}\|\|\Delta A\|}.$$

Proof Let us define the mapping $T : \mathbb{R}^n \to \mathbb{R}^n$ with $Tx = (A + \Delta A)x$, $x \in \mathbb{R}^n$. Then, we have obviously $x = A^{-1}Tx - A^{-1}(\Delta A)x$ and $\|x\| \le \|A^{-1}\|\|Tx\| + \|A^{-1}\|\|\Delta A\|\|x\|$. This means particularly

$$\|x\| \le \frac{\|A^{-1}\|}{1 - \|A^{-1}\|\|\Delta A\|}\|Tx\|,$$

which immediately leads to the injectivity and hence bijectivity of $T = A + \Delta A$ and to the stated bound.   □

Theorem 2.43 *Suppose that $A \in \mathbb{R}^{n \times n}$ is invertible and that the perturbation $\Delta A \in \mathbb{R}^{n \times n}$ satisfies $\|A^{-1}\| \|\Delta A\| < 1$. Then, for $\mathbf{b}, \Delta\mathbf{b} \in \mathbb{R}^{n}$ with $\mathbf{b} \neq \mathbf{0}$, the estimate*

$$\frac{\|\Delta\mathbf{x}\|}{\|\mathbf{x}\|} \leq \kappa(A) \left(1 - \kappa(A)\frac{\|\Delta A\|}{\|A\|}\right)^{-1} \left(\frac{\|\Delta\mathbf{b}\|}{\|\mathbf{b}\|} + \frac{\|\Delta A\|}{\|A\|}\right)$$

holds.

Proof Lemma 2.42 guarantees the invertibility of $A + \Delta A$. Hence, our findings so far together with Lemma 2.42 yield

$$\frac{\|\Delta\mathbf{x}\|}{\|\mathbf{x}\|} \leq \|(A + \Delta A)^{-1}\| \|A\| \left(\frac{\|\Delta\mathbf{b}\|}{\|\mathbf{b}\|} + \frac{\|\Delta A\|}{\|A\|}\right)$$

$$\leq \frac{\|A^{-1}\| \|A\|}{1 - \|A^{-1}\| \|\Delta A\|} \left(\frac{\|\Delta\mathbf{b}\|}{\|\mathbf{b}\|} + \frac{\|\Delta A\|}{\|A\|}\right),$$

from which the statement easily follows. □

If the number $\kappa(A)\|\Delta A\|/\|A\|$ is close to zero, the stability estimate in Theorem 2.43 takes the form

$$\frac{\|\Delta\mathbf{x}\|}{\|\mathbf{x}\|} \approx \kappa(A) \left(\frac{\|\Delta\mathbf{b}\|}{\|\mathbf{b}\|} + \frac{\|\Delta A\|}{\|A\|}\right),$$

showing that the relative input error is amplified by $\kappa(A)$ in the relative output error.

Example 2.44 Assume the condition number behaves like $\kappa(A) = O(10^{\sigma})$ and that the relative input errors behave like

$$\frac{\|\Delta A\|}{\|A\|} = O(10^{-k}), \qquad \frac{\|\Delta\mathbf{b}\|}{\|\mathbf{b}\|} = O(10^{-k})$$

with $k > \sigma$. Then, the relative error of the solution is of size

$$\frac{\|\Delta\mathbf{x}\|}{\|\mathbf{x}\|} \approx 10^{\sigma - k}.$$

In the case of the maximum norm we have to expect to lose σ digits in accuracy.

As we always have to expect errors of the size of the machine precision, the above example shows that a condition number inverse proportional to the machine precision will produce essentially unreliable results.

2.4 Stability

There is yet another way of looking at the output of an algorithm and how well it computes the solution of the original problem.

Consider again a problem $f : V \to W$ from a vector space V of data to a vector space W of solutions. A numerical algorithm can then simply be defined to be another map $\tilde{f} : V \to W$. More precisely, the given data $\mathbf{x} \in V$ will be rounded to floating point precision and then supplied to the algorithm $\tilde{f}$. We can and will, however, incorporate this rounding into the algorithm $\tilde{f}$. Hence, the actual outcome is a solution $\tilde{f}(\mathbf{x})$.

Obviously, we could call $\tilde{f}$ stable if the approximate result $\tilde{f}(\mathbf{x})$ is close to the desired result $f(\mathbf{x})$, i.e., when taking the relative point of view again, if

$$\frac{\|\tilde{f}(\mathbf{x}) - f(\mathbf{x})\|}{\|f(\mathbf{x})\|}$$

is small. Unfortunately, this is often extremely difficult to verify. Hence, a different concept has been developed. While the above concept requires the approximate result from the correct input data to be close to the correct result, we could also try to interpret the outcome $\tilde{f}(\mathbf{x})$ as the result of the original function f at a perturbed point $\tilde{\mathbf{x}} \in V$, i.e. we assume that $\tilde{f}(\mathbf{x}) = f(\tilde{\mathbf{x}})$.

Definition 2.45 The algorithm $\tilde{f}$ is called *backward-stable* for the problem f if for every $\mathbf{x} \in V$ there is an $\tilde{\mathbf{x}} \in V$ with $f(\tilde{\mathbf{x}}) = \tilde{f}(\mathbf{x})$ and .

$$\frac{\|\mathbf{x} - \tilde{\mathbf{x}}\|}{\|\mathbf{x}\|} = O(\text{eps}), \tag{2.19}$$

where eps denotes the machine precision.

In other words, this means that a backward-stable algorithm solves the problem correctly with nearly the correct input data.

The concept of backward-stability is a very powerful concept in Numerical Linear Algebra. For many algorithms it can be shown that they are backward-stable. A backward-stable algorithm computes a good approximation to the original problem provided the condition number of the original problem is of moderate size.

Theorem 2.46 Let $\tilde{f} : V \to W$ be a backward-stable algorithm to compute the problem $f : V \to W$. Then, for each $\mathbf{x} \in V$,

$$\frac{\|\tilde{f}(\mathbf{x}) - f(\mathbf{x})\|}{\|f(\mathbf{x})\|} = O(\kappa(\mathbf{x}) \, \text{eps}),$$

where $\kappa(\mathbf{x})$ denotes the relative condition number for computing $f(\mathbf{x})$.

Proof Since $\tilde{f}$ is backward-stable, we can find an $\tilde{\mathbf{x}} \in V$ with $\tilde{f}(\mathbf{x}) = f(\tilde{\mathbf{x}})$ and (2.19). The definition of the relative condition number in Definition 2.33 yields

$$\frac{\|\tilde{f}(\mathbf{x}) - f(\mathbf{x})\|}{\|f(\mathbf{x})\|} = \frac{\|f(\tilde{\mathbf{x}}) - f(\mathbf{x})\|}{\|f(\mathbf{x})\|} \le \kappa(\mathbf{x}) \frac{\|\mathbf{x} - \tilde{\mathbf{x}}\|}{\|\mathbf{x}\|} = O(\kappa(\mathbf{x}) \, \text{eps}). \qquad \square$$

Let us briefly describe how this general theory applies to our main application of solving linear systems, though we can also use it for analysing algorithms for solving least-squares or eigenvalue problems.

When solving linear systems $A\mathbf{x} = \mathbf{b}$, we may assume that the right-hand side $\mathbf{b}$ is exact. Hence, the linear mapping we are interested in is given by $f : \mathbb{R}^{n \times n} \to \mathbb{R}^n$, $f(A) := A^{-1}\mathbf{b}$. The condition number of this problem is given by Theorem 2.43 with $\Delta\mathbf{b} = \mathbf{0}$. More precisely, Theorem 2.43 yields

$$\frac{\|f(A + \Delta A) - f(A)\|}{\|f(A)\|} \Big/ \frac{\|\Delta A\|}{\|A\|} = \frac{\|\Delta\mathbf{x}\|}{\|\mathbf{x}\|} \Big/ \frac{\|\Delta A\|}{\|A\|} \le \kappa(A) \left(1 - \kappa(A) \frac{\|\Delta A\|}{\|A\|}\right)^{-1}.$$

Taking the limit $\|\Delta A\| \to 0$ as in Definition 2.33, this shows that $\kappa(f, A) \le \kappa(A) = \|A\| \, \|A^{-1}\|$.

Corollary 2.47 *Let $A \in \mathbb{R}^{n \times n}$ be invertible and $\mathbf{b} \in \mathbb{R}^n$. If $\mathbf{x} = A^{-1}\mathbf{b}$ and if $\tilde{\mathbf{x}} \in \mathbb{R}^n$ is the approximate solution computed with a backward-stable algorithm then the relative error satisfies*

$$\frac{\|\tilde{\mathbf{x}} - \mathbf{x}\|}{\|\mathbf{x}\|} = O(\kappa(A) \, \text{eps}).$$

In the next chapter, we will discuss the backward-stability of several algorithms. However, we will omit the proofs as they are usually extremely technical. Nonetheless, the reader should be very aware of this problem and may consult the books by Higham [85] and Trefethen and Bau [124].

Exercises

2.1 Consider the matrix $A = \mathbf{u}\mathbf{v}^\mathsf{T}$, where $\mathbf{u} \in \mathbb{R}^m$ and $\mathbf{v} \in \mathbb{R}^n$. Show that

$$\|A\|_2 = \|\mathbf{u}\|_2 \|\mathbf{v}\|_2.$$

2.2 Calculate $\|A\|_1, \|A\|_2$ and $\|A\|_\infty$ for the matrices

$$A = \begin{pmatrix} 1 & -2 \\ -2 & 4 \end{pmatrix}, \qquad A = \begin{pmatrix} 4 & 1 & -1 \\ 1 & 2 & 0 \\ -1 & 0 & 2 \end{pmatrix}.$$

2.3 For $A \in \mathbb{R}^{m \times n}$ show that

$$\|A\|_2 \leq \sqrt{\|A\|_\infty \|A\|_1}.$$

2.4 Let $A \in \mathbb{R}^{n \times n}$ be invertible and $1 \leq p, q \leq \infty$ with $\frac{1}{p} + \frac{1}{q} = 1$. Show that

$$\kappa_p(A) = \kappa_q(A^T).$$

2.5 Let $A \in \mathbb{R}^{m \times n}$ have the singular values $\sigma_1 \geq \sigma_2 \geq \cdots \geq \sigma_r > 0$ with $r = \text{rank}(A)$. Show that

$$\|A\|_F = \left(\sum_{j=1}^{r} \sigma_j^2 \right)^{1/2}.$$

2.6 Consider the matrix

$$A = \begin{pmatrix} 1 & 1 \\ 1 & -1 \end{pmatrix}.$$

Show that for $1 \leq p, q \leq \infty$ the norm $\|A\|_{q,p}^{\mathbb{C}}$ is given by

$$\|A\|_{q,p}^{\mathbb{C}} = \max\{2^{1-\frac{1}{p}}, 2^{\frac{1}{q}}, 2^{\frac{1}{q}-\frac{1}{p}+\frac{1}{2}}\}.$$

Show further that for $p \leq 2$ or $q \geq 2$ we also have

$$\|A\|_{q,p}^{\mathbb{C}} = \|A\|_{q,p}^{\mathbb{R}} = \max\{2^{1-\frac{1}{p}}, 2^{\frac{1}{q}}\}$$

and that for $q < 2 < p$ we have

$$\|A\|_{q,p} < 2^{\frac{1}{q}-\frac{1}{p}+\frac{1}{2}} = \|A\|_{q,p}^{\mathbb{C}}.$$

2.7 For $\epsilon > 0$ let $A_\epsilon \in \mathbb{R}^{3 \times 3}$ be given by

$$A_\epsilon := \begin{pmatrix} 1-\epsilon & -\epsilon & -\epsilon \\ -\epsilon & 1-\epsilon & -\epsilon \\ -\epsilon & -\epsilon & 1-\epsilon \end{pmatrix}.$$

Show that for $p > q \geq 1$ there exists an $\epsilon > 0$ such that $\|A_\epsilon\|_{q,p}^{\mathbb{R}} \leq \|A_\epsilon\|_{q,p}^{\mathbb{C}}$.

PART TWO

BASIC METHODS

3

Direct Methods for Solving Linear Systems

In this chapter we will discuss direct methods for solving linear systems. Direct means that the algorithms derived here will terminate after a fixed number of steps, usually n for an $n \times n$ matrix, with the solution of the system.

3.1 Back Substitution

The simplest linear system to solve is, of course, a system of the form $D\mathbf{x} = \mathbf{b}$, where $D = \text{diag}(d_{11}, \ldots, d_{nn}) \in \mathbb{R}^{n \times n}$ is a diagonal matrix with non-vanishing entries on the diagonal. The obvious solution is simply given by $x_i = b_i/d_{ii}$ for $1 \leq i \leq n$.

A slightly more complex problem is given if the matrix is a triangular matrix, i.e. we seek a solution $\mathbf{x} \in \mathbb{R}^n$ of the equation

$$R\mathbf{x} = \mathbf{b}, \tag{3.1}$$

where $\mathbf{b} \in \mathbb{R}^n$ is given and $R \in \mathbb{R}^{n \times n}$ is, for example, an upper triangular matrix, i.e. a matrix of the form

$$R = \begin{pmatrix} r_{11} & r_{12} & r_{13} & \cdots & r_{1n} \\ & r_{22} & r_{23} & \cdots & r_{2n} \\ & & \ddots & \ddots & \vdots \\ & 0 & & \ddots & \vdots \\ & & & & r_{nn} \end{pmatrix}.$$

The system has a unique solution if the determinant of R is different from zero. Since we have an upper triangular matrix, the determinant equals the product of all diagonal entries. Hence, R is invertible once again if $r_{ii} \neq 0$ for $1 \leq i \leq n$.

Assuming all of this, we see that the last equation of (3.1) is simply given by

$$r_{nn}x_n = b_n,$$

which resolves to $x_n = b_n/r_{nn}$. Next, the equation from row $n-1$ is

$$r_{n-1,n-1}x_{n-1} + r_{n-1,n}x_n = b_{n-1}.$$

In this equation, we already know x_n so that the only unknown is x_{n-1}, which we can compute as

$$x_{n-1} = (b_{n-1} - r_{n-1,n}x_n)/r_{n-1,n-1}.$$

We obviously can proceed in this way to compute successively x_{n-2}, x_{n-3} and so on until we finally compute x_1. The general algorithm for computing the solution in this situation is based upon

$$x_i = \frac{1}{r_{ii}}\left(b_i - \sum_{j=i+1}^{n} r_{ij}x_j\right), \qquad i = n-1, n-2, \ldots, 1, \tag{3.2}$$

see Algorithm 2, and is called *back substitution* or *backward substitution*.

Algorithm 2: Back substitution

Input : Upper triangular matrix $R \in \mathbb{R}^{n \times n}$, $\mathbf{b} \in \mathbb{R}^n$.
Output: Solution $\mathbf{x} \in \mathbb{R}^n$ of $R\mathbf{x} = \mathbf{b}$.

1 $x_n := b_n/r_{nn}$
2 **for** $i = n-1$ **downto** 1 **do**
3     $x_i := b_i$
4   **for** $j = i+1$ **to** n **do**
5        $x_i := x_i - r_{ij}x_j$
6     $x_i := x_i/r_{ii}$

A standard run-time analysis shows the following.

Theorem 3.1 *The system $R\mathbf{x} = \mathbf{b}$ with an invertible upper triangular matrix $R \in \mathbb{R}^{n \times n}$ can be solved in $O(n^2)$ time using back substitution.*

Proof The computational cost is mainly determined by the two for loops in Algorithm 2. The cost of line 5 is one flop, as is the cost of line 6. Hence, the total cost becomes

$$\sum_{i=1}^{n-1}\left(1 + \sum_{j=i+1}^{n} 1\right) = n-1 + \sum_{i=1}^{n-1}(n-(i+1)) = \sum_{i=1}^{n-1}(n-i) = \sum_{i=1}^{n-1} i = \frac{(n-1)n}{2}. \quad \square$$

It should be clear that we can proceed in the exactly same way when considering lower triangular matrices, starting with the computation of x_1. The corresponding solution procedure is then called *forward substitution*.

Remark 3.2 Back substitution is backward-stable. To be more precise, the computed solution $\tilde{x} \in \mathbb{R}^n$ of a non-singular upper triangular system $Rx = b$ satisfies $(R + \Delta R)\tilde{x} = b$ with $\Delta R \in \mathbb{R}^{n \times n}$ satisfying

$$|(\Delta R)_{ij}| \le n\text{eps} + O(\text{eps}^2), \qquad 1 \le i, j \le n.$$

A proof of this result can, for example, be found in Higham [85] and Trefethen and Bau [124]. According to Corollary 2.47, we can assume that back substitution allows us to compute a sufficiently accurate solution as long as $\kappa(R)$ is not too large. The same remains true for forward substitution.

3.2 Gaussian Elimination

We now turn to solving the system $Ax = b$ for arbitrary, invertible matrices $A \in \mathbb{R}^{n \times n}$. Probably the best-known and still very popular method for solving a square system $Ax = b$ is Gaussian elimination.

The aim of Gaussian elimination is to reduce a linear system of equations $Ax = b$ to an upper triangular system $Ux = c$ by applying very simple linear transformations to it, which do not change the solution.

Suppose we have a linear system of the form

$$a_{11}x_1 + a_{12}x_2 + \cdots + a_{1n}x_n = b_1,$$
$$a_{21}x_1 + a_{22}x_2 + \cdots + a_{2n}x_n = b_2,$$
$$\vdots \quad \vdots$$
$$a_{n1}x_1 + a_{n2}x_2 + \cdots + a_{nn}x_n = b_n,$$

then, assuming that $a_{11} \ne 0$, we can multiply the first row by $\frac{a_{21}}{a_{11}}$ and subtract the resulting row from the second row, which cancels the factor in front of x_1 in that row. Then, we can multiply the original first row by $\frac{a_{31}}{a_{11}}$ and subtract it from the third row, which, again, cancels the factor in front of x_1 in that row. It is important to note that this procedure does not change the solution of the system, i.e. the original system and the system modified in this way obviously have the same solution.

Continuing like this all the way down, we end up with an equivalent linear system, i.e. a system with the same solution, of the form

$$a_{11}x_1 + a_{12}x_2 + \cdots + a_{1n}x_n = b_1,$$

$$a_{22}^{(2)}x_2 + \cdots + a_{2n}^{(2)}x_n = b_2^{(2)},$$

$$\vdots \quad \vdots$$

$$a_{n2}^{(2)}x_2 + \cdots + a_{nn}^{(2)}x_n = b_n^{(2)}.$$

Assuming now that $a_{22}^{(2)} \neq 0$, we can repeat the whole process using the second row now to eliminate x_2 from row three to n, and so on. Hence, after $k - 1$ steps, $k \geq 2$, the system can be written in matrix form as

$$A^{(k)}\mathbf{x} = \begin{pmatrix} a_{11} & * & * & \cdots & * \\ 0 & a_{22}^{(2)} & * & \cdots & * \\ & & \ddots & & \\ 0 & 0 & a_{kk}^{(k)} & \cdots & a_{kn}^{(k)} \\ \vdots & \vdots & \vdots & & \vdots \\ 0 & 0 & a_{nk}^{(k)} & \cdots & a_{nn}^{(k)} \end{pmatrix} \mathbf{x} = \begin{pmatrix} b_1^{(1)} \\ b_2^{(2)} \\ \vdots \\ b_k^{(k)} \\ \vdots \\ b_n^{(k)} \end{pmatrix}. \tag{3.3}$$

If in each step $a_{kk}^{(k)}$ is different from zero, Gaussian elimination produces after $n - 1$ steps an upper triangular matrix. The final, resulting linear system can then be solved using back substitution as described in Algorithm 2.

In the next sections, we will address the questions of when all the diagonal entries $a_{kk}^{(k)}$ are different from zero and what to do if this is not the case.

For theoretical (not numerical) reasons, it is useful to rewrite this process using matrices. To this end, we need to rewrite the elementary operations we just used into matrix form. The corresponding matrices are the following elementary lower triangular matrices.

Definition 3.3 For $1 \leq k \leq n - 1$, let $\mathbf{m} \in \mathbb{R}^n$ be a vector with $\mathbf{e}_j^{\mathsf{T}}\mathbf{m} = 0$ for $1 \leq j \leq k$, meaning that $\mathbf{m}$ is of the form

$$\mathbf{m} = (0, 0, \ldots, 0, m_{k+1}, \ldots, m_n)^{\mathsf{T}}.$$

An *elementary lower triangular matrix* is a lower triangular matrix of the specific form

$$L_k(\mathbf{m}) := I - \mathbf{m}\mathbf{e}_k^T = \begin{pmatrix} 1 & & & & & \\ & \ddots & & & & \\ & & 1 & & & \\ & & -m_{k+1} & 1 & & \\ & & \vdots & & \ddots & \\ & & -m_n & & & 1 \end{pmatrix}.$$

Obviously, an elementary lower triangular matrix is a lower triangular matrix. It also is *normalised* in the sense that the diagonal entries are all 1. It is quite easy to see that an elementary lower triangular matrix has the following properties.

Lemma 3.4 *An elementary lower triangular matrix $L_k(\mathbf{m})$ has the following properties:*

1. *$\det L_k(\mathbf{m}) = 1$.*
2. *$L_k(\mathbf{m})^{-1} = L_k(-\mathbf{m})$.*
3. *Multiplying a matrix A with $L_k(\mathbf{m})$ from the left leaves the first k rows unchanged and, starting from row $j = k+1$, subtracts the row $m_j(a_{k1}, \ldots, a_{kn})$ from row j of A.*

With this notation, we see that the first step of Gaussian elimination can be described using the elementary lower triangular matrix

$$L_1 = L_1(\mathbf{m}_1) = I - \mathbf{m}_1\mathbf{e}_1^T$$

employing the vector

$$\mathbf{m}_1 = \left(0, \frac{a_{21}}{a_{11}}, \ldots, \frac{a_{n1}}{a_{11}}\right)^T.$$

The complete Gaussian elimination process can be described as follows.

Theorem 3.5 *Let $A \in \mathbb{R}^{n \times n}$ be non-singular and $\mathbf{b} \in \mathbb{R}^n$ be given. Set $A^{(1)} = A$ and $\mathbf{b}^{(1)} = \mathbf{b}$ and then for $1 \le k \le n - 1$ iteratively*

$$\mathbf{m}_k := \left(0, \ldots, 0, \frac{a_{k+1,k}^{(k)}}{a_{kk}^{(k)}}, \ldots, \frac{a_{nk}^{(k)}}{a_{kk}^{(k)}}\right)^T,$$

$$L_k := I - \mathbf{m}_k\mathbf{e}_k^T,$$

$$(A^{(k+1)}, \mathbf{b}^{(k+1)}) := L_k\left(A^{(k)}, \mathbf{b}^{(k)}\right),$$

provided that $a_{kk}^{(k)} \ne 0$. Assuming that the process does not finish prematurely, *it stops with a linear system $A^{(n)}x = b^{(n)}$ with an upper triangular matrix $A^{(n)}$, which has the same solution as the original system $Ax = b$.*

Proof Obviously, the systems have the same solution since, in each step, we multiply both sides of the equation $Ax = b$ by an invertible matrix.
We will show by induction that the matrices $A^{(k)}$, $2 \leq k \leq n$, satisfy

$$a_{ij}^{(k)} = e_i^T A^{(k)} e_j = 0 \qquad \text{for } 1 \leq j < k, \ j < i \leq n. \qquad (3.4)$$

This means particularly for $A^{(n)}$ that all sub-diagonal entries vanish.
For $k = 2$ this has been explained above. Hence, let us now assume that (3.4) holds for $k < n$. If the indices i and j satisfy $1 \leq j < k + 1$ and $j < i \leq n$ then we can conclude

$$a_{ij}^{(k+1)} = e_i^T L_k A^{(k)} e_j = e_i^T (I - m_k e_k^T) A^{(k)} e_j$$
$$= e_i^T A^{(k)} e_j - (e_i^T m_k)(e_k^T A^{(k)} e_j).$$

For $j < k$ this means particularly $a_{ij}^{(k+1)} = 0$, since both $e_i^T A^{(k)} e_j$ and $e_k^T A^{(k)} e_j$ are zero by assumption. Finally, for $j = k$ and $i > j$ we have because of

$$e_i^T m_k = \frac{a_{ik}^{(k)}}{a_{kk}^{(k)}} = \frac{e_i^T A^{(k)} e_k}{e_k^T A^{(k)} e_k}$$

also

$$a_{ij}^{(k+1)} = e_i^T A^{(k)} e_k - \frac{e_i^T A^{(k)} e_k}{e_k^T A^{(k)} e_k} e_k^T A^{(k)} e_k = 0. \qquad \square$$

An algorithmic description of Gaussian elimination is given in Algorithm 3. Note that this algorithm works *in situ*, meaning that the sequence of matrices $A^{(k)}$ all overwrite the previous matrix and no additional memory is required. Note also that Algorithm 3 does not only store the upper triangular matrix $A^{(n)}$ but even stores the essential elements of the elementary lower triangular matrices L_k, i.e. it stores the defining vectors m_k in that part of column k beneath the diagonal.

Remark 3.6 Algorithm 3 for Gaussian elimination requires $O(n^3)$ time and $O(n^2)$ space.

Proof The remark about the space is obvious. For the computational cost, we analyse the three for loops in Algorithm 3. Considering that line 2 needs one flop, lines 4 and 5 require two flops and line 7 requires again one flop, we see

---

Algorithm 3: Gaussian elimination

Input : $A \in \mathbb{R}^{n \times n}$, $\mathbf{b} \in \mathbb{R}^n$.

Output: $A^{(n)}$ upper triangular and $\mathbf{m}_1, \ldots, \mathbf{m}_{n-1}$ and $\mathbf{b}^{(n)} \in \mathbb{R}^n$.

1 **for** $k = 1$ **to** $n - 1$ **do**
2     $d := 1/a_{kk}$
3   **for** $i = k + 1$ **to** n **do**
4        $a_{ik} := a_{ik} \cdot d$
5        $b_i := b_i - b_k \cdot a_{ik}$
6   **for** $j = k + 1$ **to** n **do**
7           $a_{ij} := a_{ij} - a_{ik} \cdot a_{kj}$

---

that the time requirement is determined by

$$
\begin{aligned}
T(n) &= \sum_{k=1}^{n-1} \left(1 + \sum_{i=k+1}^{n} \left(2 + \sum_{j=k+1}^{n} 1 \right) \right) \\
&= (n - 1) + \sum_{k=1}^{n-1} \left(2(n - k) + \sum_{i=k+1}^{n} (n - k) \right) \\
&= (n - 1) + \sum_{k=1}^{n-1} \left(2k + k^2 \right) \\
&= (n - 1) + n(n - 1) + \frac{(n - 1)n(2n - 1)}{6} \\
&= \frac{1}{3} n^3 + O(n^2).
\end{aligned}
$$
□

3.3 LU Factorisation

Naturally, Gaussian elimination is **not** realised by matrix multiplication, but by programming the corresponding operations directly, as shown in Algorithm 3. This leads to an $O(n^3)$ complexity. In addition, we have an $O(n^2)$ complexity for solving the final linear system by back substitution.

However, there is another way of looking at the process. Suppose we may construct a sequence of $n - 1$ elementary lower triangular matrices $L_j = L_j(\mathbf{m}_j)$ such that

$$
L_{n-1} L_{n-2} \cdots L_2 L_1 A = U
$$

is an upper triangular matrix. Since $L_i(\mathbf{m}_i)^{-1} = L_i(-\mathbf{m}_i)$, we have

$$
\begin{aligned}
A &= L_1(-\mathbf{m}_1)L_2(-\mathbf{m}_2)\cdots L_{n-2}(-\mathbf{m}_{n-2})L_{n-1}(-\mathbf{m}_{n-1})U \\
&= (I + \mathbf{m}_1\mathbf{e}_1^{\mathrm{T}})(I + \mathbf{m}_2\mathbf{e}_2^{\mathrm{T}})\cdots(I + \mathbf{m}_{n-2}\mathbf{e}_{n-2}^{\mathrm{T}})(I + \mathbf{m}_{n-1}\mathbf{e}_{n-1}^{\mathrm{T}})U \\
&= (I + \mathbf{m}_{n-1}\mathbf{e}_{n-1}^{\mathrm{T}} + \mathbf{m}_{n-2}\mathbf{e}_{n-2}^{\mathrm{T}} + \cdots + \mathbf{m}_2\mathbf{e}_2^{\mathrm{T}} + \mathbf{m}_1\mathbf{e}_1^{\mathrm{T}})U \\
&=: LU,
\end{aligned}
$$

where L is lower triangular with unit diagonal elements

$$
L = I + \sum_{i=1}^{n-1} \mathbf{m}_i\mathbf{e}_i^{\mathrm{T}}.
$$

Definition 3.7 A matrix $L = (\ell_{ij}) \in \mathbb{R}^{n\times n}$ is called a *normalised lower triangular matrix* if $\ell_{ij} = 0$ for $i < j$ and $\ell_{ii} = 1$.

The *LU factorisation* of a matrix A is the decomposition $A = LU$ into the product of a normalised lower triangular matrix and an upper triangular matrix.

We will soon see that if an *LU* factorisation of a matrix A exists then it is unique, which explains why we can speak of *the LU* factorisation.

Sometimes, the condition on L to be normalised is relaxed and $A = LU$ with a regular lower triangular matrix L and a regular upper triangular matrix U is already called an *LU* factorisation. In this case, we will, however, lose the uniqueness of the factorisation. We will also have uniqueness if we require U to be normalised instead of L.

So far, we have assumed that Gaussian elimination does not break down, i.e. that we can divide by $a_{kk}^{(k)}$ for each k. It is now time to look at examples of matrices where this condition is guaranteed.

Theorem 3.8 *Let $A \in \mathbb{R}^{n\times n}$. Let $A_p \in \mathbb{R}^{p\times p}$ be the pth principal sub-matrix of A, i.e.*

$$
A_p = \begin{pmatrix} a_{11} & \cdots & a_{1p} \\ \vdots & & \vdots \\ a_{p1} & \cdots & a_{pp} \end{pmatrix}.
$$

If $\det(A_p) \neq 0$ for $1 \leq p \leq n$ then A has an LU factorisation. In particular, every symmetric, positive definite matrix possesses an LU factorisation.

Proof We will prove this by induction. For $k = 1$ we have $\det A_1 = a_{11} \neq 0$, hence the first step in the Gaussian elimination procedure is possible. For $k \to k + 1$ assume that our matrix is of the form as in (3.3). Then, as elementary matrix operations do not change the determinant of a matrix, we have

$$
0 \neq \det A_k = \det A_k^{(k)} = a_{11}a_{22}^{(2)}\cdots a_{kk}^{(k)},
$$

so that particularly $a_{kk}^{(k)} \neq 0$. Hence, the next step is also possible and we can proceed in this way.

A symmetric, positive definite matrix satisfies obviously $\det A_p > 0$ for all $1 \leq p \leq n$. □

Another class of matrices with an *LU* factorisation is the following one.

Definition 3.9 A matrix A is called *strictly row diagonally dominant* if

$$\sum_{\substack{k=1 \\ k \neq i}}^{n} |a_{ik}| < |a_{ii}|, \qquad 1 \leq i \leq n.$$

Theorem 3.10 *A strictly row diagonally dominant matrix $A \in \mathbb{R}^{n \times n}$ is invertible and possesses an LU factorisation.*

Proof Since $|a_{11}| > \sum_{j=2}^{n} |a_{1j}| \geq 0$, the first step of Gaussian elimination is possible. To use once again an inductive argument, it obviously suffices to show that the new matrix $A^{(2)} = (I - \mathbf{m}_1 \mathbf{e}_1^{\mathrm{T}})A$ is also strictly row diagonally dominant. Since the first row of $A^{(2)}$ coincides with that of A we only have to look at the rows with index $i = 2, \ldots, n$. For such an i, we have $a_{i1}^{(2)} = 0$ and

$$a_{ij}^{(2)} = a_{ij} - \frac{a_{i1}}{a_{11}} a_{1j}, \qquad 2 \leq j \leq n.$$

This leads to

$$\sum_{\substack{j=1 \\ j \neq i}}^{n} |a_{ij}^{(2)}| = \sum_{\substack{j=2 \\ j \neq i}}^{n} |a_{ij}^{(2)}| \leq \sum_{\substack{j=2 \\ j \neq i}}^{n} |a_{ij}| + \frac{|a_{i1}|}{|a_{11}|} \sum_{\substack{j=2 \\ j \neq i}}^{n} |a_{1j}|$$

$$< |a_{ii}| - |a_{i1}| + \frac{|a_{i1}|}{|a_{11}|} \{|a_{11}| - |a_{1i}|\}$$

$$= |a_{ii}| - \frac{|a_{i1}|}{|a_{11}|} |a_{1i}| \leq |a_{ii}^{(2)}|.$$

Thus, $A^{(2)}$ is indeed strictly row diagonally dominant and hence $a_{22}^{(2)} \neq 0$ so that we can proceed in the Gaussian elimination procedure. Continuing like this, we see that all elements $a_{kk}^{(k)}$ are different from zero, meaning that Gaussian elimination goes through all the way. It also means that the upper triangular matrix $A^{(n)}$ is non-singular and hence A too is non-singular. □

We have used Gaussian elimination to compute the *LU* factorisation of a matrix A. However, this might not be the only way of doing this. Hence, the question of whether the *LU* factorisation is unique comes up naturally. To answer this question, we need a result on triangular matrices.

Theorem 3.11   *The set of non-singular (normalised) lower (or upper) triangular matrices is a group with respect to matrix multiplication.*

Proof   If A and B are matrices of one of these sets, we have to show that also A^{-1} and AB belong to that particular set. Suppose A is a non-singular upper triangular matrix and $\mathbf{e}_k$ is, as usual, the kth unit vector in $\mathbb{R}^n$. Let $\mathbf{x}^{(k)}$ be the solution of $A\mathbf{x}^{(k)} = \mathbf{e}_k$. Then, the columns of A^{-1} are given by these $\mathbf{x}^{(k)}$. From Algorithm 2 we can inductively conclude that the components $x_{k+1}^{(k)}, \ldots, x_n^{(k)}$ are zero and that $x_k^{(k)} = 1/a_{kk}$. This shows that A^{-1} is also an upper triangular matrix. If A is normalised then this shows that A^{-1} is normalised, as well. Next, assume that B is another non-singular upper triangular matrix. Since $a_{ij} = b_{ij} = 0$ for $i > j$ we can conclude that

$$(AB)_{ij} = \sum_{k=i}^{j} a_{ik}b_{kj}, \qquad 1 \le i, j \le n,$$

which shows that AB is also an upper triangular matrix. If both A and B are normalised the above formula immediately shows that AB is also normalised. This finishes the proof for (normalised) upper triangular matrices. For (normalised) lower triangular matrices the proof is essentially the same.   □

Theorem 3.12   *If the invertible matrix A has an LU factorisation then it is unique.*

Proof   Suppose $A = L_1 U_1$ and $A = L_2 U_2$ are two LU factorisations of a non-singular matrix A. Then, we have

$$L_2^{-1}L_1 = U_2 U_1^{-1}.$$

Furthermore, $L_2^{-1}L_1$ is, as the product of two normalised lower triangular matrices, a normalised lower triangular matrix itself. However, $U_2 U_1^{-1}$ is an upper triangular matrix. Since we have equality between these matrices, this is possible only if they are the identity matrix, which shows $L_1 = L_2$ and $U_1 = U_2$.   □

As mentioned above, Algorithm 3 already overwrites A with all the information required for the LU factorisation. To be more precise, if we leave out step 5 in Algorithm 3 then we have an algorithm for computing the LU factorisation *in situ*, because we have at the end

$$\ell_{ij} = \begin{cases} a_{ij} & \text{if } i > j, \\ \delta_{ij} & \text{if } i \le j, \end{cases} \qquad u_{ij} = \begin{cases} a_{ij} & \text{if } i \le j, \\ 0 & \text{if } i > j. \end{cases}$$

There are, however, other ways of computing the LU factorisation. One other possible way of deriving an algorithm for calculating the *LU* factorisation starts with the component-wise formulation of $A = LU$, i.e.

$$a_{ij} = \sum_{k=1}^{n} \ell_{ik} u_{kj}.$$

Since U is upper triangular and L is lower triangular, the upper limit of the sum is actually given by $\min(i, j)$. Taking the two cases separately gives

$$a_{ij} = \sum_{k=1}^{j} \ell_{ik} u_{kj}, \qquad 1 \leq j < i \leq n,$$

$$a_{ij} = \sum_{k=1}^{i} \ell_{ik} u_{kj}, \qquad 1 \leq i \leq j \leq n.$$

Rearranging these equations, and using the fact that $\ell_{ii} = 1$ for all $1 \leq i \leq n$, we find that

$$\ell_{ij} = \frac{1}{u_{jj}} \left(a_{ij} - \sum_{k=1}^{j-1} \ell_{ik} u_{kj} \right), \qquad 2 \leq i \leq n,\ 1 \leq j \leq i-1, \qquad (3.5)$$

$$u_{ij} = a_{ij} - \sum_{k=1}^{i-1} \ell_{ik} u_{kj}, \qquad 1 \leq i \leq n,\ i \leq j \leq n. \qquad (3.6)$$

Thus, the elements of U in the first row are $u_{1j} = a_{1j}$, $1 \leq j \leq n$, and the elements of L in the first column are $\ell_{11} = 1$ and $\ell_{i1} = a_{i1}/u_{11}$, $2 \leq i \leq n$.

The equations (3.5) and (3.6) can now be used for the calculation of the elements ℓ_{ij} and u_{ij}. For each value of i, starting with $i = 2$, we calculate first ℓ_{ij} for $1 \leq j \leq i - 1$ in increasing order, and then the values of u_{ij} for $i \leq j \leq n$, again in increasing order. We then move on to the same calculation for $i + 1$ and so on until $i = n$. We refrain from giving the easily derived algorithm, but state the obvious result on the computational complexity.

Remark 3.13 The computational cost of computing the *LU* factorisation of a matrix $A \in \mathbb{R}^{n \times n}$ is $O(n^3)$.

We want to address a few applications of the *LU* factorisation. The first one is rather obvious.

Remark 3.14 If $A = LU$ then the linear system $\mathbf{b} = A\mathbf{x} = LU\mathbf{x}$ can be solved in two steps. First, we solve $L\mathbf{y} = \mathbf{b}$ by forward substitution and then $U\mathbf{x} = \mathbf{y}$ by back substitution. Both are possible in $O(n^2)$ time.

This means in particular that we could compute the inverse of a matrix A with *LU* factorisation by solving the n linear systems $A\mathbf{x}^{(j)} = \mathbf{e}_j$, $1 \leq j \leq n$, where

$\mathbf{e}_j$ is the jth unit vector in $\mathbb{R}^n$. Solving these n systems would cost $O(n^3)$ time and hence the computation of A^{-1} would cost $O(n^3)$ time.

Remark 3.15 A numerically reasonable way of calculating the determinant of a matrix A is to first compute the LU factorisation and then use the fact that $\det(A) = \det(LU) = \det(L)\det(U) = \det(U) = u_{11}u_{22}\cdots u_{nn}$.

In the case of a tridiagonal matrix, there is an efficient way of constructing the LU factorisation, at least under certain additional assumptions. Let the tridiagonal matrix be given by

$$A = \begin{pmatrix} a_1 & c_1 & & & 0 \\ b_2 & a_2 & c_2 & & \\ & \ddots & \ddots & \ddots & \\ & & \ddots & \ddots & c_{n-1} \\ 0 & & & b_n & a_n \end{pmatrix}. \tag{3.7}$$

Then, we have the following theorem.

Theorem 3.16 *Assume A is a tridiagonal matrix of the form (3.7) with*

$$|a_1| > |c_1| > 0,$$
$$|a_i| \geq |b_i| + |c_i|, \quad b_i, c_i \neq 0, \ 2 \leq i \leq n-1,$$
$$|a_n| \geq |b_n| > 0.$$

Then, A is invertible and has an LU factorisation of the form

$$A = \begin{pmatrix} 1 & & & 0 \\ \ell_2 & 1 & & \\ & \ddots & \ddots & \\ 0 & & \ell_n & 1 \end{pmatrix} \begin{pmatrix} u_1 & c_1 & & 0 \\ & u_2 & \ddots & \\ & & \ddots & c_{n-1} \\ 0 & & & u_n \end{pmatrix}.$$

The vectors $\boldsymbol{\ell} \in \mathbb{R}^{n-1}$ and $\mathbf{u} \in \mathbb{R}^n$ can be computed as follows: $u_1 = a_1$ and $\ell_i = b_i/u_{i-1}$ and $u_i = a_i - \ell_i c_{i-1}$ for $2 \leq i \leq n$.

Proof We show inductively for $1 \leq i \leq n-1$ that $u_i \neq 0$ and $|c_i/u_i| < 1$. From this, it follows that both $\boldsymbol{\ell}$ and $\mathbf{u}$ are well defined. By assumption, we have for $i = 1$ obviously $|u_1| = |a_1| > |c_1| > 0$. The induction step then follows from

$$|u_{i+1}| \geq |a_{i+1}| - \frac{|c_i|}{|u_i|}|b_{i+1}| > |a_{i+1}| - |b_{i+1}| \geq |c_{i+1}|.$$

This calculation also shows that $u_n \neq 0$, proving that A is invertible, provided the method really gives the LU factorisation of A. To see the latter, we first notice that for the given L and U their product LU must be a tridiagonal matrix. Simple calculations then show the statement. For example, we have $(LU)_{i,i} = \ell_i c_{i-1} + u_i = a_i$. The other two cases $(LU)_{i,i+1}$ and $(LU)_{i+1,i}$ follow just as easily. $\qquad\square$

Note that for such a system not only the calculation of the LU factorisation simplifies but also the solution of the corresponding systems by forward and back substitution. This means that in this case it is possible to solve the linear system $Ax = b$ in $O(n)$ time.

Example 3.17 For our second example in the introduction, Section 1.1.2, we see that the matrix from (1.2) satisfies the assumption of Theorem 3.16. Here, the situation is even simpler since the entries in each band are constant, i.e. if we ignore the $1/h^2$ factor then we have $a_i = 2$ and $b_i = c_i = -1$. Thus, the computation reduces to $u_1 = a_1 = 2$ and then $\ell_i = b_i/u_{i-1} = -1/u_{i-1}, 2 \le i \le n$. Inserting this into the computation of u_i yields

$$u_i = a_i - \ell_i c_{i-1} = 2 + \ell_i = 2 - \frac{1}{u_{i-1}}, \qquad 2 \le i \le n,$$

which resolve to $\mathbf{u} = \left(2, \frac{3}{2}, \frac{4}{3}, \frac{5}{4}, \ldots, \frac{n+1}{n}\right)^{\mathsf{T}}$, or $u_i = \frac{i+1}{i}$, which also determines $\ell_i = -1/u_{i-1} = -(i-1)/i$.

3.4 Pivoting

We now want to address the situation that the Gaussian elimination process breaks down prematurely. This means that there is an index k with $a_{kk}^{(k)} = 0$. For example, let us consider the simple matrix

$$A = \begin{pmatrix} 0 & 1 \\ 1 & 1 \end{pmatrix}.$$

This matrix is non-singular and well-conditioned with a condition number $\kappa_2(A) = (3 + \sqrt{5})/2$, in the 2-norm. But Gaussian elimination fails already at its first step, since $a_{11} = 0$. Note, however, that a simple exchanging of the rows gives an upper triangular matrix. Furthermore, a simple exchanging of the columns leads to a lower triangular matrix. The first action corresponds to rearranging the equations in the linear system, the latter corresponds to rearranging the unknowns.

Hence, rearranging either the rows or columns of the matrix (or both) seems to resolve the problem of a premature breakdown.

Next, let us consider the slightly perturbed matrix

$$A = \begin{pmatrix} 10^{-20} & 1 \\ 1 & 1 \end{pmatrix}.$$

Using Gaussian elimination on this matrix gives the factors

$$L = \begin{pmatrix} 1 & 0 \\ 10^{20} & 1 \end{pmatrix}, \qquad U = \begin{pmatrix} 10^{-20} & 1 \\ 0 & 1 - 10^{20} \end{pmatrix}.$$

However, we are using floating point arithmetic with machine precision $\approx$ 10^{-16}. The number $1 - 10^{20}$ will not be represented exactly, but by its nearest floating point number, let us say that this is the number -10^{20}. Using this number produces the factorisation

$$\tilde{L} = \begin{pmatrix} 1 & 0 \\ 10^{20} & 1 \end{pmatrix}, \qquad \tilde{U} = \begin{pmatrix} 10^{-20} & 1 \\ 0 & -10^{20} \end{pmatrix}.$$

The matrix $\tilde{U}$ is relatively close to the correct U, but on calculating the product we obtain

$$\tilde{L}\tilde{U} = \begin{pmatrix} 10^{-20} & 1 \\ 1 & 0 \end{pmatrix}.$$

We see that this matrix is not close to A, since a 1 has been replaced by a 0. Suppose we wish to solve $Ax = b$ with $b = (1,0)^T$ using floating point arithmetic we would obtain $\tilde{x} = (0,1)^T$ while the true answer is approximately $(-1,1)^T$. The explanation for this is that LU factorisation is not *backward-stable*.

A proof of the following result can again be found in Higham [85] or Trefethen and Bau [124]. It shows that Gaussian elimination is backward-stable if the norms of the triangular matrices L and U can be bounded. Unfortunately, as we have just seen, this may not be the case.

Remark 3.18 Let $A \in \mathbb{R}^{n \times n}$ have an LU factorisation. Then, Gaussian elimination computes matrices $\tilde{L}, \tilde{U}$ satisfying $\tilde{L}\tilde{U} = A + \Delta A$, where ΔA satisfies

$$\|\Delta A\| = O(\|L\| \|U\| \, \text{eps}).$$

But the important conclusion here is that exchanging rows or columns or both is also necessary if the element $a_{kk}^{(k)}$ is close to zero to stabilise the elimination process.

The exchange of rows or columns during the Gaussian elimination process is referred to as *pivoting*. Assume we have performed $k - 1$ steps and now have a matrix of the form

$$A^{(k)} = \begin{pmatrix} a_{11} & * & * & \cdots & * \\ 0 & a_{22}^{(2)} & * & \cdots & * \\ & & \ddots & & \\ 0 & 0 & a_{kk}^{(k)} & \cdots & a_{kn}^{(k)} \\ \vdots & \vdots & \vdots & & \vdots \\ 0 & 0 & a_{nk}^{(k)} & \cdots & a_{nn}^{(k)} \end{pmatrix}. \tag{3.8}$$

If $\det A = \det A^{(k)} \neq 0$, not all the entries in the column vector $(a_{kk}^{(k)}, \ldots, a_{nk}^{(k)})^{\mathrm{T}}$ can be zero. Hence, we can pick one entry and swap the corresponding row with the kth row. This is usually referred to as *partial (row) pivoting*. For numerical reasons it is sensible to pick a row index $\ell \in \{k, k+1, \ldots, n\}$ with

$$|a_{\ell k}| = \max_{k \leq i \leq n} |a_{ik}^{(k)}|.$$

In a similar way, *partial column pivoting* can be defined. Finally, we could use *total pivoting*, i.e. we could pick indices $\ell, m \in \{k, k+1, \ldots, n\}$ such that

$$|a_{\ell m}| = \max_{k \leq i, j \leq n} |a_{ij}^{(k)}|.$$

Usually, partial row pivoting is implemented. This, however, depends on the way the programming language used stores matrices. If a matrix is stored row by row then swapping two rows can be achieved by simply swapping two row pointers. An exchange of two columns could only be realised by really exchanging all entries in these two columns which is much more expensive.

To understand the process of pivoting in an abstract form, we once again use matrices to describe the operations. Once again, this is only for theoretical purposes and not for a numerical implementation. The required matrices to describe pivoting are permutation matrices.

Definition 3.19 A *permutation* of the set $\{1, \ldots, n\}$ is a bijective map $p : \{1, \ldots, n\} \to \{1, \ldots, n\}$. A matrix $P \in \mathbb{R}^{n \times n}$ is called a *permutation matrix* if there is a permutation p such that

$$P\mathbf{e}_j = \mathbf{e}_{p(j)}, \qquad 1 \leq j \leq n,$$

where $\mathbf{e}_j$ denotes once again the jth unit vector.

A permutation matrix is simply a matrix that results from the identity matrix by exchanging its rows (or columns). This means particularly that a permutation matrix is invertible.

Theorem 3.20 *Every permutation matrix $P \in \mathbb{R}^{n \times n}$ is orthogonal, i.e. $P^{-1} = P^{\mathrm{T}}$. Let $P = P_p \in \mathbb{R}^{n \times n}$ be a permutation matrix with permutation p. If p^{-1} is the permutation inverse to p, i.e. if $p^{-1}(p(j)) = j$ for $1 \le j \le n$, then $P_{p^{-1}} = P_p^{-1}$.*

Proof We start with the second statement. This is true since we have

$$P_{p^{-1}} P_p \mathbf{e}_j = P_{p^{-1}} \mathbf{e}_{p(j)} = \mathbf{e}_{p^{-1}(p(j))} = \mathbf{e}_j,$$

for $1 \le j \le n$. The first statement follows, for $1 \le j, k \le n$, from

$$\mathbf{e}_{p^{-1}(j)}^{\mathrm{T}} P_p^{\mathrm{T}} \mathbf{e}_k = \mathbf{e}_k^{\mathrm{T}} P_p \mathbf{e}_{p^{-1}(j)} = \mathbf{e}_k^{\mathrm{T}} \mathbf{e}_j = \delta_{jk} = \mathbf{e}_{p^{-1}(j)}^{\mathrm{T}} \mathbf{e}_{p^{-1}(k)} = \mathbf{e}_{p^{-1}(j)}^{\mathrm{T}} P_p^{-1} \mathbf{e}_k. \qquad \square$$

For partial pivoting we need to exchange exactly two rows in each step. This is realised using elementary permutation matrices.

Definition 3.21 A permutation matrix $P_{ij} \in \mathbb{R}^{n \times n}$ is called an *elementary permutation matrix* if it is of the form

$$P_{ij} = I - (\mathbf{e}_i - \mathbf{e}_j)(\mathbf{e}_i - \mathbf{e}_j)^{\mathrm{T}}.$$

This means simply that the matrix P_{ij} is an identity matrix with rows (columns) i and j exchanged.

Remark 3.22 An elementary permutation matrix has the properties

$$P_{ij}^{-1} = P_{ij} = P_{ji} = P_{ij}^{\mathrm{T}}$$

and $\det(P_{ij}) = -1$, for $i \ne j$ and $P_{ii} = I$. Pre-multiplication of a matrix A by P_{ij} exchanges rows i and j of A. Similarly post-multiplication exchanges columns i and j of A.

Theorem 3.23 *Let A be an $n \times n$ matrix. There exist elementary lower triangular matrices $L_i := L_i(\mathbf{m}_i)$ and elementary permutation matrices $P_i := P_{r_i i}$ with $r_i \ge i$, $i = 1, 2, \ldots, n - 1$, such that*

$$U := L_{n-1} P_{n-1} L_{n-2} P_{n-2} \cdots L_2 P_2 L_1 P_1 A \tag{3.9}$$

is upper triangular.

Proof This follows from the previous considerations. Note that, if the matrix is singular, we might come into a situation (3.8), where the column vector $(a_{kk}^{(k)}, \ldots, a_{nk}^{(k)})^{\mathrm{T}}$ is the zero vector. In such a situation we pick the corresponding elementary lower triangular and permutation matrices as the identity and proceed with the next column. $\qquad \square$

The permutation matrices in (3.9) can be "moved" to the right in the following sense. If P is a symmetric permutation matrix, which acts only on rows (or columns) with index larger than j then we have

$$PL_jP^{\mathrm{T}} = P(I - \mathbf{m}_j\mathbf{e}_j^{\mathrm{T}})P^{\mathrm{T}} = I - P\mathbf{m}_j(P\mathbf{e}_j)^{\mathrm{T}} = I - \tilde{\mathbf{m}}_j\mathbf{e}_j^{\mathrm{T}} = \tilde{L}_j.$$

Obviously, the first j components of $\tilde{\mathbf{m}}_j$ are also vanishing, making $\tilde{L}_j$ again an elementary lower triangular matrix. This gives in particular

$$U = L_{n-1}P_{n-1}L_{n-2}P_{n-1}^{\mathrm{T}}P_{n-1}P_{n-2}L_{n-3}\cdots L_2P_2L_1P_1A$$
$$= L_{n-1}\tilde{L}_{n-2}P_{n-1}P_{n-2}L_{n-3}\cdots L_2P_2L_1P_1A.$$

In the same way, we can move $P_{n-1}P_{n-2}$ to the right of L_{n-3}. Continuing with this procedure leads to

$$U = L_{n-1}\tilde{L}_{n-2}\cdots\tilde{L}_1P_{n-1}P_{n-2}\cdots P_1A =: L^{-1}PA,$$

which establishes the following theorem.

Theorem 3.24 *For every non-singular matrix $A \in \mathbb{R}^{n\times n}$ there is a permutation matrix P such that PA possesses an LU factorisation $PA = LU$.*

As mentioned above, permutation matrices are only used to describe the theory mathematically. When it comes to the implementation, permutations are done directly. For partial pivoting, this is described in Algorithm 4, which is a simple modification of the original Algorithm 3.

Algorithm 4: LU-factorisation with partial pivoting

Input : $A \in \mathbb{R}^{n\times n}, \mathbf{b} \in \mathbb{R}^n.$
Output: $PA = LU.$

1 **for** $k = 1, 2, \ldots, n - 1$ **do**
2   Find the pivot element a_{kr} for row k
3   Exchange row k with row r
4     $d := 1/a_{kk}$
5   **for** $i = k + 1, \ldots, n$ **do**
6        $a_{ik} := a_{ik}d$
7   **for** $j = k + 1, \ldots, n$ **do**
8           $a_{ij} := a_{ij} - a_{ik}a_{kj}$

3.5 Cholesky Factorisation

Let us assume that A has an LU factorisation $A = LU$ and that A is symmetric, i.e. $A^T = A$. Then we have

$$LU = A = A^T = U^T L^T.$$

Since U^T is a lower triangular matrix and L^T is an upper triangular matrix, we would like to use the uniqueness of the LU factorisation to conclude that $L = U^T$ and $U = L^T$. Unfortunately, this is not possible since the uniqueness requires the lower triangular matrix to be normalised, i.e. to have only ones as diagonal entries, and this may not be the case for U^T.

But if A is invertible, then we can write

$$U = D\tilde{U}$$

with a diagonal matrix $D = \mathrm{diag}(d_{11}, \ldots, d_{nn})$ and a normalised upper triangular matrix $\tilde{U}$. Then, we can conclude that $A = LD\tilde{U}$ and hence $A^T = \tilde{U}^T DL^T = LD\tilde{U}$, so that we can now apply the uniqueness result to derive $L = \tilde{U}^T$ and $U = DL^T$, which gives $A = LDL^T$.

Let us finally make the assumption that all diagonal entries of D are positive, so that we can define its square root by setting $D^{1/2} = \mathrm{diag}(\sqrt{d_{11}}, \ldots, \sqrt{d_{nn}})$, which leads to the decomposition

$$A = (LD^{1/2})(LD^{1/2})^T = \tilde{L}\tilde{L}^T.$$

Definition 3.25   A decomposition of a matrix A of the form $A = LL^T$ with a lower triangular matrix L is called a *Cholesky factorisation* of A.

It remains to verify for what kind of matrices a Cholesky factorisation exists.

Theorem 3.26   *Suppose $A = A^T$ is positive definite. Then, A possesses a Cholesky factorisation.*

Proof   A matrix A is positive definite if and only if the determinant of every upper principal sub-matrix A_p is positive. From Theorem 3.8 we can therefore conclude that $A = LU$ is possible. Since a positive definite matrix is also invertible, our previous derivation shows that $A = LDL^T$. Finally, A being positive definite also means that

$$d_{ii} = \mathbf{e}_i^T D\mathbf{e}_i = \mathbf{e}_i^T (L^{-1}AL^{-T})\mathbf{e}_i = (L^{-T}\mathbf{e}_i)^T A(L^{-T}\mathbf{e}_i) > 0,$$

where we have used the short notation L^{-T} for $(L^{-1})^T$.   □

For the numerical algorithm, it is again useful to write $A = LL^T$ component-wise taking into account that L is lower triangular. For $i \geq j$ we have

$$a_{ij} = \sum_{k=1}^{j} \ell_{ik}\ell_{jk} = \sum_{k=1}^{j-1} \ell_{ik}\ell_{jk} + \ell_{ij}\ell_{jj}.$$

This can first be resolved for $i = j$:

$$\ell_{jj} = \left(a_{jj} - \sum_{k=1}^{j-1} \ell_{jk}^2 \right)^{1/2}.$$

With this, we can successively compute the other coefficients. For $i > j$ we have

$$\ell_{ij} = \frac{1}{\ell_{jj}} \left(a_{ij} - \sum_{k=1}^{j-1} \ell_{ik}\ell_{jk} \right).$$

With these equations it is now easy to successively compute the matrix L either row-wise or column-wise. A column-oriented version of the Cholesky factorisation is given in Algorithm 5. Obviously, in a final implementation it would be appropriate to check a_{jj} for non-negativity before taking the square root in step 4. This is also a means to check whether the given matrix A is "numerically" positive definite.

Remark 3.27 The computational complexity of computing the Cholesky factorisation is given by $n^3/6 + O(n^2)$, which is about half the complexity of the standard Gaussian elimination process. However, here, we also have to take n roots.

Proof Leaving the n roots from line 4 of Algorithm 5 aside and counting one flop for each of the lines 3, 7 and 8 yields

$$T(n) = \sum_{j=1}^{n} \left(\sum_{k=1}^{j-1} 1 + \sum_{i=j+1}^{n} \left(1 + \sum_{k=1}^{j-1} 1 \right) \right).$$

After some simple calculations, similar to the ones we have done before, we see that this leads indeed to $T(n) = n^3/6 + O(n^2)$. □

Remark 3.28 In contrast to Gaussian elimination, the computation of a Cholesky factorisation is backward-stable, see again [85, 124], as long as the norm of the matrix is not too large. The computed factor $\tilde{L}$ satisfies $\tilde{L}^T\tilde{L} = A + \Delta A$ where ΔA can be bounded by $\|\Delta A\| = O(\|A\| \text{ eps})$.

Algorithm 5: Cholesky factorisation

Input : $A \in \mathbb{R}^{n \times n}$ symmetric, positive definite.
Output: $A = LL^T$ Cholesky factorisation.

1 **for** $j = 1$ **to** n **do**
2   **for** $k = 1$ **to** $j - 1$ **do**
3         $a_{jj} := a_{jj} - a_{jk} \cdot a_{jk}$
4     $a_{jj} := \sqrt{a_{jj}}$
5   **for** $i = j + 1$ **to** n **do**
6   **for** $k = 1$ **to** $j - 1$ **do**
7           $a_{ij} := a_{ij} - a_{ik} \cdot a_{jk}$
8        $a_{ij} := a_{ij}/a_{jj}$

As we already know, solving triangular systems with backward and forward substitution is also backward-stable. Hence, the solution process for solving a linear system $A\mathbf{x} = \mathbf{b}$ with A being symmetric and positive definite using the Cholesky factorisation will produce a reasonable solution as long as the condition number of A is not too large.

3.6 QR Factorisation

We have seen that we can derive an LU factorisation for every matrix A if we employ pivoting if necessary. The LU factorisation can be described by multiplying the original matrix A with elementary lower triangular matrices from the left. Unfortunately, this might change the condition number $\kappa(A) = \|A\| \|A^{-1}\|$. Though we can only say that

$$\kappa(LA) = \|LA\| \|(LA)^{-1}\| \leq \kappa(L)\kappa(A),$$

we have to expect $\kappa(LA) > \kappa(A)$ because $\kappa(L) \geq 1$. Hence, it would be better to use transformations which do not change the condition number. Candidates for this are orthogonal matrices, i.e. matrices $Q \in \mathbb{R}^{n \times n}$ with $Q^T Q = I$.

Proposition 3.29 *Let $Q \in \mathbb{R}^{n \times n}$ be orthogonal and $A \in \mathbb{R}^{n \times n}$, then $\|Q\mathbf{x}\|_2 = \|\mathbf{x}\|_2$ for all $\mathbf{x} \in \mathbb{R}^n$ and $\|QA\|_2 = \|A\|_2$.*

Proof We have

$$\|Q\mathbf{x}\|_2^2 = (Q\mathbf{x})^T(Q\mathbf{x}) = \mathbf{x}^T Q^T Q \mathbf{x} = \mathbf{x}^T \mathbf{x} = \|\mathbf{x}\|_2^2.$$

Similarly,

$$\|QA\|_2 = \sup_{\|x\|_2=1} \|QAx\|_2 = \sup_{\|x\|_2=1} \|Ax\|_2 = \|A\|_2. \qquad \square$$

The goal of this section is to prove that every matrix $A \in \mathbb{R}^{m \times n}$, $m \geq n$, has a factorisation of the form

$$A = QR,$$

where $Q \in \mathbb{R}^{m \times m}$ is orthogonal and $R \in \mathbb{R}^{m \times n}$ is an upper triangular matrix, which, because of the non-quadratic form of R, takes the form

$$R = \begin{pmatrix} * & \cdots & * \\ & * & \cdots & * \\ & & \ddots & \\ & & & * \\ \\ \\ \end{pmatrix}.$$

We will achieve this by employing specific, orthogonal matrices which are geometrically reflections. It would, however, also be possible to use rotations, which we will encounter later on.

Definition 3.30 A *Householder matrix* $H = H(\mathbf{w}) \in \mathbb{R}^{m \times m}$ is a matrix of the form

$$H(\mathbf{w}) = I - 2\mathbf{w}\mathbf{w}^{\mathrm{T}} \in \mathbb{R}^{m \times m},$$

where $\mathbf{w} \in \mathbb{R}^m$ satisfies either $\|\mathbf{w}\|_2 = 1$ or $\mathbf{w} = 0$.

A more general form of a Householder matrix is given by

$$H(\mathbf{w}) = I - 2\frac{\mathbf{w}\mathbf{w}^{\mathrm{T}}}{\mathbf{w}^{\mathrm{T}}\mathbf{w}},$$

for an arbitrary vector $\mathbf{w} \neq 0$. Here, we find both the inner product $\mathbf{w}^{\mathrm{T}}\mathbf{w} \in \mathbb{R}$ and the *outer product* $\mathbf{w}\mathbf{w}^{\mathrm{T}} \in \mathbb{R}^{m \times m}$. Householder matrices have quite a few elementary but important properties, which we want to collect now.

Lemma 3.31 *Let $H = H(\mathbf{w}) \in \mathbb{R}^{m \times m}$ be a Householder matrix.*

1. *H is symmetric.*
2. *$HH = I$ so that H is orthogonal.*
3. *$\det(H(\mathbf{w})) = -1$ if $\mathbf{w} \neq 0$.*
4. *Storing $H(\mathbf{w})$ only requires storing the m elements of $\mathbf{w}$.*
5. *The computation of the product $H\mathbf{a}$ of $H = H(\mathbf{w})$ with a vector $\mathbf{a} \in \mathbb{R}^m$ requires only $O(m)$ time.*

Proof   The first property is clear. For the second note that $w^T w = 1$ leads to

$$HH = (I - 2ww^T)(I - 2ww^T) = I - 4ww^T + 4(ww^T)(ww^T) = I.$$

For the third property, we note that H has the eigenvalues $\lambda = \pm 1$. To be more precise, we have $Hw = -w$ so that w is the corresponding eigenvector to the eigenvalue $\lambda = -1$. Every vector orthogonal to w is obviously an eigenvector to the eigenvalue $\lambda = 1$. Hence, the eigenvalue $\lambda = 1$ has multiplicity $(m - 1)$ and the eigenvalue $\lambda = -1$ has multiplicity 1. Since the determinant is the product of the eigenvalues, the determinant of H is -1.

The fourth property is clear again. For the last property we first compute the number $\lambda = a^T w$ in $O(m)$ time, then we multiply this number by each component of w to form the vector λw and finally we subtract twice this vector from the vector a. All of this can be done in $O(m)$ time.   □

Figure 3.1 demonstrates, in the case of $\mathbb{R}^2$, that a Householder matrix represents a reflection. To be more precise, suppose we want to find a reflection, i.e. an orthogonal matrix H which maps the vector $a \in \mathbb{R}^2$ onto the vector αe_1 with α to be specified. First of all, because of

$$|\alpha| = \|\alpha e_1\|_2 = \|Ha\|_2 = \|a\|_2,$$

we see that $\alpha = \pm\|a\|_2$. Next, if S_w denotes the bisector of the angle between a and e_1 and w its orthogonal vector, then we can express the transformation via

$$Ha = a - 2(w^T a)w = (I - 2ww^T)a.$$

Formalising this fact yields the following result.

Theorem 3.32   *For every vector* $a \in \mathbb{R}^m$, *there is a vector* $w \in \mathbb{R}^m$ *with* $w = 0$ *or* $\|w\|_2 = 1$, *such that* $H(w)a = \|a\|_2 e_1$.

Proof   There is nothing to show if $a = 0$ or $a = \|a\|_2 e_1$, as we can simply pick $w = 0$ in these cases. Otherwise, let us define $v = a - \|a\|_2 e_1$ and $w = v/\|v\|_2$. Then,

$$1 = w^T w = \frac{v^T v}{\|v\|_2^2} = \frac{(a - \|a\|_2 e_1)^T (a - \|a\|_2 e_1)}{\|v\|_2^2} = \frac{a^T a - 2\|a\|_2 a^T e_1 + \|a\|_2^2}{\|v\|_2^2}$$

$$= \frac{2a^T(a - \|a\|_2 e_1)}{\|v\|_2^2} = \frac{2a^T v}{\|v\|_2^2} = \frac{2a^T w}{\|v\|_2},$$

such that $\|v\|_2 = 2a^T w$. Hence, the application of $H(w)$ to a becomes

$$H(w)a = a - 2(a^T w)w = a - \|v\|_2 \frac{v}{\|v\|_2} = a - v = \|a\|_2 e_1.$$ □

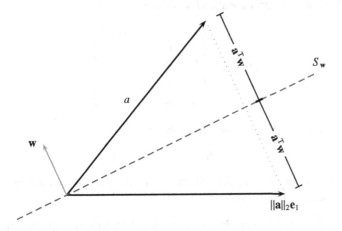

Figure 3.1 Householder transformation.

Note that we could also project onto $-\mathbf{e}_1$ by using $\mathbf{v} = \mathbf{a} + \|\mathbf{a}\|_2\mathbf{e}_1$. In general, one should pick the sign in such a way that numerical cancellation is avoided, i.e. one should use $\mathbf{v} = \mathbf{a} + \operatorname{sign}(a_1)\|\mathbf{a}\|_2\mathbf{e}_1$.

Theorem 3.33 (*QR* factorisation)   *For every $A \in \mathbb{R}^{m \times n}$, $m \geq n$, there exist an orthogonal matrix $Q \in \mathbb{R}^{m \times m}$ and an upper triangular matrix $R \in \mathbb{R}^{m \times n}$ such that $A = QR$.*

Proof   Let $\mathbf{a}_1 \in \mathbb{R}^m$ be the first column of A. We can find a Householder matrix $H_1 \in \mathbb{R}^{m \times m}$ such that

$$H_1 A = \begin{pmatrix} \alpha_1 & * & \cdots & * \\ 0 & & & \\ \vdots & & A_1 & \\ 0 & & & \end{pmatrix}$$

with an $(m-1) \times (n-1)$ matrix A_1. Considering the first column $\tilde{\mathbf{a}}_2 \in \mathbb{R}^{m-1}$ of this matrix, we can find a second Householder matrix $\tilde{H}_2 \in \mathbb{R}^{(m-1) \times (m-1)}$ such that $\tilde{H}_2 \tilde{\mathbf{a}}_2 = \alpha_2 \mathbf{e}_1 \in \mathbb{R}^{m-1}$. The matrix

$$H_2 = \begin{pmatrix} 1 & 0 & \cdots & 0 \\ 0 & & & \\ \vdots & & \tilde{H}_2 & \\ 0 & & & \end{pmatrix}$$

is easily seen to be orthogonal and we derive

$$H_2H_1A = \begin{pmatrix} \alpha_1 & * & \cdots & * \\ 0 & \alpha_2 & * & \cdots & * \\ 0 & 0 & & & \\ \vdots & \vdots & & A_2 & \\ 0 & 0 & & & \end{pmatrix},$$

and we can proceed in this form to establish

$$H_{n-1}H_{n-2}\cdots H_2H_1A = R,$$

where R is an upper triangular matrix. Since all H_j are orthogonal so is their product and also their inverse. □

Note that the proof is actually constructive and describes a numerical method for deriving the QR factorisation of a matrix A. Moreover, if we take Lemma 3.31 into account we can already determine the cost.

Remark 3.34 It takes $O(mn^2)$ time to compute the QR factorisation of an $m \times n$ matrix with $m \geq n$.

Proof In the first step we have to apply the matrix H_1 to the n columns of the matrix A. Each of these applications can be done in $O(m)$ time such that the first step of the procedure requires $O(mn)$ time. Since we have to apply $n-1$ of these steps, we see that the cost is bounded by $O(mn^2)$. □

It is not entirely possible to program the QR factorisation *in situ*, since the space of the matrix A is not enough to store all relevant information. Though we can store the R part in the upper triangular part of A we also need to store the relevant information on the transformations $H_j = I - c_j \mathbf{v}_j \mathbf{v}_j^{\mathrm{T}}$, i.e. the vectors $\mathbf{v}_j = (v_{jj}, \ldots, v_{mj})^{\mathrm{T}}$, which form a lower triangular matrix, and the coefficients c_j. We can store the vectors $\mathbf{v}_j$ in the lower triangular part of A except for v_{jj}, which we can store in an additional vector $\mathbf{v}$. For the square case $m = n$, this is given in detail in Algorithm 6.

In the case of the LU factorisation, we have seen that it might be necessary to use pivoting to continue the process all the way down. In contrast to this, a QR factorisation can always be computed without pivoting even if the matrix A is singular. We actually can compute it, even if the matrix is not square. Nonetheless, pivoting can improve the numerical stability.
As in the case of the LU factorisation (Theorem 3.12) the factors in the QR factorisation are unique. However, we have to make some additional assumptions.

Algorithm 6: *QR* factorisation

Input : $A \in \mathbb{R}^{n \times n}$.

Output: *QR* factorisation of *A*.

1 **for** $j = 1$ **to** $n - 1$ **do**
2     $\beta := 0$
3   **for** $k = j$ **to** n **do** $\beta := \beta + a_{kj} \cdot a_{kj}$
4     $\alpha := \sqrt{\beta}$
5   **if** $\alpha = 0$ **then** $v_j := 0$
6   **else**
7        $c_j := 1/(\beta + \alpha \cdot |a_{jj}|)$
8   **if** $a_{jj} < 0$ **then** $\alpha := -\alpha$
9        $v_j := a_{jj} + \alpha$
10       $a_{jj} := -\alpha$
11   **for** $k = j + 1$ **to** n **do**
12          $sum := v_j \cdot a_{jk}$
13   **for** $i = j + 1$ **to** n **do** $sum := sum + a_{ij} \cdot a_{ik}$
14          $sum := sum \cdot c_j$
15          $a_{jk} := a_{jk} - v_j \cdot sum$
16   **for** $i = j + 1$ **to** n **do** $a_{ik} := a_{ik} - a_{ij} \cdot sum$

Theorem 3.35 *The factorisation $A = QR$ of a non-singular matrix $A \in \mathbb{R}^{n \times n}$ into the product of an orthogonal matrix $Q \in \mathbb{R}^{n \times n}$ and an upper triangular matrix $R \in \mathbb{R}^{n \times n}$ is unique, if the signs of the diagonal elements of R are prescribed.*

Proof Assume there are two such factorisations $A = Q_1 R_1 = Q_2 R_2$ with orthogonal matrices Q_1, Q_2 and upper triangular matrices R_1, R_2. Then, we have $S := Q_2^{-1} Q_1 = R_2 R_1^{-1}$. This is an identity between an orthogonal matrix on the one hand and an upper triangular matrix on the other. Hence, S is an orthogonal upper triangular matrix and since $S^{-1} = S^{\mathrm{T}}$ it must be a diagonal matrix. But a diagonal orthogonal matrix can only have ± 1 as diagonal entries. Thus, if the diagonal entries of R_1 and R_2 have the same sign, we must have $S = I$. □

Remark 3.36 The *QR* factorisation is backward-stable. The computed factors $\tilde{Q}$ and $\tilde{R}$ satisfy $\tilde{Q}\tilde{R} = A + \Delta A$ with ΔA satisfying

$$\|\Delta A\| = O(\|A\| \operatorname{eps}).$$

3.7 Schur Factorisation

We want to use Householder transformations to derive yet another factorisation. Though its derivation is algorithmic again, this factorisation will only be of interest to us from a theoretical point of view. However, here we need to discuss complex matrices.

Recall that a matrix $U \in \mathbb{C}^{n \times n}$ is called *unitary* if it satisfies $\overline{U}^T U = I$, where the overbar indicates the complex conjugate. A unitary matrix is thus the complex counterpart to an orthogonal matrix.

Moreover, we can introduce complex Householder matrices $H \in \mathbb{C}^{m \times m}$ simply by defining $H = H(\mathbf{w}) = I - 2\mathbf{w}\overline{\mathbf{w}}^T$ where $\mathbf{w} \in \mathbb{C}^m$ satisfies either $\|\mathbf{w}\|_2^2 = \overline{\mathbf{w}}^T\mathbf{w} = 1$ or $\mathbf{w} = \mathbf{0}$. It is easy to see that a complex Householder matrix is unitary, that it satisfies $\overline{H}^T = H$, and that the results of the previous subsection remain true. In particular, we have the complex counterpart to Theorem 3.32.

Lemma 3.37 *For every vector* $\mathbf{a} \in \mathbb{C}^m$, *there is a vector* $\mathbf{w} \in \mathbb{C}^m$ *with* $\mathbf{w} = \mathbf{0}$ *or* $\|\mathbf{w}\|_2 = 1$ *such that* $H(\mathbf{w})\mathbf{a} = \|\mathbf{a}\|_2\mathbf{e}_1$.

We may now use the above Lemma to obtain the following Theorem.

Theorem 3.38 (Schur factorisation)   *Let* $A \in \mathbb{C}^{n \times n}$. *There exists a unitary matrix,* $U \in \mathbb{C}^{n \times n}$, *such that* $R := \overline{U}^T A U$ *is an upper triangular matrix.*

Proof   We will prove this by induction on n. Clearly the result holds for $n = 1$. Hence, let us now assume that the result holds for all $(n-1) \times (n-1)$ matrices. Since the characteristic polynomial $p(\lambda) = \det(A - \lambda I)$ factorises over $\mathbb{C}$, we can find an eigenvalue λ and a corresponding eigenvector $\mathbf{x} \in \mathbb{C}^n \setminus \{\mathbf{0}\}$, i.e. we have $A\mathbf{x} = \lambda\mathbf{x}$.

By the previous lemma there exists a Householder matrix such that

$$H(\mathbf{w}_1)\mathbf{x} = c_1\mathbf{e}_1 \quad \text{or} \quad \mathbf{x} = c_1\overline{H(\mathbf{w}_1)}^T\mathbf{e}_1 = c_1 H(\mathbf{w}_1)\mathbf{e}_1$$

with

$$|c_1| = \|\mathbf{x}\|_2 \neq 0.$$

Using the above properties we have

$$H(\mathbf{w}_1)AH(\mathbf{w}_1)\mathbf{e}_1 = H(\mathbf{w}_1)A\frac{\mathbf{x}}{c_1} = \frac{\lambda}{c_1}H(\mathbf{w}_1)\mathbf{x} = \lambda\mathbf{e}_1.$$

We may write this in the form

$$H(\mathbf{w}_1)AH(\mathbf{w}_1) = \begin{pmatrix} \lambda & \overline{\mathbf{a}}^T \\ \mathbf{0} & \tilde{A} \end{pmatrix}$$

with a vector $\mathbf{a} \in \mathbb{C}^{n-1}$ and a matrix $\tilde{A} \in \mathbb{C}^{(n-1)\times(n-1)}$. By the induction hypothesis there is a unitary matrix $V \in \mathbb{C}^{(n-1)\times(n-1)}$ such that $\overline{V}^T \tilde{A} V = T$ is an upper triangular matrix. If we now define an $n \times n$ matrix by

$$U = H(\mathbf{w}_1)\begin{pmatrix} 1 & \mathbf{0}^T \\ \mathbf{0} & V \end{pmatrix}, \qquad \overline{U}^T = \begin{pmatrix} 1 & \mathbf{0}^T \\ \mathbf{0} & \overline{V}^T \end{pmatrix} H(\mathbf{w}_1)$$

then we immediately see that $U\overline{U}^T = I$, i.e. U is unitary. Moreover, we have

$$\overline{U}^T A U = \begin{pmatrix} 1 & \mathbf{0}^T \\ \mathbf{0} & \overline{V}^T \end{pmatrix} H(\mathbf{w}_1) A H(\mathbf{w}_1) \begin{pmatrix} 1 & \mathbf{0}^T \\ \mathbf{0} & V \end{pmatrix} = \begin{pmatrix} 1 & \mathbf{0}^T \\ \mathbf{0} & \overline{V}^T \end{pmatrix} \begin{pmatrix} \lambda & \overline{\mathbf{a}}^T \\ \mathbf{0} & \tilde{A} \end{pmatrix} \begin{pmatrix} 1 & \mathbf{0}^T \\ \mathbf{0} & V \end{pmatrix}$$

$$= \begin{pmatrix} 1 & \mathbf{0}^T \\ \mathbf{0} & \overline{V}^T \end{pmatrix} \begin{pmatrix} \lambda & \overline{\mathbf{a}}^T V \\ \mathbf{0} & \tilde{A}V \end{pmatrix} = \begin{pmatrix} \lambda & \overline{\mathbf{a}}^T V \\ \mathbf{0} & \overline{V}^T \tilde{A} V \end{pmatrix}.$$

Hence, $\overline{U}^T A U$ is also an upper triangular matrix, which completes the induction and the proof. $\square$

In the situation of a real matrix with complex eigenvalues, we cannot achieve this result using only orthogonal transformations. However, each complex eigenvalue λ of a real matrix comes in pairs, i.e. also the complex conjugate of λ is an eigenvalue. Indeed, if $A\mathbf{x} = \lambda\mathbf{x}$ with $\mathbf{x} \neq \mathbf{0}$ then $\overline{\lambda}\overline{\mathbf{x}} = \overline{A\mathbf{x}} = A\overline{\mathbf{x}}$. This allows us to derive the following analogue to Theorem 3.38.

Theorem 3.39 (Real Schur factorisation) *To $A \in \mathbb{R}^{n\times n}$ there is an orthogonal matrix $Q \in \mathbb{R}^{n\times n}$ such that*

$$Q^T A Q = \begin{pmatrix} R_{11} & R_{12} & \cdots & R_{1m} \\ 0 & R_{22} & \cdots & R_{2m} \\ \vdots & \vdots & \ddots & \vdots \\ 0 & 0 & \cdots & R_{mm} \end{pmatrix},$$

where the diagonal blocks R_{ii} are either 1×1 or 2×2 matrices. A 1×1 block corresponds to a real eigenvalue, a 2×2 block corresponds to a pair of complex conjugate eigenvalues.
If A has only real eigenvalues then it is orthogonal similar to an upper triangular matrix.

Proof Let k be the number of pairs of complex conjugate eigenvalues. We will prove the result by induction on k. If $k = 0$ then the statement is obviously correct since we can proceed as in the proof of Theorem 3.38 with real Householder matrices. Hence, let us assume that $k \geq 1$ and that the result is correct for $k-1$. Let $\lambda = \alpha + i\beta$ with $\beta \neq 0$ be a complex eigenvalue with corresponding eigenvector $\mathbf{z} = \mathbf{x} + i\mathbf{y}$ with $\mathbf{x}, \mathbf{y} \in \mathbb{R}^n$. Then, $\mathbf{y} \neq \mathbf{0}$ since the vector $A\mathbf{z}$ would otherwise be a real vector equalling the complex vector $\lambda \mathbf{x}$. Moreover, with λ also $\bar{\lambda}$ is an eigenvalue of A with corresponding eigenvector $\bar{\mathbf{z}}$.

Next, we have $A(\mathbf{x} + i\mathbf{y}) = (\alpha + i\beta)(\mathbf{x} + i\mathbf{y})$ and hence

$$A\mathbf{x} = \alpha\mathbf{x} - \beta\mathbf{y}, \qquad A\mathbf{y} = \beta\mathbf{x} + \alpha\mathbf{y},$$

which we can write in matrix form as

$$A(\mathbf{x}, \mathbf{y}) = (\mathbf{x}, \mathbf{y})\begin{pmatrix} \alpha & \beta \\ -\beta & \alpha \end{pmatrix}.$$

The real vectors $\mathbf{x}, \mathbf{y}$ must be linearly independent. Otherwise, $\mathbf{x} = c\mathbf{y}$ with $c \in \mathbb{R} \setminus \{0\}$ would mean that $\mathbf{z} = (c + i)\mathbf{y}$ and $\bar{\mathbf{z}} = (c - i)\mathbf{y}$ are linearly dependent, which contradicts the fact that they are eigenvectors to two distinct eigenvalues λ and $\bar{\lambda}$, respectively. Thus, we can choose an orthonormal basis $\{\mathbf{x}_1, \mathbf{x}_2\}$ of $\text{span}\{\mathbf{x}, \mathbf{y}\}$ and describe the coordinate transformation by a non-singular matrix $C \in \mathbb{R}^{2 \times 2}$, i.e. $(\mathbf{x}_1, \mathbf{x}_2) = (\mathbf{x}, \mathbf{y})C$. With this, we can conclude that

$$A(\mathbf{x}_1, \mathbf{x}_2) = A(\mathbf{x}, \mathbf{y})C = (\mathbf{x}, \mathbf{y})\begin{pmatrix} \alpha & \beta \\ -\beta & \alpha \end{pmatrix}C$$

$$= (\mathbf{x}_1, \mathbf{x}_2)C^{-1}\begin{pmatrix} \alpha & \beta \\ -\beta & \alpha \end{pmatrix}C =: (\mathbf{x}_1, \mathbf{x}_2)S.$$

Thus, the newly defined matrix S has also the eigenvalues $\lambda = \alpha + i\beta$ and $\bar{\lambda} = \alpha - i\beta$. If $n = 2$ we are done. Otherwise, we now extend the vectors $\{\mathbf{x}_1, \mathbf{x}_2\}$ to a full orthonormal basis $\{\mathbf{x}_1, \dots, \mathbf{x}_n\}$ of $\mathbb{R}^n$ and define the orthogonal matrix $(\mathbf{x}_1, \dots, \mathbf{x}_n) =: (\mathbf{x}_1, \mathbf{x}_2, W)$ with $W = (\mathbf{x}_3, \dots, \mathbf{x}_n) \in \mathbb{R}^{n \times (n-2)}$ to see that

$$(\mathbf{x}_1, \mathbf{x}_2, W)^T A(\mathbf{x}_1, \mathbf{x}_2, W) = \begin{pmatrix} \mathbf{x}_1^T \\ \mathbf{x}_2^T \\ W^T \end{pmatrix}((\mathbf{x}_1, \mathbf{x}_2)S, AW) = \begin{pmatrix} S & (\mathbf{x}_1, \mathbf{x}_2)^T AW \\ 0 & W^T AW \end{pmatrix}.$$

The matrix $W^T AW$ has less than k complex conjugate eigenvalue pairs. Hence, by the induction assumption, there is an orthogonal matrix $\tilde{Q} \in \mathbb{R}^{(n-2) \times (n-2)}$ so that the matrix $\tilde{Q}^T(W^T AW)\tilde{Q}$ has the desired form. Finally, the orthogonal matrix

$$Q := (\mathbf{x}_1, \dots, \mathbf{x}_n)\begin{pmatrix} I & 0 \\ 0 & \tilde{Q} \end{pmatrix},$$

with I being the 2×2 identity matrix, is the required orthogonal matrix, which transforms A to the described quasi-triangular form. $\qquad\square$

3.8 Solving Least-Squares Problems

We now want to deal with the problem of solving an over-determined system of the form

$$Ax = b, \tag{3.10}$$

where $A \in \mathbb{R}^{m \times n}$ and $\mathbf{b} \in \mathbb{R}^m$ are given and $m > n$. The latter means that we have more equations than unknowns, which makes the system over-determined. Hence, we cannot expect a solution to (3.10) and may instead try to change the problem to solving the *least-squares problem*

$$\min_{\mathbf{x} \in \mathbb{R}^n} \|A\mathbf{x} - \mathbf{b}\|_2. \tag{3.11}$$

For the time being, we will assume that the rank of the matrix rank(A) is rank(A) = n, i.e. the matrix has full rank. Then, to solve (3.11) we can look for critical points of the function

$$f(\mathbf{x}) := \|A\mathbf{x} - \mathbf{b}\|_2^2 = \mathbf{x}^T A^T A\mathbf{x} - 2\mathbf{b}^T A\mathbf{x} + \mathbf{b}^T \mathbf{b}.$$

Setting the gradient to zero yields

$$\mathbf{0} = \nabla f(\mathbf{x}) = 2A^T A\mathbf{x} - 2A^T \mathbf{b}.$$

Since rank(A) = n, we also have rank($A^T A$) = n (see (1.6)) which means that the matrix $A^T A \in \mathbb{R}^{n \times n}$ is invertible. Thus we have in principle the following result.

Theorem 3.40 (Normal Equations) *The solution of the least-squares problem (3.11) with a matrix $A \in \mathbb{R}^{m \times n}$ with $m \geq n =$ rank(A) is the unique solution of the* Normal Equations

$$(A^T A)\mathbf{x} = A^T \mathbf{b}. \tag{3.12}$$

Proof The solution to the normal equations is indeed a critical point. Furthermore, since the Hessian of the function f is given by the positive definite matrix $A^T A$, we have a local minimum, which is actually a global one, as it is the only critical point. □

The normal equations are not a good way of computing the solution to the least-squares problem since the involved matrix $A^T A$ is usually badly conditioned.

Nonetheless, we notice that we can use this result to better understand the pseudo-inverse. By looking at (3.12) and (1.10) We can immediately read off the following result.

Corollary 3.41   *Let $A \in \mathbb{R}^{m \times n}$ with* rank$(A) = n$ *be given. Then, for a given* $\mathbf{b} \in \mathbb{R}^n$, *the solution of the least-squares problem (3.11) is given by* $\mathbf{x} = A^+ \mathbf{b}$.

We are now going to investigate two better ways of computing the solution to the least-squares problem. The first way is based on the QR factorisation of the matrix A and the second way is based upon the singular value decomposition $A = U \Sigma V^T$ from Theorem 1.18. In both cases, orthogonal matrices play an important role.

Let us start by using the QR factorisation from Theorem 3.33. Hence, we can represent our matrix $A \in \mathbb{R}^{m \times n}$ as $A = QR$ with an orthogonal matrix $Q \in \mathbb{R}^{m \times m}$ and an upper triangular matrix $R \in \mathbb{R}^{m \times n}$. Using the fact that orthogonal transformations leave the Euclidean norm invariant, we see that we can now produce a solution by noting that

$$\|A\mathbf{x} - \mathbf{b}\|_2^2 = \|QR\mathbf{x} - \mathbf{b}\|_2^2 = \|R\mathbf{x} - \mathbf{c}\|_2^2 = \left\| \begin{pmatrix} R_1 \\ O \end{pmatrix} \mathbf{x} - \begin{pmatrix} \mathbf{c}_1 \\ \mathbf{c}_2 \end{pmatrix} \right\|_2$$

$$= \|R_1 \mathbf{x} - \mathbf{c}_1\|_2^2 + \|\mathbf{c}_2\|_2^2,$$

where we have set $\mathbf{c} = Q^T \mathbf{b} \in \mathbb{R}^m$ and where $R_1 \in \mathbb{R}^{n \times n}$ denotes the upper part of the upper triangular matrix R.

The solution to the least-squares problem is therefore given by the solution of

$$R_1 \mathbf{x} = \mathbf{c}_1,$$

where $R_1 \in \mathbb{R}^{n \times n}$ is a square upper-triangular matrix. This system can be solved quite easily using back substitution, as we have seen at the beginning of this chapter.

Proposition 3.42   *Let $A \in \mathbb{R}^{m \times n}$ with $m \geq n$ and* rank$(A) = n$ *be given. Then, the solution of the least-squares problem (3.11) can be computed as follows:*

1. *Compute the QR factorisation of A,*
2. *Let $R_1 \in \mathbb{R}^{n \times n}$ be the upper square part of the upper triangular matrix $R \in \mathbb{R}^{m \times n}$, $\mathbf{c} = Q^T \mathbf{b} \in \mathbb{R}^m$ and $\mathbf{c}_1 \in \mathbb{R}^n$ be the upper part of $\mathbf{c}$.*
3. *Compute $R_1 \mathbf{x} = \mathbf{c}_1$ by back substitution.*

The method also works if A does not have full rank, i.e. if rank$(A) < n$. In this case the diagonal of R_1 has additional zeros. But splitting R and $\mathbf{c}$ up appropriately will also lead to the solution in this case.

If A does not have full rank then we cannot solve the normal equations directly, since the matrix $A^T A$ is not invertible. However, we can still compute the pseudo-inverse of A using the singular value decomposition. Hence, we will now discuss how to use the singular value decomposition $A = U \Sigma V^T$ with orthogonal matrices $U \in \mathbb{R}^{m \times m}$ and $V \in \mathbb{R}^{n \times n}$ and a diagonal matrix $\Sigma \in \mathbb{R}^{m \times n}$ for solving the least-squares problem and also generalise Corollary 3.41. We will describe this now already in the case of a matrix that is not necessarily of full rank.

The following observation is helpful. Let r denote the rank of the matrix A and hence the number of singular values. If we set $\mathbf{y} := V^T \mathbf{x} \in \mathbb{R}^n$ and $\mathbf{c} := U^T \mathbf{b} \in \mathbb{R}^m$, then

$$\|\mathbf{b} - A\mathbf{x}\|_2^2 = \|UU^T\mathbf{b} - U\Sigma V^T\mathbf{x}\|_2^2 = \|\mathbf{c} - \Sigma\mathbf{y}\|_2^2 = \sum_{j=1}^{r}(c_j - \sigma_j y_j)^2 + \sum_{j=r+1}^{m} c_j^2,$$

i.e. the residual is given by

$$\|\mathbf{b} - A\mathbf{x}\|_2^2 = \sum_{j=1}^{r}|\sigma_j \mathbf{v}_j^T\mathbf{x} - \mathbf{u}_j^T\mathbf{b}|^2 + \sum_{j=r+1}^{m}|\mathbf{u}_j^T\mathbf{b}|^2. \tag{3.13}$$

This means, we have to choose $\mathbf{x}$ such that $y_j = \mathbf{v}_j^T\mathbf{x} = \mathbf{u}_j^T\mathbf{b}/\sigma_j$ for $1 \le j \le r$. The remaining variables y_j, $r + 1 \le j \le n$ are free to choose. Hence, we have the following result

Theorem 3.43 *The general solution to the least-squares problem (3.11) is given by*

$$\mathbf{x} = \sum_{j=1}^{r}\frac{\mathbf{u}_j^T\mathbf{b}}{\sigma_j}\mathbf{v}_j + \sum_{j=r+1}^{n}\alpha_j\mathbf{v}_j =: \mathbf{x}^+ + \sum_{j=r+1}^{n}\alpha_j\mathbf{v}_j.$$

Here, σ_j denote the singular values of the matrix A, $\mathbf{v}_j \in \mathbb{R}^n$ are the columns of the matrix V and $\mathbf{u}_j \in \mathbb{R}^m$ are the columns of the matrix U from the singular value decomposition. The coefficients α_j are free to choose. From all possible solutions, the solution $\mathbf{x}^+$ is the solution having minimal Euclidean norm.

Proof The representation of the general form follows by expressing $\mathbf{x}$ in the orthonormal basis $\mathbf{v}_1, \ldots, \mathbf{v}_n$, having coefficients $\mathbf{v}_j^T\mathbf{x} = \mathbf{u}_j^T\mathbf{b}/\sigma_j$. The solution $\mathbf{x}^+$ has minimal norm, since we have for a general solution $\mathbf{x} \in \mathbb{R}^n$ that

$$\|\mathbf{x}\|_2^2 = \|\mathbf{x}^+\|_2^2 + \sum_{j=r+1}^{n}\alpha_j^2 \ge \|\mathbf{x}^+\|_2^2,$$

using the fact that the $\mathbf{v}_j$ form an orthonormal system. $\qquad\square$

With this result, it is now easy to see that the norm minimal solution is given by applying the pseudo-inverse A^+ to the right-hand side $\mathbf{b}$. Indeed, The representation $A^+ = V\Sigma^+U^T$ from (1.7) shows that

$$A^+\mathbf{b} = V\Sigma^+U^T\mathbf{b} = V\Sigma^+\mathbf{c} = \mathbf{x}^+.$$

Hence, we have the following generalisation of Corollary 3.41.

Corollary 3.44 *Let $A \in \mathbb{R}^{m \times n}$ with $m \geq n$ be given. Then, the pseudo-inverse $A^+ \in \mathbb{R}^{n \times m}$ maps every vector $\mathbf{b} \in \mathbb{R}^m$ to its norm-minimal least-squares solution $\mathbf{x}^+ \in \mathbb{R}^n$, i.e.*

$$A^+\mathbf{b} = \min \left\{ \|\mathbf{x}\|_2 : \mathbf{x} \in \mathbb{R}^n \text{ solves } \min_{\mathbf{z}} \|A\mathbf{z} - \mathbf{b}\|_2 \right\}.$$

Next, we want to analyse the condition number of the least-squares process. Since the Euclidean norm is the natural choice here, we will give all estimates in it. As in the analysis of solving linear systems, the condition number of the matrix will play a crucial role. We will continue to assume that $A \in \mathbb{R}^{m \times n}$ with $m \geq n$. Hence, according to Definition 2.24, the condition number is given by

$$\kappa_2(A) = \frac{\sigma_1}{\sigma_r} = \|A\|_2 \|A^+\|_2,$$

where σ_1 and σ_r are the largest and smallest singular value of A, respectively, and A^+ denotes the pseudo-inverse of A.

We start with a simple perturbation result, where the right-hand side $\mathbf{b}$ but not the matrix A is perturbed. The result employs the orthogonal projection P onto range(A), which is, according to Lemma 1.24, given by $P = AA^+$.

Proposition 3.45 *Let $A \in \mathbb{R}^{m \times n}$ with $m \geq n$ be given. Let $\mathbf{b}, \Delta\mathbf{b} \in \mathbb{R}^m$. If $\mathbf{x} \in \mathbb{R}^n$ and $\Delta\mathbf{x} \in \mathbb{R}^n$ denote the norm-minimal solutions of the least-squares problem (3.11) with data $(A, \mathbf{b})$ and $(A, \mathbf{b} + \Delta\mathbf{b})$, respectively, then*

$$\frac{\|\Delta\mathbf{x}\|_2}{\|\mathbf{x}\|_2} \leq \kappa_2(A) \frac{\|P\Delta\mathbf{b}\|_2}{\|P\mathbf{b}\|_2},$$

where $P := AA^+$ is the orthogonal projection of $\mathbb{R}^m$ onto range(A).

Proof By Corollary 3.44 we have $\mathbf{x} = A^+\mathbf{b}$ and $\mathbf{x} + \Delta\mathbf{x} = A^+(\mathbf{b} + \Delta\mathbf{b}) = \mathbf{x} + A^+ \Delta\mathbf{b}$. This means $\Delta\mathbf{x} = A^+ \Delta\mathbf{b} = A^+AA^+ \Delta\mathbf{b}$, where we have used (1.8) in the last equality. From this, it immediately follows that

$$\|\Delta\mathbf{x}\|_2 \leq \|A^+\|_2 \|AA^+ \Delta\mathbf{b}\|_2 = \|A^+\|_2 \|P\Delta\mathbf{b}\|_2.$$

Using the full singular value factorisation $A = U\Sigma V^{\mathrm{T}}$, we have

$$\mathbf{x} = A^+\mathbf{b} = A^+AA^+\mathbf{b} = A^+P\mathbf{b} = \sum_{i=1}^{r} \frac{\mathbf{u}_i^{\mathrm{T}}P\mathbf{b}}{\sigma_i}\mathbf{v}_i,$$

where $r = \text{rank}(A)$ and $\sigma_1 \geq \sigma_2 \geq \cdots \geq \sigma_r > 0$ are the singular values of A. The orthonormality of the columns $\mathbf{u}_i$ and $\mathbf{v}_i$ of U and V, respectively, shows

$$\|\mathbf{x}\|_2^2 = \sum_{i=1}^{r} \left| \frac{\mathbf{u}_i^{\mathrm{T}}P\mathbf{b}}{\sigma_i} \right|^2 \geq \frac{1}{\sigma_1^2} \sum_{i=1}^{r} |\mathbf{u}_i^{\mathrm{T}}P\mathbf{b}|^2 = \frac{1}{\sigma_1^2}\|P\mathbf{b}\|_2^2,$$

where we have used that $Pb \in \text{range}(A) = \text{span}\{u_1, \ldots, u_r\}$. Employing finally $\sigma_1 = \|A\|_2$ yields $\|x\|_2 \geq \|Pb\|_2 / \|A\|_2$ and hence

$$\frac{\|\Delta x\|_2}{\|x\|_2} \leq \|A^+\|_2 \|A\|_2 \frac{\|P\Delta b\|_2}{\|Pb\|_2}. \qquad \square$$

For the general perturbation result, where b as well as A can be perturbed we need two auxiliary statements. The first one is a generalisation of the perturbation Lemma 2.42.

Lemma 3.46 *Let $A \in \mathbb{R}^{m \times n}$ be given with $\text{rank}(A) = n \leq m$. Let $\Delta A \in \mathbb{R}^{m \times n}$ be a perturbation with $\|A^+\|_2 \|\Delta A\|_2 < 1$. Then, $A + \Delta A$ has also rank n and satisfies the bound*

$$\|(A + \Delta A)^+\|_2 \leq \frac{\|A^+\|_2}{1 - \|A^+\|_2 \|\Delta A\|_2}.$$

Proof We start by showing that $A + \Delta A$ has rank n. Let $x \in \ker(A + \Delta A)$, which means $Ax = -\Delta A\, x$ and, after multiplication by A^T, also $A^\mathrm{T} A x = -A^\mathrm{T} \Delta A\, x$. As $A^\mathrm{T} A$ is invertible, (1.10) gives $x = -(A^\mathrm{T} A)^{-1} A^\mathrm{T} \Delta A\, x = -A^+ \Delta A\, x$. and the condition $\|A^+\|_2 \|\Delta A\|_2 < 1$ shows $x = 0$. From this we can conclude that the columns of $A + \Delta A$ are linearly independent and hence the rank of $A + \Delta A$ is n. Next, let λ_n be the smallest eigenvalue of $(A + \Delta A)^\mathrm{T}(A + \Delta A)$ and let $x \in \mathbb{R}^n$ be a corresponding eigenvector with $\|x\|_2 = 1$. Then we have

$$\frac{1}{\|(A + \Delta A)^+\|_2} = \lambda_n^{1/2} = \left[x^\mathrm{T} (A + \Delta A)^\mathrm{T} (A + \Delta A) x \right]^{1/2}$$

$$= \|(A + \Delta A)x\|_2 \geq \|Ax\|_2 - \|\Delta A\, x\|_2$$

$$\geq (x^\mathrm{T} A^\mathrm{T} A x)^{1/2} - \|\Delta A\|_2 = \sigma_n(A) - \|\Delta A\|_2$$

$$= \frac{1}{\|A^+\|_2} - \|\Delta A\|_2 = \frac{1 - \|A^+\|_2 \|\Delta A\|_2}{\|A^+\|_2}.$$

The latter expression is positive by assumption, from which the statement then follows. $\qquad \square$

The result remains essentially true if A does not have full rank, as long as $\text{rank}(A + \Delta A) \leq \text{rank}(A)$ is satisfied. However, we will restrict ourselves to the case $\text{rank}(A) = n$ from now on.

Lemma 3.47 *Let $A, B \in \mathbb{R}^{m \times n}$ with $\text{rank}(A) = \text{rank}(B) = n$. Then,*

$$\|BB^+(I - AA^+)\|_2 = \|AA^+(I - BB^+)\|_2.$$

Proof Let $A = U\Sigma V^\mathrm{T}$ and $B = \tilde{U}\tilde{\Sigma}\tilde{V}^\mathrm{T}$ be the full singular value decompositions of A and B, respectively. Then, we have $AA^+ = U\Sigma V^\mathrm{T} V \Sigma^+ U^\mathrm{T} = U\Sigma\Sigma^+ U^\mathrm{T} = UDU^\mathrm{T}$ with the diagonal matrix $D = \text{diag}(1, \ldots, 1, 0, \ldots, 0) \in$

$\mathbb{R}^{m \times m}$ having exactly n times a 1 and $m - n$ times a 0 on the diagonal. In the same way we have $BB^{+} = \tilde{U}D\tilde{U}^{\mathrm{T}}$ with the same diagonal matrix. If we define

$$W := \tilde{U}^{\mathrm{T}} U = \begin{pmatrix} W_{11} & W_{12} \\ W_{21} & W_{22} \end{pmatrix} \in \mathbb{R}^{m \times m}$$

with block matrices $W_{11} \in \mathbb{R}^{n \times n}$, $W_{12} \in \mathbb{R}^{n \times (m-n)}$, $W_{21} \in \mathbb{R}^{(m-n) \times n}$ and $W_{22} \in \mathbb{R}^{(m-n) \times (m-n)}$ then, using the invariance of the Euclidean norm under orthogonal transformations, we find

$$\|BB^{+}(I - AA^{+})\|_2 = \|\tilde{U}D\tilde{U}^{\mathrm{T}}(I - UDU^{\mathrm{T}})\|_2 = \|DW(I - D)\|_2 = \|W_{12}\|_2$$

and, in the same way,

$$\|AA^{+}(I - BB^{+})\|_2 = \|W_{21}^{\mathrm{T}}\|_2.$$

Hence, it remains to show that $\|W_{12}\|_2 = \|W_{21}^{\mathrm{T}}\|_2$ holds. Note that the transpose is irrelevant as the Euclidean norm is invariant under forming the transpose. To see this, let $\mathbf{z} \in \mathbb{R}^{m-n}$ be given and let $\mathbf{x} = (\mathbf{0}^{\mathrm{T}}, \mathbf{z}^{\mathrm{T}})^{\mathrm{T}} \in \mathbb{R}^m$ be its prolongation. Using again the invariance of the Euclidean norm, we find

$$\|\mathbf{z}\|_2^2 = \|\mathbf{x}\|_2^2 = \|\tilde{U}^{\mathrm{T}} U\mathbf{x}\|_2^2 = \|W\mathbf{x}\|_2^2 = \|W_{12}\mathbf{z}\|_2^2 + \|W_{22}\mathbf{z}\|_2^2,$$

which gives the norm

$$\|W_{12}\|_2^2 = \max_{\|\mathbf{z}\|_2=1} \|W_{12}\mathbf{z}\|_2^2 = 1 - \min_{\|\mathbf{z}\|_2=1} \|W_{22}\mathbf{z}\|_2^2 = 1 - \lambda_{\min}(W_{22}^{\mathrm{T}} W_{22}),$$

where we have also used that $\|W_{22}\mathbf{z}\|_2^2 = \mathbf{z}^{\mathrm{T}} W_{22}^{\mathrm{T}} W_{22}\mathbf{z} = \langle W_{22}^{\mathrm{T}} W_{22}\mathbf{z}, \mathbf{z} \rangle_2$ so that (2.13) applies to the symmetric and positive semi-definite matrix $W_{22}^{\mathrm{T}} W_{22}$. In the same way, we can conclude from

$$\|\mathbf{z}\|_2^2 = \|\mathbf{x}\|_2^2 = \|(\tilde{U}^{\mathrm{T}} U)^{\mathrm{T}}\mathbf{x}\|_2^2 = \|W^{\mathrm{T}}\mathbf{x}\|_2^2 = \|W_{21}^{\mathrm{T}}\mathbf{z}\|_2^2 + \|W_{22}^{\mathrm{T}}\mathbf{z}\|_2^2$$

that

$$\|W_{21}^{\mathrm{T}}\|^2 = \max_{\|\mathbf{z}\|_2=1} \|W_{21}^{\mathrm{T}}\mathbf{z}\|_2^2 = 1 - \min_{\|\mathbf{z}\|_2=1} \|W_{22}^{\mathrm{T}}\mathbf{z}\|_2^2 = 1 - \lambda_{\min}(W_{22} W_{22}^{\mathrm{T}}).$$

However, as we have seen when deriving the singular value decomposition, the smallest eigenvalue of $W_{22}^{\mathrm{T}} W_{22}$ coincides with the smallest eigenvalue of $W_{22} W_{22}^{\mathrm{T}}$. □

After this, we can state and prove our main perturbation result.

Theorem 3.48 *Let $A \in \mathbb{R}^{m \times n}$ with rank$(A) = n$ be given. Let $\Delta A \in \mathbb{R}^{m \times n}$ be a perturbation with $\|A^{+}\|_2\|\Delta A\|_2 < 1$. Let $\mathbf{b}, \Delta\mathbf{b} \in \mathbb{R}^m$. Finally, let $\mathbf{x}, \mathbf{x} + \Delta\mathbf{x} \in$*

$\mathbb{R}^n$ *be the solutions of the least-squares problem (3.11) with data $(A, \mathbf{b})$ and $(A + \Delta A, \mathbf{b} + \Delta \mathbf{b})$, respectively. Then,*

$$\frac{\|\Delta \mathbf{x}\|_2}{\|\mathbf{x}\|_2} \leq \frac{\kappa_2(A)}{1 - \kappa_2(A)\|\Delta A\|_2/\|A\|_2} \left[\frac{\|\Delta A\|_2}{\|A\|_2} \left(1 + \kappa_2(A) \frac{\|A\mathbf{x} - \mathbf{b}\|_2}{\|A\|_2 \|\mathbf{x}\|_2} \right) + \frac{\|\Delta \mathbf{b}\|_2}{\|A\|_2 \|\mathbf{x}\|_2} \right].$$

Proof From $\mathbf{x} = A^+ \mathbf{b}$ and $\mathbf{x} + \Delta \mathbf{x} = (A + \Delta A)^+ (\mathbf{b} + \Delta \mathbf{b})$ it follows that

$$\Delta \mathbf{x} = (A + \Delta A)^+ (\mathbf{b} + \Delta \mathbf{b}) - A^+ \mathbf{b} = [(A + \Delta A)^+ - A^+] \mathbf{b} + (A + \Delta A)^+ \Delta \mathbf{b}.$$

We will now bound the norms of both terms on the right-hand side separately. To this end, we have to rewrite the first term. As A has rank n, its pseudo-inverse is given by (1.10) as $A^+ = (A^\mathsf{T} A)^{-1} A^\mathsf{T}$ which means $A^+ A = I$. As $A + \Delta A$ also has rank n, we also have $(A + \Delta A)^+ (A + \Delta A) = I$. With this, we derive

$$\begin{aligned}
(A + \Delta A)^+ - A^+ &= (A + \Delta A)^+ (I - AA^+) + (A + \Delta A)^+ AA^+ - A^+ \\
&= (A + \Delta A)^+ (I - AA^+) + (A + \Delta A)^+ AA^+ \\
&\quad - (A + \Delta A)^+ (A + \Delta A) A^+ \\
&= (A + \Delta A)^+ (I - AA^+) - (A + \Delta A)^+ (\Delta A) A^+.
\end{aligned}$$

Applying this to $\mathbf{b}$ and using $A^+ \mathbf{b} = \mathbf{x}$ and $(I - AA^+)A = A - AA^+ A = 0$ gives

$$\begin{aligned}
[(A + \Delta A)^+ - A^+] \mathbf{b} &= (A + \Delta A)^+ (I - AA^+) \mathbf{b} - (A + \Delta A)^+ (\Delta A) A^+ \mathbf{b} \\
&= (A + \Delta A)^+ (I - AA^+)(\mathbf{b} - A\mathbf{x}) - (A + \Delta A)^+ (\Delta A) \mathbf{x}.
\end{aligned}$$

Setting $B := (A + \Delta A)$ in Lemma 3.47 shows

$$\begin{aligned}
\|(A + \Delta A)^+ (I - AA^+)\|_2 &= \|B^+ (I - AA^+)\|_2 = \|B^+ BB^+ (I - AA^+)\|_2 \\
&\leq \|B^+\|_2 \|BB^+ (I - AA^+)\|_2 \\
&= \|B^+\|_2 \|AA^+ (I - BB^+)\|_2 \\
&= \|B^+\|_2 \|(AA^+)^\mathsf{T} (I - BB^+)\|_2 \\
&= \|B^+\|_2 \|(A^+)^\mathsf{T} A^\mathsf{T} (I - BB^+)\|_2 \\
&= \|B^+\|_2 \|(A^+)^\mathsf{T} (A^\mathsf{T} - B^\mathsf{T})(I - BB^+)\|_2 \\
&= \|B^+\|_2 \|(A^+)^\mathsf{T} (\Delta A)^\mathsf{T} (I - BB^+)\|_2 \\
&\leq \|B^+\|_2 \|A^+\|_2 \|\Delta A\|_2 \|I - BB^+\|_2,
\end{aligned}$$

where we have also used $B^\mathsf{T} (I - BB^+) = B^\mathsf{T} - B^\mathsf{T} BB^+ = 0$ and $B - A = \Delta A$ and the fact that the Euclidean norm of a matrix equals the Euclidean norm of its transpose.

If $B = U \Sigma V^\mathsf{T}$ is this time the full singular value decomposition of B, we have with $B^+ = V \Sigma^+ U^\mathsf{T}$ that $BB^+ = U \Sigma \Sigma^+ U^\mathsf{T}$. As $\Sigma \Sigma^+ \in \mathbb{R}^{m \times m}$ is a diagonal matrix with n entries equal to 1 and $m - n$ entries equal to 0 on the diagonal and as the Euclidean norm is invariant under orthogonal transformations, we see that

$$\|I - BB^+\|_2 = \|I - \Sigma\Sigma^+\|_2 = \begin{cases} 1 & \text{if } m > n, \\ 0 & \text{if } m = n. \end{cases}$$

Thus, we can conclude that

$$\|(A + \Delta A)^+(I - AA^+)\|_2 \leq \|(A + \Delta A)^+\|_2\|A^+\|_2\|\Delta A\|_2.$$

Finally, this allows us to finish the proof. We have

$$\|\Delta \mathbf{x}\|_2 \leq \|[(A + \Delta A)^+ - A^+]\mathbf{b}\|_2 + \|(A + \Delta A)^+\|_2\|\Delta \mathbf{b}\|_2$$

$$\leq \|(A + \Delta A)^+(I - AA^+)\|_2\|\mathbf{b} - A\mathbf{x}\|_2 + \|(A + \Delta A)^+\|_2\|\Delta A\|_2\|\mathbf{x}\|_2$$
$$+ \|(A + \Delta A)^+\|_2\|\Delta \mathbf{b}\|_2$$

$$\leq \|(A + \Delta A)^+\|_2\left[\|\Delta A\|_2\|A^+\|_2\|A\mathbf{x} - \mathbf{b}\|_2 + \|\Delta A\|_2\|\mathbf{x}\|_2 + \|\Delta \mathbf{b}\|_2\right]$$

$$\leq \frac{\|A^+\|_2}{1 - \|A^+\|_2\|\Delta A\|_2}\left[\|\Delta A\|_2\|A^+\|_2\|A\mathbf{x} - \mathbf{b}\|_2 + \|\Delta A\|_2\|\mathbf{x}\|_2 + \|\Delta \mathbf{b}\|_2\right]$$

$$= \frac{\kappa_2(A)}{1 - \kappa_2(A)\|\Delta A\|_2/\|A\|_2}\left[\frac{\|\Delta A\|_2}{\|A\|_2}(\|A^+\|_2\|A\mathbf{x} - \mathbf{b}\|_2 + \|\mathbf{x}\|_2) + \frac{\|\Delta \mathbf{b}\|_2}{\|A\|_2}\right]$$

$$= \frac{\kappa_2(A)}{1 - \kappa_2(A)\|\Delta A\|_2/\|A\|_2}\left[\frac{\|\Delta A\|_2}{\|A\|_2}\left(\kappa_2(A)\frac{\|A\mathbf{x} - \mathbf{b}\|_2}{\|A\|_2} + \|\mathbf{x}\|_2\right) + \frac{\|\Delta \mathbf{b}\|_2}{\|A\|_2}\right]$$

and dividing by $\|\mathbf{x}\|_2$ gives the stated result.   □

Theorem 3.48 remains true, even if A is not of full rank, as long as the perturbation does not lead to a reduced rank, i.e. as long as the perturbed matrix $A + \Delta A$ has the same rank as A, see for example Björck [20].

We note that a large defect $\|A\mathbf{x} - \mathbf{b}\|_2$ becomes the dominant error term as it is multiplied by a factor of $\kappa_2(A)^2$. If the defect $\|A\mathbf{x} - \mathbf{b}\|_2$ is small the sensitivity of the least-squares problem is determined by the factor $\kappa_2(A)$, instead.

In the case of a quadratic matrix $A \in \mathbb{R}^{n \times n}$ with full rank, the defect $\|A\mathbf{x} - \mathbf{b}\|_2$ is zero. As we also have $\|\mathbf{b}\|_2 \leq \|A\|_2\|\mathbf{x}\|_2$, the bound from the above Theorem 3.48 is exactly the one from Theorem 2.43 for the Euclidean norm.

If the smallest singular value of A is close to zero then this *rank deficiency* leads obviously to a large condition number. In this situation it is better to reduce the rank of A numerically by setting the smallest singular value – and any other which is considered to be too small – to zero and solve the resulting least-squares problem. If $A = U\Sigma V^T$ is the original singular value decomposition of A with singular values $\sigma_1 \geq \sigma_2 \geq \cdots \geq \sigma_r > 0$ and if we set $\sigma_{k+1} = \cdots = \sigma_r = 0$ for a fixed $k < r$ then this means that we actually minimise the expression

$\|A_k \mathbf{x} - \mathbf{b}\|_2$, where $A_k \in \mathbb{R}^{m \times n}$ is given by

$$A_k = \sum_{j=1}^{k} \sigma_j \mathbf{u}_j \mathbf{v}_j^{\mathrm{T}}.$$

If $\mathbf{x}_k^+ = A_k^+ \mathbf{b}$ denotes the solution to this problem and if $\mathbf{x}^+ = A^+ \mathbf{b}$ denotes the solution to the original least-squares problem (3.11) then (3.13) shows that the residual $\mathbf{b} - A\mathbf{x}_k^+$ is given by

$$\|\mathbf{b} - A\mathbf{x}_k^+\|_2^2 = \sum_{j=k+1}^{m} |\mathbf{u}_j^{\mathrm{T}}\mathbf{b}|^2 = \|\mathbf{b} - A\mathbf{x}^+\|_2^2 + \sum_{j=k+1}^{r} |\mathbf{u}_j^{\mathrm{T}}\mathbf{b}|^2,$$

which is manageable as long as the components of $\mathbf{b}$ in the direction of these $\mathbf{u}_j$, $k + 1 \le j \le r$, are not too large. However, from the representations of $\mathbf{x}^+$ and $\mathbf{x}_k^+$, we can also read off that the actual error is given by

$$\|\mathbf{x}^+ - \mathbf{x}_k^+\|_2^2 = \sum_{j=k+1}^{r} \left| \frac{\mathbf{u}_j^{\mathrm{T}}\mathbf{b}}{\sigma_j} \right|^2,$$

which is problematic as we are concerned with small singular values σ_j, $k+1 \le j \le r$.

Hence, we are now going to look at a different way of dealing with the problem of numerical rank deficiency.

Definition 3.49   Let $A \in \mathbb{R}^{m \times n}$, $\mathbf{b} \in \mathbb{R}^m$ and $\tau > 0$. Then, the *Tikhonov regularisation* of the least-squares problem (3.11) with *regularisation parameter* $\tau > 0$ is

$$\min_{\mathbf{x} \in \mathbb{R}^n} \|A\mathbf{x} - \mathbf{b}\|_2^2 + \tau \|\mathbf{x}\|_2^2. \tag{3.14}$$

The term $\tau \|\mathbf{x}\|_2^2$ is also called a *penalty term* and the problem a *penalised least-squares problem*. The penalty term is sometimes replaced by a more general expression of the form $\tau \|L\mathbf{x}\|_2^2$, where L is a given matrix. Here, however, we will restrict ourselves to the case of $L = I$.

The penalised least-squares problem (3.14) is equivalent to a standard least-squares problem as we have

$$\|A\mathbf{x} - \mathbf{b}\|_2^2 + \tau \|\mathbf{x}\|_2^2 = \left\| \begin{pmatrix} A \\ \sqrt{\tau}I \end{pmatrix} \mathbf{x} - \begin{pmatrix} \mathbf{b} \\ 0 \end{pmatrix} \right\|_2^2 =: \|A_\tau \mathbf{x} - \tilde{\mathbf{b}}\|_2^2,$$

where $A_\tau \in \mathbb{R}^{(m+n) \times n}$ and $\tilde{\mathbf{b}} \in \mathbb{R}^{m+n}$. Obviously, the new matrix A_τ has full rank n, as its last n rows are linearly independent. Thus it has a unique solution and so has (3.14) even if $\mathrm{rank}(A) = r < n$. Moreover, we can use once again the singular value decomposition to represent the solution.

Theorem 3.50   *Let $A \in \mathbb{R}^{m \times n}$ be given with rank$(A) = r \leq n \leq m$. Let $A = \hat{U}\hat{\Sigma}\hat{V}^T$ be a reduced singular value decomposition of $A \in \mathbb{R}^{m \times n}$, where $\hat{\Sigma} \in \mathbb{R}^{r \times r}$ is a diagonal matrix with diagonal entries $\sigma_1 \geq \sigma_2 \geq \cdots \geq \sigma_r > 0$ and where $\hat{U} \in \mathbb{R}^{m \times r}$ and $\hat{V} \in \mathbb{R}^{n \times r}$ have orthonormal columns.*

The penalised least-squares problem (3.14) has for each $\tau > 0$ a unique solution $\mathbf{x}_\tau^+$ which is given by

$$\mathbf{x}_\tau^+ = \sum_{j=1}^{r} \frac{\sigma_j \mathbf{u}_j^T \mathbf{b}}{\sigma_j^2 + \tau} \mathbf{v}_j. \tag{3.15}$$

For $\tau \to 0$ the solution $\mathbf{x}_\tau^+$ converges to $\mathbf{x}^+ := A^+\mathbf{b}$, the norm-minimal solution of the least-squares problem (3.11). The error between $\mathbf{x}_\tau^+$ and $\mathbf{x}^+$ can be bounded by

$$\|\mathbf{x}^+ - \mathbf{x}_\tau^+\|_2 \leq \frac{\tau}{\sigma_r(\sigma_r^2 + \tau)} \|\mathbf{b}\|_2.$$

The condition number of the associated matrix $A_\tau \in \mathbb{R}^{(m+n) \times n}$ is

$$\kappa_2(A_\tau) = \|A_\tau\|_2 \|A_\tau^+\|_2 = \left(\frac{\sigma_1^2 + \tau}{\sigma_r^2 + \tau} \right)^{1/2}. \tag{3.16}$$

Proof   From the definition of A_τ and $\tilde{\mathbf{b}}$ it immediately follows that

$$A_\tau^T A_\tau = A^T A + \tau I, \qquad A_\tau^T \tilde{\mathbf{b}} = A^T \mathbf{b}.$$

Using the reduced singular value decomposition and Corollary 3.41 in combination with (1.10) we can derive

$$\mathbf{x}_\tau^+ = A_\tau^+ \tilde{\mathbf{b}} = (A_\tau^T A_\tau)^{-1} A_\tau^T \tilde{\mathbf{b}} = (A^T A + \tau I)^{-1} A^T \mathbf{b}$$

$$= [\hat{V}(\hat{\Sigma}^2 + \tau I)\hat{V}^T]^{-1} \hat{V}\hat{\Sigma}\hat{U}^T \mathbf{b} = \hat{V}(\hat{\Sigma}^2 + \tau I)^{-1} \hat{\Sigma} U^T \mathbf{b} = \sum_{j=1}^{r} \frac{\sigma_j \mathbf{u}_j^T \mathbf{b}}{\sigma_j^2 + \tau} \mathbf{v}_j.$$

For the error between $\mathbf{x}^+$ and $\mathbf{x}_\tau^+$ we note that

$$\mathbf{x}^+ - \mathbf{x}_\tau^+ = \sum_{j=1}^{r} \mathbf{u}_j^T \mathbf{b} \left[\frac{1}{\sigma_j} - \frac{\sigma_j}{\sigma_j^2 + \tau} \right] \mathbf{v}_j = \sum_{j=1}^{r} \mathbf{u}_j^T \mathbf{b} \frac{\tau}{\sigma_j(\sigma_j^2 + \tau)} \mathbf{v}_j.$$

As the $\mathbf{v}_j$ are orthonormal, we immediately can conclude that

$$\|\mathbf{x}^+ - \mathbf{x}_\tau^+\|_2^2 = \sum_{j=1}^{r} |\mathbf{u}_j^T \mathbf{b}|^2 \left[\frac{\tau}{\sigma_j(\sigma_j^2 + \tau)} \right]^2 \leq \left[\frac{\tau}{\sigma_r(\sigma_r^2 + \tau)} \right]^2 \sum_{j=1}^{r} |\mathbf{u}_j^T \mathbf{b}|^2$$

$$\leq \left[\frac{\tau}{\sigma_r(\sigma_r^2 + \tau)} \right]^2 \|\mathbf{b}\|_2^2.$$

For the condition number $\kappa_2(A_\tau) = \|A_\tau\|_2 \|A_\tau^+\|_2$ we start with

$$\|A_\tau\|_2^2 = \lambda_{\max}(A_\tau^T A_\tau) = \lambda_{\max}(A^T A + \tau I) = \lambda_{\max}(\hat{\Sigma}^2 + \tau I) = \sigma_1^2 + \tau. \quad (3.17)$$

For the remaining $\|A_\tau^+\|_2$ we use $\|A_\tau^+\|_2 = \|(A_\tau^+)^T\|_2$ and then $A_\tau^+ = (A_\tau^T A_\tau)^{-1} A_\tau^T$ to derive

$$A_\tau^+ (A_\tau^+)^T = (A_\tau^T A_\tau)^{-1} A_\tau^T [(A_\tau^T A_\tau)^{-1} A_\tau^T]^T = (A_\tau^T A_\tau)^{-1} A_\tau^T A_\tau (A_\tau^T A_\tau)^{-1}$$
$$= (A_\tau^T A_\tau)^{-1} = (A^T A + \tau I)^{-1} = \hat{V}(\hat{\Sigma}^2 + \tau I)^{-1} \hat{V}^T.$$

Thus, we can conclude

$$\|A_\tau^+\|_2^2 = \lambda_{\max}((\hat{\Sigma}^2 + \tau I)^{-1}) = \frac{1}{\sigma_r^2 + \tau},$$

which gives, together with (3.17), the condition number. $\qquad\qquad\square$

From (3.15) it obviously follows that $\mathbf{x}_\tau^+$ tends with $\tau \to 0$ to the solution $\mathbf{x}^+$ of the standard least-squares problem. This is not too surprising since the penalised least-squares problem (3.14) becomes the least-squares problem (3.11) for $\tau = 0$. From (3.15) we see that the parameter τ is indeed regularising the problem since it moves the singular values away from zero.

The remaining question is how to choose the regularisation parameter $\tau > 0$. Obviously, a smaller τ means that the least-squares part becomes more significant and the solution vector tries mainly to minimise this. For a larger τ, the penalty term $\tau \|\mathbf{x}\|_2^2$ is dominant and the solution vector will try to achieve a small norm. This becomes particularly important if the given data is corrupted. Let us assume that the right-hand side $\mathbf{b}$ is perturbed by some noise $\Delta\mathbf{b}$ to $\mathbf{b} + \Delta\mathbf{b}$.

If we denote the solution to this perturbed Tikhonov problem by $\mathbf{x}_\tau^\Delta$, then we see that

$$\mathbf{x}_\tau^\Delta = \sum_{j=1}^r \frac{\sigma_j \mathbf{u}_j^T (\mathbf{b} + \Delta\mathbf{b})}{\sigma_j^2 + \tau} \mathbf{v}_j = \mathbf{x}_\tau^+ + \sum_{j=1}^r \frac{\sigma_j \mathbf{u}_j^T \Delta\mathbf{b}}{\sigma_j^2 + \tau} \mathbf{v}_j,$$

where the latter summand is just the solution of the Tikhonov problem with data $\Delta\mathbf{b}$. Hence, we can bound the error between $\mathbf{x}_\tau^\Delta$ and the solution of the original least-squares problem $\mathbf{x}^+ = A^+ \mathbf{b}$ by

$$\|\mathbf{x}^+ - \mathbf{x}_\tau^\Delta\|_2 \le \|\mathbf{x}^+ - \mathbf{x}_\tau^+\|_2 + \left\| \sum_{j=1}^r \frac{\sigma_j \mathbf{u}_j^T \Delta\mathbf{b}}{\sigma_j^2 + \tau} \mathbf{v}_j \right\|_2$$
$$\le \frac{\tau}{\sigma_r(\sigma_r^2 + \tau)} \|\mathbf{b}\|_2 + \max_{1 \le j \le r} \frac{\sigma_j}{\sigma_j^2 + \tau} \|\Delta\mathbf{b}\|_2.$$

This shows how the error is split up into an *approximation error*, which goes to zero with $\tau \to 0$, and a *data error*. It would be desirable to choose τ to minimise the overall error. This is, however, in general not possible.

There are various ways to choose τ. Often, a statistical method called *cross validation* or *generalised cross validation* is used. Generalised cross validation is based on the idea that a good value of the regularisation parameter should help to predict missing data values. Hence, the parameter τ is chosen as the minimiser of

$$G(\tau) := \frac{\|A\mathbf{x}_\tau - \mathbf{b}\|_2^2}{[\operatorname{tr}(I - A(A^T A + \tau I)^{-1} A^T)]^2},$$

see for example Golub *et al.* [67] or Hansen [81]. Another method is the so-called *Morozov discrepancy principle* (see [97]), which we want to describe now and which is based on the strategy of choosing τ in such a way that the defect $\|A\mathbf{x}_\tau^\Delta - \mathbf{b}\|_2$ equals the data error $\|\Delta\mathbf{b}\|_2$. We will show that this is always possible. As before let $\mathbf{x}_\tau^+$ be the minimiser of

$$\mu_\tau(\mathbf{x}) := \|A\mathbf{x} - \mathbf{b}\|_2^2 + \tau\|\mathbf{x}\|_2^2.$$

As we are now interested in the behaviour of the defect, we define the function

$$J(\tau) := \|A\mathbf{x}_\tau^+ - \mathbf{b}\|_2^2.$$

Lemma 3.51 *Let* $\mathbf{b} \in \operatorname{range}(A)$ *with* $\mathbf{b} \neq \mathbf{0}$ *be given. Then, the function* $J(\tau)$ *is continuous on* $[0, \infty)$ *and strictly monotonically increasing with range* $[0, \|\mathbf{b}\|_2^2)$.

Proof The continuity of $\tau \mapsto \mathbf{x}_\tau^+$ follows immediately from the representation (3.15). From this, the continuity of $J(\tau)$ is obvious. Moreover, our assumptions yield that $\mathbf{x}_\tau^+ \neq \mathbf{0}$ for each $\tau > 0$, as $\mathbf{x}_\tau^+ = \mathbf{0}$ means by (3.15) that $\mathbf{u}_j^T \mathbf{b} = 0$ for $1 \leq j \leq r$, which contradicts $\mathbf{0} \neq \mathbf{b} \in \operatorname{range}(A) = \operatorname{span}\{\mathbf{u}_1, \ldots, \mathbf{u}_r\}$.

Next, let $K(\tau) := \|\mathbf{x}_\tau^+\|_2^2$ so that we have the decomposition

$$\mu_\tau(\mathbf{x}_\tau^+) = J(\tau) + \tau K(\tau).$$

Let us assume that $0 < \tau_1 < \tau_2$. We will first show that $\mathbf{x}_{\tau_1}^+ \neq \mathbf{x}_{\tau_2}^+$. To see this, we note that they satisfy the equations

$$(A^T A + \tau_1 I)\mathbf{x}_{\tau_1}^+ = A^T \mathbf{b}, \qquad (A^T A + \tau_2 I)\mathbf{x}_{\tau_2}^+ = A^T \mathbf{b}.$$

Subtracting these equations yields

$$A^T A(\mathbf{x}_{\tau_1}^+ - \mathbf{x}_{\tau_2}^+) + \tau_1(\mathbf{x}_{\tau_1}^+ - \mathbf{x}_{\tau_2}^+) = (\tau_2 - \tau_1)\mathbf{x}_{\tau_2}^+. \tag{3.18}$$

From this, we can conclude that $\mathbf{x}_{\tau_1}^+ = \mathbf{x}_{\tau_2}^+$ would imply $(\tau_2 - \tau_1)\mathbf{x}_{\tau_2}^+ = \mathbf{0}$. But as $\mathbf{x}_{\tau_2}^+ \neq \mathbf{0}$ we have the contradiction $\tau_1 = \tau_2$.

With this, we can show that $K(\tau)$ is strictly monotonically decreasing. Indeed, multiplying (3.18) by $(\mathbf{x}_{\tau_1}^+ - \mathbf{x}_{\tau_2}^+)^T$ from the left gives

$$\|A(\mathbf{x}_{\tau_1}^+ - \mathbf{x}_{\tau_2}^+)\|_2^2 + \tau_1\|\mathbf{x}_{\tau_1}^+ - \mathbf{x}_{\tau_2}^+\|_2^2 = (\tau_2 - \tau_1)\langle\mathbf{x}_{\tau_1}^+ - \mathbf{x}_{\tau_2}^+, \mathbf{x}_{\tau_2}^+\rangle_2.$$

Since $\mathbf{x}_{\tau_1}^+ \neq \mathbf{x}_{\tau_2}^+$, we see that the left-hand side is positive and as $\tau_2 > \tau_1$ we can conclude that

$$\langle\mathbf{x}_{\tau_1}^+ - \mathbf{x}_{\tau_2}^+, \mathbf{x}_{\tau_2}^+\rangle_2 > 0,$$

showing

$$\|\mathbf{x}_{\tau_2}^+\|_2^2 < \langle\mathbf{x}_{\tau_1}^+, \mathbf{x}_{\tau_2}^+\rangle_2 \leq \|\mathbf{x}_{\tau_1}^+\|_2\|\mathbf{x}_{\tau_2}^+\|_2,$$

i.e. $K(\tau_2) < K(\tau_1)$. Finally, still under the assumption of $0 < \tau_1 < \tau_2$, we can conclude that $J(\tau_1) < J(\tau_2)$ because $J(\tau_2) \leq J(\tau_1)$ would imply that

$$\mu_{\tau_1}(\mathbf{x}_{\tau_2}^+) = J(\tau_2) + \tau_1 K(\tau_2) < J(\tau_1) + \tau_1 K(\tau_1) = \mu_{\tau_1}(\mathbf{x}_{\tau_1}^+),$$

which contradicts the fact that $\mathbf{x}_{\tau_1}^+$ minimises μ_{τ_1}.

Finally, it remains to show that the range of J is given by $[0, \|\mathbf{b}\|_2)$. On the one hand, we have $J(0) = 0$ as $\mathbf{b} \in \text{range}(A)$. On the other hand, we know that J is continuous and monotonically increasing, which means that the range of J is an interval with an upper bound given by the limit of $J(\tau)$ for $\tau \to \infty$. To determine this limit, we use that (3.15) yields $\mathbf{x}_\tau^+ \to \mathbf{0}$ for $\tau \to \infty$. This, however, implies $J(\mathbf{x}_\tau^+) \to \|\mathbf{b}\|_2^2$ for $\tau \to 0$. □

Hence, for each $s \in (0, \|\mathbf{b}\|_2)$ there exists a unique $\tau > 0$ such that $J(\tau) = s$. As we can apply this also to $J^\Delta(\tau) = \|A\mathbf{x}_\tau^\Delta - (\mathbf{b} + \Delta\mathbf{b})\|_2^2$, this proves the following result.

Theorem 3.52 (Morozov's discrepancy principle) *Let $A \in \mathbb{R}^{m\times n}$ with $m \geq n$. Let $\mathbf{b} \neq \mathbf{0}$ be in the range of A. Let the perturbation $\Delta\mathbf{b} \in \mathbb{R}^m$ satisfy $0 < \|\Delta\mathbf{b}\|_2 < \|\mathbf{b}\|_2$. Then, there exists a unique $\tau > 0$ such that the unique solution $\mathbf{x}_\tau^\Delta$ which minimises $\|A\mathbf{x} - (\mathbf{b} + \Delta\mathbf{b})\|_2^2 + \tau\|\mathbf{x}\|_2^2$ over all $\mathbf{x} \in \mathbb{R}^n$ satisfies*

$$\|A\mathbf{x}_\tau^\Delta - (\mathbf{b} + \Delta\mathbf{b})\|_2 = \|\Delta\mathbf{b}\|_2.$$

The above result only guarantees the existence of a unique τ with this property. Its numerical determination is often based upon the so-called *L-curve principle*. As we know that the function $K(\tau)$ is monotonically decreasing and the function $J(\tau)$ is monotonically increasing, we see that the function K is monotonically decreasing as a function of J, i.e. if the curve $(K(\tau), J(\tau))$ is monotonically decreasing in the first quadrant. In many cases this curve has the shape of an L with a prominent *corner*, particularly in a logarithmic plot. The parameter τ corresponding to this corner often yields a good choice of the penalisation parameter. Details can be found, for example, in Hansen [81].

Exercises

3.1   Let $A \in \mathbb{R}^{n \times n}$ be a symmetric matrix and assume that Gaussian elimination without pivoting is possible. Show that after $k - 1$ steps, the lower right $(n - k + 1) \times (n - k + 1)$ block in $A^{(k)}$ from (3.8) is symmetric.

3.2   Denote the columns of $A \in \mathbb{R}^{n \times n}$ by $\mathbf{a}_1, \ldots, \mathbf{a}_n \in \mathbb{R}^n$. Use the QR factorisation of A to show $|\det A| \leq \|\mathbf{a}_1\|_2 \cdots \|\mathbf{a}_n\|_2$.

3.3   Let data $\{y_1, \ldots, y_m\}$ at positions $\{x_1, \ldots, x_m\}$ be given.

- Use the least-squares approach to determine the linear polynomial $y(x) = ax + b$ which fits these data best, i.e. find the linear polynomial which minimises

$$\sum_{j=1}^{m} |y_j - y(x_j)|^2. \tag{3.19}$$

- Find the function $y(x) = ae^{\lambda(x-\mu)}$ which minimises (3.19) for $a, \lambda, \mu \in \mathbb{R}$.

3.4   A *Givens rotation* is an $n \times n$ matrix of the form

$$J(i, j, \theta) = I + (\cos(\theta) - 1)(\mathbf{e}_j\mathbf{e}_j^T + \mathbf{e}_i\mathbf{e}_i^T) + \sin(\theta)(\mathbf{e}_j\mathbf{e}_i^T - \mathbf{e}_i\mathbf{e}_j^T).$$

- Show that a Givens rotation is orthogonal.
- Show that for $\mathbf{x} \in \mathbb{R}^n$ there is an angle θ such that $y_k = 0$ for $\mathbf{y} = J(i, k, \theta)\mathbf{x}$. Use this to show that the QR factorisations of a tridiagonal matrix $A \in \mathbb{R}^{n \times n}$ can be achieved in $O(n)$ time using Givens rotations.
- Show that in $\mathbb{R}^{2 \times 2}$ an orthogonal matrix is either a Householder matrix or a Givens rotation.

3.5   Let $A \in \mathbb{R}^{m \times n}$ with $m \geq n$ and let $\mathbf{b}, \Delta\mathbf{b} \in \mathbb{R}^m$ with $\mathbf{b} \notin$ range(A). Let $\mathbf{x}$ and $\mathbf{x} + \Delta\mathbf{x}$ be the minimal norm solutions of the least-squares problem with data $(A, \mathbf{b})$ and $(A, \mathbf{b} + \Delta\mathbf{b})$, respectively. Show

$$\frac{\|\Delta\mathbf{x}\|_2}{\|\mathbf{x}\|_2} \leq \kappa_2(A)\frac{\|\Delta\mathbf{b}\|_2}{\|A\|_2\|\mathbf{x}\|_2} \leq \kappa_2(A)\frac{\|\Delta\mathbf{b}\|_2}{\|AA^+\mathbf{b}\|_2}.$$

3.6   Let $A \in \mathbb{R}^{m \times n}$ with rank(A) = n and $\mathbf{b} \in \mathbb{R}^m$ be given. Determine the condition number of solving the least-squares problem $\min_\mathbf{x} \|A\mathbf{x} - \mathbf{b}\|_2$ under the assumption that $\mathbf{b}$ is exact, i.e. determine the condition number of the function $f : \{A \in \mathbb{R}^{m \times n} : \text{rank}(A) = n\} \rightarrow \mathbb{R}^n$, $f(A) := \mathbf{x}^+$.

3.7   Let $A \in \mathbb{R}^{n \times n}$ be a symmetric, positive definite matrix. Let $\tau > 0$ and $\mathbf{b} \in \mathbb{R}^n$ be given. Show that the function $\mathbf{x} \mapsto \|A\mathbf{x} - \mathbf{b}\|_2^2 + \tau\mathbf{x}^T A\mathbf{x}$ has a unique minimum $\mathbf{x}_\tau^* \in \mathbb{R}^n$ which solves the linear system $(A + \tau I)\mathbf{x} = \mathbf{b}$.

4

Iterative Methods for Solving Linear Systems

4.1 Introduction

We have seen that a direct algorithm for solving an $n \times n$ linear system

$$Ax = b$$

generally requires $O(n^3)$ time. For larger n, this becomes quite quickly impractical. The basic idea behind iterative methods is to produce a way of approximating the application of the inverse of A to b so that the amount of work required is substantially less than $O(n^3)$. To achieve this, a sequence of approximate solutions is generated, which is supposed to converge to the solution. The computation of each iteration usually costs $O(n^2)$ time so that the method becomes computationally interesting only if a sufficiently good approximation can be achieved in far fewer than n steps.

To understand the general concept, let us write the matrix A as $A = A - B + B$ with an invertible matrix B at our disposal. Then, the equation $Ax = b$ can be reformulated as $b = Ax = (A - B)x + Bx$ and hence as

$$x = B^{-1}(B - A)x + B^{-1}b =: Cx + c =: F(x), \tag{4.1}$$

so that $x \in \mathbb{R}^n$ solves $Ax = b$ if and only if it is the only *fixed point* of the mapping F, i.e. it satisfies $F(x) = x$. To calculate the fixed point of F, we can use the following simple iterative process. We first pick a starting point x_0 and then form

$$x_{j+1} := F(x_j) = Cx_j + c, \qquad j = 0, 1, 2, \dots. \tag{4.2}$$

Noting that this particular F is continuous, we see that if this sequence converges then the limit has to be the fixed point of F and hence the solution of $Ax = b$.

We can, however, also start with an iteration of the form (4.2). If C and $\mathbf{c}$ have the form (4.1) and if (4.2) converges the limit must be the solution of $A\mathbf{x} = \mathbf{b}$.

Definition 4.1 An iterative method (4.2) is called *consistent* with the linear system $A\mathbf{x} = \mathbf{b}$ if the *iteration matrix* C and vector $\mathbf{c}$ are of the form $C = I - B^{-1}A$ and $\mathbf{c} = B^{-1}\mathbf{b}$ with an invertible matrix B.

In the next section, we will discuss possible choices of B and conditions for the convergence of the iterative method.

4.2 Banach's Fixed Point Theorem

We will start by deriving a general convergence theory for an iteration process of the form (4.2) even with a more general, not necessarily linear $F : \mathbb{R}^n \to \mathbb{R}^n$.

Definition 4.2 A mapping $F : \mathbb{R}^n \to \mathbb{R}^n$ is called a *contraction mapping* with respect to a norm $\|\cdot\|$ on $\mathbb{R}^n$ if there is a constant $0 \le q < 1$ such that

$$\|F(\mathbf{x}) - F(\mathbf{y})\| \le q\|\mathbf{x} - \mathbf{y}\|$$

for all $\mathbf{x}, \mathbf{y} \in \mathbb{R}^n$.

A contraction mapping is Lipschitz continuous with Lipschitz constant $q < 1$.

Theorem 4.3 (Banach) *If $F : \mathbb{R}^n \to \mathbb{R}^n$ is a contraction mapping then F has exactly one fixed point $\mathbf{x}^* \in \mathbb{R}^n$. The sequence $\mathbf{x}_{j+1} := F(\mathbf{x}_j)$ converges for every starting point $\mathbf{x}_0 \in \mathbb{R}^n$ to $\mathbf{x}^*$. Furthermore, we have the error estimates*

$$\|\mathbf{x}^* - \mathbf{x}_j\| \le \frac{q}{1-q}\|\mathbf{x}_j - \mathbf{x}_{j-1}\| \qquad \text{(a posteriori)},$$

$$\|\mathbf{x}^* - \mathbf{x}_j\| \le \frac{q^j}{1-q}\|\mathbf{x}_1 - \mathbf{x}_0\| \qquad \text{(a priori)}.$$

Proof First, let us assume that F has two different fixed points $\mathbf{x}^*, \tilde{\mathbf{x}} \in \mathbb{R}^n$. Then, the contraction property of F yields

$$\|\mathbf{x}^* - \tilde{\mathbf{x}}\| = \|F(\mathbf{x}^*) - F(\tilde{\mathbf{x}})\| \le q\|\mathbf{x}^* - \tilde{\mathbf{x}}\| < \|\mathbf{x}^* - \tilde{\mathbf{x}}\|,$$

which is a contradiction. Hence, if existent, the fixed point is unique.

In the next step, we will show that the sequence $\{\mathbf{x}_j\}$ is a Cauchy sequence. The completeness of $\mathbb{R}^n$ then proves its convergence to a point $\mathbf{x}^* \in \mathbb{R}^n$. Since F is continuous, this limit point $\mathbf{x}^*$ has to be the fixed point of F.

For arbitrary j and k from $\mathbb{N}_0$, we can use the contraction property j times to derive

$$\|\mathbf{x}_{j+k} - \mathbf{x}_j\| = \|F(\mathbf{x}_{j+k-1}) - F(\mathbf{x}_{j-1})\| \leq q\|\mathbf{x}_{j+k-1} - \mathbf{x}_{j-1}\|$$
$$\leq q^j\|\mathbf{x}_k - \mathbf{x}_0\|.$$

The distance between $\mathbf{x}_k$ and $\mathbf{x}_0$ can then be estimated using a telescoping sum argument:

$$\|\mathbf{x}_k - \mathbf{x}_0\| \leq \|\mathbf{x}_k - \mathbf{x}_{k-1}\| + \|\mathbf{x}_{k-1} - \mathbf{x}_{k-2}\| + \cdots + \|\mathbf{x}_1 - \mathbf{x}_0\|$$
$$\leq \left(q^{k-1} + q^{k-2} + \cdots + 1\right)\|\mathbf{x}_1 - \mathbf{x}_0\|$$
$$\leq \frac{1}{1-q}\|\mathbf{x}_1 - \mathbf{x}_0\|,$$

using the geometric series for $0 \leq q < 1$. Hence, we have

$$\|\mathbf{x}_{j+k} - \mathbf{x}_j\| \leq \frac{q^j}{1-q}\|\mathbf{x}_1 - \mathbf{x}_0\|, \tag{4.3}$$

and this expression becomes smaller than any given $\epsilon > 0$, provided j is large enough. This proves that $\{\mathbf{x}_j\}$ is indeed a Cauchy sequence.

Finally, letting $k \to \infty$ in (4.3) and using the continuity of the norm yields the a priori estimate. Since this estimate is valid for each starting point, we can restart the iteration with $\mathbf{y}_0 = \mathbf{x}_{j-1}$ and the a priori estimate for the first two terms $\mathbf{y}_0 = \mathbf{x}_{j-1}$ and $\mathbf{y}_1 = F(\mathbf{y}_0) = \mathbf{x}_j$ gives the a posteriori estimate. $\quad\square$

If we apply this theorem to our specific iteration function $F(\mathbf{x}) = C\mathbf{x} + \mathbf{c}$, where C is the *iteration matrix*, then we see that

$$\|F(\mathbf{x}) - F(\mathbf{y})\| = \|C\mathbf{x} + \mathbf{c} - (C\mathbf{y} + \mathbf{c})\| = \|C(\mathbf{x} - \mathbf{y})\| \leq \|C\|\,\|\mathbf{x} - \mathbf{y}\|,$$

so that we have convergence if $\|C\| < 1$. Unfortunately, this depends on the chosen vector and hence matrix norm, while, since all norms on $\mathbb{R}^n$ are equivalent, the fact that the sequence converges does not depend on the norm.

In other words, having a specific compatible matrix norm with $\|C\| < 1$ is sufficient for convergence but not necessary. A sufficient and necessary condition can be stated using the spectral radius of the iteration matrix.

Definition 4.4 Let $A \in \mathbb{R}^{n \times n}$ with eigenvalues $\lambda_1, \lambda_2, \ldots, \lambda_n$ ordered so that $|\lambda_1| \geq |\lambda_2| \geq \cdots \geq |\lambda_n|$. The *spectral radius* of A is given by $\rho(A) := |\lambda_1|$.

We have encountered the spectral radius before. In Theorem 2.19 we have seen that the 2-norm of a matrix A is given by the square root of the largest eigenvalue of $A^{\mathrm{T}}A$, which we can now write as $\|A\|_2 = \rho(A^{\mathrm{T}}A)^{1/2}$.

Note that, if λ is an eigenvalue of A with eigenvector $\mathbf{x}$, then λ^k is an eigenvalue of A^k, $k = 1, 2, 3, \ldots$ with eigenvector $\mathbf{x}$. Hence, $\rho(A)^k \leq \rho(A^k)$.

In the proof of the following theorem we have to be a little careful since a real matrix $A \in \mathbb{R}^{n \times n}$ might easily have eigenvectors $\mathbf{x}$ in $\mathbb{C}^n$ and hence $A\mathbf{x} \in \mathbb{C}^n$.

Theorem 4.5 *1. If $\|\cdot\| : \mathbb{R}^{n \times n} \to \mathbb{R}$ is a compatible matrix norm then $\rho(A) \leq \|A\|$ for all matrices $A \in \mathbb{R}^{n \times n}$.*

2. For any $A \in \mathbb{R}^{n \times n}$ and any $\epsilon > 0$ there exists a compatible matrix norm $\|\cdot\| : \mathbb{R}^{n \times n} \to \mathbb{R}$ such that $\rho(A) \leq \|A\| \leq \rho(A) + \epsilon$.

Proof 1. Suppose $\lambda \in \mathbb{C}$ is an eigenvalue of A with corresponding eigenvector $\mathbf{x} \in \mathbb{C}^n \setminus \{\mathbf{0}\}$. If we have $\lambda \in \mathbb{R}$ then we can choose the corresponding eigenvector $\mathbf{x} \in \mathbb{R}^n$. To see this note that with $\mathbf{x} \in \mathbb{C}^n$ also $\bar{\mathbf{x}} \in \mathbb{C}^n$ and hence the real part $\mathfrak{R}(\mathbf{x}) \in \mathbb{R}^n$ are eigenvectors of A to the eigenvalue λ. Hence, for such an $\mathbf{x} \in \mathbb{R}^n$ we immediately have

$$|\lambda| \|\mathbf{x}\| = \|\lambda \mathbf{x}\| = \|A\mathbf{x}\| \leq \|A\| \|\mathbf{x}\|$$

and hence $|\lambda| \leq \|A\|$. Next, let $\lambda = \mu e^{i\theta} \in \mathbb{C}$ be a complex-valued eigenvalue with $\mu = |\lambda| > 0$ and $\theta \neq 0$ with corresponding normalised eigenvector $\mathbf{x} \in \mathbb{C}^n$. With $\mathbf{x}$ also each vector $\mathbf{y} := e^{i\phi}\mathbf{x}$ is obviously an eigenvector of A to the eigenvalue λ. Thus, we can choose the angle ϕ such that $\mathbf{y}$ has an imaginary part $\mathfrak{I}(\mathbf{y})$ satisfying $\|\mathfrak{I}(\mathbf{y})\| \leq \|\mathfrak{I}(e^{i\theta}\mathbf{y})\|$. Then, we have $A(\mathfrak{I}(\mathbf{y})) = \mathfrak{I}(A\mathbf{y}) = \mathfrak{I}(\lambda \mathbf{y}) = \mu \mathfrak{I}(e^{i\theta}\mathbf{y})$ and hence

$$\|A\| \geq \frac{\|A\mathfrak{I}(\mathbf{y})\|}{\|\mathfrak{I}(\mathbf{y})\|} = \mu \frac{\|\mathfrak{I}(e^{i\theta}\mathbf{y})\|}{\|\mathfrak{I}(\mathbf{y})\|} \geq \mu = |\lambda|.$$

Since λ was an arbitrary eigenvalue this means $\rho(A) \leq \|A\|$.

2. From Theorem 3.38, Schur's factorisation, we know that there exists a unitary matrix W such that $\overline{W}^{\mathrm{T}} A W$ is an upper triangular matrix, with the eigenvalues of A as the diagonal elements:

$$\overline{W}^{\mathrm{T}} A W = \begin{pmatrix} \lambda_1 & r_{12} & \cdots & r_{1n} \\ 0 & \lambda_2 & \cdots & r_{2n} \\ \vdots & \vdots & \ddots & \vdots \\ 0 & 0 & \cdots & \lambda_n \end{pmatrix}.$$

Let D be a diagonal matrix with diagonal elements $1, \delta, \ldots, \delta^{n-1}$, where

$0 < \delta < \min(1, \epsilon/(r + \epsilon))$ with $r = \max |r_{ij}|$ and $\epsilon > 0$. Let $S = WD$, then

$$S^{-1}AS = D^{-1}\overline{W}^{T}AWD = \begin{pmatrix} \lambda_1 & \delta r_{12} & \cdots & \delta^{n-1}r_{1n} \\ 0 & \lambda_2 & \cdots & \delta^{n-2}r_{2n} \\ \vdots & \vdots & \ddots & \vdots \\ 0 & 0 & \cdots & \lambda_n \end{pmatrix}.$$

Furthermore, using Theorem 2.19 and Remark 2.25, we see that

$$\|S^{-1}AS\|_{\infty} = \max_{1 \le i \le n} \sum_{j=1}^{n} |(S^{-1}AS)_{ij}| \le \rho(A) + \delta r(1 + \delta + \cdots + \delta^{n-2}),$$

which is a geometric progression. Hence, we have

$$\|S^{-1}AS\|_{\infty} \le \rho(A) + \delta r \left(\frac{1 - \delta^{n-1}}{1 - \delta} \right) \le \rho(A) + \frac{\delta r}{1 - \delta} \le \rho(A) + \epsilon.$$

Since $A \mapsto \|S^{-1}AS\|_{\infty}$ is the (complex) matrix norm induced by the (complex) vector norm $\mathbf{x} \mapsto \|S^{-1}\mathbf{x}\|_{\infty}$, see Example 2.29 and the remarks right after it, we know that these norms are compatible when restricted to the real numbers, which completes the proof. $\qquad\square$

Note that the proof of the above theorem, as well as the proof of the next theorem, simplifies significantly if a complex set-up is used. Nonetheless, it is worth knowing that everything works out even in an entirely real set-up.

Theorem 4.6 *Let $C \in \mathbb{R}^{n\times n}$ and $\mathbf{c} \in \mathbb{R}^n$ be given. The iteration $\mathbf{x}_{j+1} = C\mathbf{x}_j + \mathbf{c}$ converges for every starting point $\mathbf{x}_0 \in \mathbb{R}^n$ if and only if $\rho(C) < 1$.*

Proof Assume first that $\rho(C) < 1$. Then, we can pick an $\epsilon > 0$ such that $\rho(C) + \epsilon < 1$ and, by Theorem 4.5, we can find a compatible matrix norm $\| \cdot \|$ such that $\|C\| \le \rho(C) + \epsilon < 1$, which gives convergence.

Assume now that the iteration converges to $\mathbf{x}^*$ for every starting point $\mathbf{x}_0$. This particularly means that if we pick two arbitrary starting points $\mathbf{x}_0, \mathbf{y}_0 \in \mathbb{R}^n$ then the sequences $\mathbf{x}_{j+1} := C\mathbf{x}_j + \mathbf{c}$ and $\mathbf{y}_{j+1} := C\mathbf{y}_j + \mathbf{c}$ both converge to $\mathbf{x}^* \in \mathbb{R}^n$. Hence, the sequence

$$\mathbf{z}_{j+1} := \mathbf{x}_{j+1} + i\mathbf{y}_{j+1} = C(\mathbf{x}_j + i\mathbf{y}_j) + (1 + i)\mathbf{c} = C\mathbf{z}_j + \tilde{\mathbf{c}}$$

converges for every starting point $\mathbf{z}_0 = \mathbf{x}_0 + i\mathbf{y}_0 \in \mathbb{C}^n$ to $\mathbf{z}^* = (1 + i)\mathbf{x}^*$, which satisfies $\mathbf{z}^* = C\mathbf{z}^* + \tilde{\mathbf{c}}$. If we pick the starting point $\mathbf{z}_0$ such that $\mathbf{z} = \mathbf{z}_0 - \mathbf{z}^*$ is an eigenvector of C with eigenvalue λ, then

$$\mathbf{z}_j - \mathbf{z}^* = C(\mathbf{z}_{j-1} - \mathbf{z}^*) = \cdots = C^j(\mathbf{z}_0 - \mathbf{z}^*) = \lambda^j(\mathbf{z}_0 - \mathbf{z}^*).$$

Since the expression on the left-hand side tends to zero for $j \to \infty$, so does the expression on the right-hand side. This, however, is possible only if $|\lambda| < 1$. Since λ was an arbitrary eigenvalue of C, this shows that $\rho(C) < 1$.   □

4.3 The Jacobi and Gauss–Seidel Iterations

After this general discussion, we return to the question of how to choose the iteration matrix C. Our initial approach is based upon a splitting

$$C = B^{-1}(B - A) = I - B^{-1}A, \qquad \mathbf{c} = B^{-1}\mathbf{b}$$

with a matrix B, which should be sufficiently close to A but also easily invertible.

From now on, we will assume that the diagonal elements of A are all non-zero. This can be achieved by exchanging rows and/or columns as long as A is non-singular. Next, we decompose A in its lower-left sub-diagonal part, its diagonal part and its upper-right super-diagonal part, i.e.

$$A = L + D + R$$

with

$$L = \begin{cases} a_{ij} & \text{if } i > j, \\ 0 & \text{else,} \end{cases} \qquad D = \begin{cases} a_{ij} & \text{if } i = j, \\ 0 & \text{else,} \end{cases} \qquad R = \begin{cases} a_{ij} & \text{if } i < j, \\ 0 & \text{else.} \end{cases}$$

The simplest possible approximation to A is then given by picking its diagonal part D for B so that the iteration matrix becomes

$$C_J = I - B^{-1}A = I - D^{-1}(L + D + R) = -D^{-1}(L + R),$$

with entries

$$c_{ik} = \begin{cases} -a_{ik}/a_{ii} & \text{if } i \neq k, \\ 0 & \text{else.} \end{cases} \tag{4.4}$$

This means that we can write the iteration defined by

$$\mathbf{x}^{(j+1)} = -D^{-1}(L + R)\mathbf{x}^{(j)} + D^{-1}\mathbf{b}$$

component-wise as follows.

Definition 4.7   The iteration defined by

$$x_i^{(j+1)} = \frac{1}{a_{ii}}\left(b_i - \sum_{\substack{k=1 \\ k \neq i}}^{n} a_{ik}x_k^{(j)} \right), \qquad 1 \leq i \leq n, \tag{4.5}$$

is called the *Jacobi method*.

Note that we wrote the iteration index as an upper index, which we will continue to do from now on. An algorithmic formulation is given in Algorithm 7. Here we have realised the iteration with just two vectors $\mathbf{x}$ and $\mathbf{y}$, where $\mathbf{x}$ represents the "old" iteration and $\mathbf{y}$ represents the new, next iteration.

We also need a stopping criterion here. Unfortunately, we cannot use the error $\mathbf{x}^* - \mathbf{x}^{(j)}$ since we do not know the exact solution $\mathbf{x}^*$. But there are at least two possibilities. The easiest one is to choose a maximum number of iteration steps for which we are willing to run the iteration. The advantage of this stopping criterion is that we will finish after the prescribed number of iterations. However, we might have a good approximation $\mathbf{x}^{(j)}$ already after a few steps and would thereafter do more iterations than necessary. But we might also have a bad approximation, and would then need to perform additional iterations.

A better stopping criterion is to look at the residual $A\mathbf{x}^* - A\mathbf{x}^{(j)} = \mathbf{b} - A\mathbf{x}^{(j)}$ and to stop if the norm of the residual falls below a given threshold. Unfortunately, computing the residual is an $O(n^2)$ operation for a full matrix. Another, widely used stopping criterion is to look at the difference of two iterations $\mathbf{x}^{(j+1)} - \mathbf{x}^{(j)}$. If the norm of this difference falls below a certain threshold, the process stops. This is computationally cheaper as it costs only $O(n)$ time.

Algorithm 7: Jacobi iteration

Input : $A \in \mathbb{R}^{n \times n}$ invertible, $\mathbf{b} \in \mathbb{R}^n$, $\mathbf{x}^{(0)} \in \mathbb{R}^n$.
Output: Approximate solution of $A\mathbf{x} = \mathbf{b}$.

1 Compute $r := \|\mathbf{b} - A\mathbf{x}^{(0)}\|$
2 **while** $r \geq \epsilon$ **do**
3   **for** $i = 1$ **to** n **do**
4          $y_i := b_i$
5   **for** $k = 1$ **to** $i - 1$ **do**
6             $y_i := y_i - a_{ik} x_k$
7   **for** $k = i + 1$ **to** n **do**
8             $y_i := y_i - a_{ik} x_k$
9          $y_i := y_i / a_{ii}$
10      $\mathbf{x} := \mathbf{y}$
11      $r := \|\mathbf{b} - A\mathbf{x}\|$

It is easy to calculate the computational cost. As is typical for an iterative method, we only give the computational cost for one step of the iteration, so the total cost becomes this cost times the number of iterations.

Remark 4.8   Let $A \in \mathbb{R}^{n \times n}$ be a full matrix. Then, one step of the Jacobi method costs $O(n^2)$ time.

Note that the computational cost drops to $O(n)$ if the matrix A is sparse and has only a constant number of non-zero entries per row.

Obviously, one can expect convergence of the Jacobi method if the original matrix A resembles a diagonal matrix, i.e. if the entries on the diagonal dominate the other entries in that row. Recall that a matrix A is strictly row diagonally dominant if

$$\sum_{\substack{k=1 \\ k \neq i}}^{n} |a_{ik}| < |a_{ii}|, \qquad 1 \leq i \leq n.$$

Theorem 4.9   *The Jacobi method converges for every starting point if the matrix A is strictly row diagonally dominant.*

Proof   We use the row sum norm to calculate the norm of the iteration matrix C_J as

$$\|C_J\|_{\infty} = \max_{1 \leq i \leq n} \sum_{k=1}^{n} |c_{ik}| = \max_{1 \leq i \leq n} \sum_{\substack{k=1 \\ k \neq i}}^{n} \frac{|a_{ik}|}{|a_{ii}|} < 1.$$

Hence, we have convergence.   □

The latter criterion can be weakened in a way which we will describe now.

Definition 4.10   A matrix $A \in \mathbb{R}^{n \times n}$ is called *weakly (row) diagonally dominant*, if, for $1 \leq i \leq n$,

$$\sum_{\substack{k=1 \\ k \neq i}}^{n} |a_{ik}| \leq |a_{ii}| \tag{4.6}$$

is satisfied and if there is at least one index i for which (4.6) holds with a strict lower sign.

If the matrix A is invertible and weakly diagonally dominant, the diagonal elements of A have to be different from zero. To see this, let us assume that there is an i with $a_{ii} = 0$. In that case the whole row i would be zero, which contradicts the non-singularity of A.

Being weakly diagonally dominant is not enough for the Jacobi method to achieve convergence. We also need that the matrix is not reducible in the following sense.

Definition 4.11 A matrix $A \in \mathbb{R}^{n \times n}$ is called *reducible* if there are non-empty subsets N_1 and N_2 of $N := \{1, 2, \ldots, n\}$ with

1. $N_1 \cap N_2 = \emptyset$,
2. $N_1 \cup N_2 = N$,
3. for each $i \in N_1$ and each $k \in N_2$ we have $a_{ik} = 0$.

The matrix A is called *irreducible* if it is not reducible.

For a linear system $A\mathbf{x} = \mathbf{b}$ with reducible matrix $A \in \mathbb{R}^{n \times n}$ we can split the system into two smaller, independent systems. If, for example, N_1 contains exactly $m < n$ elements, then we can first solve the m equations

$$\sum_{k=1}^{n} a_{ik} x_k = \sum_{k \in N_1} a_{ik} x_k = b_i, \qquad i \in N_1.$$

This gives us the m components x_k of the solution $\mathbf{x}$ with index $k \in N_1$. Having these components, we can rewrite the equations for the other indices $i \in N_2$ as

$$\sum_{k \in N_2} a_{ik} x_k = b_i - \sum_{k \in N_1} a_{ik} x_k, \qquad i \in N_2.$$

Hence, without restriction, we can assume that our matrix is irreducible.

Theorem 4.12 *If the matrix $A \in \mathbb{R}^{n \times n}$ is irreducible and weakly diagonally dominant then the Jacobi method converges for every starting point.*

Proof First of all, we note that all diagonal elements of A are different from zero. Otherwise, the sets $N_1 := \{i \in N : a_{ii} = 0\}$ and $N_2 := \{i \in N : a_{ii} \neq 0\}$ would give a non-trivial decomposition of N. To see this, note that N_1 is non-empty by this assumption and N_2 also contains at least one element by the fact that A is weakly diagonally dominant. The union of the two sets obviously gives N. Furthermore, for $i \in N_1$ the weakly diagonal dominance of A ensures that also all a_{ij} for $j \neq i$ have to vanish, in particular for those $j \in N_2$.

From A being weakly diagonally dominant and Theorem 4.5 we immediately have $\rho(C_J) \leq \|C_J\|_\infty \leq 1$ for the iteration matrix C_J of the Jacobi method. Hence, it remains to ensure that there is no eigenvalue of C_J with absolute value one. Hence, let us assume there is such an eigenvalue $\lambda \in \mathbb{C}$ of C_J with $|\lambda| = 1$ and corresponding eigenvector $\mathbf{x} \in \mathbb{C}^n$, which we normalise to satisfy $\|\mathbf{x}\|_\infty = 1$. Then we can form the sets $N_1 := \{i \in N : |x_i| = 1\} \neq \emptyset$ and

$N_2 = N \setminus N_1$. The set N_2 is also not empty since

$$|x_i| = |\lambda||x_i| = |(C_J \mathbf{x})_i| = \frac{1}{|a_{ii}|} \left| \sum_{\substack{k=1 \\ k \neq i}}^{n} a_{ik} x_k \right| \leq \frac{1}{|a_{ii}|} \sum_{\substack{k=1 \\ k \neq i}}^{n} |a_{ik} x_k| \leq \frac{1}{|a_{ii}|} \sum_{\substack{k=1 \\ k \neq i}}^{n} |a_{ik}| \leq 1$$

(4.7)

shows that for $i \in N_1$ we must have equality here, meaning particularly

$$|a_{ii}| = \sum_{\substack{k=1 \\ k \neq i}}^{n} |a_{ik}|, \qquad i \in N_1.$$

Hence, since A is weakly diagonally dominant, there must be at least one index $i \notin N_1$, which shows that N_2 cannot be empty.

Since A is irreducible there is at least one $i \in N_1$ and one $k_0 \in N_2$ with $a_{ik_0} \neq 0$. For this $k_0 \in N_2$ we have particularly $|a_{ik_0} x_{k_0}| < |a_{ik_0}|$, so that we have a strict inequality in (4.7). This, however, is a contradiction to $i \in N_1$. □

If the matrix A is strictly diagonally dominant, we have $\|C_J\|_\infty < 1$. If the matrix A is irreducible and weakly diagonally dominant we only have $\rho(C_J) < 1$. We will have $\|C_J\|_\infty = 1$ whenever there is at least one index i with equality in (4.6).

A closer inspection of the Jacobi method shows that the computation of $x_i^{(j+1)}$ is independent of any other $x_\ell^{(j+1)}$. This means that on a parallel or vector computer all components of the new iteration $\mathbf{x}^{(j+1)}$ can be computed simultaneously.

However, it also gives us the possibility to improve the process. For example, to calculate $x_2^{(j+1)}$ we could already employ the newly computed $x_1^{(j+1)}$. Then, for computing $x_3^{(j+1)}$ we could use $x_1^{(j+1)}$ and $x_2^{(j+1)}$ and so on. This leads to the following iterative scheme.

Definition 4.13 The *Gauss–Seidel* method is given by the iterative scheme

$$x_i^{(j+1)} = \frac{1}{a_{ii}} \left(b_i - \sum_{k=1}^{i-1} a_{ik} x_k^{(j+1)} - \sum_{k=i+1}^{n} a_{ik} x_k^{(j)} \right), \qquad 1 \leq i \leq n. \qquad (4.8)$$

As usual, the algorithm is given in Algorithm 8. Once, again we use the residual as the stopping criterion. This time, we have an *in situ* algorithm, i.e. we can store each iteration directly over the previous one.

As in the case of the Jacobi method, the computational cost of the Gauss–Seidel iteration is easily derived.

Remark 4.14 The computational cost of one iteration of the Gauss–Seidel

---

Algorithm 8: Gauss–Seidel iteration

Input : $A \in \mathbb{R}^{n \times n}$ invertible, $\mathbf{b} \in \mathbb{R}^n$, $\mathbf{x}^{(0)} \in \mathbb{R}^n$.

Output: Approximate solution of $A\mathbf{x} = \mathbf{b}$.

1   Compute $r := \|\mathbf{b} - A\mathbf{x}^{(0)}\|$

2   **while** $r \geq \epsilon$ **do**

3   **for** $i = 1$ **to** n **do**

4         $x_i := b_i$

5   **for** $k = 1$ **to** $i - 1$ **do**

6            $x_i := x_i - a_{ik}x_k$

7   **for** $k = i + 1$ **to** n **do**

8            $x_i := x_i - a_{ik}x_k$

9         $x_i := x_i/a_{ii}$

10      $r := \|\mathbf{b} - A\mathbf{x}\|$

---

method is $O(n^2)$. This reduces to $O(n)$ if we have a sparse matrix with only $O(n)$ non-zero entries.

To see that this scheme is consistent and to analyse its convergence, we have to find $C = I - B^{-1}A = B^{-1}(B - A)$ and $\mathbf{c} = B^{-1}\mathbf{b}$. To this end, we rewrite (4.8) as

$$a_{ii}x_i^{(j+1)} + \sum_{k=1}^{i-1} a_{ik}x_k^{(j+1)} = b_i - \sum_{k=i+1}^{n} a_{ik}x_k^{(j)},$$

which translates into $(L + D)\mathbf{x}^{(j+1)} = -R\mathbf{x}^{(j)} + \mathbf{b}$. Hence, if we define $B = (L + D)^{-1}$ and use $B - A = -R$, we note that the scheme is indeed consistent and that the iteration matrix of the Gauss–Seidel method is given by

$$C_{GS} = -(L + D)^{-1}R.$$

Later on, we will prove a more general version of the following theorem.

Theorem 4.15 *If $A \in \mathbb{R}^{n \times n}$ is symmetric, positive definite then the Gauss–Seidel method converges.*

Our motivation for introducing the Gauss–Seidel method was to improve the Jacobi method. Under certain assumptions it is indeed possible to show that the Gauss–Seidel method converges faster than the Jacobi method.

Theorem 4.16 (Sassenfeld) *Let $A \in \mathbb{R}^{n \times n}$. Assume that the diagonal elements* *of A are different from zero. Define recursively*

$$s_i = \frac{1}{|a_{ii}|}\left(\sum_{k=1}^{i-1}|a_{ik}|s_k + \sum_{k=i+1}^{n}|a_{ik}|\right), \qquad 1 \le i \le n.$$

Then, we have for the iteration matrix $C_{GS} = -(L+D)^{-1}R$ of the Gauss–Seidel method the bound

$$\|C_{GS}\|_\infty \le \max_{1 \le i \le n} s_i =: s,$$

and the Gauss–Seidel method converges if $s < 1$. If A is a strictly row diagonally dominant matrix, we also have

$$\|C_{GS}\|_\infty \le s \le \|C_J\|_\infty < 1,$$

where $C_J = -D^{-1}(L+R)$ is the iteration matrix of the Jacobi method.

Proof Let $\mathbf{y} \in \mathbb{R}^n$. We have to show that $\|C_{GS}\mathbf{y}\|_\infty \le s\|\mathbf{y}\|_\infty$. From this, $\|C_{GS}\|_\infty \le s$ immediately follows. Let $\mathbf{z} = C_{GS}\mathbf{y}$. For the components $z_1, \ldots, z_n$ of $\mathbf{z}$ we can conclude that

$$z_i = -\frac{1}{a_{ii}}\left(\sum_{k=1}^{i-1}a_{ik}z_k + \sum_{k=i+1}^{n}a_{ik}y_k\right), \qquad 1 \le i \le n.$$

In particular for $i = 1$ this means

$$|z_1| \le \frac{1}{|a_{11}|}\sum_{k=2}^{n}|a_{1k}||y_k| \le \frac{1}{|a_{11}|}\sum_{k=2}^{n}|a_{1k}|\,\|\mathbf{y}\|_\infty = s_1\|\mathbf{y}\|_\infty \le s\|\mathbf{y}\|_\infty.$$

If, for $1 \le j \le i-1$ the statement $|z_j| \le s_j\|\mathbf{y}\|_\infty$ is correct, then we can, by induction, conclude that

$$\begin{aligned}
|z_i| &\le \frac{1}{|a_{ii}|}\left(\sum_{k=1}^{i-1}|a_{ik}||z_k| + \sum_{k=i+1}^{n}|a_{ik}||y_k|\right)\\
&\le \frac{\|\mathbf{y}\|_\infty}{|a_{ii}|}\left(\sum_{k=1}^{i-1}|a_{ik}|s_k + \sum_{k=i+1}^{n}|a_{ik}|\right)\\
&= \|\mathbf{y}\|_\infty s_i.
\end{aligned}$$

Hence, we have proven the first part of the theorem. Now suppose that A is a strictly row diagonally dominant matrix. Then, it follows that

$$K := \|C_J\|_\infty = \max_{1 \le i \le n}\frac{1}{|a_{ii}|}\sum_{\substack{k=1\\k\ne i}}^{n}|a_{ik}| < 1$$

and particularly $s_1 \leq K < 1$. We can now continue by induction and may assume that $s_j \leq K < 1$ for all $1 \leq j \leq i - 1$. With this, we can conclude that

$$s_i = \frac{1}{|a_{ii}|} \left(\sum_{k=1}^{i-1} |a_{ik}| s_k + \sum_{k=i+1}^{n} |a_{ik}| \right) \leq \frac{1}{|a_{ii}|} \left(K \sum_{k=1}^{i-1} |a_{ik}| + \sum_{k=i+1}^{n} |a_{ik}| \right)$$

$$\leq \frac{1}{|a_{ii}|} \sum_{\substack{k=1 \\ k \neq i}}^{n} |a_{ik}| \leq K < 1,$$

meaning also $s \leq \|C_J\|_\infty$. □

As an example, let us have a look at the discretisation of the boundary value problem described in Section 1.1.2. Essentially, we have to solve a linear system with a matrix of the form

$$A = \begin{pmatrix} 2 & -1 & & & & 0 \\ -1 & 2 & -1 & & & \\ & -1 & 2 & -1 & & \\ & & \ddots & \ddots & \ddots & \\ & & & -1 & 2 & -1 \\ 0 & & & & -1 & 2 \end{pmatrix} = L + D + R, \qquad (4.9)$$

where $D = 2I$, L is a matrix with -1 on the sub-diagonal and R is a matrix with -1 on the super-diagonal. All other entries of R and L are zero. This means that the Jacobi method computes the new iteration $u^{(j+1)}$ component-wise as

$$u_i^{(j+1)} = \frac{1}{2} h^2 f_i + \frac{1}{2} \begin{cases} u_2^{(j)} & \text{if } i = 1, \\ u_{i-1}^{(j)} + u_{i+1}^{(j)} & \text{if } 2 \leq i \leq n - 1, \\ u_{n-1}^{(j)} & \text{if } i = n \end{cases} \qquad (4.10)$$

and the Gauss–Seidel method calculates it as

$$u_i^{(j+1)} = \frac{1}{2} h^2 f_i + \frac{1}{2} \begin{cases} u_2^{(j)} & \text{if } i = 1, \\ u_{i-1}^{(j+1)} + u_{i+1}^{(j)} & \text{if } 2 \leq i \leq n - 1, \\ u_{n-1}^{(j+1)} & \text{if } i = n. \end{cases} \qquad (4.11)$$

Note that we have used **u** rather than **x** to denote the iterations since this is more natural in this context.

To analyse the convergence, we need to determine the iteration matrices. Unfortunately, the matrix A is not strictly row diagonally dominant but only weakly diagonally dominant and irreducible. Nonetheless, we can have a look at the iteration matrices and their $\| \cdot \|_\infty$ norms.

For the Jacobi method the iteration matrix is given by

$$
C_J = -D^{-1}(L+R) = \begin{pmatrix} \frac{1}{2} & & & \\ & \frac{1}{2} & & \\ & & \ddots & \\ & & & \frac{1}{2} \\ & & & & \frac{1}{2} \end{pmatrix} \begin{pmatrix} 0 & 1 & & & \\ 1 & 0 & 1 & & \\ & \ddots & \ddots & \ddots & \\ & & 1 & 0 & 1 \\ & & & 1 & 0 \end{pmatrix}
$$

$$
= \begin{pmatrix} 0 & \frac{1}{2} & & & \\ \frac{1}{2} & 0 & \frac{1}{2} & & \\ & \ddots & \ddots & \ddots & \\ & & \frac{1}{2} & 0 & \frac{1}{2} \\ & & & \frac{1}{2} & 0 \end{pmatrix}, \tag{4.12}
$$

showing that $\|C_J\|_\infty = 1$, as expected, so that we cannot conclude convergence from this. The situation is slightly better when it comes to the Gauss–Seidel method. Here, we first have to compute

$$
(L+D)^{-1} = \begin{pmatrix} 2 & & & \\ -1 & 2 & & \\ & -1 & 2 & \\ & & \ddots & \ddots & \\ 0 & & & -1 & 2 \end{pmatrix}^{-1} = \begin{pmatrix} \frac{1}{2} & & & & 0 \\ \frac{1}{4} & \frac{1}{2} & & & \\ \frac{1}{8} & \frac{1}{4} & \frac{1}{2} & & \\ \vdots & \vdots & & \ddots & \\ \frac{1}{2^n} & \frac{1}{2^{n-1}} & \cdots & \frac{1}{4} & \frac{1}{2} \end{pmatrix}.
$$

Note that there is a *fill in* when computing the inverse. We cannot expect that the inverse of a sparse matrix is sparse again. Here, however, we know that the inverse at least has to be a lower triangular matrix.

With this, we can compute the iteration matrix of the Gauss–Seidel method:

$$
C_{GS} = -(L+D)^{-1}R = \begin{pmatrix} 0 & \frac{1}{2} & & & \\ 0 & \frac{1}{4} & \frac{1}{2} & & \\ 0 & \frac{1}{8} & \frac{1}{4} & \ddots & \\ 0 & \vdots & \vdots & \ddots & \frac{1}{2} \\ 0 & \frac{1}{2^n} & \frac{1}{2^{n-1}} & \cdots & \frac{1}{4} \end{pmatrix}, \tag{4.13}
$$

since multiplying by this R from the right means shifting all columns to the right and filling the first column up with zeros. This gives

$$
\|C_{GS}\|_\infty = \frac{1}{4} + \frac{1}{8} + \cdots + \frac{1}{2^n} = \frac{1}{4} \sum_{i=0}^{n-2} 2^{-i} = \frac{1}{2}(1 - 2^{-n+1}) < 1. \tag{4.14}
$$

This shows that the Gauss–Seidel method converges for our problem. However, the bound on the right-hand side becomes arbitrarily close to 1 if n tends to infinity. Hence, we might expect that convergence slows down for larger n, which is quite unfortunate since a larger n already means a higher computational cost per iteration.

To determine the convergence of the Jacobi method, we need to compute the spectral radius and hence the eigenvalues of the iteration matrices. Since the iteration matrix is given by $C_J = I - D^{-1}A$ we see that every eigenvector of A is also an eigenvector of C_J. To be more precise, if $Ax = \lambda x$, then

$$C_J x = x - D^{-1}Ax = x - \lambda D^{-1}x = x - \frac{\lambda}{2}x = \left(1 - \frac{\lambda}{2}\right)x.$$

Hence, it suffices to determine the eigenvalues of A.

Remark 4.17 The matrix $A \in \mathbb{R}^{n \times n}$ defined by (4.9) has the eigenvalues $\lambda_j = 2(1 - \cos\theta_j) = 4\sin^2(\theta_j/2)$ with corresponding eigenvectors

$$x_j = (\sin\theta_j, \sin(2\theta_j), \ldots, \sin(n\theta_j))^T$$

for $1 \le j \le n$ with $\theta_j = j\pi/(n+1)$.

Proof To verify this, it is helpful to recall the identity

$$\sin(\alpha + \beta) + \sin(\alpha - \beta) = 2\sin\alpha\cos\beta \qquad (4.15)$$

for the trigonometric functions. Now, using the above-defined quantities yields

$$(Ax_j)_i = \begin{cases} 2\sin\theta_j - \sin(2\theta_j) & \text{for } i = 1, \\ -\sin((i-1)\theta_j) + 2\sin(i\theta_j) - \sin((i+1)\theta_j) & \text{for } 2 \le i \le n-1, \\ -\sin((n-1)\theta_j) + 2\sin(n\theta_j) & \text{for } i = n. \end{cases}$$

Taking $\sin(0\theta_j) = 0$ and $\sin(n+1)\theta_j = \sin(j\pi) = 0$ into account, this can uniformly be written as

$$(Ax_j)_i = 2\sin(i\theta_j) - [\sin(i-1)\theta_j + \sin(i+1)\theta_j], \qquad 1 \le i \le n.$$

Using (4.15) with $\alpha = i\theta_j$ and $\beta = \theta_j$ then gives

$$(Ax_j)_i = 2\sin(i\theta_j) - 2\sin(i\theta_j)\cos\theta_j = \lambda_j \sin(i\theta_j) = \lambda_j(x_j)_i. \qquad \square$$

From this remark and the above we can conclude the following.

Remark 4.18 The iteration matrix C_J, given in (4.12), of the Jacobi method has the eigenvalues

$$\mu_j = 1 - \frac{\lambda_j}{2} = 1 - 2\sin^2\left(\frac{j\pi}{2(n+1)}\right) = \cos\left(\frac{j\pi}{n+1}\right), \qquad 1 \le j \le n.$$

The eigenvectors are the same as in Remark 4.17.

Note that in both remarks we have used the identity $\cos(2\alpha) = 1 - 2\sin^2\alpha$. Taking the graph of the cos into account, we see that

$$\rho(C_J) = \cos\left(\frac{\pi}{n+1}\right) < 1. \tag{4.16}$$

Hence, as expected, the Jacobi method converges. However, a Taylor expansion of cos reveals

$$\rho(C_J) = 1 - \frac{\pi^2}{2(n+1)^2} + \frac{\pi^4}{4!(n+1)^4} - \cdots,$$

which means that the convergence also slows down for larger n. If we compare this with (4.14), it seems to be better and hence convergence of the Jacobi method should be faster. But this is not true since in (4.14) we have only looked at an upper bound for $\rho(C_{GS})$. To have a real comparison of both methods we must compute $\rho(C_{GS})$, as well. This is slightly more complicated than computing $\rho(C_J)$, but the following can be shown.

Remark 4.19   The iteration matrix C_{GS} given in (4.13) has the eigenvalues $\lambda_j = \cos^2\theta_j$ with corresponding eigenvectors

$$\mathbf{x}_j = (\cos(\theta_j)\sin(\theta_j), \cos^2(\theta_j)\sin(2\theta_j), \ldots, \cos^n(\theta_j)\sin(n\theta_j))^{\mathsf{T}},$$

where $\theta_j = j\pi/(n+1)$.

This means that we have the relation $\lambda_j = \mu_j^2$ between the eigenvalues λ_j of C_{GS} and μ_j of C_J, leading also to $\rho(C_{GS}) = \rho(C_J)^2$. Hence, the Gauss–Seidel method converges faster than the Jacobi method.

The above relation between the spectral radius of the Gauss–Seidel method and the spectral radius of the Jacobi method is always given if the matrix A is *consistently ordered*. We will discuss this in more detail at the end of the next section.

4.4 Relaxation

A further improvement of both methods can sometimes be achieved by *relaxation*. We start by looking at the Jacobi method. Here, the iterations can be written as

$$\mathbf{x}^{(j+1)} = D^{-1}\mathbf{b} - D^{-1}(L+R)\mathbf{x}^{(j)} = \mathbf{x}^{(j)} + D^{-1}\mathbf{b} - D^{-1}(L+R+D)\mathbf{x}^{(j)}$$
$$= \mathbf{x}^{(j)} + D^{-1}(\mathbf{b} - A\mathbf{x}^{(j)}).$$

The latter equality shows that the new iteration $\mathbf{x}^{(j+1)}$ is given by the old iteration $\mathbf{x}^{(j)}$ corrected by the D^{-1}-multiple of the *residual* $\mathbf{b} - A\mathbf{x}^{(j)}$. In practice, one often notices that the correction term is off the correct correction term by a fixed factor. Hence, it makes sense to introduce a *relaxation parameter* ω and to form the new iteration rather as

$$\mathbf{x}^{(j+1)} = \mathbf{x}^{(j)} + \omega D^{-1}(\mathbf{b} - A\mathbf{x}^{(j)}), \tag{4.17}$$

which is a consistent splitting with $B = B(\omega) = \frac{1}{\omega}D$.

Definition 4.20 The *Jacobi relaxation* is given by

$$x_i^{(j+1)} = x_i^{(j)} + \frac{\omega}{a_{ii}}\left(b_i - \sum_{k=1}^{n} a_{ik}x_k^{(j)}\right), \qquad 1 \le i \le n.$$

In algorithmic form this is detailed in Algorithm 9. Similarly to Algorithm 7, we use two vectors to realise the iteration. Obviously, to compute one iteration requires $O(n^2)$ time for a full matrix A.

Algorithm 9: Jacobi relaxation

Input : $A \in \mathbb{R}^{n \times n}$ invertible, $\mathbf{b} \in \mathbb{R}^n$, $\mathbf{x}^{(0)} \in \mathbb{R}^n$, $\omega \in \mathbb{R}$.
Output: Approximate solution of $A\mathbf{x} = \mathbf{b}$.

1 Compute $r := \|\mathbf{b} - A\mathbf{x}^{(0)}\|$
2 **while** $r \ge \epsilon$ **do**
3 $\quad$ **for** $i = 1$ **to** n **do**
4 $\quad\quad$ $y_i := b_i$
5 $\quad\quad$ **for** $k = 1$ **to** n **do**
6 $\quad\quad\quad$ $y_i := y_i - a_{ik}x_k$
7 $\quad\quad$ $y_i := x_i + \omega \cdot y_i/a_{ii}$
8 $\quad$ $\mathbf{x} := \mathbf{y}$
9 $\quad$ $r := \|\mathbf{b} - A\mathbf{x}\|$

Of course, the relaxation parameter should be chosen such that the convergence improves compared with the original Jacobi method. It follows from

$$\mathbf{x}^{(j+1)} = \mathbf{x}^{(j)} + \omega D^{-1}\mathbf{b} - \omega D^{-1}(L + D + R)\mathbf{x}^{(j)}$$
$$= [(1 - \omega)I - \omega D^{-1}(L + R)]\mathbf{x}^{(j)} + \omega D^{-1}\mathbf{b} \tag{4.18}$$

that the iteration matrix is given by

$$C_J(\omega) = [(1 - \omega)I - \omega D^{-1}(L + R)] = (1 - \omega)I + \omega C_J, \tag{4.19}$$

which shows that $C_J(1) = C_J$ corresponds to the classical Jacobi method.

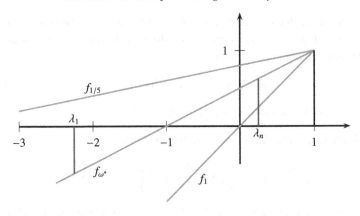

Figure 4.1 Determination of the relaxation parameter.

Theorem 4.21 *Assume that $C_J = -D^{-1}(L+R)$ has only real eigenvalues $\lambda_1 \leq \lambda_2 \leq \cdots \leq \lambda_n < 1$ with corresponding eigenvectors $z_1, \ldots, z_n$. Then, $C_J(\omega)$ has the same eigenvectors $z_1, \ldots, z_n$, but with eigenvalues $\mu_j = 1 - \omega + \omega\lambda_j$ for $1 \leq j \leq n$. The spectral radius of $C_J(\omega)$ is minimised by choosing*

$$\omega^* = \frac{2}{2 - \lambda_1 - \lambda_n}. \tag{4.20}$$

In the case of $\lambda_1 \neq -\lambda_n$ relaxation converges faster than the Jacobi method.

Proof For every eigenvector z_j of C_J it follows that

$$C_J(\omega)z_j = (1 - \omega)z_j + \omega\lambda_j z_j = (1 - \omega + \omega\lambda_j)z_j,$$

i.e. z_j is an eigenvector of $C_J(\omega)$ for the eigenvalue $1 - \omega + \omega\lambda_j =: \mu_j(\omega)$. Thus, the spectral radius of $C_J(\omega)$ is given by

$$\rho(C_J(\omega)) = \max_{1 \leq j \leq n} |\mu_j(\omega)| = \max_{1 \leq j \leq n} |1 - \omega + \omega\lambda_j|,$$

which should be minimised. For a fixed ω let us have a look at the function $f_\omega(\lambda) := 1 - \omega + \omega\lambda$, which is, as a function of λ, a straight line with $f_\omega(1) = 1$. For different choices of ω we thus have a collection of such lines (see Figure 4.1) and it follows that the maximum in the definition of $\rho(C_J(\omega))$ can only be attained for the indices $j = 1$ and $j = n$. Moreover, it follows that ω is optimally chosen if $f_\omega(\lambda_1) = -f_\omega(\lambda_n)$ or

$$1 - \omega + \omega\lambda_1 = -(1 - \omega + \omega\lambda_n).$$

This gives (4.20). Finally, we have the Jacobi method if and only if $\omega^* = 1$, which is equivalent to $\lambda_1 = -\lambda_n$. □

Example 4.22 Let us have another look at the second example from the introduction. We were concerned with solving a boundary value problem with finite differences. The resulting system has been stated in Section 1.1.2. In the last section, we have seen that the iteration matrix of the Jacobi method has eigenvalues

$$\mu_j = \cos\left(\frac{j\pi}{n+1}\right), \qquad 1 \le j \le n.$$

Hence, the biggest eigenvalue is $\mu_1 = \cos(\pi/(n+1))$ and the smallest eigenvalue is given by $\mu_n = \cos(n\pi/(n+1))$.

This means that the relaxation of the Jacobi method has an iteration matrix with eigenvalues

$$\mu_j(\omega) = 1 - \omega + \omega \cos\left(\frac{j\pi}{n+1}\right).$$

However, since we have $\mu_n = -\mu_1$, Theorem 4.21 tells us that the optimal relaxation parameter is $\omega^* = 1$ and hence the classical Jacobi method cannot be sped up using relaxation.

An alternative interpretation of the Jacobi relaxation can be derived from

$$\mathbf{x}^{(j+1)} = (1 - \omega)\mathbf{x}^{(j)} + \omega C_J \mathbf{x}^{(j)} + \omega D^{-1} \mathbf{b}$$
$$= (1 - \omega)\mathbf{x}^{(j)} + \omega (C_J \mathbf{x}^{(j)} + D^{-1} \mathbf{b}).$$

Hence, if we define $\mathbf{z}^{(j+1)} = C_J \mathbf{x}^{(j)} + D^{-1} \mathbf{b}$, which is one step of the classical Jacobi method, the next iteration of the Jacobi relaxation method is

$$\mathbf{x}^{(j+1)} = (1 - \omega)\mathbf{x}^{(j)} + \omega \mathbf{z}^{(j+1)},$$

which is a linear interpolation between the old iteration and the new Jacobi iteration.

This idea can be used to introduce relaxation for the Gauss–Seidel method, as well. We start by looking at $D\mathbf{x}^{(j+1)} = \mathbf{b} - L\mathbf{x}^{(j+1)} - R\mathbf{x}^{(j+1)}$ and replace the iteration on the left-hand side by $\mathbf{z}^{(j+1)}$ and then use linear interpolation again. Hence, we set

$$D\mathbf{z}^{(j+1)} = \mathbf{b} - L\mathbf{x}^{(j+1)} - R\mathbf{x}^{(j+1)},$$
$$\mathbf{x}^{(j+1)} = (1 - \omega)\mathbf{x}^{(j)} + \omega \mathbf{z}^{(j+1)}.$$

Multiplying the second equation by D and inserting the first one yields

$$D\mathbf{x}^{(j+1)} = (1 - \omega)D\mathbf{x}^{(j)} + \omega \mathbf{b} - \omega L\mathbf{x}^{(j+1)} - \omega R\mathbf{x}^{(j)}$$

and hence

$$(D + \omega L)\mathbf{x}^{(j+1)} = [(1 - \omega)D - \omega R]\,\mathbf{x}^{(j)} + \omega \mathbf{b}.$$

Thus, the iteration matrix of the relaxed Gauss–Seidel method is given by

$$C_{GS}(\omega) = (D + \omega L)^{-1}[(1 - \omega)D - \omega R]. \tag{4.21}$$

We can rewrite this component-wise.

Definition 4.23　The *Gauss–Seidel Relaxation* or *Successive Over-relaxation (SOR)* method is given by

$$x_i^{(j+1)} = x_i^{(j)} + \frac{\omega}{a_{ii}}\left(b_i - \sum_{k=1}^{i-1} a_{ik}x_k^{(j+1)} - \sum_{k=i}^{n} a_{ik}x_k^{(j)}\right), \qquad 1 \le i \le n.$$

The algorithmic description is given in Algorithm 10.

Algorithm 10: SOR

   Input　: $A \in \mathbb{R}^{n \times n}$ invertible, $\mathbf{b} \in \mathbb{R}^n$, $\mathbf{x}^{(0)} \in \mathbb{R}^n$, $\omega \in \mathbb{R}$.
   Output: Approximate solution of $A\mathbf{x} = \mathbf{b}$.

1　Compute $r := \|\mathbf{b} - A\mathbf{x}^{(0)}\|$
2　**while** $r \ge \epsilon$ **do**
3　 **for** $i = 1$ **to** n **do**
4　 $x_i := b_i$
5　 **for** $k = 1$ **to** n **do**
6　 $x_i := x_i - a_{ik}x_k$
7　 $x_i := x_i + \omega \cdot x_i/a_{ii}$
8　 $r := \|\mathbf{b} - A\mathbf{x}\|$

Again, we have to deal with the question of how to choose the relaxation parameter. The next result shows that we do not have much of a choice.

Theorem 4.24　*The spectral radius of the iteration matrix $C_{GS}(\omega)$ of SOR satisfies*

$$\rho(C_{GS}(\omega)) \ge |\omega - 1|.$$

Hence, convergence is only possible if $\omega \in (0, 2)$.

Proof　The iteration matrix $C_{GS}(\omega)$ can be written in the form

$$C_{GS}(\omega) = (I + \omega D^{-1}L)^{-1}[(1 - \omega)I - \omega D^{-1}R].$$

The first matrix in this product is a normalised lower triangular matrix and the second matrix is an upper triangular matrix with diagonal entries all equal to

$1 - \omega$. Since the determinant of a matrix equals the product of its eigenvalues, the result follows from

$$|1 - \omega|^n = |\det C_{GS}(\omega)| \le \rho(C_{GS}(\omega))^n.$$ □

We will now show that for a positive definite matrix, $\omega \in (0, 2)$ is also sufficient for convergence. Since $\omega = 1$ gives the classical Gauss–Seidel method, we also cover Theorem 4.15. The proof of the following theorem also shows that the method is always consistent.

Theorem 4.25 *Let $A \in \mathbb{R}^{n \times n}$ be symmetric and positive definite. Then, the SOR method converges for every relaxation parameter $\omega \in (0, 2)$.*

Proof We have to show that $\rho(C_{GS}(\omega)) < 1$. To this end, we rewrite the iteration matrix $C_{GS}(\omega)$ in the form

$$C_{GS}(\omega) = (D + \omega L)^{-1}[D + \omega L - \omega(L + D + R)]$$
$$= I - \omega(D + \omega L)^{-1}A = I - \left(\frac{1}{\omega}D + L\right)^{-1}A$$
$$= I - B^{-1}A,$$

with $B := \frac{1}{\omega}D + L$. Let $\lambda \in \mathbb{C}$ be an eigenvalue of $C_{GS}(\omega)$ with corresponding eigenvector $\mathbf{x} \in \mathbb{C}^n$, which we assume to be normalised by $\|\mathbf{x}\|_2 = 1$. Then, we have $C_{GS}(\omega)\mathbf{x} = (I - B^{-1}A)\mathbf{x} = \lambda \mathbf{x}$ or $A\mathbf{x} = (1 - \lambda)B\mathbf{x}$. Since A is positive definite, we must have $\lambda \ne 1$. Hence, we can conclude

$$\frac{1}{1 - \lambda} = \frac{\bar{\mathbf{x}}^T B \mathbf{x}}{\bar{\mathbf{x}}^T A \mathbf{x}}.$$

Since A is symmetric, we can also conclude that $B + B^T = (\frac{2}{\omega} - 1)D + A$, such that the real part of $1/(1 - \lambda)$ satisfies

$$\mathfrak{R}\left(\frac{1}{1 - \lambda}\right) = \frac{1}{2} \frac{\bar{\mathbf{x}}^T(B + B^T)\mathbf{x}}{\bar{\mathbf{x}}^T A \mathbf{x}} = \frac{1}{2}\left\{\left(\frac{2}{\omega} - 1\right)\frac{\bar{\mathbf{x}}^T D \mathbf{x}}{\bar{\mathbf{x}}^T A \mathbf{x}} + 1\right\} > \frac{1}{2},$$

because, on account of $\omega \in (0, 2)$, the expression $2/\omega - 1$ is positive, as also is $\bar{\mathbf{x}}^T D \mathbf{x}/\bar{\mathbf{x}}^T A \mathbf{x}$. The latter follows since the diagonal entries of a positive definite matrix have to be positive. If we write $\lambda = u + iv$ then we can conclude that

$$\frac{1}{2} < \mathfrak{R}\left(\frac{1}{1 - \lambda}\right) = \frac{1 - u}{(1 - u)^2 + v^2}$$

and hence $|\lambda|^2 = u^2 + v^2 < 1$. □

To find an optimal parameter ω^* is in general difficult. However, the situation is better if the matrix is *consistently ordered*. We have mentioned the term *consistently ordered* before, namely in the situation following Remark 4.19. There, we have seen that in the specific situation of our boundary value model problem from Section 1.1.2, we have the relation $\rho(C_J)^2 = \rho(C_{GS})$ between the spectral radii of the Jacobi and Gauss–Seidel methods. We pointed out that this always holds when A is consistently ordered. Hence, it is now time to make this more precise.

Definition 4.26   The matrix $A = L + D + R \in \mathbb{R}^{n \times n}$ is called *consistently ordered* if the eigenvalues of the matrix

$$C(\alpha) := -(\alpha D^{-1}L + \alpha^{-1}D^{-1}R) = -D^{-1}(\alpha L + \alpha^{-1}R)$$

are independent of the parameter α.

Note that we require the diagonal elements of A to be non-zero to make this definition meaningful. This condition has already been imposed throughout this entire section. Note also that all the matrices $C(\alpha)$ have the same eigenvalues as the matrix

$$C(1) = -D^{-1}(L + R) = C_J,$$

i.e. as the iteration matrix of the Jacobi method, provided that A is consistently ordered.

Example 4.27   Any tridiagonal matrix

$$A = \begin{pmatrix} a_1 & c_1 & & & 0 \\ b_2 & a_2 & c_2 & & \\ & \ddots & \ddots & \ddots & \\ & & \ddots & \ddots & c_{n-1} \\ 0 & & & b_n & a_n \end{pmatrix} \in \mathbb{R}^{n \times n}$$

with $a_i \neq 0$ for $1 \leq i \leq n$ is consistently ordered. To see this, note that

$$C(1) = -D^{-1}(L + R) = \begin{pmatrix} 0 & r_1 & & & 0 \\ \ell_2 & 0 & r_2 & & \\ & \ddots & \ddots & \ddots & \\ & & \ddots & \ddots & r_{n-1} \\ 0 & & & \ell_n & 0 \end{pmatrix}$$

with $r_i = -c_i/a_i$ and $\ell_i = -b_i/a_i$. Hence, if we define a diagonal matrix $S(\alpha) = \text{diag}(1, \alpha, \alpha^2, \ldots, \alpha^{n-1})$ with $\alpha \neq 0$, we see that $C(\alpha) = S(\alpha)C(1)S^{-1}(\alpha)$, which has the same eigenvalues as $C(1)$.

The following theorem shows that there is an intrinsic relation between the eigenvalues of the iteration matrices of the SOR method and the Jacobi method. It also shows that, for consistently ordered matrices, the Gauss–Seidel method converges faster than the Jacobi method, as long as the Jacobi method converges.

Theorem 4.28 *Let $A \in \mathbb{R}^{n \times n}$ be consistently ordered. Let $C_{GS}(\omega)$, $\omega \in (0, 2)$, denote the iteration matrix of the SOR method and C_J denote the iteration matrix of the Jacobi method. Then, $\mu \in \mathbb{C} \setminus \{0\}$ is an eigenvalue of $C_{GS}(\omega)$ if and only if*

$$\lambda = \frac{\mu + \omega - 1}{\omega \sqrt{\mu}}$$

is an eigenvalue of C_J. In particular, we have

$$\rho(C_{GS}) = \rho(C_j)^2.$$

Proof By (4.21) the iteration matrix of SOR is given by

$$C_{GS}(\omega) = (D + \omega L)^{-1}[(1 - \omega)D - \omega R].$$

For $\mu \in \mathbb{C} \setminus \{0\}$ we thus have

$$
\begin{aligned}
(I + \omega D^{-1}L)(\mu I - C_{GS}(\omega)) &= \mu(I + \omega D^{-1}L) - (I + \omega D^{-1}L)C_{GS}(\omega) \\
&= \mu(I + \omega D^{-1}L) - D^{-1}(D + \omega L)C_{GS}(\omega) \\
&= \mu(I + \omega D^{-1}L) - D^{-1}[(1 - \omega)D - \omega R] \\
&= (\mu - (1 - \omega))I + \omega D^{-1}(\mu L + R) \\
&= (\mu - (1 - \omega))I + \omega \mu^{1/2} D^{-1} \left(\mu^{1/2}L + \mu^{-1/2}R \right).
\end{aligned}
$$

Since the determinant of $I + \omega D^{-1}L$ is one, we can conclude from this that $\mu \neq 0$ is an eigenvalue of $C_{GS}(\omega)$ if and only if

$$\det \left[(\mu - (1 - \omega))I + \omega \mu^{1/2} D^{-1} \left(\mu^{1/2}L + \mu^{-1/2}R \right) \right] = 0,$$

i.e. if

$$\lambda := \frac{\mu - (1 - \omega)}{\omega \mu^{1/2}}$$

is an eigenvalue of $-D^{-1} \left(\mu^{1/2}L + \mu^{-1/2}R \right)$. But since A is consistently ordered the eigenvalues of the latter matrix coincide with the eigenvalues of C_J.

Finally, we have for Gauss–Seidel $C_{GS} = C_{GS}(1)$, i.e. $\omega = 1$ and hence $\mu \neq 0$ is an eigenvalue of C_{GS} if and only if $\sqrt{\mu}$ is an eigenvalue of C_J. Thus we have $\rho(C_{GS}) = \rho(C_J)^2$. □

If the matrix A is *consistently ordered* then it is even possible to show that the optimal parameter is given by

$$\omega^* = \frac{2}{1 + \sqrt{1 - \rho(C_J)^2}},$$

where C_J is the iteration matrix of the Jacobi method, for details see Young [140]. Note that this means that $\omega^* \in (1, 2)$, justifying the name successive *over* relaxation.

Usually, $\rho(C_J)$ is unknown. A possible remedy to this is to use one of the methods to compute the largest eigenvalue, which we will discuss in the next chapter, particularly the so-called *power method* to compute an approximation to $\rho(C_J)$.

Example 4.29   Coming back to our boundary value problem from Section 1.1.2, we know from Remark 4.18 and (4.16) that $\rho(C_J) = \cos\left(\frac{\pi}{n+1}\right) = \cos(\pi h)$ with $h = 1/(n + 1)$. A Taylor expansion then yields

$$\omega^* = \frac{2}{1 + \sqrt{1 - \cos^2(\pi h)}} = \frac{2}{1 + \sin(\pi h)}$$

$$= 2 - 2\pi h + 2(\pi h)^2 - \frac{5}{3}(\pi h)^3 + \frac{4}{3}(\pi h)^4 + O(h^5)$$

$$= 2 - \frac{2\pi}{n + 1} + O\left(\frac{1}{(n + 1)^2}\right).$$

Note that this comes arbitrarily close to 2 with n becoming large. Nonetheless, because of Theorem 4.24 we cannot simply choose $\omega = 2$.

Example 4.30   Let us stick with our second model problem from Section 1.1.2. We already know from (4.10) and (4.11) what the Jacobi and Gauss–Seidel methods look like. It is similarly easy to see that the relaxed versions become

$$u_i^{(j+1)} = (1 - \omega)u_i^{(j)} + \frac{\omega}{2}h^2 f_i + \frac{\omega}{2}\begin{cases} u_2^{(j)} & \text{if } i = 1, \\ u_{i-1}^{(j)} + u_{i+1}^{(j)} & \text{if } 2 \leq i \leq n - 1, \\ u_{n-1}^{(j)} & \text{if } i = n \end{cases}$$

for the relaxation of the Jacobi iteration and

$$u_i^{(j+1)} = (1 - \omega)u_i^{(j)} + \frac{\omega}{2}h^2 f_i + \frac{\omega}{2}\begin{cases} u_2^{(j)} & \text{if } i = 1, \\ u_{i-1}^{(j+1)} + u_{i+1}^{(j)} & \text{if } 2 \leq i \leq n - 1, \\ u_{n-1}^{(j+1)} & \text{if } i = n \end{cases}$$

for the SOR method.

Let us now assume that we want to solve the original problem $-u'' = f$ on $(0, 1)$

with $u(0) = u(1) = 0$ and now the right-hand side $f(x) = \sin(\pi x)$. Then, the true solution is given by $u(x) = \frac{1}{\pi^2}\sin(\pi x)$. Let us run our simulations with $n = 10$. Since we know that in this situation relaxation of the Jacobi method does not improve convergence, we restrict ourselves to the Jacobi, Gauss–Seidel and SOR methods. For the latter, we know that the best relaxation parameter is, with $h = 1/(n + 1)$, given by

$$\omega^* = \frac{2}{1 + \sin(\pi h)} \approx 1.5603879\ldots.$$

In Figure 4.2 we have plotted the residual $\|Ax^{(j)} - \mathbf{b}\|_2$ for these three methods. Clearly, as predicted, the Gauss–Seidel method converges faster than the Jacobi method, but the SOR method is by far the fastest method. Nonetheless, each method needs significantly more than $n = 10$ steps to reach machine precision.

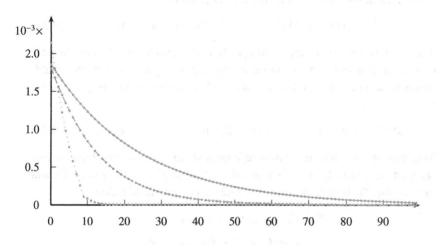

Figure 4.2 The convergence of the Jacobi, Gauss–Seidel (dashed) and SOR (dotted) methods. The number of iterations is on the x-axis, while the residual is on the y-axis.

4.5 Symmetric Methods

We started discussing iterative methods for linear systems by using the iteration

$$\mathbf{x}^{(j+1)} = B^{-1}(B - A)\mathbf{x}^{(j)} + B^{-1}\mathbf{b} = \mathbf{x}^{(j)} + B^{-1}(\mathbf{b} - A\mathbf{x}^{(j)}) \tag{4.22}$$

and our goal was to choose the matrix B as an easy computable approximation to the inverse of A. If the initial matrix A is symmetric and positive definite, it would hence be good to choose B also as symmetric and positive definite.

Definition 4.31   A splitting iteration of the form (4.22) is called *symmetric* if for a symmetric (and positive definite) matrix $A \in \mathbb{R}^{n \times n}$ the matrix B is also symmetric (and positive definite).

This will become even more important later on. Obviously, the matrix $B = D$ of the Jacobi method is symmetric but the matrix $B = L + D$ of the Gauss–Seidel method is not, unless the strict lower part L of A is completely zero. Both statements are also true for the relaxed versions of the Jacobi and Gauss–Seidel method.

It is now our goal to derive a symmetric version of the Gauss–Seidel method. We recall that the Gauss–Seidel iteration is given by

$$\mathbf{x}^{(j+1)} = -(D+L)^{-1} R \mathbf{x}^{(j)} + (D+L)^{-1} \mathbf{b} =: C_{GS} \mathbf{x}^{(j)} + \mathbf{c}_{GS}, \qquad (4.23)$$

if $A = L + D + R$ is the usual decomposition of A into its strictly sub-diagonal part L, its diagonal part D and its strictly upper-diagonal part R. We could, however, also define a *backward Gauss–Seidel* method by iterating according to

$$\mathbf{x}^{(j+1)} = -(D+R)^{-1} L \mathbf{x}^{(j)} + (D+R)^{-1} \mathbf{b} =: C_{BGS} \mathbf{x}^{(j)} + \mathbf{c}_{BGS}. \qquad (4.24)$$

This does also not lead to a symmetric method but we could combine the two steps into one step. Hence, if we first do a "half step" according to (4.23) and then another "half step" according to (4.24), we have the iteration

$$\begin{aligned}
\mathbf{x}^{(j+1)} &= C_{BGS} \left[C_{GS} \mathbf{x}^{(j)} + \mathbf{c}_{GS} \right] + \mathbf{c}_{BGS} \\
&= C_{BGS} C_{GS} \mathbf{x}^{(j)} + (C_{BGS} \mathbf{c}_{GS} + \mathbf{c}_{BGS}) \\
&= C_{SGS} \mathbf{x}^{(j)} + \mathbf{c}_{SGS}
\end{aligned}$$

with the iteration matrix C_{SGS} and vector $\mathbf{c}_{SGS}$ given by

$$\begin{aligned}
C_{SGS} &:= C_{BGS} C_{GS} = (D+R)^{-1} L (D+L)^{-1} R, \\
\mathbf{c}_{SGS} &:= C_{BGS} \mathbf{c}_{GS} + \mathbf{c}_{BGS} \\
&= -(D+R)^{-1} L (D+L)^{-1} \mathbf{b} + (D+R)^{-1} \mathbf{b} \\
&= (D+R)^{-1} \left[I - L(D+L)^{-1} \right] \mathbf{b} \\
&= (D+R)^{-1} D (D+L)^{-1} \mathbf{b}.
\end{aligned}$$

To see that this is indeed a symmetric method, we have to rewrite this iteration in the form of (4.22), i.e. we need to find the associated matrix $B = B_{SGS}$.

Before that, we will introduce the relaxation of this method. It is simply defined to be the just-introduced combination of the relaxed Gauss–Seidel and backward Gauss–Seidel methods. The latter is relaxed in exactly the same way as the Gauss–Seidel method is. Hence, the relevant matrices and vectors are given as

$$C_{GS}(\omega) = (D + \omega L)^{-1}[(1 - \omega)D - \omega R] = \left(\frac{1}{\omega}D + L\right)^{-1}\left[\left(\frac{1}{\omega} - 1\right)D - R\right],$$

$$C_{BGS}(\omega) = (D + \omega R)^{-1}[(1 - \omega)D - \omega L] = \left(\frac{1}{\omega}D + R\right)^{-1}\left[\left(\frac{1}{\omega} - 1\right)D - L\right],$$

$$\mathbf{c}_{GS}(\omega) = (D + \omega L)^{-1}\omega \mathbf{b} = \left(\frac{1}{\omega}D + L\right)^{-1}\mathbf{b},$$

$$\mathbf{c}_{BGS}(\omega) = (D + \omega R)^{-1}\omega \mathbf{b} = \left(\frac{1}{\omega}D + R\right)^{-1}\mathbf{b}.$$

Definition 4.32 The *symmetric Gauss–Seidel relaxation* for solving the linear system $A\mathbf{x} = \mathbf{b}$ is given by

$$\mathbf{x}^{(j+1)} = C_{SGS}(\omega)\mathbf{x}^{(j)} + \mathbf{c}_{SGS}(\omega),$$

where

$$C_{SGS}(\omega) := C_{BGS}(\omega)C_{GS}(\omega),$$
$$\mathbf{c}_{SGS}(\omega) := C_{BGS}(\omega)\mathbf{c}_{GS}(\omega) + \mathbf{c}_{BGS}(\omega).$$

In the case of a symmetric matrix A, the method is also called the *symmetric successive over-relaxation (SSOR) method*.

Obviously, the symmetric Gauss–Seidel method makes mainly sense for symmetric matrices. In this case, the notation further simplifies since we have $R = L^T$. Nonetheless, for the time being we will stick to the general notation. The first step in understanding this method is to show that it is indeed an iterative method of the form (4.22), i.e. we have to find the defining matrix $B = B_{SGS}(\omega)$ and to show that $C_{SGS}(\omega) = I - B_{SGS}^{-1}(\omega)A$. To find B_{SGS} we have to investigate the iteration vector $\mathbf{c}_{SGS}(\omega)$ which has to be given by $\mathbf{c}_{SGS}(\omega) = B_{SGS}^{-1}(\omega)\mathbf{b}$. With

$$B_{GS}(\omega) = \frac{1}{\omega}D + L \qquad \text{and} \qquad B_{BGS}(\omega) = \frac{1}{\omega}D + R$$

we obviously have

$$C_{GS}(\omega) = I - B_{GS}^{-1}(\omega)A \qquad \text{and} \qquad C_{BGS}(\omega) = I - B_{BGS}^{-1}(\omega)A,$$

which is easily verified and shows again that both methods are of the form (4.22). Furthermore, we have from the definition of $\mathbf{c}_{SGS}(\omega)$ that

$$\mathbf{c}_{SGS}(\omega) = C_{BGS}(\omega)\mathbf{c}_{GS}(\omega) + \mathbf{c}_{BGS}(\omega) = \left[C_{BGS}(\omega)B_{GS}^{-1}(\omega) + B_{BGS}^{-1}(\omega)\right]\mathbf{b}$$

which implies

$$B_{SGS}^{-1}(\omega) = C_{BGS}(\omega)B_{GS}^{-1}(\omega) + B_{BGS}^{-1}(\omega),$$

as long as the matrix on the right-hand side is invertible. In this situation, we can conclude that the symmetric Gauss–Seidel method is indeed a splitting scheme of the form (4.22) since

$$
\begin{aligned}
I - B_{SGS}^{-1}(\omega)A &= I - \left(C_{BGS}(\omega)B_{GS}^{-1}(\omega) + B_{BGS}^{-1}(\omega)\right)A \\
&= I - B_{BGS}^{-1}(\omega)A - C_{BGS}(\omega)B_{GS}^{-1}(\omega)A \\
&= C_{BGS}(\omega) - C_{BGS}(\omega)(I - C_{GS}(\omega)) \\
&= C_{BGS}(\omega)C_{GS}(\omega) = C_{SGS}(\omega).
\end{aligned}
$$

Finally, we have to verify that all the previous operations are justified. To this end, we note that we have for $\omega \neq 2$ that

$$
\begin{aligned}
\mathbf{c}_{SGS}(\omega) &= C_{BGS}(\omega)\mathbf{c}_{GS}(\omega) + \mathbf{c}_{BGS}(\omega) \\
&= B_{BGS}^{-1}(\omega)\left[\left(\frac{1}{\omega} - 1\right)D - L\right]B_{GS}^{-1}(\omega)\mathbf{b} + B_{BGS}^{-1}(\omega)\mathbf{b} \\
&= \left(\frac{1}{\omega}D + R\right)^{-1}\left[\left(\left(\frac{1}{\omega} - 1\right)D - L\right)\left(\frac{1}{\omega}D + L\right)^{-1} + I\right]\mathbf{b} \\
&= \left(\frac{1}{\omega}D + R\right)^{-1}\left[\left(\frac{1}{\omega}D - D - L\right)\left(\frac{1}{\omega}D + L\right)^{-1} + \left(\frac{1}{\omega}D + L\right)\left(\frac{1}{\omega}D + L\right)^{-1}\right]\mathbf{b} \\
&= \left(\frac{1}{\omega}D + R\right)^{-1}\left[\frac{1}{\omega}D - D - L + \frac{1}{\omega}D + L\right]\left(\frac{1}{\omega}D + L\right)^{-1}\mathbf{b} \\
&= \left(\frac{2}{\omega} - 1\right)\left(\frac{1}{\omega}D + R\right)^{-1}D\left(\frac{1}{\omega}D + L\right)^{-1}\mathbf{b},
\end{aligned}
$$

from which we can conclude that

$$
\begin{aligned}
B_{SGS}(\omega) &= \frac{\omega}{2 - \omega}\left(\frac{1}{\omega}D + L\right)D^{-1}\left(\frac{1}{\omega}D + R\right) \\
&= \frac{\omega}{2 - \omega}B_{GS}(\omega)D^{-1}B_{BGS}(\omega). \quad\quad\quad (4.25)
\end{aligned}
$$

This has several further consequences, which we will collect now.

Proposition 4.33 *Let $A \in \mathbb{R}^{n \times n}$ be symmetric with positive diagonal entries.*

For each $\omega \in (0, 2)$, *the SSOR method is well-defined and a symmetric splitting method.*

Proof As we have already seen, the matrix $B_{SGS}(\omega)$ is well-defined for $\omega \in (0, 2)$. Furthermore, since A is symmetric, we have $B_{GS}(\omega) = B_{BGS}^{\mathrm{T}}(\omega)$. Hence, (4.25) implies that $B_{SGS}(\omega)$ is symmetric. Since D is a diagonal matrix with positive entries, (4.25) also implies that $B_{SGS}(\omega)$ is positive definite. $\square$

We finally want to prove convergence of the SSOR method. To this end, it is helpful to recall the following context. If the matrix A is positive definite and symmetric it possesses a square root $A^{1/2}$ which is also positive definite and symmetric and satisfies $A = A^{1/2}A^{1/2}$. According to Example 2.29, the induced matrix norm of the vector norm $\mathbf{x} \mapsto \|A^{1/2}\mathbf{x}\|_2$ is given by $\|C\|_{A^{1/2}} = \|A^{1/2}CA^{-1/2}\|_2$.

Theorem 4.34 *Let $A \in \mathbb{R}^{n \times n}$ be symmetric and positive definite. Then, the symmetric Gauss–Seidel relaxation converges for each $\omega \in (0, 2)$ and*

$$\rho(C_{SGS}(\omega)) = \|C_{SGS}(\omega)\|_{A^{1/2}} = \|C_{GS}(\omega)\|_{A^{1/2}}^2 < 1.$$

Proof The matrix $C_{SGS}(\omega) = C_{BGS}(\omega)C_{GS}(\omega)$ has the same eigenvalues as the matrix

$$A^{1/2}C_{SGS}(\omega)A^{-1/2} = \left[A^{1/2}C_{BGS}(\omega)A^{-1/2}\right]\left[A^{1/2}C_{GS}(\omega)A^{-1/2}\right].$$

Since we have $B_{BGS}^{\mathrm{T}}(\omega) = B_{GS}(\omega)$ we can conclude that

$$A^{1/2}C_{BGS}(\omega)A^{-1/2} = A^{1/2}\left[I - B_{BGS}^{-1}(\omega)A\right]A^{-1/2} = I - A^{1/2}B_{BGS}^{-1}(\omega)A^{1/2}$$
$$= \left[I - A^{1/2}B_{GS}^{-1}(\omega)A^{1/2}\right]^{\mathrm{T}} = \left[A^{1/2}C_{GS}(\omega)A^{-1/2}\right]^{\mathrm{T}},$$

which shows

$$A^{1/2}C_{SGS}(\omega)A^{-1/2} = \left[A^{1/2}C_{GS}(\omega)A^{-1/2}\right]^{\mathrm{T}}\left[A^{1/2}C_{GS}(\omega)A^{-1/2}\right].$$

From this, we can conclude that $A^{1/2}C_{SGS}(\omega)A^{-1/2}$ is symmetric and positive definite and has therefore only non-negative eigenvalues. Furthermore, with Example 2.29 and Corollary 2.21 we find

$$\rho(C_{SGS}(\omega)) = \rho(A^{1/2}C_{SGS}(\omega)A^{-1/2})$$
$$= \|A^{1/2}C_{SGS}(\omega)A^{-1/2}\|_2 = \|C_{SGS}(\omega)\|_{A^{1/2}}$$
$$= \left\|\left[A^{1/2}C_{GS}(\omega)A^{-1/2}\right]^{\mathrm{T}}\left[A^{1/2}C_{GS}(\omega)A^{-1/2}\right]\right\|_2$$
$$= \|A^{1/2}C_{GS}(\omega)A^{-1/2}\|_2^2 = \|C_{GS}(\omega)\|_{A^{1/2}}^2.$$

It remains to show that the spectral radius is less than one, i.e., we have to show that $\|A^{1/2}C_{GS}(\omega)A^{-1/2}\|_2 < 1$. Since the $\|\cdot\|_2$-norm of the matrix $C(\omega) := A^{1/2}C_{GS}(\omega)A^{-1}$ is given by the square root of the maximum eigenvalue of $C(\omega)^{\mathrm{T}}C(\omega)$, we have to compute the latter. To this end, we use again that $B_{GS}^{\mathrm{T}}(\omega) = B_{BGS}(\omega)$,

$$B_{GS}(\omega) + B_{BGS}(\omega) = A + \left(\frac{2}{\omega} - 1\right)D$$

and

$$C(\omega) = A^{1/2}C_{GS}(\omega)A^{-1/2} = A^{1/2}\left[I - B_{GS}^{-1}(\omega)A\right]A^{-1/2} = I - A^{1/2}B_{GS}^{-1}(\omega)A^{1/2}$$

to derive

$$\begin{aligned}
C(\omega)^{\mathrm{T}}C(\omega) &= \left[I - A^{1/2}B_{GS}^{-1}(\omega)A^{1/2}\right]^{\mathrm{T}}\left[I - A^{1/2}B_{GS}^{-1}(\omega)A^{1/2}\right] \\
&= \left[I - A^{1/2}B_{BGS}^{-1}(\omega)A^{1/2}\right]\left[I - A^{1/2}B_{GS}^{-1}(\omega)A^{1/2}\right] \\
&= I - A^{1/2}\left[B_{BGS}^{-1}(\omega) + B_{GS}^{-1}(\omega)\right]A^{1/2} + A^{1/2}B_{BGS}^{-1}(\omega)AB_{GS}^{-1}(\omega)A^{1/2} \\
&= I - A^{1/2}B_{BGS}^{-1}(\omega)\left[A + \left(\frac{2}{\omega} - 1\right)D\right]B_{GS}^{-1}(\omega)A^{1/2} \\
&\quad + A^{1/2}B_{BGS}^{-1}(\omega)AB_{GS}^{-1}(\omega)A^{1/2} \\
&= I - A^{1/2}B_{BGS}^{-1}(\omega)DB_{GS}^{-1}(\omega)A^{1/2}\left(\frac{2}{\omega} - 1\right) \\
&=: I - \left(\frac{2}{\omega} - 1\right)B(\omega).
\end{aligned}$$

The newly introduced matrix $B(\omega)$ is, because of

$$B(\omega) := A^{1/2}B_{BGS}^{-1}(\omega)DB_{GS}^{-1}(\omega)A^{1/2} = \left[D^{1/2}B_{GS}^{-1}(\omega)A^{1/2}\right]^{\mathrm{T}}\left[D^{1/2}B_{GS}^{-1}(\omega)A^{1/2}\right],$$

symmetric and positive definite. If $\lambda \in \mathbb{R}$ is an eigenvalue of $C(\omega)^{\mathrm{T}}C(\omega)$ with corresponding eigenvector $\mathbf{x} \in \mathbb{R}^n$ satisfying $\|\mathbf{x}\|_2 = 1$ then $\omega \in (0, 2)$ implies

$$0 \le \lambda = \mathbf{x}^{\mathrm{T}}C(\omega)^{\mathrm{T}}C(\omega)\mathbf{x} = 1 - \left(\frac{2}{\omega} - 1\right)\mathbf{x}^{\mathrm{T}}B(\omega)\mathbf{x} < 1. \qquad \square$$

Exercises

4.1   Let $F : \mathbb{R}^n \to \mathbb{R}^n$ be a contraction mapping with contraction number $q \in (0, 1)$ and fixed point $\mathbf{x}^* \in \mathbb{R}^n$. Let $G : \mathbb{R}^n \to \mathbb{R}^n$ be a mapping satisfying $\|F(\mathbf{x}) - G(\mathbf{x})\| \le \epsilon$ for all $\mathbf{x} \in \mathbb{R}^n$. Show that the iteration $\mathbf{y}_{j+1} := G(\mathbf{y}_j)$ satisfies the error bound

$$\|\mathbf{x}^* - \mathbf{y}_j\| \le \frac{1}{1 - q}\left(\epsilon + q^j\|\mathbf{y}_0 - \mathbf{y}_1\|\right).$$

4.2 Show that the following modification of Banach's fixed point theorem is true. Let $D \subseteq \mathbb{R}^n$ be a compact set. Let $F : D \to D$ be a contraction mapping. Then, F has exactly one fixed point $\mathbf{x}^* \in D$ and the sequence $\mathbf{x}_{j+1} := F(\mathbf{x}_j)$ converges to $\mathbf{x}^*$ for each starting point $\mathbf{x}_0 \in D$.

Use Banach's fixed point theorem to show that the following functions have a fixed point $f(x) = \sqrt{2 + x}$, $x \geq 0$, $f(x) = e^{-x}$, $x \in \mathbb{R}$, $f(x_1, x_2) :=$ $\left(\frac{1}{5}(x_1^2 + x_2^2), \frac{1}{2}e^{-x_1}\right)^{\mathrm{T}}$, $\mathbf{x} = (x_1, x_2) \in \mathbb{R}^2$. Compute the fixed point for the first function and show that the sequence $x_{j+1} = f(x_j)$ converges for every $x_0 \in \mathbb{R}$ in the case of the second function.

4.3 Show that a matrix $A \in \mathbb{R}^{n \times n}$ is reducible if and only if there are a permutation matrix $P \in \mathbb{R}^{n \times n}$, an index $k \in \{1, \ldots, n-1\}$ and matrices $B \in \mathbb{R}^{k \times k}$, $C \in \mathbb{R}^{(n-k) \times k}$ and $D \in \mathbb{R}^{(n-k) \times (n-k)}$ such that

$$P^{\mathrm{T}} A P = \begin{pmatrix} B & O \\ C & D \end{pmatrix}.$$

4.4 Show that a matrix $A \in \mathbb{R}^{n \times n}$ is irreducible if and only if we can find for each pair of indices $i, j \in \{1, \ldots, n\}$ a *chain* $j_0, \ldots, j_k \in \{1, \ldots, n\}$ with $j_0 = i$, $j_k = j$ and $a_{j_\ell, j_{\ell+1}} \neq 0$ for $0 \leq \ell \leq k - 1$.

4.5 Let $A \in \mathbb{R}^{n \times n}$ satisfy $a_{ii} > 0$ and $a_{ij} \leq 0$ for $i \neq j$. Let $C_J = -D^{-1}(L + R)$ be the iteration matrix of the Jacobi method for $A = L + D + R$. Show that $\rho(C_J) < 1$ if and only if A has an inverse with non-negative entries (such a matrix is called an M-matrix).

4.6 Let $A \in \mathbb{R}^{n \times n}$ be symmetric, irreducible and weakly diagonally dominant. Assume that all diagonal elements of A are positive. Show that A is positive definite.

4.7 Let $A \in \mathbb{R}^{n \times n}$ with $n \geq 2$ have diagonal elements $a_{ii} = 1$ and off-diagonal elements $a_{ij} = a$, $i \neq j$.

- Determine the iteration matrix C_{GS} of the Gauss–Seidel method for A. Calculate the eigenvalues of C_{GS} and A.
- Determine those $a \in \mathbb{R}$, for which the Gauss–Seidel method converges. For which $a \in \mathbb{R}$ is A positive definite?

4.8 A simple *residual correction* method to solve $A\mathbf{x} = \mathbf{b}$ is the so-called *Richardson iteration*, given by $\mathbf{x}_{j+1} = (I - A)\mathbf{x}_j + \mathbf{b} = \mathbf{x}_j + (\mathbf{b} - A\mathbf{x}_j)$. Its relaxation is given by $\mathbf{x}_{j+1} = \mathbf{x}_j + \omega(\mathbf{b} - A\mathbf{x}_j)$. Determine the iteration matrix $C(\omega)$ of this method. Assume that A has only real eigenvalues. Determine $\rho(C(\omega))$ and the optimal relaxation parameter.

5

Calculation of Eigenvalues

Particularly when analysing vibrations in mechanical or electrical systems, we are mathematically confronted with eigenvalue problems. Initially, these are eigenvalue problems for certain differential operators but via discretisation they can be recast as eigenvalue problems for linear systems. We have also seen that eigenvalues play an important role when studying the conditioning of linear systems. Hence, in this chapter we are interested in finding solutions to the problem

$$Ax = \lambda x,$$

where $A \in \mathbb{R}^{n \times n}$ is given and the eigenvalue $\lambda \in \mathbb{C}$ and the eigenvector $x \in \mathbb{C}^n \setminus \{0\}$ are what we are looking for.

Recall from linear algebra that the eigenvalues of A are the zeros of the *characteristic polynomial*

$$p(\lambda) := \det(A - \lambda I).$$

In the applications mentioned above, the root of an eigenvalue represents a frequency of the vibration of the mechanical system. The corresponding eigenvector gives the corresponding shape mode or mode of vibration.

There are different eigenvalue problems depending on the nature of the underlying problem. For each of them, there are different solution techniques. Typical problems are as follows.

1. Computation of the largest (or smallest) eigenvalue without the corresponding eigenvector.
2. Computation of all eigenvalues without the corresponding eigenvectors.
3. Computation of one eigenvalue together with a corresponding eigenvector.
4. Computation of several (or all) eigenvalues and the corresponding eigenvectors.

132

The numerical methods also depend on the special form of the matrix. Particularly, whether the matrix A is symmetric (or Hermitian) or not. In this book, we will mainly concentrate on symmetric matrices since methods for computing the eigenvalues and eigenvectors are much easier in this case. Moreover, eigenvalues and eigenvectors are real in this situation.

As in the case of solving linear systems, one can distinguish between direct and iterative methods. In direct methods, first the characteristic polynomial and then its zeros are determined. However, more popular are iterative methods, which try to compute successive approximations to the eigenvectors and eigenvalues without computing the characteristic polynomial.

Before discussing methods for computing eigenvalues and eigenvectors, we will address basic localisation techniques. They sometimes already give good approximations of the eigenvalues.

5.1 Basic Localisation Techniques

The first way of estimating the location of all eigenvalues works for an arbitrary matrix.

Theorem 5.1 (Gershgorin) *The eigenvalues of a matrix $A \in \mathbb{R}^{n \times n}$ are contained in the union of the discs*

$$D_j = \left\{ \lambda \in \mathbb{C} : |\lambda - a_{jj}| \leq \sum_{\substack{k=1 \\ k \neq j}}^{n} |a_{jk}| \right\}, \qquad 1 \leq j \leq n.$$

Proof For every eigenvalue $\lambda \in \mathbb{C}$ of A we can choose an eigenvector $\mathbf{x} \in \mathbb{C}^n \setminus \{\mathbf{0}\}$ with $\|\mathbf{x}\|_\infty = \max_{1 \leq j \leq n} |x_j| = 1$. From $A\mathbf{x} - \lambda\mathbf{x} = \mathbf{0}$ we can conclude that

$$(a_{jj} - \lambda)x_j + \sum_{\substack{k=1 \\ k \neq j}}^{n} a_{jk}x_k = 0, \qquad 1 \leq j \leq n.$$

If we pick an index j with $|x_j| = 1$ then the statement follows via

$$|a_{jj} - \lambda| = |(a_{jj} - \lambda)x_j| = \left| \sum_{\substack{k=1 \\ k \neq j}}^{n} a_{jk}x_k \right| \leq \sum_{\substack{k=1 \\ k \neq j}}^{n} |a_{jk}| \, |x_k| \leq \sum_{\substack{k=1 \\ k \neq j}}^{n} |a_{jk}|. \qquad \square$$

Corollary 5.2 *Let $A \in \mathbb{R}^{n \times n}$ be symmetric and strictly row diagonally dominant with positive diagonal elements. Then, A is positive definite.*

Proof Since A is symmetric, all eigenvalues λ of A are real. Since A is strictly row diagonally dominant with positive diagonal elements, we have

$$r_j := \sum_{\substack{k=1 \\ k \neq j}}^{n} |a_{jk}| < a_{jj}, \qquad 1 \leq j \leq n.$$

According to Gershgorin's theorem we have for every eigenvalue $\lambda \in \mathbb{R}$ of A an index j with $|\lambda - a_{jj}| \leq r_j$ and hence

$$0 < a_{jj} - r_j \leq \lambda. \qquad \qquad \square$$

It is possible to derive an improved version of Gershgorin's theorem.

Theorem 5.3 (Gershgorin) *If all the discs D_j are disjoint, then each of them contains exactly one eigenvalue of A. If p discs D_j form a connected set P which is disjoint to all other discs, then P contains exactly p eigenvalues of A.*

Proof The first statement follows immediately from the second one. Hence, we will concentrate on the second statement. Let r_j denote the radius of D_j, i.e. $r_j = \sum_{k \neq j} |a_{jk}|$. Let P' denote the union of the remaining discs D_j which are disjoint to P. Then, both P and P' are closed, disjoint subsets of $\mathbb{C}$ and hence there is an $\epsilon_0 > 0$ such that for all $x \in P$ and all $y \in P'$ we have $|x - y| > \epsilon_0$. Next we define for $t \in [0, 1]$ the matrix $A(t) = (a_{ij}(t))$ by setting $a_{ii}(t) = a_{ii}$ and $a_{ij}(t) = t a_{ij}$ if $i \neq j$. Obviously, we have $A(1) = A$ and $A(0) = \mathrm{diag}(a_{11}, \ldots, a_{nn})$. Furthermore, the Gershgorin discs $D_j(t)$ associated with this matrix $A(t)$ are also centred at a_{jj} but have radius $t r_j$, which means $D_j(t) \subseteq D_j$ for all $t \in [0, 1]$ and hence $P(t) \subseteq P$ and $P'(t) \subseteq P'$. Here, $P(t)$ denotes the union of the p discs $D_j(t)$ corresponding to those in P. Note that Theorem 5.1 states that all eigenvalues of $A(t)$ must be contained in the union of $P(t)$ and $P'(t)$.

Let us now define

$$t_0 := \sup\{t \in [0, 1] : P(t) \text{ contains exactly } p \text{ eigenvalues of } A(t)\}. \qquad (5.1)$$

For every t in that set, we also have that $P'(t)$ contains exactly $n - p$ eigenvalues. Our proof is finished once we have shown that $t_0 = 1$. We immediately see that 0 belongs to the set since $A(0)$ is a diagonal matrix and $P(0)$ contains exactly p elements, the eigenvalues of $A(0)$. Hence, the set in (5.1) is not empty. Next, notice that $A(t)$ depends continuously on t. Since the eigenvalues of $A(t)$ are the zeros of the corresponding characteristic polynomial, they also depend continuously on t. Hence, to every $\epsilon > 0$ there is a $\delta > 0$ such that $|\lambda_j(t) - \lambda_j(t_0)| < \epsilon$ for all $t \in [0, 1]$ with $|t - t_0| < \delta$ and $1 \leq j \leq n$, provided we sort the eigenvalues consistently. We will use this for the above given $\epsilon = \epsilon_0$.

The definition of t_0 allows us to pick a $t \in [0, 1]$ with $t_0 - \delta < t < t_0$ such that $P(t)$ contains exactly p eigenvalues of $A(t)$ and $P'(t)$ contains the remaining $n - p$ eigenvalues. The definition of ϵ_0 and the choice of δ now guarantee that also $P(t_0)$ contains exactly p eigenvalues of $A(t_0)$ and $P'(t_0)$ contains the remaining $n - p$ eigenvalues. Hence, the supremum in (5.1) is actually a maximum, i.e. t_0 belongs to the set in (5.1).

Let us now assume $t_0 < 1$. Then, we can again choose $\epsilon = \epsilon_0$ and a corresponding $\delta > 0$ as above. This means, however, that for every $t \in [0, 1]$ with $t_0 < t < t_0 + \delta$ we have $|\lambda_j(t) - \lambda_j(t_0)| < \epsilon_0$ for every $1 \leq j \leq n$. The choice of ϵ_0 guarantees once again that we now also have exactly p eigenvalues of $A(t)$ in $P(t)$, which contradicts the definition of t_0. Hence, $t_0 = 1$ and $P = P(1)$ contains exactly p eigenvalues of $A = A(1)$. $\qquad\square$

In this section, we want to address two additional questions. How does a small change in the elements of the matrix A change the eigenvalues of A? What can we say about the location of an eigenvalue if we have an approximate eigenvalue?

To answer these questions we need sharper estimates on the eigenvalues, which we will discuss now. To derive them, we will restrict ourselves mainly to symmetric matrices. Most of the results also carry immediately over to Hermitian matrices and normal matrices, i.e. matrices which satisfy $A\overline{A}^T = \overline{A}^T A$. In all other cases the situation is more complicated and, though the eigenvalues still depend continuously on the matrix entries, it is very likely that a small perturbation of the matrix may lead to significant changes in its eigenvalues.

Theorem 5.4 (Rayleigh) *Let $A \in \mathbb{R}^{n \times n}$ be symmetric with eigenvalues $\lambda_1 \geq \lambda_2 \geq \cdots \geq \lambda_n$ and corresponding orthonormal eigenvectors $\mathbf{w}_1, \ldots, \mathbf{w}_n \in \mathbb{R}^n$. For $1 \leq j \leq n$ let $W_j := \mathrm{span}\{\mathbf{w}_1, \ldots, \mathbf{w}_j\}$ and $W_j^\perp := \mathrm{span}\{\mathbf{w}_{j+1}, \ldots, \mathbf{w}_n\}$. Let also $W_0^\perp := \mathbb{R}^n$. Then,*

$$\lambda_j = \max_{\substack{\mathbf{x} \in W_{j-1}^\perp \\ \mathbf{x} \neq 0}} \frac{\mathbf{x}^T A \mathbf{x}}{\mathbf{x}^T \mathbf{x}}, \tag{5.2}$$

$$\lambda_j = \min_{\substack{\mathbf{x} \in W_j \\ \mathbf{x} \neq 0}} \frac{\mathbf{x}^T A \mathbf{x}}{\mathbf{x}^T \mathbf{x}} \tag{5.3}$$

for $1 \leq j \leq n$.

Proof Every $\mathbf{x} \in \mathbb{R}^n$ has a representation of the form $\mathbf{x} = \sum_{k=1}^n c_k \mathbf{w}_k$ with $c_k = \mathbf{x}^T \mathbf{w}_k$. This means particularly $\mathbf{x}^T \mathbf{x} = \sum_{k=1}^n |c_k|^2$, $A\mathbf{x} = \sum_{k=1}^n c_k \lambda_k \mathbf{w}_k$ and $\mathbf{x}^T A \mathbf{x} = \sum_{k=1}^n |c_k|^2 \lambda_k$.

If $\mathbf{x} \in W_{j-1}^\perp = \mathrm{span}\{\mathbf{w}_j, \ldots, \mathbf{w}_n\}$ then we have particularly $c_1 = \cdots = c_{j-1} = 0$

such that, provided $\mathbf{x} \neq \mathbf{0}$,

$$\frac{\mathbf{x}^T A \mathbf{x}}{\mathbf{x}^T \mathbf{x}} = \frac{\sum_{k=j}^n |c_k|^2 \lambda_k}{\mathbf{x}^T \mathbf{x}} \leq \frac{\lambda_j \mathbf{x}^T \mathbf{x}}{\mathbf{x}^T \mathbf{x}} = \lambda_j. \tag{5.4}$$

Hence, the maximum of the quotient over all $\mathbf{x} \in W_{j-1}^\perp$ is less than or equal to λ_j. However, the maximum is attained for $\mathbf{x} = \mathbf{w}_j \in W_{j-1}^\perp$, which shows (5.2). If, however, $\mathbf{x} \in W_j = \text{span}\{\mathbf{w}_1, \ldots, \mathbf{w}_j\}$ then we have this time $c_{j+1} = \cdots = c_n = 0$ and hence, again under the assumption that $\mathbf{x} \neq \mathbf{0}$,

$$\frac{\mathbf{x}^T A \mathbf{x}}{\mathbf{x}^T \mathbf{x}} = \frac{\sum_{k=1}^j |c_k|^2 \lambda_k}{\mathbf{x}^T \mathbf{x}} \geq \frac{\lambda_j \mathbf{x}^T \mathbf{x}}{\mathbf{x}^T \mathbf{x}} = \lambda_j. \tag{5.5}$$

This shows that the minimum of the quotient over all $\mathbf{x} \in W_j$ is greater than or equal to λ_j and since the minimum is attained for $\mathbf{x} = \mathbf{w}_j$, we have the equality (5.3).   □

An immediate consequence of this result is the following minimum maximum principle.

Theorem 5.5 (Courant–Fischer)   *Let $A \in \mathbb{R}^{n \times n}$ be symmetric with eigenvalues $\lambda_1 \geq \lambda_2 \geq \ldots \geq \lambda_n$. For $1 \leq j \leq n$ let M_j denote the set of all linear subspaces of $\mathbb{R}^n$ of dimension j. Then,*

$$\lambda_j = \min_{U \in M_{n+1-j}} \max_{\substack{\mathbf{x} \in U \\ \mathbf{x} \neq 0}} \frac{\mathbf{x}^T A \mathbf{x}}{\mathbf{x}^T \mathbf{x}}, \tag{5.6}$$

$$\lambda_j = \max_{U \in M_j} \min_{\substack{\mathbf{x} \in U \\ \mathbf{x} \neq 0}} \frac{\mathbf{x}^T A \mathbf{x}}{\mathbf{x}^T \mathbf{x}} \tag{5.7}$$

for $1 \leq j \leq n$.

Proof   We will only prove (5.6) since the second equality is proven in a very similar fashion.

Let $\mathbf{w}_j$, W_j and $W_j^\perp$ be defined as in Theorem 5.4. Let us denote the right-hand side of (5.6) with ρ_j. Since $W_{j-1}^\perp = \text{span}\{\mathbf{w}_j, \ldots, \mathbf{w}_n\} \in M_{n-j+1}$ we immediately have $\rho_j \leq \lambda_j$. Moreover, the space $W_j = \text{span}\{\mathbf{w}_1, \ldots, \mathbf{w}_j\}$ obviously has dimension j and an arbitrary $U \in M_{n+1-j}$ has dimension $n + 1 - j$. Thus, the dimension formula yields

$$\dim\left(W_j \cap U\right) = \dim(W_j) + \dim(U) - \dim\left(W_j + U\right) \geq 1.$$

Hence, for each $U \in M_{n+1-j}$ there is an $\mathbf{x} \in W_j \cap U$, $\mathbf{x} \neq \mathbf{0}$. This means that this $\mathbf{x}$ has the representation $\mathbf{x} = \sum_{k=1}^j c_k \mathbf{w}_k$, and we can derive, as before,

$$\frac{\mathbf{x}^T A \mathbf{x}}{\mathbf{x}^T \mathbf{x}} = \frac{\sum_{k=1}^j |c_k|^2 \lambda_k}{\mathbf{x}^T \mathbf{x}} \geq \lambda_j$$

and therefore also $\rho_j \geq \lambda_j$. $\qquad\qquad\qquad\qquad\qquad\qquad\qquad\qquad\qquad\square$

A first consequence of this min–max principle is Sylvester's theorem of inertia. The *inertia* of a symmetric matrix $A \in \mathbb{R}^{n \times n}$ is a triple (n_+, n_0, n_-) with $n_+ + n_- + n_0 = n$, where n_+, n_-, n_0 denote the numbers of positive, negative and zero eigenvalues of A. The result will be of importance for us later on, when discussing preconditioning.

Theorem 5.6 (Sylvester) *Let $A \in \mathbb{R}^{n \times n}$ be symmetric and $S \in \mathbb{R}^{n \times n}$ be non-singular. Then, A and $B := S^T A S$ have the same inertia, i.e. the same numbers of positive, negative and zero eigenvalues.*

Proof We start by noting that the matrix $S^T S$ is positive definite and denote its largest and its smallest eigenvalues by $\lambda_{\max}(S^T S)$ and $\lambda_{\min}(S^T S)$, respectively. Both are positive; they are the squares of the largest and smallest singular values of S and satisfy

$$\lambda_{\min}(S^T S) = \min_{\mathbf{x} \neq 0} \frac{\mathbf{x}^T S^T S \mathbf{x}}{\mathbf{x}^T \mathbf{x}} = \min_{\mathbf{y} \neq 0} \frac{\mathbf{y}^T \mathbf{y}}{\mathbf{y}^T S^{-T} S^{-1} \mathbf{y}},$$

$$\lambda_{\max}(S^T S) = \max_{\mathbf{x} \neq 0} \frac{\mathbf{x}^T S^T S \mathbf{x}}{\mathbf{x}^T \mathbf{x}} = \max_{\mathbf{y} \neq 0} \frac{\mathbf{y}^T \mathbf{y}}{\mathbf{y}^T S^{-T} S^{-1} \mathbf{y}}$$

due to Theorem 5.4.

Next, let us denote the eigenvalues of A and B by $\lambda_1(A) \geq \lambda_2(A) \geq \cdots \geq \lambda_n(A)$ and $\lambda_1(B) \geq \lambda_2(B) \geq \cdots \geq \lambda_n(B)$.

By (5.7), we have

$$\lambda_j(B) = \max_{U \in \mathcal{M}_j} \min_{\substack{\mathbf{x} \in U \\ \mathbf{x} \neq 0}} \frac{\mathbf{x}^T S^T A S \mathbf{x}}{\mathbf{x}^T \mathbf{x}} = \max_{U \in \mathcal{M}_j} \min_{\substack{\mathbf{y} \in S(U) \\ \mathbf{y} \neq 0}} \frac{\mathbf{y}^T A \mathbf{y}}{\mathbf{y}^T S^{-T} S^{-1} \mathbf{y}}$$

using the substitution $\mathbf{y} = S\mathbf{x}$ again and noting that $S(U)$ is also in $\mathcal{M}_j$. Thus, if $\mathbf{w}_1, \ldots, \mathbf{w}_n$ denote once again an orthonormal basis consisting of the eigenvectors to the eigenvalues of A and setting again $W_j = \mathrm{span}\{\mathbf{w}_1, \ldots, \mathbf{w}_j\}$, we can choose $U := S^{-1}(W_j) \in \mathcal{M}_j$. This, together with (5.5), consequently yields

$$\lambda_j(B) \geq \min_{\substack{\mathbf{y} \in W_j \\ \mathbf{y} \neq 0}} \frac{\mathbf{y}^T A \mathbf{y}}{\mathbf{y}^T \mathbf{y}} \frac{\mathbf{y}^T \mathbf{y}}{\mathbf{y}^T S^{-T} S^{-1} \mathbf{y}} \geq \lambda_j(A) \min_{\substack{\mathbf{y} \in W_j \\ \mathbf{y} \neq 0}} \frac{\mathbf{y}^T \mathbf{y}}{\mathbf{y}^T S^{-T} S^{-1} \mathbf{y}}$$

$$\geq \lambda_j(A) \min_{\mathbf{y} \neq 0} \frac{\mathbf{y}^T \mathbf{y}}{\mathbf{y}^T S^{-T} S^{-1} \mathbf{y}} = \lambda_j(A) \min_{\mathbf{x} \neq 0} \frac{\mathbf{x}^T S^T S \mathbf{x}}{\mathbf{x}^T \mathbf{x}}$$

$$= \lambda_j(A) \lambda_{\min}(S^T S),$$

since $\mathbf{y}^T \mathbf{y} / \mathbf{y}^T S^{-T} S^{-1} \mathbf{y} = \|\mathbf{y}\|_2^2 / \|S^{-1}\mathbf{y}\|_2^2 > 0$.

In the same way, we can use (5.6) and (5.4) to derive

$$\lambda_j(B) = \min_{\substack{U \in \mathcal{M}_{n+1-j} \\ }} \max_{\substack{\mathbf{x} \in U \\ \mathbf{x} \neq 0}} \frac{\mathbf{x}^T S^T A S \mathbf{x}}{\mathbf{x}^T \mathbf{x}} = \min_{\substack{U \in \mathcal{M}_{n+1-j} \\ }} \max_{\substack{\mathbf{y} \in S(U) \\ \mathbf{y} \neq 0}} \frac{\mathbf{y}^T A \mathbf{y}}{\mathbf{y}^T S^{-T} S^{-1} \mathbf{y}}$$

$$\leq \max_{\substack{\mathbf{y} \in W^{\perp}_{j-1} \\ \mathbf{y} \neq 0}} \frac{\mathbf{y}^T A \mathbf{y}}{\mathbf{y}^T \mathbf{y}} \frac{\mathbf{y}^T \mathbf{y}}{\mathbf{y}^T S^{-T} S^{-1} \mathbf{y}} \leq \lambda_j(A) \max_{\substack{\mathbf{y} \in W^{\perp}_{j-1} \\ \mathbf{y} \neq 0}} \frac{\mathbf{y}^T \mathbf{y}}{\mathbf{y}^T S^{-T} S^{-1} \mathbf{y}}$$

$$\leq \lambda_j(A) \max_{\mathbf{y} \neq 0} \frac{\mathbf{y}^T \mathbf{y}}{\mathbf{y}^T S^T S^{-1} \mathbf{y}}$$

$$= \lambda_j(A) \lambda_{\max}(S^T S).$$

Both bounds together yield

$$\lambda_{\min}(S^T S) \lambda_j(A) \leq \lambda_j(B) \leq \lambda_{\max}(S^T S) \lambda_j(A) \tag{5.8}$$

and since $\lambda_{\min}(S^T S)$ and $\lambda_{\max}(S^T S)$ are both positive, $\lambda_j(A)$ and $\lambda_j(B)$ must have the same sign. $\qquad\square$

The proof we have just given actually shows more than we have stated, namely (5.8), which is also called *Ostrowski's quantitative version of Sylvester's theorem*, see for example [98] and Wimmer [136].

Another consequence of Theorem 5.5 is that it allows us to give a stability result on the eigenvalues of a symmetric matrix.

Corollary 5.7 *Let $A \in \mathbb{R}^{n \times n}$ and $B \in \mathbb{R}^{n \times n}$ be two symmetric matrices with eigenvalues $\lambda_1(A) \geq \lambda_2(A) \geq \cdots \geq \lambda_n(A)$ and $\lambda_1(B) \geq \lambda_2(B) \geq \cdots \geq \lambda_n(B)$. Then,*

$$|\lambda_j(A) - \lambda_j(B)| \leq \|A - B\|$$

for every compatible matrix norm.

Proof Using the Cauchy–Schwarz inequality, we have

$$\mathbf{x}^T(A\mathbf{x} - B\mathbf{x}) \leq \|A\mathbf{x} - B\mathbf{x}\|_2 \|\mathbf{x}\|_2 \leq \|A - B\|_2 \|\mathbf{x}\|_2^2,$$

meaning particularly

$$\frac{\mathbf{x}^T A \mathbf{x}}{\mathbf{x}^T \mathbf{x}} \leq \frac{\mathbf{x}^T B \mathbf{x}}{\mathbf{x}^T \mathbf{x}} + \|A - B\|_2$$

for $\mathbf{x} \neq \mathbf{0}$. Thus, Theorem 5.5 yields $\lambda_j(A) \leq \lambda_j(B) + \|A - B\|_2$. Exchanging the roles of A and B finally gives

$$|\lambda_j(A) - \lambda_j(B)| \leq \|A - B\|_2 = \rho(A - B) \leq \|A - B\|,$$

where we have used Theorems 4.5 and 2.19 and the fact that the matrix $A - B$ is symmetric. $\qquad\square$

As mentioned earlier, the situation is not so favourable if A is not a symmetric or Hermitian matrix. This is demonstrated in the next theorem, which is a generalisation of the above corollary.

Theorem 5.8 (Bauer–Fike) *Let $A \in \mathbb{C}^{n \times n}$ be given, and let $B = A + \Delta A \in \mathbb{C}^{n \times n}$ be a perturbation of A. If $\mu \in \mathbb{C}$ is an eigenvalue of B and $A = S D S^{-1}$ with $D = \mathrm{diag}(\lambda_1, \ldots, \lambda_n)$ then*

$$\min_{1 \le j \le n} |\lambda_j - \mu| \le \kappa_p(S) \|\Delta A\|_p.$$

Here, $\| \cdot \|_p$, $1 \le p \le \infty$, is the ℓ_p-norm and $\kappa_p(S)$ is the condition number of the matrix S in the induced norm.

Proof If μ is an eigenvalue of A this is obviously true. Hence, assume that μ is not an eigenvalue of A. Since μ is an eigenvalue of $B = A + \Delta A$, the matrix $S^{-1}(A + \Delta A - \mu I)S$ is singular, i.e. there is an $\mathbf{x} \in \mathbb{C}^n \setminus \{\mathbf{0}\}$ with $S^{-1}(A + \Delta A - \mu I)S\mathbf{x} = \mathbf{0}$. We can rearrange this to $(D - \mu I)\mathbf{x} = -S^{-1}(\Delta A)S\mathbf{x}$ and then to

$$\mathbf{x} = -(D - \mu I)^{-1}S^{-1}(\Delta A)S\mathbf{x}.$$

Taking the norm immediately leads to

$$1 = \|(D - \mu I)^{-1}S^{-1}(\Delta A)S\|_p \le \|(D - \mu I)^{-1}\|_p \|S^{-1}\|_p \|\Delta A\|_p \|S\|_p$$
$$\le \max_{1 \le j \le n} \frac{1}{|\lambda_j - \mu|} \kappa_p(S) \|\Delta A\|_p. \qquad \square$$

This theorem shows that the perturbation ΔA is magnified by the condition number of the transformation matrix S. If S is orthogonal or unitary then $\kappa_2(S) = 1$ and this is the best we can hope for. However, a unitary transformation is possible only if A is normal. Hence, in all other cases this will very probably lead to problems.

We now return to the situation of real eigenvalues and real eigenvectors of real matrices. Assume that we already have an approximation λ of an eigenvalue and an approximation $\mathbf{x}$ of a corresponding eigenvector. Then, we can try to use this information to derive a better estimate for the eigenvalue. To this end, let us assume that all components x_j of $\mathbf{x}$ are different from zero. Then, all the quotients

$$q_j := \frac{(A\mathbf{x})_j}{x_j} = \frac{\mathbf{e}_j^{\mathrm{T}} A \mathbf{x}}{\mathbf{e}_j^{\mathrm{T}} \mathbf{x}} \tag{5.9}$$

should be about the same and coincide approximately with the eigenvalue.

Lemma 5.9 *If all the components x_j of $\mathbf{x} \in \mathbb{R}^n$ are different from zero and if Q denotes the diagonal matrix $Q = \mathrm{diag}(q_1, \ldots, q_n) \in \mathbb{R}^{n \times n}$ with diagonal* *components given by (5.9) then we have for an arbitrary vector norm and a compatible matrix norm*

1. $1 \leq \|(A - pI)^{-1}\| \, \|(Q - pI)\mathbf{x}\| / \|\mathbf{x}\|,$
2. $1 \leq \|(A - pI)^{-1}\| \, \|Q - pI\|$

for every $p \in \mathbb{R}$ for which $A - pI$ is non-singular.

Proof The definition of the q_j yields for our fixed vector $\mathbf{x}$ the equation $A\mathbf{x} = Q\mathbf{x}$ so that $(A - pI)\mathbf{x} = (Q - pI)\mathbf{x}$ follows. This means

$$\mathbf{x} = (A - pI)^{-1}(Q - pI)\mathbf{x},$$

from which the stated inequalities immediately follow.   □

As a special case of Lemma 5.9 we have the following *quotient theorem*.

Theorem 5.10   *Let $A \in \mathbb{R}^{n \times n}$ be symmetric. Let q_j be defined by (5.9). Then, for every $p \in \mathbb{R}$ there is an eigenvalue λ of A satisfying*

$$|\lambda - p| \leq \max_{1 \leq j \leq n} |q_j - p|.$$

Proof If p is an eigenvalue of A the inequality is obviously satisfied. If p is not an eigenvalue of A then the matrix $A - pI$ is invertible and $(A - pI)^{-1}$ has the eigenvalues $1/(\lambda_j - p)$, if λ_j, $1 \leq j \leq n$, denote the eigenvalues of A. Since $(A - pI)^{-1}$ is symmetric its matrix norm induced by the Euclidean vector norm and its spectral radius are the same. Thus,

$$\|(A - pI)^{-1}\|_2 = \rho((A - pI)^{-1}) = \max_{1 \leq j \leq n} \frac{1}{|\lambda_j - p|} = \frac{1}{\min_{1 \leq j \leq n} |\lambda_j - p|}. \quad (5.10)$$

In the same way, we can derive

$$\|Q - pI\|_2 = \rho(Q - pI) = \max_{1 \leq j \leq n} |q_j - p|$$

and the second statement of Lemma 5.9 yields

$$\min_{1 \leq j \leq n} |\lambda_j - p| \leq \max_{1 \leq j \leq n} |q_j - p|.$$ □

Corollary 5.11   *There is at least one eigenvalue λ of A satisfying*

$$q_{\min} := \min_{1 \leq j \leq n} q_j \leq \lambda \leq q_{\max} := \max_{1 \leq j \leq n} q_j.$$

Proof If we define $p = (q_{\min} + q_{\max})/2$ then we have

$$\max_{1 \leq j \leq n} |q_j - p| = \max_{1 \leq j \leq n} \left| q_j - \frac{q_{\min} + q_{\max}}{2} \right| = \frac{1}{2} |q_{\max} - q_{\min}|.$$

Hence, we can conclude from Theorem 5.10 that there is at least one eigenvalue λ with

$$\left| \lambda - \frac{q_{max} + q_{min}}{2} \right| \leq \frac{1}{2} |q_{max} - q_{min}|,$$

which means that λ must be in the given interval. □

5.2 The Power Method

The first numerical method we want to discuss is for computing the largest eigenvalue of a matrix $A \in \mathbb{R}^{n \times n}$ and a corresponding eigenvector. It is designed for matrices A with one *dominant* eigenvalue λ_1, i.e. we assume in this section that the eigenvalues of A satisfy

$$|\lambda_1| > |\lambda_2| \geq |\lambda_3| \geq \cdots \geq |\lambda_n|. \tag{5.11}$$

We will not assume that A is symmetric but we will assume that it has real eigenvalues and that there is a basis $\mathbf{w}_1, \ldots, \mathbf{w}_n$ of $\mathbb{R}^n$ consisting of eigenvectors of A. Then, we can represent every $\mathbf{x}$ as $\mathbf{x} = \sum_{j=1}^{n} c_j \mathbf{w}_j$ with certain coefficients c_j. Using (5.11) shows that

$$A^m \mathbf{x} = \sum_{j=1}^{n} c_j \lambda_j^m \mathbf{w}_j = \lambda_1^m \left(c_1 \mathbf{w}_1 + \sum_{j=2}^{n} \left(\frac{\lambda_j}{\lambda_1} \right)^m \mathbf{w}_j \right) =: \lambda_1^m (c_1 \mathbf{w}_1 + \mathbf{R}_m) \tag{5.12}$$

defines a vector sequence $\{\mathbf{R}_m\}$ with $\mathbf{R}_m \to \mathbf{0}$ for $m \to \infty$. This means that if $c_1 \neq 0$ that

$$A^m \mathbf{x} / \lambda_1^m \to c_1 \mathbf{w}_1, \qquad m \to \infty.$$

The latter is an eigenvector of A to the eigenvalue λ_1. Of course, this is only of limited use since we do not know the eigenvalue λ_1 and hence cannot form the quotient $A^m \mathbf{x} / \lambda_1^m$. Another problem comes from the fact that the norm of $A^m \mathbf{x}$ converges to zero if $|\lambda_1| < 1$ and to infinity if $|\lambda_1| > 1$. Both problems can be resolved by normalisation. For example, if we take the Euclidean norm of $A^m \mathbf{x}$ then

$$\|A^m \mathbf{x}\|_2 = \left(\sum_{i,j=1}^{n} c_i c_j \lambda_i^m \lambda_j^m \mathbf{w}_i^T \mathbf{w}_j \right)^{1/2} =: |\lambda_1|^m (|c_1| \|\mathbf{w}_1\|_2 + r_m) \tag{5.13}$$

with $\mathbb{R} \ni r_m \to 0$ for $m \to \infty$. From this we can conclude that

$$\frac{\|A^{m+1} \mathbf{x}\|_2}{\|A^m \mathbf{x}\|_2} = \frac{\|A^{m+1} \mathbf{x}\|_2}{|\lambda_1|^{m+1}} \frac{|\lambda_1|^m}{\|A^m \mathbf{x}\|_2} |\lambda_1| \to |\lambda_1|, \qquad m \to \infty, \tag{5.14}$$

which gives λ_1 up to its sign. To determine also its sign and a corresponding eigenvector, we refine the method as follows.

Definition 5.12 The *power method* or *von Mises iteration* is defined in the following way. First, we pick a start vector $\mathbf{y}_0 = \sum_{j=1}^{n} c_j \mathbf{w}_j$ with $c_1 \neq 0$ and set $\mathbf{x}_0 = \mathbf{y}_0 / \|\mathbf{y}_0\|_2$. Then, for $m = 1, 2, \ldots$ we define

1. $\mathbf{y}_m = A\mathbf{x}_{m-1}$,
2. $\mathbf{x}_m = \frac{\sigma_m \mathbf{y}_m}{\|\mathbf{y}_m\|_2}$, where the sign $\sigma_m \in \{-1, 1\}$ is chosen such that $\mathbf{x}_m^T \mathbf{x}_{m-1} \geq 0$.

Since the algorithm can directly be derived from this definition, we refrain from stating it explicitly. Each step costs $O(n^2)$ time, which is mainly given by the involved matrix–vector multiplication.

The choice of the sign means that the angle between $\mathbf{x}_{m-1}$ and $\mathbf{x}_m$ is in $[0, \pi/2]$, which means that we are avoiding a "jump" in the orientation when moving from $\mathbf{x}_{m-1}$ to $\mathbf{x}_m$.

The condition $c_1 \neq 0$ is usually satisfied simply because of numerical rounding errors and is hence no real restriction.

Theorem 5.13 *Let $A \in \mathbb{R}^{n \times n}$ be a diagonalisable matrix with real eigenvalues and eigenvectors with one dominant eigenvalue λ_1. The iterations of the power method satisfy*

1. *$\|\mathbf{y}_m\|_2 \to |\lambda_1|$ for $m \to \infty$,*
2. *$\mathbf{x}_m$ converges to an eigenvector of A to the eigenvalue λ_1,*
3. *$\sigma_m \to \text{sign}(\lambda_1)$ for $m \to \infty$, i.e. $\sigma_m = \text{sign}(\lambda_1)$ for sufficiently large m.*

Proof We have

$$
\mathbf{x}_m = \sigma_m \frac{A\mathbf{x}_{m-1}}{\|A\mathbf{x}_{m-1}\|_2} = \sigma_m \frac{A\left(\sigma_{m-1} \frac{A\mathbf{x}_{m-2}}{\|A\mathbf{x}_{m-2}\|_2}\right)}{\left\|\sigma_{m-1} \frac{A^2\mathbf{x}_{m-2}}{\|A\mathbf{x}_{m-2}\|_2}\right\|_2}
$$

$$
= \sigma_m \sigma_{m-1} \frac{A^2\mathbf{x}_{m-2}}{\|A^2\mathbf{x}_{m-2}\|_2} = \sigma_m \sigma_{m-1} \cdots \sigma_1 \frac{A^m\mathbf{x}_0}{\|A^m\mathbf{x}_0\|_2}
$$

$$
= \sigma_m \sigma_{m-1} \cdots \sigma_1 \frac{A^m\mathbf{y}_0}{\|A^m\mathbf{y}_0\|_2}
$$

for $m = 1, 2, \ldots$. From this, we can conclude

$$
\mathbf{y}_{m+1} = A\mathbf{x}_m = \sigma_m \cdots \sigma_1 \frac{A^{m+1}\mathbf{y}_0}{\|A^m\mathbf{y}_0\|_2},
$$

such that (5.14) immediately leads to

$$
\|\mathbf{y}_{m+1}\|_2 = \frac{\|A^{m+1}\mathbf{y}_0\|_2}{\|A^m\mathbf{y}_0\|_2} \to |\lambda_1|, \qquad m \to \infty.
$$

For the rest of the proof we may assume, without restriction, that $\|\mathbf{w}_1\|_2 = 1$. Using the representations (5.12) and (5.13) yields

$$\mathbf{x}_m = \sigma_m \cdots \sigma_1 \frac{\lambda_1^m (c_1 \mathbf{w}_1 + \mathbf{R}_m)}{|\lambda_1|^m (|c_1| \|\mathbf{w}_1\|_2 + r_m)}$$
$$= \sigma_m \cdots \sigma_1 \operatorname{sign}(\lambda_1)^m \operatorname{sign}(c_1) \mathbf{w}_1 + \boldsymbol{\rho}_m$$

with $\boldsymbol{\rho}_m \to \mathbf{0}$ for $m \to \infty$. From this we can conclude that $\mathbf{x}_m$ indeed converges to an eigenvector of A to the eigenvalue λ_1, provided that $\sigma_m = \operatorname{sign}(\lambda_1)$ for all $m \geq m_0$ sufficiently large. The latter follows from

$$0 \leq \mathbf{x}_{m-1}^{\mathrm{T}} \mathbf{x}_m = \sigma_m \sigma_{m-1}^2 \cdots \sigma_1^2 \frac{\lambda_1^{2m-1}(c_1 \mathbf{w}_1^{\mathrm{T}} + \mathbf{R}_{m-1}^{\mathrm{T}})(c_1 \mathbf{w}_1 + \mathbf{R}_m)}{|\lambda_1|^{2m-1}(|c_1| + r_{m-1})(|c_1| + r_m)}$$
$$= \sigma_m \operatorname{sign}(\lambda_1) \frac{|c_1|^2 + c_1 \mathbf{w}_1^{\mathrm{T}} \mathbf{R}_m + c_1 \mathbf{R}_{m-1}^{\mathrm{T}} \mathbf{w}_1 + \mathbf{R}_{m-1}^{\mathrm{T}} \mathbf{R}_m}{|c_1|^2 + |c_1|(r_{m-1} + r_m) + r_m r_{m-1}},$$

because the fraction involved converges to one for $m \to \infty$. □

The Euclidean norm involved in the normalisation process can be replaced by any other norm without changing the convergence result. Often, the maximum norm is used, since it is cheaper to compute. Also, we do not need all eigenvalues to be real. It suffices that the dominant eigenvalue is real. Even if the dominant eigenvalue is complex, we can still apply the method and have at least $\|\mathbf{y}_m\| \to |\lambda_1|$.

It follows from (5.12) that the convergence rate of the power method is mainly determined by the quotient $|\lambda_2/\lambda_1| < 1$. Obviously, the convergence will be slow if λ_2 is close to λ_1.

5.3 Inverse Iteration by von Wielandt and Rayleigh

We now want to discuss a specific application of the power method. To this end, let us assume that A has a simple eigenvalue $\lambda_j \in \mathbb{R}$ and that we already have an approximation $\lambda \in \mathbb{R}$ to this eigenvalue. Then, obviously, we may assume that

$$|\lambda - \lambda_j| < |\lambda - \lambda_i|$$

for all other eigenvalues $\lambda_i \neq \lambda_j$ of A. If our approximation λ is not an eigenvalue of A itself then we can invert $A - \lambda I$ and $(A - \lambda I)^{-1}$ has the eigenvalues $1/(\lambda_i - \lambda) =: \tilde{\lambda}_i$. Moreover, we have

$$\lambda_j = \lambda + \frac{1}{\tilde{\lambda}_j}$$

such that a good approximation to $\tilde{\lambda}_j$ allows us to improve our approximation to λ_j. From

$$\frac{1}{|\lambda - \lambda_i|} < \frac{1}{|\lambda - \lambda_j|} \qquad \text{for all } i \neq j$$

we can conclude that $\tilde{\lambda}_j$ is a dominant eigenvalue of $(A - \lambda I)^{-1}$ such that the power method applied to $(A - \lambda I)^{-1}$ should give good results. This is the idea behind the inverse iteration method by von Wielandt.

Definition 5.14 For the *inverse iteration method* or *von Wielandt iteration* for computing an eigenvalue of a symmetric matrix $A \in \mathbb{R}^{n \times n}$ we assume that we have an approximation $\lambda \in \mathbb{R}$, which is not an eigenvalue, and that we have a start vector $\mathbf{y}_0 \neq \mathbf{0}$. Then, we compute $\mathbf{x}_0 := \mathbf{y}_0 / \|\mathbf{y}_0\|_2$ and then, for $m = 1, 2, \ldots$, we obtain

$$\mathbf{y}_m = (A - \lambda I)^{-1} \mathbf{x}_{m-1},$$
$$\mathbf{x}_m = \frac{\mathbf{y}_m}{\|\mathbf{y}_m\|_2}.$$

The computation of $\mathbf{y}_m$ thus requires solving the linear system

$$(A - \lambda I)\mathbf{y}_m = \mathbf{x}_{m-1}.$$

To this end, we determine, *before* the iteration starts, an *LU* factorisation of A (or a *QR* factorisation) using column pivoting, i.e. we compute

$$P(A - \lambda I) = LU,$$

with a permutation matrix P, an upper triangular matrix U and a normalised lower triangular matrix L. Then, we can use forward and back substitution to solve

$$LU\mathbf{y}_m = P\mathbf{x}_{m-1}.$$

This reduces the complexity necessary in each step to $O(n^2)$ and requires only $O(n^3)$ once to compute the *LU* decomposition.

The approximation λ can be given by any other method. From this point of view, inverse iteration is in particular interesting for improving the results of other methods.

Obviously, we could and should adapt the sign as we have done in the power method. Here, however, we want to discuss a different strategy for symmetric matrices, where it is possible to improve the convergence dramatically by adapting λ in each step. To this end, let us recall the Rayleigh quotient, which we have encountered already several times.

Definition 5.15   The *Rayleigh quotient* of a vector $\mathbf{x} \in \mathbb{R}^n$ with respect to a real matrix $A \in \mathbb{R}^{n \times n}$ is the scalar

$$r(\mathbf{x}) := \frac{\mathbf{x}^T A \mathbf{x}}{\mathbf{x}^T \mathbf{x}}, \qquad \mathbf{x} \neq \mathbf{0}.$$

Obviously, if $\mathbf{x}$ is an eigenvector then $r(\mathbf{x})$ gives the corresponding eigenvalue of A. Moreover, we have the following two immediate properties of the Rayleigh quotient for symmetric matrices.

Lemma 5.16   *Let $A \in \mathbb{R}^{n \times n}$ be symmetric.*

1. If $\lambda_{\min}(A)$ and $\lambda_{\max}(A)$ denote the minimum and maximum eigenvalues of A, respectively, then

$$\lambda_{\min}(A) \leq r(\mathbf{x}) \leq \lambda_{\max}(A), \qquad \mathbf{x} \in \mathbb{R}^n \setminus \{\mathbf{0}\}.$$

2. For $\mathbf{x} \in \mathbb{R}^n$ the function $f : \mathbb{R} \to \mathbb{R}$ defined by $f(\lambda) := \|(A - \lambda I)\mathbf{x}\|_2^2$ becomes minimal for $\lambda = r(\mathbf{x})$ with value

$$f(r(\mathbf{x})) = \|A\mathbf{x}\|_2^2 - r(\mathbf{x})^2 \|\mathbf{x}\|_2^2.$$

Proof The first statement follows directly from Theorem 5.4. The second property follows from differentiating the function

$$f(\lambda) = \|A\mathbf{x} - \lambda \mathbf{x}\|_2^2 = \|A\mathbf{x}\|_2^2 - 2\lambda \mathbf{x}^T A \mathbf{x} + \lambda^2 \|\mathbf{x}\|_2^2. \tag{5.15}$$

The only root of the derivative is given by $\lambda = r(\mathbf{x})$ and inserting this into (5.15) yields the stated function value. It is a minimum as $f''(\lambda) = 2\|\mathbf{x}\|_2^2 > 0$.   □

The idea of the Rayleigh iteration is based upon using the Rayleigh quotient as an approximation to an eigenvalue. If $\mathbf{x}$ is sufficiently close to an eigenvector $\mathbf{z}$ then, by continuity, $r(\mathbf{x})$ is close to $r(\mathbf{z})$ which is an eigenvalue.

Thus, changing the parameter λ in the inverse iteration method in each step leads to Algorithm 11.

Algorithm 11: Rayleigh iteration

   Input : $A \in \mathbb{R}^{n \times n}$, $\mathbf{y}_0 \in \mathbb{R}^n \setminus \{\mathbf{0}\}$.
   Output: Approximate eigenvalue and eigenvector.

1 $\mathbf{x}_0 := \mathbf{y}_0 / \|\mathbf{y}_0\|_2$
2 **for** $m = 0, 1, 2, \ldots$ **do**
3     $\mu_m := \mathbf{x}_m^T A \mathbf{x}_m$
4     $\mathbf{y}_{m+1} := (A - \mu_m I)^{-1} \mathbf{x}_m$
5     $\mathbf{x}_{m+1} := \mathbf{y}_{m+1} / \|\mathbf{y}_{m+1}\|_2$

Some remarks need to be made concerning Algorithm 11. First of all, $\mathbf{y}_{m+1}$ is computed only if μ_m is not an eigenvalue of A, otherwise the method stops. An indication for this is that $\|\mathbf{y}_{m+1}\|_2$ becomes too large, which can be used as a stopping criterion. Although, for $m \to \infty$, the matrices $A - \mu_m I$ become singular, there are usually no problems with the computation of $\mathbf{y}_{m+1}$, provided that one terminates the computation of the LU- or QR-decomposition of $A - \mu_m I$ in time.

Note that this time we have to compute an LU factorisation in each step. This additional computational cost has to be compensated for by a faster convergence. This is, fortunately, given in most cases, as we will see soon. We start with a simpler stability result.

Proposition 5.17 *Let $A \in \mathbb{R}^{n \times n}$ be symmetric. Let the sequence $\{(\mathbf{x}_m, \mu_m)\}$ be generated by the Rayleigh iteration. Then,*

$$\|(A - \mu_{m+1}I)\mathbf{x}_{m+1}\|_2 \le \|(A - \mu_m I)\mathbf{x}_m\|_2, \qquad m = 0, 1, 2, \dots.$$

Here, equality holds if and only if $\mu_m = \mu_{m+1}$ and if $\mathbf{x}_m$ is an eigenvector of $(A - \mu_m I)^2$.

Proof We know from Lemma 5.16 that the Rayleigh quotient μ_{m+1} minimises $f(\lambda) = \|(A - \lambda I)\mathbf{x}_{m+1}\|_2^2$, which means that we have

$$\|(A - \mu_{m+1}I)\mathbf{x}_{m+1}\|_2 \le \|(A - \mu_m I)\mathbf{x}_{m+1}\|_2.$$

By construction, we have $\mathbf{x}_m = (A - \mu_m I)\mathbf{x}_{m+1}\|\mathbf{y}_{m+1}\|_2$ and $\|\mathbf{x}_m\|_2 = 1$, which means

$$\mathbf{x}_m = \frac{(A - \mu_m I)\mathbf{x}_{m+1}}{\|(A - \mu_m I)\mathbf{x}_{m+1}\|_2}.$$

Thus, we can conclude that

$$\|(A - \mu_{m+1}I)\mathbf{x}_{m+1}\|_2 \le \|(A - \mu_m I)\mathbf{x}_{m+1}\|_2 = |\mathbf{x}_m^\mathrm{T}(A - \mu_m I)\mathbf{x}_{m+1}|$$
$$= |\mathbf{x}_{m+1}^\mathrm{T}(A - \mu_m I)\mathbf{x}_m| \le \|(A - \mu_m I)\mathbf{x}_m\|_2,$$

using again that $\|\mathbf{x}_{m+1}\|_2 = 1$. Equality can hold only if it holds in both of the inequalities above. The first inequality means $\mu_{m+1} = \mu_m$ since the Rayleigh quotient gives the unique minimum of the above function f. The second equality is an equality in the Cauchy–Schwarz inequality. Hence, we must in this case have that $(A - \mu_m I)\mathbf{x}_m$ is a multiple of $\mathbf{x}_{m+1}$, say $(A - \mu_m I)\mathbf{x}_m = \alpha_m \mathbf{x}_{m+1}$ with $\alpha_m \ne 0$. This shows that

$$\mathbf{x}_{m+1} = \frac{(A - \mu_m I)^{-1}\mathbf{x}_m}{\|(A - \mu_m I)^{-1}\mathbf{x}_m\|_2} \tag{5.16}$$

implies that

$$(A - \mu_m I)^2 \mathbf{x}_m = \alpha_m (A - \mu_m I) \mathbf{x}_{m+1} = \frac{\alpha_m}{\|(A - \mu_m I)^{-1} \mathbf{x}_m\|_2} \mathbf{x}_m,$$

proving that $\mathbf{x}_m$ is indeed an eigenvector of $(A - \mu_m I)^2$.   □

Next, let us come back to the claimed fast convergence of the Rayleigh method. We will show that if the method converges it converges cubically. We need, however, the following auxiliary result.

Lemma 5.18 *Let $A \in \mathbb{R}^{n \times n}$ be symmetric with eigenvalues $\lambda_1, \ldots, \lambda_n \in \mathbb{R}$ and associated orthonormal eigenvectors $\mathbf{w}_1, \ldots, \mathbf{w}_n$. Let λ be one of the eigenvalues and let $J := \{j \in \{1, \ldots, n\} : \lambda_j \neq \lambda\}$. If $\mathbf{u} \in \mathrm{span}\{\mathbf{w}_j : j \in J\}$ with $\|\mathbf{u}\|_2 = 1$ and if $\mu \in \mathbb{R}$ is not an eigenvalue of A then*

$$\|(A - \mu I)^{-1} \mathbf{u}\|_2 \leq \frac{1}{\min_{j \in J} |\lambda_j - \mu|}.$$

Proof We can expand $\mathbf{u}$ as $\mathbf{u} = \sum_{j \in J} \alpha_j \mathbf{w}_j$. Since $\|\mathbf{u}\|_2 = 1$, we have $\sum_{j \in J} \alpha_j^2 = 1$ and hence

$$\|(A - \mu I)^{-1} \mathbf{u}\|_2 = \left(\sum_{j \in J} \frac{\alpha_j^2}{(\lambda_j - \mu)^2} \right)^{1/2} \leq \frac{1}{\min_{j \in J} |\lambda_j - \mu|}. \qquad \square$$

Theorem 5.19 *Let $A \in \mathbb{R}^{n \times n}$ be symmetric and let $\{\mathbf{x}_m\}$, $\{\mu_m\}$ be the sequences generated by the Rayleigh iteration. Assume that $\{\mathbf{x}_m\}$ converges to an eigenvector $\mathbf{w} \in \mathbb{R}^n$ with $\|\mathbf{w}\|_2 = 1$ associated with the eigenvalue $\lambda \in \mathbb{R}$ of A. Then, the convergence of $\{\mathbf{x}_m\}$ is cubic, i.e. there is a constant $C > 0$ such that*

$$\|\mathbf{x}_{m+1} - \mathbf{w}\|_2 \leq C \|\mathbf{x}_m - \mathbf{w}\|_2^3, \qquad m = 0, 1, 2, \ldots.$$

Furthermore, there is a constant $c > 0$ such that

$$|\mu_m - \lambda| \leq c \|\mathbf{x}_m - \mathbf{w}\|_2^2, \qquad m = 0, 1, 2, \ldots.$$

Proof The proof is based on the idea of studying the behaviour of the angle ϕ_m between $\mathbf{x}_m$ and $\mathbf{w}$. Since both vectors have norm one, the angle is given by $\cos \phi_m = \langle \mathbf{x}_m, \mathbf{w} \rangle_2$. From

$$\|\mathbf{x}_m - \mathbf{w}\|_2^2 = \|\mathbf{x}_m\|_2^2 + \|\mathbf{w}\|_2^2 - 2\langle \mathbf{x}_m, \mathbf{w} \rangle_2 = 2(1 - \cos \phi_m) = 4 \sin^2(\phi_m/2) \quad (5.17)$$

we see that it suffices to show that $2 \sin(\phi_m/2)$ or, equivalently, $\sin \phi_m$ converges cubically. As we have $\mathbb{R}^n = \mathrm{span}\{\mathbf{w}\} \oplus \mathrm{span}\{\mathbf{w}\}^\perp$, we can find for each $\mathbf{x}_m$ a vector $\mathbf{u}_m \in \mathbb{R}^n$ with $\|\mathbf{u}_m\|_2 = 1$ and $\mathbf{u}_m^T \mathbf{w} = 0$ such that $\mathbf{x}_m = \alpha_m \mathbf{w} + \beta_m \mathbf{u}_m$ with

$\alpha_m = \langle \mathbf{w}, \mathbf{x}_m \rangle_2 = \cos \phi_m$. From $1 = \|\mathbf{x}_m\|_2^2 = \cos^2 \phi_m + \beta_m^2$ we find $\beta_m = \sin \phi_m$, i.e. we have the representation

$$\mathbf{x}_m = \cos \phi_m \, \mathbf{w} + \sin \phi_m \, \mathbf{u}_m. \tag{5.18}$$

Multiplying this by $(A - \mu_m I)^{-1}$ yields

$$\mathbf{y}_{m+1} = (A - \mu_m I)^{-1} \mathbf{x}_m = \frac{\cos \phi_m}{\lambda - \mu_m} \mathbf{w} + \sin \phi_m (A - \mu_m I)^{-1} \mathbf{u}_m$$

and because of $\mathbf{x}_{m+1} = \mathbf{y}_{m+1}/\|\mathbf{y}_{m+1}\|_2$ also

$$
\begin{aligned}
\mathbf{x}_{m+1} &= \frac{\cos \phi_m}{(\lambda - \mu_m)\|\mathbf{y}_{m+1}\|_2} \mathbf{w} + \frac{\sin \phi_m}{\|\mathbf{y}_{m+1}\|_2} (A - \mu_m I)^{-1} \mathbf{u}_m \\
&= \frac{\cos \phi_m}{(\lambda - \mu_m)\|\mathbf{y}_{m+1}\|_2} \mathbf{w} + \frac{\sin \phi_m \|(A - \mu_m I)^{-1} \mathbf{u}_m\|_2}{\|\mathbf{y}_{m+1}\|_2} \frac{(A - \mu_m I)^{-1} \mathbf{u}_m}{\|(A - \mu_m I)^{-1} \mathbf{u}_m\|_2}.
\end{aligned}
$$

Noticing that $\mathbf{w}$ is also an eigenvector of $(A - \mu_m I)^{-1}$ we find that $\mathbf{w}^{\mathrm{T}}(A - \mu_m I)^{-1} \mathbf{u}_m = 0$. Hence, we can choose $\mathbf{u}_{m+1}$ as

$$\mathbf{u}_{m+1} = \frac{(A - \mu_m I)^{-1} \mathbf{u}_m}{\|(A - \mu_m I)^{-1} \mathbf{u}_m\|_2} \tag{5.19}$$

and comparing coefficients yields

$$\cos \phi_{m+1} = \frac{\cos \phi_m}{(\lambda - \mu_m)\|\mathbf{y}_{m+1}\|_2}, \qquad \sin \phi_{m+1} = \frac{\sin \phi_m \|(A - \mu_m I)^{-1} \mathbf{u}_m\|_2}{\|\mathbf{y}_{m+1}\|_2}.$$

From (5.18) we find $A\mathbf{x}_m = \lambda \cos \phi_m \, \mathbf{w} + \sin \phi_m \, A\mathbf{u}_m$ and hence

$$
\begin{aligned}
\mu_m = \mathbf{x}_m^{\mathrm{T}} A \mathbf{x}_m &= \lambda \cos^2 \phi_m + \sin^2 \phi_m \, \mathbf{u}_m^{\mathrm{T}} A \mathbf{u}_m \\
&= \lambda - \sin^2 \phi_m [\lambda - r(\mathbf{u}_m)]
\end{aligned}
\tag{5.20}
$$

with the Rayleigh quotient $r(\mathbf{u}_m) = \mathbf{u}_m^{\mathrm{T}} A \mathbf{u}_m$. Inserting this into the formula of $\cos \phi_{m+1}$ from above yields

$$
\begin{aligned}
\tan \phi_{m+1} = \frac{\sin \phi_{m+1}}{\cos \phi_{m+1}} &= (\lambda - \mu_m)\|(A - \mu_m I)^{-1} \mathbf{u}_m\|_2 \tan \phi_m \\
&= [\lambda - r(\mathbf{u}_m)]\|(A - \mu_m I)^{-1} \mathbf{u}_m\|_2 \tan \phi_m \sin^2 \phi_m.
\end{aligned}
\tag{5.21}
$$

Since the Rayleigh quotient is bounded from above and below we know that the term $\lambda - r(\mathbf{u}_m)$ in the above expression is bounded. To show that $\|(A - \mu_m I)^{-1} \mathbf{u}_m\|_2$ is also bounded independently of m, we will apply Lemma 5.18. Using the notation established in that lemma, we have to show that $\mathbf{u}_m \in \mathrm{span}\{\mathbf{w}_j : j \in J\}$ for all m, where $J = \{j \in \{1, \ldots, n\} : \lambda_j \neq \lambda\}$. This is clear if λ is a simple eigenvalue. If this is not the case then we have to work harder. We know from (5.19) that $\mathbf{u}_{m+1}$ is a scalar multiple of $(A - \mu_m I)^{-1} \mathbf{u}_m$. As $A - \mu_m I$ maps $\mathrm{span}\{\mathbf{w}_j : j \in J\}$ onto itself, we see that $\mathbf{u}_m \in \mathrm{span}\{\mathbf{w}_j :$

$j \in J\}$ implies $\mathbf{u}_{m+1} \in \text{span}\{\mathbf{w}_j : j \in J\}$ and it hence suffices to show that $\mathbf{u}_0 \in \text{span}\{\mathbf{w}_j : j \in J\}$. Let $M := \text{span}\{\mathbf{w}_j : j \notin J\}$ and denote the orthogonal projection from $\mathbb{R}^n$ to M by P_M. Then, we have to show that $P_M(\mathbf{u}_0) = \mathbf{0}$. This is done, as follows. First of all, we show that $\mathbf{w}$ is a multiple of $P_M(\mathbf{x}_0)$. To see this, note that if $\mathbf{x}_m$ has the representation

$$\mathbf{x}_m = \sum_{j \notin J} \alpha_j \mathbf{w}_j + \sum_{j \in J} \alpha_j \mathbf{w}_j = P_M(\mathbf{x}_m) + \sum_{j \in J} \alpha_j \mathbf{w}_j,$$

then $\mathbf{x}_{m+1}$ has, as a normalised vector, the representation

$$
\begin{aligned}
\mathbf{x}_{m+1} &= \frac{1}{\|(A - \mu_m I)^{-1}\mathbf{x}_m\|_2}(A - \mu_m I)^{-1}\mathbf{x}_m \\
&= \frac{1}{\|(A - \mu_m I)^{-1}\mathbf{x}_m\|_2(\lambda - \mu_m)} \sum_{j \notin J} \alpha_j \mathbf{w}_j \\
&\quad + \frac{1}{\|(A - \mu_m I)^{-1}\mathbf{x}_m\|_2} \sum_{j \in J} \frac{\alpha_j}{\lambda_j - \mu_m} \mathbf{w}_j
\end{aligned}
$$

and hence we can conclude that

$$P_M(\mathbf{x}_{m+1}) = \frac{1}{\|(A - \mu_m I)^{-1}\mathbf{x}_m\|_2(\lambda - \mu_m)} P_M(\mathbf{x}_m),$$

which shows that $P_M(\mathbf{x}_m)$ is a scalar multiple of $P_M(\mathbf{x}_0)$. Since we assume that $\mathbf{x}_m$ converges to the eigenvector $\mathbf{w} \in M$, we can conclude by the continuity of the orthogonal projection that $\mathbf{w}$ is also a scalar multiple of $P_M(\mathbf{x}_0)$, i.e. there is an $\alpha \in \mathbb{R} \setminus \{0\}$ such that $\mathbf{w} = \alpha P_M(\mathbf{x}_0)$. Now, if $\mathbf{x}_0 = \cos \phi_0 \, \mathbf{w} + \sin \phi_0 \, \mathbf{u}_0$ then we may assume that $\sin \phi_0 \neq 0$ because otherwise $\mathbf{x}_0$ would already be an eigenvector. The linearity of the orthogonal projection gives

$$
\begin{aligned}
P_M(\mathbf{x}_0) &= \cos \phi_0 \, P_M(\mathbf{w}) + \sin \phi_0 \, P_M(\mathbf{u}_0) = \cos \phi_0 \, \mathbf{w} + \sin \phi_0 \, P_M(\mathbf{u}_0) \\
&= \alpha \cos \phi_0 \, P_M(\mathbf{x}_0) + \sin \phi_0 \, P_M(\mathbf{u}_0) = P_M(\mathbf{x}_0) + \sin \phi_0 \, P_M(\mathbf{u}_0),
\end{aligned}
$$

where in the last step we have used that $\mathbf{w} \in M$ implies

$$1 = \|\mathbf{w}\|_2^2 = \alpha P_M(\mathbf{x}_0)^{\mathrm{T}}\mathbf{w} = \alpha \mathbf{x}_0^{\mathrm{T}}\mathbf{w} = \alpha \cos \phi_0.$$

Hence, we have $P_M(\mathbf{u}_0) = \mathbf{0}$ and Lemma 5.18 can indeed be applied, yielding

$$\|(A - \mu_m I)^{-1}\mathbf{u}_m\|_2 \leq \frac{1}{\min_{j \in J} |\lambda_j - \mu_m|}$$

for all m. Let us now define $\gamma := \min_{j \in J} |\lambda_j - \lambda| > 0$. As $\mathbf{x}_m \to \mathbf{w}$ implies $\mu_m \to \lambda$, we have for sufficiently large m that $\min_{j \in J} |\lambda_j - \mu_m| \geq \gamma/2$ and thus

$$\|(A - \mu_m I)^{-1}\mathbf{u}_m\|_2 \leq \frac{2}{\gamma}$$

for all such m sufficiently large. Next, $\mathbf{x}_m \to \mathbf{w}$ also implies $\cos \phi_m \to 1$ such that $\cos \phi_m \geq 1/2$ for all sufficiently large m. This means, using (5.21), that there is a $c > 0$ such that

$$\sin \phi_{m+1} \leq |\lambda - r(\mathbf{u}_m)| \|(A - \mu_m I)^{-1} \mathbf{u}_m\|_2 \sin^3 \phi_m \frac{\cos \phi_{m+1}}{\cos \phi_m} \leq c \sin^3 \phi_m$$

for all sufficiently large m. As $\sin \phi_m$ behaves like ϕ_m and hence $2 \sin(\phi_m/2)$ behaves like $\sin \phi_m$ for small ϕ_m, we see that we can conclude, with (5.17), that also

$$\|\mathbf{x}_{m+1} - \mathbf{w}\|_2 \leq c \|\mathbf{x}_m - \mathbf{w}\|_2^3.$$

Finally, combining (5.20) with (5.17) yields

$$|\lambda - \mu_m| \leq |\lambda - r(\mathbf{u}_m)| \sin \phi_m^2 \leq C \|\mathbf{x}_m - \mathbf{w}\|_2^2. \qquad \square$$

The actual proof of convergence is even more difficult. Here, we will prove only a partial, easier result. By Proposition 5.17, we know that the sequence $\{\|(A - \mu_m I)\mathbf{x}_m\|_2\}$ is non-increasing and obviously bounded from below such that it converges. Let τ be the limit of this sequence, i.e.

$$\tau := \lim_{m \to \infty} \|(A - \mu_m I)\mathbf{x}_m\|_2. \tag{5.22}$$

Theorem 5.20 *Let $\{\mathbf{x}_m\}$ and $\{\mu_m\}$ be the sequences generated by the Rayleigh iteration. Let τ be defined by (5.22). Then, the following results hold.*

1. *The sequence $\{\mu_m\}$ converges.*
2. *If $\tau = 0$ then the sequence $\{\mathbf{x}_m\}$ converges to an eigenvector of A and $\{\mu_m\}$ converges to the corresponding eigenvalue.*

Proof We start by showing that $\{\mu_m\}$ always converges, though not necessarily to an eigenvalue of A. This is done in two steps. First, we will show that $\mu_{m+1} - \mu_m$ converges to zero. Second, we will show that $\{\mu_m\}$ has at most a finite number of accumulation points. From this, it follows that $\{\mu_m\}$ converges. To see this, let $\{\rho_1, \ldots, \rho_L\}$ be the set of distinct accumulation points and assume that $L > 1$. Let $\delta := \min_{i \neq j} |\rho_i - \rho_j| > 0$. Then, for sufficiently large m each μ_m must be within a distance of $\delta/4$ of one of the ρ_i, since, otherwise, the bound-edness of the sequence would yield another accumulation point. Hence, there is an $m_0 > 0$ such that we have for $m \geq m_0$ on the one hand $|\mu_{m+1} - \mu_m| < \delta/4$ and on the other hand $|\mu_m - \rho_j| < \delta/4$ for a certain $j = j(m) \in \{1, \ldots, L\}$. But this means

$$|\mu_{m+1} - \rho_i| \geq |\rho_j - \rho_i| - \left(|\rho_j - \mu_m| + |\mu_m - \mu_{m+1}| \right) \geq \delta - 2\delta/4 = \delta/2$$

for all $i \neq j$. But since μ_{m+1} must also be in the $\delta/4$ neighbourhood of an accumulation point, this accumulation point can only be ρ_j. This means that all μ_m, $m \geq m_0$, are within a distance $\delta/4$ of ρ_j, which contradicts the fact that we have $L > 1$. Thus the sequence has only one accumulation point, i.e. it converges.

To see that $\mu_{m+1} - \mu_m$ converges to zero, let us set $\mathbf{r}_m := (A - \mu_m I)\mathbf{x}_m$ and let us define θ_m by $\cos \theta_m := \mathbf{r}_m^T \mathbf{x}_{m+1}/\|\mathbf{r}_m\|_2$. Then,

$$
\begin{aligned}
\|\mathbf{r}_{m+1}\|_2^2 &= \|(A - \mu_m I)\mathbf{x}_{m+1} + (\mu_m - \mu_{m+1})\mathbf{x}_{m+1}\|_2^2 \\
&= \|(A - \mu_m I)\mathbf{x}_{m+1}\|_2^2 + 2(\mu_m - \mu_{m+1})\mathbf{x}_{m+1}^T(A - \mu_m I)\mathbf{x}_{m+1} + (\mu_m - \mu_{m+1})^2 \\
&= \|(A - \mu_m I)\mathbf{x}_{m+1}\|_2^2 + 2(\mu_m - \mu_{m+1})(\mu_{m+1} - \mu_m) + (\mu_m - \mu_{m+1})^2 \\
&= |\mathbf{x}_m^T(A - \mu_m I)\mathbf{x}_{m+1}|^2 - (\mu_{m+1} - \mu_m)^2 \\
&= \|\mathbf{r}_m\|_2^2 \cos^2 \theta_m - (\mu_{m+1} - \mu_m)^2,
\end{aligned}
$$

where we have used ideas from the beginning of the proof of Proposition 5.17. This means in particular

$$(\mu_{m+1} - \mu_m)^2 \leq \|\mathbf{r}_m\|_2^2 - \|\mathbf{r}_{m+1}\|_2^2. \tag{5.23}$$

However, we know from Proposition 5.17 that the sequence $\{\|\mathbf{r}_m\|_2\}$ converges to τ so that the right-hand side of (5.23) converges to zero, which shows $\mu_{m+1} - \mu_m \to 0$ for $m \to \infty$.

Next, we need to show that $\{\mu_m\}$ has only finitely many accumulation points. If $\tau = 0$ then each accumulation point has to be an eigenvalue of A and since A has only a finite number of eigenvalues, we only have to consider the case $\tau > 0$. In this situation, let ρ be an accumulation point. Using $\|\mathbf{r}_m\|_2 \to \tau$ and $\mu_{m+1} - \mu_m \to 0$ together with

$$\|\mathbf{r}_{m+1}\|_2^2 = \|\mathbf{r}_m\|_2^2 \cos^2 \theta_m - (\mu_{m+1} - \mu_m)^2$$

allows us to conclude that $\cos^2 \theta_m \to 1$. With (5.16) we can conclude from

$$\|\mathbf{r}_m\|_2 \cos \theta_m = \mathbf{r}_m^T \mathbf{x}_{m+1} = \frac{1}{\|(A - \mu_m I)^{-1}\mathbf{x}_m\|_2} > 0 \tag{5.24}$$

that even $\cos \theta_m \to 1$ for $m \to \infty$. This, however, lets us conclude that

$$\|\mathbf{r}_m - \|\mathbf{r}_m\|_2 \mathbf{x}_{m+1}\|_2^2 = 2\|\mathbf{r}_m\|_2^2(1 - \cos \theta_m) \to 0.$$

Finally, combining (5.24) with (5.16) yields $(A - \mu_m I)\mathbf{x}_{m+1} = \|\mathbf{r}_m\|_2 \cos \theta_m \mathbf{x}_m$ and thus we have

$$
\begin{aligned}
\left\|[(A - \mu_m I)^2 - \|\mathbf{r}_m\|_2^2 \cos \theta_m I]\mathbf{x}_m\right\|_2 &= \|(A - \mu_m I)(\mathbf{r}_m - \|\mathbf{r}_m\|_2 \mathbf{x}_{m+1})\|_2 \\
&\leq \|A - \mu_m I\|_2 \|\mathbf{r}_m - \|\mathbf{r}_m\|_2 \mathbf{x}_{m+1}\|_2 \\
&\to 0.
\end{aligned}
$$

Now assume that $\{\mu_{m_j}\}$ converges to our accumulation point ρ. Then, as the sub-sequence $\{\mathbf{x}_{m_j}\}$ is also bounded, it must also have an accumulation point $\mathbf{w}$ with $\|\mathbf{w}\|_2 = 1$. Taking a sub-sequence of the sub-sequence $\{m_j\}$ which we will denote with $\{m_j\}$ again, we see that $\mu_{m_j} \to \rho$ and $\mathbf{x}_{m_j} \to \mathbf{w}$. This all then leads to $\|[(A - \rho I)^2 - \tau^2 I]\mathbf{w}\|_2 = 0$ and hence the accumulation point is a zero of the polynomial $p(t) = \det((A - tI)^2 - \tau^2 I)$, but, since any polynomial has only a finite number of different zeros, we only have a finite number of accumulation points. This finishes the proof of the first part.

For the second part, we assume that $\tau = 0$. Let $(\lambda, \mathbf{w})$ be an accumulation point of the sequence $\{(\mu_m, \mathbf{x}_m)\}$. Then, $\tau = 0$ implies that $(A - \lambda I)\mathbf{w} = \mathbf{0}$ and, since $\mathbf{w}$ has norm one, it follows that $\mathbf{w}$ is an eigenvector of A to the eigenvalue λ. As we know from the first part that $\{\mu_m\}$ converges, it must converge to λ. Finally, if $\{\mathbf{x}_{m_j}\}$ is the sequence that converges to $\mathbf{w}$, then for each $\epsilon > 0$ there is a j_0 such that $\|\mathbf{x}_{m_{j_0}} - \mathbf{w}\|_2 < \epsilon$. If we choose $\epsilon > 0$ so small that $C\epsilon^2 < 1$ with C from Theorem 5.19 then we have

$$\|\mathbf{x}_{m_{j_0}+1} - \mathbf{w}\|_2 \leq C\|\mathbf{x}_{m_{j_0}} - \mathbf{w}\|_2^3 < C\epsilon^3 < \epsilon.$$

From this it immediately follows that $\|\mathbf{x}_m - \mathbf{w}\|_2 < \epsilon$ for all $m \geq m_{j_0}$, i.e. the sequence $\{\mathbf{x}_m\}$ converges to $\mathbf{w}$. □

The case $\tau > 0$ is somewhat more complicated. It is possible to show that in this situation we have $\mathbf{x}_{2m} \to \mathbf{w}_+$ and $\mathbf{x}_{2m+1} \to \mathbf{w}_-$ linearly, where $\mathbf{w}_+$ and $\mathbf{w}_-$ are the bisectors of a pair of eigenvectors whose eigenvalues have mean $\rho = \lim \mu_m$, though this case is unstable under perturbations of $\mathbf{x}_m$. Details can be found in Parlett [100].

To finish this discussion, we want to give one more result on the Rayleigh quotient. As we have seen in Theorem 5.19, the sequence of Rayleigh quotients $\mu_m = r(\mathbf{x}_m)$ satisfies $|\mu_m - \lambda| \leq c\|\mathbf{x}_m - \mathbf{w}\|_2^2$, if the Rayleigh iteration converges. Interestingly, this quadratic dependence is not restricted to the sequence $\{\mathbf{x}_m\}$ generated by the Rayleigh iteration.

Theorem 5.21 *Suppose $A \in \mathbb{R}^{n \times n}$ is symmetric. Assume that we have a sequence $\{\mathbf{x}_m\}$ with $\|\mathbf{x}_m\|_2 = 1$, which converges to an eigenvector $\mathbf{w}$. Then we have*

$$|r(\mathbf{x}_m) - r(\mathbf{w})| = O(\|\mathbf{x}_m - \mathbf{w}\|_2^2), \qquad \mathbf{x}_m \to \mathbf{w}.$$

Proof As before let $\lambda_1 \geq \cdots \geq \lambda_n$ be the eigenvalues of A and $\mathbf{w}_1, \ldots, \mathbf{w}_n$ be the corresponding orthonormal eigenvectors, i.e. we have $A\mathbf{w}_j = \lambda_j \mathbf{w}_j$ and $\mathbf{w}_j^\mathsf{T} \mathbf{w}_k = \delta_{jk}$. Without restriction, we may assume that there is a $j \in \{1, \ldots, n\}$ such that $\mathbf{w} = \mathbf{w}_j$.

The representation $\mathbf{x}_m = \sum_k c_k \mathbf{w}_k$, suppressing the fact that $c_k = c_k^{(m)}$ depends also on m, gives $A\mathbf{x}_m = \sum_k c_k \lambda_k \mathbf{w}_k$ and, since $\|\mathbf{x}_m\|_2 = 1$,

$$r(\mathbf{x}_m) = \mathbf{x}_m^T A \mathbf{x}_m = \sum_{k=1}^{n} \lambda_k c_k^2.$$

This shows

$$r(\mathbf{x}_m) - r(\mathbf{w}) = \sum_{k=1}^{n} \lambda_k c_k^2 - \lambda_j = \lambda_j(c_j^2 - 1) + \sum_{k \neq j} \lambda_k c_k^2.$$

If we set $\epsilon = \|\mathbf{x}_m - \mathbf{w}\|_2^2$ then it obviously suffices to show that $c_j^2 - 1 = O(\epsilon^2)$ and $c_k = O(\epsilon)$ for $k \neq j$ and $m \to \infty$. The first property follows from

$$\epsilon^2 = \|\mathbf{x}_m - \mathbf{w}\|_2^2 = \|\mathbf{x}_m\|_2^2 + \|\mathbf{w}\|_2^2 - 2\mathbf{w}^T\mathbf{x}_m = 2(1 - c_j)$$

and hence

$$|c_j^2 - 1| = |(c_j - 1)(c_j + 1)| \le 2|c_j - 1| = \epsilon^2,$$

using $c_j^2 \le \sum_k c_k^2 = 1$. The second property then follows for all $k \neq j$, as we can conclude from $\sum_k c_k^2 = 1$ that

$$c_k^2 \le \sum_{\ell \neq j} c_\ell^2 = 1 - c_j^2 = |1 - c_j^2| \le \epsilon^2. \qquad \square$$

5.4 The Jacobi Method

Another iterative method goes back to Jacobi, who developed an algorithm for dealing with the eigenvalue problem for symmetric $n \times n$ matrices, which is still feasible if the matrices are not too big.

Certain versions of this algorithm can run in parallel (see for example Golub and Van Loan [66]), so that it sometimes outperforms on parallel computers even the otherwise superior QR method. It computes *all* eigenvalues and if necessary also all eigenvectors. It is based upon the following easy fact.

Lemma 5.22 *Let $A \in \mathbb{R}^{n \times n}$ be a symmetric matrix. For every orthogonal matrix $Q \in \mathbb{R}^{n \times n}$ both A and $Q^T A Q$ have the same Frobenius norm. If $\lambda_1, \ldots, \lambda_n$ are the eigenvalues of A then*

$$\sum_{j=1}^{n} |\lambda_j|^2 = \sum_{k,j=1}^{n} |a_{jk}|^2.$$

Proof The square of the Frobenius norm of A equals $\sum_{j,k} |a_{jk}|^2$ and this is precisely the trace of AA^T, see also Corollary 2.31. Since the trace of AB is the same as the trace of BA for two arbitrary matrices, we can conclude that

$$\|Q^T A Q\|_F^2 = \text{tr}(Q^T A Q Q^T A^T Q) = \text{tr}(Q^T A A^T Q)$$
$$= \text{tr}(A^T Q Q^T A) = \|A\|_F^2.$$

For a symmetric matrix A there is an orthogonal matrix Q, such that $Q^T A Q = D$ is a diagonal matrix having the eigenvalues of A as diagonal entries.   □

If we define the *outer norm*, which is not really a norm in the strict sense of Definition 1.6, by

$$N(A) := \sum_{j \neq k} |a_{jk}|^2,$$

then, Lemma 5.22 gives the decomposition

$$\sum_{j=1}^n |\lambda_j|^2 = \sum_{j=1}^n |a_{jj}|^2 + N(A). \tag{5.25}$$

Since the left-hand side is invariant to orthogonal transformations, it is now our goal to diminish $N(A)$ by choosing appropriate orthogonal transformations and thus by increasing $\sum |a_{jj}|^2$ to transform A into a diagonal matrix. To this end, we choose an element $a_{ij} \neq 0$ with $i \neq j$ and perform a transformation in the plane spanned by $\mathbf{e}_i$ and $\mathbf{e}_j$, which maps a_{ij} to zero. We can choose this transformation in $\mathbb{R}^2$ as a rotation with angle α. The resulting matrix

$$\begin{pmatrix} b_{ii} & b_{ij} \\ b_{ij} & b_{jj} \end{pmatrix} = \begin{pmatrix} \cos \alpha & \sin \alpha \\ -\sin \alpha & \cos \alpha \end{pmatrix} \begin{pmatrix} a_{ii} & a_{ij} \\ a_{ij} & a_{jj} \end{pmatrix} \begin{pmatrix} \cos \alpha & -\sin \alpha \\ \sin \alpha & \cos \alpha \end{pmatrix} \tag{5.26}$$

is a diagonal matrix if the non-diagonal element b_{ij} satisfies

$$0 = b_{ij} = a_{ij}(\cos^2 \alpha - \sin^2 \alpha) + (a_{jj} - a_{ii}) \cos \alpha \sin \alpha$$
$$= a_{ij} \cos(2\alpha) + (a_{jj} - a_{ii}) \frac{1}{2} \sin(2\alpha).$$

From $a_{ij} \neq 0$ we can conclude that the angle α is given by

$$\cot(2\alpha) = \frac{a_{ii} - a_{jj}}{2a_{ij}}. \tag{5.27}$$

For the implementation, it is better to avoid the calculation of the angle α by taking the inverse $\cot^{-1}$ in this formula and then its sine and cosine. Instead, one can first only compute

$$\theta := \frac{a_{ii} - a_{jj}}{2a_{ij}}.$$

Then, since we have the trigonometric identity $\tan^2\alpha + 2\cot(2\alpha)\tan\alpha = 1$, we see that $t := \tan\alpha$ satisfies the quadratic equation

$$t^2 + 2\theta t = 1,$$

which has two solutions $t_{1,2} = -\theta \pm \sqrt{1 + \theta^2}$. Considering numerical issues we should pick the one with smaller absolute value in a cancellation-avoiding form

$$t := -\theta + \text{sign}(\theta)\sqrt{1 + \theta^2} = \frac{\text{sign}(\theta)}{|\theta| + \sqrt{1 + \theta^2}}.$$

With this, we can compute all relevant quantities without using trigonometric functions,

$$c := \frac{1}{\sqrt{1 + t^2}} = \cos\alpha,$$
$$s := ct = \sin\alpha,$$
$$\tau := \frac{s}{1 + c} = \tan\left(\frac{\alpha}{2}\right),$$

where τ will be required later on. This solves the problem for 2×2 matrices. The general case is dealt with using Givens rotations.

Definition 5.23 Let $i, j \in \{1, \ldots, n\}$ and an angle α be given. Let $c = \cos\alpha$ and $s = \sin\alpha$. A *Givens rotation* $G_{ij}(\alpha) \in \mathbb{R}^{n\times n}$ is a matrix of the form

$$G_{ij}(\alpha) = I + (c - 1)(\mathbf{e}_j\mathbf{e}_j^\mathrm{T} + \mathbf{e}_i\mathbf{e}_i^\mathrm{T}) + s(\mathbf{e}_j\mathbf{e}_i^\mathrm{T} - \mathbf{e}_i\mathbf{e}_j^\mathrm{T})$$

$$= \begin{pmatrix} 1 & \vdots & & \vdots & \\ \cdots & c & \cdots & -s & \cdots \\ & \vdots & 1 & \vdots & \\ \cdots & s & \cdots & c & \cdots \\ & \vdots & & \vdots & 1 \end{pmatrix}.$$

Note that in the last equation of this definition we have assumed that $j > i$ to show what the Givens rotation looks like. This is, of course, not required.

Proposition 5.24 Let $A \in \mathbb{R}^{n\times n}$ be symmetric and $a_{ij} \neq 0$ for a pair $i \neq j$. If $B = G_{ij}^\mathrm{T}(\alpha)AG_{ij}(\alpha)$ with α determined by (5.27) then $b_{ij} = b_{ji} = 0$ and $N(B) = N(A) - 2|a_{ij}|^2$.

Proof The first part is clear. For the second part, we use the invariance property of the Frobenius norm twice. On the one hand, we have $\|A\|_F = \|B\|_F$. On the other hand, we also have equality of the norms for the small matrices in (5.26), which means

$$|a_{ii}|^2 + |a_{jj}|^2 + 2|a_{ij}|^2 = |b_{ii}|^2 + |b_{jj}|^2,$$

since $b_{ij} = 0$. From this, we can conclude that

$$N(B) = \|B\|_F^2 - \sum_{k=1}^n |b_{kk}|^2 = \|A\|_F^2 - \sum_{k=1}^n |b_{kk}|^2$$

$$= N(A) + \sum_{k=1}^n \left(|a_{kk}|^2 - |b_{kk}|^2 \right) = N(A) - 2|a_{ij}|^2,$$

since $a_{kk} = b_{kk}$ for all $k \neq i, j$. $\qquad\qquad\square$

The iteration of this process gives the classical Jacobi method for computing the eigenvalues of a symmetric matrix.

Definition 5.25 Let $A \in \mathbb{R}^{n \times n}$ be symmetric. The classical *Jacobi method* for computing the eigenvalues defines $A^{(0)} = A$ and then proceeds for $m = 0, 1, 2, \ldots$, as follows

1. Determine $i \neq j$ with $|a_{ij}^{(m)}| = \max_{\ell \neq k} |a_{\ell k}^{(m)}|$ and determine $G^{(m)} = G_{ij}$.
2. Set $A^{(m+1)} = G^{(m)T} A G^{(m)}$.

For practical computations we will again avoid matrix multiplication and code the transformations directly, see Algorithm 12. Furthermore, we will use the following identities to compute the ith and jth row and column, which follow after some trigonometric manipulations from (5.26). We have $b_{ij} = b_{ji} = 0$ and

$$b_{ii} = a_{ii} - t a_{ij},$$
$$b_{jj} = a_{jj} + t a_{ij},$$
$$b_{i\ell} = b_{\ell i} = c a_{i\ell} + s a_{j\ell} = a_{i\ell} + s(a_{j\ell} - \tau a_{i\ell}), \qquad \ell \neq i, j,$$
$$b_{j\ell} = b_{\ell j} = -s a_{i\ell} + c a_{j\ell} = a_{j\ell} - s(a_{i\ell} + \tau a_{j\ell}), \qquad \ell \neq i, j,$$

where we have used the previous abbreviations $s = \sin \alpha$, $c = \cos \alpha$, $t = \tan \alpha$ and $\tau = \tan(\alpha/2)$, which can be computed without using trigonometric functions, as explained above. In the implementation in Algorithm 12 we have used two additional vectors $\mathbf{b}i$ and $\mathbf{b}j$ to store the relevant update information temporarily before overwriting the old matrix.

Note that an element which has been mapped to zero in an earlier step might be changed again in later steps.

Theorem 5.26 *The classical Jacobi method converges linearly in the outer norm.*

Algorithm 12: Jacobi method for computing eigenvalues

Input : $A \in \mathbb{R}^{n \times n}$.

Output: Approximate eigenvalues of A.

1   $norm := N(A)$

2   **while** $norm > \epsilon$ **do**

3   Determine (i, j) with $|a_{ij}| = \max_{\ell \neq k} |a_{\ell k}|$

4   **if** $|a_{ij}| \neq 0$ **then**

5         $\theta := 0.5 \cdot (a_{ii} - a_{jj})/a_{ij}$

6         $t := \text{sign}(\theta)/(|\theta| + \sqrt{1 + \theta \cdot \theta})$

7         $c := 1/\sqrt{1 + t \cdot t}, \quad s := c \cdot t$

8         $bi_j := 0, \quad bj_i := 0$

9         $bi_i := a_{ii} - t \cdot a_{ij}, \quad bj_j := a_{jj} + t \cdot a_{ij}$

10   **for** $\ell = 1$ **to** n **do**

11   **if** $\ell \neq i$ **and** $\ell \neq j$ **then**

12             $bi_\ell := c \cdot a_{i\ell} + s \cdot a_{j\ell}$

13             $bj_\ell := -s \cdot a_{i\ell} + c \cdot a_{j\ell}$

14        $norm := norm - 2 \cdot a_{ij} \cdot a_{ij}$

15   **for** $\ell = 1$ **to** n **do**

16           $a_{i\ell} := a_{\ell i} := bi_\ell$

17           $a_{j\ell} := a_{\ell j} := bj_\ell$

Proof We have to look at one step of the method, i.e. at the transformation from A to $B = G_{ij}^{\text{T}} A G_{ij}$. Since $|a_{ij}| \geq |a_{\ell k}|$ for all $\ell \neq k$, we have

$$N(A) = \sum_{\ell \neq k} |a_{\ell k}|^2 \leq n(n - 1)|a_{ij}|^2.$$

Thus, we can bound the outer norm by

$$N(B) = N(A) - 2|a_{ij}|^2 \leq N(A) - \frac{2}{n(n-1)} N(A) = \left(1 - \frac{2}{n(n-1)}\right) N(A),$$

which means linear convergence.   □

Convergence in the outer norm does not necessarily mean convergence of the eigenvalues, since the elements on the diagonal can still permute. However, every convergent sub-sequence converges to a diagonal matrix having the eigenvalues of A as its diagonal entries. Another way of formulating this is as follows.

Corollary 5.27 *If $\lambda_1 \geq \lambda_2 \geq \cdots \geq \lambda_n$ are the eigenvalues of the symmetric matrix A and if $\tilde{a}_{11}^{(m)} \geq \tilde{a}_{22}^{(m)} \geq \cdots \geq \tilde{a}_{nn}^{(m)}$ is an appropriate permutation of the diagonal elements of $A^{(m)}$ then*

$$|\lambda_i - \tilde{a}_{ii}^{(m)}| \leq \sqrt{N(A^{(m)})} \to 0, \qquad for \ 1 \leq i \leq n \ and \ m \to \infty.$$

Proof If we define $B = \mathrm{diag}(\tilde{a}_{11}^{(m)}, \ldots, \tilde{a}_{nn}^{(m)})$ then we have by Corollary 5.7 the estimate

$$|\lambda_j - \tilde{a}_{jj}^{(m)}| = |\lambda_j(A) - \lambda_j(B)| \leq \|A - B\|_F = \|A^{(m)} - B\|_F = N(A^{(m)})^{1/2}. \quad \square$$

Remark 5.28 One step of the classical Jacobi method takes $O(n^2)$ time to find the maximum element and then $O(n)$ time to update the matrix.

Since the cost for finding the maximum element is critical, there are cheaper versions. For example, the *cyclic Jacobi method* visits all non-diagonal entries regardless of their sizes in a cyclic way, i.e. the index pair (i, j) is cyclically chosen as $(1, 2), (1, 3), \ldots, (1, n), (2, 3), \ldots, (2, n), (3, 4), \ldots$ and then the process starts again with $(1, 2)$ and so on. A transformation only takes place if $a_{ij} \neq 0$. The cyclic version is convergent and in the case of pairwise distinct eigenvalues even quadratically convergent if one complete cycle is considered to be one step (see Henrici [82]).
For small values of a_{ij} it is not efficient to perform a transformation. Thus, we can restrict ourselves to elements a_{ij} having a square above a certain threshold, for example $N(A)/(2n^2)$. Since then

$$N(B) \leq N(A)\left(1 - \frac{1}{n^2}\right)$$

we still have linear convergence in the outer norm for the cyclic Jacobi method with thresholding.
Finally, let us have a look at the eigenvectors. Since the matrices

$$A^{(m+1)} = G^{(m)\mathrm{T}} A^{(m)} G^{(m)} = G^{(m)\mathrm{T}} \cdots G^{(1)\mathrm{T}} A G^{(1)} \cdots G^{(m)} =: Q_m^\mathrm{T} A Q_m$$

are, at least for sufficiently large m, almost diagonal, we see that the columns of Q_m define approximate eigenvectors of A.

Corollary 5.29 *If the columns of Q_m are sorted as proposed in Corollary 5.27 and if the eigenvalues of A are pairwise distinct, then the columns of Q_m converge to a complete basis of orthonormal eigenvectors of A. If the eigenvalues are not pairwise distinct then every accumulation point gives an orthonormal basis of eigenvectors.*

5.5 Householder Reduction to Hessenberg Form

In the next section, we want to use the QR factorisation of a matrix A from Section 3.6 to compute its eigenvalues in an iterative process. As we have to use in this process similarity transformations which do not change the eigenvalues, our transformations have to be of the form QAQ^T with orthogonal Q. The first, immediate idea, however, faces the following problem.

Suppose we choose a Householder matrix $H = H(\mathbf{w})$ such that the first column of A is mapped to a multiple of the first unit vector, i.e. $HA\mathbf{e}_1 = \alpha_1\mathbf{e}_1$. Then, HAH^T will in general be full again, i.e. all the zeros created by pre-multiplication with H are destroyed again by the post-multiplication with H. This simply comes from the fact that multiplication from the right particularly means that the first column is replaced by linear combinations of all columns. Hence we have to modify this approach. To this end, let us write

$$A = \begin{pmatrix} a_{11} & \mathbf{b}^T \\ \tilde{\mathbf{a}}_1 & \tilde{A} \end{pmatrix}$$

with $a_{11} \in \mathbb{R}$, $\tilde{\mathbf{a}}_1, \mathbf{b} \in \mathbb{R}^{n-1}$ and $\tilde{A} \in \mathbb{R}^{(n-1)\times(n-1)}$. Then, we can choose a Householder matrix $\tilde{H}_1 \in \mathbb{R}^{(n-1)\times(n-1)}$ with $\tilde{H}_1\tilde{\mathbf{a}}_1 = \alpha_1\mathbf{e}_1$, and define the orthogonal and symmetric matrix

$$H_1 = \begin{pmatrix} 1 & \mathbf{0}^T \\ \mathbf{0} & \tilde{H}_1 \end{pmatrix}.$$

This time, pre- and post-multiplication with H_1 yields

$$H_1 A H_1 = \begin{pmatrix} 1 & \mathbf{0}^T \\ \mathbf{0} & \tilde{H}_1 \end{pmatrix}\begin{pmatrix} a_{11} & \mathbf{b}^T \\ \tilde{\mathbf{a}}_1 & \tilde{A} \end{pmatrix}\begin{pmatrix} 1 & \mathbf{0}^T \\ \mathbf{0} & \tilde{H}_1 \end{pmatrix} = \begin{pmatrix} a_{11} & \mathbf{b}^T \\ \alpha_1\mathbf{e}_1 & \tilde{H}_1\tilde{A} \end{pmatrix}\begin{pmatrix} 1 & \mathbf{0}^T \\ \mathbf{0} & \tilde{H}_1 \end{pmatrix}$$

$$= \begin{pmatrix} a_{11} & \mathbf{b}^T\tilde{H}_1 \\ \alpha_1\mathbf{e}_1 & \tilde{H}_1\tilde{A}\tilde{H}_1 \end{pmatrix} = \begin{pmatrix} a_{11} & \mathbf{b}^T\tilde{H}_1 \\ \alpha_1\mathbf{e}_1 & A_2 \end{pmatrix}$$

with $A_2 \in \mathbb{R}^{(n-1)\times(n-1)}$. This means we have kept almost all the zeros in the first column except for the one directly under the diagonal. If we proceed like this now, we derive in the next step a transformation of the form

$$H_2 H_1 A H_1 H_2 = \begin{pmatrix} * & * & & \cdots & * \\ * & * & * & \cdots & * \\ 0 & * & & & \\ 0 & 0 & & & \\ \vdots & \vdots & & & \\ 0 & 0 & & & \end{pmatrix},$$

and continuing all the way down finally yields a representation

$$H_{n-2} \cdots H_1 A H_1 \cdots H_{n-2} = \begin{pmatrix} * & \cdots & \cdots & * \\ * & \ddots & & \vdots \\ & \ddots & \ddots & \vdots \\ 0 & & * & * \end{pmatrix}.$$

Such a matrix is almost an upper triangular matrix. We have only one sub-diagonal band which might be different from zero. A matrix of this form is called a Hessenberg matrix or a matrix in Hessenberg form. We can define this even for non-square matrices.

Definition 5.30 A matrix $B \in \mathbb{R}^{m \times n}$ is of *Hessenberg form* if $b_{ij} = 0$ for all $i > j + 1$.

Hence, the above contemplations give the following result.

Theorem 5.31 *Any matrix* $A \in \mathbb{R}^{n \times n}$ *can be transformed into a Hessenberg matrix using* $n - 2$ *Householder transformations in* $O(n^3)$ *time.*

Proof We only have to analyse the computational cost. In the kth step, we have to multiply a Householder matrix $H_k \in \mathbb{R}^{(n-k) \times (n-k)}$ by the significant part of the current matrix both from the left and from the right. According to Lemma 3.31, this can be done in $O((n-k)^2)$ time. Hence, the total time required is given by

$$\sum_{k=1}^{n-2} O((n-k)^2) = O(n^3). \qquad \square$$

We can easily construct the algorithm from the above proof. As we have done before, we want to overwrite the matrix A with its Hessenberg form $H = H_{n-2} \cdots H_1 A H_1 \cdots H_{n-2}$ during the process. In step k we have the relevant information given by $H_k = \mathrm{diag}(I_k, \tilde{H}_k)$, where $I_k \in \mathbb{R}^{k \times k}$ denotes the identity on $\mathbb{R}^k$ and $\tilde{H}_k = I_{n-k} - \beta_k \mathbf{u}_k \mathbf{u}_k^{\mathrm{T}}$ with $\mathbf{u}_k = (u_{k+1}^{(k)}, u_{k+2}^{(k)}, \dots, u_n^{(k)})^{\mathrm{T}}$ is a Householder matrix. As in the case of the QR factorisation, there is not enough space in A to store all the relevant information.

A possible way of using the available space is as follows. We can store the partial vector $(u_{k+2}^{(k)}, \dots, u_n^{(k)})$ within the free $n-k-1$ positions of the kth column of A and $u_{k+1}^{(k)}$ and β_k for $1 \le k \le n - 2$ as the kth component of new vectors $\mathbf{d}$ and β in $\mathbb{R}^{n-2}$. Details are given in Algorithm 13, where lines 2 to 9 represent the computation of $\tilde{H}_k$ and the remaining lines deal with the actual update step.

Algorithm 13: Hessenberg reduction

Input : $A \in \mathbb{R}^{n \times n}$.

Output: Hessenberg form of A.

1   **for** $k = 1$ **to** $n - 2$ **do**

2      $norm := \max_{k+1 \leq i \leq n} |a_{ik}|$

3   **if** $norm = 0$ **then** $d_k := 0, \quad \beta_k := 0$

4   **else**

5         $\alpha := 0$

6   **for** $i = k + 1$ **to** n **do**

7            $a_{ik} := a_{ik}/norm, \quad \alpha := \alpha + a_{ik} \cdot a_{ik}$

8         $\alpha := \sqrt{\alpha}, \quad \beta_k := 1/[\alpha(\alpha + |a_{k+1,k}|)]$

9         $d_k := -\text{sign}(a_{k+1,k})\alpha \cdot norm, \quad a_{k+1,k} := \text{sign}(a_{k+1,k})\alpha$

10   **for** $j = k + 1$ **to** n **do**

11           $s := \beta_k \cdot \sum_{i=k+1}^{n} a_{ik} \cdot a_{ij}$

12   **for** $i = k + 1$ **to** n **do** $a_{ij} := a_{ij} - s \cdot a_{ik}$

13   **for** $i = 1$ **to** n **do**

14           $s := \beta_k \cdot \sum_{j=k+1}^{n} a_{ij} \cdot a_{jk}$

15   **for** $j = k + 1$ **to** n **do** $a_{ij} := a_{ij} - s \cdot a_{jk}$

16   Exchange $a_{k+1,k}$ and d_k

At the end of the algorithm, the matrix A and the vectors $\mathbf{d}, \beta$ have the following form

$$
A = \begin{pmatrix}
h_{11} & h_{12} & \cdots & \cdots & h_{1,n-1} & h_{1n} \\
h_{21} & h_{22} & \cdots & \cdots & h_{2,n-1} & h_{2n} \\
u_3^{(1)} & h_{32} & \cdots & \cdots & h_{3,n-1} & h_{3n} \\
u_4^{(1)} & u_4^{(2)} & \ddots & \cdots & h_{4,n-1} & h_{4n} \\
\vdots & \vdots & \ddots & \ddots & \vdots & \vdots \\
u_n^{(1)} & u_n^{(2)} & \cdots & u_n^{(n-2)} & h_{n,n-1} & h_{nn}
\end{pmatrix}, \quad
\mathbf{d} = \begin{pmatrix}
u_2^{(1)} \\
u_3^{(2)} \\
\vdots \\
u_{n-1}^{(n-2)}
\end{pmatrix}, \quad
\beta = \begin{pmatrix}
\beta_1 \\
\beta_2 \\
\vdots \\
\beta_{n-2}
\end{pmatrix},
$$

from which all the relevant information can be retrieved.

We now want to have a closer look at the situation when $A \in \mathbb{R}^{n \times n}$ is symmetric. In this case its Hessenberg form must be a tridiagonal matrix. It is hence quite natural to assume that the reduction of a symmetric matrix to its Hessenberg form is significantly cheaper than the general case.

Let us assume that $A = A^{\mathrm{T}} \in \mathbb{R}^{n \times n}$ has already been transformed using the $k - 1$

Householder matrices $H_1, \ldots, H_{k-1}$, i.e. we have

$$H_{k-1} \cdots H_1 A H_1 \cdots H_{k-1} = \begin{pmatrix} A_k & & O^{\mathrm{T}} \\ & & \mathbf{a}_k^{\mathrm{T}} \\ O & \mathbf{a}_k & C_k \end{pmatrix},$$

where A_k is a $k \times k$ tridiagonal matrix, C_k is a $(n-k) \times (n-k)$ matrix, $\mathbf{a}_k \in \mathbb{R}^{n-k}$ and O represents a zero matrix of dimension $(n-k) \times (k-1)$. Then, we can pick a Householder matrix $\tilde{H}_k \in \mathbb{R}^{(n-k) \times (n-k)}$, set $H_k := \mathrm{diag}(I_k, \tilde{H}_k)$ and derive

$$H_k \cdots H_1 A H_1 \cdots H_k = \begin{pmatrix} A_k & & O^{\mathrm{T}} \\ & & \mathbf{a}_k^{\mathrm{T}} \tilde{H}_k \\ O & \tilde{H}_k \mathbf{a}_k & \tilde{H}_k C_k \tilde{H}_k \end{pmatrix}.$$

Obviously, we will pick $\tilde{H}_k$ such that $\tilde{H}_k \mathbf{a}_k$ is again a multiple of the first unit vector. We can now use the symmetry to compute the product $\tilde{H}_k C_k \tilde{H}_k$ efficiently. Assume that $\tilde{H}_k = I - \beta_k \mathbf{u}_k \mathbf{u}_k^{\mathrm{T}}$ with $\beta_k = 2/\|\mathbf{u}_k\|_2^2$. If we now define the vector $\mathbf{p}_k := \beta_k C_k \mathbf{u}_k$, we find

$$\begin{aligned} \tilde{H}_k C_k \tilde{H}_k &= [I - \beta_k \mathbf{u}_k \mathbf{u}_k^{\mathrm{T}}] C_k [I - \beta_k \mathbf{u}_k \mathbf{u}_k^{\mathrm{T}}] \\ &= [I - \beta_k \mathbf{u}_k \mathbf{u}_k^{\mathrm{T}}][C_k - \mathbf{p}_k \mathbf{u}_k^{\mathrm{T}}] \\ &= C_k - \mathbf{u}_k \mathbf{p}_k^{\mathrm{T}} - \mathbf{p}_k \mathbf{u}_k^{\mathrm{T}} + \beta_k \mathbf{u}_k^{\mathrm{T}} \mathbf{p}_k \mathbf{u}_k \mathbf{u}_k^{\mathrm{T}} \\ &= C_k - \mathbf{u}_k \mathbf{w}_k^{\mathrm{T}} - \mathbf{w}_k \mathbf{u}_k^{\mathrm{T}} \end{aligned}$$

with

$$\mathbf{w}_k = \mathbf{p}_k - \frac{\beta_k \mathbf{u}_k^{\mathrm{T}} \mathbf{p}_k}{2} \mathbf{u}_k.$$

Using this, we can derive an algorithm as given in Algorithm 14. Here, we store the diagonal elements and the sub-diagonal elements in two vectors $\boldsymbol{\delta} = (\delta_1, \ldots, \delta_n)^{\mathrm{T}} \in \mathbb{R}^n$ and $\boldsymbol{\gamma} = (\gamma_1, \ldots, \gamma_{n-1})^{\mathrm{T}} \in \mathbb{R}^{n-1}$. The information on the Householder transformation $\tilde{H}_k = I - \beta_k \mathbf{u}_k \mathbf{u}_k^{\mathrm{T}}$ can be stored in the kth column of A by storing β_k as the kth diagonal element and $\mathbf{u}_k \in \mathbb{R}^{n-k}$ in the part of the kth column below the diagonal.

5.6 The QR Algorithm

This method aims at computing all eigenvalues of a given matrix $A \in \mathbb{R}^{n \times n}$ simultaneously. It benefits from the Hessenberg form of a matrix and can be accelerated by shifts. It is extremely efficient, particularly for symmetric matrices. It is also possible to derive the eigenvectors by accumulating certain transformation matrices. It goes back to Francis [56, 57].

Algorithm 14: Hessenberg reduction of a symmetric matrix

Input : $A = A^T \in \mathbb{R}^{n \times n}$.

Output: Tridiagonal matrix.

1 **for** $k = 1$ **to** $n - 2$ **do**

2     $\delta_k := a_{kk}$

3     $norm := \max_{k+1 \le i \le n} |a_{ik}|$

4   **if** $norm = 0$ **then** $a_{kk} := 0, \quad \gamma_k := 0$

5   **else**

6        $\alpha := 0$

7   **for** $i = k + 1$ **to** n **do**

8           $a_{ik} := a_{ik}/norm, \quad \alpha := \alpha + a_{ik} \cdot a_{ik}$

9        $\alpha := \sqrt{\alpha}, \quad a_{kk} := 1/[\alpha(\alpha + |a_{k+1,k}|)]$

10       $\gamma_k := -\text{sign}(a_{k+1,k}) \cdot \alpha \cdot norm, \quad a_{k+1,k} := a_{k+1,k} + \text{sign}(a_{k+1,k}) \cdot \alpha$

11       $s := 0$

12   **for** $i = k + 1$ **to** n **do**

13          $\gamma_i := a_{kk} \left(\sum_{j=k+1}^{i} a_{ij} \cdot a_{jk} + \sum_{j=i+1}^{n} a_{ji} \cdot a_{jk} \right)$

14          $s := s + \gamma_i \cdot a_{ik}$

15       $s := 0.5 \cdot a_{kk} \cdot s$

16   **for** $i = k + 1$ **to** n **do** $\gamma_i := \gamma_i - s \cdot a_{ik}$

17   **for** $i = k + 1$ **to** n **do**

18   **for** $j = k + 1$ **to** i **do**

19             $a_{ij} := a_{ij} - a_{ik} \cdot \gamma_j - a_{jk} \cdot \gamma_i$

20 $\delta_{n-1} := a_{n-1,n-1}, \quad \delta_n := a_{nn}, \quad \gamma_{n-1} := a_{n,n-1}$

Definition 5.32 (*QR* method) Let $A_0 := A \in \mathbb{R}^{n \times n}$. For $m = 0, 1, \ldots$ decompose A_m in the form $A_m = Q_m R_m$ with an orthogonal matrix Q_m and an upper triangular matrix R_m. Then, form the swapped product

$$A_{m+1} := R_m Q_m.$$

Since $Q_m^T A_m = R_m$ we obviously have

$$A_{m+1} = Q_m^T A_m Q_m, \tag{5.28}$$

showing that all matrices A_m have the same eigenvalues as $A_0 = A$.

For the analysis of the convergence of the *QR* method, we need to recall that the *QR* factorisation of a matrix is unique if the signs of the diagonal elements of

R are prescribed, see Theorem 3.35. This means particularly that the mapping $A \to Q$ is continuous.

Lemma 5.33   *For $A \in \mathbb{R}^{n \times n}$ invertible let $A = QR$ be the unique QR factorisation with orthogonal $Q \in \mathbb{R}^{n \times n}$ and upper triangular $R \in \mathbb{R}^{n \times n}$ with positive diagonal entries. Then, the mapping $A \mapsto Q$ is continuous.*

Proof   We start by looking at the Cholesky factorisation of a symmetric and positive definite matrix $B \in \mathbb{R}^{n \times n}$, i.e. $B = LL^{\mathrm{T}}$ with a lower triangular matrix L. We will show that this factorisation is unique and that the mapping $B \mapsto L$ is continuous.

In the process of deriving the Cholesky factorisation, we have seen that the LU factorisation can be written as $B = LDL^{\mathrm{T}}$ with a diagonal matrix D with positive elements. This means that the factors L and $U = DL^{\mathrm{T}}$ are uniquely determined by the uniqueness of the LU factorisation. Hence, D is uniquely determined and if we take the positive square root, we see that $\tilde{L} = LD^{1/2}$ is the unique L matrix with positive elements of the Cholesky factorisation of B. To see that $B \mapsto L$ is continuous we use induction by n. For $n = 1$, we have $B = (\beta)$ with $\beta > 0$ and $L = (\sqrt{\beta})$ which obviously depends continuously on β. Hence, let us assume that the statement is true for all symmetric and positive definite $(n - 1) \times (n - 1)$ matrices. We decompose B and L into

$$B = \begin{pmatrix} \beta & \mathbf{b}^{\mathrm{T}} \\ \mathbf{b} & \hat{B} \end{pmatrix}, \qquad L = \begin{pmatrix} \gamma & \mathbf{0}^{\mathrm{T}} \\ \boldsymbol{\ell} & \hat{L} \end{pmatrix}$$

with $\hat{B} \in \mathbb{R}^{(n-1) \times (n-1)}$ symmetric and positive definite, $\hat{L} \in \mathbb{R}^{(n-1) \times (n-1)}$ lower triangular with positive diagonal elements and $\mathbf{b}, \boldsymbol{\ell} \in \mathbb{R}^{n-1}, \beta, \gamma \in \mathbb{R}$. With this notation the equation $B = LL^{\mathrm{T}}$ immediately gives $\gamma = \sqrt{\beta}$ and $\boldsymbol{\ell} = \mathbf{b}/\gamma = \mathbf{b}/\sqrt{\beta}$ which shows that both depend continuously on B. We also have $\hat{B} = \hat{L}\hat{L}^{\mathrm{T}} + \boldsymbol{\ell}\boldsymbol{\ell}^{\mathrm{T}}$ so that $B \mapsto \hat{L}\hat{L}^{\mathrm{T}} = \hat{B} - \boldsymbol{\ell}\boldsymbol{\ell}^{\mathrm{T}} = \hat{B} - \mathbf{b}\mathbf{b}^{\mathrm{T}}/\beta$ maps continuously into the set of symmetric and positive definite $(n-1) \times (n-1)$ matrices. By induction we know that the mapping $\hat{L}\hat{L}^{\mathrm{T}} \to \hat{L}$ is continuous and hence the mapping $B \to L$ is continuous.

Finally, let $A \in \mathbb{R}^{n \times n}$ be a non-singular matrix with unique QR factorisation $A = QR$, where R has positive diagonal entries. Then the matrix $B = A^{\mathrm{T}}A$ is symmetric and positive definite and has hence a unique Cholesky factorisation $A^{\mathrm{T}}A = LL^{\mathrm{T}} = \hat{R}^{\mathrm{T}}\hat{R}$ with a unique upper triangular matrix $\hat{R} = L^{\mathrm{T}}$ with positive diagonal elements. From this uniqueness and $A^{\mathrm{T}}A = (QR)^{\mathrm{T}}(QR) = R^{\mathrm{T}}R$ we can conclude that $R = \hat{R}$ depends continuously on A. Finally, $A \mapsto Q = AR^{-1}$ is also continuous, as $R \mapsto R^{-1}$ obviously is.   □

Obviously, the proof of the previous lemma also showed the uniqueness of the Cholesky factorisation of a symmetric and positive definite matrix.

Lemma 5.34 *Let $D := \text{diag}(d_1, \ldots, d_n) \in \mathbb{R}^{n \times n}$ be a diagonal matrix with*

$$|d_j| > |d_{j+1}| > 0, \qquad 1 \le j \le n - 1,$$

and let $L = (\ell_{ij}) \in \mathbb{R}^{n \times n}$ be a normalised lower triangular matrix. Let L_m^* denote the lower triangular matrix with entries $\ell_{ij} d_i^m / d_j^m$ for $i \ge j$. Then, we have

$$D^m L = L_m^* D^m, \qquad m \in \mathbb{N}_0.$$

Furthermore, L_m^* converges linearly to the identity matrix for $m \to \infty$. The asymptotic error coefficient is at most $\max_{2 \le i \le n} |d_i| / |d_{i-1}|$, i.e.

$$\|L_m^* - I\|_\infty \le \left(\max_{2 \le i \le n} \left| \frac{d_i}{d_{i-1}} \right| \right)^m \|L - I\|_\infty.$$

Proof The identity $D^m L = L_m^* D$ immediately follows from the fact that multiplication by a diagonal matrix from the left means scaling the rows while multiplication from the right means scaling the columns. Moreover, as L is normalised, we have

$$\|L_m^* - I\|_\infty = \max_{1 \le i \le n} \sum_{j=1}^i \left| \frac{\ell_{ij} d_i^m}{d_j^m} - 1 \right| = \max_{2 \le i \le n} \sum_{j=1}^{i-1} \left| \ell_{ij} \frac{d_i^m}{d_j^m} \right|$$

$$\le \max_{2 \le i \le n} \left| \frac{d_i}{d_{i-1}} \right|^m \sum_{j=1}^{i-1} |\ell_{ij}| \le \max_{2 \le i \le n} \left| \frac{d_i}{d_{i-1}} \right|^m \|L - I\|_\infty,$$

from which the convergence result follows. $\square$

With this result at hand, we can now prove convergence of the *QR* method for computing the eigenvalues of a matrix under some additional assumptions. These assumptions mean in particular that A has only simple eigenvalues. For a real matrix this also means that all eigenvalues are real. The latter is not too surprising, as in the situation of complex eigenvalues, Theorem 3.39 tells us that we cannot expect to find an orthogonal matrix $Q \in \mathbb{R}^{n \times n}$ with $Q^T A Q$ being upper triangular.

Theorem 5.35 *Assume that the eigenvalues of the matrix $A \in \mathbb{R}^{n \times n}$ can be sorted as $|\lambda_1| > |\lambda_2| > \cdots > |\lambda_n| > 0$. Let T be the matrix of corresponding eigenvectors of A. Assume that T^{-1} possesses an LU factorisation without pivoting. Then, the matrices $A_m = (a_{ij}^{(m)})$ created by the QR algorithm satisfy the following conditions.*

- *The sub-diagonal elements converge to zero, i.e. $a_{ij}^{(m)} \to 0$ for $m \to \infty$ for all $i > j$.*
- *The diagonal elements converge to the eigenvalues, i.e. $a_{ii}^{(m)} \to \lambda_i$ for $m \to \infty$ for all $1 \le i \le n$.*
- *The sequences $\{A_{2m}\}$ and $\{A_{2m+1}\}$ converge to upper triangular matrices.*

Furthermore, the sequence $\{Q_m\}$ converges to an orthogonal diagonal matrix, i.e. to an diagonal matrix having only 1 or -1 on the diagonal.

Proof We already know that all generated matrices A_m have the same eigenvalues as A. If we use the notation $R_{m...0} = R_m \cdots R_0$ and $Q_{0...m} = Q_0 \cdots Q_m$, then we have

$$A_m = Q_{m-1}^T A_{m-1} Q_{m-1} = Q_{m-1}^T Q_{m-2}^T A_{m-2} Q_{m-2} Q_{m-1} = \cdots = Q_{0...m-1}^T A Q_{0...m-1}.$$

By induction we can also show that the powers of A have a similar decomposition. To be more precise, we have $A^m = Q_{0...m-1} R_{m-1...0}$. This is clear for $m = 1$ and for $m + 1$ it follows via

$$A^{m+1} = A A^m = A Q_{0...m-1} R_{m-1...0} = Q_{0...m-1} A_m R_{m-1...0} = Q_{0...m} R_{m...0}.$$

However, this QR factorisation $A^m = Q_{0...m-1} R_{m-1...0}$ is, by Theorem 3.35, unique provided that A^m is non-singular and that we assume that all upper triangular matrices R_i have, for example, positive diagonal elements.

If we define $D = \mathrm{diag}(\lambda_1, \ldots, \lambda_n)$, we have the relation $AT = TD$, which leads to $A^m = TD^m T^{-1}$. By assumption, we have an LU factorisation of T^{-1}, i.e. $T^{-1} = LR$ with a normalised lower triangular matrix L and an upper triangular matrix R. This gives to

$$A^m = TD^m LR.$$

By Lemma 5.34, there is a sequence $\{L_m^*\}$ of lower triangular matrices, which converges to I and which satisfy $D^m L = L_m^* D^m$, which yields the representation

$$A^m = T L_m^* D^m R.$$

Using a QR factorisation $T = \tilde{Q}\tilde{R}$ of T with positive diagonal elements in $\tilde{R}$ finally gives

$$A^m = \tilde{Q}\tilde{R} L_m^* D^m R. \tag{5.29}$$

Since the matrices L_m^* converge to I, the matrices $\tilde{R} L_m^*$ have to converge to $\tilde{R}$. If we now compute a QR factorisation of $\tilde{R} L_m^*$ as $\tilde{R} L_m^* = Q_m^{**} R_m^{**}$, again with positive diagonal elements in R_m^{**} then we can conclude that $Q_m^{**} R_m^{**}$ converges to $\tilde{R}$

so that Lemma 5.33 shows that Q_m^{**} converges to the identity matrix. Equation (5.29) can hence be rewritten as

$$A^m = \tilde{Q} Q_m^{**} R_m^{**} D^m R.$$

Next, let us introduce diagonal matrices $\Delta_m := \text{diag}(s_1^{(m)}, \ldots, s_n^{(m)})$ with entries $s_i^{(m)} := \text{sign}(\lambda_i^m r_{ii})$, where r_{ii} are the diagonal elements of R. Then, because of $\Delta_m^2 = I$, we can rewrite the representation of A^m as

$$A^m = (\tilde{Q} Q_m^{**} \Delta_m)(\Delta_m R_m^{**} D^m R). \tag{5.30}$$

Since the signs of the diagonal elements of the upper triangular matrix $R_m^{**} D^m R$ coincide with those of $D^m R$ and hence with those of Δ_m, we see that (5.30) is a QR factorisation of A^m with positive diagonal elements in the upper triangular matrix.

If we compare this QR factorisation to the factorisation $A^m = Q_{0\ldots m-1} R_{m-1\ldots 0}$ we can thus conclude that

$$Q_{0\ldots m-1} = \tilde{Q} Q_m^{**} \Delta_m. \tag{5.31}$$

Since Q_m^{**} converges to the identity matrix, the matrices $Q_{0\ldots m}$ must become constant for sufficiently large m and up to the sign of the columns. From $A_m = Q_{0\ldots m-1}^T A Q_{0\ldots m-1}$ and (5.31) we can derive

$$A_m = Q_{0\ldots m-1}^{-1} A\, Q_{0\ldots m-1} = \Delta_m Q_m^{**-1} \tilde{Q}^{-1} A \tilde{Q} Q_m^{**} \Delta_m$$
$$= \Delta_m \underbrace{Q_m^{**-1}}_{\to I} \underbrace{\tilde{R} T^{-1} A T \tilde{R}^{-1}}_{=D} \underbrace{Q_m^{**}}_{\to I} \Delta_m.$$

If m tends to infinity then, because of $\Delta_{2m} = \Delta_0$ and $\Delta_{2m+1} = \Delta_1$, we can conclude the convergence of $\{A_{2m}\}$ and $\{A_{2m+1}\}$ to $\Delta_0 \tilde{R} D \tilde{R}^{-1} \Delta_0$ and $\Delta_1 \tilde{R} D \tilde{R}^{-1} \Delta_1$, respectively. Since both limit matrices have the form

$$\begin{pmatrix} \lambda_1 & * & \cdots & & * \\ & \lambda_n & & & \vdots \\ & & \ddots & & * \\ & & & & \lambda_n \end{pmatrix}$$

we have also proven the first two statements.

Finally, using the convergence of Q_m^{**} to the identity matrix again and

$$Q_m = Q_{0\ldots m-1}^{-1} Q_{0\ldots m} = \Delta_m^{-1} (Q_m^{**})^{-1} \tilde{Q}^{-1} \tilde{Q} Q_{m+1}^{**} \Delta_{m+1}$$

we see that Q_m converges to Δ_1. $\qquad\square$

There are several things to mention here. Obviously, we have the following computational cost. In each step, we have to compute a QR factorisation, which will cost us $O(n^3)$ time. Then, we have to form the new iteration A_{m+1} which is done by multiplying two full matrices, which also costs $O(n^3)$ time. Both are too expensive if a large number of steps is required or the matrix dimension n is too large.

As already indicated in the last section, it is possible to improve this performance significantly by reducing the matrix A first to its Hessenberg form. This still may cost $O(n^3)$ time but it is required only once.

After this pre-processing step, it is important to see that the QR algorithm respects the specific form and that we can compute both the QR factorisation and the product RQ in each step efficiently. We will explain how this works with special emphasis on symmetric Hessenberg matrices, i.e. tridiagonal matrices.

Theorem 5.36 *Suppose $A_m \in \mathbb{R}^{n \times n}$ is a symmetric tridiagonal matrix. Then, it is possible to compute the QR factorisation of $A_m = Q_m R_m$ in $O(n)$ time. The next iteration of the QR algorithm $A_{m+1} = R_m Q_m$ is also a symmetric tridiagonal matrix and can be computed in linear time, as well.*

Proof The symmetry of A_{m+1} follows immediately from (5.28). Suppose A_m has the form

$$A_m = \begin{pmatrix} * & * & 0 & \cdots & 0 \\ * & * & * & & \vdots \\ 0 & \ddots & \ddots & \ddots & 0 \\ \vdots & & * & * & * \\ 0 & \cdots & 0 & * & * \end{pmatrix}.$$

We will again proceed in an iterative way. We first concentrate on the upper-left 2×2 block of A and determine a 2×2 Householder matrix $\tilde{H}(1,2)$, which transforms the vector $(a_{11}, a_{21})^T$ into a multiple of $(1,0)$. This matrix $\tilde{H}(1,2)$ can be "filled-up" to give an $n \times n$ orthogonal matrix $H(1,2)$ in the usual way. Important here is that the computation of $H(1,2)A$ costs only constant time since it involves only changing the first two rows and, because of the tridiagonal structure, only the first three columns. Continuing like this, we can use the index pairs $(2,3), (3,4), \ldots, (n-1, n)$ to create the QR factorisation

$$R = H(n-1, n)H(n-2, n) \cdots H(1,2)A,$$

such that, because of the symmetry of the Householder matrices,

$$Q = H(1,2)H(2,3) \cdots H(n-1, n).$$

In each step, at most six entries are changed. Thus the computational cost is $O(n)$.

This can be visualised as follows:

$$
\begin{pmatrix}
* & * & 0 & 0 & 0 \\
* & * & * & 0 & 0 \\
0 & * & * & * & 0 \\
0 & 0 & * & * & * \\
0 & 0 & 0 & * & *
\end{pmatrix}
\overset{(1,2)}{\to}
\begin{pmatrix}
* & * & * & 0 & 0 \\
0 & * & * & 0 & 0 \\
0 & * & * & * & 0 \\
0 & 0 & * & * & * \\
0 & 0 & 0 & * & *
\end{pmatrix}
\overset{(2,3)}{\to}
\begin{pmatrix}
* & * & * & 0 & 0 \\
0 & * & * & * & 0 \\
0 & 0 & * & * & 0 \\
0 & 0 & * & * & * \\
0 & 0 & 0 & * & *
\end{pmatrix}
$$

$$
\overset{(3,4)}{\to}
\begin{pmatrix}
* & * & * & 0 & 0 \\
0 & * & * & * & 0 \\
0 & 0 & * & * & * \\
0 & 0 & 0 & * & * \\
0 & 0 & 0 & * & *
\end{pmatrix}
\overset{(4,5)}{\to}
\begin{pmatrix}
* & * & * & 0 & 0 \\
0 & * & * & * & 0 \\
0 & 0 & * & * & * \\
0 & 0 & 0 & * & * \\
0 & 0 & 0 & 0 & *
\end{pmatrix}.
$$

Next, to compute the new iteration $A_{m+1} = R_m Q_m = R_m H(1,2) H(2,3) \cdots H(n-1,n)$ we see that the first matrix $H(1,2)$ acts only on the first two columns, the next matrix $H(2,3)$ on columns 2 and 3 and so on:

$$
\begin{pmatrix}
* & * & * & 0 & 0 \\
0 & * & * & * & 0 \\
0 & 0 & * & * & * \\
0 & 0 & 0 & * & * \\
0 & 0 & 0 & 0 & *
\end{pmatrix}
\overset{(1,2)}{\to}
\begin{pmatrix}
* & * & * & 0 & 0 \\
* & * & * & * & 0 \\
0 & 0 & * & * & * \\
0 & 0 & 0 & * & * \\
0 & 0 & 0 & 0 & *
\end{pmatrix}
\overset{(2,3)}{\to}
\begin{pmatrix}
* & * & * & 0 & 0 \\
* & * & * & * & 0 \\
0 & * & * & * & * \\
0 & 0 & 0 & * & * \\
0 & 0 & 0 & 0 & *
\end{pmatrix}
$$

$$
\overset{(3,4)}{\to}
\begin{pmatrix}
* & * & * & * & 0 \\
* & * & * & * & 0 \\
0 & * & * & * & * \\
0 & 0 & * & * & * \\
0 & 0 & 0 & 0 & *
\end{pmatrix}
\overset{(4,5)}{\to}
\begin{pmatrix}
* & * & * & * & * \\
* & * & * & * & * \\
0 & * & * & * & * \\
0 & 0 & * & * & * \\
0 & 0 & 0 & * & *
\end{pmatrix}.
$$

The new matrix is indeed a Hessenberg matrix again. But since it is also symmetric, all entries above the super-diagonal have to be zero. This ensures that the new matrix is a tridiagonal matrix and that the computation can again be done in linear time.   □

Let us note two consequences, which follow from the above proof immediately. The first one regards tridiagonal matrices.

Corollary 5.37 *If $A \in \mathbb{R}^{n \times n}$ is a tridiagonal matrix, then the upper triangular matrix $R \in \mathbb{R}^{n \times n}$ has at most three non-zero entries in each row, which are $r_{ii}, r_{i,i+1}$ and $r_{i,i+2}$.*

The second consequence will be important later on. The algorithm described above yields for a non-symmetric Hessenberg matrix the following.

Corollary 5.38   *If $A \in \mathbb{R}^{n \times n}$ is a Hessenberg matrix then its QR factorisation can be computed in $O(n^2)$ time.*

Proof   This follows from the proof of the previous theorem. The only difference is that, in each step, we have to apply the 2×2 matrices $H(i, i+1)$ to all entries in rows i and $i+1$ and columns $i+1 \le k \le n$.   □

A further improvement can be achieved by introducing shifts into the algorithm. Instead of decomposing the matrix A_m, we now decompose the matrix $A_m - \mu_m I$ with a certain shift parameter $\mu_m \in \mathbb{R}$. Thus, one step of the *QR method with shifts* consists of

- form the QR factorisation of $A_m - \mu_m I = Q_m R_m$,
- set $A_{m+1} = R_m Q_m + \mu_m I$.

From $Q_m^T A_m - \mu_m Q_m^T = R_m$ it again follows easily that

$$A_{m+1} = Q_m^T A_m Q_m - \mu_m Q_m^T Q_m + \mu_m I = Q_m^T A_m Q_m = \cdots = Q_{0\ldots m}^T A Q_{0\ldots m},$$

such that all of the matrices involved have again the same eigenvalues as A. It also follows that

$$Q_{0\ldots m} R_m = Q_{0\ldots m-1} Q_m R_m = Q_{0\ldots m-1}(A_m - \mu_m I)$$
$$= A Q_{0\ldots m-1} - \mu_m Q_{0\ldots m-1}$$
$$= (A - \mu_m I) Q_{0\ldots m-1}.$$

If we form the transpose of this equation we can conclude that

$$Q_{0\ldots m-1} R_m^T = (A^T - \mu_m I) Q_{0\ldots m}.$$

Hence, if we define $\rho_m := e_n^T R_m e_n$ to be the bottom diagonal element of R_m then

$$Q_{0\ldots m-1} R_m^T e_n = \rho_m Q_{0\ldots m-1} e_n = (A^T - \mu_m I) Q_{0\ldots m} e_n,$$

and with $v^{(m+1)} := Q_{0\ldots m} e_n$ we derive

$$\rho_m v^{(m)} = (A^T - \mu_m I) v^{(m+1)},$$

which is one step of the inverse iteration. Thus, in this case it is possible to apply the convergence results on the power method and the inverse iteration to derive convergence results for the smallest eigenvalue of A and an associated eigenvector. In the best case, it is possible to establish cubic convergence again.

In particular, if we simply use the shift $a_{n,n}^{(m-1)}$, we will, in almost all cases, have rapid convergence leading to

$$A_m = \begin{pmatrix} T_m & \mathbf{0} \\ \mathbf{0}^T & \lambda \end{pmatrix},$$

where $T_m \in \mathbb{R}^{(n-1)\times(n-1)}$ is tridiagonal and symmetric, and λ is an eigenvalue of A_1. Inductively, once this form has been found, the QR algorithm with shift can be concentrated only on the $(n-1) \times (n-1)$ leading sub-matrix T_m. This process is called *deflation*.

Taking this all into account, the final algorithm for calculating the eigenvalues of an $n \times n$ symmetric matrix is given in Algorithm 15.

Algorithm 15: QR algorithm with shifts

Input : $A = A^T \in \mathbb{R}^{n\times n}$.
Output: Approximate eigenvalues and eigenvectors.

1   Reduce A to tridiagonal form
2   **for** $k = n$ **downto** 2 **do**
3   **while** $|a_{k-1,k}| > \epsilon$ **do**
4   Compute $QR = A - a_{kk}I$
5   Set $A := RQ + a_{kk}I$
6   Record eigenvalue $\lambda_k = a_{kk}$
7   Replace A by its leading $k-1$ by $k-1$ sub-matrix
8   Record eigenvalue $\lambda_1 = a_{11}$

5.7 Computing the Singular Value Decomposition

In this section we want to discuss numerical methods to compute the singular value decomposition

$$A = U\Sigma V^T \tag{5.32}$$

of a matrix $A \in \mathbb{R}^{m\times n}$ with $m \geq n$. Here, the matrices $U \in \mathbb{R}^{m\times m}$ and $V \in \mathbb{R}^{n\times n}$ are orthogonal and $\Sigma \in \mathbb{R}^{m\times n}$ is a diagonal matrix with diagonal entries $\sigma_i \geq 0$ for $1 \leq i \leq n$. We restrict ourselves to the case $m \geq n$ since it is the more important case and since in the the case $m < n$ we can simply consider A^T instead of A.

As mentioned before, the factorisation (5.32) is also called the *full singular value decomposition* since it computes square matrices $U \in \mathbb{R}^{m \times m}$ and $V \in \mathbb{R}^{n \times n}$. However, the essential information is already given by a reduced singular value decomposition, see Section 1.5. Sometimes a reduced singular value decomposition for $A \in \mathbb{R}^{m \times n}$ with $m \geq n$ employs matrices $U \in \mathbb{R}^{m \times n}$ with $U^T U = I$, $V \in \mathbb{R}^{n \times n}$ orthogonal and a diagonal matrix $\Sigma \in \mathbb{R}^{n \times n}$ with $A = U\Sigma V^T$. In any case, we have

$$A^T A = V\Sigma^T \Sigma V^T$$

and $S := \Sigma^T \Sigma \in \mathbb{R}^{n \times n}$ is a diagonal matrix with diagonal entries σ_j^2, $1 \leq i \leq n$, and that the singular values σ_i are the square roots of the positive eigenvalues of $A^T A$.

This, of course, immediately gives rise to a numerical scheme. We could first compute the matrix $\tilde{A} := A^T A$ and then use one of the methods of the previous sections to compute the eigenvalues and eigenvectors of $\tilde{A}$. Taking the square roots of the eigenvalues gives us the singular values. Moreover, if we have the eigenvalue decomposition $\tilde{A} = VSV^T$ we can solve for $U\Sigma = AV$, for example using a QR factorisation to compute the missing orthogonal matrix U.

This is, unfortunately, though quite obvious, not advisable. First of all, the computational cost expended to form the matrix $A^T A$ is already $O(mn^2)$, but this is not the main problem. The main problem is that the condition number will be the square of the condition number of the matrix A. It can be shown that this leads to problems, particularly for computing the small singular values of A, see for example Trefethen and Bau [124].

Hence, the general idea is to use the fact that the singular values are the positive roots of the positive eigenvalues of $A^T A$ without computing $A^T A$.

As in the case of computing the eigenvalues of a symmetric matrix using the QR method, we will achieve this by first transferring our matrix to a more suitable form. This time, it will be a *bidiagonal form*.

Definition 5.39   A matrix $B = (b_{ij}) \in \mathbb{R}^{m \times n}$ with $m \geq n$ is in (upper) *bidiagonal form* if $b_{ij} = 0$ for all $j \neq i, i + 1$, i.e. B is of the form

$$B = \begin{pmatrix} * & * & & & \\ & * & * & & \\ & & * & \ddots & \\ & & & \ddots & * \\ & & & & * \\ & & & & \end{pmatrix}.$$

To compute the bidiagonal form of A we proceed similarly to what we did to compute the Hessenberg form of a matrix. However, this time we are more flexible. In the case of constructing the Hessenberg form of A, we had to use transformations of the form $Q^T A Q$ with Q orthogonal to keep the same eigenvalues. Here, we want to keep the same singular values, which allows us to use transformations of the form $U^T A V$ with orthogonal matrices U and V since we have:

Remark 5.40 Let $A \in \mathbb{R}^{m \times n}$ with $m \geq n$ be given. If $B \in \mathbb{R}^{m \times n}$ is defined by $B = U^T A V$ with orthogonal matrices $U \in \mathbb{R}^{m \times m}$ and $V \in \mathbb{R}^{n \times n}$ then A and B have the same singular values.

Proof The singular values of B are the square roots of the positive eigenvalues of $B^T B$. Since

$$B^T B = (U^T A V)^T (U^T A V) = V^T A^T U U^T A V = V^T A^T A V,$$

$B^T B$ and $A^T A$ have the same positive eigenvalues. $\qquad\square$

Hence, we can start with a Householder matrix $U_1 \in \mathbb{R}^{m \times m}$ which transforms the first column of A into a multiple of the first unit vector. We then want to choose a Householder matrix V_1 to transform the first row of $U_1 A$ into a multiple of the transpose of the first unit vector. However, as explained in the context of deriving the Hessenberg form, this would destroy the previously created zeros in the first column. Hence, we have to transform the row vector consisting of $((U_1 A)_{12}, \ldots (U_1 A)_{1n})$ into a multiple of the first row unit vector in $\mathbb{R}^{n-1}$. Continuing this way, this looks schematically like

$$
\begin{pmatrix}
* & * & * & * \\
* & * & * & * \\
* & * & * & * \\
* & * & * & * \\
* & * & * & * \\
* & * & * & *
\end{pmatrix}
\xrightarrow{U_1^T}
\begin{pmatrix}
* & * & * & * \\
0 & * & * & * \\
0 & * & * & * \\
0 & * & * & * \\
0 & * & * & * \\
0 & * & * & *
\end{pmatrix}
\xrightarrow{V_1}
\begin{pmatrix}
\bullet & * & 0 & 0 \\
0 & * & * & * \\
0 & * & * & * \\
0 & * & * & * \\
0 & * & * & * \\
0 & * & * & *
\end{pmatrix}
\xrightarrow{U_2^T}
\begin{pmatrix}
\bullet & \bullet & 0 & 0 \\
0 & * & * & * \\
0 & 0 & * & * \\
0 & 0 & * & * \\
0 & 0 & * & * \\
0 & 0 & * & *
\end{pmatrix}
$$

$$
\xrightarrow{V_2}
\begin{pmatrix}
\bullet & \bullet & 0 & 0 \\
0 & \bullet & * & 0 \\
0 & 0 & * & * \\
0 & 0 & * & * \\
0 & 0 & * & * \\
0 & 0 & * & *
\end{pmatrix}
\xrightarrow{U_3^T}
\begin{pmatrix}
\bullet & \bullet & 0 & 0 \\
0 & \bullet & \bullet & 0 \\
0 & 0 & * & * \\
0 & 0 & 0 & * \\
0 & 0 & 0 & * \\
0 & 0 & 0 & *
\end{pmatrix}
\xrightarrow{U_4^T}
\begin{pmatrix}
\bullet & \bullet & 0 & 0 \\
0 & \bullet & \bullet & 0 \\
0 & 0 & \bullet & \bullet \\
0 & 0 & 0 & * \\
0 & 0 & 0 & 0 \\
0 & 0 & 0 & 0
\end{pmatrix},
$$

where the U^T matrices are multiplied from the left and the V matrices are multiplied from the right. In the above diagram, elements that do not change anymore are denoted by a •; those elements that change are denoted by a ∗. Note that we need to apply n Householder matrices from the left and $n - 2$ Householder transformations from the right. The method described here is called *Householder* bidiagonalisation and goes back to Golub and Kahan [64]. A possible realisation is given in Algorithm 16. To analyse its numerical cost, we recall that multiplying a Householder matrix $U \in \mathbb{R}^{m \times m}$ to a vector $\mathbf{a} \in \mathbb{R}^m$ costs $O(m)$ time, see Lemma 3.31.

Lemma 5.41 *A matrix $A \in \mathbb{R}^{m \times n}$ with $m \geq n$ can be transformed into a bidiagonal form using the Householder bidiagonalisation method in $O(mn^2)$ time.*

Proof We can represent the U matrix of step i by an $(m - 1 + i) \times (m - 1 + i)$ matrix, which we then have to apply to $n - i + 1$ partial columns of A. Hence this multiplication can be done in $O((n - i + 1)(m - i + 1))$ time and we have to do it for $1 \leq i \leq n$, so that the total cost for multiplying with all U matrices is

$$\sum_{i=1}^{n} O((n - i + 1)(m - i + 1)) = O(n^2 m).$$

Furthermore, we can represent the V matrix of step i by an $(n-i) \times (n-i)$ matrix which has to be applied to $m - i + 1$ partial row vectors of A, for $1 \leq i \leq n - 2$. Hence, the total cost for all these operations becomes

$$\sum_{i=1}^{n-2} O((n - i)(m - i + 1)) = O(n^2 m). \qquad \square$$

Algorithm 16: Householder bidiagonalisation

Input : $A \in \mathbb{R}^{m \times n}$.
Output: $B = U A V^{\mathrm{T}}$ bidiagonal.

1 **for** $i = 1$ **to** n **do**
2   Determine Householder matrix $\tilde{U}_i \in \mathbb{R}^{(m-i+1) \times (m-i+1)}$ such that
      $\tilde{U}_i(a_{ii}, a_{i+1,m}, \ldots, a_{mi})^{\mathrm{T}} = (*, 0, \ldots, 0)^{\mathrm{T}}$.
3   Let $U_i := \mathrm{diag}(I_{i-1}, \tilde{U}_i)$ and compute $A := U_i A$
4   **if** $i \leq n - 2$ **then**
5   Determine Householder matrix $\tilde{V}_i \in \mathbb{R}^{(n-i) \times (n-i)}$ such that
          $(a_{i,i+1}, a_{i,i+2}, \ldots, a_{in})\tilde{V}_i^{\mathrm{T}} = (*, 0, \ldots, 0)$
6   Let $V_i^{\mathrm{T}} := \mathrm{diag}(I_i, \tilde{V}_i^{\mathrm{T}})$ and compute $A := A V_i^{\mathrm{T}}$

As mentioned above, the matrix–matrix multiplications in Lines 3 and 6 of Algorithm 16 have to be carried out using the special structure of the Householder matrices. Furthermore, we can also store these matrices efficiently. The Householder matrix $\tilde{U}_i \in \mathbb{R}^{(m-i+1)\times(m-i+1)}$ can be represented by $\tilde{U}_i = I_{m-i+1} - 2\mathbf{u}_i\mathbf{u}_i^T$, i.e. by a vector $\mathbf{u}_i \in \mathbb{R}^{m-i+1}$. Similarly, the matrix $\tilde{V}_i \in \mathbb{R}^{(n-i)\times(n-i)}$ can be represented by a vector $\mathbf{v}_i \in \mathbb{R}^{n-i}$. Hence, when it comes to an actual implementation of Algorithm 16 we could store most of the information in the original matrix as follows. The vector associated with U_i can be stored in the lower triangular part of A while the Householder vector associated with V_i can be stored in the upper triangular portion of A. For details, see the similar Algorithm 6. Hence, we only need to store the diagonal and super-diagonal entries of the transformed matrix.

In the case of m being much larger than n, the method will produce a large number of unnecessary zeros. To avoid this, we could first compute a QR factorisation of A and then the Householder bidiagonalisation $B = URV^T$ of the upper triangular matrix R. The advantage here is that the bidiagonalisation process then only needs to be carried out on the upper $n \times n$ part of R. A thorough analysis of the computational cost (see for example Trefethen and Bau [124]) shows that the QR factorisation can be done in about half the time $T_H(m,n)$ of the bidiagonalisation of A. The bidiagonalisation process on the small $n \times n$ part of R costs $O(n^3)$ so that the total cost of this method will be

$$T(m,n) = \frac{1}{2}T_H(m,n) + O(n^3),$$

which turns out to be better if at least $m > (5/3)n$.

After the transformation to an upper bidiagonal matrix, the transformed matrix has the upper bidiagonal form

$$\tilde{B} = \begin{pmatrix} d_1 & f_2 & 0 & \cdots & 0 \\ & d_2 & f_3 & \ddots & \vdots \\ & & \ddots & \ddots & 0 \\ & & & \ddots & f_n \\ & & & & d_n \\ 0 & & \cdots & & 0 \\ \vdots & & & & \vdots \\ 0 & & \cdots & & 0 \end{pmatrix} = \begin{pmatrix} B \\ 0 \cdots 0 \\ \vdots \quad \vdots \\ 0 \cdots 0 \end{pmatrix} \tag{5.33}$$

with $B \in \mathbb{R}^{n\times n}$, and we have matrices $U \in \mathbb{R}^{m\times n}$ and $V \in \mathbb{R}^{n\times n}$ such that $A = UBV^T$. The singular values of A are the square roots of the positive eigenvalues of the matrix $C := B^T B$, which is a tridiagonal matrix with diagonal entries

$c_{11} = d_1^2$ and $c_{ii} = d_i^2 + f_i^2$ for $2 \leq i \leq n$. The off-diagonal entries are given by $c_{i,i+1} = c_{i+1,i} = d_i f_{i+1}$ for $1 \leq i \leq n-1$.

Hence, the matrix $C = B^{\mathrm{T}} B$ is irreducible (see Definition 4.11) if and only if $d_1 \cdots d_{n-1} \neq 0$ and $f_2 \cdots f_n \neq 0$.

If the matrix is reducible, the calculation of the singular values of B can be reduced to the calculation of two lower-dimensional matrices. This is detailed in the following lemma, where we have to distinguish between the two cases characterised by whether one of the d_i or one of the f_i vanishes.

Lemma 5.42 *Let $B \in \mathbb{R}^{n \times n}$ be a bidiagonal matrix with diagonal elements $d_1, \ldots, d_n$ and super-diagonal elements $f_2, \ldots, f_n$.*

1. *If there is a $1 \leq k \leq n-1$ with $f_{k+1} = 0$ then the matrix B can be split into*

$$B = \begin{pmatrix} B_1 & O \\ O & B_2 \end{pmatrix}$$

with $B_1 \in \mathbb{R}^{k \times k}$ and $B_2 \in \mathbb{R}^{(n-k) \times (n-k)}$. If $B_1 = U_1 \Sigma_1 V_1^{\mathrm{T}}$ and $B_2 = U_2 \Sigma_2 V_2^{\mathrm{T}}$ are singular value decompositions of B_1 and B_2, respectively, then

$$B = \begin{pmatrix} U_1 & O \\ O & U_2 \end{pmatrix} \begin{pmatrix} \Sigma_1 & O \\ O & \Sigma_2 \end{pmatrix} \begin{pmatrix} V_1 & O \\ O & V_2 \end{pmatrix}^{\mathrm{T}}$$

is a singular value decomposition of B.

2. *If there is a $1 \leq k \leq n-1$ with $d_k = 0$ and $f_{k+1} \neq 0$ then we can choose $n-k$ Givens rotations $G_{k,k+1}, \ldots, G_{k,n}$ such that $\tilde{B} = (\tilde{b}_{ij}) := G_{k,n} \cdots G_{k,k+1} B$ is a bidiagonal matrix with $\tilde{b}_{k,k+1} = 0$. Hence, the matrix $\tilde{B}$ satisfies the assumptions of the first case.*

Proof The first part of the lemma simply follows by straightforward calculations. For the second part, we will use Givens rotations to move the non-vanishing f_{k+1} along the kth row to the right until it disappears, as described schematically in

Here, unchanging entries are again denoted by a • and changing entries by a
*. The precise proof follows the same pattern and is left to the reader, see also
Algorithm 17. □

Algorithm 17: Transformation of reducible bidiagonal matrix

Input : $B \in \mathbb{R}^{n \times n}$ upper bidiagonal, i.e. of the form (5.33), index k with
$d_k = 0$ and $f_{k+1} \neq 0$, matrix $U \in \mathbb{R}^{m \times n}$ so that $A = UBV^T$.
Output: $\tilde{B}$ upper bidiagonal with $\tilde{f}_{k+1} = 0$.

1   $c := 0, \quad s := 1$
2   **for** $j = k + 1$ **to** n **do**
3      $f := sf_j, \quad f_j := cf_j, \quad u := (f^2 + d_j^2)^{1/2}$
4      $c := d_j/u, \quad s := -f/u, \quad d_j := u$
5   **for** $i = 1$ **to** m **do**
6          $(u_{ik}, u_{ij}) := (u_{ik}, u_{ij}) \begin{pmatrix} c & -s \\ s & c \end{pmatrix}$

At the end of Algorithm 17 we have an upper bidiagonal matrix $\tilde{B} \in \mathbb{R}^{n \times n}$,
which can be split as described, and a new matrix $\tilde{U}$ which satisfy $A = \tilde{U}\tilde{B}V^T$.
We can repeat this until we only have to deal with blocks B with $B^T B$ irreducible.

It remains to derive a method for computing the singular values of an upper
bidiagonal matrix B with irreducible $B^T B$. Here, the idea of Golub and Reinsch
[65] is to compute the eigenvalues of $B^T B$ with the shifted QR method without
actually computing $B^T B$. We will now describe a method which transforms B
to a new bidiagonal matrix $\tilde{B}$ which should have a much smaller off-diagonal
element $\tilde{b}_{n-1,n}$ than the original matrix B. Hence, after a few steps it should be
possible to use deflation to reduce the problem to an $(n-1) \times (n-1)$ matrix.
We start by selecting the shift parameter $\mu \in \mathbb{R}$ as the eigenvalue of the lower
block

$$\begin{pmatrix} d_{n-1}^2 + f_{n-1}^2 & d_{n-1}f_n \\ d_{n-1}f_n & d_n^2 + f_n^2 \end{pmatrix}$$

of $B^T B$ which is closest to $d_n^2 + f_n^2$. Then, we determine a Givens rotation
$V_{12} = V_{12}(c, s)$ satisfying

$$\begin{pmatrix} c & s \\ -s & c \end{pmatrix} \begin{pmatrix} d_1^2 - \mu \\ d_1 f_2 \end{pmatrix} = \begin{pmatrix} * \\ 0 \end{pmatrix},$$

i.e. V_{12} transforms the first column of $B^T B - \mu I$ into a multiple of the first unit vector. This means that the first column of V_{12} coincides with the first column of the orthogonal matrix Q of a QR factorisation of $B^T B - \mu I$.

If we apply this directly to B, i.e. if we form BV_{12}^T with dimensions appropriately adapted, we only change the upper 2×2 block of B according to

$$\begin{pmatrix} d_1 & f_2 \\ 0 & d_2 \end{pmatrix}\begin{pmatrix} c & -s \\ s & c \end{pmatrix} = \begin{pmatrix} d_1 c + f_2 s & -d_1 s + f_2 c \\ d_2 s & d_2 c \end{pmatrix},$$

which means that the upper bidiagonal form is destroyed by the element $d_2 s$ in position $(2,1)$. We will now use successive Givens rotations from the left and from the right to move this element out of the matrix. This idea can be depicted as follows:

where $V_{k,k+1}^T$ is multiplied from the right and hence acts only on columns k and $k + 1$, while $U_{k,k+1}$ is multiplied from the left and hence acts on rows k and $k + 1$. All other rows and columns are left unchanged. As before, we indicated non-changing values with $\bullet$ and those which change with $*$, unless they are transformed to zero.

The result of this procedure is a matrix

$$\tilde{B} = U_{n-1,n} \cdots U_{12} B V_{12}^T \cdots V_{n-1,n}^T$$

which is also upper bidiagonal and has the same singular values as B but should, one hopes, have a smaller entry $\tilde{b}_{n-1,n}$ than B. The full algorithm of this step is given in Algorithm 18.

Algorithm 18 not only gives a new upper bidiagonal matrix $\tilde{B}$ but also overwrites the matrices $U \in \mathbb{R}^{m \times n}$ and $V \in \mathbb{R}^{n \times n}$ with

$$\tilde{U} = U U_{12}^T \cdots U_{n-1,n}^T, \qquad \tilde{V} = V V_{12}^T \cdots V_{n-1,n}^T,$$

so that we also have $\tilde{U} \tilde{B} \tilde{V}^T = UBV^T$. To see the connection to the shifted QR

Algorithm 18: *QR* Golub–Kahan SVD step

Input : $B \in \mathbb{R}^{n \times n}$ bidiagonal matrix of the form (5.33) with $B^T B$
irreducible, matrices $U \in \mathbb{R}^{m \times n}$ and $V \in \mathbb{R}^{n \times n}$.

Output: Upper bidiagonal matrix $\tilde{B} \in \mathbb{R}^{n \times n}$, matrices $\tilde{U} \in \mathbb{R}^{m \times n}$ and
$\tilde{V} \in \mathbb{R}^{n \times n}$ with $\tilde{U} \tilde{B} \tilde{V}^T = U B V^T$.

1 Determine $\mu \in \mathbb{R}$ as the eigenvalue of

$$\begin{pmatrix} d_{n-1}^2 + f_{n-1}^2 & d_{n-1} f_n \\ d_{n-1} f_n & d_n^2 + f_n^2 \end{pmatrix},$$

which is closest to $d_n^2 + f_n^2$.

2 Determine Givens rotation $V_{12} = V_{12}(c, s)$ with

$$\begin{pmatrix} c & s \\ -s & c \end{pmatrix} \begin{pmatrix} d_1^2 - \mu \\ d_1 f_2 \end{pmatrix} = \begin{pmatrix} * \\ 0 \end{pmatrix}.$$

Set $B := B V_{12}^T$ and $V := V V_{12}^T$.

3 **for** $k = 1$ **to** $n - 1$ **do**

4   Determine Givens rotation $U_{k,k+1} = U_{k,k+1}(c, s)$ with

$$\begin{pmatrix} c & s \\ -s & c \end{pmatrix} \begin{pmatrix} b_{kk} \\ b_{k+1,k} \end{pmatrix} = \begin{pmatrix} * \\ 0 \end{pmatrix}.$$

5   Set $B := U_{k,k+1} B$ and $U := U U_{k,k+1}^T$.

6   **if** $k < n - 1$ **then**

7   Determine Givens rotation $V_{k+1,k+2} = V_{k+1,k+2}(c, s)$ with

$$\begin{pmatrix} c & s \\ -s & c \end{pmatrix} \begin{pmatrix} b_{k,k+1} \\ b_{k,k+2} \end{pmatrix} = \begin{pmatrix} * \\ 0 \end{pmatrix}.$$

8   Set $B := B V_{k+1,k+2}^T$ and $V := V V_{k+1,k+2}^T$.

---

method applied to $B^T B$, we note that, with the just-introduced matrices, we also have

$$\tilde{B}^T \tilde{B} = V_{n-1,n} \cdots V_{12} B^T B V_{12}^T \cdots V_{n-1,n}^T.$$

As we have

$$(V_{n-1,n} \cdots V_{12})^T \mathbf{e}_1 = V_{12}^T \cdots V_{n-1,n}^T \mathbf{e}_1 = V_{12}^T \mathbf{e}_1$$

we see that the first column of $(V_{n-1,n} \cdots V_{1,2})^T$ coincides with the first column of V_{12}^T which coincides with the first column of Q the orthogonal matrix in the QR factorisation of $B^T B - \mu I$. This means that we have indeed implicitly applied one step of the shifted QR method and our considerations there allow us now to expect a new matrix $\tilde{B}$ with considerably smaller super-diagonal element f_n.

It should be clear by now how to implement these algorithms and how to combine them to create a working algorithm for computing the singular value decomposition. After each step $B \mapsto \tilde{B}$ it should be checked whether the last super-diagonal falls below a given threshold.

Exercises

5.1   • Let $A \in \mathbb{R}^{n \times n}$ be a tridiagonal matrix with diagonal entries $5j$, $1 \le j \le n$, and sub- and super-diagonal entries ± 1. Use Gershgorin's theorem to give as tight bounds on the eigenvalues of A as possible. Show that A is invertible.

     • Let $\mathbf{x}_0 \in \mathbb{R}^n$ and define for $k \in \mathbb{N}$ $\mathbf{x}_k$ by $A\mathbf{x}_k = \mathbf{x}_{k-1}$, where A is the matrix from the first part. Show that there is a constant $C > 0$ such that the components $\mathbf{e}_j^T \mathbf{x}_k$ of $\mathbf{x}_k$ satisfy $|\mathbf{e}_j \mathbf{x}_k| \le 4^{-k} C$.

5.2   Let $A, B \in \mathbb{R}^{n \times n}$ be symmetric with eigenvalues $\lambda_1 \ge \cdots \ge \lambda_n$ and $\mu_1 \ge \cdots \ge \mu_n$, respectively. Let $\nu_1 \ge \cdots \ge \nu_n$ be the eigenvalues of $A + B$ Show $\lambda_j + \mu_n \le \nu_j \le \lambda_j + \mu_1$ for $1 \le j \le n$.

5.3   Let $A \in \mathbb{R}^{n \times n}$ be symmetric with eigenvalues $\lambda_1, \ldots, \lambda_n$. Show, for every $\lambda \in \mathbb{R}$ and $\mathbf{x} \in \mathbb{R}^n \setminus \{\mathbf{0}\}$,

$$\min_{1 \le j \le n} |\lambda - \lambda_j| \le \frac{\|\lambda \mathbf{x} - A\mathbf{x}\|_2}{\|\mathbf{x}\|_2}.$$

5.4   Let $A \in \mathbb{R}^{m \times n}$ with $m \ge n$. Let $\sigma_1 \ge \cdots \ge \sigma_n$ be the singular values of A. Show

$$\sigma_j = \min_{U \in \mathcal{M}_{n+1-j}} \max_{\substack{\mathbf{x} \in U \\ \mathbf{x} \ne \mathbf{0}}} \frac{\|A\mathbf{x}\|_2}{\|\mathbf{x}\|_2}, \qquad 1 \le j \le n,$$

where $\mathcal{M}_j$ is the set of all j-dimensional subspaces of $\mathbb{R}^n$.

5.5   Let $A, B \in \mathbb{R}^{m \times n}$ with $m \ge n$ and singular values $\sigma_1 \ge \cdots \ge \sigma_n$ and $\tau_1 \ge \cdots \ge \tau_n$. Show

$$|\sigma_j - \tau_j| \le \|A - B\|_2, \qquad 1 \le j \le n.$$

5.6   Show that every irreducible, symmetric tridiagonal matrix $A \in \mathbb{R}^{n \times n}$ has pairwise distinct eigenvalues.

PART THREE

ADVANCED METHODS

6

Methods for Large Sparse Systems

In this chapter, we will concentrate on iterative methods which are particularly suited for large sparse systems, though they can also be applied to non-sparse matrices. We will discuss multigrid methods but our main focus will be on so-called Krylov subspace methods. For such methods, the main operation within one step of the iteration is the calculation of one or at most two matrix–vector products. If the matrix is sparse with only $O(n)$ non-zero entries then this operation can be done in $O(n)$ time. For a general, non-sparse matrix the cost becomes $O(n^2)$, which might still be acceptable if only a very small number of steps is required and n is not too large.

6.1 The Conjugate Gradient Method

We start by constructing an iterative method for symmetric positive definite matrices, which was introduced in [83] by Hestenes and Stiefel. Let $A \in \mathbb{R}^{n \times n}$ be symmetric, positive definite and $\mathbf{b} \in \mathbb{R}^n$. We wish to solve the linear system

$$A\mathbf{x} = \mathbf{b}.$$

Associated with this system we have a function $f : \mathbb{R}^n \to \mathbb{R}$ given by

$$f(\mathbf{x}) := \frac{1}{2}\mathbf{x}^{\mathrm{T}}A\mathbf{x} - \mathbf{x}^{\mathrm{T}}\mathbf{b}, \qquad \mathbf{x} \in \mathbb{R}^n.$$

We can calculate the first-order and second-order derivatives as

$$\nabla f(\mathbf{x}) = A\mathbf{x} - \mathbf{b},$$
$$Hf(\mathbf{x}) = A.$$

Here $\nabla f = (\partial_1 f, \ldots, \partial_n f)^{\mathrm{T}}$ is the gradient of f and $Hf = (\partial^2_{ij} f)_{ij}$ is its Hessian matrix. Since all higher-order derivatives vanish, we can rewrite f as its Taylor polynomial of degree two as

$$f(\mathbf{x}) = f(\mathbf{y}) + (\mathbf{x} - \mathbf{y})^{\mathrm{T}} \nabla f(\mathbf{y}) + \frac{1}{2}(\mathbf{x} - \mathbf{y})^{\mathrm{T}} H f(\mathbf{y})(\mathbf{x} - \mathbf{y})$$

$$= f(\mathbf{y}) + (\mathbf{x} - \mathbf{y})^{\mathrm{T}}(A\mathbf{y} - \mathbf{b}) + \frac{1}{2}(\mathbf{x} - \mathbf{y})^{\mathrm{T}} A(\mathbf{x} - \mathbf{y})$$

$$\geq f(\mathbf{y}) + (\mathbf{x} - \mathbf{y})^{\mathrm{T}}(A\mathbf{y} - \mathbf{b}),$$

where, in the last step, we have used that A is positive definite. Thus, if $\mathbf{y} = \mathbf{x}^*$ solves $A\mathbf{x} = \mathbf{b}$, we see that $f(\mathbf{x}) \geq f(\mathbf{x}^*)$, i.e. $\mathbf{x}^*$ minimises f. On the other hand, every minimiser $\mathbf{y}$ of f has to satisfy the necessary condition $\mathbf{0} = \nabla f(\mathbf{y}) = A\mathbf{y} - \mathbf{b}$. This is only possible for $\mathbf{y} = \mathbf{x}^*$.

Theorem 6.1 *Let $A \in \mathbb{R}^{n \times n}$ be symmetric and positive definite. The solution of the system $A\mathbf{x} = \mathbf{b}$ is the unique minimum of the function $f(\mathbf{y}) := \frac{1}{2}\mathbf{y}^{\mathrm{T}} A\mathbf{y} - \mathbf{y}^{\mathrm{T}}\mathbf{b}$.*

We will now try to find the minimum of f by a simple iterative procedure of the form

$$\mathbf{x}_{j+1} = \mathbf{x}_j + \alpha_j \mathbf{p}_j.$$

Here, $\mathbf{x}_j$ is our current position. From this position we want to move in the direction of $\mathbf{p}_j$. The step-length of our move is determined by α_j. Of course, it will be our goal to select the direction $\mathbf{p}_j$ and the step-length α_j in such a way that

$$f(\mathbf{x}_{j+1}) \leq f(\mathbf{x}_j).$$

Given a new direction $\mathbf{p}_j$, the best possible step-length in that direction can be determined by looking at the minimum of f along the line $\mathbf{x}_j + \alpha \mathbf{p}_j$. Hence, if we set $\phi(\alpha) = f(\mathbf{x}_j + \alpha \mathbf{p}_j)$ the necessary condition for a minimum yields

$$0 = \phi'(\alpha) = \mathbf{p}_j^{\mathrm{T}} \nabla f(\mathbf{x}_j + \alpha \mathbf{p}_j) = \mathbf{p}_j^{\mathrm{T}}[A(\mathbf{x}_j + \alpha \mathbf{p}_j) - \mathbf{b}] = \mathbf{p}_j^{\mathrm{T}} A\mathbf{x}_j + \alpha \mathbf{p}_j^{\mathrm{T}} A\mathbf{p}_j - \mathbf{p}_j^{\mathrm{T}}\mathbf{b}.$$

Resolving this for α gives the new step-length as

$$\alpha_j = \frac{\mathbf{p}_j^{\mathrm{T}}(\mathbf{b} - A\mathbf{x}_j)}{\mathbf{p}_j^{\mathrm{T}} A\mathbf{p}_j} = \frac{\mathbf{p}_j^{\mathrm{T}}\mathbf{r}_j}{\mathbf{p}_j^{\mathrm{T}} A\mathbf{p}_j} = \frac{\langle \mathbf{r}_j, \mathbf{p}_j \rangle_2}{\langle A\mathbf{p}_j, \mathbf{p}_j \rangle_2},$$

where we have defined the residual of the jth step as $\mathbf{r}_j := \mathbf{b} - A\mathbf{x}_j$. Thus we have a generic algorithm as outlined in Algorithm 19.

Note that we pick α_j in such a way that

$$0 = \mathbf{p}_j^{\mathrm{T}}(A\mathbf{x}_{j+1} - \mathbf{b}) = -\langle \mathbf{r}_{j+1}, \mathbf{p}_j \rangle_2, \tag{6.1}$$

showing that $\mathbf{p}_j$ and $\mathbf{r}_{j+1}$ are orthogonal.

Algorithm 19: Generic minimisation

Input : $A = A^T \in \mathbb{R}^{n \times n}$ positive definite, $\mathbf{b} \in \mathbb{R}^n$.

Output: Approximate solution of $A\mathbf{x} = \mathbf{b}$.

1 Choose $\mathbf{x}_0$ and $\mathbf{p}_0$.
2 Compute $\mathbf{r}_0 := \mathbf{b} - A\mathbf{x}_0$ and set $j := 0$.
3 **while** $\|\mathbf{r}_j\| > \epsilon$ **do**
4    $\quad \alpha_j := \dfrac{\langle \mathbf{r}_j, \mathbf{p}_j \rangle_2}{\langle A\mathbf{p}_j, \mathbf{p}_j \rangle_2}$
5    $\quad \mathbf{x}_{j+1} := \mathbf{x}_j + \alpha_j \mathbf{p}_j$
6    $\quad \mathbf{r}_{j+1} := \mathbf{b} - A\mathbf{x}_{j+1}$
7    $\quad$ Choose next direction $\mathbf{p}_{j+1}$
8    $\quad j := j + 1$

Obviously, we still have to determine how to choose the search directions. One possible way is to pick the direction of *steepest descent*. It is easy to see and known from analysis that this direction is given by the negative gradient of the target function, i.e. by

$$\mathbf{p}_j = -\nabla f(\mathbf{x}_j) = -(A\mathbf{x}_j - \mathbf{b}) = \mathbf{r}_j.$$

This gives the steepest descent algorithm shown in Algorithm 20.

Algorithm 20: Steepest descent

Input : $A = A^T \in \mathbb{R}^{n \times n}$ positive definite, $\mathbf{b} \in \mathbb{R}^n$.

Output: Approximate solution of $A\mathbf{x} = \mathbf{b}$.

1 Choose $\mathbf{x}_0$.
2 Set $\mathbf{p}_0 := \mathbf{b} - A\mathbf{x}_0$ and $j := 0$
3 **while** $\|\mathbf{p}_j\| > \epsilon$ **do**
4    $\quad \alpha_j := \dfrac{\langle \mathbf{p}_j, \mathbf{p}_j \rangle_2}{\langle A\mathbf{p}_j, \mathbf{p}_j \rangle_2}$
5    $\quad \mathbf{x}_{j+1} := \mathbf{x}_j + \alpha_j \mathbf{p}_j$
6    $\quad \mathbf{p}_{j+1} := \mathbf{b} - A\mathbf{x}_{j+1}$
7    $\quad j := j + 1$

The relation (6.1) now becomes $\langle \mathbf{p}_{j+1}, \mathbf{p}_j \rangle_2 = 0$, which means that two successive search directions are orthogonal.

To see that the method of steepest descent converges and to determine its convergence speed, we recall that a symmetric and positive definite matrix $A \in \mathbb{R}^{n \times n}$ has n positive eigenvalues $0 < \lambda_1 \le \lambda_2 \le \cdots \le \lambda_n$ and $\mathbb{R}^n$ has an orthonormal basis $\mathbf{w}_1, \ldots, \mathbf{w}_n$ satisfying $A\mathbf{w}_j = \lambda_j \mathbf{w}_j$ for $1 \le j \le n$. We need the following lemma.

Lemma 6.2 (Kantorovich inequality) *Let λ_1 and λ_n be the smallest and largest eigenvalues of the symmetric and positive definite matrix $A \in \mathbb{R}^{n \times n}$. Then,*

$$\frac{\langle A\mathbf{x}, \mathbf{x} \rangle_2}{\langle \mathbf{x}, \mathbf{x} \rangle_2} \frac{\langle A^{-1}\mathbf{x}, \mathbf{x} \rangle_2}{\langle \mathbf{x}, \mathbf{x} \rangle_2} \le \frac{(\lambda_1 + \lambda_n)^2}{4\lambda_1 \lambda_n}, \qquad \mathbf{x} \in \mathbb{R}^n \setminus \{\mathbf{0}\}.$$

Proof Without restriction we may assume that $\langle \mathbf{x}, \mathbf{x} \rangle_2 = \|\mathbf{x}\|_2^2 = 1$. Using the notation introduced above, we can expand such an $\mathbf{x} \in \mathbb{R}^n$ as $\mathbf{x} = \sum_{j=1}^n x_j \mathbf{w}_j$ with

$$\langle A\mathbf{x}, \mathbf{x} \rangle_2 = \mathbf{x}^T A \mathbf{x} = \sum_{j=1}^n \lambda_j x_j^2, \qquad \langle A^{-1}\mathbf{x}, \mathbf{x} \rangle_2 = \mathbf{x}^T A^{-1} \mathbf{x} = \sum_{j=1}^n \lambda_j^{-1} x_j^2.$$

Noticing that $x_j^2 \in [0, 1]$ with $\sum x_j^2 = 1$, we see that

$$\lambda := \sum_{j=1}^n \lambda_j x_j^2 = \langle A\mathbf{x}, \mathbf{x} \rangle_2$$

is a convex combination of the eigenvalues of A and hence we have $\lambda \in [\lambda_1, \lambda_n]$. Next, let us define the points $P_j := (\lambda_j, 1/\lambda_j)$ for $1 \le j \le n$ and $P := (\lambda, \sum_j \lambda_j^{-1} x_j^2)$. The points P_j lie on the graph of the function $f(t) = 1/t$, which is a convex function. Thus, all P_j for $2 \le j \le n-1$ lie under the straight line connecting P_1 and P_n. The point P can be written as $P = \sum_j x_j^2 P_j$ and is therefore a convex combination of the points P_j and thus contained in the convex hull of $P_1, \ldots, P_n$. Hence, P cannot be above the straight line through P_1 and P_n. Since this line is given by $g(t) = (\lambda_1 + \lambda_n - t)/(\lambda_1 \lambda_n)$, we see that

$$\langle A^{-1}\mathbf{x}, \mathbf{x} \rangle_2 = \sum_{j=1}^n \lambda_j^{-1} x_j^2 \le g(\lambda) = \frac{\lambda_1 + \lambda_n - \lambda}{\lambda_1 \lambda_n}$$

and hence

$$\langle A\mathbf{x}, \mathbf{x} \rangle_2 \langle A^{-1}\mathbf{x}, \mathbf{x} \rangle_2 \le \lambda \frac{\lambda_1 + \lambda_n - \lambda}{\lambda_1 \lambda_n}. \tag{6.2}$$

The expression on the right-hand side is a quadratic polynomial in λ which attains its global maximum in $[\lambda_1, \lambda_n]$ at $\lambda = (\lambda_1 + \lambda_n)/2$. Inserting this into (6.2) gives the desired result. $\square$

With this, we can prove convergence of the method of steepest descent. To formulate it, we introduce the inner product

$$\langle \mathbf{x}, \mathbf{y} \rangle_A := \mathbf{y}^T A \mathbf{x} = \langle A\mathbf{x}, \mathbf{y} \rangle_2 = \langle \mathbf{x}, A\mathbf{y} \rangle_2 = \langle A\mathbf{y}, \mathbf{x} \rangle_2 \qquad (6.3)$$

with associated norm $\|\mathbf{x}\|_A := \sqrt{\langle \mathbf{x}, \mathbf{x} \rangle_A}$, $\mathbf{x} \in \mathbb{R}^n$.

Theorem 6.3 *Let $A \in \mathbb{R}^{n \times n}$ be symmetric and positive definite. Then, for a given right-hand side $\mathbf{b} \in \mathbb{R}^n$, the method of steepest descent converges for every starting point $\mathbf{x}_0 \in \mathbb{R}^n$ to the solution $\mathbf{x}^* \in \mathbb{R}^n$ of $A\mathbf{x} = \mathbf{b}$. Moreover, if $\mathbf{x}_j$ denotes the jth iteration, the error can be bounded by*

$$\|\mathbf{x}^* - \mathbf{x}_j\|_A \le \left(\frac{\kappa_2(A) - 1}{\kappa_2(A) + 1} \right)^j \|\mathbf{x}^* - \mathbf{x}_0\|_A, \qquad (6.4)$$

where $\kappa_2(A) = \|A\|_2 \|A^{-1}\|_2$ denotes the condition number of A with respect to the Euclidean norm.

Proof Let us write $\mathbf{e}_j := \mathbf{x}^* - \mathbf{x}_j$. Then, we have the following two relations:

$$\mathbf{e}_{j+1} = \mathbf{x}^* - \mathbf{x}_j - \alpha_j \mathbf{p}_j = \mathbf{e}_j - \alpha_j \mathbf{p}_j,$$
$$\mathbf{p}_{j+1} = \mathbf{b} - A\mathbf{x}_{j+1} = A(\mathbf{x}^* - \mathbf{x}_{j+1}) = A\mathbf{e}_{j+1}.$$

The first one leads to

$$\|\mathbf{e}_{j+1}\|_A^2 = \langle \mathbf{e}_{j+1}, \mathbf{e}_j - \alpha_j \mathbf{p}_j \rangle_A = \langle \mathbf{e}_{j+1}, \mathbf{e}_j \rangle_A - \alpha_j \langle \mathbf{e}_{j+1}, \mathbf{p}_j \rangle_A.$$

The orthogonality of $\mathbf{p}_j$ and $\mathbf{p}_{j+1}$ and the fact that $\mathbf{p}_{j+1} = A\mathbf{e}_{j+1}$ shows

$$\langle \mathbf{e}_{j+1}, \mathbf{p}_j \rangle_A = \langle A\mathbf{e}_{j+1}, \mathbf{p}_j \rangle_2 = \langle \mathbf{p}_{j+1}, \mathbf{p}_j \rangle_2 = 0,$$

which allows us to derive

$$\|\mathbf{e}_{j+1}\|_A^2 = \langle \mathbf{e}_{j+1}, \mathbf{e}_j \rangle_A = \langle A\mathbf{e}_j, \mathbf{e}_{j+1} \rangle_2 = \langle \mathbf{p}_j, \mathbf{e}_{j+1} \rangle_2 = \langle \mathbf{p}_j, \mathbf{e}_j - \alpha_j \mathbf{p}_j \rangle_2$$
$$= \langle \mathbf{p}_j, \mathbf{e}_j \rangle_2 - \alpha_j \langle \mathbf{p}_j, \mathbf{p}_j \rangle_2 = \langle A\mathbf{e}_j, \mathbf{e}_j \rangle_2 - \alpha_j \langle \mathbf{p}_j, \mathbf{p}_j \rangle_2$$
$$= \langle A\mathbf{e}_j, \mathbf{e}_j \rangle_2 \left(1 - \alpha_j \frac{\langle \mathbf{p}_j, \mathbf{p}_j \rangle_2}{\langle A\mathbf{e}_j, \mathbf{e}_j \rangle_2} \right)$$
$$= \|\mathbf{e}_j\|_A^2 \left(1 - \frac{\langle \mathbf{p}_j, \mathbf{p}_j \rangle_2}{\langle A\mathbf{p}_j, \mathbf{p}_j \rangle_2} \frac{\langle \mathbf{p}_j, \mathbf{p}_j \rangle_2}{\langle \mathbf{p}_j, A^{-1}\mathbf{p}_j \rangle_2} \right)$$
$$\le \|\mathbf{e}_j\|_A^2 \left(1 - \frac{4\lambda_1 \lambda_n}{(\lambda_1 + \lambda_n)^2} \right)$$
$$= \|\mathbf{e}_j\|_A^2 \frac{(\lambda_n - \lambda_1)^2}{(\lambda_n + \lambda_1)^2},$$

using the Kantorovich inequality. From this, we can conclude that

$$\|e_{j+1}\|_A \leq \frac{\kappa_2(A) - 1}{\kappa_2(A) + 1} \|e_j\|_A$$

and iterating this argument gives the stated error bound and convergence.   □

The predicted error bound shows that the convergence is best if the condition number of A is close to 1 and that the convergence will be arbitrarily slow if the condition number is large. We can even estimate the number of iterations that we would need to reduce the initial error $\|x^* - x_0\|_A$ to a given $\epsilon > 0$, though this estimate is true only when one is working in exact arithmetic.

Corollary 6.4   *Let $A \in \mathbb{R}^{n \times n}$ be symmetric and positive definite. If $\{x_j\}$ denotes the iterations of the steepest descent method then we have*

$$\frac{\|x^* - x_j\|_A}{\|x^* - x_0\|_A} \leq \epsilon$$

after at most $j \geq \frac{1}{2}\kappa_2(A) \log(1/\epsilon)$ steps.

Proof   Let us write $\kappa := \kappa_2(A)$. It follows from (6.4) that the relative error drops below ϵ if

$$\left(\frac{\kappa + 1}{\kappa - 1}\right)^j > \frac{1}{\epsilon}.$$

Taking the logarithm of both sides shows that we need

$$j \geq \frac{\log(1/\epsilon)}{\log\left(\frac{\kappa+1}{\kappa-1}\right)}. \tag{6.5}$$

Since $\kappa \geq 1$, we can use the expansion

$$\log\left(\frac{\kappa + 1}{\kappa - 1}\right) = 2 \sum_{k=0}^{\infty} \frac{1}{2k + 1} \kappa^{-2k-1} = 2\left[\frac{1}{\kappa} + \frac{1}{3\kappa^3} + \frac{1}{5\kappa^5} + \cdots\right] \geq \frac{2}{\kappa}$$

to see that (6.5) is satisfied if $j \geq \frac{1}{2}\kappa \log(1/\epsilon)$.   □

The next example shows that the error bound of the previous theorem can be sharp, showing also that even for moderately conditioned matrices the convergence of the steepest descent method becomes unacceptably slow.

Example 6.5   Let us choose the following matrix, right-hand side and initial position:

$$A = \begin{pmatrix} 1 & 0 \\ 0 & 9 \end{pmatrix}, \quad b = \begin{pmatrix} 0 \\ 0 \end{pmatrix}, \quad x_0 = \begin{pmatrix} 9 \\ 1 \end{pmatrix}.$$

It is not too difficult to see that the method of steepest descent produces the iterations

$$\mathbf{x}_j = (0.8)^j (9, (-1)^j)^{\mathrm{T}},$$

which are depicted in Figure 6.1.

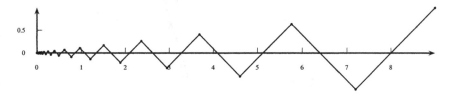

Figure 6.1 Steepest descent for the example.

Since the solution $\mathbf{x}^*$ is obviously given by $\mathbf{x}^* = \mathbf{0}$, we can easily compute all relevant quantities from Theorem 6.3. First of all we have $\kappa_2(A) = 9$ and hence the convergence factor is $(\kappa_2(A) - 1)/(\kappa_2(A) + 1) = 0.8$. Moreover, we have $\|\mathbf{x}_0 - \mathbf{x}^*\|_A = \|\mathbf{x}_0\|_A = \sqrt{90}$ and

$$\|\mathbf{x}_j - \mathbf{x}^*\|_A^2 = (0.8)^{2j}(9, (-1)^j) \begin{pmatrix} 1 & 0 \\ 0 & 9 \end{pmatrix} \begin{pmatrix} 9 \\ (-1)^j \end{pmatrix} = (0.8)^{2j} 90 = 0.8^{2j} \|\mathbf{x}_0 - \mathbf{x}^*\|_A^2.$$

Thus, we have equality in equation (6.4).

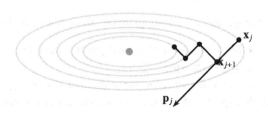

Figure 6.2 The steepest descent method, level curves.

The problem of the previous example becomes more apparent if we look at the level curves of the corresponding quadratic function $f(\mathbf{x}) = \mathbf{x}^{\mathrm{T}} A \mathbf{x} = \frac{1}{2}(x_1^2 + 9x_2^2)$, which are ellipses, see Figure 6.2. Since the new search direction has to be orthogonal to the previous one, we are always tangential to the level curves, and hence the new direction does not point towards the centre of the ellipses, which is our solution vector.

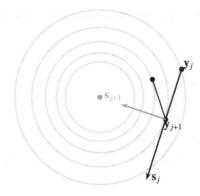

Figure 6.3 The steepest descent method, level curves after scaling.

Thus, it would make sense to introduce a new coordinate system by setting $\mathbf{y} := A^{1/2}\mathbf{x}$, in which the function becomes $g(\mathbf{y}) = f(A^{-1/2}\mathbf{y}) = \frac{1}{2}\mathbf{y}^T\mathbf{y}$. Following this idea, we transform the positions by setting $\mathbf{y}_j := A^{1/2}\mathbf{x}_j$ and the directions by $\mathbf{s}_j := A^{1/2}\mathbf{p}_j$. If the new search directions are orthogonal as shown in Figure 6.3, we find the minimum in two steps. Moreover, being orthogonal now translates back into $0 = \mathbf{s}_j^T\mathbf{s}_{j+1} = \mathbf{p}_j^T A\mathbf{p}_{j+1} = \langle A\mathbf{p}_j, \mathbf{p}_{j+1}\rangle_2$.
Following these ideas, we make the following definition.

Definition 6.6   The search directions $\mathbf{p}_0, \ldots, \mathbf{p}_{n-1} \in \mathbb{R}^n \setminus \{0\}$ are called *A-conjugate* for a given positive definite and symmetric matrix $A \in \mathbb{R}^{n \times n}$ if $\langle A\mathbf{p}_k, \mathbf{p}_j\rangle_2 = 0$ for all $0 \le j \ne k \le n - 1$.

The following properties of A-conjugate directions can easily be verified.

Remark 6.7   • Since A is symmetric and positive definite, we have for each $\mathbf{p} \ne 0$ that $\langle A\mathbf{p}, \mathbf{p}\rangle_2 = \langle \mathbf{p}, A\mathbf{p}\rangle_2 > 0$.
  • As in (6.3), we can introduce an inner product via $\langle \mathbf{x}, \mathbf{y}\rangle_A := \langle A\mathbf{x}, \mathbf{y}\rangle_2 = \langle \mathbf{x}, A\mathbf{y}\rangle_2$. With respect to this inner product, the search directions are orthogonal.
  • A-conjugate directions are always linearly independent.

For A-conjugate directions it turns out that the generic algorithm, Algorithm 19, terminates after n steps, so that the method is actually a direct method. Of course, we hope to have an acceptable approximation after significantly fewer iterations. However, in some cases, due to numerical contamination, the algorithm might even require more than n steps.

Theorem 6.8   *Let $A \in \mathbb{R}^{n \times n}$ be symmetric and positive definite. Let $\mathbf{x}_0 \in \mathbb{R}^n$*

be given and assume that the search directions $\mathbf{p}_0, \ldots, \mathbf{p}_{n-1} \in \mathbb{R}^n \setminus \{0\}$ *are A-conjugate. The generic Algorithm 19 terminates after at most n steps with the solution* $\mathbf{x}^*$ *of* $A\mathbf{x} = \mathbf{b}$.

Proof Since the search directions form a basis of $\mathbb{R}^n$ we can represent the vector $\mathbf{x}^* - \mathbf{x}_0$ in this basis, which means that we can find $\beta_0, \ldots, \beta_{n-1}$ with

$$\mathbf{x}^* = \mathbf{x}_0 + \sum_{j=0}^{n-1} \beta_j \mathbf{p}_j.$$

Furthermore, from the generic algorithm, we can conclude that the iterations have the representation

$$\mathbf{x}_i = \mathbf{x}_0 + \sum_{j=0}^{i-1} \alpha_j \mathbf{p}_j, \qquad 0 \le i \le n. \tag{6.6}$$

Hence, it is sufficient to show that $\alpha_i = \beta_i$ for all $0 \le i \le n - 1$. We know that

$$\alpha_i = \frac{\langle \mathbf{r}_i, \mathbf{p}_i \rangle_2}{\langle A\mathbf{p}_i, \mathbf{p}_i \rangle_2}.$$

To compute the β_i, we first observe that

$$\mathbf{b} - A\mathbf{x}_0 = A(\mathbf{x}^* - \mathbf{x}_0) = \sum_{j=0}^{n-1} \beta_j A\mathbf{p}_j$$

and hence

$$\langle \mathbf{b} - A\mathbf{x}_0, \mathbf{p}_i \rangle_2 = \sum_{j=0}^{n-1} \beta_j \langle A\mathbf{p}_j, \mathbf{p}_i \rangle_2 = \beta_i \langle A\mathbf{p}_i, \mathbf{p}_i \rangle_2,$$

because the directions are A-conjugate. This gives the explicit representation

$$\beta_i = \frac{\langle \mathbf{b} - A\mathbf{x}_0, \mathbf{p}_i \rangle_2}{\langle A\mathbf{p}_i, \mathbf{p}_i \rangle_2} = \frac{\langle \mathbf{r}_0, \mathbf{p}_i \rangle_2}{\langle A\mathbf{p}_i, \mathbf{p}_i \rangle_2}, \qquad 0 \le i \le n - 1,$$

which differs, at first sight, from the α_i in the numerator. Fortunately, from (6.6) we can conclude that

$$\mathbf{r}_i = \mathbf{b} - A\mathbf{x}_i = \mathbf{r}_0 - \sum_{j=0}^{i-1} \alpha_j A\mathbf{p}_j,$$

which allows us to derive

$$\langle \mathbf{r}_i, \mathbf{p}_i \rangle_2 = \langle \mathbf{r}_0, \mathbf{p}_i \rangle_2 - \sum_{j=0}^{i-1} \alpha_j \langle A\mathbf{p}_j, \mathbf{p}_i \rangle_2 = \langle \mathbf{r}_0, \mathbf{p}_i \rangle_2,$$

employing again the fact that the directions are A-conjugate. Thus we have $\alpha_i = \beta_i$ for all i. $\qquad\square$

It remains to answer the question regarding how the search directions are actually determined. Obviously, we do not want to determine them a priori but while we iterate, hoping that our iteration will terminate significantly before the iteration step becomes n.

Assume we already have created directions $\mathbf{p}_0, \ldots, \mathbf{p}_j$. In the case of $A\mathbf{x}_{j+1} = \mathbf{b}$ we can terminate the algorithm and hence do not need to compute another direction. Otherwise, we could try to compute the next direction by setting

$$\mathbf{p}_{j+1} = \mathbf{b} - A\mathbf{x}_{j+1} + \sum_{k=0}^{j} \beta_{jk}\mathbf{p}_k = \mathbf{r}_{j+1} + \sum_{k=0}^{j} \beta_{jk}\mathbf{p}_k,$$

where we can determine the coefficients from the $j+1$ conditions

$$0 = \langle A\mathbf{p}_i, \mathbf{p}_{j+1}\rangle_2 = \langle A\mathbf{p}_i, \mathbf{r}_{j+1}\rangle_2 + \sum_{k=0}^{j} \beta_{jk}\langle A\mathbf{p}_i, \mathbf{p}_k\rangle_2$$

$$= \langle A\mathbf{p}_i, \mathbf{r}_{j+1}\rangle_2 + \beta_{ji}\langle A\mathbf{p}_i, \mathbf{p}_i\rangle_2, \qquad 0 \le i \le j,$$

as

$$\beta_{ji} = -\frac{\langle A\mathbf{p}_i, \mathbf{r}_{j+1}\rangle_2}{\langle A\mathbf{p}_i, \mathbf{p}_i\rangle_2}, \qquad 0 \le i \le j.$$

Surprisingly, $\beta_{j0}, \ldots, \beta_{j,j-1}$ vanish automatically, as we will see soon, so that only the coefficient

$$\beta_{j+1} := \beta_{jj} = -\frac{\langle A\mathbf{p}_j, \mathbf{r}_{j+1}\rangle_2}{\langle A\mathbf{p}_j, \mathbf{p}_j\rangle_2}$$

remains and the new direction is given by

$$\mathbf{p}_{j+1} = \mathbf{r}_{j+1} + \beta_{j+1}\mathbf{p}_j.$$

This gives the first preliminary version of the *conjugate gradient (CG) method*, Algorithm 21.

It is now time to show that the so-defined directions are indeed A-conjugate.

Theorem 6.9 *If the CG method does not stop prematurely, the introduced vectors satisfy the following equations:*

$$\langle A\mathbf{p}_j, \mathbf{p}_i\rangle_2 = 0, \qquad\qquad 0 \le j \le i-1, \qquad (6.7)$$

$$\langle \mathbf{r}_j, \mathbf{r}_i\rangle_2 = 0, \qquad\qquad 0 \le j \le i-1, \qquad (6.8)$$

$$\langle \mathbf{r}_j, \mathbf{p}_j\rangle_2 = \langle \mathbf{r}_j, \mathbf{r}_j\rangle_2, \qquad 0 \le j \le i. \qquad (6.9)$$

The CG method terminates with an index $i \le n$ and $\mathbf{r}_i = \mathbf{b} - A\mathbf{x}_i = \mathbf{0} = \mathbf{p}_i$. Hence, it needs at most n steps to compute the solution $\mathbf{x}^*$ of $A\mathbf{x} = \mathbf{b}$.

Algorithm 21: CG method, preliminary version

Input : $A = A^T \in \mathbb{R}^{n \times n}$ positive definite, $\mathbf{b} \in \mathbb{R}^n$.
Output: Approximate solution of $A\mathbf{x} = \mathbf{b}$.

1 Choose $\mathbf{x}_0 \in \mathbb{R}^n$.
2 Set $\mathbf{p}_0 := \mathbf{r}_0 := \mathbf{b} - A\mathbf{x}_0$ and $j := 0$.
3 **while** $\mathbf{r}_j \neq \mathbf{0}$ **do**
4     $\alpha_j := \langle \mathbf{r}_j, \mathbf{p}_j \rangle_2 / \langle A\mathbf{p}_j, \mathbf{p}_j \rangle_2$
5     $\mathbf{x}_{j+1} := \mathbf{x}_j + \alpha_j \mathbf{p}_j$
6     $\mathbf{r}_{j+1} := \mathbf{b} - A\mathbf{x}_{j+1}$
7     $\beta_{j+1} := -\langle A\mathbf{p}_j, \mathbf{r}_{j+1} \rangle_2 / \langle A\mathbf{p}_j, \mathbf{p}_j \rangle_2$
8     $\mathbf{p}_{j+1} := \mathbf{r}_{j+1} + \beta_{j+1} \mathbf{p}_j$
9     $j := j + 1$

Proof We will prove (6.7) to (6.9) by induction. For $i = 0$ there is nothing to show for (6.7) and (6.8); (6.9) follows immediately from $\mathbf{p}_0 = \mathbf{r}_0$.

Let us now assume everything is satisfied for an arbitrary $i \geq 0$. We will first show that then (6.8) follows for $i + 1$. By definition, we have

$$\mathbf{r}_{i+1} = \mathbf{b} - A\mathbf{x}_{i+1} = \mathbf{b} - A\mathbf{x}_i - \alpha_i A\mathbf{p}_i = \mathbf{r}_i - \alpha_i A\mathbf{p}_i. \qquad (6.10)$$

Thus, by the induction hypothesis, we have for $j \leq i - 1$ immediately

$$\langle \mathbf{r}_j, \mathbf{r}_{i+1} \rangle_2 = \langle \mathbf{r}_j, \mathbf{r}_i \rangle_2 - \alpha_i \langle A\mathbf{r}_j, \mathbf{p}_i \rangle_2 = \langle \mathbf{r}_j, \mathbf{r}_i \rangle_2 - \alpha_i \langle A(\mathbf{p}_j - \beta_j \mathbf{p}_{j-1}), \mathbf{p}_i \rangle_2$$
$$= \langle \mathbf{r}_j, \mathbf{r}_i \rangle_2 - \alpha_i \langle A\mathbf{p}_j, \mathbf{p}_i \rangle_2 + \alpha_i \beta_j \langle A\mathbf{p}_{j-1}, \mathbf{p}_i \rangle_2 = 0.$$

For $j = i$ we can use the definition of α_i, equation (6.10) and

$$\langle A\mathbf{r}_i, \mathbf{p}_i \rangle_2 = \langle A(\mathbf{p}_i - \beta_i \mathbf{p}_{i-1}), \mathbf{p}_i \rangle_2 = \langle A\mathbf{p}_i, \mathbf{p}_i \rangle_2$$

and the third induction hypothesis to conclude that

$$\langle \mathbf{r}_i, \mathbf{r}_{i+1} \rangle_2 = \langle \mathbf{r}_i, \mathbf{r}_i \rangle_2 - \alpha_i \langle A\mathbf{r}_i, \mathbf{p}_i \rangle_2 = \langle \mathbf{r}_i, \mathbf{r}_i \rangle_2 - \frac{\langle \mathbf{r}_i, \mathbf{p}_i \rangle_2}{\langle A\mathbf{p}_i, \mathbf{p}_i \rangle_2} \langle A\mathbf{r}_i, \mathbf{p}_i \rangle_2$$
$$= \langle \mathbf{r}_i, \mathbf{r}_i \rangle_2 - \langle \mathbf{r}_i, \mathbf{p}_i \rangle_2 = 0,$$

which finishes the induction step for (6.8). Similarly, we proceed for (6.7). First of all, we have

$$\langle A\mathbf{p}_j, \mathbf{p}_{i+1} \rangle_2 = \langle A\mathbf{p}_j, (\mathbf{r}_{i+1} + \beta_{i+1}\mathbf{p}_i) \rangle_2 = \langle A\mathbf{p}_j, \mathbf{r}_{i+1} \rangle_2 + \beta_{i+1} \langle A\mathbf{p}_j, \mathbf{p}_i \rangle_2.$$

In the case of $j = i$ this leads to

$$\langle A\mathbf{p}_i, \mathbf{p}_{i+1} \rangle_2 = \langle A\mathbf{p}_i, \mathbf{r}_{i+1} \rangle_2 - \frac{\langle A\mathbf{p}_i, \mathbf{r}_{i+1} \rangle_2}{\langle A\mathbf{p}_i, \mathbf{p}_i \rangle_2} \langle A\mathbf{p}_i, \mathbf{p}_i \rangle_2 = 0.$$

In the case of $j \leq i - 1$ we have $\langle A\mathbf{p}_j, \mathbf{p}_{i+1}\rangle_2 = \langle A\mathbf{p}_j, \mathbf{r}_{i+1}\rangle_2$. Moreover, $\alpha_j = 0$ particularly means $\langle \mathbf{r}_j, \mathbf{p}_j\rangle_2 = \langle \mathbf{r}_j, \mathbf{r}_j\rangle_2 = 0$, which is equivalent to $\mathbf{r}_j = \mathbf{0}$. Thus if $\alpha_j = 0$ then the iteration would have stopped before. We hence may assume that $\alpha_j \neq 0$ such that we can use (6.10) to gain the representation $A\mathbf{p}_j = (\mathbf{r}_j - \mathbf{r}_{j+1})/\alpha_j$. Together with (6.8) for $i + 1$ this leads to

$$\langle A\mathbf{p}_j, \mathbf{p}_{i+1}\rangle_2 = \langle A\mathbf{p}_j, \mathbf{r}_{i+1}\rangle_2 = \frac{1}{\alpha_j}\langle \mathbf{r}_j - \mathbf{r}_{j+1}, \mathbf{r}_{i+1}\rangle_2 = 0.$$

This proves (6.7) for $i + 1$. Finally, for (6.9) we use (6.1) from the generic minimisation, which holds for any index, in the form $\langle \mathbf{r}_{i+1}, \mathbf{p}_i\rangle_2 = 0$. From this, we can conclude that

$$\langle \mathbf{r}_{i+1}, \mathbf{p}_{i+1}\rangle_2 = \langle \mathbf{r}_{i+1}, \mathbf{r}_{i+1}\rangle_2 + \beta_{i+1}\langle \mathbf{r}_{i+1}, \mathbf{p}_i\rangle_2 = \langle \mathbf{r}_{i+1}, \mathbf{r}_{i+1}\rangle_2,$$

which finalises our induction step.

For the computation of the next iteration step, we need $\mathbf{p}_{i+1} \neq \mathbf{0}$. If this is not the case then the method terminates. Since $0 = \langle \mathbf{r}_{i+1}, \mathbf{p}_{i+1}\rangle_2 = \|\mathbf{r}_{i+1}\|_2^2$ and hence $\mathbf{r}_{i+1} = \mathbf{0} = \mathbf{b} - A\mathbf{x}_{i+1}$ we have produced a solution. If the method does not terminate early then, after n steps, we have created n conjugate directions and Theorem 6.8 shows that $\mathbf{x}_n$ is the true solution $\mathbf{x}^*$. □

It is possible to improve the preliminary version of the CG method. First of all, we can get rid of the matrix–vector multiplication in the definition of $\mathbf{r}_{j+1}$ by using (6.10). Moreover, from (6.10) it also follows that $A\mathbf{p}_j = \frac{1}{\alpha_j}(\mathbf{r}_j - \mathbf{r}_{j+1})$ such that

$$\begin{aligned}
\beta_{j+1} &= -\frac{\langle A\mathbf{p}_j, \mathbf{r}_{j+1}\rangle_2}{\langle A\mathbf{p}_j, \mathbf{p}_j\rangle_2} = -\frac{1}{\alpha_j}\frac{\langle \mathbf{r}_j, \mathbf{r}_{j+1}\rangle_2 - \langle \mathbf{r}_{j+1}, \mathbf{r}_{j+1}\rangle_2}{\langle A\mathbf{p}_j, \mathbf{p}_j\rangle_2} \\
&= \frac{\langle \mathbf{r}_{j+1}, \mathbf{r}_{j+1}\rangle}{\langle A\mathbf{p}_j, \mathbf{p}_j\rangle_2}\frac{\langle A\mathbf{p}_j, \mathbf{p}_j\rangle_2}{\langle \mathbf{r}_j, \mathbf{p}_j\rangle_2} = \frac{\|\mathbf{r}_{j+1}\|_2^2}{\|\mathbf{r}_j\|_2^2}.
\end{aligned}$$

This leads to a version of the CG method which can easily be run on a parallel computer, and which contains only one matrix–vector multiplication and three inner products and three scalar–vector multiplications, as detailed in Algorithm 22.

In the following theorems we will show some of the properties of the CG algorithm. In particular, we will investigate convergence in the *energy norm* $\|\mathbf{x}\|_A := \sqrt{\langle \mathbf{x}, \mathbf{x}\rangle_A}$, $\mathbf{x} \in \mathbb{R}^n$.

Definition 6.10 Let $A \in \mathbb{R}^{n\times n}$ and $\mathbf{r} \in \mathbb{R}^n$ be given. For $i \in \mathbb{N}$ we define the ith *Krylov space* to A and $\mathbf{r}$ as

$$\mathcal{K}_i(A, \mathbf{r}) = \text{span}\{\mathbf{r}, A\mathbf{r}, \ldots, A^{i-1}\mathbf{r}\}.$$

Algorithm 22: CG method

Input : $A = A^{\mathrm{T}} \in \mathbb{R}^{n \times n}$ positive definite, $\mathbf{b} \in \mathbb{R}^n$.
Output: Approximate solution of $A\mathbf{x} = \mathbf{b}$.

1 Choose $\mathbf{x}_0 \in \mathbb{R}^n$.
2 Set $\mathbf{p}_0 := \mathbf{r}_0 := \mathbf{b} - A\mathbf{x}_0$ and $j := 0$.
3 **while** $\|\mathbf{r}_j\|_2 > \epsilon$ **do**
4 $\quad$ $\mathbf{t}_j := A\mathbf{p}_j$
5 $\quad$ $\alpha_j := \|\mathbf{r}_j\|_2^2 / \langle \mathbf{t}_j, \mathbf{p}_j \rangle_2$
6 $\quad$ $\mathbf{x}_{j+1} := \mathbf{x}_j + \alpha_j \mathbf{p}_j$
7 $\quad$ $\mathbf{r}_{j+1} := \mathbf{r}_j - \alpha_j \mathbf{t}_j$
8 $\quad$ $\beta_{j+1} := \|\mathbf{r}_{j+1}\|_2^2 / \|\mathbf{r}_j\|_2^2$
9 $\quad$ $\mathbf{p}_{j+1} := \mathbf{r}_{j+1} + \beta_{j+1} \mathbf{p}_j$
10 $\quad$ $j := j + 1$

In general, we only have dim $\mathcal{K}_i(A, \mathbf{r}) \leq i$, since $\mathbf{r}$ could, for example, be from the null space of A. Fortunately, in our situation things are much better.

Lemma 6.11 *Let $A \in \mathbb{R}^{n \times n}$ be symmetric and positive definite. Let $\mathbf{p}_i$ and $\mathbf{r}_i$ be the vectors created during the CG iterations. Then,*

$$\mathcal{K}_i(A, \mathbf{r}_0) = \mathrm{span}\{\mathbf{r}_0, \dots, \mathbf{r}_{i-1}\} = \mathrm{span}\{\mathbf{p}_0, \dots, \mathbf{p}_{i-1}\}$$

for $1 \leq i \leq n$. In particular, we have dim $\mathcal{K}_i(A, \mathbf{r}_0) = i$.

Proof The proof is again by induction on i. For $i = 1$ this follows immediately as we have $\mathbf{p}_0 = \mathbf{r}_0$. For the induction step $i \to i + 1$ we assume that we have not stopped prematurely. By construction, we have $\mathbf{p}_i = \mathbf{r}_i + \beta_i \mathbf{p}_{i-1}$ with $\beta_i \neq 0$ as we would have stopped before otherwise. This shows $\mathbf{p}_i \in \mathrm{span}\{\mathbf{r}_i, \mathbf{p}_{i-1}\}$ and hence by induction span$\{\mathbf{p}_0, \dots, \mathbf{p}_i\} \subseteq \mathrm{span}\{\mathbf{r}_0, \dots, \mathbf{r}_i\}$. As the A-conjugate directions $\mathbf{p}_0, \dots, \mathbf{p}_i$ are linearly independent, comparing the dimensions shows that we actually have span$\{\mathbf{p}_0, \dots, \mathbf{p}_i\} = \mathrm{span}\{\mathbf{r}_0, \dots, \mathbf{r}_i\}$.
Using $\mathbf{r}_i = \mathbf{r}_{i-1} - \alpha_{i-1} A\mathbf{p}_{i-1}$, where we again may assume that $\alpha_{i-1} \neq 0$, we find $\mathbf{r}_i \in \mathrm{span}\{\mathbf{r}_{i-1}, A\mathbf{p}_{i-1}\} \subseteq \mathcal{K}_i(A, \mathbf{r}_0) + A\mathcal{K}_i(A, \mathbf{r}_0) = \mathcal{K}_{i+1}(A, \mathbf{r}_0)$ and thus span$\{\mathbf{r}_0, \dots, \mathbf{r}_i\} \subseteq \mathcal{K}_{i+1}(A, \mathbf{r}_0)$ and a comparison of the dimensions shows equality again. $\qquad\square$

Recall that the true solution $\mathbf{x}^*$ of $A\mathbf{x} = \mathbf{b}$ and the iterations $\mathbf{x}_i$ of the CG method can be written as

$$\mathbf{x}^* = \mathbf{x}_0 + \sum_{j=0}^{n-1} \alpha_j \mathbf{p}_j \quad \text{and} \quad \mathbf{x}_i = \mathbf{x}_0 + \sum_{j=0}^{i-1} \alpha_j \mathbf{p}_j.$$

Moreover, by Lemma 6.11, it is possible to represent an arbitrary element $\mathbf{x} \in \mathbf{x}_0 + \mathcal{K}_i(A, \mathbf{r}_0)$ by

$$\mathbf{x} = \mathbf{x}_0 + \sum_{j=0}^{i-1} \gamma_j \mathbf{p}_j$$

with certain numbers $\gamma_0, \ldots, \gamma_{i-1} \in \mathbb{R}$. Let us define $d_j = \langle A\mathbf{p}_j, \mathbf{p}_j \rangle_2$. Since the directions are A-conjugate, we can conclude that

$$\|\mathbf{x}^* - \mathbf{x}_i\|_A^2 = \left\| \sum_{j=i}^{n-1} \alpha_j \mathbf{p}_j \right\|_A^2 = \sum_{j,k=i}^{n-1} \alpha_j \alpha_k \langle A\mathbf{p}_k, \mathbf{p}_j \rangle_2 = \sum_{j=i}^{n-1} d_j |\alpha_j|^2$$

$$\leq \sum_{j=i}^{n-1} d_j |\alpha_j|^2 + \sum_{j=0}^{i-1} d_j |\alpha_j - \gamma_j|^2 = \left\| \sum_{j=i}^{n-1} \alpha_j \mathbf{p}_j + \sum_{j=0}^{i-1} (\alpha_j - \gamma_j) \mathbf{p}_j \right\|_A^2$$

$$= \left\| \mathbf{x}^* - \mathbf{x}_0 - \sum_{j=0}^{i-1} \gamma_j \mathbf{p}_j \right\|_A^2 = \|\mathbf{x}^* - \mathbf{x}\|_A^2.$$

Since this holds for an arbitrary $\mathbf{x} \in \mathbf{x}_0 + \mathcal{K}_i(A, \mathbf{r}_0)$ we have proven the following theorem.

Theorem 6.12   *Let $A \in \mathbb{R}^{n \times n}$ be symmetric and positive definite. The iteration $\mathbf{x}_i$ from the CG method gives the best approximation to the solution $\mathbf{x}^*$ of $A\mathbf{x} = \mathbf{b}$ from the affine space $\mathbf{x}_0 + \mathcal{K}_i(A, \mathbf{r}_0)$ with respect to the energy norm $\| \cdot \|_A$, i.e.*

$$\|\mathbf{x}^* - \mathbf{x}_i\|_A \leq \|\mathbf{x}^* - \mathbf{x}\|_A, \qquad \mathbf{x} \in \mathbf{x}_0 + \mathcal{K}_i(A, \mathbf{r}_0).$$

The same idea shows that the iteration sequence is monotone.

Corollary 6.13   *The sequence of iterations of the CG method is monotone in the energy norm, i.e. for all i we have*

$$\|\mathbf{x}^* - \mathbf{x}_{i+1}\|_A \leq \|\mathbf{x}^* - \mathbf{x}_i\|_A.$$

Proof   Using the same notation as in the theorem, we find

$$\mathbf{x}_i \in \mathbf{x}_0 + \mathcal{K}_i(A, \mathbf{r}_0) \subseteq \mathbf{x}_0 + \mathcal{K}_{i+1}(A, \mathbf{r}_0).$$

Since $\mathbf{x}_{i+1}$ minimises $\mathbf{x} \mapsto \|\mathbf{x}^* - \mathbf{x}\|_A$ over $\mathbf{x}_0 + \mathcal{K}_{i+1}(A, \mathbf{r}_0)$, the statement follows immediately.   □

Next, let us rewrite this approximation problem in the original basis of the Krylov space. We will use the following notation. We denote the set of all polynomials of degree less than or equal to n by $\pi_n = \pi_n(\mathbb{R})$.

For a polynomial $P(t) = \sum_{j=0}^{i-1} \gamma_j t^j \in \pi_{i-1}$, a matrix $A \in \mathbb{R}^{n \times n}$ and $\mathbf{x} \in \mathbb{R}^n$ we will write

$$P(A) = \sum_{j=0}^{i-1} \gamma_j A^j, \qquad P(A)\mathbf{x} = \sum_{j=0}^{i-1} \gamma_j A^j \mathbf{x}.$$

If $\mathbf{x}$ is an eigenvector of A with eigenvalue λ then

$$P(A)\mathbf{x} = \sum_{j=0}^{i-1} \gamma_j \lambda^j \mathbf{x} = P(\lambda)\mathbf{x}.$$

Theorem 6.14 *Let $A \in \mathbb{R}^{n \times n}$ be symmetric and positive definite, having the eigenvalues $0 < \lambda_1 \leq \cdots \leq \lambda_n$. If $\mathbf{x}^*$ denotes the solution of $A\mathbf{x} = \mathbf{b}$ and if $\mathbf{x}_i$ denotes the ith iteration of the CG method, then*

$$\|\mathbf{x}^* - \mathbf{x}_i\|_A \leq \min_{\substack{P \in \pi_i \\ P(0)=1}} \max_{1 \leq j \leq n} |P(\lambda_j)| \, \|\mathbf{x}^* - \mathbf{x}_0\|_A. \tag{6.11}$$

Proof Let us express an arbitrary $\mathbf{x} \in \mathbf{x}_0 + \mathcal{K}_i(A, \mathbf{r}_0)$ as

$$\mathbf{x} = \mathbf{x}_0 + \sum_{j=0}^{i-1} \gamma_j A^j \mathbf{r}_0 =: \mathbf{x}_0 + Q(A)\mathbf{r}_0,$$

introducing the polynomial $Q(t) = \sum_{j=0}^{i-1} \gamma_j t^j \in \pi_{i-1}$, where we set $Q = 0$ for $i = 0$. This gives with $\mathbf{r}_0 = A(\mathbf{x}^* - \mathbf{x}_0)$ and $P(A) := I - Q(A)A$ the representation

$$\mathbf{x}^* - \mathbf{x} = \mathbf{x}^* - \mathbf{x}_0 - Q(A)\mathbf{r}_0 = \mathbf{x}^* - \mathbf{x}_0 - Q(A)A(\mathbf{x}^* - \mathbf{x}_0)$$
$$= (I - Q(A)A)(\mathbf{x}^* - \mathbf{x}_0) = P(A)(\mathbf{x}^* - \mathbf{x}_0)$$

and hence

$$\|\mathbf{x}^* - \mathbf{x}\|_A = \|P(A)(\mathbf{x}^* - \mathbf{x}_0)\|_A.$$

For the polynomial P we have

$$P(t) = 1 - \sum_{j=0}^{i-1} \gamma_j t^{j+1} = 1 - \sum_{j=1}^{i} \gamma_{j-1} t^j$$

showing $P \in \pi_i$ with $P(0) = 1$. However, if, vice versa, $P \in \pi_i$ with $P(0) = 1$ is given then we can define $Q(t) = (P(t) - 1)/t \in \pi_{i-1}$, which leads to an element from $\mathbf{x}_0 + \mathcal{K}_i(A, \mathbf{r}_0)$, for which the calculation above holds. Thus, Theorem 6.12 yields

$$\|\mathbf{x}^* - \mathbf{x}_i\|_A \leq \min_{\substack{P \in \pi_i \\ P(0)=1}} \|P(A)(\mathbf{x}^* - \mathbf{x}_0)\|_A. \tag{6.12}$$

Next, let $\mathbf{w}_1, \ldots, \mathbf{w}_n$ be an orthonormal basis of $\mathbb{R}^n$ consisting of eigenvectors of A associated with the eigenvalues $\lambda_1, \ldots, \lambda_n$. These vectors satisfy

$$\langle \mathbf{w}_j, \mathbf{w}_k \rangle_A = \langle A\mathbf{w}_j, \mathbf{w}_k \rangle_2 = \lambda_j \langle \mathbf{w}_j, \mathbf{w}_k \rangle_2 = \lambda_j \delta_{jk}.$$

Moreover, we can represent every vector using this basis and with such a representation $\mathbf{x}^* - \mathbf{x}_0 = \sum \rho_j \mathbf{w}_j$ we can conclude that

$$P(A)(\mathbf{x}^* - \mathbf{x}_0) = \sum_{j=1}^{n} \rho_j P(\lambda_j) \mathbf{w}_j$$

holds, which leads to

$$\|P(A)(\mathbf{x}^* - \mathbf{x}_0)\|_A^2 = \sum_{j=1}^{n} \rho_j^2 \lambda_j P(\lambda_j)^2 \leq \max_{1 \leq j \leq n} P(\lambda_j)^2 \sum_{j=1}^{n} \rho_j^2 \lambda_j$$

$$= \max_{1 \leq j \leq n} P(\lambda_j)^2 \|\mathbf{x}^* - \mathbf{x}_0\|_A^2.$$

Plugging this into (6.12) gives the desired inequality.   □

Hence, we have converted the weighted ℓ_2-approximation problem into a discrete ℓ_∞-approximation problem. Recall that by Theorem 6.8 the CG method converges after at most n steps. This can also directly be concluded from (6.11), since for $i = n$ we can pick a polynomial $P^* \in \pi_n$ with $P^*(0) = 1$ and $P^*(\lambda_j) = 0$ for $1 \leq j \leq n$, such that (6.11) gives

$$\|\mathbf{x}^* - \mathbf{x}_n\|_A \leq \min_{\substack{P \in \pi_n \\ P(0)=1}} \max_{1 \leq j \leq n} |P(\lambda_j)| \, \|\mathbf{x}^* - \mathbf{x}_0\|_A \leq \max_{1 \leq j \leq n} |P^*(\lambda_j)| \, \|\mathbf{x}^* - \mathbf{x}_0\|_A = 0.$$

This result can obviously be generalised in the following sense.

Corollary 6.15 *Assume that $A \in \mathbb{R}^{n \times n}$ is symmetric and positive definite and has $1 \leq d \leq n$ distinct eigenvalues. Then, the CG method terminates with the solution $\mathbf{x}^* \in \mathbb{R}^n$ of $A\mathbf{x} = \mathbf{b}$ after at most d steps.*

Since the eigenvalues are in general unknown, we need to convert the discrete ℓ_∞ problem into a continuous L_∞ approximation problem by further estimating

$$\|\mathbf{x}^* - \mathbf{x}_i\|_A \leq \min_{\substack{P \in \pi_i \\ P(0)=1}} \|P\|_{L_\infty[\lambda_1, \lambda_n]} \|\mathbf{x}^* - \mathbf{x}_0\|_A,$$

where $\|P\|_{L_\infty[a,b]} = \max_{x \in [a,b]} |P(x)|$. Note that λ_1 and λ_n can be replaced by estimates $\tilde{\lambda}_1 \leq \lambda_1$ and $\tilde{\lambda}_n \geq \lambda_n$.

The solution of this approximation problem can be computed explicitly. It involves the classical *Chebyshev polynomials*.

Definition 6.16 The *Chebyshev polynomial* of degree $n \in \mathbb{N}_0$ is defined by

$$T_n(t) = \cos(n \arccos(t)), \qquad t \in [-1, 1].$$

It is easy to see that we have $T_0(t) = 1$, $T_1(t) = t$ and

$$T_{n+1}(t) = 2tT_n(t) - T_{n-1}(t). \tag{6.13}$$

From this, it follows immediately that T_n is indeed a polynomial of degree n. We also need some further elementary properties of the Chebyshev polynomials, which we will collect in the next lemma.

Lemma 6.17 *The Chebyshev polynomials have the following properties.*

1. For every $t \in [0, 1)$, we have

$$\frac{1}{2}\left(\frac{1+\sqrt{t}}{1-\sqrt{t}}\right)^n \leq T_n\left(\frac{1+t}{1-t}\right).$$

2. For every $t \in [-1, 1]$ we have $|T_n(t)| \leq 1$.
3. On $[-1, 1]$, the Chebyshev polynomial T_n attains its extreme values ± 1 at $t_k = \cos(\pi k/n)$, $0 \leq k \leq n$. To be more precise we have $T_n(t_k) = (-1)^k$.

Proof The second property follows immediately from the definition. The third property follows from the second one and by simple computation. For the first property it is helpful to show that for $|x| \geq 1$, we have the representation

$$T_n(x) = \frac{1}{2}\left(\left(x + \sqrt{x^2 - 1}\right)^n + \left(x - \sqrt{x^2 - 1}\right)^n\right).$$

This is clear for $n = 0$ and $n = 1$ and for general n it follows if we can show that the right-hand side follows the same recursion (6.13) as the Chebyshev polynomials, which is easily done. If we now set $x = \frac{1+t}{1-t}$ with $t \in [0, 1)$ we have $x \geq 1$ and hence

$$T_n\left(\frac{1+t}{1-t}\right) \geq \frac{1}{2}\left(x + \sqrt{x^2 - 1}\right)^n = \frac{1}{2}\left(\frac{1+\sqrt{t}}{1-\sqrt{t}}\right)^n. \qquad \square$$

With this at hand, we can continue with bounding the error for the conjugate gradient method.

Theorem 6.18 *Let $\lambda_n > \lambda_1 > 0$. The problem*

$$\min\{\|P\|_{L_\infty[\lambda_1, \lambda_n]} : P \in \pi_i, P(0) = 1\}$$

has the solution

$$P^*(t) = T_i\left(\frac{\lambda_n + \lambda_1 - 2t}{\lambda_n - \lambda_1}\right) \bigg/ T_i\left(\frac{\lambda_n + \lambda_1}{\lambda_n - \lambda_1}\right), \qquad t \in [\lambda_1, \lambda_n].$$

Proof   Setting $\gamma = \lambda_1/\lambda_n \in (0, 1)$ shows

$$\frac{\lambda_n + \lambda_1}{\lambda_n - \lambda_1} = \frac{1 + \gamma}{1 - \gamma} \geq 1.$$

This means that the denominator of P^* is positive and P^* is hence a feasible candidate for the minimum.

Noting that

$$t \mapsto \frac{\lambda_n + \lambda_1 - 2t}{\lambda_n - \lambda_1}, \qquad t \in [\lambda_1, \lambda_n]$$

maps $[\lambda_1, \lambda_n]$ linearly to $[-1, 1]$, we can conclude from Lemma 6.17 that there are $i + 1$ different points $s_j \in [\lambda_1, \lambda_n]$ on which P^* attains its extreme value

$$M := \frac{1}{T_i\left(\frac{\lambda_n + \lambda_1}{\lambda_n - \lambda_1}\right)}$$

on $[\lambda_1, \lambda_n]$ with alternating signs.

Now, assume that P^* is not the solution to the minimisation problem, i.e. that there is a $Q \in \pi_i$ with $Q(0) = 1$ and $|Q(t)| < M$ for all $t \in [\lambda_1, \lambda_n]$. Then, $P^* - Q$ must have alternating signs in the s_j, which means that $P^* - Q$ must have at least i zeros in $[\lambda_1, \lambda_n]$. However, $P^* - Q$ is also zero at $0 \notin [\lambda_1, \lambda_n]$, which means that $P^* - Q$ must have at least $i + 1$ different zeros. But since $P^* - Q \in \pi_i$ this means $P^* = Q$ by the fundamental theorem of algebra. This is, however, a contradiction to our assumption on Q.   □

This altogether gives the final estimate on the convergence of the CG method. We have, again with $\gamma = \lambda_1/\lambda_n$, the bound

$$\|\mathbf{x}^* - \mathbf{x}_i\|_A \leq \min_{\substack{P \in \pi_i \\ P(0)=1}} \|P\|_{L_\infty[\lambda_1, \lambda_n]} \|\mathbf{x}^* - \mathbf{x}_0\|_A$$

$$\leq \max_{t \in [\lambda_1, \lambda_n]} \frac{\left|T_i\left(\frac{\lambda_n + \lambda_1 - 2t}{\lambda_n - \lambda_1}\right)\right|}{T_i\left(\frac{\lambda_n + \lambda_1}{\lambda_n - \lambda_1}\right)} \|\mathbf{x}^* - \mathbf{x}_0\|_A$$

$$\leq \frac{1}{T_i\left(\frac{1+\gamma}{1-\gamma}\right)} \|\mathbf{x}^* - \mathbf{x}_0\|_A$$

$$\leq 2\left(\frac{1 - \sqrt{\gamma}}{1 + \sqrt{\gamma}}\right)^i \|\mathbf{x}^* - \mathbf{x}_0\|_A.$$

Finally using the fact that $1/\gamma = \kappa_2(A)$ shows that we have the following result.

Theorem 6.19   *Let $A \in \mathbb{R}^{n \times n}$ be symmetric and positive definite. The sequence* *of iterations $\{x_i\}$ generated by the CG method satisfies the estimate*

$$\|x^* - x_i\|_A \le 2\|x^* - x_0\|_A \left(\frac{1 - \sqrt{\gamma}}{1 + \sqrt{\gamma}}\right)^i \le 2\|x^* - x_0\|_A \left(\frac{\sqrt{\kappa_2(A)} - 1}{\sqrt{\kappa_2(A)} + 1}\right)^i, \quad (6.14)$$

where $\gamma = 1/\kappa_2(A) = \lambda_1/\lambda_n$.

As in the case of the method of steepest descent we can determine the expected number of iterations necessary to reduce the initial error to a given $\epsilon > 0$. The proof of the following result is the same as the proof of Corollary 6.4.

Corollary 6.20 *Let $A \in \mathbb{R}^{n \times n}$ be symmetric and positive definite. If $\{x_j\}$ denotes the iterations of the conjugate gradient method then we have*

$$\frac{\|x^* - x_j\|_A}{\|x^* - x_0\|_A} \le \epsilon$$

after at most $j \ge \frac{1}{2}\sqrt{\kappa_2(A)} \log(1/\epsilon)$ steps.

If we compare this result with $j \ge \frac{1}{2}\kappa_2(A)\log(1/\epsilon)$, which is required for the steepest descent method and note that $\sqrt{\kappa_2(A)} \le \kappa_2(A)$ we see that the CG method is significantly faster than the steepest descent method.

In specific situations, the estimate (6.14) can further be improved. As a matter of fact, (6.14) is useful only if the condition number is small and if the eigenvalues are more or less quasi-uniformly distributed over $[\lambda_1, \lambda_n]$. If the eigenvalues are clustered, it is possible to choose better polynomials.

For example, let us assume that A has an isolated largest eigenvalue, i.e. we have $\lambda_1 \le \lambda_2 \le \cdots \le \lambda_{n-1} \ll \lambda_n$. Then, with each polynomial $\tilde{P} \in \pi_{i-1}$ with $\tilde{P}(0) = 1$ we can define a polynomial $P \in \pi_i$ by

$$P(t) := \left(\frac{\lambda_n - t}{\lambda_n}\right)\tilde{P}(t), \qquad t \in [\lambda_1, \lambda_n],$$

which also satisfies $P(0) = 1$ but also $P(\lambda_n) = 0$ and, since the first factor has absolute value less than or equal to one on $[\lambda_1, \lambda_n]$, we also have $|P(\lambda_j)| \le |\tilde{P}(\lambda_j)|$. Thus, using (6.11) and then the ideas leading to (6.14), we can derive

$$\|x^* - x_i\|_A \le \min_{\substack{P \in \pi_i \\ P(0)=1}} \max_{1 \le j \le n} |P(\lambda_j)| \, \|x^* - x_0\|_A \le \min_{\substack{P \in \pi_{i-1} \\ P(0)=1}} \max_{1 \le j \le n-1} |P(\lambda_j)| \, \|x^* - x_0\|_A$$

$$\le \max_{t \in [\lambda_1, \lambda_{n-1}]} \frac{\left|T_{i-1}\left(\frac{\lambda_{n-1} + \lambda_1 - 2t}{\lambda_{n-1} - \lambda_1}\right)\right|}{T_{i-1}\left(\frac{\lambda_{n-1} + \lambda_1}{\lambda_{n-1} - \lambda_1}\right)} \|x^* - x_0\|_A \le \frac{1}{T_{i-1}\left(\frac{1+\gamma}{1-\gamma}\right)}\|x^* - x_0\|_A$$

$$\le 2\left(\frac{1 - \sqrt{\gamma}}{1 + \sqrt{\gamma}}\right)^{i-1} \|x^* - x_0\|_A$$

with $\gamma = \lambda_1/\lambda_{n-1}$. Hence, we have eliminated the largest eigenvalue and expressed convergence using the *reduced* condition number $\kappa_{n-1} := \lambda_{n-1}/\lambda_1$ at the cost of one factor. Obviously, this result can be generalised in such a way that the d largest eigenvalues are discarded.

Corollary 6.21 *If $A \in \mathbb{R}^{n \times n}$ is symmetric and positive definite with eigenvalues $0 < \lambda_1 \le \cdots \le \lambda_{n-d} \ll \lambda_{n-d+1} \le \cdots \le \lambda_n$, then we have for $i \ge d$ the estimate*

$$\|\mathbf{x}^* - \mathbf{x}_i\|_A \le 2\left(\frac{\sqrt{\kappa_{n-d}} - 1}{\sqrt{\kappa_{n-d}} + 1}\right)^{i-d} \|\mathbf{x}^* - \mathbf{x}_0\|_A,$$

with the reduced condition number $\kappa_{n-d} = \lambda_{n-d}/\lambda_1$.

Similarly, we can deal with an isolated smallest eigenvalue. However, the situation here is somewhat worse, in the following sense. If we proceed as above then, for a polynomial $\tilde{P} \in \pi_{i-1}$ with $\tilde{P}(0) = 1$, we define the polynomial $P \in \pi_i$ by

$$P(t) = \left(\frac{\lambda_1 - t}{\lambda_1}\right)\tilde{P}(t), \qquad t \in [\lambda_1, \lambda_n].$$

We still have $P(0) = 1$ and $P(\lambda_1) = 0$. But at the other eigenvalues λ_j the absolute value of the first factor can only be bounded by $(\lambda_j - \lambda_1)/\lambda_1 \le (\lambda_n - \lambda_1)/\lambda_1 = \tilde{\kappa}_1 - 1$ with the (original) condition number $\tilde{\kappa}_1 = \kappa_2(A) = \lambda_n/\lambda_1$. Hence, this time we only have

$$\|\mathbf{x}^* - \mathbf{x}_i\|_A \le 2(\tilde{\kappa}_1 - 1)\left(\frac{\sqrt{\tilde{\kappa}_2} - 1}{\sqrt{\tilde{\kappa}_2} + 1}\right)^{i-1} \|\mathbf{x}^* - \mathbf{x}_0\|_A$$

with $\tilde{\kappa}_2 = \lambda_n/\lambda_2$. This can still be an improvement over the standard estimate since the condition number enters only as a constant factor but the convergence forcing term can significantly improve. Of course, we can iterate this process, as well.

Corollary 6.22 *If $A \in \mathbb{R}^{n \times n}$ is symmetric and positive definite with eigenvalues $0 < \lambda_1 \le \cdots \le \lambda_d \ll \lambda_{d+1} \le \cdots \le \lambda_n$, then we have for $i \ge d$ the estimate*

$$\|\mathbf{x}^* - \mathbf{x}_i\|_A \le 2\prod_{j=1}^{d}(\tilde{\kappa}_j - 1)\left(\frac{\sqrt{\tilde{\kappa}_{d+1}} - 1}{\sqrt{\tilde{\kappa}_{d+1}} + 1}\right)^{i-d} \|\mathbf{x}^* - \mathbf{x}_0\|_A,$$

with the reduced condition number $\tilde{\kappa}_j = \lambda_n/\lambda_j$.

This also shows that the method still converges if the matrix is almost singular, i.e. if $\lambda_1 \approx \cdots \approx \lambda_d \approx 0$, but it might take some time for the convergence to become effective. The convergence rate depends then on $[\lambda_{d+1}, \lambda_n]$. Hence, one should try to use appropriate matrix manipulations to reduce the condition number of A. If the matrix A is almost singular one should try to find a transformation of the smallest eigenvalues to zero and of the bigger eigenvalues to an interval of the form $(\lambda, \lambda(1 + \varepsilon)) \subset (0, \infty)$ with ε as small as possible.

In general it does not matter if, during this process, the rank of the matrix is reduced. Generally, this leads only to a small additional error but also to a significant increase in the convergence rate of the CG method.

6.2 GMRES and MINRES

We are now going to discuss how to solve the linear system $A\mathbf{x} = \mathbf{b}$ for arbitrary matrices $A \in \mathbb{R}^{n \times n}$ using ideas similar to those we applied in the CG method.

One possibility would be to look at the normal equations $A^T A \mathbf{x} = A^T \mathbf{b}$, which lead to the same solution, provided the matrix A is invertible. Since $A^T A$ is symmetric and positive definite, we can use the CG method to solve this problem. If $\mathbf{x}^*$ is the solution and $\mathbf{x}_j \in \mathbf{x}_0 + \mathcal{K}_j(A^T A, A^T \mathbf{r}_0)$ is a typical iteration then we have the identity

$$\|\mathbf{x}^* - \mathbf{x}_j\|^2_{A^T A} = (\mathbf{x}^* - \mathbf{x}_j)^T A^T A (\mathbf{x}^* - \mathbf{x}_j) = (A\mathbf{x}^* - A\mathbf{x}_j)^T (A\mathbf{x}^* - A\mathbf{x}_j)$$
$$= \|\mathbf{b} - A\mathbf{x}_j\|^2_2.$$

This is the reason why this method is also called the CGNR method, where CGNR stands for *Conjugate Gradient on the Normal equation to minimise the Residual*.

However, the method is only of limited use since we know that we have to expect a condition number which is the square of the original condition number. Nonetheless, we can generalise this idea in the following way.

Definition 6.23 Assume $A \in \mathbb{R}^{n \times n}$ is invertible and $\mathbf{b} \in \mathbb{R}^n$. Let $\mathbf{x}_0 \in \mathbb{R}^n$ and $\mathbf{r}_0 := \mathbf{b} - A\mathbf{x}_0$. The jth iteration of the *GMRES* (Generalised Minimum Residual) method is defined to be the solution of

$$\min\{\|\mathbf{b} - A\mathbf{x}\|_2 : \mathbf{x} \in \mathbf{x}_0 + \mathcal{K}_j(A, \mathbf{r}_0)\}. \tag{6.15}$$

If $A \in \mathbb{R}^{n \times n}$ is symmetric, then the method generating the sequence $\{\mathbf{x}_j\}$ by minimising (6.15) is called *MINRES* (Minimum Residual).

The difference between MINRES and GMRES is two-fold. First of all, in the case of GMRES, an actual algorithm for creating the sequence $\{\mathbf{x}_j\}$ needs to work for *all* non-singular matrices $A \in \mathbb{R}^{n \times n}$, while in the case of MINRES such an algorithm can exploit the fact that it will only be used for *symmetric* matrices. We will soon see that this makes a significant difference in designing such algorithms. Secondly, there is a difference in analysing the algorithms. For MINRES we can use the fact that the matrix is diagonalisable with only real eigenvalues and a corresponding orthonormal basis consisting of eigenvectors. We cannot do this when analysing GMRES. Finally, historically, MINRES was introduced in [99] by Paige and Saunders long before GMRES was presented in [105] by Saad and Schultz, but this is obviously of no consequence for us. Despite these differences, the starting point for analysing GMRES and MINRES is the same and very similar to the analysis of the CG method. Since every $\mathbf{x} \in \mathbf{x}_0 + \mathcal{K}_j(A, \mathbf{r}_0)$ can be written as $\mathbf{x} = \mathbf{x}_0 + \sum_{k=0}^{j-1} a_k A^k \mathbf{r}_0$, we can conclude that

$$\mathbf{b} - A\mathbf{x} = \mathbf{b} - A\mathbf{x}_0 - \sum_{k=0}^{j-1} a_k A^{k+1} \mathbf{r}_0 = \mathbf{r}_0 - \sum_{k=1}^{j} a_{k-1} A^k \mathbf{r}_0 =: P(A)\mathbf{r}_0$$

with a polynomial $P \in \pi_j$ satisfying $P(0) = 1$. Hence, minimising over all such $\mathbf{x}$ is equivalent to minimising over all these P.

Theorem 6.24 *If $A \in \mathbb{R}^{n \times n}$ is invertible (and symmetric) and if $\{\mathbf{x}_j\}$ denote the iterations of the GMRES (MINRES) method then*

$$\|\mathbf{b} - A\mathbf{x}_j\|_2 = \min_{\substack{P \in \pi_j \\ P(0)=1}} \|P(A)\mathbf{r}_0\|_2.$$

Moreover, the method needs at most n steps to terminate with the solution of $A\mathbf{x} = \mathbf{b}$.

Proof It remains to show that the method stops with the solution $\mathbf{x}^*$. To see this, let $p(t) = \det(A - tI)$ be the characteristic polynomial of A. Then, $p \in \pi_n$ and, since A is invertible, $p(0) = \det A \neq 0$. Hence, we can choose the polynomial $P := p/p(0)$ in the last step. However, the Cayley–Hamilton theorem gives $p(A) = 0$ and hence $P(A) = 0$ so that we must have $\mathbf{b} = A\mathbf{x}_n$, unless the method terminates before. □

In the case of the CG method, we then used the fact that there is a basis of $\mathbb{R}^n$ consisting of orthonormal eigenvectors of A. This is the point where the analyses of MINRES and GMRES diverge. Since the analysis of MINRES is closer to that one of CG we will first look at MINRES.

Hence, for the time being, let $A = A^{\mathrm{T}} \in \mathbb{R}^{n \times n}$ be symmetric. Then, A has real eigenvalues $\lambda_j \in \mathbb{R}$, $1 \leq j \leq n$, which are due to the invertibility of A all different from zero. Moreover, we can choose an orthonormal basis $\mathbf{w}_1, \ldots, \mathbf{w}_n \in \mathbb{R}^n$ of $\mathbb{R}^n$ consisting of eigenvectors of A, i.e. $A\mathbf{w}_j = \lambda_j \mathbf{w}_j$. With this we can continue as in the analysis of the CG method and expand $\mathbf{x} \in \mathbb{R}^n$ with $\|\mathbf{x}\|_2 = 1$ as

$\mathbf{x} = \sum x_j \mathbf{w}_j$ which then gives $P(A)\mathbf{x} = \sum x_j P(\lambda_j) \mathbf{w}_j$ and hence

$$\|P(A)\|_2^2 = \sup_{\|\mathbf{x}\|_2=1} \|P(A)\mathbf{x}\|_2^2 = \sup_{\|\mathbf{x}\|_2=1} \sum_{j=1}^n x_j^2 P^2(\lambda_j) \leq \max_{1\leq j\leq n} P^2(\lambda_j).$$

Thus, we have the following version of Theorem 6.14.

Proposition 6.25 *Let $A \in \mathbb{R}^{n \times n}$ be symmetric and invertible, having the eigenvalues $\lambda_1 \leq \cdots \leq \lambda_n$. Let $\mathbf{x}^* \in \mathbb{R}^n$ denote the solution of $A\mathbf{x} = \mathbf{b}$ and let $\{\mathbf{x}_i\}$ denote the iterations from MINRES, then the residuals $\mathbf{r}_i := \mathbf{b} - A\mathbf{x}_i$ satisfy*

$$\|\mathbf{r}_i\|_2 \leq \min_{\substack{P\in\pi_i \\ P(0)=1}} \max_{1\leq j\leq n} |P(\lambda_j)| \, \|\mathbf{r}_0\|_2. \tag{6.16}$$

In contrast to the situation of the CG method, now the eigenvalues of A, though still real numbers, will be negative and positive, which makes the analysis somewhat more complicated. In this context, it is usual to assume that the eigenvalues of A are contained in $[a,b] \cup [c,d]$ with $a < b < 0 < c < d$ such that $d - c$ and $b - a$ are as small as possible. Ideally, a, b, c, d are given by eigenvalues of A. However, for the purpose of the analysis it makes things easier to assume that $b - a = d - c$, which can be achieved by shifting some of the values and increasing the size of one of the intervals if necessary.

Since we now have both positive and negative eigenvalues we must expect a slower convergence than when we only have positive (or negative) eigenvalues. Nonetheless, using ideas similar to those in the analysis of the CG method, we can derive the following result.

Theorem 6.26 *Let $A \in \mathbb{R}^{n \times n}$ be symmetric and invertible. Let the eigenvalues of A be contained in $[a,b] \cup [c,d]$ with $a < b < 0 < c < d$ and $b - a = d - c$. Then, the residual $\mathbf{r}_i = \mathbf{b} - A\mathbf{x}_i$ between the true solution $\mathbf{x}^* \in \mathbb{R}^n$ of $A\mathbf{x} = \mathbf{b}$ and the ith iteration $\mathbf{x}_i$ of MINRES can be bounded by*

$$\|\mathbf{r}_i\|_2 \leq 2 \left(\frac{\sqrt{|ad|} - \sqrt{|bc|}}{\sqrt{|ad|} + \sqrt{|bc|}} \right)^{\lfloor i/2 \rfloor} \|\mathbf{r}_0\|_2.$$

Proof As we want to use our ideas on Chebyshev polynomials, we need to map the intervals $[a,b]$ and $[c,d]$ simultaneously to $[-1,1]$. Since they have the same length, we can do this by a polynomial of degree two. It is not too difficult to see that this polynomial is given by

$$q(t) = 1 + 2\frac{(t-b)(t-c)}{ad - bc}, \qquad t \in [a,b] \cup [c,d].$$

Next, we have

$$q(0) = \frac{ad + bc}{ad - bc} = \frac{|ad| + |bc|}{|ad| - |bc|} = \frac{1+\gamma}{1-\gamma} > 1,$$

with $\gamma = |bc|/|ad| \in (0, 1)$. Thus

$$P^*(t) := \frac{T_{\lfloor i/2 \rfloor}(q(t))}{T_{\lfloor i/2 \rfloor}(q(0))} \in \pi_i$$

is well-defined and satisfies $P^*(0) = 1$. Thus, we can bound

$$\|\mathbf{r}_i\|_2 \leq \min_{\substack{P \in \pi_i \\ P(0)=1}} \max_{1 \leq j \leq n} |P(\lambda_j)| \|\mathbf{r}_0\|_2 \leq \min_{\substack{P \in \pi_i \\ P(0)=1}} \max_{t \in [a,b] \cup [c,d]} |P(t)| \|\mathbf{r}_0\|_2$$

$$\leq \max_{t \in [a,b] \cup [c,d]} |P^*(t)| \|\mathbf{r}_0\|_2 \leq \frac{1}{T_{\lfloor i/2 \rfloor}(q(0))} \|\mathbf{r}_0\|_2$$

$$= \frac{1}{T_{\lfloor i/2 \rfloor}\left(\frac{1+\gamma}{1-\gamma}\right)} \|\mathbf{r}_0\|_2 \leq 2 \left(\frac{1 - \sqrt{\gamma}}{1 + \sqrt{\gamma}}\right)^{\lfloor i/2 \rfloor} \|\mathbf{r}_0\|_2,$$

where we have used Lemma 6.17. The result follows using $\gamma = |bc|/|ad|$.   □

In the case where the intervals $[a, b]$ and $[c, d]$ are symmetric with respect to the origin, i.e. in the case of $a = -d$ and $b = -c$, we have $\gamma = |bc|/|ad| = c^2/d^2 \leq \kappa_2(A)^2$ and hence

$$\|\mathbf{r}_i\|_2 \leq 2 \left(\frac{\kappa_2(A) - 1}{\kappa_2(A) + 1}\right)^{\lfloor i/2 \rfloor} \|\mathbf{r}_0\|_2.$$

Finally, if MINRES is applied to a positive definite and symmetric matrix, then obviously we can proceed exactly as in the analysis of the CG method, yielding an estimate of the form

$$\|\mathbf{r}_i\|_2 \leq 2 \left(\frac{\sqrt{\kappa_2(A)} - 1}{\sqrt{\kappa_2(A)} + 1}\right)^i \|\mathbf{r}_0\|_2.$$

Also results similar to those in Corollaries 6.21 and 6.22 regarding large and small isolated eigenvalues remain valid if the $\| \cdot \|_A$-norm there is replaced by the $\| \cdot \|_2$-norm.

Next, let us return to the analysis of the more general GMRES method. Hence, we are back at the representation

$$\|\mathbf{b} - A\mathbf{x}_j\|_2 = \min_{\substack{P \in \pi_j \\ P(0)=1}} \|P(A)\mathbf{r}_0\|_2. \tag{6.17}$$

Since $A \in \mathbb{R}^{n \times n}$ is a general invertible matrix, we cannot expect anymore to have an orthonormal basis of $\mathbb{R}^n$ consisting of eigenvectors of A.

Nonetheless, let us assume that the matrix A is at least diagonalisable, i.e. that there is a matrix $V \in \mathbb{C}^{n \times n}$ and a diagonal matrix $D = \text{diag}(\lambda_1, \ldots, \lambda_n) \in \mathbb{C}^{n \times n}$, such that

$$A = VDV^{-1}.$$

The diagonal elements of D are the eigenvalues of A. However, from now on, we have to work with complex matrices.

If $P \in \pi_j$ is of the form $P(t) = 1 + \sum_{k=1}^{j} a_k t^k$ then we can conclude that

$$P(A) = P(VDV^{-1}) = 1 + \sum_{k=1}^{j} a_k (VDV^{-1})^k = 1 + \sum_{k=1}^{j} a_k VD^k V^{-1}$$
$$= VP(D)V^{-1},$$

and we derive the following error estimate, which is, compared with the corresponding result of the CG method, worse by a factor $\kappa_2(V)$.

Corollary 6.27 *Assume the matrix $A \in \mathbb{R}^{n \times n}$ is similar to a diagonal matrix with eigenvalues $\lambda_k \in \mathbb{C}$. The jth iteration of the GMRES method satisfies the error bound*

$$\|\mathbf{b} - A\mathbf{x}_j\|_2 \leq \kappa_2(V) \min_{\substack{P \in \pi_j \\ P(0)=1}} \max_{1 \leq k \leq n} |P(\lambda_k)| \, \|\mathbf{b} - A\mathbf{x}_0\|_2. \tag{6.18}$$

Note that, in contrast to the corresponding minimisation problem of the CG or the MINRES method, here, the eigenvalues λ_k can be complex, which complicates matters. Even more, the role of the matrix V is problematic. Estimate (6.18) is useful only if $\kappa_2(V) \approx 1$. For example, if A is a normal matrix, then V is unitary and hence $\kappa_2(V) = 1$. In this situation, (6.18) is optimal. However, if $\kappa_2(V)$ is large, then the error estimate (6.18) is not useful and it is unclear whether in such a situation GMRES converges only poorly or whether estimate (6.18) is simply too pessimistic. If the condition number of V is sufficiently small, then it is possible to use complex Chebyshev polynomials to derive bounds similar to those of the CG method. Details can, for example, be found in Saad's book [104].

Moreover, in some situations the convergence of GMRES is difficult to predict from the eigenvalues of A alone. To see this, let us have a look at the following example.

Example 6.28 Let A be a matrix of the form

$$\begin{pmatrix} 0 & * & 0 & \dots & 0 \\ 0 & * & * & \dots & 0 \\ \vdots & \vdots & \vdots & \ddots & \\ 0 & * & * & \dots & * \\ * & * & * & \dots & * \end{pmatrix},$$

where a $*$ denotes a non-zero entry, and let $\mathbf{x}_0$ be such that $\mathbf{r}_0 = \mathbf{b} - A\mathbf{x}_0$ is a multiple of $\mathbf{e}_1$. Then we see that $A\mathbf{r}_0$ is a multiple of $\mathbf{e}_n$, $A^2 \mathbf{r}_0$ is a linear combination of e_n and e_{n-1} and so on. Hence, all vectors $A^k r_0$ for $1 \le k \le n-1$ are orthogonal to r_0.

Since we can write x_j as $x_j = x_0 + y_j$, where y_j minimises $\|r_0 - Ay\|_2$ over all $y \in \mathcal{K}_j(A, r_0)$, we see that this minimising of $\|r_0 - Ay\|_2$ over all $y \in \mathcal{K}_j(A, r_0)$ will always produce $y_j = 0$ as long as $j \le n - 1$, i.e. we will have $x_j = x_0$ and hence no progress for $1 \le j \le n - 1$.

Typical matrices of the form given in the example are *companion matrices*, i.e. matrices of the form

$$A = \begin{pmatrix} 0 & 1 & 0 & \dots & 0 \\ 0 & 0 & 1 & \dots & 0 \\ \vdots & \vdots & \vdots & \ddots & \vdots \\ 0 & 0 & 0 & \dots & 1 \\ a_0 & a_1 & a_2 & \dots & a_{n-1} \end{pmatrix}.$$

The eigenvalues are the roots of the polynomial $t^n - \sum_{j=0}^{n-1} a_j t^j$, which shows that matrices of the above form can occur with any desired eigenvalue distribution. We will not further pursue this here. Instead we will look at a different possible approach.

To describe this, we need to broaden our perspective a little. First of all, it is easy to see that for a real matrix $A \in \mathbb{R}^{n \times n}$, the GMRES iteration x_j satisfies (6.17) even if we allow polynomials $P \in \pi_j$ with complex coefficients. This follows because such a polynomial would have the form $P(t) = Q(t) + iR(t)$ with real polynomials $Q, R \in \pi_j$ satisfying $Q(0) = 1$ and $R(0) = 0$ and from

$$\|P(A)r_0\|_2 = \left(\|Q(A)r_0\|_2^2 + \|R(A)r_0\|_2^2 \right)^{1/2}$$

we see that any nonzero R would only increase this norm.

In the case of a complex matrix $A \in \mathbb{C}^{n \times n}$ we would define the GMRES iteration by looking at complex Krylov spaces and hence would immediately use polynomials with complex coefficients in (6.17). Hence, for the time being let us work in the complex setting.

For a symmetric matrix we know that the maximum of the Rayleigh quotient defines its maximum eigenvalue. The same is true for normal matrices. For a general matrix we can generalise this concept as follows.

Definition 6.29 For a matrix $A \in \mathbb{C}^{n \times n}$, the *field of values* of A is defined to be

$$\mathcal{F}(A) := \left\{ \bar{x}^T A x : x \in \mathbb{C}^n, \bar{x}^T x = 1 \right\}.$$

The *numerical radius* of A is defined as

$$v(A) := \max\{|z| : z \in \mathcal{F}(A)\}.$$

Since the function $\mathbf{x} \mapsto \overline{\mathbf{x}}^T A \mathbf{x}$ is continuous, the field of values $\mathcal{F}(A)$ is compact and hence the numerical radius is well-defined. Moreover, by Corollary 2.28 we know that in the case of a normal matrix A the numerical radius coincides with the 2-norm, i.e. $v(A) = \|A\|_2$. For a general matrix we have $\lambda \in \mathcal{F}(A)$ for every eigenvalue of A because if $\mathbf{x} \in \mathbb{C}^n$ denotes a corresponding, normalised eigenvector then we obviously have $\overline{\mathbf{x}}^T A \mathbf{x} = \lambda$. We have the following properties.

Lemma 6.30 *Let $A \in \mathbb{C}^{n \times n}$ and $\alpha \in \mathbb{C}$. Then,*

1. $\mathcal{F}(A + \alpha I) = \mathcal{F}(A) + \alpha$,
2. $\mathcal{F}(\alpha A) = \alpha \mathcal{F}(A)$,
3. $\frac{1}{2}\|A\|_2 \le v(A) \le \|A\|$,
4. $v(A^m) \le [v(A)]^m$, $m = 1, 2, \ldots$.

Proof The first two properties follow from

$$\overline{\mathbf{x}}^T(A + \alpha I)\mathbf{x} = \overline{\mathbf{x}}^T A \mathbf{x} + \alpha, \qquad \overline{\mathbf{x}}^T \alpha A \mathbf{x} = \alpha \overline{\mathbf{x}}^T A \mathbf{x}$$

which hold for all $\overline{\mathbf{x}}^T \mathbf{x} = 1$. For the third property we first note that

$$\overline{\mathbf{x}}^T A \mathbf{x} \le \|\mathbf{x}\|_2 \|A\mathbf{x}\|_2 \le \|A\|_2,$$

which gives the right inequality. For the left inequality we split A into $A = H + N$ with $H = (A + \overline{A}^T)/2$ and $N = (A - \overline{A}^T)/2$. Since both matrices are normal, we have

$$\|A\|_2 \le \|H\|_2 + \|N\|_2 = v(H) + v(N)$$
$$= \frac{1}{2}\left(\sup_{\|\mathbf{x}\|_2=1} |\overline{\mathbf{x}}^T(A + \overline{A}^T)\mathbf{x}| + \sup_{\|\mathbf{x}\|_2=1} |\overline{\mathbf{x}}^T(A - \overline{A}^T)\mathbf{x}| \right)$$
$$\le \frac{1}{2}\left(2 \sup_{\|\mathbf{x}\|_2=1} |\overline{\mathbf{x}}^T A \mathbf{x}| + \sup_{\|\mathbf{x}\|_2=1} |\overline{\mathbf{x}}^T \overline{A}^T \mathbf{x}| \right)$$
$$= 2v(A).$$

For the last property, $v(A^m) \le [v(A)]^m$, we have to work a little harder. First note that because of the second property we have $v(\alpha A) = |\alpha| v(A)$. Thus, if we can show that $v(A) \le 1$ implies $v(A^m) \le 1$ for all $m \in \mathbb{N}$, then we will have for an arbitrary $A \in \mathbb{C}^{n \times n}$ with $\alpha = 1/v(A)$ that $v(\alpha A) \le 1$ and hence $v((\alpha A)^m) \le 1$, i.e.

$$v((\alpha A)^m) = \alpha^m v(A^m) = \frac{1}{v(A)^m} v(A^m) \le 1.$$

To see that $\nu(A) \leq 1$ implies $\nu(A^m) \leq 1$, let us introduce the roots of unity $\omega_k := \exp(2\pi i k/m)$ for $k \in \mathbb{Z}$. Obviously, there are only m different roots of unity, for example for $1 \leq k \leq m$. Nonetheless, whenever necessary, we will use them in this periodic form. In particularly, we will use that $\omega_m = \omega_0$. In this sense, the linear polynomial $\ell_k(z) = 1 - \omega_k z$ satisfies $\ell_k(\omega_{m-k}) = 0$ for all k so that we can factorise the polynomial $1 - z^m$ as

$$1 - z^m = \prod_{k=1}^{m} \ell_k(z) = \prod_{k=1}^{m}(1 - \omega_k z). \tag{6.19}$$

Next, let $\pi_m(\mathbb{C})$ denote the space of complex polynomials of degree at most m and let us define the Lagrange functions $L_j \in \pi_{m-1}(\mathbb{C})$, $1 \leq j \leq m$ via

$$L_j(z) := \prod_{\substack{k=1 \\ k \neq j}}^{m} \frac{\ell_k(z)}{\ell_k(\omega_{m-j})} = \prod_{\substack{k=1 \\ k \neq j}}^{m} \frac{1 - \omega_k z}{1 - \omega_{k+m-j}} = \frac{1}{m} \prod_{\substack{k=1 \\ k \neq j}}^{m}(1 - \omega_k z).$$

In the last step, we have used that the denominator can be significantly simplified employing the identities

$$\prod_{\substack{k=1 \\ k \neq j}}^{m}(1 - \omega_{k+m-j}) = \prod_{k=1}^{m-1}(1 - \omega_k) = \lim_{z \to 1} \prod_{k=1}^{m-1}(1 - \omega_k z)$$

$$= \lim_{z \to 1} \frac{1}{1 - \omega_m z} \prod_{k=1}^{m}(1 - \omega_k z) = \lim_{z \to 1} \frac{1 - z^m}{1 - z}$$

$$= m.$$

As we well know, these Lagrangian functions form a very specific basis of the polynomials of degree less than m as they obviously satisfy $L_j(\omega_{m-k}) = \delta_{jk}$ for $1 \leq j, k \leq m$. In particular, we can reconstruct the constant function 1 by its interpolant

$$1 = \sum_{j=1}^{m} 1 \cdot L_j(z) = \frac{1}{m} \sum_{j=1}^{m} \prod_{\substack{k=1 \\ k \neq j}}^{m}(1 - \omega_k z). \tag{6.20}$$

Equations (6.19) and (6.20) remain obviously valid if z is replaced by a matrix $B \in \mathbb{C}^{n \times n}$.

For $\mathbf{x} \in \mathbb{C}^n$ with $\|\mathbf{x}\|_2 = 1$, we define the vectors

$$\mathbf{x}_j := \left[\prod_{\substack{k=1 \\ k \neq j}}^{m}(I - \omega_k B) \right] \mathbf{x}, \qquad 1 \leq j \leq m,$$

and use (6.19) and (6.20) to derive

$$\frac{1}{m} \sum_{j=1}^{m} \|\mathbf{x}_j\|_2^2 \left[1 - \omega_j \left\langle \frac{B\mathbf{x}_j}{\|\mathbf{x}_j\|_2}, \frac{\mathbf{x}_j}{\|\mathbf{x}_j\|_2} \right\rangle_2 \right]$$

$$= \frac{1}{m} \sum_{j=1}^{m} \langle (I - \omega_j B)\mathbf{x}_j, \mathbf{x}_j \rangle_2 = \frac{1}{m} \sum_{j=1}^{m} \left\langle \left[\prod_{k=1}^{m} (I - \omega_k B) \right] \mathbf{x}, \mathbf{x}_j \right\rangle_2$$

$$= \frac{1}{m} \sum_{j=1}^{m} \langle (I - B^m)\mathbf{x}, \mathbf{x}_j \rangle_2 = \left\langle (I - B^m)\mathbf{x}, \frac{1}{m} \sum_{j=1}^{m} \mathbf{x}_j \right\rangle_2$$

$$= \left\langle (I - B^m)\mathbf{x}, \frac{1}{m} \sum_{j=1}^{m} \left(\prod_{\substack{k=1 \\ k \neq j}}^{m} (I - \omega_k B) \right) \mathbf{x} \right\rangle_2$$

$$= \langle (I - B^m)\mathbf{x}, \mathbf{x} \rangle_2 = 1 - \langle B^m \mathbf{x}, \mathbf{x} \rangle_2.$$

If we now set $B = e^{i\theta} A$ with $\theta \in \mathbb{R}$ chosen such that $e^{im\theta} \langle A^m \mathbf{x}, \mathbf{x} \rangle_2 = |\langle A^m \mathbf{x}, \mathbf{x} \rangle_2|$ we thus have

$$1 - |\langle A^m \mathbf{x}, \mathbf{x} \rangle_2| = 1 - e^{im\theta} \langle A^m \mathbf{x}, \mathbf{x} \rangle_2$$

$$= \frac{1}{m} \sum_{j=1}^{m} \|\mathbf{x}_j\|_2^2 \left[1 - \omega_j e^{i\theta} \left\langle \frac{A\mathbf{x}_j}{\|\mathbf{x}_j\|_2}, \frac{\mathbf{x}_j}{\|\mathbf{x}_j\|_2} \right\rangle_2 \right]$$

$$= \frac{1}{m} \sum_{j=1}^{m} \|\mathbf{x}_j\|_2^2 \left[1 - \Re \left(\omega_j e^{i\theta} \left\langle \frac{A\mathbf{x}_j}{\|\mathbf{x}_j\|_2}, \frac{\mathbf{x}_j}{\|\mathbf{x}_j\|_2} \right\rangle_2 \right) \right]$$

$$\geq \frac{1}{m} \sum_{j=1}^{m} \|\mathbf{x}_j\|_2^2 \left[1 - \left| \left\langle \frac{A\mathbf{x}_j}{\|\mathbf{x}_j\|_2}, \frac{\mathbf{x}_j}{\|\mathbf{x}_j\|_2} \right\rangle_2 \right| \right] \geq 0$$

since $\nu(A) \leq 1$ implies that the term in the brackets on the right-hand side of the last line is non-negative. Thus we have $|\langle A^m \mathbf{x}, \mathbf{x} \rangle_2| \leq 1$ for all normalised vectors $\mathbf{x} \in \mathbb{C}^n$ showing $\nu(A^m) \leq 1$. □

Let us see how we can use the concept of the numerical radius to provide possible convergence estimates for GMRES.

Theorem 6.31 *Suppose that $\mathcal{F}(A)$ is contained in the disc $D := \{z \in \mathbb{C} : |z - c| \leq s\}$ and assume that $0 \notin D$, i.e. that $s < |c|$. Then the residuals of the GMRES method satisfy*

$$\|\mathbf{r}_j\|_2 \leq 2 \left(\frac{s}{|c|} \right)^j \|\mathbf{r}_0\|_2.$$

Proof Let us define $P(z) = (1 - z/c)^j$. Then, Lemma 6.30, yields

$$\frac{\|\mathbf{r}_j\|_2}{\|\mathbf{r}_0\|_2} \le \|P(A)\|_2 \le 2\nu(P(A)) = 2\nu\left(\left(I - \frac{1}{c}A\right)^j\right) \le 2\left[\nu\left(I - \frac{1}{c}A\right)\right]^j.$$

Furthermore, if $\mathbf{x} \in \mathbb{C}^n$ satisfies $\|\mathbf{x}\|_2 = 1$ then we know by assumption that $z := \bar{\mathbf{x}}^T A\mathbf{x}$ satisfies $|z - c| \le s$ or $|1 - z/c| \le s/|c|$. Hence,

$$\nu\left(I - \frac{1}{c}A\right) = \max_{\|\mathbf{x}\|_2=1}\left|\bar{\mathbf{x}}^T\left(I - \frac{1}{c}A\right)\mathbf{x}\right| = \max_{\|\mathbf{x}\|_2=1}\left|1 - \frac{1}{c}\bar{\mathbf{x}}^T A\mathbf{x}\right| \le \frac{s}{|c|},$$

which completes the proof.   □

Now, we will have a look at a possible implementation for both GMRES and MINRES.

We start by deriving an algorithm for GMRES and will then work out how the algorithm can be changed for MINRES.

The implementation is based upon the idea to find an orthonormal basis for $\mathcal{K}_j(A, \mathbf{r}_0)$ and then to solve the minimisation problem within this basis.

We can use the Gram–Schmidt orthogonalisation method (see Lemma 1.9) to compute an orthogonal basis of $\mathcal{K}_j(A, \mathbf{r}_0)$. Recall that the idea of the Gram–Schmidt method is to compute orthogonal vectors successively, starting with a vector $\mathbf{v}_1 \in \mathbb{R}^n$ with $\|\mathbf{v}_1\|_2 = 1$. Next, provided that $\{\mathbf{v}_1, \ldots, \mathbf{v}_k\}$ are already orthonormal and that $\mathbf{v} \notin \text{span}\{\mathbf{v}_1, \ldots, \mathbf{v}_k\}$, the Gram–Schmidt procedure calculates

$$\tilde{\mathbf{v}}_{k+1} := \mathbf{v} - \sum_{\ell=1}^{k}\langle \mathbf{v}, \mathbf{v}_\ell\rangle_2 \mathbf{v}_\ell,$$

$$\mathbf{v}_{k+1} := \tilde{\mathbf{v}}_{k+1}/\|\tilde{\mathbf{v}}_{k+1}\|_2.$$

We will use this by setting $\mathbf{r}_0 = \mathbf{b} - A\mathbf{x}_0$ and $\mathbf{v}_1 = \mathbf{r}_0/\|\mathbf{r}_0\|_2$ and then choose $\mathbf{v}$ as $\mathbf{v} = A\mathbf{v}_k$. This gives

$$\tilde{\mathbf{v}}_{k+1} = A\mathbf{v}_k - \sum_{\ell=1}^{k}\langle A\mathbf{v}_k, \mathbf{v}_\ell\rangle_2 \mathbf{v}_\ell = A\mathbf{v}_k - \sum_{\ell=1}^{k}h_{\ell k}\mathbf{v}_\ell, \tag{6.21}$$

$$\mathbf{v}_{k+1} = \tilde{\mathbf{v}}_{k+1}/\|\tilde{\mathbf{v}}_{k+1}\|_2 = \tilde{\mathbf{v}}_{k+1}/h_{k+1,k}, \tag{6.22}$$

where we have defined $h_{\ell k} = \langle A\mathbf{v}_k, \mathbf{v}_\ell\rangle_2$ for $1 \le \ell \le k$ and $h_{k+1,k} = \|\tilde{\mathbf{v}}_{k+1}\|_2$. This method is called the *Arnoldi method* and was introduced in [2]. We will analyse it in this simple form. However, from a numerical point of view, a more stable version can be derived as follows. Since $\mathbf{v}_1, \ldots, \mathbf{v}_k$ are orthogonal, we see that we have for arbitrary numbers c_i, $1 \leq i \leq k$, the equivalent formulation

$$\tilde{\mathbf{v}}_{k+1} = A\mathbf{v}_k - \sum_{\ell=1}^{k} h_{\ell k}\mathbf{v}_\ell$$

$$= A\mathbf{v}_k - \sum_{\ell=1}^{k}\langle A\mathbf{v}_k, \mathbf{v}_\ell\rangle_2\mathbf{v}_\ell - \sum_{\ell=1}^{k}\sum_{i=1}^{\ell-1} c_i\langle \mathbf{v}_i, \mathbf{v}_\ell\rangle_2\mathbf{v}_\ell$$

$$= A\mathbf{v}_k - \sum_{\ell=1}^{k}\left\langle A\mathbf{v}_k - \sum_{i=1}^{\ell-1} c_i\mathbf{v}_i, \mathbf{v}_\ell\right\rangle_2\mathbf{v}_\ell.$$

Choosing $c_i = \langle A\mathbf{v}_k, \mathbf{v}_i\rangle_2$ gives an algorithm which is in general not only much more stable than the basic algorithm but also can easily be implemented. This modified Arnoldi method is given in Algorithm 23.

Algorithm 23: Arnoldi method (modified Gram–Schmidt)

Input : $A \in \mathbb{R}^{n \times n}$, $\mathbf{x}_0 \in \mathbb{R}^n$.
Output: Orthonormal basis $\{\mathbf{v}_1, \ldots, \mathbf{v}_j\}$ of $\mathcal{K}_j(A, \mathbf{r}_0)$.

1   $\mathbf{r}_0 := \mathbf{b} - A\mathbf{x}_0$, $\mathbf{v}_1 := \mathbf{r}_0/\|\mathbf{r}_0\|$
2   **for** $k = 1, 2, \ldots, j-1$ **do**
3      $\mathbf{w}_k := A\mathbf{v}_k$
4   **for** $\ell = 1$ **to** k **do**
5          $h_{\ell k} := \langle \mathbf{w}_k, \mathbf{v}_\ell\rangle_2$
6          $\mathbf{w}_k := \mathbf{w}_k - h_{\ell k}\mathbf{v}_\ell$
7      $h_{k+1,k} := \|\mathbf{w}_k\|_2$
8   **if** $h_{k+1,k} = 0$ **then break**
9   **else** $\mathbf{v}_{k+1} := \mathbf{w}_k/h_{k+1,k}$

Obviously, the Arnoldi method can produce an orthonormal basis only if it does not stop prematurely. Hence, for the time being, let us assume that always $\mathbf{w}_k = \tilde{\mathbf{v}}_{k+1} \neq \mathbf{0}$.

Lemma 6.32 *If the Arnoldi method is well-defined up to step j then $\mathbf{v}_1, \ldots, \mathbf{v}_j$ form an orthonormal basis of $\mathcal{K}_j(A, \mathbf{r}_0)$.*

Proof It is easy to check that $\{\mathbf{v}_k\}$ forms an orthonormal set. That the elements actually form a basis for $\mathcal{K}_j(A, \mathbf{r}_0)$ can be proven by induction on j. Obviously, for $j = 1$ there is nothing to show. For the induction step note that the definition gives $\mathbf{v}_{j+1} \in \text{span}\{\mathbf{v}_1, \ldots, \mathbf{v}_j, A\mathbf{v}_j\}$ and the induction hypothesis leads to $\mathbf{v}_{j+1} \in \mathcal{K}_{j+1}(A, \mathbf{r}_0)$. Equality of the spaces follows on comparing the dimensions. $\square$

To further analyse Arnoldi's method and to see how it can be used for an implementation of GMRES, we stick to the original formulation (6.21), (6.22). If we want to compute a basis for $\mathcal{K}_j(A, \mathbf{r}_0)$ we need to compute up to j orthogonal vectors. As before, let us define $h_{\ell k} = \langle A\mathbf{v}_k, \mathbf{v}_\ell\rangle_2$ for $1 \le \ell \le k$ and $1 \le k \le j$ and $h_{k+1,k} = \|\tilde{\mathbf{v}}_{k+1}\|_2$ for $1 \le k \le j$. Then, using (6.22), equation (6.21) can be rewritten as

$$A\mathbf{v}_k = \sum_{\ell=1}^{k+1} h_{\ell k}\mathbf{v}_\ell. \tag{6.23}$$

If we now set additionally $h_{\ell k} = 0$ for $1 \le k \le j-1$ and $k+2 \le \ell \le j+1$, this defines a non-square Hessenberg matrix

$$H_j := (h_{\ell k}) = \begin{pmatrix} h_{11} & h_{12} & \cdots & \cdots & h_{1j} \\ h_{21} & h_{22} & \cdots & \cdots & h_{2j} \\ & h_{32} & \ddots & & \vdots \\ & & \ddots & \ddots & \vdots \\ & & & h_{j,j-1} & h_{jj} \\ & & & & h_{j+1,j} \end{pmatrix} \in \mathbb{R}^{(j+1)\times j}.$$

If we further define the matrix $V_j = (\mathbf{v}_1, \ldots, \mathbf{v}_j) \in \mathbb{R}^{n \times j}$ then we can use (6.23) to derive

$$AV_j = \left(A\mathbf{v}_1, \ldots, A\mathbf{v}_j\right)$$

$$= \left(\sum_{\ell=1}^{2} h_{\ell 1}\mathbf{v}_\ell, \sum_{\ell=1}^{3} h_{\ell 2}\mathbf{v}_\ell, \ldots, \sum_{\ell=1}^{j+1} h_{\ell j}\mathbf{v}_\ell\right)$$

$$= \sum_{\ell=1}^{j+1} \left(h_{\ell 1}\mathbf{v}_\ell, h_{\ell 2}\mathbf{v}_\ell, \ldots, h_{\ell j}\mathbf{v}_\ell\right),$$

i.e. the matrix $AV_j \in \mathbb{R}^{n \times j}$ has entries

$$(AV_j)_{ik} = \sum_{\ell=1}^{j+1} h_{\ell k}(\mathbf{v}_\ell)_i = \sum_{\ell=1}^{j+1} h_{\ell k}(V_{j+1})_{i\ell} = (V_{j+1}H_j)_{ik}, \qquad 1 \le i \le n, 1 \le k \le j.$$

Moreover, if $\tilde{H}_j \in \mathbb{R}^{j \times j}$ is the matrix H_j without its last row then we can rewrite this as

$$(AV_j)_{ik} = \sum_{\ell=1}^{j+1} h_{\ell k}(\mathbf{v}_\ell)_i = \sum_{\ell=1}^{j} h_{\ell k}(\mathbf{v}_\ell)_i + h_{j+1,k}(\mathbf{v}_{j+1})_i$$

$$= (V_j\tilde{H}_j)_{ik} + h_{j+1,k}(\mathbf{v}_{j+1})_i = (V_j\tilde{H}_j)_{ik} + \delta_{kj}\|\tilde{\mathbf{v}}_{j+1}\|_2(\mathbf{v}_{j+1})_i$$

$$= (V_j\tilde{H}_j)_{ik} + \delta_{kj}(\tilde{\mathbf{v}}_{j+1})_i = (V_j\tilde{H}_j)_{ik} + (\tilde{\mathbf{v}}_{j+1}\mathbf{e}_j^{\mathsf{T}})_{ik},$$

where we have particularly used that $h_{j+1,k} = 0$ for $k \neq j$. Hence, we can summarise this as

$$AV_j = V_{j+1}H_j = V_j\tilde{H}_j + \tilde{v}_{j+1}e_j^T. \tag{6.24}$$

Lemma 6.33 *Assume that A is invertible. If the Arnoldi method stops with iteration j, then the solution x^* of $Ax = b$ is contained in $x_0 + \mathcal{K}_j(A, r_0)$.*

Proof That the method stops with iteration j means that $\tilde{v}_{j+1} = 0$. Hence, equation (6.24) implies $AV_j = V_j\tilde{H}_j$, which means that the space $\mathcal{K}_j(A, r_0)$ is invariant under A. Next, since A is invertible, we also must have that $\tilde{H}_j$ is invertible. For each $x \in x_0 + \mathcal{K}_j(A, r_0)$ there is a vector $y \in \mathbb{R}^j$ with $x - x_0 = V_j y$. Moreover, we have $r_0 = \beta v_1 = \beta V_j e_1$ with $\beta = \|r_0\|_2$. This leads to

$$\|b - Ax\|_2 = \|r_0 - A(x - x_0)\|_2 = \|r_0 - AV_j y\|_2 = \|V_j(\beta e_1 - \tilde{H}_j y)\|_2$$
$$= \|\beta e_1 - \tilde{H}_j y\|_2,$$

where we also have used the orthogonality of the columns of V_j. Since $\tilde{H}_j$ is invertible we can set $y = \beta \tilde{H}_j^{-1} e_1$, which leads to $x^* = x_0 + V_j y \in x_0 + \mathcal{K}_j(A, r_0)$. □

Algorithm 24: GMRES(j)

Input : $A \in \mathbb{R}^{n \times n}$, $b \in \mathbb{R}^n$, $x_0 \in \mathbb{R}^n$, $j \in \{1, \ldots, n\}$.
Output: Approximate solution of $Ax = b$.

1   $r_0 := b - Ax_0$, $\beta := \|r_0\|_2$, $v_1 := r_0/\beta$
2   **for** $k = 1, 2, \ldots, j$ **do**
3      $\lfloor$ Compute v_{k+1} and $h_{\ell k}$ for $1 \leq \ell \leq k + 1$ using Arnoldi's method
4   Compute y_j as the solution of $\|\beta e_1 - H_j y\|_2$
5   $x_j = x_0 + V_j y_j$

The proof of Lemma 6.33 gives a constructive way of computing the iterations of the GMRES method. Equation (6.24) implies, with $\beta = \|r_0\|_2$ and $x = x_0 + V_j y \in x_0 + \mathcal{K}_j(A, r_0)$, as before,

$$b - Ax = r_0 - AV_j y = \beta V_{j+1}e_1 - V_{j+1}H_j y = V_{j+1}(\beta e_1 - H_j y).$$

Hence, we see that $x_j = x_0 + V_j y_j$, where y_j minimises $\|\beta e_1 - H_j y\|_2$. This leads to Algorithm 24.

The GMRES method can stop prematurely. The only possible reason for this is that the Arnoldi method stops prematurely, i.e. if $h_{k+1,k} = 0$ for a $k < j$. According to Lemma 6.33 this means that $x^* \in x_0 + \mathcal{K}_k(A, r_0)$ and hence, by definition, $x_k = x^*$.

Remark 6.34 The solution of the least-squares problem $\|\beta e_1 - H_j y\|_2$ can be computed using a QR factorisation, see Section 3.8. This can be done in $O(j^2)$ time since H_j is a Hessenberg matrix, see Corollary 5.38.

There is another consequence of this process, which we want to mention here, though it is not related to solving linear systems but rather to computing the eigenvalues of the matrix A. Recall from Section 5.5 that it is desirable to reduce A to a Hessenberg matrix and then to compute the eigenvalues of this Hessenberg matrix. The following remark is a simple consequence of (6.24).

Remark 6.35 If the Arnoldi method does not stop prematurely then, after n steps, $v_1, \ldots, v_n$ form an orthonormal basis of $\mathbb{R}^n$ and $V_n = (v_1, \ldots, v_n)$ transforms A into the Hessenberg matrix $\tilde{H}_n = V_n^T A V_n$ having the same eigenvalues as A.

In the present form, the GMRES algorithm does not compute an approximate solution in each step, i.e. for each Krylov space $\mathcal{K}_j(A, r_0)$. Instead, we first compute the orthonormal basis of $\mathcal{K}_j(A, r_0)$ and after that the approximate solution x_j. Since one usually does not know beforehand which iteration has to be computed to achieve a desired accuracy, one could compute iterations always after a fixed number of steps of the Arnoldi method. Another possibility is to produce an iteration in each step of the Arnoldi method by computing the QR factorisation of H_{j+1}, which is necessary for computing a new iteration x_{j+1}, by exploiting the already-computed QR factorisation of H_j. Finally, we can use this repeated updating of the QR factorisation to compute only an approximate solution if a prescribed accuracy is achieved. We will describe this now in more detail, covering also the solution of the least-squares problem.

The idea for this comes from the proofs of Corollary 5.38 or Theorem 5.36, where we have successively removed the sub-diagonal entries using 2×2 Householder matrices. Instead of Householder matrices, we can of course also use Givens rotations. As usual, we describe the idea using full matrices of the form

$$G_i := \begin{pmatrix} I_{i-1} & & \\ & c_i & s_i \\ & -s_i & c_i \\ & & & I_{j-i} \end{pmatrix} = \begin{pmatrix} I_{i-1} & & \\ & \tilde{G}_i & \\ & & I_{j-i} \end{pmatrix} \in \mathbb{R}^{(j+1)\times(j+1)},$$

where I_{i-1} and I_{j-i} are the identities matrices of size $(i-1) \times (i-1)$ and $(j-i) \times (j-i)$, respectively.

As described in the proof of Theorem 5.36, j such orthogonal matrices suffice to reduce H_j to upper triangular form

$$
G_j G_{j-1} \cdots G_1
\begin{pmatrix}
h_{11} & h_{12} & \cdots & \cdots & h_{1j} \\
h_{21} & h_{22} & \cdots & \cdots & h_{2j} \\
 & h_{32} & \ddots & & \vdots \\
 & & \ddots & \ddots & \vdots \\
 & & & h_{j,j-1} & h_{jj} \\
 & & & & h_{j+1,j}
\end{pmatrix}
=
\begin{pmatrix}
r_{11} & r_{12} & \cdots & \cdots & r_{1j} \\
0 & r_{22} & \cdots & \cdots & r_{2j} \\
 & & \ddots & & \vdots \\
 & & & \ddots & \ddots & \vdots \\
 & & & & r_{jj} \\
 & & & & 0
\end{pmatrix}.
$$

$$(6.25)$$

From this, we can conclude two things. First of all, defining $Q_j^{\mathrm{T}} := G_j \cdots G_1 \in \mathbb{R}^{(j+1)\times(j+1)}$ and $R_j = Q_j^{\mathrm{T}} H_j \in \mathbb{R}^{(j+1)\times j}$ allows us to transform $\|\beta e_1 - H_j y\|_2$ as usual. To this end, let us define $\mathbf{q}_j := Q_j^{\mathrm{T}} e_1 \in \mathbb{R}^{j+1}$ and write $\mathbf{q}_j = (\tilde{\mathbf{q}}_j, q_{j+1})^{\mathrm{T}}$ with $\tilde{\mathbf{q}}_j \in \mathbb{R}^j$. Then, we have

$$
\begin{aligned}
\|\beta e_1 - H_j y\|_2^2 &= \|\beta e_1 - Q_j R_j y\|_2^2 \\
&= \|\beta Q_j^{\mathrm{T}} e_1 - R_j y\|_2^2 \\
&= \|\beta \mathbf{q}_j - R_j y\|_2^2 \\
&= \|\beta \tilde{\mathbf{q}}_j - \tilde{R}_j y\|_2^2 + |\beta q_{j+1}|^2,
\end{aligned}
$$

where $\tilde{R}_j \in \mathbb{R}^{j\times j}$ is R_j without its last row. The solution y_j, which minimises the latter expression, is hence given by

$$
y_j := \beta \tilde{R}_j^{-1} \tilde{\mathbf{q}}_j. \tag{6.26}
$$

Obviously, we can compute $\mathbf{q}_j = Q_j^{\mathrm{T}} e_1$ step by step by applying the rotations $\tilde{G}_j \in \mathbb{R}^{2\times 2}$ to the corresponding entries of the right-hand side. From this, it also immediately follows that the previously computed components do not change from now on. To be more precise, when going over from $\mathbf{q}_j \in \mathbb{R}^{j+1}$ to $\mathbf{q}_{j+1} \in \mathbb{R}^{j+2}$ we only have to apply the 2×2 matrix $\tilde{G}_{j+1}$ to the last two components of $(\mathbf{q}_j, 0)^{\mathrm{T}} = (\tilde{\mathbf{q}}_j, q_{j+1}, 0)^{\mathrm{T}}$, i.e. we have

$$
\mathbf{q}_{j+1} =
\begin{pmatrix}
\tilde{\mathbf{q}}_j \\
\tilde{G}_{j+1}\begin{pmatrix} q_{j+1} \\ 0 \end{pmatrix}
\end{pmatrix}
=
\begin{pmatrix}
\tilde{\mathbf{q}}_j \\
* \\
*
\end{pmatrix}
=:
\begin{pmatrix}
\tilde{\mathbf{q}}_{j+1} \\
q_{j+2}
\end{pmatrix}. \tag{6.27}
$$

Next, assume that we have already computed the rotations $G_1, \ldots, G_j$ and applied them to H_j. Since H_j is the upper left sub-matrix of H_{j+1}, this means that we only have to apply $G_1, \ldots, G_j$ (after adjusting their dimensions) to the last column of H_{j+1}, to obtain

$$G_j G_{j-1} \cdots G_1 H_{j+1} = \begin{pmatrix} r_{11} & r_{12} & \cdots & \cdots & r_{1j} & r_{1,j+1} \\ 0 & r_{22} & \cdots & \cdots & r_{2j} & r_{2,j+1} \\ & & \ddots & & \vdots & \vdots \\ & & & \ddots & \ddots & \vdots & \vdots \\ & & & & r_{jj} & r_{j,j+1} \\ & & & & 0 & d \\ & & & & 0 & h \end{pmatrix}. \tag{6.28}$$

Here, the entry h in the last row and column is simply given by $h = h_{j+2,j+1}$. Thus, besides these applications to the last column, we only need one additional rotation G_{j+1} to eliminate this entry. This can be done by choosing

$$c_{j+1} = |d|/\sqrt{d^2 + h^2}, \qquad s_{j+1} = c_{j+1} h/d$$

if $d \neq 0$ and $c_{j+1} = 0$, $s_{j+1} = 1$ if $d = 0$. Taking this all into account, we can state the final version of the GMRES algorithm. In principle, after initialisation, which also contains the initialisation of $\xi = \beta e_1$, the method consists in each iteration of the following steps.

1. Compute v_{k+1} and $h_{\ell k}$ using Arnoldi's method.
2. Apply the rotations $G_1, \ldots, G_{k-1}$ to the last column of H.
3. Compute the kth rotation to eliminate $h_{k+1,k}$.
4. Apply the kth rotation to ξ and to the last column of H.

The iteration stops if the residual norm estimate $|\xi_{k+1}|$ becomes sufficiently small. Algorithm 25 contains all these steps in detail.

Even in this form, the GMRES method suffers from two problems. First of all, the computational cost increases from iteration to iteration since the cost is still $O(k^2)$ in the kth iteration. Moreover, with increasing k, the memory requirement grows. In each step we have to store the vectors $v_1, \ldots, v_k \in \mathbb{R}^n$. For this alone we need $O(nk)$ space and that is even the case if the original matrix A was sparse.

An often-suggested remedy to this problem is the restarted GMRES method, which stops after a fixed number of orthogonalisation steps, computes an approximate solution and then restarts the algorithm using this approximate solution as the new initialisation, see Algorithm 26.

As for the CG method it is easy to see that the iterations of the GMRES (and also MINRES) method yield a decreasing sequence of residuals $\{r_k\}$, this time, however, in the ℓ_2-norm. This remains obviously true for the restarted GMRES method. Unfortunately, while we have (at least theoretical) convergence after

---

Algorithm 25: GMRES

Input : $A \in \mathbb{R}^{n \times n}, \mathbf{b} \in \mathbb{R}^n, \mathbf{x}_0 \in \mathbb{R}^n, \epsilon > 0$.

Output: Approximate solution of $A\mathbf{x} = \mathbf{b}$.

1   $\mathbf{r}_0 := \mathbf{b} - A\mathbf{x}_0, \quad \beta := \|\mathbf{r}_0\|_2, \quad \mathbf{v}_1 := \mathbf{r}_0/\beta, \quad \xi = (\beta, 0, \ldots, 0)^{\mathrm{T}}$

2   **for** $k = 1, 2, \ldots,$ **do**

3      $\mathbf{w}_k := A\mathbf{v}_k$

4   **for** $\ell = 1$ **to** k **do**

5         $h_{\ell k} := \langle \mathbf{w}_k, \mathbf{v}_\ell \rangle_2$

6         $\mathbf{w}_k := \mathbf{w}_k - h_{\ell k}\mathbf{v}_\ell$

7      $h_{k+1,k} := \|\mathbf{w}_k\|_2$

8   **for** $i = 1, \ldots, k-1$ **do**

9         $\begin{pmatrix} h_{ik} \\ h_{i+1,k} \end{pmatrix} := \begin{pmatrix} c_i & s_i \\ -s_i & c_i \end{pmatrix} \begin{pmatrix} h_{ik} \\ h_{i+1,k} \end{pmatrix}$

10      $\gamma := (h_{kk}^2 + h_{k+1,k}^2)^{1/2}, \quad c_k := h_{kk}/\gamma, \quad s_k := c_k h_{k+1,k}/h_{kk}$

11      $\begin{pmatrix} \xi_k \\ \xi_{k+1} \end{pmatrix} := \begin{pmatrix} c_k & s_k \\ -s_k & c_k \end{pmatrix} \begin{pmatrix} \xi_k \\ 0 \end{pmatrix}$

12      $h_{kk} := \gamma, \quad h_{k+1,k} := 0$

13   **if** $|\xi_{k+1}| < \epsilon$ **then**

14   **for** $\ell = k, k-1, \ldots, 1$ **do**

15            $y_\ell := \frac{1}{h_{\ell\ell}} \left(\xi_\ell - \sum_{i=\ell+1}^{k} h_{\ell i} y_i \right)$

16         $\mathbf{x}_k := \mathbf{x}_0 + \sum_{i=1}^{k} y_k \mathbf{v}_k$

17   **break**

18   **else**

19         $\mathbf{v}_{k+1} := \mathbf{w}_k/h_{k+1,k}$

---

n steps for GMRES, this may not be true for the restarted GMRES. As a matter of fact, it can happen that the sequence $\{\|\mathbf{r}_k\|_2\}$ "levels out", i.e. becomes stationary with $k \to \infty$. However, in the case of a positive definite but not necessarily symmetric matrix A, the following result shows that the restarted GMRES method converges. The matrix A is positive definite if $\mathbf{x}^{\mathrm{T}}A\mathbf{x} > 0$ for all $\mathbf{x} \neq \mathbf{0}$. Since $\mathbf{x}^{\mathrm{T}}A\mathbf{x} = \mathbf{x}^{\mathrm{T}}A^{\mathrm{T}}\mathbf{x}$, we have that the smallest eigenvalue μ of the symmetric matrix $(A + A^{\mathrm{T}})/2$ is positive by Theorem 5.4:

$$\mu := \min_{\mathbf{x} \neq 0} \frac{1}{2} \frac{\mathbf{x}^{\mathrm{T}}(A^{\mathrm{T}} + A)\mathbf{x}}{\mathbf{x}^{\mathrm{T}}\mathbf{x}} = \min_{\mathbf{x} \neq 0} \frac{\mathbf{x}^{\mathrm{T}}A\mathbf{x}}{\mathbf{x}^{\mathrm{T}}\mathbf{x}} > 0.$$

Also, if $\mathbf{x}_0$ is a corresponding eigenvector to the eigenvalue μ of $(A + A^{\mathrm{T}})/2$

Algorithm 26: GMRES restarted

Input : $A \in \mathbb{R}^{n \times n}$, $\mathbf{b} \in \mathbb{R}^n$, $\mathbf{x}_0 \in \mathbb{R}^n$, $j \in \mathbb{N}$, $\epsilon > 0$.
Output: Approximate solution of $A\mathbf{x} = \mathbf{b}$.

1 $\mathbf{r}_0 := \mathbf{b} - A\mathbf{x}_0, \quad \beta := \|\mathbf{r}_0\|_2$
2 **while** $\beta > \epsilon$ **do**
3 $\quad$ Compute the GMRES approximation $\mathbf{x}_j$ using Algorithm 24
4 $\quad$ Set $\mathbf{x}_0 := \mathbf{x}_j, \quad \mathbf{r}_0 := \mathbf{b} - A\mathbf{x}_0, \quad \beta := \|\mathbf{r}_0\|_2$

---

with $\|\mathbf{x}_0\|_2 = 1$ then

$$\mu = \frac{1}{2}\mathbf{x}_0^{\mathrm{T}}(A + A^{\mathrm{T}})\mathbf{x}_0 = \mathbf{x}_0^{\mathrm{T}}A\mathbf{x}_0 \leq \|A\mathbf{x}_0\|_2 \leq \|A\|_2.$$

Proposition 6.36 *Let $A \in \mathbb{R}^{n \times n}$ be positive definite. Let $\mathbf{x}_j \in \mathbf{x}_0 + \mathcal{K}_j(A, \mathbf{r}_0)$ be the jth iteration of the GMRES method. Then, the residual $\mathbf{r}_j = \mathbf{b} - A\mathbf{x}_j$ satisfies*

$$\|\mathbf{r}_j\|_2 \leq \left(1 - \frac{\mu^2}{\sigma^2}\right)^{j/2} \|\mathbf{r}_0\|_2,$$

where μ is the smallest eigenvalue of $(A + A^{\mathrm{T}})/2$ and $\sigma = \|A\|_2$.

Proof From Theorem 6.24 we know that

$$\|\mathbf{r}_j\|_2 \leq \min_{\substack{P \in \pi_j \\ P(0)=1}} \|P(A)\|_2 \|\mathbf{r}_0\|_2.$$

If we now define $p \in \pi_1$ by $p(t) := 1 - \alpha t$ with $\alpha \in \mathbb{R}$ then we have $P = p^j \in \pi_j$ with $P(0) = 1$ such that $\|P(A)\|_2 = \|p^j(A)\|_2 \leq \|p(A)\|_2^j$ gives an upper bound on the minimum above. Next, we want to choose α in the definition of p to have a bound on $\|p(A)\|_2$. To this end, note that, for a fixed $\mathbf{x} \in \mathbb{R}^n \setminus \{0\}$,

$$\|p(A)\mathbf{x}\|_2^2 = \|\mathbf{x} - \alpha A\mathbf{x}\|_2^2 = \|\mathbf{x}\|_2^2 - 2\alpha\mathbf{x}^{\mathrm{T}}A\mathbf{x} + \alpha^2\|A\mathbf{x}\|_2^2$$

becomes minimal for $\alpha = \mathbf{x}^{\mathrm{T}}A\mathbf{x}/\|A\mathbf{x}\|_2^2$, see also the second part of Lemma 5.16 for a similar argument, with value

$$\|p(A)\mathbf{x}\|_2^2 = \|\mathbf{x}\|_2^2 - \left(\frac{\mathbf{x}^{\mathrm{T}}A\mathbf{x}}{\|A\mathbf{x}\|_2}\right)^2 = \|\mathbf{x}\|_2^2\left[1 - \left(\frac{\mathbf{x}^{\mathrm{T}}A\mathbf{x}}{\|\mathbf{x}\|_2^2}\right)^2\left(\frac{\|\mathbf{x}\|_2}{\|A\mathbf{x}\|_2}\right)^2\right]$$

$$\leq \|\mathbf{x}\|_2^2\left(1 - \frac{\mu^2}{\sigma^2}\right),$$

where we have used that $\mathbf{x}^T A \mathbf{x}/\|\mathbf{x}\|_2^2 \geq \mu$ and $\|\mathbf{x}\|_2/\|A\mathbf{x}\|_2 \geq 1/\sigma$. This yields

$$\|p(A)\|_2^2 \leq 1 - \frac{\mu^2}{\sigma^2}$$

and hence the overall statement. $\square$

As mentioned above, this means that the restarted GMRES method converges.

Corollary 6.37 *If $A \in \mathbb{R}^{n \times n}$ is positive definite then the restarted GMRES(j) method converges for every $j \geq 1$.*

Further improvements of GMRES can be achieved by preconditioning, which we will discuss later on, and by replacing the Gram–Schmidt process by a more stable Householder variant. Details can, for example, be found in Saad [104]. To see how things change when going from GMRES to MINRES, we first note that in the case of a symmetric matrix A, most entries computed in the Arnoldi method are actually zero.

Lemma 6.38 *Let $A \in \mathbb{R}^{n \times n}$ be symmetric. Let $\{\mathbf{v}_\ell\}$ be the sequence of vectors computed by the Arnoldi method and let $h_{\ell k} = \langle A\mathbf{v}_k, \mathbf{v}_\ell \rangle_2$ for $1 \leq \ell \leq k$ and $h_{k+1,k} = \|\tilde{\mathbf{v}}_{k+1}\|_2$. Then,*

$$h_{\ell k} = 0 \qquad 1 \leq \ell < k - 1,$$
$$h_{k,k+1} = h_{k+1,k}.$$

Proof From the fact that $\text{span}\{\mathbf{v}_1, \ldots, \mathbf{v}_\ell\} = \mathcal{K}_\ell(A, \mathbf{r}_0)$ we see that $A\mathbf{v}_\ell \in \mathcal{K}_{\ell+1}(A, \mathbf{r}_0) = \text{span}\{\mathbf{v}_1, \ldots, \mathbf{v}_{\ell+1}\}$. Thus, using the symmetry of A yields

$$h_{\ell k} = \langle A\mathbf{v}_k, \mathbf{v}_\ell \rangle_2 = \langle \mathbf{v}_k, A\mathbf{v}_\ell \rangle_2 = 0$$

for all $\ell + 1 < k$. For the second property note that the orthogonality of $\tilde{\mathbf{v}}_{k+1}$ to $\mathbf{v}_1, \ldots, \mathbf{v}_k$ gives

$$h_{k,k+1} = \langle A\mathbf{v}_{k+1}, \mathbf{v}_k \rangle_2 = \langle \mathbf{v}_{k+1}, A\mathbf{v}_k \rangle_2 = \frac{1}{\|\tilde{\mathbf{v}}_{k+1}\|_2} \langle \tilde{\mathbf{v}}_{k+1}, A\mathbf{v}_k \rangle_2$$

$$= \frac{1}{\|\tilde{\mathbf{v}}_{k+1}\|_2} \left\langle \tilde{\mathbf{v}}_{k+1}, A\mathbf{v}_k - \sum_{\ell=1}^{k} \langle A\mathbf{v}_k, \mathbf{v}_\ell \rangle_2 \mathbf{v}_\ell \right\rangle_2 = \|\tilde{\mathbf{v}}_{k+1}\|_2$$

$$= h_{k+1,k}. \qquad \square$$

Thus, the previously defined matrix $\tilde{H}_j = (h_{\ell k}) \in \mathbb{R}^{j \times j}$ reduces to a symmetric tridiagonal matrix with diagonal entries $\alpha_k := h_{kk}$ and sub- and super-diagonal entries $\beta_k := h_{k,k+1} = h_{k+1,k}$:

$$
\tilde{H}_j = \begin{pmatrix}
\alpha_1 & \beta_1 & & \\
\beta_1 & \ddots & \ddots & \\
& \ddots & \ddots & \beta_{j-1} \\
& & \beta_{j-1} & \alpha_j
\end{pmatrix}.
$$

Taking this new notation into account, we see that the Arnoldi algorithm, Algorithm 23, reduces to the algorithm given in Algorithm 27, which is the *Lanczos orthogonalisation method* for symmetric matrices, see [89, 90].

Algorithm 27: Lanczos method

Input : $A = A^T \in \mathbb{R}^{n \times n}$, $\mathbf{x}_0 \in \mathbb{R}^n$, $j \in \{1, \ldots, n\}$.
Output: Orthonormal basis $\{\mathbf{v}_1, \ldots, \mathbf{v}_j\}$ of $\mathcal{K}_j(A, \mathbf{r}_0)$.

1   $\mathbf{r}_0 := \mathbf{b} - A\mathbf{x}_0$, $\mathbf{v}_0 := \mathbf{0}$, $\mathbf{v}_1 := \mathbf{r}_0/\|\mathbf{r}_0\|_2$, $\beta_0 := 0$
2   **for** $k = 1, 2, \ldots, j - 1$ **do**
3      $\mathbf{w}_k := A\mathbf{v}_k - \beta_{k-1}\mathbf{v}_{k-1}$
4      $\alpha_k := \langle \mathbf{w}_k, \mathbf{v}_k \rangle_2$
5      $\mathbf{w}_k := \mathbf{w}_k - \alpha_k\mathbf{v}_k$
6      $\beta_k := \|\mathbf{w}_k\|_2$
7   **if** $\beta_k = 0$ **then break**
8   **else** $\mathbf{v}_{k+1} := \mathbf{w}_k/\beta_k$

It is interesting to note that we could derive the CG method from Lanczos' method. We will not do this here, but later on, when we discuss biorthogonalisation methods, we will derive a method similar to the CG method from a two-sided or biorthogonal Lanczos method.

As in the non-symmetric case, we now also have an alternative method for reducing A to a tridiagonal matrix having the same eigenvalues as A.

Remark 6.39 If the Lanczos method does not stop prematurely, the orthogonal matrix $V = (\mathbf{v}_1, \ldots, \mathbf{v}_n)$ transforms the symmetric matrix A into the tridiagonal matrix $V_n^T A V_n = \tilde{H}_n$ having the same eigenvalues as A.

We will now work out the details of a possible implementation of MINRES. As in the case of GMRES, we use Givens rotations to transform the matrix H_j to an upper triangular matrix R_j. However, by Corollary 5.37, we know that row i of R has at most non-zero entries r_{ii}, $r_{i,i+1}$ and $r_{i,i+2}$. Hence, applying the

Givens rotations G_1 to G_{j-1} to H_{j-1} leads to the $j \times (j-1)$ matrix

$$G_{j-1} \cdots G_1 H_{j-1} = \begin{pmatrix} r_{11} & r_{12} & r_{13} & 0 & \cdots & 0 \\ & \ddots & \ddots & \ddots & \ddots & \vdots \\ & & \ddots & \ddots & \ddots & 0 \\ & & & \ddots & \ddots & r_{j-3,j-1} \\ & & & & \ddots & r_{j-2,j-1} \\ & & & & & r_{j-1,j-1} \\ & & & & & 0 \end{pmatrix}.$$

The next step is to carry this over to H_j. This means we have to add the jth column and and $(j + 1)$st row and then apply $G_{j-1} \cdots G_1$ to the jth column. However, since the $j$the column of H_j has only the entries β_{j-1}, α_j and β_j in rows $j - 1$, j and $j + 1$, respectively, and since each G_i acts only on rows i and $i + 1$, we see that we only have to apply G_{j-2} and then G_{j-1} to the new jth column. This essentially means that we have to form

$$\begin{pmatrix} r_{j-2,j} \\ \tilde{r}_{j-1,j} \end{pmatrix} = \begin{pmatrix} c_{j-2} & s_{j-2} \\ -s_{j-2} & c_{j-2} \end{pmatrix} \begin{pmatrix} 0 \\ \beta_{j-1} \end{pmatrix},$$

$$\begin{pmatrix} r_{j-1,j} \\ \tilde{r}_{jj} \end{pmatrix} = \begin{pmatrix} c_{j-1} & s_{j-1} \\ -s_{j-1} & c_{j-1} \end{pmatrix} \begin{pmatrix} \tilde{r}_{j-1,j} \\ \alpha_j \end{pmatrix},$$

which leads to the representation

$$G_{j-1} \cdots G_1 H_j = \begin{pmatrix} r_{11} & r_{12} & r_{13} & 0 & \cdots & 0 & 0 \\ & \ddots & \ddots & \ddots & \ddots & \vdots & \vdots \\ & & \ddots & \ddots & \ddots & 0 & \vdots \\ & & & \ddots & \ddots & r_{j-3,j-1} & 0 \\ & & & & \ddots & r_{j-2,j-1} & r_{j-2,j} \\ & & & & & r_{j-1,j-1} & r_{j-1,j} \\ & & & & & 0 & \tilde{r}_{jj} \\ & & & & & 0 & \beta_j \end{pmatrix}.$$

Then, we have to determine a final rotation to remove the β_j from the last column and row, i.e. we determine c_j and s_j such that

$$\begin{pmatrix} c_j & s_j \\ -s_j & c_j \end{pmatrix} \begin{pmatrix} \tilde{r}_{jj} \\ \beta_j \end{pmatrix} = \begin{pmatrix} r_{jj} \\ 0 \end{pmatrix}.$$

Obviously, we can choose $c_j = \tilde{r}_{jj} / \sqrt{\tilde{r}_{jj}^2 + \beta_j^2}$ and $s_j = \beta_j / \sqrt{\tilde{r}_{jj}^2 + \beta_j^2}$, but see also the discussion about numerical stability in this context just before Definition 5.23. We will see that we do not even have to save the numbers $r_{j-2,j}$, $r_{j-1,j}$ and r_{jj} since we do not need them in the next iteration. Hence, we can compute all relevant quantities by

$$\gamma_0 := \tilde{r}_{jj} = -s_{j-1}\tilde{r}_{j-1,j} + c_{j-1}\alpha_j$$
$$= -s_{j-1}c_{j-2}\beta_{j-1} + c_{j-1}\alpha_j,$$
$$\gamma_1 := \sqrt{\gamma_0^2 + \beta_j^2},$$
$$\gamma_2 := r_{j-1,j} = c_{j-1}\tilde{r}_{j-1,j} + s_{j-1}\alpha_j$$
$$= s_{j-1}\alpha_j + c_{j-1}c_{j-2}\beta_{j-1},$$
$$\gamma_3 := r_{j-2,j} = s_{j-2}\beta_{j-1},$$
$$c_j := \gamma_0/\gamma_1, \quad s_j := \beta_j/\gamma_1,$$

using the above considerations. Moreover, we also have $r_{jj} = c_j\tilde{r}_{jj} + s_j\beta_j = \gamma_1$. As in the case of GMRES, we can write the iteration $x_k = x_0 + V_k y$, where $y \in \mathbb{R}^k$ minimises $\|\beta e_1 - H_k y\|_2$. However, for MINRES it is not necessary to save the orthonormal basis, i.e. the matrix V_k. Thus we need a different approach to actually compute the iteration x_k. According to (6.26), we can express the iteration as

$$x_k = x_0 + \beta V_k \tilde{R}_k^{-1} \tilde{q}_k = x_0 + \beta P_k \tilde{q}_k$$

if we define the matrix $P_k := V_k \tilde{R}_k^{-1}$, where $\tilde{R}_k$ is again the upper $k \times k$ block of the matrix $R_k \in \mathbb{R}^{(k+1)\times k}$, which is the upper triangular matrix from the QR factorisation of $H_k = Q_k R_k$. Since the upper $k \times k$ block $\tilde{H}_k$ of H_k is now a tridiagonal matrix, the only entries r_{ij} of R_k in row i which might be non-zero are r_{ii}, $r_{i,i+1}$ and $r_{i,i+2}$. We also know from our previous considerations that when going over from $R_k \in \mathbb{R}^{(k+1)\times k}$ to $R_{k+1} \in \mathbb{R}^{(k+2)\times(k+1)}$ we keep R_k as the upper left part of R_{k+1}. This altogether means that we can compute the columns of $P_k \in \mathbb{R}^{n\times k}$ iteratively. If we set $P_k = (p_1, \ldots, p_k)$ and $V_k = (v_1, \ldots, v_k)$ then the relation $P_k \tilde{R}_k = V_k$ yields

$$v_1 = r_{11}p_1, \qquad v_2 = r_{12}p_1 + r_{22}p_2$$

and then

$$v_j = r_{j-2,j}p_{j-2} + r_{j-1,j}p_{j-1} + r_{jj}p_j, \qquad 3 \le j \le k.$$

Noting that $r_{jj} \ne 0$ as long as the Lanczos method does not break down, this can be rearranged and, using the notation above, rewritten as

$$\mathbf{p}_j = \frac{1}{r_{jj}}(\mathbf{v}_j - r_{j-1,j}\mathbf{p}_{j-1} - r_{j-2,j}\mathbf{p}_{j-2}) \qquad (6.29)$$

$$= \frac{1}{\gamma_1}(\mathbf{v}_j - \gamma_2\mathbf{p}_{j-1} - \gamma_3\mathbf{p}_{j-2}), \qquad 1 \le j \le k,$$

where we have set $\mathbf{p}_0 = \mathbf{p}_{-1} = \mathbf{0}$ and recall that the constants $\gamma_1, \gamma_2, \gamma_3$ have to be computed in each iteration, i.e. for each j.

A consequence of these considerations is that we can update the iterations in the following form. We have

$$\mathbf{x}_k = \mathbf{x}_0 + \beta P_k \tilde{\mathbf{q}}_k = \mathbf{x}_0 + \beta \sum_{j=1}^{k} q_j \mathbf{p}_j = \mathbf{x}_0 + \beta \sum_{j=1}^{k-1} q_j \mathbf{p}_j + \beta q_k \mathbf{p}_k$$

$$= \mathbf{x}_{k-1} + \beta q_k \mathbf{p}_k. \qquad (6.30)$$

From this, we can also conclude that we do not need the whole vector $\tilde{\mathbf{q}}_k$ but only the scalar $\delta := \beta q_k$ to update the iteration. Since $\beta \mathbf{q}_k = \beta Q_k^{\mathsf{T}} \mathbf{e}_1 = G_k \cdots G_1(\beta \mathbf{e}_1)$ we compute with each application of a G_j two new entries q_j and $\tilde{q}_{j+1}$ of which the first one is not changed by the following updates while the latter one is changed only by the next update. This can be expressed by

$$\begin{pmatrix} q_j \\ \tilde{q}_{j+1} \end{pmatrix} = \tilde{G}_j \begin{pmatrix} \tilde{q}_j \\ 0 \end{pmatrix} = \begin{pmatrix} c_j & s_j \\ -s_j & c_j \end{pmatrix}\begin{pmatrix} \tilde{q}_j \\ 0 \end{pmatrix} = \begin{pmatrix} c_j\tilde{q}_j \\ -s_j\tilde{q}_j \end{pmatrix},$$

which is started with $\tilde{q}_1 = \beta$, which means that we are "absorbing" β into $\mathbf{q}_k$. Hence, if we have computed $\delta := \tilde{q}_k$, then we need $q_k = c_k \delta$ to update $\mathbf{x}_k = \mathbf{x}_{k-1} + c_k \delta \mathbf{p}_k$ and we need to replace δ by $-s_k \delta$ to prepare the next iteration. This altogether shows that we can implement MINRES as given in Algorithm 28.

Let us make a few more remarks. First of all, as we know, the residual of the kth iteration satisfies

$$\|\mathbf{b} - A\mathbf{x}_k\|_2^2 = \|\beta \mathbf{e}_1 - \tilde{H}_k \mathbf{y}_k\|_2^2 = \|\beta \tilde{\mathbf{q}}_k - \tilde{R}_k \mathbf{y}_k\|_2^2 + |\beta q_{k+1}|^2 = |\beta q_{k+1}|^2$$

or, if we again absorb β into $\mathbf{q}_k$ as described above then we simply have $\|\mathbf{b} - A\mathbf{x}_k\|_2 = |q_{k+1}|$. The algorithm described above shows that $|q_{k+1}| = |c_{k+1}\tilde{q}_{k+1}| = |c_{k+1}s_k\tilde{q}_k|$ is at hand at any time during the algorithm without any additional cost, which can be used as a stopping criterion.

There is an alternative to MINRES in the case of symmetric matrices, which we only want to mention here. The method is called *SYMMLQ*. Here the iteration $\mathbf{x}_k \in \mathbf{x}_0 + A\mathcal{K}_k(A, \mathbf{r}_0)$ is computed as the minimiser of $\|\mathbf{x}^* - \mathbf{x}\|_2$ over $\mathbf{x}_0 + A\mathcal{K}_k(A, \mathbf{r}_0)$, where $\mathbf{x}^*$ is again the solution to $A\mathbf{x} = \mathbf{b}$. Details can be found in Paige and Saunders [99].

Algorithm 28: MINRES

Input : $A \in \mathbb{R}^{n \times n}$ symmetric, $\mathbf{b} \in \mathbb{R}^n$, $\mathbf{x}_0 \in \mathbb{R}^n$.

Output: Approximate solution of $Ax = \mathbf{b}$.

1 $\beta_0 := 0, \quad s_{-1} = s_0 = 0, \quad c_{-1} = c_0 = 1$

2 $\mathbf{p}_{-1} := \mathbf{p}_0 := \mathbf{v}_0 = \mathbf{0}$

3 $\mathbf{r}_0 := \mathbf{b} - A\mathbf{x}_0, \quad \delta := \|\mathbf{r}_0\|_2, \quad \mathbf{v}_1 := \mathbf{r}_0/\delta$

4 **for** $k = 1, 2, \ldots,$ **do**

5 $\quad$ $\mathbf{w}_k := A\mathbf{v}_k - \beta_{k-1}\mathbf{v}_{k-1}$

6 $\quad$ $\alpha_k := \langle \mathbf{w}_k, \mathbf{v}_k \rangle_2$

7 $\quad$ $\mathbf{w}_k := \mathbf{w}_k - \alpha_k\mathbf{v}_k$

8 $\quad$ $\beta_k := \|\mathbf{w}_k\|_2$

9 $\quad$ **if** $\beta_k = 0$ **then** stop

10 $\quad$ $\gamma_0 := c_{k-1}\alpha_k - s_{k-1}c_{k-2}\beta_{k-1}$

11 $\quad$ $\gamma_1 := \sqrt{\gamma_0^2 + \beta_k^2}$

12 $\quad$ $\gamma_2 := s_{k-1}\alpha_k + c_{k-1}c_{k-2}\beta_{k-1}$

13 $\quad$ $\gamma_3 := s_{k-2}\beta_{k-1}$

14 $\quad$ $c_k := \gamma_0/\gamma_1 \quad s_k := \beta_k/\gamma_1$

15 $\quad$ $\mathbf{p}_k := [\mathbf{v}_k - \gamma_2\mathbf{p}_{k-1} - \gamma_3\mathbf{p}_{k-2}]/\gamma_1$

16 $\quad$ $\mathbf{x}_k := \mathbf{x}_{k-1} + c_k\delta\mathbf{p}_k$

17 $\quad$ $\delta := -s_k\delta$

18 $\quad$ $\mathbf{v}_{k+1} := \mathbf{w}_k/\beta_k$

6.3 Biorthogonalisation Methods

For symmetric, sparse matrices $A \in \mathbb{R}^{n \times n}$, the Krylov subspace method of choice would be MINRES if the matrix is indefinite and either CG or MINRES if the matrix is definite.

For non-symmetric matrices, GMRES often works well but has the disadvantage of an increasing memory and time requirement. Moreover, though the restarted GMRES avoids this increase in required resources, it might not converge but only level out. Hence, in the case of non-symmetric matrices it makes sense to look for alternative Krylov subspace methods.

Recall that both MINRES and GMRES were based upon an orthogonalisation of the Krylov space $\mathcal{K}_k(A, \mathbf{r}_0)$. In the case of MINRES this was given by Lanczos' method, which essentially boils down to the three-term recursion

$$\tilde{\mathbf{v}}_{j+1} = A\mathbf{v}_j - \alpha_j\mathbf{v}_j - \beta_{j-1}\mathbf{v}_{j-1},$$

$$\mathbf{v}_{j+1} = \tilde{\mathbf{v}}_{j+1}/\|\tilde{\mathbf{v}}_{j+1}\|_2$$

and leads to orthonormal vectors $\mathbf{v}_1, \ldots, \mathbf{v}_k \in \mathbb{R}^n$, which form a basis of the Krylov space $\mathcal{K}_k(A, \mathbf{r}_0)$. In the case of GMRES the construction of an orthonormal basis $\mathbf{v}_1, \ldots, \mathbf{v}_k$ of $\mathcal{K}_k(A, \mathbf{r}_0)$ was based upon Arnoldi's method and could not be reduced to such a simple three-term recursion.

This naturally raises the question of whether it is in general possible to find a short recurrence relation for computing an orthonormal basis of the Krylov space of an arbitrary matrix $A \in \mathbb{R}^{n \times n}$. The answer, in general, is negative as shown in [49] by Faber and Manteuffel.

Hence, to have a memory-efficient orthogonalisation procedure also in the case of a non-symmetric matrix, we will now relax the idea of orthonormality. Instead of having a set of orthonormal basis vectors $\mathbf{v}_1, \ldots, \mathbf{v}_k$ we will construct two sets $\mathbf{v}_1, \ldots, \mathbf{v}_k$ and $\mathbf{w}_1, \ldots, \mathbf{w}_k$ which are biorthogonal, i.e. satisfy $\langle \mathbf{v}_i, \mathbf{w}_j \rangle_2 = 0$ for all $i \neq j$ and which are bases for

$$\mathcal{K}_k(A, \mathbf{r}_0) = \operatorname{span}\{\mathbf{r}_0, A\mathbf{r}_0, \ldots A^{k-1}\mathbf{r}_0\},$$
$$\mathcal{K}_k(A^{\mathrm{T}}, \hat{\mathbf{r}}_0) = \operatorname{span}\{\hat{\mathbf{r}}_0, A^{\mathrm{T}}\hat{\mathbf{r}}_0, \ldots, (A^{\mathrm{T}})^{k-1}\hat{\mathbf{r}}_0\},$$

respectively.

The corresponding procedure is the Lanczos biorthogonalisation method, also called the two-sided Lanczos method, and is given in detail in Algorithm 29.

Algorithm 29: Two-sided Lanczos method

Input : $A \in \mathbb{R}^{n \times n}$, $\mathbf{r}_0, \hat{\mathbf{r}}_0 \in \mathbb{R}^n$ with $\langle \mathbf{r}_0, \hat{\mathbf{r}}_0 \rangle_2 \neq 0$.
Output: Biorthogonal bases of $\mathcal{K}_k(A, \mathbf{r}_0)$ and $\mathcal{K}_k(A, \hat{\mathbf{r}}_0)$.

1 $\mathbf{v}_1 = \mathbf{r}_0/\|\mathbf{r}_0\|_2$, $\mathbf{w}_1 = \hat{\mathbf{r}}_0/\langle \hat{\mathbf{r}}_0, \mathbf{v}_1 \rangle_2$, $\beta_0 := \gamma_0 := 0$, $\mathbf{v}_0 = \mathbf{w}_0 = \mathbf{0}$.
2 **for** $j = 1, 2, \ldots, k$ **do**
3 $\quad$ $\alpha_j := \langle A\mathbf{v}_j, \mathbf{w}_j \rangle_2$
4 $\quad$ $\tilde{\mathbf{v}}_{j+1} := A\mathbf{v}_j - \alpha_j \mathbf{v}_j - \beta_{j-1}\mathbf{v}_{j-1}$
5 $\quad$ $\tilde{\mathbf{w}}_{j+1} := A^{\mathrm{T}}\mathbf{w}_j - \alpha_j \mathbf{w}_j - \gamma_{j-1}\mathbf{w}_{j-1}$
6 $\quad$ $\gamma_j := \|\tilde{\mathbf{v}}_{j+1}\|_2$
7 $\quad$ $\mathbf{v}_{j+1} := \tilde{\mathbf{v}}_{j+1}/\gamma_j$
8 $\quad$ $\beta_j := \langle \mathbf{v}_{j+1}, \tilde{\mathbf{w}}_{j+1} \rangle_2$
9 $\quad$ $\mathbf{w}_{j+1} := \tilde{\mathbf{w}}_{j+1}/\beta_j$

The two-sided Lanczos method in Algorithm 29 requires two matrix–vector products per iteration, one with A and one with A^{T}. It does indeed compute biorthogonal vectors, as long as it does not stop prematurely. This and further properties are given in the next proposition, which will help us to define Krylov subspace methods based upon this biorthogonalisation technique.

Proposition 6.40 *Assume that the two-sided Lanczos method does not terminate prematurely. Then, we have* $\|\mathbf{v}_j\|_2 = 1$ *and* $\langle \mathbf{v}_j, \mathbf{w}_j \rangle_2 = 1$ *for* $1 \leq j \leq k$ *and*

$$\langle \mathbf{v}_i, \mathbf{w}_j \rangle_2 = 0, \qquad 1 \leq i \neq j \leq k. \tag{6.31}$$

Furthermore, we have

$$\mathcal{K}_k(A, \mathbf{r}_0) = \text{span}\{\mathbf{v}_1, \dots, \mathbf{v}_k\}, \text{ and } \mathcal{K}_k(A^\mathsf{T}, \hat{\mathbf{r}}_0) = \text{span}\{\mathbf{w}_1, \dots, \mathbf{w}_k\}.$$

Finally, if $V_k := (\mathbf{v}_1, \dots, \mathbf{v}_k) \in \mathbb{R}^{n \times k}$ *and* $W_k := (\mathbf{w}_1, \dots, \mathbf{w}_k) \in \mathbb{R}^{n \times k}$ *then*

$$AV_k = V_k T_k + \gamma_k \mathbf{v}_{k+1} \mathbf{e}_k^\mathsf{T}, \tag{6.32}$$

$$A^\mathsf{T} W_k = W_k T_k^\mathsf{T} + \beta_k \mathbf{w}_{k+1} \mathbf{e}_k^\mathsf{T}, \tag{6.33}$$

$$W_k^\mathsf{T} A V_k = T_k, \tag{6.34}$$

where $T_k \in \mathbb{R}^{k \times k}$ *is the tridiagonal matrix*

$$T_k := \begin{pmatrix} \alpha_1 & \beta_1 & & & \\ \gamma_1 & \alpha_2 & \beta_2 & & \\ & \ddots & \ddots & \ddots & \\ & & \ddots & \ddots & \beta_{k-1} \\ & & & \gamma_{k-1} & \alpha_k \end{pmatrix}. \tag{6.35}$$

Proof We will show the first three properties by induction on k. For $k = 1$ we have $\|\mathbf{v}_1\|_2 = 1$ and $\langle \mathbf{v}_1, \mathbf{w}_1 \rangle_2 = \langle \mathbf{v}_1, \hat{\mathbf{r}}_0 \rangle_2 / \langle \mathbf{v}_1, \hat{\mathbf{r}}_0 \rangle_2 = 1$ by definition and there is nothing to show for (6.31). Let us now assume that we have biorthogonal vectors $\mathbf{v}_1, \dots, \mathbf{v}_k$ and $\mathbf{w}_1, \dots, \mathbf{w}_k$ normalised in the stated way. Then, obviously, we also have $\|\mathbf{v}_{k+1}\|_2 = 1$ and $\langle \mathbf{v}_{k+1}, \mathbf{w}_{k+1} \rangle_2 = \langle \mathbf{v}_{k+1}, \tilde{\mathbf{w}}_{k+1} \rangle_2 / \beta_k = 1$. Hence, it remains to show that $\mathbf{v}_{k+1}$ is orthogonal to $\mathbf{w}_1, \dots, \mathbf{w}_k$ and that $\mathbf{w}_{k+1}$ is orthogonal to $\mathbf{v}_1, \dots, \mathbf{v}_k$. Since these two claims are verified in very similar ways, we will show the reasoning just for the first property. Here, we start with

$$\langle \mathbf{v}_{k+1}, \mathbf{w}_k \rangle_2 = \frac{1}{\gamma_k} \left[\langle A\mathbf{v}_k, \mathbf{w}_k \rangle_2 - \alpha_k \langle \mathbf{v}_k, \mathbf{w}_k \rangle_2 - \beta_{k-1} \langle \mathbf{v}_{k-1}, \mathbf{w}_k \rangle_2 \right]$$

$$= \frac{1}{\gamma_k} \left[\langle A\mathbf{v}_k, \mathbf{w}_k \rangle_2 - \langle A\mathbf{v}_k, \mathbf{w}_k \rangle_2 \langle \mathbf{v}_k, \mathbf{w}_k \rangle_2 \right] = 0,$$

using the orthogonality of $\mathbf{v}_{k-1}$ to $\mathbf{w}_k$, the definition of α_k and the fact that $\langle \mathbf{v}_k, \mathbf{w}_k \rangle_2 = 1$.

Next, let $j < k$. Then we have

$$
\begin{aligned}
\langle \mathbf{v}_{k+1}, \mathbf{w}_j \rangle_2 &= \frac{1}{\gamma_k} \left[\langle A\mathbf{v}_k, \mathbf{w}_j \rangle_2 - \alpha_k \langle \mathbf{v}_k, \mathbf{w}_j \rangle_2 - \beta_{k-1} \langle \mathbf{v}_{k-1}, \mathbf{w}_j \rangle_2 \right] \\
&= \frac{1}{\gamma_k} \left[\langle \mathbf{v}_k, A^{\mathrm{T}} \mathbf{w}_j \rangle_2 - \beta_{k-1} \langle \mathbf{v}_{k-1}, \mathbf{w}_j \rangle_2 \right] \\
&= \frac{1}{\gamma_k} \left[\langle \mathbf{v}_k, \beta_j \mathbf{w}_{j+1} + \alpha_j \mathbf{w}_j + \gamma_{j-1} \mathbf{w}_{j-1} \rangle_2 - \beta_{k-1} \langle \mathbf{v}_{k-1}, \mathbf{w}_j \rangle_2 \right] \\
&= \frac{1}{\gamma_k} \left[\beta_j \langle \mathbf{v}_k, \mathbf{w}_{j+1} \rangle_2 - \beta_{k-1} \langle \mathbf{v}_{k-1}, \mathbf{w}_j \rangle_2 \right],
\end{aligned}
$$

using the orthogonality relation that we have by the induction hypothesis and the definition of $\mathbf{w}_{j+1}$. Now, if even $j < k - 1$ then the last two remaining terms on the right-hand side also vanish, which shows orthogonality in this case. If, however, $j = k - 1$, this becomes

$$
\langle \mathbf{v}_{k+1}, \mathbf{w}_j \rangle_2 = \frac{1}{\gamma_k} \left[\beta_{k-1} \langle \mathbf{v}_k, \mathbf{w}_k \rangle_2 - \beta_{k-1} \langle \mathbf{v}_{k-1}, \mathbf{w}_{k-1} \rangle_2 \right] = 0
$$

since $\langle \mathbf{v}_k, \mathbf{w}_k \rangle_2 = \langle \mathbf{v}_{k-1}, \mathbf{w}_{k-1} \rangle_2 = 1$. This establishes the biorthogonality relation (6.31). Equation (6.32) follows from

$$
\begin{aligned}
AV_k &= \left(A\mathbf{v}_1, \ldots, A\mathbf{v}_j, \ldots, A\mathbf{v}_k \right) \\
&= \left(\alpha_1 \mathbf{v}_1 + \gamma_1 \mathbf{v}_2, \ldots, \beta_{j-1} \mathbf{v}_{j-1} + \alpha_j \mathbf{v}_j + \gamma_j \mathbf{v}_{j+1}, \ldots, \beta_{k-1} \mathbf{v}_{k-1} + \alpha_k \mathbf{v}_k + \gamma_k \mathbf{v}_{k+1} \right) \\
&= V_k T_k + \gamma_k \mathbf{v}_{k+1} \mathbf{e}_k^{\mathrm{T}},
\end{aligned}
$$

and equation (6.33) can be proven in the same way. Finally, equation (6.34) follows from (6.32) and the fact that $W_k^{\mathrm{T}} V_k = I$ and $W_k^{\mathrm{T}} \mathbf{v}_{k+1} = \mathbf{0}$. □

To simplify the presentation of the algorithm, we have left out any test for division by zero. However, it can happen that either γ_j or β_j become zero and in this case the corresponding vectors $\mathbf{v}_{j+1}$ or $\mathbf{w}_{j+1}$ become undefined and the algorithm in this form will stop prematurely.

Such a premature ending can happen for various reasons. First of all, we could have that either $\tilde{\mathbf{v}}_{j+1} = \mathbf{0}$ or $\tilde{\mathbf{w}}_{j+1} = \mathbf{0}$. These cases are usually referred to as *regular termination*. The Lanczos process has found an invariant subspace. If $\tilde{\mathbf{v}}_{j+1} = \mathbf{0}$ then the vectors $\mathbf{v}_1, \ldots, \mathbf{v}_j$, which have been created so far, form an A-invariant space. If $\tilde{\mathbf{w}}_{j+1} = \mathbf{0}$ then the vectors $\mathbf{w}_1, \ldots, \mathbf{w}_j$ form an A^{T}-invariant space. More problematic is the situation when both vectors $\tilde{\mathbf{v}}_{j+1}$ and $\tilde{\mathbf{w}}_{j+1}$ are different from the zero vector but are orthogonal, i.e. satisfy $\langle \tilde{\mathbf{v}}_{j+1}, \tilde{\mathbf{w}}_{j+1} \rangle_2 = 0$. This situation is called a *serious breakdown*. It means that there are no vectors $\mathbf{v}_{j+1} \in \mathcal{K}_{j+1}(A, \mathbf{r}_0)$ and $\mathbf{w}_{j+1} \in \mathcal{K}_{j+1}(A^{\mathrm{T}}, \hat{\mathbf{r}}_0)$ with $\langle \mathbf{v}_{j+1}, \mathbf{w}_i \rangle_2 = 0$ and $\langle \mathbf{v}_i, \mathbf{w}_{j+1} \rangle_2 = 0$ for all $1 \leq i \leq j$. However, this does not necessarily mean that later on, say for $k > j + 1$, there are such vectors $\mathbf{v}_k \in \mathcal{K}_k(A, \mathbf{r}_0)$ orthogonal to $\mathcal{K}_{k-1}(A^T, \hat{\mathbf{r}}_0)$ and $\mathbf{w}_k \in \mathcal{K}_k(A^T, \hat{\mathbf{r}}_0)$ orthogonal to $\mathcal{K}_{k-1}(A, \mathbf{r}_0)$. In this case, a remedy to the problem is to simply skip those steps in the algorithm which lead to undefined Lanczos vectors and to continue with those steps, where these vectors are well-defined. Such a method is called a *look-ahead* Lanczos method.

After having a procedure for computing the biorthogonal bases for the Krylov spaces $\mathcal{K}_k(A, \mathbf{r}_0)$ and $\mathcal{K}_k(A^T, \hat{\mathbf{r}}_0)$ we have to address the question of how to compute a possible approximation $\mathbf{x}_k \in \mathcal{K}_k(A, \mathbf{r}_0)$. Naturally, we will write

$$\mathbf{x}_k = \mathbf{x}_0 + V_k \mathbf{y}_k$$

and could, for example, determine $\mathbf{y}_k$ such that the residual $\mathbf{r}_k = \mathbf{b} - A\mathbf{x}_k = \mathbf{r}_0 - AV_k \mathbf{y}_k$ is orthogonal to $\mathcal{K}_k(A^T, \hat{\mathbf{r}}_0)$, i.e.

$$0 = W_k^T \mathbf{r}_k = W_k^T \mathbf{r}_0 - W_k^T A V_k \mathbf{y}_k = \|\mathbf{r}_0\|_2 \mathbf{e}_1 - T_k \mathbf{y}_k,$$

where we have also used that $\mathbf{v}_1 = \mathbf{r}_0 / \|\mathbf{r}_0\|_2$ and $\langle \mathbf{v}_1, \mathbf{w}_1 \rangle_2 = 1$. Thus, if the tridiagonal matrix T_k is invertible, we have a unique solution $\mathbf{y}_k \in \mathbb{R}^k$, which then defines an iteration $\mathbf{x}_k \in \mathbb{R}^n$.

Definition 6.41 Under the assumption that the Lanczos biorthogonalisation process is defined and the tridiagonal matrix T_k is invertible, the *biconjugate gradient (BiCG) method* computes the iteration $\mathbf{x}_k \in \mathbf{x}_0 + \mathcal{K}_k(A, \mathbf{r}_0)$ as

$$\mathbf{x}_k = \mathbf{x}_0 + V_k T_k^{-1} (\beta \mathbf{e}_1),$$

where $\beta = \|\mathbf{r}_0\|_2$.

Note, however, that we have encountered another possible situation, where the iteration $\mathbf{x}_k$ might not be well-defined, namely if the matrix T_k is not invertible. This situation is different from the previously described breakdowns of the bi-Lanczos process.

To derive an algorithmic description of the BiCG method, we will now derive characteristic properties, which can then be used for stating the algorithm. Let us assume that the tridiagonal matrix $T_k \in \mathbb{R}^{k \times k}$ from (6.35) has an *LU*-factorisation $T_k = L_k U_k$. According to Theorem 3.16 the factors have the form

$$L_k = \begin{pmatrix} 1 & & & 0 \\ \ell_2 & 1 & & \\ & \ddots & \ddots & \\ 0 & & \ell_k & 1 \end{pmatrix}, \quad U_k = \begin{pmatrix} u_1 & \beta_1 & & 0 \\ & u_2 & \ddots & \\ & & \ddots & \beta_{k-1} \\ 0 & & & u_k \end{pmatrix},$$

where the components u_i and ℓ_i are defined recursively as $u_1 = \alpha_1$ and $\ell_i =$

γ_{i-1}/u_{i-1} and $u_i = \alpha_i - \ell_i\beta_{i-1}$ for $2 \leq i \leq k$. Defining $P_k := V_k U_k^{-1}$ and denoting the columns of P_k as $P_k = (\mathbf{p}_0, \ldots, \mathbf{p}_{k-1})$, we can rewrite the iteration $\mathbf{x}_k$ in an update form as

$$\mathbf{x}_k = \mathbf{x}_0 + V_k T_k^{-1}(\beta \mathbf{e}_1) = \mathbf{x}_0 + V_k U_k^{-1} L_k^{-1}(\beta \mathbf{e}_1)$$

$$= \mathbf{x}_0 + P_k \mathbf{a}_k = \mathbf{x}_0 + \sum_{j=0}^{k-1} a_j \mathbf{p}_j$$

$$= \mathbf{x}_{k-1} + a_{k-1}\mathbf{p}_{k-1}$$

with $\mathbf{a}_k = (a_0, \ldots, a_{k-1})^{\mathrm{T}} := L_k^{-1}(\beta \mathbf{e}_1)$. For the residual $\mathbf{r}_k = \mathbf{b} - A\mathbf{x}_k$ we have on the one hand

$$\mathbf{r}_k = \mathbf{b} - A\mathbf{x}_{k-1} - a_{k-1}A\mathbf{p}_{k-1} = \mathbf{r}_{k-1} - a_{k-1}A\mathbf{p}_{k-1}$$

and on the other hand, using (6.32) and the fact that $\mathbf{e}_k^{\mathrm{T}} T_k^{-1} \mathbf{e}_1 \in \mathbb{R}$,

$$\mathbf{r}_k = \mathbf{b} - A\mathbf{x}_0 - AV_k T_k^{-1}(\beta \mathbf{e}_1) = \mathbf{r}_0 - (V_k T_k + \gamma_k \mathbf{v}_{k+1}\mathbf{e}_k^{\mathrm{T}})T_k^{-1}(\beta \mathbf{e}_1)$$

$$= \mathbf{r}_0 - \|\mathbf{r}_0\|_2 \mathbf{v}_1 - \delta_k \mathbf{v}_{k+1} = \delta_k \mathbf{v}_{k+1}$$

with a certain constant $\delta_k \in \mathbb{R}$. This means that the residual $\mathbf{r}_k$ is always parallel to $\mathbf{v}_{k+1}$ and hence orthogonal to $\mathbf{w}_1, \ldots, \mathbf{w}_k$. Next, from $P_k = V_k U_k^{-1}$ or $P_k U_k = V_k$ we find $\mathbf{v}_k = \beta_{k-1}\mathbf{p}_{k-2} + u_k \mathbf{p}_{k-1}$ and hence

$$\mathbf{p}_{k-1} = \frac{1}{u_k}(\mathbf{v}_k - \beta_{k-1}\mathbf{p}_{k-2}) = \frac{1}{u_k}\left(\frac{1}{\delta_{k-1}}\mathbf{r}_{k-1} - \beta_{k-1}\mathbf{p}_{k-2}\right), \tag{6.36}$$

i.e. we can reconstruct $\mathbf{p}_k$ recursively from $\mathbf{p}_{k-1}$ and $\mathbf{r}_k$. Finally, if we define $\hat{P}_k = (\hat{\mathbf{p}}_0, \ldots, \hat{\mathbf{p}}_{k-1}) := W_k L_k^{-\mathrm{T}}$, then we see that

$$\hat{P}_k^{\mathrm{T}} A P_k = L_k^{-1} W_k^{\mathrm{T}} A V_k U_k^{-1} = L_k^{-1} T_k U_k^{-1} = L_k^{-1} L_k = I,$$

i.e. the vectors $\mathbf{p}_j$ and $\hat{\mathbf{p}}_i$ are A-orthogonal.

Finally, the vectors generated by the biorthogonal Lanczos method can also be used to solve the adjoint linear system $A^{\mathrm{T}}\mathbf{x} = \hat{\mathbf{b}}$, if $\hat{\mathbf{r}}_0$ is defined as $\hat{\mathbf{r}}_0 := \hat{\mathbf{b}} - A\hat{\mathbf{x}}_0$. As a matter of fact, we can define a sequence of approximations and residuals

$$\hat{\mathbf{x}}_k := \hat{\mathbf{x}}_0 + W_k \mathbf{z}_k,$$

$$\hat{\mathbf{r}}_k := \hat{\mathbf{b}} - A^{\mathrm{T}}\hat{\mathbf{x}}_k = \hat{\mathbf{r}}_0 - A^{\mathrm{T}} W_k \mathbf{z}_k,$$

where $\mathbf{z}_k \in \mathbb{R}^k$ is determined by the orthogonality condition

$$0 = V_k^{\mathrm{T}}\hat{\mathbf{r}}_k = V_k^{\mathrm{T}}\hat{\mathbf{r}}_0 - V_k^{\mathrm{T}} A^{\mathrm{T}} W_k \mathbf{z}_k = \langle \hat{\mathbf{r}}_0, \mathbf{v}_1 \rangle_2 \mathbf{e}_1 - T_k^{\mathrm{T}}\mathbf{z}_k,$$

i.e. $\mathbf{z}_k = T_k^{-\mathrm{T}}(\hat{\beta}\mathbf{e}_1)$ with $\hat{\beta} := \langle \hat{\mathbf{r}}_0, \mathbf{v}_1 \rangle_2$. Using this and the above definition

$\hat{P}_k = W_k L_k^{-T}$, we can rewrite the iterations as

$$\hat{\mathbf{x}}_k = \hat{\mathbf{x}}_0 + W_k T_k^{-T}(\hat{\beta}\mathbf{e}_1) = \hat{\mathbf{x}}_0 + W_k L_k^{-T} U_k^{-T}(\hat{\beta}\mathbf{e}_1)$$
$$= \hat{\mathbf{x}}_0 + \hat{P}_k \hat{\mathbf{a}}_k = \hat{\mathbf{x}}_{k-1} + \hat{a}_{k-1}\hat{\mathbf{p}}_{k-1},$$

where we have set $\hat{\mathbf{a}}_k = (\hat{a}_0, \ldots, \hat{a}_{k-1})^T := U_k^{-T}(\hat{\beta}\mathbf{e}_1)$.

Using (6.33) and the definition of $\mathbf{w}_1$ gives again that $\hat{\mathbf{r}}_k$ and $\mathbf{w}_{k+1}$ are parallel:

$$\hat{\mathbf{r}}_k = \hat{\mathbf{r}}_0 - A^T W_k \mathbf{z}_k = \hat{\mathbf{r}}_0 - \left(W_k T_k^T + \beta_k \mathbf{w}_{k+1}\mathbf{e}_k^T\right)\mathbf{z}_k$$
$$= \hat{\mathbf{r}}_0 - \left(W_k T_k^T + \beta_k \mathbf{w}_{k+1}\mathbf{e}_k^T\right)T_k^{-T}(\hat{\beta}\mathbf{e}_1)$$
$$= \hat{\mathbf{r}}_0 - W_k(\hat{\beta}\mathbf{e}_1) - \beta_k\hat{\beta}(\mathbf{e}_k^T T_k^{-T}\mathbf{e}_1)\mathbf{w}_{k+1}$$
$$=: \hat{\delta}_k \mathbf{w}_{k+1}.$$

From the relation $\hat{P}_k L_k^T = W_k$ we can also conclude that $\mathbf{w}_k = \ell_k \hat{\mathbf{p}}_{k-2} + \hat{\mathbf{p}}_{k-1}$ or

$$\hat{\mathbf{p}}_{k-1} = \mathbf{w}_k - \ell_k \hat{\mathbf{p}}_{k-2} = \frac{1}{\hat{\delta}_{k-1}}\hat{\mathbf{r}}_{k-1} - \ell_k \hat{\mathbf{p}}_{k-2}. \tag{6.37}$$

So far, we have update formulas for all vectors. However, we can simplify the update formulas for the "search directions" $\mathbf{p}_k$ and $\hat{\mathbf{p}}_k$ if we rescale them. To be more precise, if we replace $\mathbf{p}_k$ by $u_{k+1}\delta_k\mathbf{p}_k$, then (6.36) shows that the new $\mathbf{p}_k$ satisfies a recursion of the form $\mathbf{p}_{k-1} = \mathbf{r}_{k-1} - \tilde{\beta}_{k-1}\mathbf{p}_{k-2}$. In a similar way, we can rescale $\hat{\mathbf{p}}_k$ such that the coefficient in front of $\hat{\mathbf{r}}_{k-1}$ in the update formula (6.37) can be chosen to be one. Of course, this also changes the coefficients in the other update formulas and the normalisation, but the general form and the biorthogonality will not be modified. In conclusion we have the following result.

Proposition 6.42   *If the Lanczos biorthogonalisation process does not stop prematurely and if the matrix T_k is invertible, the process generates sequences of vectors satisfying the relations*

$$\mathbf{x}_{j+1} = \mathbf{x}_j + \alpha_j \mathbf{p}_j, \qquad\qquad \hat{\mathbf{x}}_{j+1} = \hat{\mathbf{x}}_j + \hat{\alpha}_j \hat{\mathbf{p}}_j,$$
$$\mathbf{r}_{j+1} = \mathbf{r}_j - \alpha_j A\mathbf{p}_j, \qquad\qquad \hat{\mathbf{r}}_{j+1} = \hat{\mathbf{r}}_j - \hat{\alpha}_j A^T\hat{\mathbf{p}}_j,$$
$$\mathbf{p}_{j+1} = \mathbf{r}_{j+1} + \beta_{j+1}\mathbf{p}_j, \qquad\qquad \hat{\mathbf{p}}_{j+1} = \hat{\mathbf{r}}_{j+1} + \hat{\beta}_{j+1}\hat{\mathbf{p}}_j$$

with certain constants $\alpha_j, \beta_{j+1}, \hat{\alpha}_j, \hat{\beta}_{j+1} \in \mathbb{R}$. Moreover, we have the biorthogonalities

$$\langle \mathbf{r}_j, \hat{\mathbf{r}}_i \rangle_2 = 0, \quad \langle A\mathbf{p}_j, \hat{\mathbf{p}}_i \rangle_2 = 0, \qquad i \neq j. \tag{6.38}$$

Finally, we have the alternative bases

$$\mathcal{K}_j(A, \mathbf{r}_0) = \text{span}\{\mathbf{r}_0, \ldots, \mathbf{r}_{j-1}\} = \text{span}\{\mathbf{p}_0, \ldots, \mathbf{p}_{j-1}\},$$
$$\mathcal{K}_j(A^T, \hat{\mathbf{r}}_0) = \text{span}\{\hat{\mathbf{r}}_0, \ldots, \hat{\mathbf{r}}_{j-1}\} = \text{span}\{\hat{\mathbf{p}}_0, \ldots, \hat{\mathbf{p}}_{j-1}\}.$$

Proof The recursion formulas and the biorthogonalities (6.38) follow directly from the derivation above. Hence, the only things that remain to be proven are the identities regarding the Krylov spaces at the end of the proposition. This, however, follows from the recurrence relations for $\mathbf{r}_{j+1}$ and $\mathbf{p}_{j+1}$ on the one hand and for $\hat{\mathbf{r}}_{j+1}$ and $\hat{\mathbf{p}}_{j+1}$ on the other hand, once we have established that $\mathbf{p}_0$ and $\mathbf{r}_0$ (and $\hat{\mathbf{p}}_0$ and $\hat{\mathbf{r}}_0$) are parallel. This can be seen as follows. Taking the above-mentioned rescaling into account, $\mathbf{p}_0$ is given by

$$\mathbf{p}_0 = u_1 \delta_0 V_k U_k^{-1} \mathbf{e}_1.$$

Since U_k is an upper triangular matrix, so is U_k^{-1} and we can conclude that $U_k^{-1} \mathbf{e}_1 = (1/u_1) \mathbf{e}_1$ and hence that $\mathbf{p}_0 = \delta_0 V_k \mathbf{e}_1 = \delta_0 \mathbf{v}_1 = \mathbf{r}_0$. $\qquad\square$

We can also start with the recursion formulas above and use the biorthogonalities (6.38) to determine the coefficients in Proposition 6.42. First of all, from $\hat{\mathbf{p}}_j = \hat{\mathbf{r}}_j + \hat{\beta}_j \hat{\mathbf{p}}_{j-1}$ we can conclude that

$$\langle A\mathbf{p}_j, \hat{\mathbf{r}}_j \rangle_2 = \langle A\mathbf{p}_j, \hat{\mathbf{p}}_j - \hat{\beta}_j \hat{\mathbf{p}}_{j-1} \rangle_2 = \langle A\mathbf{p}_j, \hat{\mathbf{p}}_j \rangle_2.$$

Then, from $\mathbf{r}_{j+1} = \mathbf{r}_j - \alpha_j A\mathbf{p}_j$ it follows that

$$0 = \langle \mathbf{r}_{j+1}, \hat{\mathbf{r}}_j \rangle_2 = \langle \mathbf{r}_j, \hat{\mathbf{r}}_j \rangle_2 - \alpha_j \langle A\mathbf{p}_j, \hat{\mathbf{r}}_j \rangle_2,$$

i.e. the coefficient α_j must have the form

$$\alpha_j = \frac{\langle \mathbf{r}_j, \hat{\mathbf{r}}_j \rangle_2}{\langle A\mathbf{p}_j, \hat{\mathbf{r}}_j \rangle_2} = \frac{\langle \mathbf{r}_j, \hat{\mathbf{r}}_j \rangle_2}{\langle A\mathbf{p}_j, \hat{\mathbf{p}}_j \rangle_2}.$$

In the same way we can conclude that $\hat{\alpha}_j$ must have the form

$$\hat{\alpha}_j = \frac{\langle \mathbf{r}_j, \hat{\mathbf{r}}_j \rangle_2}{\langle \mathbf{r}_j, A^{\mathsf{T}}\hat{\mathbf{p}}_j \rangle_2} = \frac{\langle \mathbf{r}_j, \hat{\mathbf{r}}_j \rangle_2}{\langle \mathbf{p}_j, A^{\mathsf{T}}\hat{\mathbf{p}}_j \rangle_2} = \frac{\langle \mathbf{r}_j, \hat{\mathbf{r}}_j \rangle_2}{\langle A\mathbf{p}_j, \hat{\mathbf{p}}_j \rangle_2} = \alpha_j.$$

From $\mathbf{p}_{j+1} = \mathbf{r}_{j+1} + \beta_{j+1} \mathbf{p}_j$ we have

$$0 = \langle \mathbf{p}_{j+1}, A^{\mathsf{T}}\hat{\mathbf{p}}_j \rangle_2 = \langle \mathbf{r}_{j+1}, A^{\mathsf{T}}\hat{\mathbf{p}}_j \rangle_2 + \beta_{j+1} \langle \mathbf{p}_j, A^{\mathsf{T}}\hat{\mathbf{p}}_j \rangle_2$$

which resolves to

$$\beta_{j+1} = -\frac{\langle \mathbf{r}_{j+1}, A^{\mathsf{T}}\hat{\mathbf{p}}_j \rangle_2}{\langle \mathbf{p}_j, A^{\mathsf{T}}\hat{\mathbf{p}}_j \rangle_2}.$$

Taking $\alpha_j = \hat{\alpha}_j$ and $A^{\mathsf{T}}\hat{\mathbf{p}}_j = -(\hat{\mathbf{r}}_{j+1} - \hat{\mathbf{r}}_j)/\hat{\alpha}_j$ into account, we can simplify the formula for β_{j+1} to

$$\beta_{j+1} = -\frac{\langle \mathbf{r}_{j+1}, A^{\mathsf{T}}\hat{\mathbf{p}}_j \rangle_2}{\langle \mathbf{p}_j, A^{\mathsf{T}}\hat{\mathbf{p}}_j \rangle_2} = \frac{1}{\alpha_j} \frac{\langle \mathbf{r}_{j+1}, \hat{\mathbf{r}}_{j+1} - \hat{\mathbf{r}}_j \rangle_2}{\langle \mathbf{p}_j, A^{\mathsf{T}}\hat{\mathbf{p}}_j \rangle_2} = \frac{\langle \mathbf{r}_{j+1}, \hat{\mathbf{r}}_{j+1} \rangle_2}{\langle \mathbf{r}_j, \hat{\mathbf{r}}_j \rangle_2}.$$

The symmetry of the argument also shows that we once again have $\hat{\beta}_{j+1} = \beta_{j+1}$.

Thus, we have determined all the coefficients and the final algorithm for the BiCG method is stated in Algorithm 30.

Algorithm 30: BiCG method

Input : $A \in \mathbb{R}^{n \times n}$, $\mathbf{b} \in \mathbb{R}^n$.
Output: Approximate solution of $A\mathbf{x} = \mathbf{b}$.

1 Choose $\mathbf{x}_0 \in \mathbb{R}^n$.
2 Set $\mathbf{r}_0 := \mathbf{p}_0 = \mathbf{b} - A\mathbf{x}_0$ and $j := 0$.
3 Choose $\hat{\mathbf{p}}_0 = \hat{\mathbf{r}}_0$ such that $\langle \mathbf{r}_0, \hat{\mathbf{r}}_0 \rangle_2 \neq 0$
4 **while** $\|\mathbf{r}_j\|_2 > \epsilon$ **do**
5 $\quad$ $\alpha_j := \langle \mathbf{r}_j, \hat{\mathbf{r}}_j \rangle_2 / \langle A\mathbf{p}_j, \hat{\mathbf{p}}_j \rangle_2$
6 $\quad$ $\mathbf{x}_{j+1} := \mathbf{x}_j + \alpha_j \mathbf{p}_j$
7 $\quad$ $\mathbf{r}_{j+1} := \mathbf{r}_j - \alpha_j A\mathbf{p}_j$
8 $\quad$ $\hat{\mathbf{r}}_{j+1} := \hat{\mathbf{r}}_j - \alpha_j A^T \hat{\mathbf{p}}_j$
9 $\quad$ $\beta_{j+1} := \langle \mathbf{r}_{j+1}, \hat{\mathbf{r}}_{j+1} \rangle_2 / \langle \mathbf{r}_j, \hat{\mathbf{r}}_j \rangle_2$
10 $\quad$ $\mathbf{p}_{j+1} := \mathbf{r}_{j+1} + \beta_{j+1} \mathbf{p}_j$
11 $\quad$ $\hat{\mathbf{p}}_{j+1} := \hat{\mathbf{r}}_{j+1} + \beta_{j+1} \hat{\mathbf{p}}_j$
12 $\quad$ $j := j + 1$

Technically, we must check whether these necessary conditions to compute the coefficients indeed lead to sequences of vectors with the desired properties. This can, however, be done as in the proof of Theorem 6.9.

When choosing $\hat{\mathbf{r}}_0 = \mathbf{r}_0$, the BiCG algorithm reduces for a symmetric matrix $A = A^T$ to the standard CG algorithm (Algorithm 22), though all vectors are computed twice, since in this case we obviously have $\mathbf{x}_j = \hat{\mathbf{x}}_j$, $\mathbf{r}_j = \hat{\mathbf{r}}_j$ and $\mathbf{p}_j = \hat{\mathbf{p}}_j$. If the matrix is in addition positive definite then we will also have convergence.

As mentioned above, the BiCG algorithm can also be used to solve a system of the form $A^T \mathbf{x} = \hat{\mathbf{b}}$ simultaneously. To this end, we only have to define $\hat{\mathbf{r}}_0 := \hat{\mathbf{b}} - A^T \hat{\mathbf{x}}_0$ and compute $\hat{\mathbf{x}}_{j+1} = \hat{\mathbf{x}}_j + \alpha_j \hat{\mathbf{p}}_j$ after step 6 of Algorithm 30.

As mentioned above, the BiCG method can fail to produce a new iteration if the two-sided Lanczos process terminates early or if the matrix T_k is not invertible. The latter can be dealt with by changing the actual idea of computing the iteration to a more GMRES-like method without the drawback of increasing memory requirements.

Recall from (6.32) that we have the relation

$$AV_k = V_k T_k + \gamma_k \mathbf{v}_{k+1} \mathbf{e}_k^T = V_{k+1} H_k, \qquad H_k = \begin{pmatrix} T_k \\ \gamma_k \mathbf{e}_k^T \end{pmatrix} \in \mathbb{R}^{(k+1) \times k}, \qquad (6.39)$$

which corresponds to the GMRES representation (6.24). Thus, as before, we can write our iteration as $x_k = x_0 + V_k y$ with a corresponding residual

$$\mathbf{r}_k := \mathbf{b} - A\mathbf{x}_k = \mathbf{b} - A(\mathbf{x}_0 + V_k \mathbf{y}) = \mathbf{r}_0 - AV_k \mathbf{y} = \beta \mathbf{v}_1 - V_{k+1} H_k \mathbf{y} = V_{k+1}(\beta \mathbf{e}_1 - H_k \mathbf{y}),$$

where we have used that $\mathbf{v}_1 = \mathbf{r}_0 / \|\mathbf{r}_0\|_2$. Minimising the ℓ_2-norm of $\mathbf{r}_k$ would be equivalent to minimising the ℓ_2-norm of $\beta \mathbf{e}_1 - H_k \mathbf{y}$ if the columns of V_{k+1} were orthonormal. In general this will not be the case but it is still a possible option to just find a minimiser for $\|\beta \mathbf{e}_1 - H_k \mathbf{y}\|_2$, particularly since T_k and hence H_k have a tridiagonal structure.

Definition 6.43 Under the assumption that the Lanczos biorthogonalisation process is defined, the *quasi-minimal residual (QMR) method* computes the iteration $\mathbf{x}_k \in \mathbf{x}_0 + \mathcal{K}_k(A, \mathbf{r}_0)$ as $\mathbf{x}_k = \mathbf{x}_0 + V_k \mathbf{y}_k$, where $\mathbf{y}_k \in \mathbb{R}^k$ solve

$$\min_{\mathbf{y} \in \mathbb{R}^k} \|\beta \mathbf{e}_1 - H_k \mathbf{y}\|_2,$$

with $\beta = \|\mathbf{r}_0\|_2$.

In an algorithmic description of the QMR method, we can proceed as in the case of the MINRES method and avoid the need to save the Lanczos vectors. As for MINRES (see equation (6.25)), we use successive Givens rotations to transform H_k into an upper triangular matrix. However, this time $H_k \in \mathbb{R}^{(k+1) \times k}$ is a tridiagonal matrix and thus the transformed matrix has the band structure

$$G_k G_{k-1} \cdots G_1 \begin{pmatrix} \alpha_1 & \beta_1 & & & \\ \gamma_1 & \alpha_2 & \beta_2 & & \\ & \ddots & \ddots & \ddots & \\ & & \ddots & \ddots & \beta_{k-1} \\ & & & \gamma_{k-1} & \alpha_k \\ & & & & \gamma_k \end{pmatrix} = \begin{pmatrix} r_{11} & r_{12} & r_{13} & & \\ & r_{22} & \ddots & & \ddots \\ & & \ddots & \ddots & r_{k-2,k} \\ & & & \ddots & r_{k-1,k} \\ & & & & r_{kk} \\ & & & & 0 \end{pmatrix}.$$

As in the case of MINRES, we can now easily compute the solution of the minimisation problem and also update the QR factorisation. If we define again $Q_k^T := G_k \cdots G_1$ and $R_k := Q_k^T H_k \in \mathbb{R}^{(k+1) \times k}$ then we can transform $\|\beta \mathbf{e}_1 - H_k \mathbf{y}\|_2$ as before. Recalling the definitions $\mathbf{q}_k := Q_k^T \mathbf{e}_k \in \mathbb{R}^{k+1}$, $\mathbf{q}_k = (\tilde{\mathbf{q}}_k, q_{k+1})^T$ with $\tilde{\mathbf{q}}_k \in \mathbb{R}^k$ and $\tilde{R}_k \in \mathbb{R}^{k \times k}$ as the upper $k \times k$ block of R_k, equation (6.26) shows that the minimiser of $\|\beta \mathbf{e}_1 - H_k \mathbf{y}\|_2$ is given by

$$\mathbf{y}_k := \beta \tilde{R}_k^{-1} \tilde{\mathbf{q}}_k.$$

Furthermore, when using the rotations G_j appropriately, we see that (6.28) becomes

$$
G_k G_{k-1} \cdots G_1 H_{k+1} =
\begin{pmatrix}
r_{11} & r_{12} & r_{13} & & & \\
& r_{22} & \ddots & & \ddots & \\
& & \ddots & \ddots & & r_{k-2,k} \\
& & & \ddots & r_{k-1,k} & r_{k-1,k+1} \\
& & & & r_{kk} & r_{k,k+1} \\
& & & & 0 & d \\
& & & & 0 & h
\end{pmatrix},
$$

from which we can again determine the next iteration G_{k+1}, as before. Setting finally again $P_k = (\mathbf{p}_1, \ldots, \mathbf{p}_k) = V_k \tilde{R}_k^{-1}$ we can compute the iterations via

$$
\mathbf{x}_k = \mathbf{x}_0 + V_k \mathbf{y}_k = \mathbf{x}_0 + \beta P_k \tilde{\mathbf{q}}_k = \mathbf{x}_{k-1} + \beta q_k \mathbf{p}_k,
$$

see equation (6.30) for details. Taking this all into account, gives the final algorithm for QMR depicted in Algorithm 31, where the first 10 lines cover the two-sided Lanczos method.

There is an obvious connection between QMR and GMRES/MINRES. To see this, recall that the iterations of GMRES $\mathbf{x}_k^G$ are defined in such a way that the residual $\mathbf{r}_k^G = \mathbf{b} - A\mathbf{x}_k^G$ satisfies

$$
\|\mathbf{r}_k^G\|_2 = \min\{\|\mathbf{b} - A\mathbf{x}\|_2 : \mathbf{x} \in \mathbf{x}_0 + \mathcal{K}_k(A, \mathbf{r}_0)\}.
$$

As before, we can use actually any basis $\mathbf{v}_1, \ldots, \mathbf{v}_k$ of $\mathcal{K}_k(A, \mathbf{r}_0)$ to express $\mathbf{x}_k^G$ as $\mathbf{x}_k^G = \mathbf{x}_0 + V_k \mathbf{y}_k^G$ with $\mathbf{y}_k^G \in \mathbb{R}^k$. If we use the basis constructed by the bi-Lanczos process, this leads to

$$
\|\mathbf{r}_k^G\|_2 = \|\mathbf{b} - A\mathbf{x}_0 - AV_k \mathbf{y}_k^G\|_2 = \|V_{k+1}(\beta \mathbf{e}_1 - H_k \mathbf{y}_k^G)\|_2
$$
$$
\geq \sigma_{k+1} \|\beta \mathbf{e}_1 - H_k \mathbf{y}_k^G\|_2,
$$

using (6.39) and Corollary 2.20 with the matrix $V_{k+1} \in \mathbb{R}^{n \times (k+1)}$ having full rank $k + 1$ and smallest singular value $\sigma_{k+1} > 0$. Moreover, we can bound the residual of the QMR method by

$$
\|\mathbf{r}_k^Q\|_2 = \|V_{k+1}(\beta \mathbf{e}_1 - H_k \mathbf{y}_k^Q)\|_2 \leq \|V_{k+1}\|_2 \|\beta \mathbf{e}_1 - H_k \mathbf{y}_k^Q\|_2
$$
$$
\leq \|V_{k+1}\|_2 \|\beta \mathbf{e}_1 - H_k \mathbf{y}_k^G\|_2 \leq \frac{\sigma_1}{\sigma_{k+1}} \|\mathbf{r}_k^G\|_2,
$$

using also that $\|V_{k+1}\|_2 = \sigma_1$, the largest singular value of V_{k+1}. This means that the residual of QMR does not deviate too much from the optimal residual of GMRES as long as V_k remains well-conditioned.

Algorithm 31: QMR (quasi-minimum residual)

Input : $A \in \mathbb{R}^{n \times n}$, $\mathbf{b} \in \mathbb{R}^n$, $\mathbf{x}_0 \in \mathbb{R}^n$.

Output: Approximate solution of $A\mathbf{x} = \mathbf{b}$.

1 $\mathbf{r}_0 := \mathbf{b} - A\mathbf{x}_0$, $\beta := \|\mathbf{r}_0\|_2$, $\mathbf{v}_1 := \mathbf{r}_0/\beta$, $\xi = (\beta, 0, \ldots, 0)^{\mathrm{T}}$

2 Choose $\hat{\mathbf{r}}_0$ with $\langle \mathbf{r}_0, \hat{\mathbf{r}}_0 \rangle_2 \neq 0$ and set $\mathbf{w}_1 := \hat{\mathbf{r}}_0/\langle \mathbf{r}_0, \hat{\mathbf{r}}_0 \rangle_2$

3 **for** $k = 1, 2, \ldots,$ **do**

4 $\qquad h_{kk} := \langle A\mathbf{v}_k, \mathbf{w}_k \rangle_2$

5 $\qquad \tilde{\mathbf{v}}_{k+1} := A\mathbf{v}_k - h_{kk}\mathbf{v}_k - h_{k-1,k}\mathbf{v}_{k-1}$ (undefined terms are zero)

6 $\qquad \tilde{\mathbf{w}}_{k+1} := A^{\mathrm{T}}\mathbf{w}_k - h_{kk}\mathbf{w}_k - h_{k,k-1}\mathbf{w}_{k-1}$ (undefined terms are zero)

7 $\qquad h_{k+1,k} := \|\tilde{\mathbf{v}}_{k+1}\|_2$

8 $\qquad \mathbf{v}_{k+1} := \tilde{\mathbf{v}}_{k+1}/h_{k+1,k}$

9 $\qquad h_{k,k+1} := \langle \mathbf{v}_{k+1}, \tilde{\mathbf{w}}_{k+1} \rangle_2$

10 $\qquad \mathbf{w}_{k+1} := \tilde{\mathbf{w}}_{k+1}/h_{k,k+1}.$

11 $\qquad$ **if** $k > 2$ **then**

12 $\qquad\qquad \begin{pmatrix} h_{k-2,k} \\ h_{k-1,k} \end{pmatrix} := \begin{pmatrix} c_{k-2} & s_{k-2} \\ -s_{k-2} & c_{k-2} \end{pmatrix} \begin{pmatrix} 0 \\ h_{k-1,k} \end{pmatrix}$

13 $\qquad$ **if** $k > 1$ **then**

14 $\qquad\qquad \begin{pmatrix} h_{k-1,k} \\ h_{k,k} \end{pmatrix} := \begin{pmatrix} c_{k-1} & s_{k-1} \\ -s_{k-1} & c_{k-1} \end{pmatrix} \begin{pmatrix} h_{k-1,k} \\ h_{kk} \end{pmatrix}$

15 $\qquad \gamma := (h_{kk}^2 + h_{k+1,k}^2)^{1/2}$, $c_k := h_{kk}/\gamma$, $s_k := c_k h_{k+1,k}/h_{kk}$

16 $\qquad \begin{pmatrix} \xi_k \\ \xi_{k+1} \end{pmatrix} := \begin{pmatrix} c_k & s_k \\ -s_k & c_k \end{pmatrix} \begin{pmatrix} \xi_k \\ 0 \end{pmatrix}$

17 $\qquad h_{kk} := \gamma$, $h_{k+1,k} := 0$

18 $\qquad \mathbf{p}_k := [\mathbf{v}_k - h_{k-1,k}\mathbf{p}_{k-1} - h_{k-2,k}\mathbf{p}_{k-2}]/h_{kk}$ (undefined terms are zero)

19 $\qquad \mathbf{x}_k := \mathbf{x}_{k-1} + \xi_k \mathbf{p}_k$

Lemma 6.44 *Provided that the bi-Lanczos process does not stop prematurely, the residuals of the QMR and GMRES method satisfy*

$$\|\mathbf{r}_k^Q\|_2 \leq \kappa_2(V_{k+1})\|\mathbf{r}_k^G\|_2,$$

where $\kappa_2(V_{k+1})$ is the condition number of the matrix V_{k+1} consisting of the basis constructed by the bi-Lanczos process.

Both the BiCG method and the QMR method require a matrix–vector multiplication with A and a matrix–vector multiplication with A^{T}. This can be avoided, though only at the price of an additional matrix–vector multiplication with the original matrix. One possible way of achieving this is based on the following observation. If we look at the iterations defined by the BiCG method closely, we see that, as usual in the context of Krylov subspace methods, we can write the direction $\mathbf{p}_j = \mathbf{r}_j + \beta_j \mathbf{p}_{j-1}$ as

$$\mathbf{p}_j = P_j(A)\mathbf{r}_0$$

with $P \in \pi_j$. In the same way, we can express the residuals $\mathbf{r}_j = \mathbf{r}_{j-1} - \alpha_{j-1} A \mathbf{p}_{j-1}$ as

$$\mathbf{r}_j = R_j(A)\mathbf{r}_0$$

with $R_j \in \pi_j$ satisfying $R_j(0) = 1$. Furthermore, the dual directions and residuals are defined by the same polynomials, i.e. we have

$$\hat{\mathbf{p}}_j = P_j(A^{\mathrm{T}})\hat{\mathbf{r}}_0 = (P_j(A))^{\mathrm{T}}\hat{\mathbf{r}}_0, \qquad \hat{\mathbf{r}}_j = R_j(A^{\mathrm{T}})\hat{\mathbf{r}}_0 = (R_j(A))^{\mathrm{T}}\hat{\mathbf{r}}_0.$$

With this, the defining coefficients can be expressed as

$$\alpha_j = \frac{\langle \mathbf{r}_j, \hat{\mathbf{r}}_j \rangle_2}{\langle A\mathbf{p}_j, \hat{\mathbf{p}}_j \rangle_2} = \frac{\langle R_j(A)\mathbf{r}_0, R_j(A^{\mathrm{T}})\hat{\mathbf{r}}_0 \rangle_2}{\langle AP_j(A)\mathbf{r}_0, P_j(A^{\mathrm{T}})\hat{\mathbf{r}}_0 \rangle_2} = \frac{\langle R_j^2(A)\mathbf{r}_0, \hat{\mathbf{r}}_0 \rangle_2}{\langle AP_j^2(A)\mathbf{r}_0, \hat{\mathbf{r}}_0 \rangle_2}, \quad (6.40)$$

$$\beta_{j+1} = \frac{\langle \mathbf{r}_{j+1} \hat{\mathbf{r}}_{j+1} \rangle_2}{\langle \mathbf{r}_j, \hat{\mathbf{r}}_j \rangle_2} = \frac{\langle R_{j+1}^2(A)\mathbf{r}_0, \hat{\mathbf{r}}_0 \rangle_2}{\langle R_j^2(A), \mathbf{r}_0, \hat{\mathbf{r}}_0 \rangle_2}. \quad (6.41)$$

Hence, if we can somehow compute $R_j^2(A)\mathbf{r}_0$ and $AP_j^2(A)\mathbf{r}_0$, then we will be able to compute these coefficients directly. The defining polynomials satisfy the recurrence

$$P_j(t) = R_j(t) + \beta_j P_{j-1}(t), \quad (6.42)$$

$$R_j(t) = R_{j-1}(t) - \alpha_{j-1} t P_{j-1}(t). \quad (6.43)$$

Squaring these equations yields

$$P_j^2(t) = R_j^2(t) + 2\beta_j P_{j-1}(t) R_j(t) + \beta_j^2 P_{j-1}^2(t),$$

$$R_j^2(t) = R_{j-1}^2(t) - 2\alpha_{j-1} t P_{j-1}(t) R_{j-1}(t) + \alpha_{j-1}^2 t^2 P_{j-1}^2(t),$$

which would be update formulas for the squared terms $\tilde{P}_j := P_j^2$ and $\tilde{R}_j = R_j^2$ if there were no mixed terms. To remove these mixed terms, we will simply introduce a third quantity $\tilde{Q}_j := P_{j-1} R_j$. To derive recursion formulas for all three quantities, let us multiply (6.42) by R_j, which gives

$$P_j(t) R_j(t) = R_j^2(t) + \beta_j P_{j-1}(t) R_j(t). \quad (6.44)$$

If we further multiply (6.43) by P_{j-1} then we find

$$P_{j-1}(t) R_j(t) = P_{j-1}(t) R_{j-1}(t) - \alpha_{j-1} t P_{j-1}^2(t)$$

$$= R_{j-1}^2(t) + \beta_{j-1} P_{j-2}(t) R_{j-1}(t) - \alpha_{j-1} t P_{j-1}^2(t).$$

With this, we immediately find the recurrence relations for the three quantities $\tilde{P}_j := P_j^2$, $\tilde{R}_j := R_j^2$ and $\tilde{Q}_j := P_{j-1}R_j$:

$$\tilde{Q}_j(t) = \tilde{R}_{j-1}(t) + \beta_{j-1}\tilde{Q}_{j-1}(t) - \alpha_{j-1}t\tilde{P}_{j-1}(t),$$

$$\tilde{R}_j(t) = \tilde{R}_{j-1}(t) - 2\alpha_{j-1}t\left(\tilde{R}_{j-1}(t) + \beta_{j-1}\tilde{Q}_{j-1}(t)\right) + \alpha_{j-1}^2 t^2 \tilde{P}_{j-1}(t),$$

$$\tilde{P}_j(t) = \tilde{R}_j(t) + 2\beta_j\tilde{Q}_j(t) + \beta_j^2\tilde{P}_{j-1}(t).$$

These recurrence relations can now be used to define recurrence relations for the vectors defined by

$$\mathbf{r}_j := \tilde{R}_j(A)\mathbf{r}_0, \quad \mathbf{p}_j := \tilde{P}_j(A)\mathbf{r}_0, \quad \mathbf{q}_{j-1} := \tilde{Q}_j(A)\mathbf{r}_0.$$

Note, however, that these vectors are not identical with those defined in the BiCG method. For the final derivation of our new algorithm, let us also introduce the quantity $\mathbf{u}_j := \mathbf{r}_j + \beta_j\mathbf{q}_{j-1}$. Then, we have the update formulas

$$\begin{aligned}
\mathbf{q}_{j-1} &= \mathbf{r}_{j-1} + \beta_{j-1}\mathbf{q}_{j-2} - \alpha_{j-1}A\mathbf{p}_{j-1} \\
&= \mathbf{u}_{j-1} - \alpha_{j-1}A\mathbf{p}_{j-1}, \\
\mathbf{r}_j &= \mathbf{r}_{j-1} - \alpha_{j-1}A(2\mathbf{r}_{j-1} + 2\beta_{j-1}\mathbf{q}_{j-2} - \alpha_{j-1}A\mathbf{p}_{j-1}) \\
&= \mathbf{r}_{j-1} - \alpha_{j-1}A(2\mathbf{u}_{j-1} - \alpha_{j-1}A\mathbf{p}_{j-1}) \\
&= \mathbf{r}_{j-1} - \alpha_{j-1}A(\mathbf{u}_{j-1} + \mathbf{q}_{j-1}), \\
\mathbf{p}_j &= \mathbf{r}_j + 2\beta_j\mathbf{q}_{j-1} + \beta_j^2\mathbf{p}_{j-1} \\
&= \mathbf{u}_j + \beta_j(\mathbf{q}_{j-1} + \beta_j\mathbf{p}_{j-1}).
\end{aligned}$$

To finalise the algorithm, we only have to note two more things. First of all, from (6.40) and (6.41) we see that we can compute the coefficients α_j and β_{j+1} as

$$\alpha_j = \frac{\langle \mathbf{r}_j, \hat{\mathbf{r}}_0 \rangle_2}{\langle A\mathbf{p}_j, \hat{\mathbf{r}}_0 \rangle_2}, \qquad \beta_{j+1} = \frac{\langle \mathbf{r}_{j+1}, \hat{\mathbf{r}}_0 \rangle_2}{\langle \mathbf{r}_j, \hat{\mathbf{r}}_0 \rangle_2}$$

and from $\mathbf{r}_{j+1} = \mathbf{r}_j - \alpha_j A(\mathbf{u}_j + \mathbf{q}_j)$ we can conclude that the next iteration is defined by

$$\mathbf{x}_{j+1} := \mathbf{x}_j + \alpha_j(\mathbf{u}_j + \mathbf{q}_j).$$

This procedure gives a method called the *Conjugate Gradient Squared (CGS)* method. The complete algorithm is given in Algorithm 32. This method does not require us to form a matrix–vector product using the transpose A^T of A. However, it requires us to form two matrix–vector products with the matrix A instead. Hence, the computational cost is still comparable to the cost of the BiCG method.

The CGS method has a residual vector which can be described by $R_j^2(A)\mathbf{r}_0$ while $R_j(A)\mathbf{r}_0$ is the residual vector of the BiCG method. This means that,

---

Algorithm 32: CGS method

Input : $A \in \mathbb{R}^{n \times n}$, $\mathbf{b} \in \mathbb{R}^n$.

Output: Approximate solution of $A\mathbf{x} = \mathbf{b}$.

1 Choose $\mathbf{x}_0 \in \mathbb{R}^n$ and $\hat{\mathbf{r}}_0 \in \mathbb{R}^n \setminus \{\mathbf{0}\}$
2 Set $\mathbf{r}_0 := \mathbf{u}_0 := \mathbf{p}_0 := \mathbf{b} - A\mathbf{x}_0$
3 Set $j := 0$.
4 **while** $\|\mathbf{r}_j\|_2 > \epsilon$ **do**
5 $\quad$ $\alpha_j := \langle \mathbf{r}_j, \hat{\mathbf{r}}_0 \rangle_2 / \langle A\mathbf{p}_j, \hat{\mathbf{r}}_0 \rangle_2$
6 $\quad$ $\mathbf{q}_j := \mathbf{u}_j - \alpha_j A\mathbf{p}_j$
7 $\quad$ $\mathbf{x}_{j+1} := \mathbf{x}_j + \alpha_j(\mathbf{u}_j + \mathbf{q}_j)$
8 $\quad$ $\mathbf{r}_{j+1} := \mathbf{r}_j - \alpha_j A(\mathbf{u}_j + \mathbf{q}_j)$
9 $\quad$ $\beta_{j+1} := \langle \mathbf{r}_{j+1}, \hat{\mathbf{r}}_0 \rangle_2 / \langle \mathbf{r}_j, \hat{\mathbf{r}}_0 \rangle_2$
10 $\quad$ $\mathbf{u}_{j+1} := \mathbf{r}_{j+1} + \beta_{j+1}\mathbf{q}_j$
11 $\quad$ $\mathbf{p}_{j+1} := \mathbf{u}_{j+1} + \beta_{j+1}(\mathbf{q}_j + \beta_{j+1}\mathbf{p}_j)$
12 $\quad$ $j := j + 1$

---

in the case of convergence, we can expect that the CGS method converges approximately twice as fast as the BiCG method. However, it also means that the effect of rounding errors will be worse in CGS than in BiCG.

A possible remedy to this is to change the residual polynomial once again. The idea here is to use the additional degrees of freedom to possibly smooth the error. To this end, we will write the residual vector $\mathbf{r}_j$ and the direction $\mathbf{p}_j$ now in the form

$$\mathbf{r}_j := \chi_j(A)R_j(A)\mathbf{r}_0,$$
$$\mathbf{p}_j := \chi_j(A)P_j(A)\mathbf{r}_0,$$

where $\chi_j \in \pi_j$ is a polynomial defined by $\chi_0(t) := 1$ and

$$\chi_j(t) = \prod_{i=1}^{j}(1 - \omega_i t) = (1 - \omega_j t)\chi_{j-1}(t),$$

with certain weights ω_i, which we will discuss later on. Moreover, we still expect the polynomials P_j and R_j to satisfy the recurrence relations (6.42) and (6.43), i.e.

$$P_j(t) = R_j(t) + \beta_j P_{j-1}(t), \tag{6.45}$$
$$R_j(t) = R_{j-1}(t) - \alpha_{j-1}t P_{j-1}(t). \tag{6.46}$$

For the vectors $\mathbf{p}_j$ and $\mathbf{r}_j$ these recurrence relations lead to the recursion

$$\mathbf{r}_j = (I - \omega_j A)\chi_{j-1}(A)R_j(A)\mathbf{r}_0$$
$$= (I - \omega_j A)\chi_{j-1}(A)[R_{j-1}(A) - \alpha_{j-1}AP_{j-1}(A)]\mathbf{r}_0$$
$$= (I - \omega_j A)[\mathbf{r}_{j-1} - \alpha_{j-1}A\mathbf{p}_{j-1}],$$
$$\mathbf{p}_j = \chi_j(A)[R_j(A) + \beta_j P_{j-1}(A)]\mathbf{r}_0$$
$$= \mathbf{r}_j + \beta_j(I - \omega_j A)\mathbf{p}_{j-1}.$$

Note that recurrence relations (6.45) and (6.46) mean that the vectors $P_j(A)\mathbf{r}_0$ and $R_j(A)\mathbf{r}_0$ are the original directions and residuals of the BiCG method. Hence, we can use the biorthogonality from Proposition 6.42, which means in particular

$$R_j(A)\mathbf{r}_0 \perp \mathcal{K}_j(A^T, \hat{\mathbf{r}}_0), \qquad AP_j(A)\mathbf{r}_0 \perp \mathcal{K}_j(A^T, \hat{\mathbf{r}}_0).$$

From this, using also (6.45) and (6.46), we can conclude that

$$\langle R_j(A)\mathbf{r}_0, R_j(A^T)\hat{\mathbf{r}}_0\rangle_2 = \langle R_j(A)\mathbf{r}_0, [R_{j-1}(A^T) - \alpha_{j-1}A^T P_{j-1}(A^T)]\hat{\mathbf{r}}_0\rangle_2$$
$$= -\alpha_{j-1}\langle R_j(A)\mathbf{r}_0, A^T P_{j-1}(A)\hat{\mathbf{r}}_0\rangle_2$$
$$= -\alpha_{j-1}\langle R_j(A)\mathbf{r}_0, A^T[R_{j-1}(A^T) + \beta_{j-1}P_{j-2}(A^T)]\hat{\mathbf{r}}_0\rangle_2$$
$$= -\alpha_{j-1}\langle R_j(A)\mathbf{r}_0, A^T R_{j-1}(A^T)\hat{\mathbf{r}}_0\rangle_2$$
$$= \cdots$$
$$= (-1)^j\alpha_{j-1}\alpha_{j-2}\cdots\alpha_0\langle R_j(A)\mathbf{r}_0, (A^T)^j\hat{\mathbf{r}}_0\rangle_2 \qquad (6.47)$$

and also in the same fashion that

$$\langle AP_j(A)\mathbf{r}_0, P_j(A^T)\hat{\mathbf{r}}_0\rangle_2 = \langle AP_j(A)\mathbf{r}_0, [R_j(A^T) + \beta_j P_{j-1}(A^T)]\hat{\mathbf{r}}_0\rangle_2$$
$$= \langle AP_j(A)\mathbf{r}_0, R_j(A^T)\hat{\mathbf{r}}_0\rangle_2$$
$$= (-1)^j\alpha_{j-1}\alpha_{j-2}\cdots\alpha_0\langle AP_j(A)\mathbf{r}_0, (A^T)^j\hat{\mathbf{r}}_0\rangle_2.$$

Hence, we can rewrite the coefficient α_j from (6.40) as

$$\alpha_j = \frac{\langle R_j(A)\mathbf{r}_0, R_j(A^T)\hat{\mathbf{r}}_0\rangle_2}{\langle AP_j(A)\mathbf{r}_0, P_j(A^T)\hat{\mathbf{r}}_0\rangle_2} = \frac{\langle R_j(A)\mathbf{r}_0, (A^T)^j\hat{\mathbf{r}}_0\rangle_2}{\langle AP_j(A)\mathbf{r}_0, (A^T)^j\hat{\mathbf{r}}_0\rangle_2}, \qquad (6.48)$$

which is not yet what we want, since we still do not use the newly defined vectors $\mathbf{r}_j$ and $\mathbf{p}_j$. However, these vectors satisfy

$$\langle \mathbf{r}_j, \hat{\mathbf{r}}_0\rangle_2 = \langle \chi_j(A)R_j(A)\mathbf{r}_0, \hat{\mathbf{r}}_0\rangle_2 = \langle R_j(A)\mathbf{r}_0, \chi_j(A^T)\hat{\mathbf{r}}_0\rangle_2$$
$$= \langle R_j(A)\mathbf{r}_0, (I - \omega_j A^T)\chi_{j-1}(A^T)\hat{\mathbf{r}}_0\rangle_2$$
$$= -\omega_j\langle R_j(A)\mathbf{r}_0, A^T\chi_{j-1}(A^T)\hat{\mathbf{r}}_0\rangle_2$$
$$= \cdots$$
$$= (-1)^j\omega_j\cdots\omega_1\langle R_j(A)\mathbf{r}_0, (A^T)^j\hat{\mathbf{r}}_0\rangle_2 \qquad (6.49)$$

and also

$$\langle A\mathbf{p}_j, \hat{\mathbf{r}}_0\rangle_2 = \langle A\chi_j(A)P_j(A)\mathbf{r}_0, \hat{\mathbf{r}}_0\rangle_2 = \langle AP_j(A)\mathbf{r}_0, \chi_j(A^T)\hat{\mathbf{r}}_0\rangle_2$$
$$= (-1)^j \omega_j \cdots \omega_1 \langle AP_j(A)\mathbf{r}_0, (A^T)^j \hat{\mathbf{r}}_0\rangle_2.$$

Hence, we can express (6.48) as

$$\alpha_j = \frac{\langle \mathbf{r}_j, \hat{\mathbf{r}}_0\rangle_2}{\langle A\mathbf{p}_j, \hat{\mathbf{r}}_0\rangle_2}.$$

Moreover, (6.47) and (6.49) allow us also to express β_{j+1} from (6.41) now as

$$\beta_{j+1} = \frac{\langle R_{j+1}(A)\mathbf{r}_0, R_{j+1}(A^T)\hat{\mathbf{r}}_0\rangle_2}{\langle R_j(A)\mathbf{r}_0, R_j(A)\hat{\mathbf{r}}_0\rangle_2} = \frac{\alpha_j}{\omega_{j+1}} \frac{\langle \mathbf{r}_{j+1}, \hat{\mathbf{r}}_0\rangle_2}{\langle \mathbf{r}_j, \hat{\mathbf{r}}_0\rangle_2}.$$

Thus, the only parameters that we have not yet determined are the weights ω_j.

Definition 6.45   If the coefficients ω_j are in each step determined in such a way that $\mathbf{r}_j$ minimises its 2-norm, i.e. if $\omega_j \in \mathbb{R}$ minimises

$$\omega \mapsto \|(I - \omega A)\chi_{j-1}(A)R_j(A)\mathbf{r}_0\|_2$$

then the resulting method is called the *stabilised BiCG (BiCGSTAB)* method.

Fortunately, the parameters can be determined directly. To this end, let us set $\mathbf{s}_j := \chi_{j-1}(A)R_j(A)\mathbf{r}_0$ and define the function

$$f_j(\omega) = \|(I - \omega A)\mathbf{s}_j\|_2^2 = \|\mathbf{s}_j\|_2^2 - 2\omega\langle \mathbf{s}_j, A\mathbf{s}_j\rangle_2 + \omega^2 \|A\mathbf{s}_j\|_2^2.$$

Then, taking the derivative shows that

$$\omega_j = \frac{\langle \mathbf{s}_j, A\mathbf{s}_j\rangle_2}{\|A\mathbf{s}_j\|_2^2}$$

is a critical point and, because of $f_j''(\omega) = 2\|A\mathbf{s}_j\|_2^2$, this critical point is a minimum, at least if $\mathbf{s}_j \neq \mathbf{0}$. If $\mathbf{s}_j = \mathbf{0}$, it does not matter how we choose ω_j since the next iteration $\mathbf{x}_{j+1}$ will be the solution of our initial linear system, as we will see soon. The final details that we need to write down the complete algorithm are a recursion formula for $\mathbf{s}_j$ and an update formula for the actual iterations $\mathbf{x}_j$. The first one follows immediately from

$$\mathbf{s}_j = \chi_{j-1}(A)R_j(A)\mathbf{r}_0 = \chi_{j-1}(A)[R_{j-1}(A) - \alpha_{j-1}AP_{j-1}(A)]\mathbf{r}_0$$
$$= \mathbf{r}_{j-1} - \alpha_{j-1}A\mathbf{p}_{j-1}.$$

The update formula for $\mathbf{x}_j$ follows from that for $\mathbf{r}_j$ since we have

$$\mathbf{r}_j = (I - \omega_j A)[\mathbf{r}_{j-1} - \alpha_{j-1}A\mathbf{p}_{j-1}] = (I - \omega_j A)\mathbf{s}_j$$
$$= \mathbf{r}_{j-1} - \alpha_{j-1}A\mathbf{p}_{j-1} - \omega_j A\mathbf{s}_j,$$

so we can conclude that

$$\mathbf{x}_j = \mathbf{x}_{j-1} + \alpha_{j-1}\mathbf{p}_{j-1} + \omega_j \mathbf{s}_j.$$

The final algorithm is given in Algorithm 33. Clearly, we once again have to compute two matrix–vector products per iteration, namely $\mathbf{v}_j := A\mathbf{p}_j$ and $\mathbf{t}_{j+1} := A\mathbf{s}_{j+1}$.

Algorithm 33: BiCGSTAB

Input : $A \in \mathbb{R}^{n \times n}$, $\mathbf{b} \in \mathbb{R}^n$, $\mathbf{x}_0 \in \mathbb{R}^n$.
Output: Approximate solution of $A\mathbf{x} = \mathbf{b}$.

1 $\mathbf{r}_0 := \mathbf{b} - A\mathbf{x}_0, \quad \mathbf{p}_0 := \mathbf{r}_0, \quad j := 0$
2 Choose $\hat{\mathbf{r}}_0$ with $\langle \mathbf{r}_0, \hat{\mathbf{r}}_0 \rangle_2 \neq 0$
3 **while** $\|\mathbf{r}_j\|_2 \geq \epsilon$ **do**
4 $\quad$ $\mathbf{v}_j := A\mathbf{p}_j$
5 $\quad$ $\alpha_j := \langle \mathbf{r}_j, \hat{\mathbf{r}}_0 \rangle_2 / \langle \mathbf{v}_j, \hat{\mathbf{r}}_0 \rangle_2$
6 $\quad$ $\mathbf{s}_{j+1} := \mathbf{r}_j - \alpha_j \mathbf{v}_j$
7 $\quad$ $\mathbf{t}_{j+1} := A\mathbf{s}_{j+1}$
8 $\quad$ $\omega_{j+1} := \langle \mathbf{s}_{j+1}, \mathbf{t}_{j+1} \rangle_2 / \langle \mathbf{t}_{j+1}, \mathbf{t}_{j+1} \rangle_2$
9 $\quad$ $\mathbf{x}_{j+1} := \mathbf{x}_j + \alpha_j \mathbf{p}_j + \omega_{j+1} \mathbf{s}_{j+1}$
10 $\quad$ $\mathbf{r}_{j+1} := \mathbf{s}_{j+1} - \omega_{j+1} \mathbf{t}_{j+1}$
11 $\quad$ $\beta_{j+1} := (\alpha_j / \omega_{j+1}) \times (\langle \mathbf{r}_{j+1}, \hat{\mathbf{r}}_0 \rangle_2 / \langle \mathbf{r}_j, \hat{\mathbf{r}}_0 \rangle_2)$
12 $\quad$ $\mathbf{p}_{j+1} := \mathbf{r}_{j+1} + \beta_{j+1}(\mathbf{p}_j - \omega_{j+1}\mathbf{v}_j)$
13 $\quad$ $j := j + 1$

Note that $\omega_{j+1} = 0$ means $\mathbf{r}_{j+1} = \mathbf{0}$ and hence $\mathbf{x}_{j+1}$ is the solution of $A\mathbf{x} = \mathbf{b}$. Hence, in this case the algorithm terminates with the solution.

Over the years, several other Krylov subspace methods have been introduced. For example, in [112] the BiCGSTAB method was generalised by Sleijpen and Fokkema by replacing the linear polynomial factor $(1 - \omega_j t)$ by a degree ℓ polynomial. As the BiCGSTAB method can be seen as a combination of BiCG and GMRES(1), their method is a certain combination of BiCG and GMRES(ℓ).

Similarly as we have derived the transpose-free CGS method from the BiCG method, which uses a multiplication by the transpose of the system matrix, it is also possible to derive a transpose-free version of the QMR method, called *transpose-free QMR*, or TFQMR, which was introduced by Freund in [58, 59]. The idea of employing only a quasi-minimisation as in QMR and TFQMR can also be combined with the BiCGSTAB method, which results in a method called QMRCGSTAB and was introduced by Chan *et al.* in [34].

Since all these Krylov subspace methods are based on the bi-Lanzcos process they have the intrinsic problem of a premature breakdown. For this reason, a theoretical convergence theory is hardly possible. Some results in this direction together with so-called *superlinear* convergence for standard Krylov subspace methods can be found in the surveys [110, 111] by Simoncini and Szyld. A theoretical connection between methods based upon the Arnoldi process like GMRES and methods based upon the bi-Lanczos process like QMR and BiCG was given by Cullum in [40].

6.4 Multigrid

The method we want to discuss now has particularly been designed to solve linear systems which are based on a discretisation which depends on a grid and where it is possible to have different instances of linear systems stemming from different underlying grids.

Our finite difference discretisation of the boundary value problem from Section 1.1.2 will hence serve us here as the perfect example.

Let us recall our findings regarding the Jacobi method and its relaxation for solving the linear system. From Remarks 4.17 and 4.18, we know that the eigenvalues of the iteration matrix of the Jacobi method are given by

$$\mu_k = \cos(k\pi h), \qquad 1 \le k \le n,$$

and the corresponding eigenvectors are given by

$$\mathbf{x}_k = (\sin(k\pi h), \sin(2k\pi h), \dots, \sin(nk\pi h))^{\mathrm{T}}, \qquad 1 \le k \le n, \qquad (6.50)$$

with $h = 1/(n + 1)$. As a consequence, we have noticed that the convergence of the Jacobi method becomes worse for larger n since the spectral radius approaches 1 in this situation.

In Example 4.22, we have also seen that the eigenvalues of the relaxation of the Jacobi method are given by

$$\mu_k(\omega) = 1 - \omega + \omega\mu_k = 1 - \omega + \omega \cos(k\pi h), \qquad 1 \le k \le n,$$

having the same eigenvectors. Moreover, we have seen that relaxation does not lead to an improved convergence, since, in this case, the optimal relaxation parameter is $\omega^* = 1$.

Though convergence is slow, we now want to understand what makes it actually slow. Recall that the iterations of the Jacobi method are given by $\mathbf{u}^{(j)} = C_J \mathbf{u}^{(j-1)} + \mathbf{c}$ and that the solution $\mathbf{u}$ of the linear system is a fixed point, i.e. it

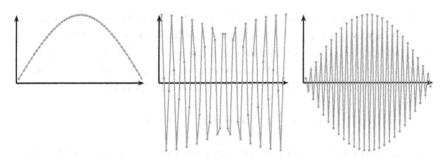

Figure 6.4 The eigenvectors of C_J with $n = 50$. From left to right: x_1, x_{25} and x_{50}.

satisfies $C_J\mathbf{u} + \mathbf{c} = \mathbf{u}$. This leads to

$$\mathbf{u} - \mathbf{u}^{(j)} = C_J(\mathbf{u} - \mathbf{u}^{(j-1)}) = \cdots = C_J^j(\mathbf{u} - \mathbf{u}^{(0)}).$$

This is not new to us. It has been an important idea in understanding the convergence of such iterative methods. To understand what dominates the error, we now expand $\mathbf{u} - \mathbf{u}^{(0)}$ in the basis consisting of the eigenvectors of C_J given in (6.50):

$$\mathbf{u} - \mathbf{u}^{(0)} = \sum_{k=1}^{n} \alpha_k \mathbf{x}_k$$

with certain coefficients $\alpha_k \in \mathbb{R}$, $1 \le k \le n$. This gives for the error after j steps

$$\mathbf{u} - \mathbf{u}^{(j)} = \sum_{k=1}^{n} \alpha_k \mu_k^j \mathbf{x}_k$$

and we can conclude the following.

- If $|\mu_k|$ is small then the component of $\mathbf{u} - \mathbf{u}^{(j)}$ in the direction of $\mathbf{x}_k$ vanishes quickly.
- After only a few iterations, the error is dominated by those components in direction $\mathbf{x}_k$, where $|\mu_k| \approx 1$. In particular, the error in direction $\mathbf{x}_1$ and direction $\mathbf{x}_n$ is large.

To understand this better, let us have a look at some of these eigenvectors. In Figure 6.4 we have depicted the eigenvectors $\mathbf{x}_1$, $\mathbf{x}_{25}$ and $\mathbf{x}_{50}$ of C_J with $n = 50$. Each graph shows the points $(ih, (\mathbf{x}_k)_i)$ for $1 \le i \le n$ linearly connected. This figure shows why we will call those eigenvectors $\mathbf{x}_k$ with $k \le n/2$ *low-frequency eigenvectors* and those with $k > n/2$ *high-frequency eigenvectors*.

Unfortunately, no matter how many steps in the Jacobi method we compute, the error will always contain both low-frequency and high-frequency eigenvectors. To avoid this, let us have another look at the relaxation of the Jacobi method. Since no choice of the relaxation parameter will improve the convergence, we can simply choose $\omega = 1/2$. In this case, we have the eigenvalues

$$\mu_k(1/2) = \frac{1}{2} + \frac{1}{2}\cos(k\pi h), \qquad 1 \le k \le n.$$

For large k this means that $\mu_k(1/2)$ is very close to zero, while for small k we have $\mu_k(1/2) \approx 1$. This means for the error after j iterations,

$$\mathbf{u} - \mathbf{u}^{(j)} = [C_J(1/2)]^j(\mathbf{u} - \mathbf{u}^{(0)}) = \sum_{k=1}^{n} \alpha_k[\mu_k(1/2)]^j\mathbf{x}_k,$$

that only the low-frequency eigenvectors dominate and the influence of the high-frequency eigenvectors tends to zero, showing that, in a certain way, the error is "smoothed" during the process. However, a "smoother" error can be represented using a smaller n and this gives the idea of the multigrid (or two-grid) method, as follows.

- Compute j steps of the relaxation, resulting in an error $\mathbf{e}^{(j)} = \mathbf{u} - \mathbf{u}^{(j)}$ which is much "smoother" than $\mathbf{e}^{(0)}$.
- We have $\mathbf{u} = \mathbf{u}^{(j)} + \mathbf{e}^{(j)}$ and $\mathbf{e}^{(j)}$ satisfies $A\mathbf{e}^{(j)} = A(\mathbf{u} - \mathbf{u}^{(j)}) = \mathbf{b} - A\mathbf{u}^{(j)} =: \mathbf{r}^{(j)}$. Hence, if we can solve $A\mathbf{e}^{(j)} = \mathbf{r}^{(j)}$ then the overall solution is given by $\mathbf{u} = \mathbf{u}^{(j)} + \mathbf{e}^{(j)}$.
- Since we expect the error $\mathbf{e}^{(j)}$ to be "smooth", we will solve the equation $A\mathbf{e}^{(j)} = \mathbf{r}^{(j)}$ somehow on a *coarser grid* to save computational time and transfer the solution back to the finer grid.

To describe this in more detail, we have to introduce some notation. Although, we shall do this in a more general setting, it is always good to keep the above example in mind.

We will, from now on, assume that we are given two grids; a fine grid X_h with n_h points and a coarse grid X_H with $n_H < n_h$ points. Associated with these grids are discrete solution spaces V_h and V_H. These can simply be $V_h = \mathbb{R}^{n_h}$ and $V_H = \mathbb{R}^{n_H}$ as in the example above, but may also be more complicated ones.

Next, we need two operators which transfer data between these solution spaces. We need a *prolongation* operator $I_H^h : V_H \rightarrow V_h$ which maps from coarse to fine and we need a *restriction* operator $I_h^H : V_h \rightarrow V_H$ which maps from fine to coarse.

Example 6.46 Suppose the coarse grid is given by $X_H = \{jH : 0 \le j < n_H\}$ with $n_H = 2^m + 1$, $m \in \mathbb{N}$, and $H = 1/(n_H - 1)$. Then the natural fine grid X_h would consist of X_H and all points in the middle between two points from X_H, i.e. $X_h = \{jh : 0 \le j < n_h\}$ with $h = H/2$ and $n_h = 2^{m+1} + 1$. In this case we could define the prolongation and restriction operators as follows. The prolongation $\mathbf{v}^h = I_{2h}^h \mathbf{v}^{2h}$ is defined by linear interpolation on the "in-between" points:

$$v_{2j}^h := v_j^{2h}, \qquad v_{2j+1}^h := \frac{v_j^{2h} + v_{j+1}^{2h}}{2}, \qquad 0 \le j < n_{2h}.$$

We can describe this process in matrix form by

$$\mathbf{v}^h = \frac{1}{2} \begin{pmatrix} 2 & & & \\ 1 & 1 & & \\ & 2 & & \\ & 1 & 1 & \\ & \vdots & \vdots & \\ & & & 1 & 1 \\ & & & & 2 \end{pmatrix} \mathbf{v}^{2h},$$

so that I_{2h}^h becomes a $n_h \times n_{2h}$ matrix. Note, however, that indices in this matrix start with zero.

For the restriction, $\mathbf{v}^{2h} := I_h^{2h} \mathbf{v}_h$ we could use the natural inclusion of $V_{2h} \subseteq V_h$, i.e. we could simply define $v_j^{2h} := v_{2j}^h$, $0 \le j < n_{2h}$. We could, however, also use a so-called *full weighting*, which is given by

$$v_j^{2h} = \frac{1}{4}\left(v_{2j-1}^h + 2v_{2j}^h + v_{2j+1}^h\right), \qquad 0 \le j < n_{2h},$$

where we have implicitly set $v_{-1}^h = v_{n_h}^h = 0$. In the latter case, we have the matrix representation

$$\mathbf{v}^{2h} = \frac{1}{4} \begin{pmatrix} 2 & 1 & & & \\ & 1 & 2 & 1 & \cdots \\ & & & 1 & \cdots \\ & & & & 1 \\ & & & & 1 & 2 \end{pmatrix} \mathbf{v}^h$$

and note that in matrix form $I_{2h}^h = 2\left(I_h^{2h}\right)^{\mathrm{T}}$.

The latter connection between I_{2h}^h and I_h^{2h} occurs in many applications in the form

$$I_{2h}^h = \gamma\left(I_h^{2h}\right)^{\mathrm{T}}, \qquad \gamma \in \mathbb{R} \setminus \{0\}. \tag{6.51}$$

Our goal is to solve a system $A_h \mathbf{u}^h = \mathbf{f}^h$ on the fine level, using the possibility of solving a system $A_H \mathbf{u}^H = \mathbf{f}^H$ on a coarse level. Hence, we are usually given the equation on the fine level but need A_H and $\mathbf{f}^H$ on the coarse level. These are often given quite naturally, simply by discretising the original problem on the coarse grid X_H. However, we can also use the prolongation and restriction operators to define

$$A_H := I_h^H A_h I_H^h, \tag{6.52}$$

$$\mathbf{f}^H := I_h^H \mathbf{f}^h. \tag{6.53}$$

Example 6.47 If we use the grids from Example 6.46 for our model problem from Section 1.1.2, we indeed find that a discretisation on the coarse grid leads to the same matrix A_H as (6.52). To see this, we have to take into account that the matrix $A_h = A$ in (1.2) only refers to interior nodes. Hence, we either have to delete the first and last column and row in the matrix representation of I_H^h and I_h^H, or we only look at interior points. Here, we see that A_H defined in (6.52) with $H = 2h$ has columns

$$
\begin{aligned}
A_H \mathbf{e}_j^H &= I_h^H A_h I_H^h \mathbf{e}_j^H \\
&= I_h^H A_h \left(\frac{1}{2} \mathbf{e}_{2j-1}^h + \mathbf{e}_{2j}^h + \frac{1}{2} \mathbf{e}_{2j+1}^h \right) \\
&= \frac{1}{h^2} I_h^H \left(\frac{1}{2} \left[-\mathbf{e}_{2j-2}^h + 2\mathbf{e}_{2j-1}^h - \mathbf{e}_{2j}^h \right] + \left[-\mathbf{e}_{2j-1}^h + 2\mathbf{e}_{2j}^h - \mathbf{e}_{2j+1}^h \right] \right. \\
&\qquad \left. + \frac{1}{2} \left[-\mathbf{e}_{2j}^h + 2\mathbf{e}_{2j+1}^h - \mathbf{e}_{2j+2}^h \right] \right) \\
&= \frac{1}{h^2} I_h^H \left(-\frac{1}{2} \mathbf{e}_{2j-2}^h + \mathbf{e}_{2j}^h - \frac{1}{2} \mathbf{e}_{2j+2}^h \right) \\
&= \frac{1}{4h^2} \left(-\mathbf{e}_{j-1}^{2h} + 2\mathbf{e}_j^{2h} - \mathbf{e}_{j+1}^{2h} \right) \\
&= \frac{1}{H^2} \left(-\mathbf{e}_{j-1}^H + 2\mathbf{e}_j^H - \mathbf{e}_{j+1}^H \right),
\end{aligned}
$$

which gives exactly the matrix from (1.2) for the grid X_H.

As mentioned above, we will use an iterative method as a "smoother". Recall that such a consistent iterative method for solving $A_h \mathbf{u}^h = \mathbf{f}^h$ is given by

$$\mathbf{u}_{j+1}^h = S_h(\mathbf{u}_j^h) := C_h \mathbf{u}_j + \mathbf{c}^h,$$

where the solution $\mathbf{u}^h$ of the linear system is a fixed point of S_h, i.e. it satisfies $C_h \mathbf{u}^h + \mathbf{c}^h = \mathbf{u}^h$.

If we apply $\nu \in \mathbb{N}$ iterations of such a smoother with inital data $\mathbf{u}_0^h$, it is easy to see that the result has the form

$$S_h^\nu(\mathbf{u}_0^h) = C_h^\nu \mathbf{u}_0^h + \sum_{j=0}^{\nu-1} C_h^j \mathbf{c}^h =: C_h^\nu \mathbf{u}_0^h + \mathbf{s}^h. \tag{6.54}$$

Note that we can use any consistent method as the smoother S_h. Essentially, we can use any iterative method that we have encountered so far, namely Jacobi, Gauss–Seidel, Jacobi relaxation, SOR, SSOR but also CG and GMRES and other Krylov subspace methods. The actual choice will depend on the problem we want to solve.

With this notation at hand, we can now formally state the two-grid algorithm we encountered at the beginning of this section. This is done in Algorithm 34, where we have added a post-smoothing on the fine grid at the end, as is often done.

Algorithm 34: Two-grid cycle, TGM(ν_1, ν_2)

Input : $A_h \in \mathbb{R}^{n_h \times n_h}$, $\mathbf{f}^h \in \mathbb{R}^{n_h}$, $\mathbf{u}_0^h \in \mathbb{R}^{n_h}$, $\nu_1, \nu_2 \in \mathbb{N}$.
Output: Approximation to $A_h^{-1} \mathbf{f}^h$.

1 Presmooth: $\mathbf{u}^h := S_h^{\nu_1}(\mathbf{u}_0^h)$
2 Get residual: $\mathbf{r}^h := \mathbf{f}^h - A_h \mathbf{u}^h$
3 Coarsen: $\mathbf{r}^H := I_h^H \mathbf{r}^h$
4 Solve: $\delta^H := A_H^{-1} \mathbf{r}^H$
5 Prolong: $\delta^h := I_H^h \delta^H$
6 Correct: $\mathbf{u}^h := \mathbf{u}^h + \delta^h$
7 Postsmooth: $\mathbf{u}^h := S_h^{\nu_2}(\mathbf{u}^h)$

Obviously, the two-grid method can be and usually is seen as only one cycle of a new iterative method. To analyse it, we need to express this algorithm in the typical form of an iterative method and then need to analyse the iteration matrix. To this end, let us assume that $\mathbf{u}_j^h$ is the input vector to Algorithm 34 and $\mathbf{u}_{j+1}^h$ is the resulting output vector. Then, we have to find matrices $T_h \in \mathbb{R}^{n_h \times n_h}$ and a vector $\mathbf{d}^h$ such that

$$\mathbf{u}_{j+1}^h = T_h \mathbf{u}_j^h + \mathbf{d}^h$$

and we have to convince ourselves that the method is consistent.

Going through the algorithm step by step leads to the following. With the first step $\mathbf{u}_j^h$ is mapped to $S_h^{\nu_1} \mathbf{u}_j^h$, which is the input to the second step. After the second and third steps we have $\mathbf{r}_j^H = I_h^H [\mathbf{f}^h - A_h S_h^{\nu_1} \mathbf{u}_j^h]$, which is the input for the fourth step, so that the results after the fourth and fifth steps become

$$\delta_j^H = A_H^{-1} I_h^H [\mathbf{f}^h - A_h S_h^{\nu_1} \mathbf{u}_j^h],$$

$$\delta_j^h = I_H^h A_H^{-1} I_h^H [\mathbf{f}^h - A_h S_h^{\nu_1} \mathbf{u}_j^h].$$

Applying steps 6 and 7 to this results finally in the new iteration

$$\mathbf{u}_{j+1}^h = S_h^{\nu_2} S_h^{\nu_1} \mathbf{u}_j^h + S_h^{\nu_2} I_H^h A_H^{-1} I_h^H [\mathbf{f}^h - A_h S_h^{\nu_1} \mathbf{u}_j^h]$$

$$= S_h^{\nu_2} [I - I_H^h A_H^{-1} I_h^H A_h] S_h^{\nu_1} \mathbf{u}_j^h + S_h^{\nu_2} I_H^h A_H^{-1} I_h^H \mathbf{f}^h.$$

This is not yet the required form as the operator S_h is only affine and not linear. Nonetheless, we can now derive the following result.

Lemma 6.48 *Let the consistent smoother S_h be given as $S_h \mathbf{x} = C_h \mathbf{x} + \mathbf{c}^h$. Assume that A_H is invertible. Then, the iteration matrix T_h of the two-grid method described in Algorithm 34 is given by*

$$T_h = C_h^{\nu_2} T_{h,H} C_h^{\nu_1}$$

with the coarse-grid correction operator

$$T_{h,H} = I - I_H^h A_H^{-1} I_h^H A_h.$$

Moreover, if $\mathbf{u}^h$ solves $A_h \mathbf{u}^h = \mathbf{f}^h$ then we have the error representation

$$\mathbf{u}_{j+1}^h - \mathbf{u}^h = T_h(\mathbf{u}_j^h - \mathbf{u}^h) = T_h^{j+1}(\mathbf{u}_0^h - \mathbf{u}^h),$$

showing that the method converges if the spectral radius of T_h is less than 1.

Proof Let us define $\tilde{T}_h := S_h^{\nu_2} T_{h,H} S_h^{\nu_1}$ and $\tilde{\mathbf{d}}^h = S_h^{\nu_2} I_H^h A_H^{-1} I_h^H \mathbf{f}^h$ so that the above derivation becomes $\mathbf{u}_{j+1}^h = \tilde{T}_h \mathbf{u}_j^h + \tilde{\mathbf{d}}^h$. As $\tilde{T}_h$ is only affine this is not yet the representation we want, but we can use (6.54) to find

$$\tilde{T}_h \mathbf{u} = S_h^{\nu_2} T_{h,H} S_h^{\nu_1} \mathbf{u} = S_h^{\nu_2} T_{h,H} \left[C_h^{\nu_1} \mathbf{u} + \sum_{j=0}^{\nu_1 - 1} C_h^j \mathbf{c}^h \right]$$

$$= C_h^{\nu_2} T_{h,H} C_h^{\nu_1} \mathbf{u} + C_h^{\nu_2} T_{h,H} \sum_{j=0}^{\nu_1 - 1} C_h^j \mathbf{c}^h + \sum_{j=0}^{\nu_2 - 1} C_h^j \mathbf{c}^h$$

$$=: T_h \mathbf{u} + \hat{\mathbf{d}}^h,$$

which shows $\mathbf{u}_{j+1}^h = T_h \mathbf{u}_j^h + \mathbf{d}^h$ with $\mathbf{d}^h = \hat{\mathbf{d}}^h + \tilde{\mathbf{d}}^h$. Hence, the iteration matrix is indeed given by T_h.

As S_h is consistent, we have $S_h \mathbf{u}^h = \mathbf{u}^h$ and hence

$$\tilde{T}_h \mathbf{u}^h + \tilde{\mathbf{d}}^h = S_h^{\nu_2} [I - I_H^h A_H^{-1} I_h^H A_h] \mathbf{u}^h + S_h^{\nu_2} I_H^h A_H^{-1} I_h^H \mathbf{f}^h$$

$$= \mathbf{u}^h - S_h^{\nu_2} I_H^h A_H^{-1} I_h^H \mathbf{f}^h + S_h^{\nu_2} I_H^h A_H^{-1} I_h^H \mathbf{f}^h$$

$$= \mathbf{u}^h.$$

This shows $\mathbf{u}_{j+1}^h - \mathbf{u}^h = \tilde{T}_h(\mathbf{u}_j^h) - \tilde{T}_h(\mathbf{u}^h) = T_h(\mathbf{u}_j^h - \mathbf{u}^h)$. □

If we want to apply the two-grid cycle in an iterative scheme, we hence have to show that $\rho(T_h) < 1$ to have convergence. In this context, it is obviously possible to combine the smoothing procedures.

Example 6.49 Let us return to our model problem as described in Example 6.47, i.e. to the finite difference discretisation of the one-dimensional boundary value problem using linear interpolation and full weighting for the inter-grid operations. If we use the relaxation of the Jacobi method with relaxation parameter $\omega = 1/2$ and $\nu = \nu_1 + \nu_2 \geq 1$ then it is possible to show that

$$\rho(T_h) \leq \max\left\{\chi(1-\chi)^\nu + (1-\chi)\chi^\nu : 0 \leq \chi \leq \frac{1}{2}\right\} =: \rho_\nu < 1.$$

The proof is done using Fourier transformation, see, for example, Hackbusch [74].

As this example already shows, the analysis of the iteration matrix of the two-grid method requires quite a few assumptions on the operators involved. Hence, typically, a thorough analysis will make use of these assumptions. Here, we want to give a rather generic result, which can be carried over to what is known as *algebraic multigrid*.

Suppose $\langle \cdot, \cdot \rangle$ denotes an inner product on $\mathbb{R}^n$. Recall that a linear mapping $T : \mathbb{R}^n \to \mathbb{R}^n$ is called

- a *projection* if it is idempotent, i.e. if $T^2 = T$;
- an *orthogonal projection* if $\langle x - Tx, Ty \rangle = 0$ for all $x, y \in \mathbb{R}^n$;
- *self-adjoint* if $\langle x, Ty \rangle = \langle Tx, y \rangle$ for all $x, y \in \mathbb{R}^n$.

It is easy to see that a projection is orthogonal if and only if it is self-adjoint. Moreover, if T is self-adjoint so is $I - T$ and vice versa. Finally, if T is an orthogonal projection, we have range$(T) = \ker(I - T)$.

Finally, recall that we have previously defined an inner product of the form $\langle \mathbf{x}, \mathbf{y} \rangle_A = \mathbf{x}^T A \mathbf{y}$ for a symmetric and positive definite matrix A.

Proposition 6.50 *Let A_h be symmetric and positive definite. Let the coarse grid matrix be defined by $A_H := I_h^H A_h I_H^h$ and let the prolongation and restriction operators be connected by $I_H^h = \gamma (I_h^H)^T$ with $\gamma > 0$. Finally, assume that I_H^h is injective. Then we have that the coarse-grid correction operator $T_{h,H}$ is an orthogonal projection with respect to the inner product $\langle \cdot, \cdot \rangle_{A_h}$ and the range of $T_{h,H}$ is $\langle \cdot, \cdot \rangle_{A_h}$-orthogonal to the range of I_H^h.*

Proof We start by showing that A_H is symmetric and positive definite. It is symmetric since

$$A_H^{\mathrm{T}} = (I_H^h)^{\mathrm{T}} A_h^{\mathrm{T}} (I_h^H)^{\mathrm{T}} = \gamma I_h^H A_h \frac{1}{\gamma} I_H^h = I_h^H A_h I_H^h = A_H.$$

It is positive definite since we have for $\mathbf{x} \in \mathbb{R}^{n_H} \setminus \{\mathbf{0}\}$ that $I_H^h \mathbf{x} \neq \mathbf{0}$ because of the injectivity of I_H^h and hence

$$\mathbf{x}^{\mathrm{T}} A_H \mathbf{x} = \mathbf{x}^{\mathrm{T}} I_h^H A_h I_H^h \mathbf{x} = \frac{1}{\gamma} \left(I_H^h \mathbf{x} \right)^{\mathrm{T}} A_h (I_H^h \mathbf{x}) > 0.$$

This means in particular that the coarse grid correction operator $T_{h,H}$ is well-defined. Next, let

$$Q_{h,H} := I - T_{h,H} = I_H^h A_H^{-1} I_h^H A_h,$$

which is also a mapping from $\mathbb{R}^{n_h}$ to $\mathbb{R}^{n_h}$. This is a projection since we have

$$\begin{aligned}
Q_{h,H}^2 &= (I_H^h A_H^{-1} I_h^H A_h)(I_H^h A_H^{-1} I_h^H A_h) \\
&= I_H^h A_H^{-1} (I_h^H A_h I_H^h) A_H^{-1} I_h^H A_h \\
&= I_H^h A_H^{-1} I_h^H A_h = Q_{h,H}.
\end{aligned}$$

It is also self-adjoint and hence an orthogonal projector:

$$\begin{aligned}
\langle Q_{h,H} \mathbf{x}, \mathbf{y} \rangle_{A_h} &= \mathbf{x}^{\mathrm{T}} Q_{h,H}^{\mathrm{T}} A_h \mathbf{y} = \mathbf{x}^{\mathrm{T}} A_h^{\mathrm{T}} (I_h^H)^{\mathrm{T}} (A_H^{-1})^{\mathrm{T}} (I_H^h)^{\mathrm{T}} A_h \mathbf{y} \\
&= \mathbf{x}^{\mathrm{T}} A_h \left(\frac{1}{\gamma} I_H^h \right) A_H^{-1} \gamma I_h^H A_h \mathbf{y} \\
&= \langle \mathbf{x}, I_H^h A_H^{-1} I_h^H A_h \mathbf{y} \rangle_{A_h} = \langle \mathbf{x}, Q_{h,H} \mathbf{y} \rangle_{A_h}.
\end{aligned}$$

With $Q_{h,H}$ also $T_{h,H}$ is an orthogonal projection.

It remains to show that the two ranges are orthogonal. This is true because we have

$$\begin{aligned}
\langle T_{h,H} \mathbf{x}, I_H^h \mathbf{y} \rangle_{A_h} &= \mathbf{x}^{\mathrm{T}} (I - I_H^h A_H^{-1} I_h^H A_h)^{\mathrm{T}} A_h I_H^h \mathbf{y} \\
&= \mathbf{x}^{\mathrm{T}} (A_h I_H^h - A_h I_H^h A_H^{-1} I_h^H A_h I_H^h) \mathbf{y} \\
&= \mathbf{x}^{\mathrm{T}} (A_h I_H^h - A_h I_H^h) \mathbf{y} = 0
\end{aligned}$$

for all $\mathbf{x} \in \mathbb{R}^{n_h}$ and $\mathbf{y} \in \mathbb{R}^{n_H}$. $\qquad\square$

Note that we have for $Q_{h,H} = I - T_{h,H} = I_H^h A_H^{-1} I_h^H A_h$ immediately

$$\ker(T_{h,H}) = \text{range}(Q_{h,H}) \subseteq \text{range}(I_H^h).$$

We even have equality, as can be seen from the following argument. If $\mathbf{z} \in \text{range}(I_H^h)$ then $\mathbf{z} = I_H^h \mathbf{y}$ with $\mathbf{y} \in \mathbb{R}^{n_H}$ and

$$Q_{h,H} \mathbf{z} = Q_{h,H} I_H^h \mathbf{y} = I_H^h A_H^{-1} (I_h^H A_h I_H^h) \mathbf{y} = I_H^h \mathbf{y} = \mathbf{z}.$$

So, we have

$$\ker(T_{h,H}) = \text{range}(Q_{h,H}) = \text{range}(I_H^h).$$

Hence, by Proposition 6.50, we have range$(T_{h,H})$ orthogonal to $\ker(T_{h,H}) = \text{range}(Q_{h,H})$ with respect to $\langle \cdot, \cdot \rangle_{A_h}$. Hence, we have an orthogonal decomposition

$$\mathbb{R}^{n_h} = \text{range}(T_{h,H}) \oplus \ker(T_{h,H}).$$

After these rather general thoughts, we will be more concrete in analysing the iteration matrix of the two-grid iteration. Obviously, we have to make some assumptions on the smoothing process and on the inter-grid operators. We will express them using various norms besides the $\| \cdot \|_{A_h}$-norm. To this end, let D_h be the diagonal part of A_h. Since A_h is supposed to be symmetric and positive definite, so is D_h, i.e. all diagonal entries are positive. The same is true for $A_h D_h^{-1} A_h$. Note that we have

$$\|\mathbf{x}\|_{A_h D_h^{-1} A_h}^2 = \mathbf{x}^\mathrm{T} A_h D_h^{-1} A_h \mathbf{x} = \|A_h \mathbf{x}\|_{D_h^{-1}}^2.$$

Definition 6.51 1. We will say that the smoothing process S_h defined by $S_h \mathbf{x} = C_h \mathbf{x} + \mathbf{c}^h$ has the *smoothing property* if there is a constant $\alpha > 0$ such that

$$\|C_h \mathbf{e}^h\|_{A_h}^2 \le \|\mathbf{e}^h\|_{A_h}^2 - \alpha \|A_h \mathbf{e}^h\|_{D_h^{-1}}^2, \qquad \mathbf{e}^h \in \mathbb{R}^{n_h}. \tag{6.55}$$

2. We will say that the prolongation operator I_H^h has the *approximation property* if there is a constant $\beta > 0$ such that

$$\min_{\mathbf{e}^H \in \mathbb{R}^{n_H}} \|\mathbf{e}^h - I_H^h \mathbf{e}^H\|_{D_h} \le \beta \|\mathbf{e}^h\|_{A_h D_h^{-1} A_h}, \qquad \mathbf{e}^h \in \mathbb{R}^{n_h}. \tag{6.56}$$

If we leave the specific norms aside, both properties make perfect sense. The norms themselves seem arbitrary here but are quite natural in certain Galerkin approximations of differential equations.

Theorem 6.52 *Let the assumptions of Proposition 6.50 and equations (6.55) and (6.56) be satisfied. Then, we have $\alpha \le \beta$ and for the iteration matrix T_h of the two-grid method*

$$\|T_h\|_{A_h} \le \sqrt{1 - \frac{\alpha}{\beta}}.$$

Hence, as an iterative scheme, the two-grid method converges.

Proof Since range$(T_{h,H})$ is A_h-orthogonal to range(I_H^h) we have

$$\langle \mathbf{e}^h, I_H^h \mathbf{e}^H \rangle_{A_h} = 0, \qquad \mathbf{e}^h \in \text{range}(T_{h,H}), \qquad \mathbf{e}^H \in \mathbb{R}^{n_H}.$$

From this, we can conclude for all $\mathbf{e}^h \in \text{range}(T_{h,H})$ and $\mathbf{e}^H \in \mathbb{R}^{n_H}$ that

$$
\begin{aligned}
\|\mathbf{e}^h\|_{A_h}^2 &= \langle \mathbf{e}^h, \mathbf{e}^h - I_H^h \mathbf{e}^H \rangle_{A_h} = \langle A_h \mathbf{e}^h, \mathbf{e}^h - I_H^h \mathbf{e}^H \rangle_2 \\
&= \langle D_h^{-1/2} A_h \mathbf{e}^h, D_h^{1/2} (\mathbf{e}^h - I_H^h \mathbf{e}^H) \rangle_2 \\
&\leq \|D_h^{-1/2} A_h \mathbf{e}^h\|_2 \|D_h^{1/2} (\mathbf{e}^h - I_H^h \mathbf{e}^H)\|_2 \\
&= \|A_h \mathbf{e}^h\|_{D_h^{-1}} \|\mathbf{e}^h - I_H^h \mathbf{e}^H\|_{D_h}.
\end{aligned}
$$

Going over to the infimum over all $\mathbf{e}^H \in \mathbb{R}^{n_H}$ and using the approximation property (6.56) leads to

$$
\|\mathbf{e}^h\|_{A_h}^2 \leq \beta \|A_h \mathbf{e}^h\|_{D_h^{-1}} \|A_h \mathbf{e}^h\|_{D_h^{-1}}, \qquad \mathbf{e}^h \in \text{range}(T_{h,H}),
$$

or

$$
\|\mathbf{e}^h\|_{A_h} \leq \sqrt{\beta} \|A_h \mathbf{e}^h\|_{D_h^{-1}}, \qquad \mathbf{e}^h \in \text{range}(T_{h,H}),
$$

i.e.

$$
\|T_{h,H} \mathbf{e}^h\|_{A_h} \leq \sqrt{\beta} \|A_h T_{h,H} \mathbf{e}^h\|_{D_h^{-1}}, \qquad \mathbf{e}^h \in \mathbb{R}^{n_h}.
$$

Using this and the smoothing property (6.55) then leads to

$$
\begin{aligned}
0 \leq \|C_h T_{h,H} \mathbf{e}^h\|_{A_h}^2 &\leq \|T_{h,H} \mathbf{e}^h\|_{A_h}^2 - \alpha \|A_h T_{h,H} \mathbf{e}^h\|_{D_h^{-1}}^2 \\
&\leq \|T_{h,H} \mathbf{e}^h\|_{A_h}^2 - \frac{\alpha}{\beta} \|T_{h,H} \mathbf{e}^h\|_{A_h}^2 \\
&= \left(1 - \frac{\alpha}{\beta}\right) \|T_{h,H} \mathbf{e}^h\|_{A_h}^2 \\
&\leq \left(1 - \frac{\alpha}{\beta}\right) \|\mathbf{e}^h\|_{A_h}^2,
\end{aligned}
$$

where the last inequality follows from the fact that $T_{h,H}$ is an A_h-orthogonal projection. This means, first of all, $\alpha \leq \beta$ and secondly

$$
\|C_h T_{h,H}\|_{A_h} \leq \sqrt{1 - \frac{\alpha}{\beta}}.
$$

Hence, using the smoothing property twice again, we finally derive

$$
\begin{aligned}
\|T_h\|_{A_h} = \sup_{\mathbf{e}^h \neq 0} \frac{\|C_h^{\nu_2} T_{h,H} C_h^{\nu_1} \mathbf{e}^h\|_{A_h}}{\|\mathbf{e}^h\|_{A_h}} &\leq \sup_{\mathbf{e}^h \neq 0} \frac{\|C_h^{\nu_2} T_{h,H}\|_{A_h} \|C_h^{\nu_1} \mathbf{e}^h\|_{A_h}}{\|\mathbf{e}^h\|_{A_h}} \\
&\leq \|C_h^{\nu_2} T_{h,H}\|_{A_h} \leq \|C_h T_{h,H}\|_{A_h} \leq \sqrt{1 - \frac{\alpha}{\beta}}. \qquad \square
\end{aligned}
$$

The two-grid method still has the disadvantage that we have to solve a system on the coarse grid. In practical applications, this coarse grid would still be too big to allow us to solve the corresponding linear system directly. Hence, instead of solving on the coarse level, we iteratively apply the two-grid idea until we reach a coarse level which has a small enough underlying grid so that we can solve the problem directly there. The result is the so-called *V-cycle*, see Algorithm 35.

Algorithm 35: V-cycle

Input : $A_h \in \mathbb{R}^{n_h \times n_h}$, $\mathbf{u}_0^h, \mathbf{f}^h \in \mathbb{R}^{n_h}$.
Output: Approximation $\mathbf{u}^h \in \mathbb{R}^{n_h}$.

1 Presmooth: $\mathbf{u}^h := S_h^{\nu_1}(\mathbf{u}_0^h)$
2 Get residual: $\mathbf{r}^h := \mathbf{f}^h - A_h \mathbf{u}^h$
3 Coarsen: $H := 2h, \mathbf{r}^H := I_h^H \mathbf{r}^h$
4 **if** $H = h_0$ **then**
5 | Solve $A_H \delta^H = \mathbf{r}^H$
6 **else**
7 | $\delta^H :=$ V-Cycle$(A_H, \mathbf{0}, \mathbf{r}^H)$
8 Prolong: $\delta^h := I_H^h \delta^H$
9 Correct: $\mathbf{u}^h := \mathbf{u}^h + \delta^h$
10 Postsmooth: $\mathbf{u}^h := S_h^{\nu_2}(\mathbf{u}^h)$ ˙

The only difference to Algorithm 34 is in lines 4 to 7, which replace the old line 4. Here, the recursion is realised. Note that in the recursion we want to approximate the residual, which should be close to zero. Hence, we also use $\mathbf{0}$ as a starting vector.

Let us analyse the cost of the V-cycle. To this end, we have to make a few assumptions. We want the matrices $A_h \in \mathbb{R}^{n_h \times n_h}$ to be sparse; to be more precise, we want the total number m_h of non-zero entries in A_h to be linear in n_h (instead of quadratic, as in the case of a full matrix), i.e. we will assume that there is a constant $c_0 > 0$ independent of h such that $m_h \leq c_0 n_h$ for all h. We will also assume that one smoothing step costs $O(m_h) = O(n_h)$. This is not unrealistic since the main operation is the matrix–vector multiplication $C_h \mathbf{u}_j^h$. Finally, we will assume that the costs for prolongation and restriction are also bounded by $c_1 n_h$, where $c_1 > 0$ is a constant independent of h. This means that the cost is

$$T(n_h) = O((c_0(\nu_1 + \nu_2) + 2c_1 + 1)n_h) + T(n_{2h}) \leq \eta n_h + T(n_{2h})$$

with a certain constant $\eta > 0$ independent of h. Furthermore, we might assume that the cost at h_0 is a constant. To resolve this recursion, we have to specify the relation between n_h and n_{2h}. This will, of course, depend on the dimension of the underlying discretisation domain. In our model problem, this dimension is one and we have $n_{2h} = n_h/2$. Similarly, when working with grids in two dimensions we have $n_{2h} = n_h/4$ and, generally, in d dimensions we have $n_{2h} = n_h/2^d$. We can now apply Lemma 1.4 with $\alpha = 1$, $c = \eta$, $a = 1$ and $b = 2^d$. Since obviously $1 = a < b^\alpha = 2^d$, this lemma gives

$$T(n) = c\frac{b^\alpha}{b^\alpha - a}n^\alpha = \frac{2^d}{2^d - 1}\eta n.$$

Hence, the cost can be bounded by $2\eta n$ in the one-dimensional case, by $\frac{4}{3}\eta n$ in the two-dimensional case and by $\frac{8}{7}\eta n$ in the three-dimensional case. In other words, the following remark holds.

Remark 6.53 Under the assumptions made in the paragraphs above, the total computational cost of a V-cycle is $O(n_h)$.

A further improvement is given in Algorithm 36, which is the full multigrid algorithm.

Algorithm 36: Multigrid (MG)

Input : $A_h \in \mathbb{R}^{n_h \times n_h}$, $\mathbf{u}_0^h$, $\mathbf{f}^h \in \mathbb{R}^{n_h}$, $\nu_1, \nu_2, \gamma \in \mathbb{N}_0$.
Output: Approximation $\mathbf{u}^h \in \mathbb{R}^{n_h}$.

1 Presmooth: $\mathbf{u}^h := S_h^{\nu_1}(\mathbf{u}_0^h)$
2 Get residual: $\mathbf{r}^h := \mathbf{f}^h - A_h\mathbf{u}^h$
3 Coarsen: $H := 2h$, $\mathbf{r}^H := I_h^H\mathbf{r}^h$
4 **if** $H = h_0$ **then**
5 | Solve $A_H\delta^H = \mathbf{r}^H$

6 **else**
7 | $\delta^H := \mathbf{0}$
8 | **for** $j = 1$ **to** γ **do**
9 | $\delta^H := MG(A_H, \delta^H, \mathbf{r}^H, \nu_1, \nu_2, \gamma)$

10 Prolong: $\delta^h := I_H^h\delta^H$
11 Correct: $\mathbf{u}^h := \mathbf{u}^h + \delta^h$
12 Postsmooth: $\mathbf{u}^h := S_h^{\nu_2}(\mathbf{u}^h)$

The only difference to Algorithm 35 is in lines 7 to 9, which replace the old line 7, and the additional parameter γ. Obviously, $\gamma = 1$ leads to the V-cycle algorithm. It is helpful to visualise the recursion in the following way, depending on the choice of γ and how many levels there are, meaning how many grids we use, see Figure 6.5.

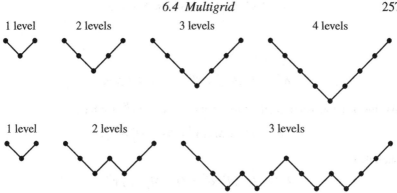

Figure 6.5 The recursion of multigrid with $\gamma = 1$ (top) and $\gamma = 2$ (bottom).

These visualisations explain why the case $\gamma = 1$ is called the V-cycle and the case $\gamma = 2$ is called the W-cycle. The case $\gamma = 3$ is hardly used in practice. Next, let us analyse the cost of multigrid. If we make the same assumptions as we made for the V-cycle, then we see that the computational cost now follows the rule

$$T(n_h) \le \eta n_h + \gamma T(n_{2h}).$$

As before, we can invoke Lemma 1.4. This time we have $c = \eta$, $\alpha = 1$, $a = \gamma$ and $b = 2^d$. Hence, the recursion breaks down to

$$T(n) = \begin{cases} \frac{2^d}{2^d-\gamma}\eta n, & \text{if } \gamma < 2^d, \\ \eta n(\log_{2^d} n + 1), & \text{if } \gamma = 2^d, \\ \frac{\gamma}{\gamma-2^d}\eta n^{\log_{2^d} \gamma}, & \text{if } \gamma > 2^d. \end{cases}$$

This gives the following special cases.

Remark 6.54 The V-cycle needs $O(n)$ time in every space dimension. The W-cycle needs $O(n)$ time in dimensions $d \ge 2$ and $O(n \log n)$ time in dimension $d = 1$.

To determine the iteration matrix M_h of the multigrid method, we start with the iteration matrix of the two-grid method

$$T_h = C_h^{\nu_2}[I - I_H^h A_H^{-1} I_h^H A_h]C_h^{\nu_1} \tag{6.57}$$

and recall that the term A_H^{-1} came from step 4 in Algorithm 34 and hence has now to be replaced by γ steps of the multigrid method on grid X_H. Before, we had $\delta^H = A_H^{-1}\mathbf{r}_H$, which is now replaced by an iteration of the form

$$\delta_0^H := \mathbf{0},$$
$$\delta_j^H := M_H \delta_{j-1}^H + \mathbf{d}^H, \qquad 1 \le j \le \gamma.$$

As this is a consistent method for solving $A_H \tilde{\delta}^H = \mathbf{r}^H$, we have

$$\tilde{\delta}^H - \delta^H = M_H^\gamma (\tilde{\delta}^H - \mathbf{0}) = M_H^\gamma \tilde{\delta}^H,$$

such that

$$\delta^H = (I - M_H^\gamma) \tilde{\delta}^H = (I - M_H^\gamma) A_H^{-1} \mathbf{r}^H.$$

Inserting this into (6.57) for A_H^{-1} yields

$$
\begin{aligned}
M_h &= C_h^{\nu_2} [I - I_H^h (I - M_H^\gamma) A_H^{-1} I_h^H A_h] C_h^{\nu_1} \\
&= C_h^{\nu_2} [I - I_H^h A_H^{-1} I_h^H A_h + I_H^h M_H^\gamma A_H^{-1} I_h^H A_h] C_h^{\nu_1} \\
&= T_h + C_h^{\nu_2} I_H^h M_H^\gamma A_H^{-1} I_h^H A_h C_h^{\nu_1},
\end{aligned}
$$

which can be seen as a perturbation of T_h. This can then be used to analyse the spectral radius of M_h, but we will not give details here. Instead we refer to [74] by Hackbusch and [125] by Trottenberg *et al.*

Though our motivation for multigrid was based upon the idea of having an underlying discretisation for various grids leading to linear systems on different refinement levels, the presentation of multigrid hardly makes use of this underlying grid. As a matter of fact, we can apply the ideas to general matrices $A = A_h$ by defining one of the inter-grid operators in an abstract way. For example, if we have an idea how to

1. define the coarse subset $\mathbb{R}^{n_H}$ from the fine set $\mathbb{R}^{n_h}$,
2. define the coarsening operator I_h^H from $\mathbb{R}^{n_h}$ to $\mathbb{R}^{n_H}$

then we can use the abstract definitions

$$I_H^h = (I_h^H)^\mathrm{T}, \qquad A_H = I_h^H A_h I_H^h, \qquad \mathbf{f}^H = I_h^H \mathbf{f}^h$$

to complete the set-up. This is known as *algebraic multigrid* (AMG). How to choose the coarse subset and the coarsening operator will obviously depend on the matrix and the application that lead to the matrix. A further discussion goes beyond the scope of this book.

Exercises

6.1   Let $A \in \mathbb{R}^{n \times n}$ be invertible with diagonal entries $a_{ii} = 1$ for $1 \le i \le n$. Let $\{\mathbf{x}_k\}$ be the sequence generated by the Jacobi relaxation. Let $\mathbf{r}_k = \mathbf{b} - A\mathbf{x}_k$

show that $\mathbf{r}_k$ can be written in the form $\mathbf{r}_k = R_k(A)\mathbf{r}_0$ with a polynomial $R_k \in \pi_k$ and conclude that $\mathbf{x}_k \in \mathbf{x}_0 + \mathcal{K}_k(A, \mathbf{r}_0)$.

6.2 Let $A \in \mathbb{R}^{n \times n}$ be symmetric and positive definite and $\mathbf{b} \in \mathbb{R}^n$. Define $f : \mathbb{R}^n \to \mathbb{R}$ by $f(\mathbf{x}) = \frac{1}{2}\mathbf{x}^{\mathsf{T}} A \mathbf{x} - \mathbf{b}^{\mathsf{T}}\mathbf{x}$. Show that for any A-conjugate directions $\mathbf{p}_1, \ldots, \mathbf{p}_n \in \mathbb{R}^n$ and $\alpha_1, \ldots, \alpha_n \in \mathbb{R}$ we have

$$f\left(\sum_{j=1}^n \alpha_j \mathbf{p}_j\right) = \sum_{j=1}^n \alpha_j f(\mathbf{p}_j).$$

6.3 The conjugate gradient method is applied to a positive definite matrix A with the result $\|\mathbf{x}^* - \mathbf{x}_1\|_A = 1$ and $\|\mathbf{x}^* - \mathbf{x}_{11}\|_A = 2 \times 2^{-10}$. Based solely on this data, what bound can you give on $\kappa_2(A)$ and on $\|\mathbf{x}^* - \mathbf{x}_{21}\|_A$?

6.4 Assume that the Arnoldi method for computing an orthogonal basis of $\mathcal{K}_j(A, \mathbf{r}_0)$ does not stop prematurely. As usual in this context, let $H_j \in \mathbb{R}^{(j+1) \times j}$ be the corresponding Hessenberg matrix and $\tilde{H}_j \in \mathbb{R}^{j \times j}$ its upper block. Assume that $\tilde{H}_j$ is invertible and let $\beta = \|\mathbf{r}_0\|_2$. Then, we can define a new iterative method by setting $\mathbf{y}_j^F := \beta \tilde{H}_j^{-1} \mathbf{e}_1$ and then $\mathbf{x}_j^F := \mathbf{x}_0 + V_j \mathbf{y}_j$, where V_j contains the orthonormal vectors. This method is called the *full orthogonal method (FOM)*. Let $\mathbf{x}_j^G$ be the iteration of GMRES and let $\mathbf{r}_j^F$ and $\mathbf{r}_j^G$ be the corresponding residuals.

- Show $\|\mathbf{r}_j^F\|_2 = |h_{j+1,j}||\mathbf{e}_j^{\mathsf{T}} \mathbf{y}_j^F|$.
- Show

$$\|\mathbf{r}_j^F\|_2 = \|\mathbf{r}_j^G\|_2 \sqrt{1 + \frac{h^2}{\xi^2}}$$

with $\xi = (G_{j-1} \cdots G_1 H_j)_{jj}$ and $h := h_{j+1,j}$.
- Show that $\mathbf{x}_j^F = \mathbf{x}_j^G$ implies $\mathbf{r}_j^F = \mathbf{r}_j^G = \mathbf{0}$, i.e. both methods yield the exact solution.

6.5 Let $A \in \mathbb{R}^{n \times n}$ be positive definite and symmetric. Let $C_J(\omega) = I - \omega D^{-1} A$ be the iteration matrix of the Jacobi relaxation, which converges for $0 < \omega < 2/\rho(D^{-1}A)$. Show that

$$\|C_J(\omega)\mathbf{e}\|_A^2 \le \|\mathbf{e}\|_A^2 - \lambda_{\min}[\omega(2I - \omega D^{-1/2} A D^{-1/2})]\|A\mathbf{e}\|_{D^{-1}}^2$$

holds for all $\mathbf{e} \in \mathbb{R}^n$. Use this to determine an $\alpha > 0$ for which the smoothing property

$$\|C_J(\omega)\mathbf{e}\|_A^2 \le \|\mathbf{e}\|_A^2 - \alpha\|A\mathbf{e}\|_{D^{-1}}^2$$

is satisfied.

7

Methods for Large Dense Systems

In Chapter 6 we discussed advanced iterative methods for solving large linear systems. Since the main operation in each iteration was one (or two) matrix–vector multiplications, these methods were clearly designed for sparse matrices, where the computational cost of such a matrix–vector multiplication is only linear. Nonetheless, they can also be used for full systems where the cost is quadratic if the number of iterations is significantly smaller than the dimension of the problem, which can sometimes be achieved using well-chosen preconditioners. The alternative that we want to discuss in this chapter is based on the idea that the original matrix $A \in \mathbb{R}^{n \times n}$ can be replaced by an approximate matrix $\tilde{A} \in \mathbb{R}^{n \times n}$ such that the cost of a typical matrix–vector product becomes significantly less than n^2. We would also like to reduce the memory requirement to store the approximate matrix and we would like to control the approximation error between A and $\tilde{A}$. To be more specific, our approximation $\tilde{A} \in \mathbb{R}^{n \times n}$ should satisfy the following criteria.

- The computational cost of a matrix–vector multiplication with the approximate matrix $\tilde{A}$ should be bounded by $O(n \log^\alpha n)$ with $\alpha \in \mathbb{N}_0$ independent of n.
- The memory required for storing and the time required for generating the approximate matrix $\tilde{A}$ should be bounded by $O(n \log^\beta n)$ with $\beta \in \mathbb{N}_0$ independent of n.
- For a given $\epsilon > 0$, and a matrix norm $\| \cdot \|$ the approximation $\tilde{A}$ satisfies $\|A - \tilde{A}\| \leq \epsilon$.

In this chapter, we want to address specific methods for solving such linear systems with a dense matrix. We will start with methods which are motivated by and are restricted to matrices from particular discretisation problems. After that, we will discuss how these methods can be generalised if less is known about the origin of the matrix.

260

7.1 Multipole Methods

We will now look at those two of the three examples given in the introduction that produce dense matrices.

In the situation of interpolation (Section 1.1.1) with radial basis functions we have data sites $\mathbf{x}_1, \ldots, \mathbf{x}_n \in \Omega \subseteq \mathbb{R}^d$ and form an interpolant of the form

$$s(\mathbf{x}) = \sum_{j=1}^{n} \alpha_j K(\mathbf{x}, \mathbf{x}_j), \qquad \mathbf{x} \in \Omega \subseteq \mathbb{R}^d, \tag{7.1}$$

with a positive definite kernel $K(\mathbf{x}, \mathbf{y}) = \Phi(\mathbf{x} - \mathbf{y}) = \phi(\|\mathbf{x} - \mathbf{y}\|_2)$. The interpolation conditions lead to a system $A\alpha = \mathbf{f}$ with the symmetric and positive definite interpolation matrix $A = (K(\mathbf{x}_i, \mathbf{x}_j))$, which is dense if Φ is not locally supported.

A very popular choice of basis function ϕ is the so-called inverse multiquadric, $\phi(r) = (r^2 + c^2)^{-1/2}$, where $c > 0$ is a fixed shape parameter. We will look at this function, as well as at the Gaussian, as a basic role model.

While in this example the matrix is dense, the computation of the matrix entries is relatively cheap. This becomes worse when looking at our second example (Section 1.1.3). Here, the matrix entries take the form

$$a_{ij} = \int_\Omega \int_\Omega K(\mathbf{x}, \mathbf{y}) \chi_j(\mathbf{y}) \chi_i(\mathbf{x}) d\mathbf{y} \, d\mathbf{x}, \qquad 1 \leq i, j \leq n, \tag{7.2}$$

where the functions χ_i, $1 \leq i \leq n$, form the basis of a given finite element space. Besides being a dense matrix, the entries of A are also expensive to calculate since the double integrals have to be discretised and things become even worse when one is looking at higher spatial dimensions. Thus, it would be useful to compute the approximate matrix $\tilde{A}$ or to give an algorithm for an approximate computation of a matrix–vector product without computing all the matrix entries.

Let us start our considerations with the first example from Section 1.1.1. Here, computing a matrix–vector product means evaluating a sum of the form (7.1) in typically n locations, namely $\mathbf{x}_1, \ldots, \mathbf{x}_n$, and each evaluation should be done in significantly less time than $O(n)$, i.e. in $O(1)$ or $O(\log n)$ time.

To get an idea how this can be achieved, assume for the time being that the kernel K is a *degenerate kernel*, i.e. it can be written in the form

$$K(\mathbf{x}, \mathbf{y}) = \sum_{k=1}^{r} \phi_k(\mathbf{x}) \psi_k(\mathbf{y}) \tag{7.3}$$

with certain, given functions ϕ_k, ψ_k, $1 \leq k \leq r$, and a fixed number $r \in \mathbb{N}$.

Then, obviously, we can rearrange the sum (7.1) by writing

$$
\sum_{j=1}^{n} \alpha_j K(\mathbf{x}, \mathbf{x}_j) = \sum_{j=1}^{n} \alpha_j \sum_{k=1}^{r} \phi_k(\mathbf{x}) \psi_k(\mathbf{x}_j)
$$

$$
= \sum_{k=1}^{r} \left(\sum_{j=1}^{n} \alpha_j \psi_k(\mathbf{x}_j) \right) \phi_k(\mathbf{x})
$$

$$
=: \sum_{k=1}^{r} \beta_k \phi_k(\mathbf{x}).
$$

As a consequence, we first need to compute the new coefficients β_k for $1 \le k \le r$; each costs us $O(n)$ time. Then each evaluation will cost $O(r)$ time. Hence, the total cost of computing all the new coefficients and then evaluating the sum n times amounts to $O(nr)$. This is significantly less than the usual $O(n^2)$ provided that r is significantly smaller than n. We can also rephrase this in terms of matrices and vectors.

Lemma 7.1 *Let $A = (K(\mathbf{x}_i, \mathbf{x}_j)) \in \mathbb{R}^{n \times n}$ be a matrix with degenerate kernel (7.3). Then, the matrix A has rank r and can be written as $A = BC^{\mathrm{T}}$ with $B = (\phi_j(\mathbf{x}_i)), C = (\psi_j(\mathbf{x}_i)) \in \mathbb{R}^{n \times r}$. Hence, $\mathbf{b} := A\alpha = BC^{\mathrm{T}}\alpha$ can be computed in $O(nr)$ time by computing first $\beta := C^{\mathrm{T}}\alpha$ and then $\mathbf{b} = B\beta$.*

Example 7.2 To see that our second example above, with a matrix with entries (7.2), leads to a very similar situation, let us again assume that the kernel K has an expansion of the form (7.3). Then, we can compute the matrix entries $\tilde{a}_{ij}$ as

$$
a_{ij} = \int_{\Omega} \int_{\Omega} \sum_{k=1}^{r} \phi_k(\mathbf{x}) \psi_k(\mathbf{y}) \chi_j(\mathbf{y}) \chi_i(\mathbf{x}) d\mathbf{y} \, d\mathbf{x}
$$

$$
= \sum_{k=1}^{r} \left(\int_{\Omega} \phi_k(\mathbf{x}) \chi_i(\mathbf{x}) d\mathbf{x} \right) \left(\int_{\Omega} \psi_k(\mathbf{y}) \chi_j(\mathbf{y}) d\mathbf{y} \right).
$$

Hence, if we define matrices $B = (b_{ik}), C = (c_{ik}) \in \mathbb{R}^{n \times r}$ by

$$
b_{ik} = \int_{\Omega} \phi_k(\mathbf{x}) \chi_i(\mathbf{x}) d\mathbf{x}, \qquad c_{ik} = \int_{\Omega} \psi_k(\mathbf{y}) \chi_i(\mathbf{y}) d\mathbf{y},
$$

we see that also in this case the matrix A can be written as $A = BC^{\mathrm{T}}$.

Unfortunately, kernels are usually not degenerate but allow only an approximate decomposition of the form (7.3), i.e.

$$
K(\mathbf{x}, \mathbf{y}) = \sum_{k=1}^{r} \phi_k(\mathbf{x}) \psi_k(\mathbf{y}) + R_r(\mathbf{x}, \mathbf{y}) \tag{7.4}
$$

with a certain remainder R_r. If we define the approximate kernel

$$K_r(\mathbf{x}, \mathbf{y}) = \sum_{j=1}^{r} \phi_k(\mathbf{x})\psi_k(\mathbf{y}) \qquad (7.5)$$

by omitting the remainder, an evaluation of the approximate sum

$$\tilde{s}(\mathbf{x}) = \sum_{j=1}^{n} \alpha_j K_r(\mathbf{x}, \mathbf{x}_j)$$

leads to an error of the form

$$|s(\mathbf{x}) - \tilde{s}(\mathbf{x})| \le \|\alpha\|_1 \max_{1 \le j \le n} |R_r(\mathbf{x}, \mathbf{x}_j)|.$$

We will discuss possible ways of computing representations of the form (7.4) later on. However, for the time being let us make the following assumption.

Assumption 7.3 For each $r \in \mathbb{N}$, the kernel K has a *far-field expansion* of the form (7.4) where the remainder satisfies $R_r(\mathbf{x}, \mathbf{y}) \to 0$ for $\mathbf{x} \ne \mathbf{y}$ and $r \to \infty$ and $R_r(\mathbf{x}, \mathbf{y}) \to 0$ for $r \in \mathbb{N}$ and $\|\mathbf{x} - \mathbf{y}\|_2 \to \infty$.

Essentially, this means that $K(\mathbf{x}, \mathbf{y})$ can be approximated by $K_r(\mathbf{x}, \mathbf{y})$ provided $\mathbf{x}$ and $\mathbf{y}$ are *well-separated* and r is chosen sufficiently large.

In the following, we will call $\mathbf{y}$ in $K(\mathbf{x}, \mathbf{y})$ a *source point* and $\mathbf{x}$ an *evaluation point*. The idea of multipole expansions is based on such a far-field expansion of K. Suppose all sources are situated in a certain region, also called a *panel*, which is centred at a point $\mathbf{y}_0$. Suppose further that we want to evaluate the function (7.1) at a point $\mathbf{x}$ that is sufficiently far away from the source panel. Figure 7.1 illustrates the situation.

Figure 7.1 Evaluation (grey) and source regions.

Then, Assumption 7.3 tells us that K_r from (7.5) is a good approximation to K and that we can approximate the sum $s(\mathbf{x})$ by $\tilde{s}(\mathbf{x})$ in $O(r)$ time.

One could say that we have averaged the items of information given at the sources x_j to one item of information given at the centre y_0 of the panel. In this sense, (7.4) is a *unipole expansion* of K.

In general, the evaluation points are close to at least a few of the centres or, as in our case, even coincide with the centres. In the next step we have to refine our approach to fit this situation. To this end, we subdivide the points into disjoint point sets.

Example 7.4 Let the source points $x_1, \ldots, x_n$ equidistantly be given by $x_j = (j-1)/(n-1) \in [0, 1]$, $1 \le j \le n$. Then, we can subdivide the interval $[0, 1]$ into equally sized sub-intervals $[0, h), [h, 2h), \ldots, [1-h, 1]$, where h is a fixed integer multiple of $1/(n-1)$. Hence, each interval contains a constant number of points which is at most $m = h/(n-1) + 1$. Two such intervals are *well-separated* if they have at least a distance of h.

We could then use the following strategy to evaluate s at a point $x \in [0, 1]$. We locate the interval $I_k := [kh, (k+1)h]$ or $[1-h, h]$ which contains x. Then, all but at most two neighbouring intervals are well-separated from this interval. For source points in I_k and these neighbouring intervals, we sum up the corresponding summands directly, which will cost $O(m)$. For all other intervals we use the far-field expansion of that interval, which will now cost $O(mr)$ for each such interval.

This means, unfortunately, that the total cost of evaluation is still $O(nr) = O(n)$ since we have $O(n/m)$ intervals.

The above example shows that a simple subdivision of the point set will not reduce the computational cost in the desired way. The remedy is a *hierarchical subdivision* of the point set – or of the region Ω of interest – into *panels or cells of sources*.

Let us explain the idea again by an example, using the same setting as in Example 7.4.

Example 7.5 Suppose all data points $x_1, \ldots, x_n$ are again equally spaced and contained in the interval $[0, 1]$. Let us hierarchically divide this interval into panels as shown, for example, in Figure 7.2. This gives us a disjoint partitioning of $[0, 1]$ on different *levels*. The panel $[0, 1]$ is on level 0, the panels $[0, 1/2)$ and $[1/2, 1]$ are on level 1 and so on.

With every source panel T at the final level we associate the part of the function s that corresponds to the sources in that panel by setting

$$s_T = \sum_{x_j \in T} \alpha_j K(\cdot, x_j).$$

Moreover, we also assign the far-field expansion $\tilde{s}_T$ of s_T to each panel T.

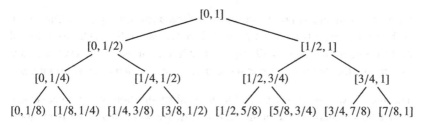

Figure 7.2 Hierarchical decomposition of $[0, 1]$.

Then, the approximation $\tilde{s}$ to the function s at evaluation point x is computed by adding the associated functions s_T for the panel that contains x itself and all neighbouring panels. Those panels that are well-separated from x contribute only by their far-field expansion $\tilde{s}_T$ to $\tilde{s}$. Here, we say that a point x is well-separated from a panel T if it lies at a distance of at least $\text{diam}(T)$ from T. A panel U is called well-separated from a panel T if all points in U are well-separated from T. Since we want to minimise the number of floating point operations we always use the largest possible source panel for the approximation.

Let us return to the example given in Figure 7.2. If we want to approximate $s(x)$ for x in the panel $[0, 1/8)$ we form

$$\tilde{s}(x) = s_{[0,\frac{1}{8})}(x) + s_{[\frac{1}{8},\frac{1}{4})}(x) + \tilde{s}_{[\frac{1}{4},\frac{3}{8})}(x) + \tilde{s}_{[\frac{3}{8},\frac{1}{2})}(x) + \tilde{s}_{[\frac{1}{2},\frac{3}{4})}(x) + \tilde{s}_{[\frac{3}{4},1]}(x).$$

Note that we use the two level-2 approximants $\tilde{s}_{[\frac{1}{2},\frac{3}{4})}$ and $\tilde{s}_{[\frac{3}{4},1]}(x)$ instead of the four level-3 approximants $\tilde{s}_{[\frac{1}{2},\frac{5}{8})}, \ldots, \tilde{s}_{[\frac{7}{8},1]}$. This halves the computational complexity in this case. We can do this because the panels $[1/2, 3/4)$ and $[3/4, 1]$ are well-separated from $[0, 1/4)$, the panel on the same level that contains x. On the other hand, we could not use the approximant $\tilde{s}_{[\frac{1}{2},1]}$ because its panel $[1/2, 1]$ is not well-separated from the panel $[0, 1/2]$, which is the panel on the same level that contains x.

Similarly, to approximately evaluate $s(x)$ in the panel $[\frac{3}{8}, \frac{1}{2})$ we would use

$$\begin{aligned}\tilde{s}(x) = &\, s_{[\frac{3}{8},\frac{1}{2})}(x) + s_{[\frac{1}{4},\frac{3}{8})}(x) + s_{[\frac{1}{2},\frac{5}{8})}(x) \\ &+ \tilde{s}_{[0,\frac{1}{8})}(x) + \tilde{s}_{[\frac{1}{8},\frac{1}{4})}(x) + \tilde{s}_{[\frac{5}{8},\frac{3}{4})}(x) + \tilde{s}_{[\frac{3}{4},1]}(x).\end{aligned}$$

To understand the computational cost, we have to continue our hierarchical decomposition until the panels on the final level contain at most m sources, where m is considered to be small and constant relative to n. Since we halve the number of sources in each panel by subdividing it into two panels on the next level, the number of sources in each panel on level ℓ is $n2^{-\ell}$ and hence the number of levels is at most $L = O(\log_2(n/m)) = O(\log n)$. On each level, we have to evaluate approximate sums $\tilde{s}_T$ for at most three panels. Since each such evaluation costs us $O(r)$ time and since we have $O(\log n)$ levels, the total cost for this is $O(r \log n) = O(\log n)$. In addition, on the finest level, we have to compute the direct sum for at most three panels, which has a constant cost.

The above example shows that a hierarchical subdivision of the point set can reduce the evaluation time in the desired way. We will call an approximation $\tilde{s}$ of s of the form described in the example a *multipole expansion* of s.

We will now extend this concept to the general situation of arbitrary source points in arbitrary dimensions.

Definition 7.6 Let $X = \{x_1, \ldots, x_n\} \subseteq \mathbb{R}^d$ be given. Let x_j have components $x_j := (x_1^{(j)}, \ldots x_d^{(j)})^{\mathrm{T}}$. The *bounding box* of X is the multivariate interval $\Omega := [\mathbf{a}, \mathbf{b}] = [a_1, b_1] \times \cdots \times [a_d, b_d]$ with

$$a_i := \min_{1 \leq j \leq n} x_i^{(j)}, \quad b_i := \max_{1 \leq j \leq n} x_i^{(j)}, \quad 1 \leq i \leq d.$$

The *separation radius* of X is given by

$$q_X := \frac{1}{2} \min_{i \neq j} \|x_i - x_j\|_\infty$$

and the *fill distance* of X in Ω is given by

$$h_X \equiv h_{X,\Omega} := \sup_{x \in \Omega} \min_{1 \leq j \leq n} \|x - x_j\|_\infty.$$

Both the separation radius and the fill distance are often defined using the Euclidean norm rather than the maximum norm. However, for our purposes the maximum norm is better suited. If our source points form a regular grid of grid width $\tilde{h}$, then we have $q_X = h_X = \tilde{h}/2$.

Obviously, two distinct source points x_j and x_k have at least a distance of $2q_X$. Moreover, for each $x \in \Omega$ there is at least one source point within a distance of h_X. The fill distance can actually be defined for arbitrary sets Ω, though we will mainly use it if Ω is the bounding box or if $X \subseteq \Omega$ with Ω convex. If $q_X = \frac{1}{2}\|x_{j_1} - x_{j_2}\|_\infty$ then $x := (x_{j_1} + x_{j_2})/2 \in \Omega$ satisfies $\|x - x_{j_1}\|_\infty = \|x - x_{j_2}\|_\infty = q_X$ and also $\min_{1 \leq j \leq n} \|x - x_j\|_\infty = q_X$, so that we have necessarily

$$q_X = \min_{1 \leq j \leq n} \|x - x_j\|_\infty \leq \sup_{z \in \Omega} \min_{1 \leq j \leq n} \|z - x_j\|_\infty = h_X.$$

The inverse inequality is in general not true, but we can always find a constant $c_{qu} \geq 1$ such that $q_X \leq h_X \leq c_{qu} q_X$. For a general set of source points X this constant can be arbitrarily large. Here, however, we are interested in point sets where this constant remains small.

Definition 7.7 A set of source points $X \subseteq \mathbb{R}^d$ is called *quasi-uniform* if there is a small constant $c_{qu} \geq 1$ such that $q_X \leq h_X \leq c_{qu}q_X$.

As pointed out above, the constant c_{qu} equals 1 if the source points form a regular grid. If we leave out only one point of such a regular grid, the constant will immediately become $c_{qu} = 2$. Hence, we will mainly work with a quasi-uniformity constant $c_{qu} \in [1, 2)$, though bigger constants are possible.

The geometric quantities q_X and $h_X = h_{X,\Omega}$ allow us to estimate the number of points. We formulate the following result only in the situation that the bounding box of X forms a regular cube, since in this situation we can determine all constants in a stricter way, but a generalisation is straightforward.

Lemma 7.8 *Let $X = \{x_1, \ldots, x_n\} \subseteq \Omega$, where Ω is an axis-parallel cube of side length 2δ. Then, the number of points in X can be bounded by*

$$\delta^d h_X^{-d} \leq n \leq \left(\frac{\delta}{q_X} + 1\right)^d. \tag{7.6}$$

Proof Without restriction, we may assume $\Omega = [-\delta, \delta]^d$. Let $B_\infty(x, \epsilon) := \{y \in \mathbb{R}^d : \|x - y\|_\infty < \epsilon\}$ be the open ℓ_∞-ball about x with radius ϵ. Then, $B_\infty(x, \epsilon)$ has volume $(2\epsilon)^d$. Moreover, by the definition of q_X we have

$$\bigcup_{j=1}^n B_\infty(x_j, q_X) \subseteq B_\infty(0, \delta + q_X)$$

and since the balls on the left-hand side are mutually disjoint, a comparison of the volumes yields $n(2q_X)^d \leq 2^d(\delta + q_X)^d$, from which the upper bound in (7.6) follows. The definition of h_X yields

$$\Omega = B_\infty(0, \delta) \subseteq \bigcup_{j=1}^n \overline{B_\infty(x_j, h_X)}$$

and we can once again compare the volumes to derive $(2\delta)^d \leq n(2h_X)^d$, from which the lower bound in (7.6) follows. $\qquad\square$

As soon as we have at least two points in X, we also have $q_X \leq \delta$ such that the upper bound in (7.6) can further be simplified to

$$n \leq 2^d \delta^d q_X^{-d}. \tag{7.7}$$

The obvious generalisation of our hierarchical splitting outlined in Example 7.5 is as follows.

Definition 7.9 Let $X = \{x_1, \ldots, x_n\} \subseteq [-\delta, \delta]^d = \Omega$. Then, a *uniform hierarchical box partitioning* of X and Ω of depth L is defined by setting $X_1^{(0)} := X$,

$\Omega_1^{(0)} := \Omega$ and then for $\ell = 1, \ldots, L$ by recursively decomposing each $\Omega_j^{(\ell-1)}$ into 2^d disjoint, equally sized sub-cubes $\Omega_i^{(\ell)}$, $2^d(j-1) \leq i \leq 2^d j$, such that

$$\Omega_j^{(\ell-1)} = \bigcup_{i=2^d(j-1)+1}^{2^d j} \Omega_i^{(\ell)}, \qquad 1 \leq j \leq 2^{d(\ell-1)}.$$

Associated with each panel $\Omega_i^{(\ell)}$ are the source points

$$X_i^{(\ell)} = X \cap \Omega_i^{(\ell)}.$$

For $d = 2$ a typical decomposition of depth 2 is depicted in Figure 7.3. As in Example 7.5, we can choose the sub-cubes semi-open but include the boundary of Ω where necessary. It is only important that on each level each source point is contained in exactly one panel. This then ensures also that we have

$$X_j^{(\ell-1)} = \bigcup_{i=2^d(j-1)+1}^{2^d j} X_i^{(\ell)}.$$

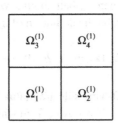

Figure 7.3 Hierarchical boxes $\Omega_j^{(\ell)}$ for $\ell = 0, 1, 2$.

In the situation of a quasi-uniform set of source points, the uniform subdivision of a panel guarantees that the source points of that panel are almost uniformly distributed among the 2^d sub-panels of this panel.

Proposition 7.10 *Let $X = \{x_1, \ldots, x_n\} \subseteq \Omega = [-\delta, \delta]^d$ be quasi-uniform with quasi-uniformity constant $c_{qu} \geq 1$ and let $\{X_j^{(\ell)}, \Omega_j^{(\ell)}\}$ be a uniform hierarchical box partitioning of depth L. Then, the number $n_j^{(\ell)} = |X_j^{(\ell)}|$ of points of each point set $X_j^{(\ell)}$ of level ℓ is bounded by*

$$\frac{1}{2^d c} n 2^{-\ell d} \leq n_j^{(\ell)} \leq c n 2^{-\ell d},$$

with $c = (2c_{qu})^d$. Moreover, if L is chosen to be at least $\log_2(cn/m)/d = O(\log n)$, then the panels on the last level contain at most m source points.

Proof We start with the following observation. Let $T \subseteq \Omega$ be an axes-parallel cube of side length $2\epsilon \geq h_{X,\Omega}$ and let $Y := T \cap X$ the source points contained in T. Then, we have

$$q_X \leq q_Y \leq h_{Y,T} \leq 2h_{X,\Omega} \leq 2c_{qu}q_X \leq 2c_{qu}q_Y, \tag{7.8}$$

which particularly means that Y is also quasi-uniform with respect to T. The first inequality follows from $Y \subseteq X$, the second has been explained above. The fourth and the fifth then follow from the quasi-uniformity of X in Ω and the the first one. Hence, the only critical one is $h_{Y,T} \leq 2h_{X,\Omega}$. To see this, let $\mathbf{t} \in T$ be arbitrary. Then, we can choose a $\tilde{\mathbf{t}} \in T$ which is at least $h_{X,\Omega}$ away from the boundary of T and satisfies $\|\mathbf{t} - \tilde{\mathbf{t}}\|_\infty \leq h_{X,\Omega}$. To this $\tilde{\mathbf{t}}$ we can choose an $\mathbf{x}_j \in X$ with $\|\tilde{\mathbf{t}} - \mathbf{x}_j\|_2 \leq h_{X,\Omega}$. However, since $\tilde{\mathbf{t}}$ is sufficiently far from the boundary of T, the source point $\mathbf{x}_j$ is also in T, i.e. $\mathbf{x}_j \in Y$. This shows that

$$\min_{\mathbf{x}_i \in Y} \|\mathbf{t} - \mathbf{x}_i\|_\infty \leq \|\mathbf{t} - \mathbf{x}_j\|_\infty \leq \|\mathbf{t} - \tilde{\mathbf{t}}\|_\infty + \|\tilde{\mathbf{t}} - \mathbf{x}_j\|_\infty \leq 2h_{X,\Omega}$$

and hence $h_{Y,T} \leq 2h_{X,\Omega}$.

Let n_Y be the number of points in Y. Then, applying (7.6) to this situation yields

$$n_Y \leq \left(\frac{\epsilon}{q_Y} + 1\right)^d \leq \left(\frac{\epsilon}{q_X} + 1\right)^d \leq \left(\frac{2\epsilon}{q_X}\right)^d \leq \left(\frac{2\epsilon c_{qu}}{h_{X,\Omega}}\right)^d,$$

where we have used $q_X \leq q_Y$ and $h_{X,\Omega} \leq c_{qu}q_X$. If T is one of the panels $\Omega_j^{(\ell)}$ on level ℓ it satisfies $\epsilon = \delta 2^{-\ell}$ and hence, using also $\delta^d h_X^{-d} \leq n$ from (7.6), we derive

$$n_Y \leq \left(\frac{2 \cdot 2^{-\ell}\delta c_{qu}}{h_{X,\Omega}}\right)^d \leq (2c_{qu})^d 2^{-\ell d} n =: cn2^{-\ell d},$$

which establishes the statement on the upper bound. For the lower bound we start again with (7.6) for Y and T and use (7.8) to derive

$$n_Y \geq \epsilon^d h_{Y,T}^{-d} \geq \epsilon^d q_X^{-d}(2c_{qu})^{-d} = \frac{1}{c}\epsilon^d q_X^{-d}.$$

For $T = \Omega_j^{(\ell)}$ at level ℓ we use again $\epsilon = \delta 2^{-\ell}$ and then $n \leq 2^d \delta^d q_X^{-d}$ from (7.7) to conclude

$$n_Y \geq \frac{1}{c}2^{-\ell d}\delta^d q_X^{-d} = \frac{1}{c2^d}2^{-\ell d}n.$$

Finally, $cn2^{-d\ell} \leq m$ is equivalent to $2^{d\ell} \geq cn/m$. Taking the logarithm shows that at level $L \geq \log_2(cn/m)/d = O(\log n)$ we have at most m source points per panel. □

Having a hierarchical partitioning of X and Ω allows us to define a fast approximation for evaluating sums of the form (7.1). Before we do this, however, it is time to introduce the data structure which is best suited to represent our hierarchical partitioning. We will use *trees* for this.

A tree is an abstract data structure which consists of *nodes* and *leaves*. A tree can be defined recursively as follows.

Definition 7.11 Let $V = \{v_1, v_2, \ldots\}$ be a set of nodes and let $B = \{b_1, b_2, \ldots\}$ be a set of leaves.

- Each element $b_i \in B$ is a *tree* and b_i is the *root* of this tree.
- If $T_1, \ldots, T_m$ are trees with pairwise distinct sets of nodes and leaves and if $v \in V$ is a new node then $(v, T_1, \ldots, T_m)$ is also a tree. The node v is the *root* of the tree, its *degree* is $\rho(v) = m$ and T_i is the ith *sub-tree*.

The following terminology is useful, when it comes to trees.

Definition 7.12 Let T be a tree with root v and sub-trees $T_1, \ldots, T_m$. Let w_i be the root of T_i. Then, w_i is called the ith *child* of v and v is called the parent of w_i.

Let v now be a leaf or a node of T. The *depth* of v in T is defined as follows. If v is the root of T then $\text{depth}(v, T) = 0$. If v is not the root of T then v belongs to one of the sub-trees T_i and $\text{depth}(v, T) := 1 + \text{depth}(v, T_i)$. The *depth of the tree T* is defined as

$$\text{depth}(T) := \max\{\text{depth}(v, T) : v \text{ is a leaf of } T\}.$$

If each node of T has degree 2 then T is called a *binary tree*. If each node of T has degree 4 then T is called a *quad-tree* and if each node of T has degree 8 then T is called an *oct-tree*.

A tree is *balanced* if the depth of each leaf v satisfies $\text{depth}(v) = \text{depth}(T) \pm 1$.

A tree is usually depicted by drawing (directed) lines – or *edges* – between a node and its children. In this sense, Figure 7.2 represents a balanced binary tree since all nodes have two children and all the leaves have the same depth. We can represent a hierarchical box partitioning of depth L by a balanced tree of depth L where each node has degree 2^d, i.e. the tree is a binary, quad- or oct-tree in dimensions 1, 2 or 3, respectively.

A tree can be traversed in different ways. For a binary tree, for example, we can traverse all the nodes and leaves in *pre-order*, where we visit first the root and then the left and right children; in *post-order*, where we visit first the left and right children and then the root; or in *symmetric order*, where we visit first the left child, then the root and then the right child. Pre- and post-order also make sense for arbitrary trees. The order chosen will depend on the actual application. A pre-order traversal corresponds to a *top-down* approach whereas a post-order traversal means a *bottom-up* approach.

Each node and leaf may also contain certain information. In our case, this information comprises the panel $T = \Omega_j^{(\ell)}$, the source points $X_j^{(\ell)}$ and the coefficients of the far-field expansion $\tilde{s}_T$. In the case of a leaf we also need to store the coefficients of the sum s_T.

To set up the data structure, we first choose the accuracy ϵ and from this the number r of necessary terms in each far-field expansion. We also choose the number m, which gives the maximum number of source points in the leaves of the tree. As mentioned above, m is considered to be a constant when compared with n and hence our tree has depth $L = O(\log n)$. Alternatively, we can simply choose the depth to be $L = O(\log n)$ knowing that the number of source points in each leaf is very small compared with n.

Then we build the tree, assigning the points to the panels. For the leaf panels we also store the coefficients of the interpolant. After this, we compute the far-field expansions. Depending on the actual far-field expansion, it might be possible to speed up the process by doing it bottom-up. The reason for this is that we might use the results from higher levels to compute the expansions for lower levels (see, for example, Exercise 7.1). For each panel we have to compute the coefficients β_k, $1 \leq k \leq r$. If we do this bottom-up every source $\mathbf{x}_j$ is considered only once so that all coefficients can be computed in $O(n)$ time. But even if we do it top-down, the complexity is bounded by $O(n \log n)$.

Lemma 7.13 *The tree data structure representing the multipole expansion of s with respect to a uniform hierarchical box partitioning can be built in $O(n \log n)$ time and requires $O(n \log n)$ space.*

Proof We know from Proposition 7.10 that our tree has depth $L = O(\log n)$. On level ℓ, a typical point set $X_j^{(\ell)}$ has less than $O(n2^{-\ell d})$ points such that the computation of the far-field expansion, i.e. the coefficients β_k, for this point set requires $O(rn2^{-\ell d})$ time. As we have $2^{d\ell}$ nodes on level ℓ the total time required on level ℓ for building the far-field expansion is $O(rn) = O(n)$. Thus, all far-field expansions can be computed in $O(n \log n)$ time.

The required space is determined by the space required for the data structure itself, which is proportional to the number of nodes and leaves, which is $O(n \log n)$ since we have $O(\log n)$ levels and on each level $O(n)$ nodes (or leaves on the last level). For each node and leaf we need to store the source points (or, better, pointers or indices) and again this costs us $O(n)$ space per level since each point is stored in exactly one panel per level, giving a total space requirement of $O(n \log n)$ for this. For each node and leaf, we have to save r coefficients for the far-field expansion and again this sums up to $O(rn \log n)$ space. Finally, for each leaf we also have to save the original coefficients α_k. But since each coefficient is only once saved, this can be done in $O(n)$ space.   □

To compute the approximation $\tilde{s}$ to s, we follow the ideas of Example 7.5 and introduce the concept of panels being well-separated.

Definition 7.14   Let $X = \{\mathbf{x}_1, \ldots, \mathbf{x}_n\} \subseteq [-\delta, \delta]^d$ with uniform hierarchical box partitioning $\{X_j^{(\ell)}\}$ and $\{\Omega_j^{(\ell)}\}$ of depth L. Two panels $\Omega_j^{(\ell)}$ and $\Omega_k^{(\ell)}$ of the same level ℓ are called *near neighbours* if they share a boundary point. They are called *well-separated* if they are not near neighbours. A point $\mathbf{x} \in \Omega$ is called *well-separated* from a panel $\Omega_j^{(\ell)}$ if the panel $\Omega_k^{(\ell)}$ of the same level which contains $\mathbf{x}$ is well-separated from $\Omega_j^{(\ell)}$.

Under the assumption that we have assigned a far-field expansion to each panel $\Omega_j^{(\ell)}$, the approximate evaluation $\tilde{s}$ of the sum s from (7.1) can be described as in Algorithm 37, which is called with the evaluation point $\mathbf{x}$ and the initial panel Ω. The idea, of course, is to go through the partitioning and use the far-field expansion as early as possible.

Formally, we must each time check whether $\mathbf{x}$ is well-separated from the current panel. This can be done either by keeping track of the panel which contains $\mathbf{x}$ at the same level as the current panel or simply by computing the distance from $\mathbf{x}$ to the panel. As a panel on level ℓ has side length $2\delta 2^{-\ell}$, the point $\mathbf{x}$ is well-separated from the given panel if it is at least this far away from the panel.

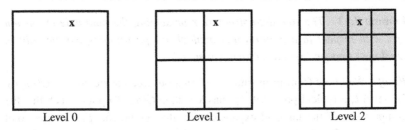

Level 0   Level 1   Level 2

Figure 7.4 Recursive subdivision of the bounding box.

Let us explain the idea behind Algorithm 37 in more detail, referring to the evaluation point $\mathbf{x}$ in Figure 7.4. On level 0 and level 1 all boxes are near neighbours, hence no far-field expansion can be used. On level 2, however, all white boxes are well-separated from the box containing $\mathbf{x}$, and for all these boxes, the far-field expansion can be used for evaluation. The light grey boxes are all near neighbours and have to be processed on the next level, see Figure 7.5.

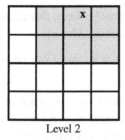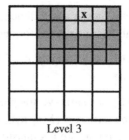

Level 2   Level 3

Figure 7.5 Refinement for evaluation.

This time, for all (dark) grey sub-boxes the far-field evaluation can be employed, while recursion has to be used for the remaining light grey boxes. Note that the dark grey boxes are exactly those boxes which result from the decomposition of the neighbour boxes of the previous level. Note also that the contributions from sources in the white boxes have already been dealt with in level 2. The recursion stops at level $L \approx \log n$; here a direct evaluation is performed.

Algorithm 37: Recursive evaluation of a multipole expansion

Input : Panel T and evaluation point $\mathbf{x}$.
Output: Approximate value $\tilde{s}(\mathbf{x})$.

1 **if** T *is well-separated from* $\mathbf{x}$ **then**
2 | Return $\tilde{s}_T(\mathbf{x})$.
3 **else**
4 | **if** T *is a leaf* **then**
5 | | Return $s_T(\mathbf{x})$.
6 | **else**
7 | | Apply this algorithm to $\mathbf{x}$ and the children of T.
8 | | Return the sum of their results.

If the evaluation of the approximation $\tilde{s}$ to the sum s is done recursively, as described in Algorithm 37 then we can estimate the computational cost of a single evaluation of $\tilde{s}$ as follows. The far-field part involves the evaluation of only a constant number of far-field expansions on each level of the tree, each consists of r coefficients. Hence, the time needed to sum up the far-field expansions is $O(r \log n)$. The direct part consists of a finite number (this number, as well as the finite number mentioned in the case of the far-field expansion, depends only on the space dimension) of panels. Thus, this takes only $O(1)$ time so that the time needed for one evaluation is $O(\log n)$.

Lemma 7.15 *One evaluation of the approximate sum $\tilde{s}$ can be performed in $O(\log n)$ time.*

Consequently, a matrix–vector product of the form $A\alpha$, where A is a kernel matrix of the form $A = (K(\mathbf{x}_i, \mathbf{x}_j))$, can be computed in $O(n \log n)$ time.

If the source points are not quasi-uniform, things become more complicated. In principle, we have two possibilities. On the one hand, we can stop using a uniform box decomposition on each level. Instead we can subdivide each box into 2^d boxes, all of which contain approximately the same number of source points. The advantage of this method is that the resulting tree will again have a depth of $O(\log n)$ and each panel at level ℓ will have $2^{-d\ell}n$ source points. The disadvantage clearly is that the panels associated with nodes of the same level may now have different sizes, such that it is not easy anymore to determine whether a point is well-separated from a panel.

On the other hand, we can still use a uniform box decomposition on each level but continue until a panel contains at most m points. The advantage here is obviously that we can continue to use our concept of well-separatedness. The disadvantage is that we cannot guarantee that the tree will have a depth of $O(\log n)$, which makes it impossible to predict how much time and space will be required. In the worst case the tree may degenerate to having an $O(n)$ depth. The subdivision strategy so far leads to 2^d children for each node, meaning that we have for $d = 2$ or $d = 3$ a large number of neighbours to check. Alternatively, we can use a bisection method to create a hierarchical partitioning.

Definition 7.16 Given a set $X = \{\mathbf{x}_1, \ldots, \mathbf{x}_n\} \subseteq [-\delta, \delta]^d = \Omega$ a *hierarchical bisectional partitioning* of X of depth L is given by setting $X_1^{(0)} := X$ and $\Omega_1^{(0)} := \Omega$ and then for $\ell = 1, \ldots, L$ recursively decomposing each $\Omega_j^{(\ell-1)}$ into two disjoint sub panels $\Omega_{2j-1}^{(\ell)}, \Omega_{2j}^{(\ell)}$ such that

$$\Omega_j^{(\ell-1)} = \Omega_{2j-1}^{(\ell)} \cup \Omega_{2j}^{(\ell)}, \qquad 1 \le j \le 2^{\ell-1}.$$

Associated with each panel $\Omega_j^{(\ell)}$ are the source points

$$X_j^{(\ell)} := X \cap \Omega_j^{(\ell)}.$$

For each panel in a hierarchical bisectional partitioning we have to decide how we want to subdivide the panel into two boxes. This can best be described by an axis-parallel hyper-plane which cuts the panel into two boxes. This hyper-plane can be described by the integer *splitting dimension* indicating the coordinate axis orthogonal to the cutting hyper-plane and the *splitting value* where the hyper-plane intersects the axis of the splitting dimension. Various rules for determining the splitting dimension and the splitting value are possible. For example, the splitting dimension can be chosen cyclic or in the direction of the widest spread of the points. The splitting value can be chosen as the mean value or median of the points. The partitioning can then be represented by a binary tree no matter what the dimension d is. Such trees are called *kd-trees*, which stands for *k*-dimensional trees. As there are obviously multiple possibilities at hand, we will skip the details here. As such trees are often used for range and nearest neighbour searches, details can in particular be found in the computational geometry literature, such as, for example, the book [43] by de Berg *et al.* or the original articles [3, 4] by Arya and Mount.

The rest of this section is devoted to the computation of a far-field expansion. Obviously, this will depend on the kernel employed. Nonetheless, we will describe three different strategies and demonstrate them for some typical kernels. Before doing so, we want to make Assumption 7.3 more precise. Having the uniform hierarchical box partitioning in mind, we can use the following definition, which easily generalises in the case of other partitionings.

Definition 7.17 Let B be a bounded domain of diameter 2η. A kernel K has a *far-field expansion* with respect to B if for each $\epsilon > 0$ there is an expansion of the form (7.4) with sufficiently large $r \in \mathbb{N}_0$ such that

$$|R_r(\mathbf{x}, \mathbf{y})| \le \epsilon$$

for each $\mathbf{y} \in B$ and each $\mathbf{x}$ with at least a distance η of B.

We start, however, with the following useful observation.

Lemma 7.18 *If the kernel K is translation-invariant, i.e. of the form $K(\mathbf{x}, \mathbf{y}) = \Phi(\mathbf{x} - \mathbf{y})$ with $\Phi : \mathbb{R}^d \to \mathbb{R}$ and if (7.4) is the far-field expansion of K with respect to $B_\infty(\mathbf{0}, \eta)$, then the far-field expansion of K with respect to $B_\infty(\mathbf{t}_0, \eta)$ is given by*

$$K(\mathbf{x}, \mathbf{y}) = \sum_{k=1}^{r} \phi_k(\mathbf{x} - \mathbf{t}_0)\psi_k(\mathbf{y} - \mathbf{t}_0) + R_r(\mathbf{x} - \mathbf{t}_0, \mathbf{y} - \mathbf{t}_0).$$

Proof This immediately follows from

$$K(\mathbf{x}, \mathbf{y}) = \Phi(\mathbf{x} - \mathbf{y}) = \Phi((\mathbf{x} - \mathbf{t}_0) - (\mathbf{y} - \mathbf{t}_0))$$
$$= \sum_{k=1}^{r} \phi_k(\mathbf{x} - \mathbf{t}_0)\psi_k(\mathbf{y} - \mathbf{t}_0) + R_r(\mathbf{x} - \mathbf{t}_0, \mathbf{y} - \mathbf{t}_0). \qquad \square$$

Hence, as almost all relevant kernels are translation-invariant, we will restrict ourselves to such kernels, meaning that we need only derive an expansion of the form (7.4) for $\mathbf{y}$ in a neighbourhood of the origin and for $\mathbf{x}$ sufficiently far away from the origin.

The first way of deriving a far-field expansion of a translation-invariant kernel $K(\mathbf{x}, \mathbf{y}) = \Phi(\mathbf{x} - \mathbf{y})$ is simply by Taylor expansion. Recall that the multivariate Taylor expansion of a function $f \in C^{r+1}(\mathbb{R}^d)$ about $\mathbf{0}$ is given by

$$f(\mathbf{y}) = \sum_{|\alpha| \le r} \frac{D^\alpha f(\mathbf{0})}{\alpha!} \mathbf{y}^\alpha + \sum_{|\alpha| = r+1} \frac{D^\alpha f(\xi)}{\alpha!} \mathbf{y}^\alpha,$$

where $\xi \in \mathbb{R}^d$ lies on the straight line connecting $\mathbf{y}$ and $\mathbf{0}$. Here, we have used the usual multi-index notation for $\alpha = (\alpha_1, \ldots, \alpha_d)^{\mathrm{T}} \in \mathbb{N}_0^d$ with $\alpha! = \alpha_1! \alpha_2! \cdots \alpha_d!$ and $|\alpha| = \alpha_1 + \cdots + \alpha_d$ and $D^\alpha = \frac{\partial^{|\alpha|}}{\partial_{x_1}^{\alpha_1} \cdots \partial_{x_d}^{\alpha_d}}$.

Hence, if $\Phi \in C^{r+1}(\mathbb{R}^d)$ and $K(\mathbf{x}, \mathbf{y}) = \Phi(\mathbf{x} - \mathbf{y})$ we can compute the Taylor expansion with respect to $\mathbf{y} \in \mathbb{R}^d$ about $\mathbf{0}$ with a fixed $\mathbf{x} \in \mathbb{R}^d$ as

$$K(\mathbf{x}, \mathbf{y}) = \Phi(\mathbf{x} - \mathbf{y}) = \sum_{|\alpha| \le r} \frac{(-1)^{|\alpha|} D^\alpha \Phi(\mathbf{x})}{\alpha!} \mathbf{y}^\alpha + \sum_{|\alpha| = r+1} \frac{(-1)^{|\alpha|} D^\alpha \Phi(\mathbf{x} - \xi)}{\alpha!} \mathbf{y}^\alpha$$

$$=: \sum_{|\alpha| \le r} \phi_\alpha(\mathbf{x}) \psi_\alpha(\mathbf{y}) + R_r(\mathbf{x}, \mathbf{y}).$$

Obviously, in this setting it makes sense to index our functions using multi-indices. Hence, the relevant basis functions are given by

$$\phi_\alpha(\mathbf{x}) = \frac{-1^{|\alpha|}}{\alpha!} D^\alpha \Phi(\mathbf{x}), \qquad \psi_\alpha(\mathbf{y}) = \mathbf{y}^\alpha.$$

If we define the cut-off kernel

$$K_r(\mathbf{x}, \mathbf{y}) = \sum_{|\alpha| \le r} \phi_\alpha(\mathbf{x}) \psi_\alpha(\mathbf{y})$$

and assume that $\mathbf{y} \in [-\eta, \eta]^d$ and $\mathbf{x} \in \mathbb{R}^d$ with $\|\mathbf{x}\|_\infty > (M + 1)\eta$ with $M \ge 1$ then the above Taylor formula gives the a priori error bound

$$|K(\mathbf{x}, \mathbf{y}) - K_r(\mathbf{x}, \mathbf{y})| = |R_r(\mathbf{x}, \mathbf{y})| \le \sum_{|\alpha| = r+1} \frac{|D^\alpha \Phi(\mathbf{x} - \xi)|}{\alpha!} \|\mathbf{y}\|_\infty^{|\alpha|}$$

$$\le C\eta^{r+1} \sup_{\substack{|\alpha| = r+1 \\ \|\xi\|_\infty \le \eta}} |D^\alpha \Phi(\mathbf{x} - \xi)|$$

$$\le C\eta^{r+1} \sup_{\substack{|\alpha| = r+1 \\ \|\mathbf{z}\|_\infty \ge M\eta}} |D^\alpha \Phi(\mathbf{z})|.$$

This bound satisfies Assumption 7.3 or Definition 7.17 if either $\eta < 1$ and the derivatives of Φ remain bounded or the derivatives of Φ decay for large arguments. We also note that it suffices to assume that $\Phi \in C^{r+1}(\mathbb{R}^d \setminus \{0\})$ to derive this far-field expansion. In conclusion, we have the following result.

Proposition 7.19 *Let* $\Phi \in C^{r+1}(\mathbb{R}^d \setminus \{0\})$ *be given. Assume that there is a* $\mu \in \mathbb{R}$ *with* $\mu \leq r + 1$ *such that*

$$|D^\alpha \Phi(\mathbf{z})| \leq C_\alpha \|\mathbf{z}\|_\infty^{\mu - r - 1}, \qquad \mathbf{z} \neq \mathbf{0}, \quad |\alpha| = r + 1. \tag{7.9}$$

Assume $M \geq 1$ *and* $\eta > 0$. *Then, for* $\mathbf{y} \in [-\eta, \eta]^d$ *and* $\mathbf{x} \in \mathbb{R}^d$ *with* $\|\mathbf{x}\|_\infty \geq (M + 1)\eta$, *the remainder* $R_r(\mathbf{x}, \mathbf{y})$ *of the Taylor expansion of* $K(\mathbf{x}, \mathbf{y}) = \Phi(\mathbf{x} - \mathbf{y})$ *satisfies*

$$|R_r(\mathbf{x}, \mathbf{y})| \leq C_r \eta^\mu M^{\mu - r - 1}$$

with a constant $C_r > 0$ *independent of* $\mathbf{x}, \mathbf{y}$.

Proof This follows directly from

$$|R_r(\mathbf{x}, \mathbf{y})| \leq C\eta^{r+1} \sup_{\substack{|\alpha| = r+1 \\ \|\mathbf{z}\|_\infty \geq M\eta}} |D^\alpha \Phi(\mathbf{z})| \leq C_r \eta^{r+1} (M\eta)^{\mu - r - 1} = C_r \eta^\mu M^{\mu - r - 1}. \qquad \square$$

In practical applications, we have usually $\mu \leq 0$ such that $r + 1 \geq \mu$ does not impose any restriction on r.

Example 7.20 Let us consider the integral equation from Section 1.1.3 once again with $d = 1$. Here, we want to find an approximation to the kernel $K(x, y) = \log(|x - y|)$ for arguments $x, y \in \mathbb{R}$ satisfying $|y| \leq \eta$ and $|x| \geq (M + 1)\eta$. Without restriction we will assume that $x \geq (M + 1)\eta$ such that K becomes $K(x, y) = \log(x - y)$. The case $x \leq -(M + 1)\eta$ can be handled in the same fashion. Since the function $\Phi(t) = \log(t)$ has the derivatives

$$\Phi^{(j)}(t) = (-1)^{j-1}(j-1)! t^{-j}, \qquad j = 1, 2, \ldots$$

we see that our approximate kernel becomes

$$K_r(x, y) = \log(x) + \sum_{j=1}^r \frac{(-1)^j \Phi^{(j)}(x)}{j!} y^j = \log(x) - \sum_{j=1}^r \frac{1}{j} x^{-j} y^j$$

and, as $x - \xi \geq M\eta$ and $|y| \leq \eta$, the remainder can be bounded by

$$|R_r(x, y)| = \left| \frac{\Phi^{(r+1)}(\xi)}{(r+1)!} y^{r+1} \right| = \frac{1}{r+1} \left| \frac{y}{x - \xi} \right|^{r+1} \leq \frac{1}{r+1} M^{-r-1}.$$

The situation becomes more elaborate in higher space dimensions. For example, in the situation of our interpolation example from Section 1.1.1, we need to compute the derivatives of a radial function, $\Phi(\mathbf{x}) = \phi(\|\mathbf{x}\|_2)$. We will give only one example here. In the case of an inverse multiquadric, i.e. $\phi(t) = (t^2 + c^2)^{-1/2}$

with $c > 0$ we can rewrite the kernel using $\psi(t) = \phi(\sqrt{t}) = (t + c^2)^{-1/2}$. This allows us to derive the following result.

Proposition 7.21   *Let* $\Phi(\mathbf{x}) = (\|\mathbf{x}\|_2^2 + c^2)^{-1/2}$, $\mathbf{x} \in \mathbb{R}^d$. *Then,* $K(\mathbf{x}, \mathbf{y}) := \Phi(\mathbf{x} - \mathbf{y})$ *has a Taylor expansion for* $\mathbf{y}$ *about* $\mathbf{0}$ *of the form*

$$K(\mathbf{x}, \mathbf{y}) = \sum_{|\alpha| \leq r} \tilde{p}_\alpha(\mathbf{x})(\|\mathbf{x}\|_2^2 + c^2)^{-|\alpha| - 1/2} \mathbf{y}^\alpha + R_r(\mathbf{x}, \mathbf{y}),$$

where $\tilde{p}_\alpha$ *is a d-variate polynomial of total degree at most* $|\alpha|$ *and where the remainder is given by*

$$R_r(\mathbf{x}, \mathbf{y}) = \sum_{|\alpha| = r+1} \tilde{p}_\alpha(\mathbf{x} - \boldsymbol{\xi})(\|\mathbf{x} - \boldsymbol{\xi}\|_2^2 + c^2)^{-r - 3/2} \mathbf{y}^\alpha,$$

with $\boldsymbol{\xi}$ *on the line between* $\mathbf{0}$ *and* $\mathbf{y}$.

Proof Let $\psi(t) = (t + c^2)^{-1/2}$. Then it is easy to see by induction that the derivatives of ψ are for $\ell \geq 1$ given by

$$\psi^{(\ell)}(t) = (-1)^\ell 2^{-\ell}(2\ell - 1)(2\ell - 3) \cdots 1(t + c^2)^{-\ell - 1/2} =: c_\ell(t + c^2)^{-\ell - 1/2}.$$

The latter expression holds obviously also for $\ell = 0$ if we define $c_0 = 1$. From this, we can conclude that

$$\psi^{(\ell)}(t) = \frac{c_\ell}{c_{\ell+1}}(t + c^2)\psi^{(\ell+1)}(t).$$

With this, we will prove by induction that the derivatives of Φ can be written as

$$D^\alpha \Phi(\mathbf{x}) = p_\alpha(\mathbf{x})\psi^{(|\alpha|)}(\|\mathbf{x}\|_2^2) \tag{7.10}$$

with a d-variate polynomial p_α of degree at most $|\alpha|$. This is obviously true for $\alpha = \mathbf{0}$. For the induction step $|\alpha| \to |\alpha| + 1$ let $\beta = \alpha + \mathbf{e}_j$. Then,

$$
\begin{aligned}
D^\beta \Phi(\mathbf{x}) &= \frac{\partial}{\partial x_j} D^\alpha \Phi(\mathbf{x}) = \frac{\partial}{\partial x_j}\left[p_\alpha(\mathbf{x})\psi^{(|\alpha|)}(\|\mathbf{x}\|_2^2)\right] \\
&= \frac{\partial p_\alpha(\mathbf{x})}{\partial x_j}\psi^{(|\alpha|)}(\|\mathbf{x}\|_2^2) + p_\alpha(\mathbf{x})2x_j\psi^{(|\alpha|+1)}(\|\mathbf{x}\|_2^2) \\
&= \left[\frac{\partial p_\alpha(\mathbf{x})}{\partial x_j}\frac{c_{|\alpha|}}{c_{|\alpha|+1}}(\|\mathbf{x}\|_2^2 + c^2) + 2x_j p_\alpha(\mathbf{x})\right]\psi^{(|\alpha|+1)}(\|\mathbf{x}\|_2^2) \\
&=: p_\beta(\mathbf{x})\psi^{(|\beta|)}(\|\mathbf{x}\|_2^2),
\end{aligned}
$$

where the new polynomial p_β indeed has at most the degree $|\beta| = |\alpha| + 1$. From this, it follows that

$$K_r(\mathbf{x}, \mathbf{y}) = \sum_{|\alpha| \le r} \frac{-1^{|\alpha|} D^\alpha \Phi(\mathbf{x})}{\alpha!} \mathbf{y}^\alpha = \sum_{|\alpha| \le r} \frac{(-1)^{|\alpha|} p_\alpha(\mathbf{x})}{\alpha!} \psi^{(|\alpha|)}(\|\mathbf{x}\|_2^2) \mathbf{y}^\alpha$$

$$=: \sum_{|\alpha| \le r} \tilde{p}_\alpha(\mathbf{x})(\|\mathbf{x}\|_2^2 + c^2)^{-|\alpha|-1/2} \mathbf{y}^\alpha,$$

and the representation of the remainder follows in the same way. □

The above proof even gives a recursion formula to compute the polynomials p_α. The given representation is indeed a far-field expansion for the inverse multiquadrics. As (7.10) implies,

$$|D^\alpha \Phi(\mathbf{z})| \le |p_\alpha(\mathbf{z})| c_{|\alpha|} (\|\mathbf{z}\|_2^2 + c^2)^{-|\alpha|-1/2} \le C\|\mathbf{z}\|_\infty^{|\alpha|} \|\mathbf{z}\|_\infty^{-2|\alpha|-1} = C\|\mathbf{z}\|_\infty^{-|\alpha|-1}$$

so that Φ satisfies the conditions of Proposition 7.19 with $\mu = -1$.

A second method for determining an approximation to the kernel K is based upon the fact that such kernels often have a natural series expansion. In particular, in the case of a translation-invariant and radial kernel $K(\mathbf{x}, \mathbf{y}) = \Phi(\mathbf{x} - \mathbf{y}) = \phi(\|\mathbf{x} - \mathbf{y}\|_2)$, such a natural series expansion can come from the fact that Φ or ϕ is the generating function of a series of orthogonal polynomials. Again, we will not discuss this in general but restrict ourselves to one important albeit simple example, which gives the foundations of the *Fast Gauss Transform*.

As mentioned in Section 1.1.1, another popular basis function is the Gaussian $\phi(r) = e^{-\alpha r^2}$ with $\alpha > 0$. For simplicity, we set $\alpha = 1$ for the time being since other values for α can be dealt with by scaling. We also restrict ourselves once again to the univariate setting.

The approximation of $K(x, y) = \exp(-(x - y)^2)$ we want to describe now is based on the generating function of the *Hermite polynomials*.

Definition 7.22 The *Hermite polynomials* H_n are defined by

$$H_n(t) := (-1)^n e^{t^2} \frac{d^n}{dt^n} e^{-t^2}.$$

The *Hermite functions* h_n are defined by $h_n(t) := e^{-t^2} H_n(t)$.

The *generating function* of the Hermite polynomials is given by

$$e^{2ts - s^2} = \sum_{n=0}^{\infty} \frac{s^n}{n!} H_n(t), \qquad s, t \in \mathbb{R}. \tag{7.11}$$

Moreover, for every $n \in \mathbb{N}_0$ and every $t \in \mathbb{R}$ the Hermite polynomials can be bounded by

$$|H_n(t)| \le 2^{n/2} \sqrt{n!} e^{t^2}. \tag{7.12}$$

The identity in (7.11) can easily be verified by considering the left-hand side as a function of the variable s and computing its Taylor expansion. The estimate (7.12) is essentially *Cramér's inequality* for Hermite polynomials. A short yet elaborate proof can be found, for example, in Wendland [133].

From (7.11) we see that we have a kernel expansion of the form

$$K(x,y) = e^{-(x-y)^2} = e^{-x^2+2xy-y^2} = e^{-x^2} \sum_{n=0}^{\infty} \frac{y^n}{n!} H_n(x) = \sum_{n=0}^{\infty} \frac{y^n}{n!} h_n(x). \quad (7.13)$$

Obviously, an approximation to K is given by K_r using only the first $r+1$ terms in the sum on the right-hand side. With Cramér's inequality (7.12) we can derive the following error estimate.

Proposition 7.23 *Let $K(x,y) = e^{-(x-y)^2}$ and let, for $r \geq 1$,*

$$K_r(x,y) = \sum_{n=0}^{r} \frac{y^n}{n!} h_n(x).$$

Then, for all $y \in \mathbb{R}$ with $\sqrt{2}|y| \leq \eta < 1$, the error between K and K_r can be bounded by

$$|K(x,y) - K_r(x,y)| \leq \frac{1}{\sqrt{(r+1)!}} \frac{\eta^{r+1}}{1-\eta}.$$

Proof Employing (7.13) and (7.12) yields

$$|K(x,y) - K_r(x,y)| = \left| \sum_{n=r+1}^{\infty} \frac{y^n}{n!} h_n(x) \right| \leq \sum_{n=r+1}^{\infty} \frac{|y|^n}{n!} 2^{n/2} \sqrt{n!}$$

$$\leq \sum_{n=r+1}^{\infty} \frac{\eta^n}{\sqrt{n!}} \leq \frac{1}{\sqrt{(r+1)!}} \frac{\eta^{r+1}}{1-\eta}. \qquad \square$$

We want to end this discussion of deriving a far-field expansion with a completely different approach, which uses only the kernel itself and the data sets X and Y from two different panels.

Definition 7.24 Let X and Y be two discrete point sets. Then, the *adaptive cross approximation (ACA)* of the kernel K is recursively defined as follows. We set $K_0(\mathbf{x}, \mathbf{y}) := 0$ and $R_0(\mathbf{x}, \mathbf{y}) = K(\mathbf{x}, \mathbf{y})$ and then, for $k = 1, 2, \ldots$,

- choose $\mathbf{x}_{i_k} \in X$ and $\mathbf{y}_{j_k} \in Y$ with $R_{k-1}(\mathbf{x}_{i_k}, \mathbf{y}_{j_k}) \neq 0$,

• define

$$R_k(\mathbf{x}, \mathbf{y}) = R_{k-1}(\mathbf{x}, \mathbf{y}) - \frac{R_{k-1}(\mathbf{x}, \mathbf{y}_{j_k}) R_{k-1}(\mathbf{x}_{i_k}, \mathbf{y})}{R_{k-1}(\mathbf{x}_{i_k}, \mathbf{y}_{j_k})},$$

$$K_k(\mathbf{x}, \mathbf{y}) = K_{k-1}(\mathbf{x}, \mathbf{y}) + \frac{R_{k-1}(\mathbf{x}, \mathbf{y}_{j_k}) R_{k-1}(\mathbf{x}_{i_k}, \mathbf{y})}{R_{k-1}(\mathbf{x}_{i_k}, \mathbf{y}_{j_k})}.$$

Later, we will discuss additional conditions, besides $R_{k-1}(\mathbf{x}_{i_k}, \mathbf{y}_{j_k}) \neq 0$, on how to choose the points. But even for this general situation, we can make some simple observations.

Lemma 7.25 *Assume that we can perform r steps of the adaptive cross approximation. Then we have for $0 \le k \le r$ that*

$$K(\mathbf{x}, \mathbf{y}) = K_k(\mathbf{x}, \mathbf{y}) + R_k(\mathbf{x}, \mathbf{y}). \tag{7.14}$$

Moreover, R_r satisfies

$$R_r(\mathbf{x}, \mathbf{y}_{j_k}) = R_r(\mathbf{x}_{i_k}, \mathbf{y}) = 0, \qquad 1 \le k \le r, \tag{7.15}$$

for all $\mathbf{x}$ and $\mathbf{y}$.

Proof The equality in (7.14) follows from the obvious equality $K_k(\mathbf{x}, \mathbf{y}) + R_k(\mathbf{x}, \mathbf{y}) = K_{k-1}(\mathbf{x}, \mathbf{y}) + R_{k-1}(\mathbf{x}, \mathbf{y})$ and $K_0(\mathbf{x}, \mathbf{y}) = 0$, $R_0(\mathbf{x}, \mathbf{y}) = K(\mathbf{x}, \mathbf{y})$.

The second statement (7.15) follows by induction. We will restrict ourselves to showing $R_r(\mathbf{x}, \mathbf{y}_{j_k}) = 0$ for $1 \le k \le r$ and all $\mathbf{x}$ as $R_r(\mathbf{x}_{i_k}, \mathbf{y}) = 0$ is proven in exactly the same way. For each $1 \le k \le r$ we obviously have

$$R_k(\mathbf{x}, \mathbf{y}_{j_k}) = R_{k-1}(\mathbf{x}, \mathbf{y}_{j_k}) - \frac{R_{k-1}(\mathbf{x}, \mathbf{y}_{j_k}) R_{k-1}(\mathbf{x}_{i_k}, \mathbf{y}_{j_k})}{R_{k-1}(\mathbf{x}_{i_k}, \mathbf{y}_{j_k})} = 0,$$

which particularly proves the statement for $r = 1$. Moreover, for the induction step $r - 1 \to r$ it means that we only need to show $R_r(\mathbf{x}, \mathbf{y}_{j_k}) = 0$ for $1 \le k \le r - 1$. This, however, directly follows from

$$R_r(\mathbf{x}, \mathbf{y}_{j_k}) = R_{r-1}(\mathbf{x}, \mathbf{y}_{j_k}) - \frac{R_{r-1}(\mathbf{x}, \mathbf{y}_{j_r}) R_{r-1}(\mathbf{x}_{i_r}, \mathbf{y}_{j_k})}{R_{r-1}(\mathbf{x}_{i_r}, \mathbf{y}_{j_r})}$$

since both $R_{r-1}(\mathbf{x}, \mathbf{y}_{j_k})$ and $R_{r-1}(\mathbf{x}_{i_r}, \mathbf{y}_{j_k})$ vanish by virtue of the induction assumption. □

Both (7.14) and (7.15) show that $K_r(\mathbf{x}, \mathbf{y}_{j_k}) = K(\mathbf{x}, \mathbf{y}_{j_k})$ for $1 \le k \le r$, i.e. $K_r(\mathbf{x}, \cdot)$ interpolates $K(\mathbf{x}, \cdot)$ in $\mathbf{y}_{j_1}, \ldots, \mathbf{y}_{j_r}$. This can be used to bound the error R_r between K and K_r.

It remains to answer the question on how to choose the data sites $\mathbf{x}_{i_k}$ and $\mathbf{y}_{j_k}$. The following result shows that a particular choice of $\mathbf{x}_{i_k}$ leads to a desired far-field expansion.

Theorem 7.26   *Let $K(\mathbf{x}, \mathbf{y}) = \Phi(\mathbf{x} - \mathbf{y})$ with $\Phi \in C^{r+1}(\mathbb{R}^d \setminus \{0\})$ satisfying the decay condition (7.9) with $\mu \leq r + 1$. Assume that the evaluation points X are contained in $[-\eta, \eta]^d$ with $\eta > 0$ and that the source points $\mathbf{y} \in Y$ satisfy $\|\mathbf{y}\|_\infty \geq (M + 1)\eta$ with $M \geq 1$. Let $n_r \in \mathbb{N}$ denote the dimension of $\pi_r(\mathbb{R}^d)$, the space of d-variate polynomials of total degree at most r. Assume that $\mathbf{x}_{i_k} \in X$, $1 \leq k \leq n_r$, is chosen such that the only polynomial from $\pi_r(\mathbb{R}^d)$ vanishing on all $\mathbf{x}_{i_1}, \ldots, \mathbf{x}_{i_{n_r}}$ is the zero polynomial. Assume, finally, that $\mathbf{y}_{j_k} \in Y$ is chosen such that*

$$|R_{k-1}(\mathbf{x}_{i_k}, \mathbf{y}_{j_k})| \geq |R_{k-1}(\mathbf{x}_{i_k}, \mathbf{y}_j)|, \qquad \mathbf{y}_j \in Y, \qquad (7.16)$$

holds for all k. Then, there is a constant $C > 0$ depending on $\mathbf{x}_1, \ldots, \mathbf{x}_{n_r}$ such that the remainder can be bounded by

$$|R_{n_r}(\mathbf{x}, \mathbf{y})| \leq C\eta^\mu M^{-r-1}, \qquad \mathbf{x} \in X, \quad \mathbf{y} \in Y.$$

We will delay the proof of this theorem until later, when we discuss a more general approach. Then, we will present this result again as Corollary 7.49, where it appears as a simple consequence of the more general theory.

Note that, in contrast to our previous results on far-field expansions, we have exchanged the assumptions on the source and evaluation points. This is, of course, irrelevant for our purposes and has been done only due to the later discussion that includes the proof of this theorem.

7.2 Hierarchical Matrices

In the last section we have seen that for specifically defined, dense matrices $A \in \mathbb{R}^{n \times n}$ and vectors $\alpha \in \mathbb{R}^n$, it is possible to compute an approximation to $A\alpha$ in $O(n \log n)$ time and space. However, the method described in the last section used a data structure which stored information on the matrix and the vector together. This was motivated by the fact that we were more interested in actually evaluating a sum of the form (7.1) maybe even in more than n points. Consequently, if we want to apply these ideas to solving a linear system $Ax = b$ in an iterative way, we have to rebuild the data structure for each new iteration. This is not as bad as it sounds since also building the data structure can be done in $O(n \log n)$ time.

It is, however, obvious that we can use the ideas of the last section to build a data structure which contains only the information on A. In the context of the last section, on looking particularly at Lemma 7.1 and Example 7.2, the only change we have to apply is storing the far-field information $\phi_j(\mathbf{x}_i)$ and $\psi_j(\mathbf{x}_i)$ in our tree rather than the coefficients α_j and β_j. This yields a hierarchical block approximation of the original matrix where the blocks are of the form BC^{T} of rank r.

In this section we want to formalise these ideas and carry them over to more general matrices. As we now do not want to rely on spatial information to derive our partitioning and our tree data structure, we start by partitioning our index sets.

Definition 7.27 A *partitioning* $P(\mathcal{J})$ of the index set $\mathcal{J} = \{1, \ldots, n\}$ is the subdivision of $\mathcal{J}$ into $p \leq n$ disjoint index sets $J_1, \ldots, J_p$ of cardinality $n_j = |J_j|$, $1 \leq j \leq p$.

This means that we have $n = n_1 + \cdots + n_p$ and that the elements J_j of the partitioning $P(\mathcal{J}) = \{J_1, \ldots, J_p\}$ satisfy

$$J_i \cap J_j = \emptyset, \quad i \neq j, \quad \text{and} \quad \bigcup_{j=1}^{p} J_j = \mathcal{J}. \tag{7.17}$$

If necessary, we can always use a permutation of the indices such that the J_j are connected, i.e., if we set $\bar{n}_0 := 0$ and $\bar{n}_j = \sum_{k=1}^{j} n_j$ then they are simply given by

$$J_j = \{1 + \bar{n}_{j-1}, \ldots, \bar{n}_j\}. \tag{7.18}$$

Having two partitionings $P_1(\mathcal{I})$ and $P_2(\mathcal{J})$ of the index sets $\mathcal{I} = \{1, \ldots, m\}$ and $\mathcal{J} = \{1, \ldots, n\}$, we can define a partitioning of $\mathcal{I} \times \mathcal{J}$ using tensor products.

Definition 7.28 The *tensor product partitioning* of the index set $\mathcal{I} \times \mathcal{J}$ induced by the partitionings $P_1(\mathcal{I})$ and $P_2(\mathcal{J})$ is defined to be

$$P(\mathcal{I} \times \mathcal{J}) := P_1(\mathcal{I}) \times P_2(\mathcal{I}) = \{I \times J : I \in P_1(\mathcal{I}), J \in P_2(\mathcal{J})\}.$$

Given a matrix $A \in \mathbb{R}^{m \times n}$, each element $I \times J \in P(\mathcal{I} \times \mathcal{J})$ defines a *block matrix* $A_{I,J} \in \mathbb{R}^{|I| \times |J|}$ which contains those elements a_{ij} of A with indices $i \in I$ and $j \in J$.

If we have $m = n$ and $\mathcal{I} = \mathcal{J}$ we can use the same partitioning $P(\mathcal{J}) = \{J_1, \ldots, J_p\}$ to define the tensor product partitioning

$$\mathcal{P}(\mathcal{J} \times \mathcal{J}) = \{J_i \times J_j : 1 \leq i, j \leq p\}.$$

In the situation of (7.18) the entries of the block matrix $A_{J_i,J_j} = (a_{\ell k}^{(J_i,J_j)}) \in \mathbb{R}^{n_i \times n_j}$ can then be written as

$$a_{\ell,k}^{(J_i,J_j)} = a_{\bar{n}_{i-1}+\ell, \bar{n}_{j-1}+k}, \quad 1 \leq \ell \leq n_i, 1 \leq k \leq n_j.$$

Example 7.29 The partitioning $P(\mathcal{J})$ of $\mathcal{J} = \{1, \ldots, 20\}$ given by the sets $\{1, 2, 3\}, \{4, 5\}, \{6\}, \{7, 8\}, \{9, 10, 11, 12\}, \{13, 14\}, \{15\}, \{16, 17, 18\}$ and $\{19, 20\}$ induces the partitioning $P(\mathcal{J} \times \mathcal{J})$ of $\mathcal{J} \times \mathcal{J}$ and hence of A visualised in Figure 7.6. The grey shaded boxes correspond to the diagonal blocks $J_i \times J_i$.

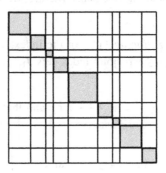

Figure 7.6 Example of a tensor product partitioning of the index set $\mathcal{I} \times \mathcal{I}$ with $\mathcal{I} = \{1, \ldots, 20\}$.

It is our goal to replace some of the matrix blocks by low-rank matrices. However, as the discussion in the last section has indicated, we have to expect to keep the diagonal blocks as they are. The following result shows that even in the ideal situation of approximating each off-diagonal block by a rank-one matrix this method is sub-optimal regarding the computational and memory cost.

Lemma 7.30 *Let $P(\mathcal{J}) = \{J_1, \ldots, J_p\}$ be a partitioning of $\mathcal{J} = \{1, \ldots, n\}$. Let $A \in \mathbb{R}^{n \times n}$ be partitioned according to the tensor product partitioning $P(\mathcal{J} \times \mathcal{J})$. Let each diagonal block A_{J_i, J_i} be stored as a full block and each off-diagonal block A_{J_i, J_j}, $i \neq j$, as a rank-one matrix. Then, the total memory requirement and the time required for computing one matrix–vector product is at least $O(n^{3/2})$.*

Proof Let us start with analysing the cost of computing the matrix–vector product $A\mathbf{x}$ with $\mathbf{x} \in \mathbb{R}^n$. If we partition the vectors $\mathbf{x}$ and $A\mathbf{x}$ using the partition $P(\mathcal{J})$ then we can compute

$$(A\mathbf{x})_{J_i} = A_{J_i, J_i}\mathbf{x}_{J_i} + \sum_{\substack{j=1 \\ j \neq i}}^{p} A_{J_i, J_j}\mathbf{x}_{J_j}, \qquad 1 \leq i \leq p.$$

The computation of $A_{J_i, J_i}\mathbf{x}_{J_i}$ costs $O(n_i^2)$ time. For $j \neq i$ we can express A_{J_i, J_j} as $A_{J_i, J_j} = \mathbf{a}^{(i)}\mathbf{b}^{(j)\mathrm{T}}$ with $\mathbf{a}^{(i)} \in \mathbb{R}^{n_i}$ and $\mathbf{b}^{(j)} \in \mathbb{R}^{n_j}$. Thus, the computation of

$A_{J_i,J_j}x_{J_j}$ costs $O(n_i + n_j)$ time and hence the computation of $(Ax)_{J_i}$ costs a constant multiple of

$$n_i^2 + \sum_{\substack{j=1 \\ j \neq i}}^{p}(n_j + n_i) = n_i^2 + (n - n_i) + (p-1)n_i = n_i^2 + n + (p-2)n_i. \quad (7.19)$$

Using (2.2), or simply the Cauchy–Schwarz inequality, yields

$$n = \sum_{j=1}^{p} n_j \leq \sqrt{p} \left(\sum_{j=1}^{p} n_j^2 \right)^{1/2}.$$

Hence, summing over all sets J_i shows that the cost for computing Ax is given by

$$\sum_{i=1}^{p} \left[n_i^2 + n + (p-2)n_i \right] = \sum_{i=1}^{n} n_i^2 + pn + (p-2)n \geq \frac{1}{p}n^2 + 2(p-1)n.$$

The latter expression becomes minimal for $p = \sqrt{n/2}$, which then leads to a lower bound of size $O(n^{3/2})$. We can argue similarly for the memory requirement. Storing each diagonal block costs $O(n_i^2)$, while storing an off-diagonal block costs $O(n_i + n_j)$, i.e. the total memory requirement is again a constant multiple of (7.19) and hence at least of size $O(n^{3/2})$. ☐

As we learnt in the last section, the remedy to these problems is to use a hierarchical decomposition of the set $\mathcal{J} = \{1, \ldots, n\}$ and hence of $\mathcal{I} \times \mathcal{J}$ and hence of A. We will start by discussing hierarchical partitionings of $\mathcal{J}$.

We saw in the last section that a uniform or balanced hierarchical decomposition, which in this context would mean that we have a partitioning of the index set $\mathcal{J}$ on each level, might not be flexible enough. Hence, we allow some non-uniformity in the definition as follows.

Definition 7.31 Let $\mathcal{J} = \{1, \ldots, n\}$. A *hierarchical partitioning* $\mathcal{P}_L(\mathcal{J})$ of $\mathcal{J}$ of depth L is a family $P_\ell(\mathcal{I}) = \{J_1^{(\ell)}, \ldots, J_{p_\ell}^{(\ell)}\}$, $0 \leq \ell \leq L$, with the following properties

1. The partitioning on level $\ell = 0$ is simply $P_0(\mathcal{J}) = \{\mathcal{J}\}$.
2. For $1 \leq \ell \leq L$ we have the following.
   - Each $J^{(\ell-1)} \in P_{\ell-1}(\mathcal{J})$ is the disjoint union of at least two sets $J^{(\ell)} \in P_\ell(\mathcal{J})$ or is disjoint with each set $J^{(\ell)}$.
   - Each $J^{(\ell)}$ is contained in exactly one $J^{(\ell-1)}$.
3. There is at least one non-empty set $J^{(L)}$ of level L.

As mentioned above, we do not require a partitioning of the whole set $\mathcal{J}$ on each level. This means that some of the sets of a given level ℓ may not be further refined on the next levels. Nonetheless, the definition ensures that the union of all the sets which are not further refined is disjoint and amounts to all of $\mathcal{J}$. This can also be described by looking at the trees that can be used to represent a hierarchical partitioning. It simply means that we might not have all the leaves at the same level, but the information stored at the leaves is disjoint and its union is all of $\mathcal{J}$. The tree associated with such a hierarchical partitioning is called a cluster tree. A cluster tree is an ordinary tree, see Definition 7.11, where the items of information stored in each node and leaf are subsets of $\mathcal{J}$ satisfying additional conditions.

Definition 7.32 Let $\mathcal{J} = \{1, \ldots, n\}$. A tree T is called a *cluster tree* of the set $\mathcal{J}$ if the nodes and leaves of T contain subsets of $\mathcal{J}$ as information such that the following holds.

- The root of the tree contains $\mathcal{J}$ as information.
- Each node has at least two children.
- Let $C(t)$ denote the children of the node t. Then the information stored at t is the disjoint union of the information stored at its children $s \in C(t)$.

The depth of a cluster tree obviously coincides with the depth of the associated hierarchical partitioning. The information stored at the leaves of a cluster tree forms a disjoint partitioning of the index set.

Example 7.33 Let $\mathcal{I} = I_1^{(0)} = \{1, 2, \ldots, 8\}$. Then, a recursive bisection of this set leads to a hierarchical partitioning $\mathcal{P}_2(\mathcal{I})$ consisting of two sets, $I_1^{(1)} = \{1, 2, \ldots, 4\}$ and $I_2^{(1)} = \{5, \ldots, 8\}$, on level 1 and of four sets, $I_1^{(2)} = \{1, 2\}$, $I_2^{(2)} = \{3, 4\}$, $I_3^{(2)} = \{5, 6\}$ and $I_4^{(2)} = \{7, 8\}$, on level 2. The corresponding cluster tree is depicted twice in Figure 7.7.

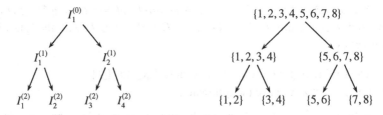

Figure 7.7 Cluster tree for Example 7.33.

The cluster tree in Figure 7.7 corresponds to a balanced partitioning where all the leaves are on the same level. However, as pointed out above, this is not necessary. Another way of looking at this is by taking the point of view of refinement or subdivision. We start with the the set $\mathcal{J} = \{1,\ldots,n\}$ on level 0. For level 1 we subdivide the set $\mathcal{J}$ into disjoint subsets. For level 2 we decide which of the level-1 subsets need further refinement and these subsets are subdivided disjointly to form subsets on level 2. Those subsets on level 1 which do not need to be subdivided will not have representatives on level 2. In this way, we proceed to level 3. This means, in particular, that we can represent a block hierarchical partitioning of level L by a tree of depth L where not all leaves are on the same level. This is in contrast to a balanced hierarchical subdivision, where all leaves are on level L. An example for this is shown in Figure 7.8.

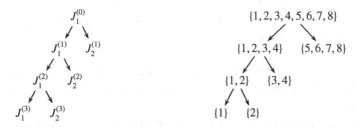

Figure 7.8 A non-balanced refined cluster tree.

Having hierarchical partitionings $\mathcal{P}_K(\mathcal{I}) = \{P_k(\mathcal{I}) : 0 \le k \le K\}$ and $\mathcal{P}_L(\mathcal{J}) = \{P_\ell(\mathcal{J}) : 0 \le \ell \le L\}$ of a set $\mathcal{I}$ and a set $\mathcal{J}$, respectively, we can introduce a partitioning for the set $\mathcal{I} \times \mathcal{J}$ as the tensor product of the hierarchical partitionings of $\mathcal{I}$ and $\mathcal{J}$, i.e.

$$\mathcal{P}(\mathcal{I} \times \mathcal{J}) := \{I \times J : I \in P_\ell(\mathcal{I}), J \in P_\ell(\mathcal{J}), 0 \le \ell \le \min\{L, K\}\}. \qquad (7.20)$$

Note that we only form tensor products of sets on the same level, though we could also allow tensor products of different levels. Consequently, in this set-up we will not use all the sets of the partitioning with the larger depth. This means, of course, that the depth of the partitioning $\mathcal{P}(\mathcal{I} \times \mathcal{J})$ is the minimum of the depths of $\mathcal{P}_K(\mathcal{I})$ and $\mathcal{P}_L(\mathcal{J})$.

The partitioning (7.20) can again be represented by a tree $T_{\mathcal{I} \times \mathcal{J}}$. If we identify the nodes and leaves with the information stored at them, then this tree has $\mathcal{I} \times \mathcal{J}$ as its root and for each $0 \le \ell \le \min(L, K)$ and each $I \in P_\ell(\mathcal{I})$ and each $J \in P_\ell(\mathcal{J})$ we define $I \times J$ as a leaf if either of I or J is a leaf in their cluster tree. Otherwise, $I \times J$ is declared a node and the children $C(I \times J)$ of $I \times J$ are defined as

$$\{I' \times J' : I' \in C(I), J' \in C(J)\}.$$

If $I \times J$ is a node the procedure is repeated for all its children.

If we use the cluster trees of Figure 7.7 and Figure 7.8 as cluster trees T_I and $T_{\mathcal{J}}$ with $\mathcal{I} = \mathcal{J} = \{1, \ldots, 8\}$ then the resulting tree $T_{I \times \mathcal{J}}$ is depicted in Figure 7.9.

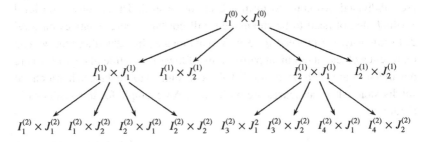

Figure 7.9 The tree $T_{I \times \mathcal{J}}$ defined by the cluster trees T_I and $T_{\mathcal{J}}$ from Figures 7.7 and 7.8, respectively.

As was the case for a cluster tree, also the leaves of $T_{I \times \mathcal{J}}$ form a regular partitioning of the index set $\mathcal{I} \times \mathcal{J}$, i.e. they are mutually disjoint and their union is all of $\mathcal{I} \times \mathcal{J}$.

In the situation that $I \in P_\ell(\mathcal{I})$ is not further refined, i.e. it is represented by a leaf in T_I, but $J \in P_\ell(\mathcal{J})$ is further refined, we declare $I \times J$ nonetheless a leaf in $T_{I \times \mathcal{J}}$. Alternatively, though we will not pursue this here, we could also declare it a node with children $I \times J'$, where J' is one of the children of J.

So far, the tree $T_{I \times \mathcal{J}}$ is entirely determined by the cluster trees of the index sets $\mathcal{I}$ and $\mathcal{J}$. In practice, it will be helpful to consider one final modification. So far, a leaf of the tree $T_{I \times \mathcal{J}}$ can only be generated by a leaf of either of the cluster trees. However, it will be useful to declare a node prematurely a leaf, either because the cardinality of the associated set is considered to be small enough or because another criterion is satisfied.

Even if we do this, the modified tree still has the property that the leaves form a disjoint partitioning of the index set $\mathcal{I} \times \mathcal{J}$.

Formally, we will achieve this with an admissible function.

Definition 7.34 Let $\mathcal{P}_K(\mathcal{I})$ and $\mathcal{P}_L(\mathcal{J})$ be hierarchical partitionings of the index sets $\mathcal{I}$ and $\mathcal{J}$, respectively. An *admissible function* for the hierarchical partitioning $\mathcal{P}(\mathcal{I} \times \mathcal{J})$ is a function

$$\text{adm} : \mathcal{P}(\mathcal{I} \times \mathcal{J}) \to \{\text{true}, \text{false}\}.$$

A set $I \times J \in \mathcal{P}(\mathcal{I} \times \mathcal{J})$ is called admissible if $\text{adm}(I \times J) = \text{true}$. A set $I \in \mathcal{P}_K(\mathcal{I})$ is called admissible with respect to $J \in \mathcal{P}_L(\mathcal{J})$ if $\text{adm}(I \times J) = \text{true}$.

We will soon give an example of a possible admissible function. However, having an abstract admissible function at hand, we can already define the *block cluster tree*.

Definition 7.35 Let T_I and T_J be cluster trees for the index sets I and J corresponding to hierarchical partitionings $\mathcal{P}_K(I)$ and $\mathcal{P}_L(J)$. Let $\mathcal{P}(I \times J)$ be the associated hierarchical partitioning of $I \times J$. Let adm : $\mathcal{P}(I \times J) \to$ {true, false} be an admissible function. Then, the associated *block cluster tree* $T_{I \times J}$ is defined recursively as follows.

1. The root of $T_{I \times J}$ is $I \times J$.
2. The recursion starts with $I \times J$ for $I = I$ and $J = J$.

   a. If either I or J is a leaf in its cluster tree, then $I \times J$ is declared a leaf.
   b. If $I \times J$ is admissible then $I \times J$ is declared a leaf.
   c. Otherwise, $I \times J$ is declared a node and the children $C(I \times J)$ of $I \times J$ are defined as

   $$\{I' \times J' : I' \in C(I), J' \in C(J)\}.$$

   d. If $I \times J$ is a node the procedure is repeated for all its children.

The recursive definition of the block cluster tree immediately leads to a possible implementation, see Algorithm 38.

Algorithm 38: BuildBlockClusterTree

Input : Index sets $I \subseteq I$ and $J \subseteq J$.
Output: Block cluster Tree $T_{I \times J}$.

1 **if** *I or J represent leaves* **then**
2   Create leaf for $I \times J$
3 **else**
4   **if** *I × J is admissible* **then**
5   Create leaf for $I \times J$
6   **else**
7   Create node for $I \times J$
8   **for** *I' child of I and J' child of J* **do**
9   Declare $I' \times J'$ a child
10   BuildBlockClusterTree(I',J')

Example 7.36 We look again at Example 7.33 of a recursive bisection of our index set. However, this time we do it more generally and let $I = \{1, \ldots, 2^L\}$.

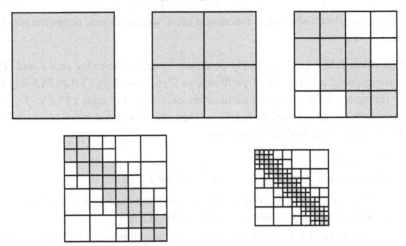

Figure 7.10 The block structure of the block cluster tree from Example 7.36 for $\ell = 0, 1, \ldots, 4$.

Hence, for $0 \leq \ell \leq L$, each set $I \in P_\ell(\mathcal{I})$ contains $2^{L-\ell}$ indices and there are exactly 2^ℓ such sets. Following the discussion of the last section, we define an admissible function on $\mathcal{P}(\mathcal{I} \times \mathcal{I})$ as follows. If $I, J \in P_\ell(\mathcal{I})$ are two index sets on the same level, then we will call them admissible if they are *well-separated*, i.e. if they have a distance which is at least their cardinality. This means that we have the admissible function

$$\text{adm}(I \times J) = \begin{cases} \text{true} & \text{if } \text{dist}(I, J) \geq 2^{L-\ell} = |I| = |J|, \quad I, J \in P_\ell(\mathcal{I}), \\ \text{false} & \text{else.} \end{cases} \tag{7.21}$$

Figure 7.10 depicts the admissible (white) and non-admissible (grey) sets of $\mathcal{P}(\mathcal{I} \times \mathcal{I})$ for $L = 4$ and the levels $\ell = 0, 1, 2, 3, 4$. Obviously, on level 0 and level 1 the index sets are not well-separated. On level 2, the index set $\{1, 2, 3, 4\}$ is well-separated from the sets $\{9, 10, 11, 12\}$ and $\{13, 14, 15, 16\}$ and the index set $\{5, 6, 7, 8\}$ is well-separated from $\{13, 14, 15, 16\}$, which gives the upper right picture in Figure 7.10. On level 3, the index set $\{1, 2\}$ is well-separated from the index sets $\{5, 6\}$ and $\{7, 8\}$ and so on, yielding the lower left picture in Figure 7.10.

The block cluster tree of the above example is a quad-tree, where the first leaves appear on level 2. The following example is similar but the first leaves of the block cluster tree already appear on level 1.

Example 7.37   Again, we consider $\mathcal{I} = \{1, \ldots, 2^L\}$ and we let $\mathcal{P}_L(\mathcal{I})$ be the hierarchical partitioning of the last example. Hence, each set of level ℓ is partitioned into two equally sized sets of level $\ell + 1$:

$$I_i^{(\ell)} = I_{2i-1}^{(\ell+1)} \cup I_{2i}^{(\ell+1)}, \qquad 1 \leq i \leq 2^\ell, \quad 0 \leq \ell \leq L - 1.$$

This time, however, on level $\ell + 1$, the sets $I_{2i-1}^{(\ell+1)}$ and $I_{2i}^{(\ell+1)}$ are considered to be admissible to each other while all other combinations are not. For $L = 3$, the resulting block cluster tree is shown in Figure 7.12 and the associated block matrix is visualised in Figure 7.11 for $L = 3$ and $L = 4$.

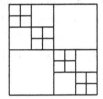
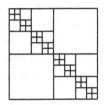

Figure 7.11 The block structure of the block cluster tree from Example 7.37.

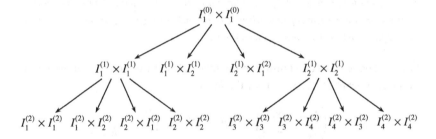

Figure 7.12 The block cluster tree from Example 7.37.

As mentioned above, the leaves of a block cluster tree represent a disjoint partitioning of the set $I \times J$. We can use this partitioning now to formally associate matrices with such a partitioning.

Definition 7.38 Let $T_{I \times J}$ be a block cluster tree for the index sets $I = \{1, \ldots, m\}$ and $J = \{1, \ldots, n\}$ based on the cluster trees T_I and T_J and an admissible function adm. A *hierarchical matrix* or $\mathcal{H}$-matrix of rank r with respect to this block cluster tree is a matrix $A \in \mathbb{R}^{m \times n}$ which satisfies

$$\text{rank}(A_{I,J}) \leq r$$

for all admissible leaves $I \times J$. Here, $A_{I,J}$ denotes the sub-matrix of A with rows and columns given by the index sets I and J, respectively. We will denote the set of all such $\mathcal{H}$-matrices by $\mathcal{H}(T_{I \times J}, r)$.

We only need to store matrix information for the leaves of an $\mathcal{H}$-matrix. If a leaf is not admissible, then we simply store the matrix block represented by the index set of this leaf in standard matrix form. If a leaf is admissible then we know from Corollary 1.20 that we can represent the matrix block for this leaf in the form BC^T with $B \in \mathbb{R}^{|I| \times r}$ and $C \in \mathbb{R}^{|J| \times r}$.

Note that the set $\mathcal{H}(T_{I \times J}, r)$ is not a linear space as the sum of two rank-r blocks might have a rank of up to $2r$.

The above examples show that the admissible function will have a crucial influence on estimating the space required to store an $\mathcal{H}$-matrix and the supporting data structure. Hence, a general estimate is obviously not possible. Here, we will give only one example, referring to the admissible function (7.21) from Example 7.36, but refer the reader to the books [77] by Hackbusch and [13] by Bebendorf for a more general discussion.

Lemma 7.39 *Let $I = \{1, \ldots, 2^L\}$ be recursively subdivided by bisection into equally sized subsets, such that $P_\ell(I)$, $0 \le \ell \le L$, consists of 2^ℓ subsets of size $2^{L-\ell}$. Let $T_{I \times I}$ be the associated block cluster tree with admissible function (7.21) and let $A \in \mathcal{H}(T_{I \times I}, r)$ be a hierarchical matrix. Then, the number of blocks required for representing A is bounded by $O(n)$ and the memory required for storing A is of size $O(rn \log n)$.*

Proof The recursive definition of the block cluster tree shows that the matrix structure at level $\ell = 2, 3, \ldots$ is of the form

$$A_\ell = \begin{pmatrix} A_{\ell-1} & N_{\ell-1} \\ N_{\ell-1}^T & A_{\ell-1} \end{pmatrix} \quad \text{with} \quad N_{\ell-1} = \begin{pmatrix} R_{\ell-2} & R_{\ell-2} \\ N_{\ell-2} & R_{\ell-2} \end{pmatrix}, \qquad (7.22)$$

where the R blocks represent leaves, which can be represented by rank-r matrices. Let a_ℓ be the number of "N blocks" generated at level ℓ. This number obviously satisfies the recursion $a_\ell = 3 + a_{\ell-1}$ which resolves to $a_\ell = 3\ell + a_0 = 3\ell + 1$. With this, we can determine the total number n_ℓ of blocks in the representation of A_ℓ as it satisfies the recursion

$$n_\ell = 2(n_{\ell-1} + a_{\ell-1}) = 2n_{\ell-1} + 2(3(\ell - 1) + 1) = 2n_{\ell-1} + 6\ell - 4$$

with initial condition $n_0 = 1$. This recursion resolves to

$$n_L = 9 \cdot 2^L - 6L - 8 = 9n - 6 \log_2(n) - 8,$$

which is easily verified by induction. To determine the required space, we use again recursion. Let $S_A(\ell)$ be the space required for storing the information of the A matrix on level ℓ. Similarly, let $S_N(\ell)$ and $S_R(\ell)$ be the space required for storing the information of the N and R matrices. Obviously, we have

$$S_A(\ell) = 2[S_A(\ell - 1) + S_N(\ell - 1)], \tag{7.23}$$

$$S_N(\ell) = 3S_R(\ell - 1) + S_N(\ell - 1). \tag{7.24}$$

As we can represent the sub-matrix associated with an R block on level ℓ by a matrix product of the form BC^T with $B, C \in \mathbb{R}^{2^\ell \times r}$, the memory requirement is given by

$$S_R(\ell) = 2r2^\ell = r2^{\ell+1}.$$

Inserting this into the recursion for S_N yields

$$S_N(L) = 3r2^L + S_N(L - 1) = 3r(2^L + 2^{L-1} + \cdots + 2^0) + S_N(0)$$
$$= 3r\frac{2^{L+1} - 1}{2 - 1} + 1 = 3r2^{L+1} = 6rn.$$

Inserting this into the recursion for S_A gives $S_A(\ell) = 2S_A(\ell - 1) + 6r2^\ell$ which resolves to

$$S_A(L) = 6rL2^L + 2^L = 6rn \log_2(n) + n,$$

which again is easily verified by induction. □

The main operation we are interested in is a matrix–vector product. For a matrix $A \in \mathcal{H}(T_{I \times I}, r)$ this can formally be done as described in Algorithm 39, which is started with initial data $I = \mathcal{I}$ and $J = \mathcal{J}$ and uses the block matrix and vector notation introduced before.

The realisation of this algorithm obviously has to take into account the different matrix structure of the block matrices stored in the leaves. If this is done properly, we can estimate the computation cost for a matrix–vector product. As this once again depends on the structure of the block cluster tree, we will do this only for the previous example.

Lemma 7.40 *Let $I = \{1, \ldots, 2^L\}$ be recursively subdivided by bisection into equally sized subsets, such that $P_\ell(I)$, $0 \le \ell \le L$, consists of 2^ℓ subsets of size $2^{L-\ell}$. Let $T_{I \times I}$ be the associated block cluster tree with admissible function (7.21) and let $A \in \mathcal{H}(T_{I \times I}, r)$ be a hierarchical matrix. Then, the computational cost for computing a matrix vector product $\mathbf{y} := A\mathbf{x}$, $\mathbf{x} \in \mathbb{R}^n$, $n = 2^L$, is of size $O(rn \log n)$.*

Proof We follow the proof of Lemma 7.39. We denote the amounts of time taken to compute a matrix–vector product for the different blocks on level ℓ by $T_A(\ell)$, $T_N(\ell)$ and $T_R(\ell)$, respectively. If we split the vector $\mathbf{x} \in \mathbb{R}^{2^\ell}$ into two parts $\mathbf{x}_1, \mathbf{x}_2 \in \mathbb{R}^{2^{\ell-1}}$ then (7.22) shows that the computation of $A_\ell \mathbf{x}$ means the computation of $A_{\ell-1}\mathbf{x}_1 + N_{\ell-1}\mathbf{x}_2$ and $N_{\ell-1}^T \mathbf{x}_1 + A_{\ell-1}\mathbf{x}_2$. Hence, T_A and T_N

follow the recursions in (7.23) and (7.24), respectively. Moreover, as we can represent the sub-matrix associated with an R block on level ℓ by a matrix product of the form BC^{T} with $B, C \in \mathbb{R}^{2^{\ell} \times r}$ we can compute $BC^{\mathrm{T}}\mathbf{x}$ by first computing $\mathbf{y} := C^{\mathrm{T}}\mathbf{x}$ and then $B\mathbf{y}$ which each costs $O(r2^{\ell})$ time. Hence, we have $T_R(\ell) = 2r2^{\ell} = r2^{\ell+1}$. This means that we have the same recursions for T_N and T_A that we had in Lemma 7.39 for S_N and S_A, which shows particularly that $T_A(L) = O(rn \log n)$. $\square$

Algorithm 39: MatrixVectorProduct

Input : Index sets $I \subseteq \mathcal{I}$ and $J \subseteq \mathcal{J}$, $\mathbf{x} \in \mathbb{R}^n$, $\mathbf{y} \in \mathbb{R}^n$.
Output: $\mathbf{y} = A\mathbf{x}$.

1 **if** *$I \times J$ has children* **then**
2   **for** *each child $I' \times J'$* **do**
3   MatrixVectorProduct(I',J', $\mathbf{x}$, $\mathbf{y}$)

4 **else**
5      $\mathbf{y}_I := A_{I,J}\mathbf{x}_J$

It is possible to introduce a complete matrix calculus on the set $\mathcal{H}(T_{\mathcal{I}\times\mathcal{J}}, r)$, i.e. to define efficient ways of computing the sum and the product of two $\mathcal{H}$-matrices and the inverse of a $\mathcal{H}$-matrix. However, as, for example, the sum of two $\mathcal{H}$-matrices will violate the rank condition, this calculus is only an approximate calculus. For the example of the sum, this means that the sum of two such matrices has be approximated by an $\mathcal{H}$-matrix of rank r which is then declared the approximate sum. We will not further pursue this here, as we are mainly interested in applications in iterative methods, but refer again to the books by Hackbusch [77] and Bebendorf [13]. It is also possible to further improve the performance by restricting consideration to a specific subclass of $\mathcal{H}(T_{\mathcal{I}\times\mathcal{I}}, r)$, the so-called $\mathcal{H}^2$-matrices, see for example Hackbusch [80, 77].

After having introduced and discussed data structures for hierarchical matrices, we are left with two questions.

The first question concerns the determination of the block cluster tree or, equivalently, the determination of the hierarchical partitioning of the index set. A good choice is obviously critical but depends on the given application. As we have seen in the last section, the index sets can often be determined by geometric information provided by the underlying problem. If nothing is known, one of the partitioning strategies introduced here can be tried.

The second question concerns the matrix itself. Usually, the matrix given cannot be represented as a $\mathcal{H}$-matrix, which means that we have to approximate those blocks which are admissible by rank-r matrices. Again, we have seen in the last section that the original problem itself gives rise to successful approximation strategies. However, for the rest of this section, we want to discuss general methods to approximate a given matrix (block) by a rank-r matrix.

We will address this issue now theoretically using the Euclidean and Frobenius norms. While the first one gives a better approximation error, the latter has the advantage of being numerically more easily accessible.

As before, to simplify the notation, we will use $A \in \mathbb{R}^{m \times n}$ to denote such a matrix block.

Theorem 7.41 *Let $A \in \mathbb{R}^{m \times n}$ be given with singular value decomposition $A = U\Sigma V^{\mathrm{T}}$, i.e. $U = (\mathbf{u}_1, \ldots, \mathbf{u}_m) \in \mathbb{R}^{m \times m}$ and $V = (\mathbf{v}_1, \ldots, \mathbf{v}_n) \in \mathbb{R}^{n \times n}$ are orthogonal matrices and $\Sigma = \mathrm{diag}(\sigma_1, \ldots, \sigma_n) \in \mathbb{R}^{m \times n}$ with $\sigma_1 \geq \sigma_2 \geq \cdots \geq \sigma_n$. Then, the matrix*

$$A_r := \sum_{j=1}^{r} \sigma_j \mathbf{u}_j \mathbf{v}_j^{\mathrm{T}}$$

gives the best approximation to A from all rank-r matrices in the Euclidean and Frobenius norm, i.e. it satisfies

$$\|A - A_r\|_2 = \min \{\|A - B\|_2 : B \in \mathbb{R}^{m \times n} \text{ with } \mathrm{rank}(B) \leq r\},$$

$$\|A - A_r\|_F = \min \{\|A - B\|_F : B \in \mathbb{R}^{m \times n} \text{ with } \mathrm{rank}(B) \leq r\}.$$

Furthermore, the norm of the best approximation errors can be expressed as

$$\|A - A_r\|_2 = \sigma_{r+1}, \qquad \|A - A_r\|_F = \left(\sum_{k=r+1}^{n} \sigma_k^2 \right)^{1/2},$$

using the singular values of A.

Proof Recall that we can write the singular value decomposition of A and hence the difference $A - A_r$ in the form

$$A = \sum_{j=1}^{n} \sigma_j \mathbf{u}_j \mathbf{v}_j^{\mathrm{T}}, \qquad A - A_r = \sum_{j=r+1}^{n} \sigma_j \mathbf{u}_j \mathbf{v}_j^{\mathrm{T}}.$$

We start with the Euclidean norm. Here, we first note that

$$(A - A_r)^{\mathrm{T}}(A - A_r) = \sum_{j,k=r+1}^{n} \sigma_j \sigma_k (\mathbf{u}_j \mathbf{v}_j^{\mathrm{T}})^{\mathrm{T}}(\mathbf{u}_k \mathbf{v}_k) = \sum_{j,k=r+1}^{n} \sigma_j \sigma_k \mathbf{v}_j \mathbf{u}_j^{\mathrm{T}} \mathbf{u}_k \mathbf{v}_k$$

$$= \sum_{j=r+1}^{n} \sigma_j^2 \mathbf{v}_j \mathbf{v}_j^{\mathrm{T}}, \qquad (7.25)$$

which shows that the matrix $(A - A_r)^{\mathrm{T}}(A - A_r)$ has σ_{r+1}^2 as its largest eigenvalue such that

$$\|A - A_r\|_2 = \sigma_{r+1}.$$

It remains to show that this is the smallest value possible. To this end, let $B \in \mathbb{R}^{m \times n}$ be an arbitrary matrix with $\mathrm{rank}(B) \leq r$. According to Corollary 1.20, we can write $B = XY^{\mathrm{T}}$ with $X \in \mathbb{R}^{m \times r}$, $Y \in \mathbb{R}^{n \times r}$. Let $\mathbf{y}_1, \ldots, \mathbf{y}_r \in \mathbb{R}^n$ be the columns of Y. Since $\dim\{\mathbf{y}_1, \ldots, \mathbf{y}_r\} \leq r$ and $\dim\{\mathbf{v}_1, \ldots, \mathbf{v}_{r+1}\} = r + 1$, there must be an $\mathbf{w} \in \mathrm{span}\{\mathbf{v}_1, \ldots, \mathbf{v}_{r+1}\}$ orthogonal to all $\mathbf{y}_j$, $1 \leq j \leq r$, i.e. we have $Y^{\mathrm{T}}\mathbf{w} = \mathbf{0}$. We may normalise $\mathbf{w}$ to satisfy $\|\mathbf{w}\|_2 = 1$. Hence, since $\mathbf{w}$ is also orthogonal to $\mathbf{v}_{r+2}, \ldots, \mathbf{v}_n$,

$$\|A - B\|_2^2 \geq \|(A - B)\mathbf{w}\|_2^2 = \|A\mathbf{w}\|_2^2 = \left\| \sum_{j=1}^{r+1} \sigma_j \mathbf{u}_j \mathbf{v}_j^{\mathrm{T}} \mathbf{w} \right\|_2^2$$

$$= \sum_{j=1}^{r+1} \sigma_j^2 (\mathbf{v}_j^{\mathrm{T}} \mathbf{w})^2 \geq \sigma_{r+1}^2 \sum_{j=1}^{r+1} (\mathbf{v}_j^{\mathrm{T}} \mathbf{w})^2 = \sigma_{r+1}^2 \|\mathbf{w}\|_2^2$$

$$= \sigma_{r+1}^2,$$

where we have used that both $\{\mathbf{u}_j\}$ and $\{\mathbf{v}_j\}$ form orthonormal bases of $\mathbb{R}^m$ and $\mathbb{R}^n$, respectively. This finishes the proof in the case of the Euclidean norm. Now, we continue by looking at the Frobenius norm. From (7.25) we find

$$\|A - A_r\|_F^2 = \mathrm{tr}((A - A_r)^{\mathrm{T}}(A - A_r)) = \sum_{j=r+1}^{n} \sigma_j^2 \, \mathrm{tr}(\mathbf{v}_j \mathbf{v}_j^{\mathrm{T}})$$

$$= \sum_{j=r+1}^{n} \sigma_j^2 \sum_{i=1}^{n} v_{ij}^2 = \sum_{j=r+1}^{n} \sigma_j^2.$$

Hence, it remains to show that for every rank-r matrix $B = XY^{\mathrm{T}} \in \mathbb{R}^{m \times n}$ we have

$$\|A - B\|_F^2 \geq \sum_{j=r+1}^{n} \sigma_j^2.$$

To see this, we proceed as in the case of the Euclidean norm. This time, however, we choose orthogonal vectors $\mathbf{w}_k \in \mathrm{span}\{\mathbf{v}_1, \ldots, \mathbf{v}_k\}$, $r + 1 \leq k \leq n$, with $Y^{\mathrm{T}}\mathbf{w}_k = \mathbf{0}$. Then, we extend $\mathbf{w}_{r+1}, \ldots, \mathbf{w}_n$ to an orthonormal basis $\mathbf{w}_1, \ldots, \mathbf{w}_n$ of $\mathbb{R}^n$ and set $W := (\mathbf{w}_1, \ldots, \mathbf{w}_n) \in \mathbb{R}^{n \times n}$, which is an orthogonal matrix. Then, we can see as above that $\|A\mathbf{w}_k\|_2^2 \geq \sigma_k^2$ for $r + 1 \leq k \leq n$ and hence, since the

Frobenius norm is invariant under orthogonal transformations,

$$\|A - B\|_F^2 = \|(A - B)W\|_F^2 = \sum_{k=1}^{n} \|(A - B)\mathbf{w}_k\|_2^2 \geq \sum_{k=r+1}^{n} \|(A - B)\mathbf{w}_k\|_2^2$$

$$= \sum_{k=r+1}^{n} \|A\mathbf{w}_k\|_2^2 \geq \sum_{k=r+1}^{n} \sigma_k^2. \qquad \square$$

In the situation of a symmetric matrix $A \in \mathbb{R}^{n \times n}$, we can choose $U = V$ in the singular value decomposition so that the singular values become the eigenvalues of A. Hence, in this situation, the previous result can be simplified as follows.

Corollary 7.42 *Let $A \in \mathbb{R}^{n \times n}$ be symmetric with eigenvalues $\lambda_1 \geq \lambda_2 \geq \cdots \geq \lambda_n$. Let $V \in \mathbb{R}^{n \times n}$ be orthogonal so that $A = VDV^{\mathsf{T}}$, where $D = \text{diag}(\lambda_1, \ldots, \lambda_n)$. Then, the matrix*

$$A_r := \sum_{j=1}^{r} \lambda_j \mathbf{v}_j \mathbf{v}_j^{\mathsf{T}}$$

gives the best approximation to A from all symmetric rank-r matrices in the Euclidean and Frobenius norm, i.e. it satisfies

$$\|A - A_r\|_2 = \min\left\{\|A - B\|_2 : B = B^{\mathsf{T}} \in \mathbb{R}^{n \times n} \text{ with } \text{rank}(B) \leq r\right\},$$

$$\|A - A_r\|_F = \min\left\{\|A - B\|_F : B = B^{\mathsf{T}} \in \mathbb{R}^{n \times n} \text{ with } \text{rank}(B) \leq r\right\}.$$

Furthermore, the norm of the best approximations can be expressed as

$$\|A - A_r\|_2 = \lambda_{r+1}, \qquad \|A - A_r\|_F = \left(\sum_{k=r+1}^{n} \lambda_k^2\right)^{1/2}.$$

While the above construction using the singular value decomposition gives the best possible rank-r approximation to a given matrix block, it becomes increasingly expensive for larger blocks.

A computationally more feasible method is based on the ideas of *adaptive cross approximation*, which we have encountered in Definition 7.24 for the approximation of a kernel. The method itself can be formulated for matrices, as follows.

Definition 7.43 Let $A \in \mathbb{R}^{m \times n}$ be given. Then, the *adaptive cross approximation (ACA)* of A is recursively defined as follows. We set $A_0 := 0$ and $R_0 := A$ and then, for $k = 1, 2, \ldots$,

- choose $i_k \in \{1, \ldots, m\}$ and $j_k \in \{1, \ldots, n\}$ such that $p_k := (R_{k-1})_{i_k, j_k} \neq 0$,

- define

$$\mathbf{u}_k := \frac{1}{p_k} R_{k-1} \mathbf{e}_{j_k}, \qquad\qquad \mathbf{v}_k^T := \mathbf{e}_{i_k}^T R_{k-1},$$

$$A_k := A_{k-1} + \mathbf{u}_k \mathbf{v}_k^T, \qquad\qquad R_k := R_{k-1} - \mathbf{u}_k \mathbf{v}_k^T.$$

After r steps of ACA, we have matrices A_r and R_r satisfying $A_r + R_r = A$ and

$$A_r = \sum_{k=1}^{r} \mathbf{u}_k \mathbf{v}_k^T =: U_r V_r^T, \qquad U_r = (\mathbf{u}_1, \dots, \mathbf{u}_r), \qquad V_r = (\mathbf{v}_1, \dots, \mathbf{v}_r)$$

The second property shows that A_r is indeed a rank-r matrix; the first, which is easily seen by induction, shows that $R_r = A - A_r$ represents the error of the approximation.

For the implementation, there are a few more things to consider. First of all, the method should stop if the error $\|R_r\|$ becomes less than a certain tolerance $\epsilon > 0$. The norm could, for example, be either the Frobenius norm or the Euclidean norm. However, even in the simpler case of the Frobenius norm, the complexity of computing the norm is not linear. Thus, in a practical application one usually looks at the difference of two errors $R_k - R_{k-1} = -\mathbf{u}_k \mathbf{v}_k^T$ and uses

$$\|R_k - R_{k-1}\|_2 = \|\mathbf{u}_k \mathbf{v}_k^T\|_2 = \|\mathbf{u}_k\|_2 \|\mathbf{v}_k\|_2,$$

which can be computed in linear complexity. Next, in each step, we need to determine the indices i_k and j_k. If no additional information is given, i_k is usually chosen either randomly or as the index satisfying

$$|\mathbf{e}_{i_k}^T \mathbf{u}_{k-1}| = \max_{1 \le i \le m} |\mathbf{e}_i^T \mathbf{u}_{k-1}|.$$

Often a better choice is possible if more is known about the origin of the matrix block. After choosing i_k, the column index j_k is usually chosen such that

$$|(R_{k-1})_{i_k, j_k}| = |\mathbf{e}_{j_k}^T \mathbf{v}_k| = \max_{1 \le j \le n} |\mathbf{e}_j^T \mathbf{v}_k| = \max_{1 \le j \le n} |(R_{k-1})_{i_k, j}|. \qquad (7.26)$$

Note that subtracting $\mathbf{u}_k \mathbf{v}_k^T$ of R_{k-1} means eliminating the i_kth row and j_kth column from R_{k-1} and leaving all other zero rows and columns of R_{k-1} unchanged, which can directly be seen from

$$(R_k)_{ij} = (R_{k-1})_{ij} - \frac{(R_{k-1})_{ij_k}(R_{k-1})_{i_k j}}{(R_{k-1})_{i_k j_k}}.$$

This means that R_k has at least k zero rows and k zero columns. It also means that $\mathbf{u}_k$ and $\mathbf{v}_k$ have at least $k - 1$ zeros.

Finally, it is not necessary to build the matrices A_k and R_k in full. As the kth step requires only the j_kth column and i_kth row of R_{k-1} to compute R_k there is no need to build the whole matrix R_k. This means particularly that not all the entries of the original matrix A have to be computed. Taking this all into account, we have Algorithm 40 as a possible implementation of ACA.

Algorithm 40: Adaptive cross approximation (ACA)

Input : $A \in \mathbb{R}^{m \times n}$, $\epsilon > 0$.
Output: $\mathbf{u}_1, \ldots, \mathbf{u}_r \in \mathbb{R}^m$, $\mathbf{v}_1, \ldots, \mathbf{v}_r \in \mathbb{R}^n$.

1 $k := 1$, $Z = \emptyset$, err $= \infty$
2 **while** err $\geq \epsilon$ and $Z \neq \{1, \ldots, m\}$ **do**
3 $\quad$ Determine i_k.
4 $\quad$ $\mathbf{v}_k^T := \mathbf{e}_{i_k}^T A$
5 $\quad$ **for** $\ell = 1$ **to** $k - 1$ **do** $\mathbf{v}_k^T := \mathbf{v}_k^T - (\mathbf{u}_\ell)_{i_k} \mathbf{v}_\ell^T$
6 $\quad$ $Z := Z \cup \{i_k\}$
7 $\quad$ **if** $\mathbf{v}_k \neq \mathbf{0}$ **then**
8 $\quad\quad$ $j_k := \arg \max_{1 \leq j \leq n} |(\mathbf{v}_k)_j|$
9 $\quad\quad$ $\mathbf{u}_k := A \mathbf{e}_{j_k}$
10 $\quad\quad$ **for** $\ell = 1$ **to** $k - 1$ **do** $\mathbf{u}_k := \mathbf{u}_k - (\mathbf{v}_\ell)_{j_k} \mathbf{u}_\ell$
11 $\quad\quad$ $\mathbf{u}_k := \mathbf{u}_k / (\mathbf{v}_k)_{j_k}$
12 $\quad\quad$ err $:= \|\mathbf{u}_k\|_2 \|\mathbf{v}_k\|_2$
13 $\quad\quad$ $k := k + 1$

To further analyse this algorithm, we will assume that $i_k = j_k = k$, which can always be achieved by permuting rows and columns. This means in particular that the first $k - 1$ entries of $\mathbf{u}_k$ and $\mathbf{v}_k$ are zero and that $(\mathbf{u}_k)_k = 1$.

We start with the following alternative way of representing the remainder matrix. To this end, we decompose the matrix $A \in \mathbb{R}^{m \times n}$ into blocks

$$A = \begin{pmatrix} A_{11} & A_{12} \\ A_{21} & A_{22} \end{pmatrix},$$

where $A_{11} \in \mathbb{R}^{k \times k}$ and the dimensions of the other blocks are defined accordingly. Note that the larger block $A_{22} \in \mathbb{R}^{(m-k) \times (n-k)}$ is not used in Algorithm 40.

Lemma 7.44 *The remainder matrix $R_k \in \mathbb{R}^{m \times n}$ has a representation of the form*

$$R_k = A - \begin{pmatrix} A_{11} \\ A_{21} \end{pmatrix} A_{11}^{-1} \begin{pmatrix} A_{11} & A_{12} \end{pmatrix} = \begin{pmatrix} O & O \\ O & C_k \end{pmatrix},$$

where $C_k := A_{22} - A_{21} A_{11}^{-1} A_{12}$ is the Schur complement of A_{11} in A.

Proof The second equality is easily verified by direct calculations. The first equality is proven by induction on k. For $k = 1$, this follows directly from the definition of $R_1 = A - \mathbf{u}_1 \mathbf{v}_1^T = A - \frac{1}{a_{11}} \mathbf{a}_1 \mathbf{a}_1^T$. Next, assume that it holds for k and let A be decomposed as

$$A = \begin{pmatrix} A_{11} & \mathbf{w} & B \\ \mathbf{v}^T & \alpha & \mathbf{y}^T \\ C & \mathbf{x} & D \end{pmatrix}$$

with $A_{11} \in \mathbb{R}^{k \times k}$ and $\mathbf{x} \in \mathbb{R}^{m-k-1}$, $\mathbf{y} \in \mathbb{R}^{n-k-1}$, $\mathbf{v}, \mathbf{w} \in \mathbb{R}^k$ and $\alpha \in \mathbb{R}$. With this notation we have by virtue of the induction assumption

$$R_k = A - \begin{pmatrix} A_{11} \\ \mathbf{v}^T \\ C \end{pmatrix} A_{11}^{-1} \begin{pmatrix} A_{11} & \mathbf{w} & B \end{pmatrix} = \begin{pmatrix} O & \mathbf{0} & O \\ \mathbf{0}^T & p_{k+1} & \mathbf{y}^T - \mathbf{v}^T A_{11}^{-1} B \\ O & \mathbf{x} - C A_{11}^{-1} \mathbf{w} & D - C A_{11}^{-1} B \end{pmatrix},$$

where O denotes a zero matrix, and then $p_{k+1} = (R_k)_{k+1,k+1} = \alpha - \mathbf{v}^T A_{11}^{-1} \mathbf{w}$ and

$$\mathbf{u}_{k+1} = \frac{1}{p_{k+1}} R_k \mathbf{e}_{k+1} = \begin{pmatrix} \mathbf{0} \\ 1 \\ \frac{1}{p_{k+1}} (\mathbf{x} - C A_{11}^{-1} \mathbf{w}) \end{pmatrix},$$

$$\mathbf{v}_{k+1}^T = \mathbf{e}_{k+1}^T R_k = \begin{pmatrix} \mathbf{0}^T & p_{k+1} & \mathbf{y}^T - \mathbf{v}^T A_{11}^{-1} B \end{pmatrix}.$$

Then, the definition of R_{k+1} yields after simple computations

$$R_{k+1} = R_k - \mathbf{u}_{k+1} \mathbf{v}_{k+1}^T = \begin{pmatrix} O & \mathbf{0} & O \\ \mathbf{0}^T & 0 & \mathbf{0}^T \\ O & \mathbf{0} & C_{k+1} \end{pmatrix}$$

with

$$C_{k+1} = D - C A_{11}^{-1} B - \frac{1}{p_{k+1}} (\mathbf{x} - C A_{11}^{-1} \mathbf{w})(\mathbf{y}^T - \mathbf{v}^T A_{11}^{-1} B)$$

$$= D - \begin{pmatrix} C & \mathbf{x} \end{pmatrix} \begin{pmatrix} A_{11}^{-1} + \frac{1}{p_{k+1}} A_{11}^{-1} \mathbf{w} \mathbf{v}^T A_{11}^{-1} & -\frac{1}{p_{k+1}} A_{11}^{-1} \mathbf{w} \\ -\frac{1}{p_{k+1}} \mathbf{v}^T A_{11}^{-1} & \frac{1}{p_{k+1}} \end{pmatrix} \begin{pmatrix} B \\ \mathbf{y}^T \end{pmatrix}.$$

However, as we have

$$\begin{pmatrix} A_{11} & \mathbf{w} \\ \mathbf{v}^T & \alpha \end{pmatrix}^{-1} = \begin{pmatrix} A_{11}^{-1} + \frac{1}{p_{k+1}} A_{11}^{-1} \mathbf{w} \mathbf{v}^T A_{11}^{-1} & -\frac{1}{p_{k+1}} A_{11}^{-1} \mathbf{w} \\ -\frac{1}{p_{k+1}} \mathbf{v}^T A_{11}^{-1} & \frac{1}{p_{k+1}} \end{pmatrix}$$

we see that C_{k+1} has the desired form

$$C_{k+1} = D - \begin{pmatrix} C & \mathbf{x} \end{pmatrix} \begin{pmatrix} A_{11} & \mathbf{w} \\ \mathbf{v}^T & \alpha \end{pmatrix}^{-1} \begin{pmatrix} B \\ \mathbf{y}^T \end{pmatrix},$$

i.e. R_{k+1} has the second stated form, and as this is equivalent to the first stated form, the induction is finished. $\qquad\square$

As mentioned above, the remainder matrix R_k has at least k zero rows and columns. However, it might very well happen that additional zero rows and columns are produced during the process. We can, once again, assume without restriction that we sort the rows in such a way that also the rows with index $k + 1, \ldots, k'$ are zero, where $k' \geq k$.

In that situation we can further split up the matrix blocks A_{21} and A_{22} as

$$A_{21} = \begin{pmatrix} \hat{A}_{21} \\ \check{A}_{21} \end{pmatrix}, \qquad A_{22} = \begin{pmatrix} \hat{A}_{22} \\ \check{A}_{22} \end{pmatrix}$$

with $\hat{A}_{21} \in \mathbb{R}^{(k'-k) \times k}$ and $\hat{A}_{22} \in \mathbb{R}^{(k'-k) \times (n-k)}$. As the upper $k' - k$ rows of C_k vanish, the representation

$$C_k = A_{22} - A_{21} A_{11}^{-1} A_{12} = \begin{pmatrix} \hat{A}_{22} \\ \check{A}_{22} \end{pmatrix} - \begin{pmatrix} \hat{A}_{21} \\ \check{A}_{21} \end{pmatrix} A_{11}^{-1} A_{12}$$

$$= \begin{pmatrix} \hat{A}_{22} - \hat{A}_{21} A_{11}^{-1} A_{12} \\ \check{A}_{22} - \check{A}_{21} A_{11}^{-1} A_{12} \end{pmatrix} =: \begin{pmatrix} O \\ \check{C}_k \end{pmatrix}$$

shows in particular that we have $\hat{A}_{22} = \hat{A}_{21} A_{11}^{-1} A_{12}$, which prepares the following auxiliary result.

Lemma 7.45 *With the notation introduced above, the matrix C_k satisfies*

$$C_k = \left\{ A_{22} - P \begin{pmatrix} A_{12} \\ \hat{A}_{22} \end{pmatrix} \right\} - \left\{ A_{21} - P \begin{pmatrix} A_{11} \\ \hat{A}_{21} \end{pmatrix} \right\} A_{11}^{-1} A_{12}$$

with any matrix $P \in \mathbb{R}^{(m-k) \times k'}$.

Proof This follows immediately from the above observation by subtracting and adding

$$P \begin{pmatrix} A_{12} \\ \hat{A}_{22} \end{pmatrix} = P \begin{pmatrix} A_{11} \\ \hat{A}_{21} \end{pmatrix} A_{11}^{-1} A_{12}$$

to the representation of C_k. □

This shows that we can bound the error R_k, which means bounding C_k by a kind of best-approximation error by taking the infimum over all matrices P. To have a valid bound, we also need to bound the matrix $A_{11}^{-1} A_{12}$. This can be done as follows.

Proposition 7.46 *If j_k, $1 \leq k \leq \min(m, n)$, is chosen according to (7.26) and if the rows and columns of A are sorted so that $i_k = j_k = k$ then the entries of the matrix $A_{11}^{-1} A_{12} \in \mathbb{R}^{k \times (n-k)}$ satisfy the bound*

$$|(A_{11}^{-1} A_{12})_{ij}| \leq 2^{k-i}, \qquad 1 \leq i \leq k, \quad 1 \leq j \leq n - k.$$

Proof If we denote the columns of A_{11} by $\mathbf{a}_i$ and the columns of A_{12} by $\mathbf{b}_i$ then Cramer's rule yields

$$(A_{11}^{-1}A_{12})_{ij} = \frac{\det(\mathbf{a}_1, \ldots, \mathbf{a}_{i-1}, \mathbf{b}_j, \mathbf{a}_{i+1}, \ldots, \mathbf{a}_k)}{\det A_{11}}. \tag{7.27}$$

Noting that both types of columns are actually given by taking the upper k entries of corresponding columns of A, we can be more specific in the notation. Let $\mathbf{a}_j^{(k)} \in \mathbb{R}^k$ be the vector consisting of the upper k entries of the jth column of A, then we have

$$A_{11} = A_{11}^{(k)} = (\mathbf{a}_1^{(k)}, \ldots, \mathbf{a}_k^{(k)})$$

and, with the definition

$$A_i^{(k)}(j) = (\mathbf{a}_1^{(k)}, \ldots, \mathbf{a}_{i-1}^{(k)}, \mathbf{a}_j^{(k)}, \mathbf{a}_{i+1}^{(k)}, \ldots \mathbf{a}_k^{(k)}) \in \mathbb{R}^{k \times k},$$

equation (7.27) becomes

$$(A_{11}^{-1}A_{12})_{ij} = \det A_i^{(k)}(k+j) / \det A_{11}^{(k)}. \tag{7.28}$$

To prove our statement we need several steps. The first one is noting that, from the initial decomposition $A = A_k + R_k$ and the fact that R_k has the first k rows as zero rows, we can conclude that the determinant of $A_{11}^{(k)}$ is given by the determinant of the upper $k \times k$ block of A_k. As $A_k = U_k V_k^T$, this upper block is the product of a normalised lower triangular matrix and an upper triangular matrix with diagonal entries $p_1, \ldots, p_k$. Hence, we have

$$\det A_{11}^{(k)} = p_1 \cdots p_k = p_k \det A_{11}^{(k-1)}.$$

Next, we note that each row of R_{k-1} is a linear combination of the rows of A. To be more precise, for each $1 \leq i \leq m$, there are coefficients $\beta_\ell^{(i,k-1)}$ such that

$$\mathbf{e}_i^T R_{k-1} = \mathbf{e}_i^T A - \sum_{\ell=1}^{k-1} \beta_\ell^{(i,k-1)} \mathbf{e}_\ell^T A.$$

This is obvious for $k = 1$ as we have $R_0 = A$. The general case follows by induction from $k-1$ to k. The construction of R_k, the definitions of $\mathbf{u}_k = R_{k-1}\mathbf{e}_k/p_k$ and $\mathbf{v}_k^T = \mathbf{e}_k^T R_{k-1}$ and then the induction hypothesis yield

$$\mathbf{e}_i^T R_k = \mathbf{e}_i^T R_{k-1} - \mathbf{e}_i^T(\mathbf{u}_k \mathbf{v}_k^T) = \mathbf{e}_i^T R_{k-1} - \frac{1}{p_k}(R_{k-1})_{ik}\mathbf{e}_k^T R_{k-1}$$

$$= \mathbf{e}_i^T A - \sum_{\ell=1}^{k-1} \beta_\ell^{(i,k-1)} \mathbf{e}_\ell^T A - \frac{1}{p_k}(R_{k-1})_{ik} \left[\mathbf{e}_k^T A - \sum_{\ell=0}^{k-1} \beta_\ell^{(k,k-1)} \mathbf{e}_\ell^T A \right]$$

$$=: \mathbf{e}_i^T A - \sum_{\ell=0}^{k} \beta_\ell^{(i,k)} \mathbf{e}_\ell^T A.$$

This means that we can exchange the kth row of A with the kth row of R_{k-1} without changing the determinant. As each matrix $A_i^{(k)}(j)$ is generated from the matrix A by exchanging the jth and ith columns and then taking the first k rows, we can also exchange the kth row of $A_i^{(k)}(j)$ with the kth row of the matrix which results from R_{k-1} by swapping columns i and j without changing the determinant. As the kth row of R_{k-1} has zero entries in the first $k-1$ columns we derive for $1 \le i < k$ that

$$
\det A_i^{(k)}(k+j) = \det \begin{pmatrix} \mathbf{a}_1^{(k-1)} & \cdots & \mathbf{a}_{i-1}^{(k-1)} & a_{k+j}^{(k-1)} & \mathbf{a}_{i+1}^{(k-1)} & \cdots & \mathbf{a}_k^{(k-1)} \\ 0 & \cdots & 0 & (R_{k-1})_{k,k+j} & 0 & \cdots & (R_{k-1})_{kk} \end{pmatrix}
$$

$$
= (-1)^{k+i}(R_{k-1})_{k,k+j} \det \begin{pmatrix} \mathbf{a}_1^{(k-1)} & \cdots & \mathbf{a}_{i-1}^{(k-1)} & \mathbf{a}_{i+1}^{(k-1)} & \cdots & \mathbf{a}_k^{(k-1)} \end{pmatrix}
$$

$$
+ (R_{k-1})_{kk} \det \begin{pmatrix} \mathbf{a}_1^{(k-1)} & \cdots & \mathbf{a}_{i-1}^{(k-1)} & \mathbf{a}_{k+j}^{(k-1)} & \mathbf{a}_{i+1}^{(k-1)} & \cdots & \mathbf{a}_{k-1}^{(k-1)} \end{pmatrix}
$$

$$
= -(R_{k-1})_{k,k+j} \det A_i^{(k-1)}(k) + p_k \det A_i^{(k-1)}(k+j),
$$

where, in the last step, we have used the definition of p_k and have also swapped the last column to position i for the first matrix. The same argument yields for $i = k$ that we have

$$
\det A_k^{(k)}(k+j) = (R_{k-1})_{k,k+j} \det \begin{pmatrix} \mathbf{a}_1^{(k-1)} & \cdots & \mathbf{a}_{k-1}^{(k-1)} \end{pmatrix} = (R_{k-1})_{k,k+j} \det A_{11}^{(k-1)}.
$$

After these preliminary observations, we can show, once again by induction on k, that we have

$$
|\det A_i^{(k)}(k+j)| \le 2^{k-i}|\det A_{11}^{(k)}|, \qquad 1 \le i \le k, \quad 1 \le j \le n-k. \tag{7.29}
$$

The choice of p_k guarantees for $i = k$ that

$$
|\det A_k^{(k)}(k+j)| = |(R_{k-1})_{k,k+j} \det A_{11}^{(k-1)}| \le |p_k \det A_{11}^{(k-1)}| = |\det A_{11}^{(k)}|,
$$

which particularly proves (7.29) for $k = 1$. The general result follows for k from $k - 1$ for $1 \le i \le k - 1$ by

$$
|\det A_i^{(k)}(k+j)| = |p_k \det A_i^{(k-1)}(k+j) - (R_{k-1})_{k,k+j} \det A_i^{(k-1)}(k)|
$$

$$
\le 2|p_k| \max \left\{ |\det A_i^{(k-1)}(k+j)|, |\det A_i^{(k-1)}(k)| \right\}
$$

$$
\le 2|p_k| 2^{k-1-i}|\det A_{11}^{(k-1)}|
$$

$$
= 2^{k-i}|\det A_{11}^{(k)}|.
$$

The statement now follows immediately by inserting (7.29) into (7.28). $\qquad \square$

The estimate itself is rather pessimistic as it grows exponentially with k. In many situations a better behaviour can be observed. Nonetheless, we have the following general approximation result.

Theorem 7.47   *Let $A \in \mathbb{R}^{m \times n}$ be given. Let A_k and $R_k = A - A_k$ be the matrices generated by the adaptive cross approximation algorithm. Let $k' \geq k$ be the number of zero rows in R_k and let the rows and columns be sorted such that R_k has the form given in Lemma 7.44. Then, $(R_k)_{ij} = 0$ for $1 \leq i \leq k'$ and $1 \leq j \leq k$ and for $k' + 1 \leq i \leq m$ and $k + 1 \leq j \leq n$, the estimate*

$$|(R_k)_{ij}| \leq 2^k \min_{P \in \mathbb{R}^{(m-k) \times k'}} \max_{\ell \in \{1,\dots,k\} \cup \{j\}} \left| a_{i\ell} - \sum_{\nu=1}^{k'} p_{i-k,\nu} a_{\nu\ell} \right|$$

holds.

Proof   By Lemma 7.45 we have, for $k + 1 \leq i \leq m$ and $k + 1 \leq j \leq n$,

$$(R_k)_{ij} = (C_k)_{i-k, j-k} = \left\{ a_{ij} - \sum_{\nu=1}^{k'} p_{i-k,\nu} a_{\nu j} \right\} - \sum_{\ell=1}^{k} \left[a_{i\ell} - \sum_{\nu=1}^{k'} p_{i-k,\nu} a_{\nu\ell} \right] (A_{11}^{-1} A_{12})_{\ell j}.$$

Hence, with Proposition 7.46, we have the bound

$$|(R_k)_{ij}| \leq \left| a_{ij} - \sum_{\nu=1}^{k'} p_{i-k,\nu} a_{\nu j} \right| + \sum_{\ell=1}^{k} 2^{k-\ell} \left| a_{i\ell} - \sum_{\nu=1}^{k'} p_{i-k,\nu} a_{\nu\ell} \right| \qquad (7.30)$$

$$\leq \left| a_{ij} - \sum_{\nu=1}^{k'} p_{i-k,\nu} a_{\nu j} \right| + \max_{1 \leq \ell \leq k} \left| a_{i\ell} - \sum_{\nu=1}^{k'} p_{i-k,\nu} a_{\nu\ell} \right| \sum_{\ell=1}^{k} 2^{k-\ell}$$

$$\leq \max_{\ell \in \{1,\dots,k\} \cup \{j\}} \left| a_{i\ell} - \sum_{\nu=1}^{k'} p_{i-k,\nu} a_{\nu\ell} \right| \left\{ 1 + \sum_{\ell=1}^{k} 2^{k-\ell} \right\}$$

and the statement follows by evaluating the geometric sum on the right-hand side and taking the minimum over all P.   □

While it is obviously difficult to derive more informative estimates for general matrices from this, the situation improves if we come back to the situation that our matrix $A \in \mathbb{R}^{m \times n}$ is given by an interpolation problem. In this context, we have $A = (K(\mathbf{x}_i, \mathbf{y}_j))$ with $\mathbf{x}_i \in X$ and $\mathbf{y}_j \in Y$ and a given kernel $K : \mathbb{R}^d \times \mathbb{R}^d \to \mathbb{R}$ and the relevant term in the estimate above becomes

$$a_{i\ell} - \sum_{\nu=1}^{k'} p_{i-k,\nu} a_{\nu\ell} = K(\mathbf{x}_i, \mathbf{y}_\ell) - \sum_{\nu=1}^{k'} p_{i-k,\nu} K(\mathbf{x}_\nu, \mathbf{y}_\ell). \qquad (7.31)$$

Thus, we need to approximate the function $f_\ell := K(\cdot, \mathbf{y}_\ell)$, or, to be more precise, its value $f_\ell(\mathbf{x}_i)$ from its values $f_\ell(\mathbf{x}_\nu)$, $1 \leq \nu \leq k'$. This can be done in a systematic way as follows. Assume that $V_{k'} \subseteq C(\mathbb{R}^d)$ is a k'-dimensional subspace of $C(\mathbb{R}^d)$. Assume further that $V_{k'}$ has a Lagrange basis with respect to

$\mathbf{x}_1, \ldots, \mathbf{x}_{k'}$, i.e. that there are functions $L_\nu \in V_{k'}$ with $L_\nu(\mathbf{x}_\mu) = \delta_{\nu\mu}$. Then, we can represent every $p \in V_{k'}$ by its interpolant

$$p = \sum_{\nu=1}^{k'} p(\mathbf{x}_\nu) L_\nu.$$

Hence, if we set $p_{i-k,\nu} = L_\nu(\mathbf{x}_i)$ for $1 \le \nu \le k'$ and $k+1 \le i \le m$, then (7.31) leads to

$$\left| K(\mathbf{x}_i, \mathbf{y}_\ell) - \sum_{\nu=1}^{k'} p_{i-k,\nu} K(\mathbf{x}_\nu, \mathbf{y}_\ell) \right| = \left| f_\ell(\mathbf{x}_i) - \sum_{\nu=1}^{k'} L_\nu(\mathbf{x}_i) f_\ell(\mathbf{x}_\nu) \right|$$

$$\le |f_\ell(\mathbf{x}_i) - p(\mathbf{x}_i)| + \sum_{\nu=1}^{k'} |f_\ell(\mathbf{x}_\nu) - p(\mathbf{x}_\nu)| |L_\nu(\mathbf{x}_i)|$$

$$\le \left(1 + \sum_{\nu=1}^{k'} |L_\nu(\mathbf{x}_i)| \right) \max_{\nu \in \{1,\ldots,k'\} \cup \{i\}} |f_\ell(\mathbf{x}_\nu) - p(\mathbf{x}_\nu)|,$$

which holds for an arbitrary $p \in V_{k'}$, i.e. we have

$$\left| f_\ell(\mathbf{x}_i) - \sum_{\nu=1}^{k'} f_\ell(\mathbf{x}_\nu) L_\nu(\mathbf{x}_i) \right| \le \Lambda_{k'}(\mathbf{x}_i) \min_{p \in V_{k'}} \|f_\ell - p\|_{\ell_\infty(X)}$$

with the *Lebesgue function*

$$\Lambda_{k'}(\mathbf{x}) := 1 + \sum_{\nu=1}^{k'} |L_\nu(\mathbf{x})|. \tag{7.32}$$

Using this in (7.30) yields

$$|(R_k)_{ij}| \le \left| f_j(\mathbf{x}_i) - \sum_{\nu=1}^{k'} f_j(\mathbf{x}_\nu) L_\nu(\mathbf{x}_i) \right| + \sum_{\ell=1}^{k} 2^{k-\ell} \left| f_\ell(\mathbf{x}_i) - \sum_{\nu=1}^{k'} f_\ell(\mathbf{x}_\nu) L_\nu(\mathbf{x}_i) \right|$$

$$\le \Lambda_{k'}(\mathbf{x}_i) \min_{p \in V_{k'}} \|f_j - p\|_{\ell_\infty(X)} + \sum_{\ell=1}^{k} 2^{k-\ell} \Lambda_{k'}(\mathbf{x}_i) \min_{p \in V_{k'}} \|f_\ell - p\|_{\ell_\infty(X)}$$

$$\le 2^k \Lambda_{k'}(\mathbf{x}_i) \max_{\ell \in \{1,\ldots,k\} \cup \{j\}} \min_{p \in V_{k'}} \|f_\ell - p\|_{\ell_\infty(X)}.$$

Hence, we have proven the following result.

Theorem 7.48 *Under the assumptions of Theorem 7.47 let the matrix A have entries $K(\mathbf{x}_i, \mathbf{y}_j)$ with $\mathbf{x}_i \in X, \mathbf{y}_j \in Y \subseteq \mathbb{R}^d$. Let $V_{k'} = \text{span}\{L_1, \ldots, L_{k'}\} \subseteq C(\mathbb{R}^d)$, where the basis functions satisfy $L_\nu(\mathbf{x}_\mu) = \delta_{\nu\mu}$, $1 \le \nu, \mu \le k'$. Then, the error $R_k = A - A_k$ can be bounded component-wise by*

$$|(R_k)_{ij}| \le 2^k \Lambda_{k'}(\mathbf{x}_i) \max_{\ell \in \{1,\ldots,k\} \cup \{j\}} \min_{p \in V_{k'}} \|K(\cdot, \mathbf{y}_\ell) - p\|_{\ell_\infty(X)},$$

where $\Lambda_{k'}(\mathbf{x}_i)$ is given by (7.32).

The Lebesgue function often grows exponentially in k' but as we have only moderately sized k' in mind this usually does not cause a problem.

This can be further refined in the situation of a translation-invariant kernel, i.e. a kernel of the form $K(\mathbf{x}, \mathbf{y}) = \Phi(\mathbf{x} - \mathbf{y})$ with $\Phi : \mathbb{R}^d \to \mathbb{R}$ satisfying the decay condition (7.9).

To this end, we assume that $k = k' = n_r = \dim \pi_r(\mathbb{R}^d)$ and hence $V_{k'} = \pi_r(\mathbb{R}^d)$ is the space of all d-variate polynomials of degree less than or equal to r. We will also assume that the selected points, after reordering, $\mathbf{x}_1, \ldots, \mathbf{x}_{n_r}$ are $\pi_r(\mathbb{R}^d)$-*unisolvent*, i.e. that the zero polynomial is the only polynomial from $\pi_r(\mathbb{R}^d)$ that vanishes on all $\mathbf{x}_1, \ldots, \mathbf{x}_{n_r}$. This is not a severe assumption and is usually satisfied in practical applications. A consequence of the latter assumption is that polynomial interpolation is uniquely possible, i.e. we have the required Lagrange functions.

If we now assume that the evaluation points X are all contained in $[-\eta, \eta]^d$ and that the source points $\mathbf{y} \in Y$ satisfy $\|\mathbf{y}\|_\infty \geq (M + 1)\eta$ with $M \geq 1$ then we can once again, as in the proof of Proposition 7.19, use a Taylor expansion

$$\Phi(\mathbf{x} - \mathbf{y}_\ell) = \sum_{|\alpha| \leq r} \frac{D^\alpha \Phi(-\mathbf{y}_\ell)}{\alpha!} \mathbf{x}^\alpha + \sum_{|\alpha| = r+1} \frac{D^\alpha \Phi(\xi - \mathbf{y}_\ell)}{\alpha!} \mathbf{x}^\alpha,$$

with $\xi \in \mathbb{R}^d$ on the line segment between $\mathbf{0}$ and $\mathbf{x}$, to derive

$$\inf_{p \in \pi_r(\mathbb{R}^d)} \|\Phi(\cdot - \mathbf{y}_\ell) - p\|_{\ell_\infty(X)} \leq C_{r+1} \eta^{r+1} (M\eta)^{\mu-r-1} = C_{r+1} \eta^\mu M^{-r-1}.$$

Hence, in this situation we have

$$|(R_{n_r})_{ij}| \leq 2^{n_r} \Lambda_{n_r}(\mathbf{x}_i) C_{r+1} \eta^\mu M^{-r-1}.$$

Corollary 7.49 *Let $A \in \mathbb{R}^{m \times n}$ be given with entries $a_{ij} = K(\mathbf{x}_i, \mathbf{y}_j) = \Phi(\mathbf{x}_i - \mathbf{x}_j)$, where $\Phi \in C^{r+1}(\mathbb{R}^d \setminus \{\mathbf{0}\})$ satisfies (7.9) with $\mu \leq r + 1$. Let the evaluation points X be contained in $[-\eta, \eta]^d$ and let the source points $\mathbf{y} \in Y$ satisfy $\|\mathbf{y}\|_\infty \geq (M + 1)\eta$ with $M \geq 1$. For $1 \leq k \leq n_r = \dim \pi_r(\mathbb{R}^d)$ let the row index i_k be chosen so that $\mathbf{x}_{i_1}, \ldots, \mathbf{x}_{i_{n_r}}$ are $\pi_r(\mathbb{R}^d)$-unisolvent. Let the column index j_k be chosen according to (7.26). Then, the remainder $R_{n_r} = A - A_{n_r}$ can be bounded by*

$$|(R_{n_r})_{ij}| \leq c_r \eta^\mu M^{-r-1}, \qquad 1 \leq i \leq m, \quad 1 \leq j \leq n,$$

where $c_r > 0$ is a constant depending on the source points.

This corollary is nothing but Theorem 7.26. To see this, we note that the remainder $R_k(\mathbf{x}, \mathbf{y})$ of the kernel $K - K_k$ and the remainder R_k of the matrix $A - A_k$

are connected via

$$(R_k)_{ij} = R_k(\mathbf{x}_i, \mathbf{y}_j),$$

which is easily seen by induction. Moreover, the choice (7.26) of the index j_k corresponds to the choice (7.16).

7.3 Domain Decomposition Methods

The idea of domain decomposition methods is simply described as follows. Instead of solving one large problem, we solve many small problems. One of the first applications was in solving partial differential equations. Here, the underlying domain is subdivided into several sub-domains and a version of the original partial differential equation is solved on each of the sub-domains with appropriate new boundary conditions on the new, interior boundaries. It is possible to subdivide the domain either in a non-overlapping or in an overlapping way; both cases have their advantages and drawbacks. Here, we will not discuss the partial differential equation related background but refer the interested reader, for example, to the books by Quarteroni and Valli [102] and Toselli and Widlund [123]. Consequently, domain decomposition methods are also frequently used for large sparse systems.

Here, however, we will follow the more abstract approach described by Griebel and Oswald [71].

Hence, we start with a different example in more detail: the interpolation problem of Section 1.1.1.

Example 7.50 Let $X = \{\mathbf{x}_1, \ldots, \mathbf{x}_n\} \subseteq \mathbb{R}^d$ be our data sites and $f_1, \ldots, f_n \in \mathbb{R}$ be our data values. For $1 \leq j \leq J$, let $X_j \subseteq X$ such that $X = \cup X_j$. The sets X_j might be mutually disjoint or they might overlap, i.e. some of the data sites can be contained in several X_j.

Instead of computing an interpolant of the form

$$I_X f = \sum_{j=1}^{n} \alpha_j K(\cdot, \mathbf{x}_j),$$

which is equivalent to solving a linear system $A_{X,K}\alpha = \mathbf{f}$ with matrix $A_{X,K} = (K(\mathbf{x}_i, \mathbf{x}_j)) \in \mathbb{R}^{n \times n}$, we can compute J interpolants $I_{X_j} f$ by solving J linear systems with coefficient matrices $A_{X_j,K} \in \mathbb{R}^{|X_j| \times |X_j|}$. The total cost for this is $O(Jq^3)$, which becomes $O(n)$ if each X_j contains only a small number of $q \ll n$ data sites and the sets X_j do not overlap too much. However, we now need a good strategy for computing the global interpolant $I_{X,K} f$ from the local interpolants $I_{X_j,K} f$, $1 \leq j \leq J$. If we define $V_j := \text{span}\{K(\cdot, \mathbf{x}) : \mathbf{x} \in X_j\}$ and

$V = \text{span}\{K(\cdot, \mathbf{x}) : \mathbf{x} \in X\}$ then we obviously have $V = V_1 + \cdots + V_J$ such that we can write $I_{X,K}f = v_1 + \cdots + v_J$ with certain functions $v_j \in V_j$. However, if the X_j are not disjoint, this representation is not unique. Moreover, even if the X_j are disjoint, we will not have $I_{X,K}f = I_{X_1,K}f + \cdots + I_{X_J,K}f$.

As the interpolation matrices in the example above are symmetric and positive definite, we can recast the problem in a matrix–vector setting. We will do this in the more general setting of an arbitrary symmetric and positive definite matrix.

Example 7.51 Let us define $V := \mathbb{R}^n$. Let us assume that we have a partitioning of $I = \{1, \ldots, n\}$ into sets $I_1, \ldots, I_J \subseteq I$ with $I = \cup I_j$, which might or might not be disjoint. Let $V_j := \text{span}\{e_k : k \in I_j\}$. For $\mathbf{x} \in V_J$ we recall the reduced vector $\mathbf{x}_{I_j} \in \mathbb{R}^{|I_j|}$ consisting only of those x_k with $k \in I_j$. Similarly, for a matrix $A \in \mathbb{R}^{n \times n}$ we have defined sub-matrices $A_{I_j} := A_{I_j, I_j} \in \mathbb{R}^{|I_j| \times |I_j|}$ by simply using only entries of A with indices in I_j. If A is symmetric and positive definite, so is each A_{I_j} and we can define inner products

$$a : V \times V \to \mathbb{R}, \quad a(\mathbf{x}, \mathbf{y}) := \langle A\mathbf{x}, \mathbf{y}\rangle_2, \qquad \mathbf{x}, \mathbf{y} \in V,$$
$$a_j : V_j \times V_j \to \mathbb{R}, \quad a_j(\mathbf{x}, \mathbf{y}) := a(\mathbf{x}, \mathbf{y}) = \langle A_{I_j}\mathbf{x}_{I_j}, \mathbf{y}_{I_j}\rangle_2, \qquad \mathbf{x}, \mathbf{y} \in V_j.$$

The solution $\alpha \in \mathbb{R}^n$ of $A\alpha = \mathbf{f}$ is then equivalently given by

$$a(\alpha, \mathbf{y}) = \langle \mathbf{f}, \mathbf{y}\rangle_2, \qquad \mathbf{y} \in V,$$

and the solution vectors $\alpha^{(j)} \in \mathbb{R}^{|I_j|}$ of $A_{I_j}\alpha^{(j)} = \mathbf{f}_{I_j}$ are similarly given by $a_j(\alpha_j, \mathbf{y}) = \langle \mathbf{f}_{I_j}, \mathbf{y}_{I_j}\rangle_2$ with $(\alpha_j)_{I_j} = \alpha^{(j)}$. Again, the question remains of how the global solution $\alpha \in \mathbb{R}^n$ can be computed using the local solutions α_j, $1 \leq j \leq J$.

After these examples, we want to describe the ideas in a more formal and general set-up as earlier. To this end, let V be a finite-dimensional space with an inner product $a : V \times V \to \mathbb{R}$, $a(u, v) = \langle u, v, \rangle_V$, i.e. a is bilinear, symmetric and positive definite. If $F : V \to \mathbb{R}$ is a linear operator then the abstract problem we want to solve is to find $u \in V$ which satisfies

$$a(u, v) = F(v), \qquad v \in V. \tag{7.33}$$

The unique solution of this problem is the Riesz representer $f \in V$ of F with respect to the a-inner product.

We assume that V is decomposed into the sum of finitely many subspaces

$$V = V_1 + \cdots + V_J,$$

i.e. each $v \in V$ has at least one representation $v = v_1 + \cdots + v_J$ with $v_j \in V_j$, $1 \leq j \leq J$. This representation does not have to be unique, which is the case if the sum above is not a direct sum. We also assume that on each V_j we have an inner product $a_j : V_j \times V_j \to \mathbb{R}$. This can simply be given by $a_j = a$, but it can also be a different inner product.

Definition 7.52 The *Schwarz operators* $P_i : V \to V_i$, $1, \le i \le J$, are defined for $u \in V$ by

$$a_i(P_i u, v_i) = a(u, v_i), \qquad v_i \in V_i. \tag{7.34}$$

The *additive Schwarz operator* $P : V \to V$ is defined as

$$P := P_1 + \cdots + P_J.$$

If we choose $a_i = a$, then (7.34) becomes

$$a(u - P_i u, v_i) = 0, \qquad v_i \in V_i,$$

which means that P_i is the a-orthogonal projection onto V_i, see Definition 1.16, and $P_i u$ is the best approximation from V_i to u in the norm induced by the a-inner product, see Proposition 1.17. In general, we have the following simple properties of the operators.

Lemma 7.53 *1. Each operator $P_i : V \to V_i$ is well-defined.*
2. The operator $P : V \to V$ is self-adjoint, i.e. it satisfies

$$a(Pu, v) = a(u, Pv), \qquad u, v \in V.$$

3. The operator $P : V \to V$ is positive definite and hence invertible, i.e.

$$a(Pu, u) > 0, \qquad u \in V \neq 0.$$

Proof If $v_1, \ldots, v_n$ is a basis of V_i then, for each $u \in V$, we can express $P_i u$ in this basis as $Pu = \sum \alpha_j v_j$. Inserting this into (7.34) yields the linear system

$$\sum_{j=1}^{n} \alpha_j a_i(v_j, v_k) = a(u, v_k), \qquad 1 \le k \le n,$$

which is uniquely solvable as the matrix with entries $(a_i(v_j, v_k))_{j,k}$ is symmetric and positive definite by definition.

To see that $P : V \to V$ is self-adjoint we use its definition and (7.34) to conclude

$$a(u, Pv) = a\left(u, \sum_{j=1}^{J} P_j v\right) = \sum_{j=1}^{J} a(u, P_j v)$$

$$= \sum_{j=1}^{J} a_j(P_j u, P_j v) = \sum_{j=1}^{J} a(P_j u, v)$$

$$= a(Pu, v)$$

for arbitrary $u, v, \in V$.

Finally, we have for $u \in V$ that

$$a(Pu, u) = \sum_{j=1}^{J} a(P_j u, u) = \sum_{j=1}^{J} a_j(P_j u, P_j u) \geq 0,$$

as each a_j is positive definite. The expression can only be zero if for all $1 \leq j \leq J$ the terms $a_j(P_j u, P_j u)$ vanish, i.e. if $P_j u = 0$ for $1 \leq j \leq J$. However, this means

$$a(u, v_j) = a_j(P_j u, v_j) = 0, \qquad v_j \in V_j,$$

for all $1 \leq j \leq J$ and hence $a(u, v) = 0$ for all $v \in V$, which shows $u = 0$. Thus, P is positive definite and injective and as a linear mapping from the finite-dimensional space V to V it is invertible. □

After this, we can give an alternative way of finding $u \in V$ solving (7.33).

Proposition 7.54 *Let V be a finite-dimensional space with finite decomposition $V = V_1 + \cdots + V_J$. Let a, a_j, P and P_j be defined as described above. Let $F : V \to \mathbb{R}$ be linear. For $1 \leq j \leq J$ let $f_j \in V_j$ be the unique element satisfying $F(v_j) = a_j(f_j, v_j)$ for all $v_j \in V_j$ and let $f = f_1 + \cdots + f_J \in V$. Then, $u \in V$ satisfies (7.33) if and only if $Pu = f$.*

Proof If $u \in V$ satisfies $a(u, v) = F(v)$ for all $v \in V$ then we have

$$a_j(P_j u, v_j) = a(u, v_j) = F(v_j) = a_j(f_j, v_j), \qquad v_j \in V_j,$$

showing that $P_j u = f_j$ and hence $Pu = f$ holds.

If, however, $u \in V$ satisfies $Pu = f$, i.e. $u = P^{-1}f$, then, as P^{-1} is also self-adjoint, we have

$$a(u, v) = a(P^{-1}f, v) = a(f, P^{-1}v) = \sum_{j=1}^{J} a(f_j, P^{-1}v)$$

$$= \sum_{j=1}^{J} a_j(f_j, P_j P^{-1}v) = \sum_{j=1}^{J} F(P_j P^{-1}v)$$

$$= F\left(\sum_{j=1}^{J} P_j P^{-1}v\right) = F(v),$$

for all $v \in V$, showing that u also satisfies (7.33). □

This proposition gives us an alternative way of solving (7.33).

Definition 7.55 The *additive Schwarz method* for finding $u \in V$ with $a(u, v) = F(v)$ for all $v \in V$ comprises the following two steps.

1. For $1 \leq j \leq J$ solve the local problems: find $f_j \in V_j$ with $a_j(f_j, v_j) = F(v_j)$ for all $v_j \in V_j$.
2. Solve $Pu = f := f_1 + \cdots + f_J$.

The success of this method depends highly on the question of how fast the system $Pu = f$ can be solved. We will now discuss some iterative methods for this. But before doing so we have a look at the condition number of P, since we know it plays a crucial role for the conditioning of the problem and the convergence of iterative solution methods.

As our problem is defined using the inner product $a : V \times V \to \mathbb{R}$, it is quite natural to define the condition number with respect to this inner product.

Definition 7.56 The maximum and minimum eigenvalues of $P = P_1 + \cdots + P_J$ are defined as

$$\lambda_{\max}(P) := \sup_{u \in V \setminus \{0\}} \frac{a(Pu, u)}{a(u, u)}, \qquad \lambda_{\min}(P) := \inf_{u \in V \setminus \{0\}} \frac{a(Pu, u)}{a(u, u)}. \tag{7.35}$$

The condition number of P is defined as

$$\kappa(P) := \frac{\lambda_{\max}(P)}{\lambda_{\min}(P)}.$$

We start by giving a lower bound for the smallest eigenvalue.

Proposition 7.57 *If there is a constant $C_2 > 0$ such that any $u \in V = V_1 + \cdots + V_J$ admits a decomposition $u = u_1 + \cdots + u_J$ with $u_j \in V_j$ satisfying*

$$\sum_{j=1}^{J} a_j(u_j, u_j) \leq C_2 a(u, u) \tag{7.36}$$

then the minimum eigenvalue of P can be bounded from below by

$$\lambda_{\min}(P) \geq C_2^{-1}.$$

Proof The definition of the operators P_j, (7.36) and the Cauchy–Schwarz inequality yield

$$a(u, u) = \sum_{j=1}^{J} a(u, u_j) = \sum_{j=1}^{J} a_j(P_j u, u_j) \leq \sum_{j=1}^{J} a_j(P_j u, P_j u)^{1/2} a_j(u_j, u_j)^{1/2}$$

$$\leq \left[\sum_{j=1}^{J} a_j(P_j u, P_j u) \right]^{1/2} \left[\sum_{j=1}^{J} a_j(u_j, u_j) \right]^{1/2}$$

$$\leq C_2^{1/2} a(u, u)^{1/2} \left[\sum_{j=1}^{J} a_j(P_j u, P_j u) \right]^{1/2}.$$

Squaring the inequality and cancelling out the common factor yields

$$a(u, u) \le C_2 \sum_{j=1}^{J} a_j(P_j u, P_j u) = C_2 \sum_{j=1}^{J} a(u, P_j u) = C_2 a(u, Pu),$$

which immediately gives the lower bound for λ_{min}. $\qquad\square$

A decomposition $V = V_1 + \cdots + V_J$ which allows a decomposition $u = u_1 + \cdots + u_J$ satisfying (7.36) is also called *a stable* decomposition.

To derive an upper bound for the maximum eigenvalue, we first note that $P : V \to V$ has, as a positive definite, self-adjoint operator on a finite-dimensional subspace, a representation as a symmetric, positive definite matrix A. This matrix has, according to Lemma 1.13, a square root $A^{1/2}$ which is also symmetric and positive definite. This square root then defines a square root $P^{1/2} : V \to V$ of P, which is also self-adjoint and positive definite. This means particularly that we have $a(Pv, w) = a(P^{1/2}v, P^{1/2}w)$ for all $v, w \in V$ and hence

$$\lambda_{max} = \sup_{v \in V \setminus \{0\}} \frac{a(Pv, v)}{a(v, v)} = \sup_{w \in V \setminus \{0\}} \frac{a(w, w)}{a(P^{-1}w, w)}. \tag{7.37}$$

Proposition 7.58 *If there is a constant $C_1 > 0$ such that for any $u \in V = V_1 + \cdots + V_J$ the decomposition $u = u_1 + \cdots + u_J$ with $u_j = P_j P^{-1} u \in V_j$ satisfies*

$$a(u, u) \le C_1 \sum_{j=1}^{J} a_j(u_j, u_j) \tag{7.38}$$

then the maximum eigenvalue of P can be bounded by

$$\lambda_{max}(P) \le C_1.$$

Moreover, we have

$$a(P^{-1}u, u) = \min\left\{ \sum_{j=1}^{J} a_j(u_j, u_j) : u = \sum_{j=1}^{J} u_j \text{ with } u_j \in V_j \right\}. \tag{7.39}$$

Proof The specific choice $u_j = P_j P^{-1} u$ obviously yields a feasible decomposition of u as we have

$$\sum_{j=1}^{J} u_j = \sum_{j=1}^{J} P_j P^{-1} u = PP^{-1} u = u,$$

which also satisfies

$$\sum_{j=1}^{J} a_j(u_j, u_j) = \sum_{j=1}^{J} a_j(P_j P^{-1} u, P_j P^{-1} u) = \sum_{j=1}^{J} a(P^{-1} u, P_j P^{-1} u) = a(P^{-1} u, u).$$

The latter gives, together with (7.37),

$$\lambda_{\max}(P) = \sup_{u \in V \setminus \{0\}} \frac{a(u, u)}{a(P^{-1}u, u)} = \sup_{u \in V \setminus \{0\}} \frac{a(u, u)}{\sum_{j=1}^{J} a_j(P_j P^{-1}u, P_j P^{-1}u)} \leq C_1.$$

Finally, if $u = u_1 + \cdots + u_J$ is any such decomposition then we have

$$a(P^{-1}u, u) = \sum_{j=1}^{J} a(P^{-1}u, u_j) = \sum_{j=1}^{J} a_j(P_j P^{-1}u, u_j)$$

$$\leq \left[\sum_{j=1}^{J} a_j(P_j P^{-1}u, P_j P^{-1}u) \right]^{1/2} \left[\sum_{j=1}^{J} a_j(u_j, u_j) \right]^{1/2}$$

$$= \left[\sum_{j=1}^{J} a(P^{-1}u, P_j P^{-1}u) \right]^{1/2} \left[\sum_{j=1}^{J} a_j(u_j, u_j) \right]^{1/2}$$

$$= \left[a(P^{-1}u, u) \right]^{1/2} \left[\sum_{j=1}^{J} a_j(u_j, u_j) \right]^{1/2},$$

which shows

$$a(P^{-1}u, u) \leq \sum_{j=1}^{J} a_j(u_j, u_j)$$

for any decomposition $u = u_1 + \cdots + u_J$, and we already know that equality is attained for $u_j = P_j P^{-1}u$, which establishes (7.39). □

Note the difference between Propositions 7.57 and 7.58 regarding the assumptions. While in Proposition 7.57 it suffices to have one decomposition $u = u_1 + \cdots + u_J$ satisfying (7.36), in Proposition 7.58 one requires (7.38) to hold for the specific choice $u_j = P_j P^{-1}u$. However, if (7.36) holds for one decomposition it certainly holds for the specific decomposition with $u_j = P_j P^{-1}u$.

Example 7.59 Let $V = V_1 + \cdots + V_J$ be an a-orthogonal sum, i.e. each $u \in V$ has exactly one representation $u = u_1 + \cdots + u_J$ with $u_j \in V_j$ and $a(u_j, u_k) = 0$ for $j \neq k$. If the local inner products a_j are defined as $a_j = a$, then we obviously have

$$a(u, u) = \sum_{j=1}^{J} a(u_j, u_j),$$

i.e. (7.36) and (7.38) are satisfied with $C_1 = C_2 = 1$.

If the conditions of both Propositions 7.57 and 7.58 are satisfied we have the bound

$$\kappa(P) = \frac{\lambda_{\max}}{\lambda_{\min}} \leq C_1 C_2$$

on the condition number of our additive Schwarz operator $P = P_1 + \cdots + P_J$. As we know from Lemma 7.53, the operator P is self-adjoint and positive definite. Hence, we can represent it by a symmetric and positive definite matrix. Thus, a natural way of solving the equation

$$Pu = f$$

is by employing the conjugate gradient method. With the above bound on the condition number, we have also all the necessary ingredients for the convergence analysis.

Hence, we will now discuss an alternative. An easy iterative way of implementing the additive Schwarz method from Definition 7.55 is a simple residual correction algorithm, as outlined in Algorithm 41 with a relaxation parameter $\omega > 0$. As we can rewrite this scheme as

$$u^{(\ell+1)} = u^{(\ell)} - \omega(Pu^{(\ell)} - f) = (I - \omega P)u^{(\ell)} + \omega f, \qquad (7.40)$$

we see that it fits into our general iterative schemes discussed in Section 4.1. If we identify all operators with their associated matrices, then it is easy to see that Theorem 4.6 also applies in this situation, which already prepares the proof of the following theorem.

Algorithm 41: Additive subspace algorithm

Input : $V = V_1 + \cdots + V_J$, $F : V \to \mathbb{R}$, $\omega > 0$, $u^{(0)}$.
Output: Approximate solution of $Pu = f$.

1 **for** $j = 1$ **to** J **do**
2   $\quad$ Compute $f_j \in V_j$ with $a_j(f_j, v_j) = F(v_j)$ for all $v_j \in V_j$.
3 **for** $\ell = 0, 1, 2, \ldots$ **do**

4   $\quad u^{(\ell+1)} := u^{(\ell)} - \omega \displaystyle\sum_{j=1}^{J} (P_j u^{(\ell)} - f_j)$

Theorem 7.60 *Let* $V = V_1 + \cdots + V_J$ *be finite-dimensional. The additive Schwarz subspace algorithm converges to the solution of* $Pu = f$ *if and only if* $0 < \omega < 2/\lambda_{\max}$. *The convergence rate is determined by*

$$\rho := \max\{|1 - \omega\lambda_{\min}|, |1 - \omega\lambda_{\max}|\},$$

which becomes minimal for $\omega^* = 2/(\lambda_{\max} + \lambda_{\min})$ with value

$$\rho^* = 1 - \frac{2}{1 + \kappa(P)}. \tag{7.41}$$

Proof As outlined above, the method converges if and only if we have

$$\rho(I - \omega P) = \max\{|1 - \omega\lambda_{\min}|, |1 - \omega\lambda_{\max}|\} < 1.$$

If $0 < \omega < 2/\lambda_{\max}$ then we have $-1 < 1 - \omega\lambda_{\max} \le 1 - \omega\lambda_{\min} < 1$ and hence $\rho(I - \omega P) < 1$. If, however, $\rho(I - \omega P) < 1$ then we have $1 > \lambda_{\max}(I - \omega P) \ge |1 - \omega\lambda_{\max}| \ge 1 - \omega\lambda_{\max}$, showing $\omega\lambda_{\max} > 0$, meaning particularly $\omega > 0$ as $\lambda_{\max} > 0$. Similarly, the relation $-1 < -\rho(I - \omega P) \le -|1 - \omega\lambda_{\max}| \le 1 - \omega\lambda_{\max}$ leads to $\omega\lambda_{\max} < 2$, i.e. $\omega < 2/\lambda_{\max}$.

The optimal value ω^* is determined much as in the proof of Theorem 4.21. It is given by the intersection of the lines $y(\omega) = \omega\lambda_{\max} - 1$ and $z(\omega) = 1 - \omega\lambda_{\min}$. This optimal ω also immediately gives (7.41). □

We want to apply this general result to the situation of Example 7.51 with $I_j = \{j\}$.

Proposition 7.61 *Let $A \in \mathbb{R}^{n \times n}$ be symmetric and positive definite. Let $V = \mathbb{R}^n$ and for $1 \le j \le n$ let $V_j := \mathrm{span}\{\mathbf{e}_j\}$. The inner products $a : V \times V \to \mathbb{R}$ and $a_j : V_j \times V_j \to \mathbb{R}$ are defined by $a(\mathbf{u}, \mathbf{v}) = a_j(\mathbf{u}, \mathbf{v}) = \langle A\mathbf{u}, \mathbf{v}\rangle_2$. The right-hand side $F : V \to \mathbb{R}$ is defined by $F(\mathbf{u}) := \langle \mathbf{b}, \mathbf{u}\rangle_2$ for a given $\mathbf{b} \in \mathbb{R}^n$. Then, Algorithm 41 for solving $a(\mathbf{u}, \mathbf{v}) = F(\mathbf{v})$ for $\mathbf{v} \in V$ is the Jacobi relaxation method given in Algorithm 9 for solving $A\mathbf{x} = \mathbf{b}$.*

Proof We start by computing the local projection operators $P_i : V \to V_i$. As $V_i = \mathrm{span}\{\mathbf{e}_i\}$ we can write $P_i\mathbf{u} = \alpha_i\mathbf{e}_i$ with $\alpha_i \in \mathbb{R}$. By definition, we have

$$\langle \alpha_i A\mathbf{e}_i, \mathbf{e}_i\rangle_2 = a(P_i\mathbf{u}, \mathbf{e}_i) = a(\mathbf{u}, \mathbf{e}_i) = \langle A\mathbf{u}, \mathbf{e}_i\rangle_2,$$

which shows $\alpha_i = \mathbf{a}_i^T\mathbf{u}/a_{ii}$ if $\mathbf{a}_i = A\mathbf{e}_i$ denotes the ith column of $A = (a_{ij})$. Hence, we have $P_i = \frac{1}{a_{ii}}\mathbf{e}_i\mathbf{a}_i^T$. From this and the symmetry of A, it immediately follows that

$$P = P_1 + \cdots + P_n = D^{-1}A$$

with $D = \mathrm{diag}(a_{11}, \ldots, a_{nn})$. Thus, if we recall the decomposition $A = L + D + R$ into the lower-left part L of A, its diagonal part D and its upper-right part R, we find that the iteration $I - \omega P$ can be written in this context as

$$I - \omega P = I - \omega D^{-1}A = I - \omega D^{-1}(D + L + R) = (1 - \omega)I - \omega D^{-1}(L + R) = C_J(\omega),$$

where $C_J(\omega)$ is the iteration matrix of the Jacobi relaxation method, see (4.19). Finally, if we write again $\mathbf{f}_j = \beta_j\mathbf{e}_j$ with $\beta_j \in \mathbb{R}$ then the definition $a(\mathbf{f}_j, \mathbf{e}_j) =$

$F(\mathbf{e}_j) = \langle \mathbf{b}, \mathbf{e}_j \rangle_2$ of $\mathbf{f}_j$ yields easily $\beta_j = b_j / a_{jj}$ and $\mathbf{f}_j = \frac{b_j}{a_{jj}} \mathbf{e}_j$ so that we have $\mathbf{f} = \mathbf{f}_1 + \cdots + \mathbf{f}_n = D^{-1} \mathbf{b}$. This shows that the iteration (7.40) becomes

$$\mathbf{u}^{(j)} = (I - \omega P)\mathbf{u}^{(\ell)} + \omega \mathbf{f} = C_J(\omega)\mathbf{u}^{(j)} + \omega D^{-1} \mathbf{b},$$

which is (4.18), i.e. the iteration scheme of the Jacobi relaxation. $\square$

In contrast to Theorem 4.1, where we have expressed the optimal relaxation parameter using the eigenvalues of the iteration matrix C_J of the Jacobi method, Theorem 7.60 expresses the optimal relaxation parameter in terms of the eigenvalues of the operator P which is here $P = D^{-1}A$. The result is, of course, the same, as λ is an eigenvalue of

$$C_J = -D^{-1}(L + R) = I - D^{-1}A = I - P$$

if and only if $1 - \lambda$ is an eigenvalue of P.

A slight modification of the situation in Proposition 7.61 yields the so-called *block Jacobi relaxation*, which we will describe now. It should be clear that many of the iterative methods we have encountered so far have block variants which are often superior to the standard version. Nonetheless, we will give only this one example of such a block variant.

Instead of defining $V_j = \text{span}\{\mathbf{e}_j\}$ we choose a partitioning $P(\mathcal{J}) = \{J_1, \ldots, J_p\}$ of $\mathcal{J} = \{1, \ldots, n\}$ (see Definition 7.27) into index sets J_j having n_j elements. Without restriction, we assume that these index sets are again of the form (7.18), i.e. $J_j = \{1 + \bar{n}_{j-1}, \ldots, \bar{n}_j\}$ with $\bar{n}_0 = 0$ and $\bar{n}_{j+1} = \bar{n}_j + n_{j+1}$, and set $V_j := \text{span}\{\mathbf{e}_j : j \in J_j\}$ for $1 \leq j \leq p$.

To describe the projection operators P and P_j we introduce the extension matrix $E_j = (\mathbf{e}_{\bar{n}_{j-1}+1}, \ldots, \mathbf{e}_{\bar{n}_j}) \in \mathbb{R}^{n \times n_j}$. Then, we can define the projection $P_j : V = \mathbb{R}^n \to V_j$ by $P_j \mathbf{u} = E_j \alpha$ with $\alpha \in \mathbb{R}^{n_j}$. The definition of the projection operator yields

$$a(P_j \mathbf{u}, \mathbf{e}_\ell) = \langle AE_j \alpha, \mathbf{e}_\ell \rangle_2 = \langle A\mathbf{u}, \mathbf{e}_\ell \rangle_2, \qquad \ell \in J_j,$$

which means $E_j^{\mathrm{T}} AE_j \alpha = E_j^{\mathrm{T}} A\mathbf{u}$ and hence

$$P_j \mathbf{u} = E_j \alpha = E_j(E_j^{\mathrm{T}} AE_j)^{-1} E_j^{\mathrm{T}} A\mathbf{u}, \qquad (7.42)$$

where we used the fact that the reduced matrix $A_{J_j, J_j} := E_j^{\mathrm{T}} AE_j \in \mathbb{R}^{n_j \times n_j}$ is symmetric and positive definite whenever A has these properties.

Writing $\mathbf{f}_j = E_j \beta$ with $\beta \in \mathbb{R}^{n_j}$ and using the definition $a(\mathbf{f}_j, \mathbf{e}_\ell) = \langle \mathbf{b}, \mathbf{e}_\ell \rangle_2$, $\ell \in J_j$ shows $E_j^{\mathrm{T}} AE_j \beta = E_j^{\mathrm{T}} \mathbf{b}$ and hence

$$\mathbf{f}_j = E_j(E_j^{\mathrm{T}} AE_j)^{-1} E_j^{\mathrm{T}} \mathbf{b}.$$

This means that the additive subspace algorithm now takes the form

$$\mathbf{u}^{(\ell+1)} = \mathbf{u}^{(\ell)} - \omega \sum_{j=1}^{p} (P_j \mathbf{u}^{(\ell)} - \mathbf{f}_j)$$

$$= \mathbf{u}^{(\ell)} - \omega \sum_{j=1}^{p} \left[E_j (E_j^{\mathrm{T}} A E_j)^{-1} E_j^{\mathrm{T}} A \mathbf{u}^{(\ell)} - E_j (E_j^{\mathrm{T}} A E_j)^{-1} E_j^{\mathrm{T}} \mathbf{b} \right]$$

$$= \mathbf{u}^{(\ell)} - \omega \sum_{j=1}^{p} E_j (E_j^{\mathrm{T}} A E_j)^{-1} E_j^{\mathrm{T}} (A \mathbf{u}^{(\ell)} - \mathbf{b}).$$

With the notation $A_{J_j,J_j} = E_j^{\mathrm{T}} A E_j$ this can be realised as described in Algorithm 42. We have derived the algorithm for symmetric positive definite matrices but it can obviously be applied to any invertible matrix $A \in \mathbb{R}^{n \times n}$ for which the sub-matrices A_{J_j,J_j} are also invertible.

The matrix E_j acts as an extension operator $E_j : \mathbb{R}^{n_j} \to \mathbb{R}^n$ and its transpose E_j^{T} acts as an restriction operator $E_j : \mathbb{R}^n \to \mathbb{R}^{n_j}$. This observation can be used to form a block Jacobi method even in the case of an overlapping decomposition of the index set. The only thing we have to change is that we need to define new restriction operators $R_j : \mathbb{R}^n \to \mathbb{R}^{n_j}$, $R_j = (\lambda_k \mathbf{e}_k : k \in J_j)$ with certain numbers $\lambda_k \in \mathbb{R}$ such that $R_j^{\mathrm{T}} E_j = I$.

Algorithm 42: Block Jacobi relaxation

Input : $A \in \mathbb{R}^{n \times n}$, $\mathbf{b} \in \mathbb{R}^n$, $\mathbf{x}^{(0)}$, $J_1, \ldots, J_p \subseteq \{1, \ldots, n\}$.
Output: Approximate solution of $A\mathbf{x} = \mathbf{b}$.

1   **for** $\ell = 1, 2, \ldots$ **do**
2   **for** $j = 1$ **to** p **do**
3   Solve $A_{J_j,J_j} \mathbf{r}_j = E_j^{\mathrm{T}} (\mathbf{b} - A\mathbf{x}^{(\ell)})$
4       $\mathbf{x}^{(\ell+1)} := \mathbf{x}^{(\ell)} + \omega E_j \mathbf{r}_j$

We will now take another look at the situation of Example 7.51 and Proposition 7.61, i.e. we define again $V_j := \mathrm{span}\{\mathbf{e}_j\}$ for $1 \leq j \leq n$. This time, however, we will not define the local inner products a_j to be a restricted to $V_j \times V_j$. Instead, we use $a_j(\mathbf{u}, \mathbf{v}) := \langle \mathbf{u}, \mathbf{v} \rangle_2$. The global inner product remains $a(\mathbf{u}, \mathbf{v}) := \langle A\mathbf{u}, \mathbf{v} \rangle_2$ and also $F(\mathbf{v}) := \langle \mathbf{b}, \mathbf{v} \rangle_2$.

In this situation the definition of the projector $P_j(\mathbf{u}) := \alpha_j \mathbf{e}_j$ and the symmetry of A yield

$$\alpha_j = \langle \alpha_j \mathbf{e}_j, \mathbf{e}_j \rangle_2 = \langle P_j \mathbf{u}, \mathbf{e}_j \rangle_2 = a_j(P_j \mathbf{u}, \mathbf{e}_j) = a(\mathbf{u}, \mathbf{e}_j) = \langle A\mathbf{u}, \mathbf{e}_j \rangle_2 = \mathbf{a}_j^{\mathrm{T}} \mathbf{u},$$

showing $P_j\mathbf{u} = \mathbf{e}_j\mathbf{a}_j^\mathsf{T}\mathbf{u}$ and hence $P\mathbf{u} = A\mathbf{u}$. In the same way, we find $\mathbf{f}_j = b_j\mathbf{e}_j$, meaning $\mathbf{f} = \mathbf{b}$ and hence the additive subspace algorithm becomes the simple residual correction algorithm also known as *Richardson iteration*

$$\mathbf{u}^{(\ell+1)} = \mathbf{u}^{(\ell)} + \omega(\mathbf{b} - A\mathbf{u}^{(\ell)}).$$

Obviously, in the light of the discussion above, also a block version of the Richardson iteration can easily be derived.

The advantage of the additive subspace algorithm in the form

$$u^{(\ell+1)} = u^{(\ell)} - \omega \sum_{j=1}^{J}(P_j u^{(\ell)} - f_j)$$

is that for each ℓ the sub-problems $P_j u^{(\ell)}$, $1 \le j \le J$, can be computed in parallel. A possible disadvantage is that already-computed sub-problems will enter the computation only at the next iteration.

Within the *multiplicative Schwarz method*, each computed projection is immediately employed and the new iterations are defined as described in Algorithm 43.

Algorithm 43: Multiplicative subspace algorithm

   Input : $V = V_1 + \cdots + V_J$, $F : V \to \mathbb{R}$, $\omega > 0$, $u^{(0)}$.
   Output: Approximate solution of $Pu = f$.

1 **for** $j = 1$ **to** J **do**
2   Compute $f_j \in V_j$ with $a_j(f_j, v_j) = F(v_j)$ for all $v_j \in V_j$
3 **for** $\ell = 0, 1, 2, \ldots$ **do**
4   **for** $j = 1$ **to** J **do**
5        $u^{(\ell+j/J)} := u^{(\ell+(j-1)/J)} - \omega(P_j u^{(\ell+(j-1)/J)} - f_j)$

This means that for deriving the new full iteration $u^{(\ell+1)}$ from the old iteration $u^{(\ell)}$, J successive steps

$$u^{(\ell+j/J)} := u^{(\ell+(j-1)/J)} - \omega(P_j u^{(\ell+(j-1)/J)} - f_j), \qquad 1 \le j \le J,$$

are necessary.

While the additive subspace algorithm is related to the Jacobi relaxation, the multiplicative subspace algorithm is related to the Gauss–Seidel relaxation. To see this, let us return to the situation of Example 7.51 and Proposition 7.61, where $V_j = \text{span}\{e_j\}$, $1 \le j \le n$, and $a_j(\mathbf{u}, \mathbf{v}) = a(\mathbf{u}, \mathbf{v}) = \langle A\mathbf{u}, \mathbf{v}\rangle_2$ with a symmetric and positive definite matrix $A \in \mathbb{R}^{n \times n}$. In this situation, we have seen that $P_i = \frac{1}{a_{ii}} \mathbf{e}_i \mathbf{a}_i^{\mathrm{T}}$ and $\mathbf{f}_i = \frac{b_i}{a_{ii}} \mathbf{e}_i$ for the given right-hand side $\mathbf{b} \in \mathbb{R}^n$. Hence, we see that the iterations become

$$
\begin{aligned}
\mathbf{u}^{(\ell+i/n)} &= \mathbf{u}^{(\ell+(i-1)/n)} - \omega(P_i \mathbf{u}^{(\ell+(i-1)/n)} - \mathbf{f}_i) \\
&= \mathbf{u}^{(\ell+(i-1)/n)} - \frac{\omega}{a_{ii}} \left(\mathbf{a}_i^{\mathrm{T}} \mathbf{u}^{(\ell+(i-1)/n)} - b_i \right) \mathbf{e}_i.
\end{aligned}
$$

From this, we see that for each $1 \leq i \leq n$ only the ith component of $\mathbf{u}^{(\ell+i/n)}$ is changed, meaning in particular

$$
u_k^{(\ell+i/n)} = \begin{cases} u_k^{(\ell+1)} & \text{if } k \leq i, \\ u_k^{(\ell)} & \text{if } k > i \end{cases} \tag{7.43}
$$

and hence

$$
\begin{aligned}
u_i^{(\ell+1)} = u_i^{(\ell+i/n)} &= u_i^{(\ell+(i-1)/n)} - \frac{\omega}{a_{ii}} \left(\mathbf{a}_i^{\mathrm{T}} \mathbf{u}^{(\ell+(i-1)/n)} - b_i \right) \\
&= u_i^{(\ell+(i-1)/n)} + \frac{\omega}{a_{ii}} \left(b_i - \sum_{k=1}^{n} a_{ik} u_k^{(\ell+(i-1)/n)} \right) \\
&= u_i^{(\ell)} + \frac{\omega}{a_{ii}} \left(b_i - \sum_{k=1}^{i-1} a_{ik} u_k^{(\ell+1)} - \sum_{k=i}^{n} a_{ik} u_k^{(i)} \right),
\end{aligned}
$$

which is exactly the Gauss–Seidel relaxation given in Definition 4.23. Thus, we have proven the following result.

Proposition 7.62 *Let $A \in \mathbb{R}^{n \times n}$ be symmetric and positive definite. Let $V = \mathbb{R}^n$ and for $1 \leq j \leq n$ let $V_j := \mathrm{span}\{\mathbf{e}_j\}$. The inner products $a : V \times V \to \mathbb{R}$ and $a_j : V_j \times V_j \to \mathbb{R}$ are defined by $a(\mathbf{u}, \mathbf{v}) = a_j(\mathbf{u}, \mathbf{v}) = \langle A\mathbf{u}, \mathbf{v} \rangle_2$. The right-hand side $F : V \to \mathbb{R}$ is defined by $F(\mathbf{u}) := \langle \mathbf{b}, \mathbf{u} \rangle_2$ for a given $\mathbf{b} \in \mathbb{R}^n$. Then, Algorithm 43 for solving $a(\mathbf{u}, \mathbf{v}) = F(\mathbf{v})$ for $\mathbf{v} \in V$ is the Gauss–Seidel relaxation or SOR method given in Algorithm 10 for solving $A\mathbf{x} = \mathbf{b}$.*

Obviously, it is easily possible to derive also a block version of the Gauss–Seidel relaxation from a multiplicative subspace algorithm, as we have done for deriving a block version of the Jacobi relaxation from an additive subspace algorithm. The details are left to the reader.

Now, we want to explain how the above ideas leading to Proposition 7.62 can be used to interpret the general multiplicative subspace algorithm as an SOR method. To this end, we define the coordinate space

$$
\tilde{V} := V_1 \times V_2 \times \cdots \times V_J
$$

and equip this space with an inner product

$$\tilde{a}(\mathbf{u}, \mathbf{v}) := \sum_{j=1}^{J} a_j(u_j, v_j), \qquad \mathbf{u} = (u_1, \ldots, u_J), \mathbf{v} = (v_1, \ldots, v_J) \in \tilde{V}.$$

The operators $P_i : V \to V_i$ define coordinate operators $P_{ij} := P_i|V_j : V_j \to V_i$, $1 \leq i, j \leq J$, which can then be used to define an operator, or a matrix, $\tilde{P} : \tilde{V} \to \tilde{V}$ by setting

$$(\tilde{P}\mathbf{u})_i := \sum_{j=1}^{J} P_{ij} u_j = \sum_{j=1}^{J} P_i u_j = P_i \left(\sum_{j=1}^{J} u_j \right), \qquad \mathbf{u} = (u_1, \ldots, u_J) \in \tilde{V},$$

and its columns as operators $\tilde{P}_i : \tilde{V} \to \tilde{V}$ given by

$$\tilde{P}_i \mathbf{u} = (\tilde{P}\mathbf{u})\mathbf{e}_i = \left(\sum_{j=1}^{J} P_{ij} u_j \right) \mathbf{e}_i = P_i \left(\sum_{j=1}^{J} u_j \right) \mathbf{e}_i. \tag{7.44}$$

It is easy to see that $\tilde{P}$ is self-adjoint with respect to $\tilde{a}$, i.e. it satisfies $\tilde{a}(\tilde{P}\mathbf{u}, \mathbf{v}) = \tilde{a}(\mathbf{u}, \tilde{P}\mathbf{v})$ for all $\mathbf{u}, \mathbf{v} \in \tilde{V}$.

Finally, we have the obvious mapping $T : \tilde{V} \to V$ defined by $\mathbf{u} \mapsto T\mathbf{u} = u_1 + \cdots + u_J$. Its adjoint $T^* : V \to \tilde{V}$ is given by $T^*u = (P_1 u, \ldots, P_J u)$ which follows directly from

$$a(T\mathbf{u}, v) = \sum_{j=1}^{J} a(u_j, v) = \sum_{j=1}^{J} a_j(u_j, P_j v) = \sum_{j=1}^{J} a_j(u_j, (T^*v)_j) = \tilde{a}(\mathbf{u}, T^*v)$$

holding for all $\mathbf{u} \in \tilde{V}$ and $v \in V$. The operators T and T^* allow us to rewrite P and $\tilde{P}$ as

$$P = TT^*, \qquad \tilde{P} = T^*T.$$

With this, we can express the multiplicative subspace algorithm entirely in the coordinate space $\tilde{V}$.

Lemma 7.63 *With the notation introduced above let $\mathbf{u}^{(0)} \in \tilde{V}$ and $u^{(0)} \in V$ be given. Moreover, let $\mathbf{f}_j := f_j \mathbf{e}_j \in \tilde{V}$ with $f_j \in V_j$. Let the sequence $\{u^{(\ell+j/J)}\}$ be defined by*

$$u^{(\ell+j/J)} = u^{(\ell+(j-1)/J)} - \omega \left(P_j u^{(\ell+(j-1)/J)} - f_j \right) \tag{7.45}$$

and let the sequence $\{\mathbf{u}^{(\ell+j/J)}\}$ be defined by

$$\mathbf{u}^{(\ell+j/J)} = \mathbf{u}^{(\ell+(j-1)/J)} - \omega \left(\tilde{P}_j \mathbf{u}^{(\ell+(j-1)/J)} - \mathbf{f}_j \right). \tag{7.46}$$

If $u^{(0)} = T\mathbf{u}^{(0)}$ then

$$u^{(\ell+j/J)} = T\mathbf{u}^{(\ell+j/J)}$$

for all $1 \leq j \leq J$ *and all* $\ell = 0, 1, 2, \ldots$.

Proof We define $v^{(\ell+j/J)} := T\mathbf{u}^{(\ell+j/J)}$. Then, the obvious relations $T\tilde{P}_j = P_j T$ and $T\mathbf{f}_j = f_j$ show that the sequence $\{v^{(\ell+j/J)}\}$ also satisfies the recurrence relation (7.45) but as $\{v^{(\ell+j/J)}\}$ and $\{u^{(\ell+j/J)}\}$ satisfy both the same recurrence and have the same initial values, they must be the same. $\quad\square$

Hence, instead of analysing the original recurrence (7.45) we can proceed with analysing the recurrence (7.46) which is closer to the classical matrix setting. As in that case, we can split the operator $\tilde{P}$ into $\tilde{P} = \tilde{L} + \tilde{D} + \tilde{R}$, where each of these operators maps $\tilde{V}$ to $\tilde{V}$ and they are given by their entries

$$\tilde{L}_{ij} = \begin{cases} P_{ij} & \text{if } i > j, \\ 0 & \text{else,} \end{cases} \qquad \tilde{R}_{ij} = \begin{cases} P_{ij} & \text{if } i < j, \\ 0 & \text{else,} \end{cases} \qquad \tilde{D}_{ij} = \begin{cases} P_{ii} & \text{if } i = j, \\ 0 & \text{else.} \end{cases}$$

The operators $\tilde{R}$ and $\tilde{L}$ are adjoint with respect to the inner product $\tilde{a}$, as we have, for $\mathbf{u}, \mathbf{v} \in \tilde{V}$,

$$\tilde{a}(\tilde{L}\mathbf{u}, \mathbf{v}) = \sum_{i=1}^{J} a_i((\tilde{L}\mathbf{u})_i, v_i) = \sum_{i=1}^{J} \sum_{j=1}^{i-1} a_i(P_{ij}u_j, v_i) = \sum_{i=2}^{J} \sum_{j=1}^{i-1} a_i(P_i u_j, v_i)$$

$$= \sum_{i=2}^{J} \sum_{j=1}^{i-1} a(u_j, v_i) = \sum_{i=2}^{J} \sum_{j=1}^{i-1} a_j(u_j, P_j v_i) = \sum_{j=1}^{J-1} \sum_{i=j+1}^{J} a_j(u_j, P_j v_i)$$

$$= \sum_{j=1}^{J} a_j\left(u_j, \sum_{i=j+1}^{J} P_{ji} v_i\right) = \sum_{j=1}^{J} a_j(u_j, (\tilde{R}\mathbf{v})_j) = \tilde{a}(\mathbf{u}, \tilde{R}\mathbf{v}).$$

Also, the operator $\tilde{D}$ is positive definite and self-adjoint with respect to $\tilde{a}$ as this time we have

$$\tilde{a}(\tilde{D}\mathbf{u}, \mathbf{u}) = \sum_{i=1}^{J} a_i(P_{ii}u_i, u_i) = \sum_{i=1}^{J} a(u_i, u_i) > 0$$

whenever $\mathbf{u} \in \tilde{V} \setminus \{\mathbf{0}\}$.

After setting up this machinery, we will now use it to show that the full iterations $\mathbf{u}^{(\ell)}$ of the sequence $\{u^{(\ell+j/J)}\}$ satisfy an SOR-like iteration.

Lemma 7.64 *With the notation above, the sequence $\{\mathbf{u}^{(\ell)}\}$ defined by (7.46) satisfies*

$$\left(\tilde{I} + \omega\tilde{L}\right)\mathbf{u}^{(\ell+1)} = \left[\tilde{I} - \omega\left(\tilde{D} + \tilde{R}\right)\right]\mathbf{u}^{(\ell)} + \omega\mathbf{f}, \qquad \ell = 0, 1, 2, \ldots,$$

where $\tilde{I}$ denotes the identity in $\tilde{V}$.

Proof The proof essentially follows the ideas outlined above for the special case $V = \mathbb{R}^n$. Using (7.44), we find from

$$\mathbf{u}^{(\ell+i/J)} = \mathbf{u}^{(\ell+(i-1)/J)} - \omega\left[\left(\sum_{k=1}^{J} P_{ik}u_k^{(\ell+(i-1)/J)}\right)\mathbf{e}_i - \mathbf{f}_i\right]$$

again that the ith step only changes the ith component of the iteration. Hence, we once again have (7.43) which leads to

$$u_i^{(\ell+1)} = u_i^{(\ell+i/J)} = u_i^{(\ell+(i-1)/J)} - \omega\left(\sum_{k=1}^{J} P_{ik}u_k^{(\ell+(i-1)/J)} - f_i\right)$$

$$= u_i^{(\ell+(i-1)/J)} - \omega\left(\sum_{k=1}^{j-1} P_{ik}u_k^{(\ell+1)} + \sum_{k=j}^{J} P_{ik}u_k^{(\ell)} - f_i\right).$$

Rewriting this in vector form and using the definitions of $\tilde{D}, \tilde{R}, \tilde{L}$ gives the desired form. □

Now we are in the situation to derive a general convergence result for the multiplicative subspace algorithm, which is similar to previous results on SOR. We will do this using the norms $\|\mathbf{u}\|_{\tilde{a}} := \tilde{a}(\mathbf{u}, \mathbf{u})^{1/2}$ and $\|u\|_a := a(u, u)^{1/2}$ on $\tilde{V}$ and V, respectively, and their induced operator norms.

Theorem 7.65 *Let $V = V_1 + \cdots + V_J$ be finite-dimensional. Let*

$$\omega_1 := \lambda_{\max}(\tilde{D}) = \max_{1 \le j \le J} \max_{u_j \in V_j} \frac{a(u_j, u_j)}{a_j(u_j, u_j)}$$

and let $\tilde{W} := \frac{1}{\omega}\tilde{I} + \tilde{L}$. Then, the iterations of the multiplicative subspace algorithm satisfy

$$u^{(\ell+1)} = [I - T\tilde{W}^{-1}T^*]u^{(\ell)} + T\tilde{W}^{-1}\mathbf{f}. \qquad (7.47)$$

They converge for $0 < \omega < 2/\omega_1$ to the solution $u \in V$ of $Pu = f$. The convergence rate is determined by the norm of the iteration matrix $C(\omega) := I - T\tilde{W}^{-1}T^*$, which can be bounded by

$$\|C(\omega)\|_a \le \left(1 - \frac{\lambda_{\min}\left(\frac{2}{\omega} - \omega_1\right)}{\|\tilde{W}\|_{\tilde{a}}^2}\right)^{1/2} \le \left(1 - \frac{\lambda_{\min}\left(\frac{2}{\omega} - \omega_1\right)}{\left(\frac{1}{\omega} + \|\tilde{L}\|_{\tilde{a}}\right)^2}\right)^{1/2}, \qquad (7.48)$$

where $\lambda_{\min} = \lambda_{\min}(P)$ is defined by (7.35). The expression on the right-hand side attains its minimum

$$\|C(\omega^*)\|_a \le \left(1 - \frac{\lambda_{\min}}{2\|\tilde{L}\|_{\tilde{a}} + \omega_1}\right)^{1/2}$$

for $\omega^* = 1/(\|\tilde{L}\|_{\tilde{a}} + \omega_1)$.

Proof We start by showing (7.47). Using the relation $u^{(\ell)} = T\mathbf{u}^{(\ell)}$ and Lemma 7.64 we have

$$
\begin{aligned}
u^{(\ell+1)} &= T(\tilde{I} + \omega\tilde{L})^{-1}[\tilde{I} - \omega(\tilde{D} + \tilde{R})]\mathbf{u}^{(\ell)} + \omega T(\tilde{I} + \omega\tilde{L})^{-1}\mathbf{f} \\
&= T[\tilde{I} - \omega(\tilde{I} + \omega\tilde{L})^{-1}\tilde{P}]\mathbf{u}^{(\ell)} + \omega T(\tilde{I} + \omega\tilde{L})^{-1}\mathbf{f} \\
&= T\left[\tilde{I} - \left(\frac{1}{\omega}\tilde{I} + \tilde{L}\right)^{-1}T^*T\right]\mathbf{u}^{(\ell)} + T\left(\frac{1}{\omega}\tilde{I} + \tilde{L}\right)^{-1}\mathbf{f} \\
&= \left[T - T\left(\frac{1}{\omega}\tilde{I} + \tilde{L}\right)^{-1}T^*T\right]\mathbf{u}^{(\ell)} + T\left(\frac{1}{\omega}\tilde{I} + \tilde{L}\right)^{-1}\mathbf{f} \\
&= \left[I - T\left(\frac{1}{\omega}\tilde{I} + \tilde{L}\right)^{-1}T^*\right]u^{(\ell)} + T\left(\frac{1}{\omega}\tilde{I} + \tilde{L}\right)^{-1}\mathbf{f},
\end{aligned}
$$

where we have also used $T\tilde{I} = IT$ and $\tilde{P} = T^*T$. Hence, the iteration matrix is indeed given by

$$
C(\omega) := I - T\left(\frac{1}{\omega}\tilde{I} + \tilde{L}\right)^{-1}T^*.
$$

To compute its norm, we first compute $C(\omega)^*C(\omega)$. Taking the discussion about the adjoint operators above into account, this becomes

$$
\begin{aligned}
C(\omega)^*C(\omega) &= \left[I - T\left(\frac{1}{\omega}\tilde{I} + \tilde{R}\right)^{-1}T^*\right]\left[I - T\left(\frac{1}{\omega}\tilde{I} + \tilde{L}\right)^{-1}T^*\right] \\
&= I - T\left(\frac{1}{\omega}\tilde{I} + \tilde{R}\right)^{-1}\left[\frac{1}{\omega}\tilde{I} + \tilde{L} + \frac{1}{\omega}\tilde{I} + \tilde{R} - T^*T\right]\left(\frac{1}{\omega}\tilde{I} + \tilde{L}\right)^{-1}T^* \\
&= I - T(\tilde{W}^{-1})^*\left[\frac{2}{\omega}\tilde{I} - \tilde{D}\right]\tilde{W}^{-1}T^*.
\end{aligned}
$$

Thus, the norm of $C(\omega)$ is given by

$$
\begin{aligned}
\|C(\omega)\|_a^2 &= \sup_{u\in V\setminus\{0\}}\frac{a(C(\omega)u, C(\omega)u)}{a(u, u)} = \sup_{u\in V\setminus\{0\}}\frac{a(C(\omega)^*C(\omega)u, u)}{a(u, u)} \\
&= \sup_{u\in V\setminus\{0\}}\left[1 - \frac{a\left(T(\tilde{W}^{-1})^*\left(\frac{2}{\omega}\tilde{I} - \tilde{D}\right)\tilde{W}^{-1}T^*u, u\right)}{a(u, u)}\right].
\end{aligned}
\tag{7.49}
$$

Before further bounding this expression, we first note that

$$
\omega_1 := \max_{1\le j\le J}\max_{u_j\in V_j}\frac{a(u_j, u_j)}{a_j(u_j, u_j)}
$$

is indeed the maximum eigenvalue of $\tilde{D}$, as we have on the one hand

$$
\begin{aligned}
\lambda_{\max}(\tilde{D}) &= \sup_{u \in \tilde{V} \setminus \{0\}} \frac{\tilde{a}(\tilde{D}\mathbf{u}, \mathbf{u})}{\tilde{a}(\mathbf{u}, \mathbf{u})} = \sup_{u \in \tilde{V} \setminus \{0\}} \frac{\sum_{j=1}^{J} a_j(P_j u_j, u_j)}{\sum_{j=1}^{J} a_j(u_j, u_j)} \\
&= \sup_{u \in \tilde{V} \setminus \{0\}} \frac{\sum_{j=1}^{J} a(u_j, u_j)}{\sum_{j=1}^{J} a_j(u_j, u_j)} \le \omega_1 \sup_{u \in \tilde{V} \setminus \{0\}} \frac{\sum_{j=1}^{J} a_j(u_j, u_j)}{\sum_{j=1}^{J} a_j(u_j, u_j)} = \omega_1.
\end{aligned}
$$

On the other hand, if we pick $1 \le k \le J$ and $u_k \in V_k$ such that $\omega_1 = a(u_k, u_k)/a_k(u_k, u_k)$ and set $\mathbf{u} = u_k \mathbf{e}_k$ then we see that also $\lambda_{\max}(\tilde{D}) \ge \omega_1$ holds. Next, we note that $P = TT^*$ and the definition of $\lambda_{\min} = \lambda_{\min}(P)$ yield

$$
a(u, u) \le \frac{1}{\lambda_{\min}} a(Pu, u) = \frac{1}{\lambda_{\min}} a(TT^*u, u) = \frac{1}{\lambda_{\min}} \tilde{a}(T^*u, T^*u)
$$

for all $u \in V$. This can now be used in

$$
\begin{aligned}
a\left(T(\tilde{W}^{-1})^* \left[\frac{2}{\omega}\tilde{I} - \tilde{D}\right] \tilde{W}^{-1} T^*u, u\right) &= \tilde{a}\left(\left[\frac{2}{\omega}\tilde{I} - \tilde{D}\right] \tilde{W}^{-1} T^*u, \tilde{W}^{-1} T^*u\right) \\
&\ge \lambda_{\min}\left(\frac{2}{\omega}\tilde{I} - \tilde{D}\right) \tilde{a}(\tilde{W}^{-1} T^*u, \tilde{W}^{-1} T^*u) \\
&\ge \left(\frac{2}{\omega} - \lambda_{\max}(\tilde{D})\right) \frac{\tilde{a}(T^*u, T^*u)}{\|\tilde{W}\|_{\tilde{a}}^2} \\
&\ge \left(\frac{2}{\omega} - \omega_1\right) \frac{\lambda_{\min}}{\|\tilde{W}\|_{\tilde{a}}^2} a(u, u),
\end{aligned}
$$

which holds as long as $\frac{2}{\omega} - \lambda_{\max}(\tilde{D}) = \frac{2}{\omega} - \omega_1 > 0$. Inserting this into (7.49) yields the first bound in (7.48). The second bound follows immediately from

$$
\|\tilde{W}\|_{\tilde{a}} = \left\|\frac{1}{\omega}\tilde{I} + \tilde{L}\right\|_{\tilde{a}} \le \frac{1}{\omega} + \|\tilde{L}\|_{\tilde{a}}.
$$

To minimise this second bound with respect to $\omega \in (0, 2/\omega_1)$ we set $x = 1/\omega$ and maximise

$$
F(x) = \frac{2x - \omega_1}{(x + \|\tilde{L}\|_{\tilde{a}})^2}
$$

over $x > \omega_1/2$. Noting $F(x) \to 0$ for $x \to \omega_1/2$ and for $x \to \infty$, we see that the only zero of $F'(x)$ which is given by $x^* = \|\tilde{L}\|_{\tilde{a}} + \omega_1$ with function value $F(x^*) = 1/(2\|\tilde{L}\|_{\tilde{a}} + \omega_1) > 0$ is the only global maximum of F. □

For the additive subspace algorithm the order of the subspaces V_j obviously does not matter as we can compute all projections simultaneously. For the multiplicative subspace algorithm, however, the order of the subspaces matters and this is reflected in the above result as the norm $\|\tilde{L}\|_{\tilde{a}}$ depends on the ordering. Nonetheless, many standard results on the convergence of the multiplicative subspace make additional assumptions which guarantee convergence rates independent of the ordering.

There is yet another way of understanding the multiplicative subspace algorithm, by looking at the recursion of the error. To this end, let us introduce the operators $Q_j = Q_j(\omega) = I - \omega P_j$. Then, we have

$$u^{(\ell+j/J)} = Q_j u^{(\ell+(j-1)/J)} + \omega f_j$$

and as the solution u of $Pu = f = f_1 + \cdots + f_J$ satisfies $P_j u = f_j$, the error $u - u^{(\ell+j/J)}$ satisfies the recursion

$$
\begin{aligned}
u - u^{(\ell+j/J)} &= u - Q_j u^{(\ell+(j-1)/J)} - \omega f_j \\
&= Q_j \left(u - u^{(\ell+(j-1)/J)} \right) + \omega P_j u - \omega f_j \\
&= Q_j \left(u - u^{(\ell+(j-1)/J)} \right)
\end{aligned}
$$

and hence

$$u - u^{(\ell+1)} = Q_J Q_{J-1} \cdots Q_1 (u - u^{(\ell)}) = \cdots = [Q_J \cdots Q_1]^{(\ell+1)} (u - u^{(0)}).$$

This means that we also have the identity

$$I - T \left(\frac{1}{\omega} \tilde{I} + \tilde{L} \right)^{-1} T^* = Q_J \cdots Q_1 = (I - \omega P_J) \cdots (I - \omega P_1),$$

which we will not exploit any further here. Instead we want to give a final convergence result for the specific situation that $a_j = a$ and $\omega = 1$. In this case, we already know that $P_j : V \to V_j$ is the orthogonal projection onto V_j. From this, it follows that $Q_j = I - P_j$ is the orthogonal projection onto the orthogonal complement $U_j := V_j^\perp = \{u \in V : a(u, v) = 0 \text{ for all } v \in V_j\}$ of V_j. The intersection $U := \cap_{j=1}^J U_j$ of all the U_j is $\{0\}$. To see this, assume that $u \in U$ then $u \in U_j$ for all $1 \le j \le J$, i.e. u is orthogonal to all V_j and hence to V but as u itself belongs to V it must be the zero element.

Consequently, the following more general result on the convergence of sequences of the form $(Q_J \cdots Q_1)^{(\ell)}$ also applies to our situation and shows convergence of the multiplicative subspace algorithm in this specific situation.

To formulate this general result, we recall that a Hilbert space is a *complete* pre-Hilbert space, i.e. all Cauchy sequences converge. We also recall that a closed subspace of a Hilbert space is complete itself and that each finite-dimensional subspace of a Hilbert space is closed. Moreover, a closed subspace U of a Hilbert space always has an orthogonal complement $U^\perp = \{v \in H : \langle u, v \rangle = 0 \text{ for all } u \in H\}$ satisfying $H = U + U^\perp$. Finally, let us introduce the concept of an angle between closed subspaces of a Hilbert space.

Definition 7.66 Let U_1 and U_2 be two closed subspaces of a Hilbert space H and denote their intersection by U. The *angle* α between U_1 and U_2 is defined by

$$\cos \alpha = \sup\{\langle u, v \rangle : u \in U_1 \cap U^\perp, v \in U_2 \cap U^\perp \text{ and } \|u\|, \|v\| \leq 1\}.$$

Theorem 7.67 *Suppose $Q_1, \ldots, Q_J$ are orthogonal projections onto closed subspaces $U_1, \ldots, U_J$ of a Hilbert space H. Let $U = \cap_{j=1}^J U_j$ and $Q : H \to U$ be the orthogonal projection onto U. Finally, let α_j be the angle between U_j and $A_j := \cap_{i=j+1}^J U_i$. Then, for any $u \in H$,*

$$\left\| (Q_J \cdots Q_1)^\ell u - Qu \right\|^2 \leq c^{2\ell} \| u - Qu \|^2,$$

where

$$c^2 \leq 1 - \prod_{j=1}^{J-1} \sin^2 \alpha_j.$$

Proof Let us set $R := Q_J \cdots Q_1$. From $Qu \in U$ it follows that $RQu = Qu$. Hence, we have

$$(Q_J \cdots Q_1)^\ell u - Qu = R^\ell u - Qu = R^\ell (u - Qu).$$

Furthermore,

$$\langle Ru, v \rangle = \langle Q_J Q_{J-1} \cdots Q_1 u, v \rangle = \langle Q_{J-1} \cdots Q_1 u, v \rangle = \cdots = \langle u, v \rangle$$

for all $u \in H$ and $v \in U$ implies $Ru \in U^\perp$ whenever $u \in U^\perp$. Since $u - Qu \in U^\perp$ it suffices to show that

$$\|Rv\|^2 \leq \left(1 - \prod_{j=1}^{J-1} \sin^2 \alpha_j \right) \|v\|^2 \qquad \text{for all } v \in U^\perp.$$

This will be done by induction on J. If $J = 1$ we have only one subspace and R is the projection onto $U = U_1$. Hence, $v \in U^\perp$ implies $Rv = 0$ and $\|Rv\| \leq \|v\|$. Now, for the induction step we set $\tilde{R} := Q_J \cdots Q_2$. We decompose an arbitrary $v \in U^\perp$ into $v = w + v_1$ with $w \in U_1$ and $v_1 \in U_1^\perp$. This gives in particular $Rv = Rw + Rv_1 = \tilde{R}w$. Next we set $w = w_1 + w_2$ with $w_1 \in A_1 = U_2 \cap \cdots \cap U_J$ and $w_2 \in A_1^\perp$ so that we can conclude $\tilde{R}w = \tilde{R}w_1 + \tilde{R}w_2 = w_1 + \tilde{R}w_2$. Since the last two elements are orthogonal we derive

$$\|\tilde{R}w\|^2 = \|w_1\|^2 + \|\tilde{R}w_2\|^2.$$

Moreover, induction gives

$$\|\tilde{R}w_2\|^2 \leq \left(1 - \prod_{j=2}^{J-1} \sin^2 \alpha_j \right) \|w_2\|^2.$$

From this we can conclude with $\|w\|^2 = \|w_1\|^2 + \|w_2\|^2$ that

$$\|\tilde{R}w\|^2 \le \left(1 - \prod_{j=2}^{J-1} \sin^2\alpha_j\right)\|w\|^2 + \|w_1\|^2 \prod_{j=2}^{J-1} \sin^2\alpha_j.$$

Now, w lies in U_1 and is orthogonal to $U = U_1 \cap A_1$ and w_1 lies in A_1 and is also orthogonal to U. Since the angle between U_1 and A_1 is α_1 we have

$$\|w_1\|^2 = \langle w_1, w \rangle \le \cos\alpha_1 \|w_1\| \|w\|,$$

giving $\|w_1\| \le \cos\alpha_1 \|w\|$. Finally, $\|w\| \le \|v\|$ allows us to derive

$$\begin{aligned}
\|Rv\|^2 &= \|\tilde{R}w\|^2 \\
&\le \left(1 - \prod_{j=2}^{J-1} \sin^2\alpha_j\right)\|v\|^2 + \|v\|^2 \cos^2\alpha_1 \prod_{j=2}^{J-1} \sin^2\alpha_j \\
&= \left(1 - \prod_{j=1}^{J-1} \sin^2\alpha_j\right)\|v\|^2,
\end{aligned}$$

which concludes the proof. □

Exercises

7.1 Let $K_r(\mathbf{x}, \mathbf{y}) = \sum_{|\alpha|\le r} \phi_\alpha(\mathbf{x})\mathbf{y}^\alpha$ the Taylor approximation to a given kernel K for $\mathbf{y} \in [-\eta, \eta]^2$ and large $\mathbf{x}$. Let us subdivide $[-\eta, \eta]^2$ into four equally sized boxes $Q_1 = [-\eta, 0] \times [-\eta, 0]$, $Q_2 = [-\eta, 0] \times [0, \eta]$, $Q_3 = [0, \eta] \times [-\eta, 0]$ and $Q_4 = [0, \eta] \times [0, \eta]$. Let $\mathbf{c}_i$ be the centre of Q_i. Let $Y = \{\mathbf{y}_1, \ldots, \mathbf{y}_n\} \subseteq [-\eta, \eta]^2$ be the source points and let $Y_i = Q_i \cap Y$ be the source points in Q_i. Show how the coefficients β_α of the far-field expansion

$$s(\mathbf{x}) = \sum_{j=1}^n c_j K_r(\mathbf{x}, \mathbf{y}) = \sum_{|\alpha|\le r} \left(\sum_{j=1}^n c_j \mathbf{y}_j^\alpha\right)\phi_\alpha(\mathbf{x}) = \sum_{|\alpha|\le r} \beta_\alpha \phi_\alpha(\mathbf{x})$$

can be computed from the coefficients

$$\beta_\alpha^{(i)} = \sum_{j:\mathbf{y}_j\in Y_i} c_j(\mathbf{y}_j - \mathbf{c}_i)^\alpha, \qquad 1 \le i \le 4,$$

of the far-field expansions of s for the boxes Q_i centred at $\mathbf{c}_i$. Determine the total cost of this bottom-up approach.

7.2   The multivariate Gaussian is defined as $\Phi(\mathbf{x}) = \exp(-\|\mathbf{x}\|_2^2)$. The univariate Hermite polynomials of Definition 7.22 yield the definition of multivariate Hermite polynomials $H_\alpha(\mathbf{x}) = H_{\alpha_1}(x_1) \cdots H_{\alpha_d}(x_d)$ for $\alpha \in \mathbb{N}_0^d$ and $\mathbf{x} \in \mathbb{R}^d$. Similarly, we can define multivariate Hermite functions as $h_\alpha(\mathbf{x}) = H_\alpha(\mathbf{x}) \exp(-\|\mathbf{x}\|_2^2)$. Use this to derive a multivariate version of Proposition 7.23. Pay particular attention to the error analysis.

7.3   Consider the integral equation from Section 1.1.3 with kernel $K(x, y) = \log(|x - y|)$, $x, y \in [0, 1]$. Use Lemma 7.18 and Example 7.20 to derive a kernel approximation $K_r(x, y)$ and an estimate for $K - K_r$ if $x \in [a, b]$ and $y \in [c, d]$. Then, use the block cluster tree of Example 7.36 and this kernel approximation to define a hierarchical matrix approximation $\tilde{A}$ to the Galerkin matrix A from Section 1.1.3. Estimate the error between A and $\tilde{A}$ in the Frobenius norm.

7.4   Consider the block cluster T tree from Example 7.37 and the associated hierarchical matrices $\mathcal{H}(T, r)$ of rank r. Show that the space required to store a matrix $A \in \mathcal{H}(T, r)$ is of size $O(n + 2rn \log_2 n)$. Determine the time necessary to form a matrix–vector product Ax for $A \in \mathcal{H}(T, r)$ and $\mathbf{x} \in \mathbb{R}^n$ with $n = 2^L$.

Set up a table for the memory required for storing A for different numbers of points $n = 2^L$ and different ranks r. In which cases is it cheaper to store the matrix as a hierarchical matrix rather than a full matrix?

7.5   Let the finite-dimensional space V be decomposed as $V = V_1 + \cdots + V_J$. Let the inner products $a : V \times V \to \mathbb{R}$ and $a_i : V_i \times V_i \to \mathbb{R}$, as well as the projection operator $P_i : V \to V_i$, be defined as described in Section 7.3. Assume that

- there are numbers $0 \le \epsilon_{ij} \le 1$, $1 \le i, j \le J$ such that

$$|a(u_i, u_j)| \le \epsilon_{ij} a(u_i, u_i)^{1/2} a(u_j, u_j)^{1/2},$$

  for $u_i \in V_i$ and $u_j \in V_j$,
- there is a $\gamma > 0$ such that

$$a(u_i, u_i) \le \gamma a_i(u_i, u_i)$$

  for all $u_i \in V_i$.

Show that in this situation we have $\|P_i\|_a \le \gamma$ and, with $P = P_1 + \cdots + P_J$,

$$a(Pu, u) \le \gamma(\rho(E) + 1) a(u, u),$$

where $\rho(E)$ is the spectral radius of $E = (\epsilon_{ij})$.

8

Preconditioning

Preconditioning is, broadly speaking, a method that transforms a linear system $A\mathbf{x} = \mathbf{b}$ into an equivalent system, i.e. a system with the same solution, $B\mathbf{x} = \mathbf{c}$, which can be solved more easily.

In a certain way, we have already encountered the idea of preconditioning, though we did not refer to it as preconditioning. In Theorem 3.24 we used a permutation matrix P to modify the given matrix A such that PA has an LU factorisation $PA = LU$; obviously, the equivalent system is given by $PA\mathbf{x} = LU\mathbf{x} = P\mathbf{b}$ which can then be solved using backward and forward substitution. Of course, P does not have to be a permutation matrix. Furthermore, we not only have the possibility of building a preconditioned system of the form

$$P_L A\mathbf{x} = P_L \mathbf{b} \tag{8.1}$$

with an invertible matrix P_L, where we will speak of *left preconditioning*, but can also construct a system of the form

$$A P_R \mathbf{y} = \mathbf{b} \tag{8.2}$$

with an invertible matrix P_R, which we will refer to as *right preconditioning*. While in the case of left preconditioning $\mathbf{x}$ solves $A\mathbf{x} = \mathbf{b}$ if and only if it solves the preconditioned system $P_L A\mathbf{x} = P_L\mathbf{b}$, the situation for right preconditioning is slightly different. Here, $\mathbf{y}$ solves $A P_R \mathbf{y} = \mathbf{b}$ if and only if $\mathbf{x} = P_R \mathbf{y}$ solves the original system $A\mathbf{x} = \mathbf{b}$. Hence, after solving the preconditioned system for $\mathbf{y}$ we also have to compute $\mathbf{x} = P_R \mathbf{y}$ which should also be easily achievable.

Finally, we also have the possibility of using both left and right preconditioning,

$$P_L A P_R \mathbf{y} = P_L \mathbf{b}, \tag{8.3}$$

which we will call *both-sided preconditioning* or *split preconditioning*. We will call a split preconditioner a *symmetric preconditioner* if $P_L = P_R^T$.

No matter which preconditioning we choose, the goal is, of course, to achieve a better-solvable system with the new matrix $A_P := P_L A P_R$. In this context, better-solvable will mainly mean that the condition number of A_P is significantly smaller than the condition number of the original matrix A, which will improve the stability and the run-time of iterative methods. For this goal, it does not matter too much whether we use a left, right or split preconditioner because of the following observation.

Lemma 8.1 *Let* $A, P, P_L, P_R \in \mathbb{R}^{n \times n}$ *be invertible with* $P = P_R P_L$. *Then, the matrices* PA, AP, *and* $P_L A P_R$ *have the same eigenvalues.*

Proof This simply follows from the identities

$$\det(PA - \lambda I) = \det(P) \det(A - \lambda P^{-1}) = \det(A - \lambda P^{-1}) \det(P) = \det(AP - \lambda I)$$

and

$$\begin{aligned}
\det(P_L A P_R - \lambda I) &= \det(P_L) \det(A - \lambda P_L^{-1} P_R^{-1}) \det(P_R) \\
&= \det(P_L) \det(A - \lambda P^{-1}) \det(P_R) \\
&= \det(P) \det(A - \lambda P^{-1}) = \det(PA - \lambda I),
\end{aligned}$$

both of which hold for any $\lambda \in \mathbb{C}$. □

We will mainly discuss left preconditioners. However, for problems with a symmetric matrix A, the preconditioned matrix $P_L A$ is in general no longer symmetric even if P_L is symmetric. In such a situation it is sometimes still possible to reformulate the solver so that we still can precondition with P_L whilst preserving symmetry of the method. Another possibility is to use a symmetric preconditioner of the form $P_L A P_L^T$ which results in a new matrix, which is also symmetric provided A is symmetric.

Besides the property of symmetry, a successfully built preconditioner will require as much information about the matrix as possible. This includes information on how the linear system has been derived and how the system should be solved. For example, when it comes to a symmetric, positive definite, sparse matrix, the conjugate gradient method is the method of choice for solving the linear system. To precondition such a system, we do not only have to make sure that the preconditioned system can still be solved with the CG method. We also want to reduce the condition number such that the CG method requires as few steps as possible to achieve a given accuracy. Also, the matrix–vector multiplication involved in each step of the CG method should remain as cheap as possible.

Eventually, not all goals that we would like to achieve with preconditioning are achievable. This is easiest seen when looking at (8.1). The two obvious goals that the preconditioner should satisfy are that

1. the preconditioned system $P_L A \mathbf{x} = P_L \mathbf{b}$ should be more easily solvable than the original system,
2. the new right-hand side $P_L \mathbf{b}$ needs to be easily computable.

These two goals are in competition with each other. The extreme cases are choosing $P_L = A^{-1}$ or $P_L = I$, respectively. In the first case the preconditioned system is easy to solve, having the matrix $P_L^{-1} P_L = I$, but leaves us with the original problem when computing the new right-hand side $P_L \mathbf{b} = A^{-1} \mathbf{b}$. In the second case, the new right-hand side is simply the old right-hand side, while the preconditioned system is as bad as the original one.

In the rest of this chapter we will pursue two goals. The first goal is to describe the current techniques for building preconditioners. The second goal is to describe how some of the iterative methods we have encountered so far have to be altered to work efficiently with the preconditioner. Often, there are better ways than just applying the iterative method to the preconditioned matrix.

8.1 Scaling and Preconditioners Based on Splitting

The easiest way of preconditioning a linear system is by multiplying it by a diagonal matrix. If used as a left preconditioner, this means that we simply scale each row of the linear system, which is sometimes called *equilibration* or *Jacobi preconditioning*. Hence, instead of solving $A\mathbf{x} = \mathbf{b}$ we are solving $DA\mathbf{x} = D\mathbf{b}$ with a diagonal matrix $D \in \mathbb{R}^{n \times n}$ with the goal of reducing the condition number of the system. It turns out that scaling the rows of A in such a way that they all have the same norm is optimal in the following sense.

Theorem 8.2 *Assume that the invertible matrix $A \in \mathbb{R}^{n \times n}$ is scaled in such a way that*

$$\sum_{j=1}^{n} |a_{ij}| = 1, \qquad 1 \le i \le n.$$

Then, for each invertible diagonal matrix D the condition number with respect to the maximum norm satisfies the inequality

$$\kappa_\infty(DA) \ge \kappa_\infty(A).$$

Proof Let $D = \mathrm{diag}(d_{ii})$ be invertible. Using Theorem 2.19, we have

$$\|DA\|_\infty = \max_{1 \le i \le n} \left\{ |d_{ii}| \sum_{j=1}^n |a_{ij}| \right\} = \max_{1 \le i \le n} |d_{ii}| = \|A\|_\infty \max_{1 \le i \le n} |d_{ii}|$$

and, if we denote the entries of A^{-1} by $\tilde{a}_{ij}$ then we also have

$$\|(DA)^{-1}\|_\infty = \|A^{-1} D^{-1}\|_\infty = \max_{1 \le i \le n} \sum_{j=1}^n |\tilde{a}_{ij}|/|d_{jj}| \ge \|A^{-1}\|_\infty \min_{1 \le j \le n} 1/|d_{jj}|.$$

Both together yield

$$\kappa_\infty(DA) = \|DA\|_\infty \|(DA)^{-1}\|_\infty \ge \|A\|_\infty \|A^{-1}\|_\infty \max_{1 \le i \le n} |d_{ii}| \min_{1 \le i \le n} 1/|d_{ii}|$$

$$= \|A\|_\infty \|A^{-1}\|_\infty = \kappa(A),$$

which we wanted to prove.   □

Obviously, we can alternatively also scale the columns of A, which corresponds to multiplying the matrix A from the right by a diagonal matrix D, i.e. to forming AD. This means we now have a right preconditioner, and since $\|A\|_\infty = \|A^{\mathrm{T}}\|_1$, we immediately have the following conclusion.

Corollary 8.3 *Assume that the invertible matrix $A \in \mathbb{R}^{n \times n}$ is scaled such that*

$$\sum_{i=1}^n |a_{ij}| = 1, \qquad 1 \le j \le n.$$

Then, for each invertible diagonal matrix D the condition number with respect to the ℓ_1-norm satisfies

$$\kappa_1(AD) \ge \kappa_1(A).$$

Since the condition number is invariant with respect to multiplying a matrix by a positive scalar, we see that it is important only that the absolute values of the entries of each row (or column) sum up to the same number.

When it comes to other ℓ_p-norms, the situation is not so good. Here, we only deal with the case $1 < p < \infty$ since we have dealt with the cases $p = 1, \infty$ above. The proof of the following result relies on the following simple observation.

For a given matrix $B \in \mathbb{R}^{n \times n}$, its columns $B\mathbf{e}_j$ satisfy

$$
\begin{aligned}
\|B\|_p &= \sup_{\mathbf{x} \neq 0} \frac{\|B\mathbf{x}\|_p}{\|\mathbf{x}\|_p} = \sup_{\mathbf{x} \neq 0} \frac{\left\|\sum_{j=1}^n x_j B\mathbf{e}_j\right\|_p}{\|\mathbf{x}\|_p} \\
&\leq \sup_{\mathbf{x} \neq 0} \frac{\sum_{j=1}^n |x_j|}{\|\mathbf{x}\|_p} \max_{1 \leq j \leq n} \|B\mathbf{e}_j\|_p \\
&\leq \max_{1 \leq j \leq n} \|B\mathbf{e}_j\|_p \sup_{\mathbf{x} \neq 0} \frac{\|\mathbf{x}\|_1}{\|\mathbf{x}\|_p} \\
&\leq n^{1-1/p} \max_{1 \leq j \leq n} \|B\mathbf{e}_j\|_p,
\end{aligned}
$$

where we have used (2.2) in the last step.

In the next theorem, we immediately deal with both cases, left preconditioning and right preconditioning. The result below can be extended in various ways. It is possible to have a similar result for a both-sided preconditioner and even for non-square matrices if the condition number is replaced by $\kappa(A) = \|A\| \|A^+\|$ using the pseudo-inverse of A. However, we will not pursue this here.

Theorem 8.4 *Let* $1 \leq p \leq \infty$. *Assume that the invertible matrix* $A \in \mathbb{R}^{n \times n}$ *is scaled such that*

$$
\sum_{i=1}^n |a_{ij}|^p = 1, \qquad 1 \leq j \leq n,
$$

i.e. all the columns of A *have* ℓ_p-*norm 1. Then, for each invertible diagonal matrix* D *the condition number with respect to the* ℓ_p-*norm satisfies*

$$
\kappa_p(A) \leq n^{1-1/p} \kappa_p(AD).
$$

If, however, the rows of A *are scaled such that they have an* ℓ_p-*norm of one, then for each invertible diagonal matrix* D *the condition number with respect to the* ℓ_p-*norm satisfies*

$$
\kappa_p(A) \leq n^{1/p} \kappa(DA).
$$

Proof We only have to deal with $1 < p < \infty$. Since all the columns are normalised to have an ℓ_p-norm of one, the above considerations show that $\|A\|_p \leq n^{1-1/p}$. Since we also have

$$
\|A^{-1}\|_p = \|DD^{-1}A^{-1}\|_p \leq \|D\|_p \|(AD)^{-1}\|_p
$$

and, with $k \in \{1, \ldots, n\}$ satisfying $k = \max_j |d_{jj}|$, also

$$
\|D\|_p = \sup_{\mathbf{x} \neq 0} \frac{\|D\mathbf{x}\|_p}{\|\mathbf{x}\|_p} = \sup_{\mathbf{x} \neq 0} \frac{\left(\sum_{j=1}^n |d_{jj} x_j|^p\right)^{1/p}}{\|\mathbf{x}\|_p}
$$

$$
\leq \max_{1 \leq j \leq n} |d_{jj}| \leq |d_{kk}| \|A\mathbf{e}_k\|_p
$$

$$
= |d_{kk}| \left(\sum_{i=1}^n |a_{ik}|^p\right)^{1/p} = \left(\sum_{i=1}^n |a_{ik} d_{kk}|^p\right)^{1/p}
$$

$$
= \|AD\mathbf{e}_k\|_p \leq \|AD\|_p,
$$

we find that $\kappa_p(A) = \|A\|_p \|A^{-1}\|_p \leq n^{1-1/p} \|AD\|_p \|(AD)^{-1}\|_p = n^{1-1/p} \kappa_p(AD)$ for all invertible diagonal matrices.

The second statement follows from the fact that $\kappa_p(A) = \kappa_q(A^T)$ where $\frac{1}{p} + \frac{1}{q} = 1$, see Exercise 2.4. □

In particular, this means that the condition number in the Euclidean norm satisfies

$$
\kappa_2(A) \leq n^{1/2} \kappa(DA), \qquad \kappa_2(A) \leq n^{1/2} \kappa(AD)
$$

for all invertible diagonal matrices D, provided that either the rows or the columns of A have Euclidean length 1, respectively. Another way of stating this is that we have for an arbitrary, invertible matrix $A \in \mathbb{R}^{n \times n}$ the bounds

$$
\kappa_2(D_L A) \leq n^{1/2} \kappa(A), \qquad \kappa_2(A D_R) \leq n^{1/2} \kappa(A)
$$

if D_L and D_R are the diagonal matrices with diagonal entries

$$
d_{ii}^L = \left(\sum_{j=1}^n |a_{ij}|^2\right)^{-1/2}, \qquad d_{jj}^R = \left(\sum_{i=1}^n |a_{ij}|^2\right)^{-1/2}.
$$

Unfortunately, the upper bound is only of limited use since it grows with the number of unknowns n.

Preconditioning by scaling is a special case of *preconditioning by splitting*. In Chapter 4 we discussed iterative methods which were based upon a splitting of the form

$$
\mathbf{x} = B^{-1}(B - A)\mathbf{x} + B^{-1}\mathbf{b}
$$

with an invertible matrix B. The goals we formulated at that time for determining the matrix B (or B^{-1}) are not so different from the goals that we now require from our preconditioner. We wanted the matrix B to be sufficiently close to A that the iteration matrix $C = B^{-1}(A - B)$ had a small spectral radius but we also needed that B^{-1} was easy to compute. We can now use this to define a general class of preconditioners.

Definition 8.5 The matrix $P := B^{-1}$ is called the *associated preconditioner* of the consistent iteration $\mathbf{x}_{j+1} := B^{-1}(B - A)\mathbf{x}_j + B^{-1}\mathbf{b}$.

As in Chapter 4, we can decompose our matrix A into $A = D + L + R$, where D is the diagonal, L is the lower left and R is the upper right part of A, respectively. Then, each of the methods introduced in Chapter 4 leads to an associated preconditioner, as follows:

$$
\begin{aligned}
\text{Jacobi:} \quad & P = D^{-1}, \\
\text{Gauss–Seidel:} \quad & P = (D + L)^{-1}, \\
\text{SOR:} \quad & P(\omega) = \omega(D + \omega L)^{-1}, \\
\text{Symmetric Gauss–Seidel} \quad & P = (D + R)^{-1}D(D + L)^{-1}, \\
\text{SSOR:} \quad & P(\omega) = \omega(2 - \omega)(D + \omega R)^{-1}D(D + \omega L)^{-1}.
\end{aligned}
$$

Other associated preconditioners are, of course, possible. The ones listed above allow at least a simple calculation of $P\mathbf{b}$ since they require only the inversion of a diagonal matrix, a triangular matrix or a product of triangular matrices.
In the case of the SOR and SSOR methods, the success of the preconditioner depends obviously on the choice of the regularisation parameter ω. This, however, depends on the matrix A. We give one possible result for the SSOR preconditioner.

Theorem 8.6 *Let $A \in \mathbb{R}^{n \times n}$ be symmetric and positive definite. Then, the eigenvalues of the matrix $P(\omega)A$, where*

$$
P(\omega) = (2 - \omega)(\hat{D} + R)^{-1}\hat{D}(\hat{D} + L)^{-1}
$$

with $\hat{D} = \frac{1}{\omega}D$, $\omega \in (0, 2)$, are contained in the interval

$$
\left[(2 - \omega) \middle/ \left(1 + \omega \left(\frac{1}{\omega} - \frac{1}{2} \right)^2 \delta^{-1} + \omega\gamma \right), 1 \right], \tag{8.4}
$$

where

$$
\delta = \min_{\mathbf{x} \neq 0} \frac{\mathbf{x}^T A \mathbf{x}}{\mathbf{x}^T D \mathbf{x}}, \qquad \gamma = \max_{\mathbf{x} \neq 0} \frac{\mathbf{x}^T (LD^{-1}R - \frac{1}{4}D)\mathbf{x}}{\mathbf{x}^T A \mathbf{x}}.
$$

Proof Since both matrices A and $P(\omega)$ are symmetric and positive definite, we know from Theorem 1.15 that the matrix $P(\omega)A$ has only real, positive eigenvalues. If $\lambda > 0$ is such an eigenvalue and $\mathbf{v} \in \mathbb{R}^n$ a corresponding eigenvector then λ and $\mathbf{v}$ also satisfy $\mathbf{v}^T A \mathbf{v} = \lambda \mathbf{v}^T B(\omega)\mathbf{v}$ with $B(\omega) = P(\omega)^{-1}$. This means in particular,

$$
\min_{\mathbf{x} \neq 0} \frac{\mathbf{x}^T A \mathbf{x}}{\mathbf{x}^T B(\omega)\mathbf{x}} \leq \lambda_{\min}, \qquad \max_{\mathbf{x} \neq 0} \frac{\mathbf{x}^T A \mathbf{x}}{\mathbf{x}^T B(\omega)\mathbf{x}} \geq \lambda_{\max},
$$

where $\lambda_{\min}$ and $\lambda_{\max}$ are the minimum and maximum eigenvalues of $P(\omega)A$, respectively. Simple calculations show that we can rewrite $B(\omega)$ in the form

$$
\begin{aligned}
B(\omega) &= \frac{1}{2-\omega}\left(\frac{1}{\omega}D+L\right)\left(\frac{1}{\omega}D\right)^{-1}\left(\frac{1}{\omega}D+R\right) \\
&= \frac{1}{2-\omega}\left(\frac{1}{\omega}D+L\right)\left(I+\omega D^{-1}R\right) \\
&= \frac{1}{2-\omega}\left[\frac{1}{\omega}D+L+R+\omega LD^{-1}R\right] \\
&= \frac{1}{2-\omega}\left[A+\left(\frac{1}{\omega}-1\right)D+\omega LD^{-1}R\right] \\
&= \frac{1}{2-\omega}\left[A+\omega\left(\frac{1}{\omega}-\frac{1}{2}\right)^2 D+\omega\left(LD^{-1}R-\frac{1}{4}D\right)\right].
\end{aligned}
$$

Using the definitions of δ and γ shows that we have for an arbitrary $\mathbf{x} \in \mathbb{R}^n$ the bound

$$
\begin{aligned}
\mathbf{x}^T B(\omega)\mathbf{x} &= \frac{1}{2-\omega}\left[\mathbf{x}^T A\mathbf{x}+\omega\left(\frac{1}{\omega}-\frac{1}{2}\right)^2 \mathbf{x}^T D\mathbf{x}+\omega\mathbf{x}^T\left(LD^{-1}R-\frac{1}{4}D\right)\mathbf{x}\right] \\
&\leq \frac{1}{2-\omega}\left[1+\frac{\omega}{\delta}\left(\frac{1}{\omega}-\frac{1}{2}\right)^2+\omega\gamma\right]\mathbf{x}^T A\mathbf{x}.
\end{aligned}
$$

Since $\omega \in (0,2)$ and both $B(\omega)$ and A are positive definite, this shows particularly that the expression in brackets on the right-hand side is positive. Thus, we can establish the lower bound by

$$
\lambda_{\min} \geq \min_{\mathbf{x}\neq 0} \frac{\mathbf{x}^T A\mathbf{x}}{\mathbf{x}^T B(\omega)\mathbf{x}} \geq (2-\omega)\Big/\left(1+\frac{\omega}{\delta}\left(\frac{1}{\omega}-\frac{1}{2}\right)^2+\omega\gamma\right).
$$

If we finally introduce the notation

$$
H = H(\omega) = \left(1-\frac{1}{\omega}\right)D+L, \qquad V = V(\omega) = \left(\frac{2}{\omega}-1\right)D,
$$

then it is easy to see that we can rewrite $B(\omega)$ as

$$
\begin{aligned}
B(\omega) &= (V+H)V^{-1}(V+H^T) = (V+H)(I+V^{-1}H^T) \\
&= V+H+H^T+HV^{-1}H^T = A+HV^{-1}H^T.
\end{aligned}
$$

Since the matrix $HV^{-1}H^T$ is also symmetric and positive semi-definite, we see that $\mathbf{x}^T B(\omega)\mathbf{x} \geq \mathbf{x}^T A\mathbf{x}$, showing $\lambda_{\max} \leq 1$. $\qquad\square$

Obviously, the condition number of $P(\omega)A$ is dominated by the lower bound in (8.4), i.e. the best possible ω should maximise the lower bound or minimise its inverse

$$f(\omega) = \frac{1}{2-\omega}\left(1 + \omega\left(\frac{1}{\omega} - \frac{1}{2}\right)^2 \delta^{-1} + \omega\gamma\right).$$

Standard but tedious calculations show that this is achieved for

$$\omega^* = \frac{2}{1 + 2\left[\left(\frac{1}{2} + \gamma\right)\delta\right]^{1/2}}$$

with

$$f(\omega^*) = \frac{1}{2} + \left[\left(\frac{1}{2} + \gamma\right)\delta^{-1}\right]^{1/2},$$

see, for example, Axelsson and Barker [7]. Obviously, the bound in (8.4) depends on δ and γ. The following example shows that in certain situations, these can be estimated reasonably.

Example 8.7 If we consider our finite difference example from Section 1.1.2, i.e. the linear system (1.2) then it suffices to look at the matrix (4.9), i.e. at

$$A = \begin{pmatrix} 2 & -1 & & & & 0 \\ -1 & 2 & -1 & & & \\ & -1 & 2 & -1 & & \\ & & \ddots & \ddots & \ddots & \\ & & & -1 & 2 & -1 \\ 0 & & & & -1 & 2 \end{pmatrix} = L + D + R.$$

From Remark 4.17 we know that the eigenvalues of A are given by $\lambda_j = 2(1 - \cos\theta_j) = 4\sin^2(\theta_j/2)$, $1 \le j \le n$ with $\theta_j = j\pi h$, $h = 1/(n+1)$. From this, we can conclude that the condition number of A with respect to the ℓ_2-norm is

$$\kappa_2(A) = \frac{\lambda_{\max}}{\lambda_{\min}} = \frac{\sin^2(n\pi h/2)}{\sin^2(\pi h/2)} = O(n^2) = O(h^{-2}).$$

To find the eigenvalue interval of $P(\omega)A$, we need to concentrate on the smallest eigenvalue and hence have to determine δ and γ. The first one is rather simple since we have $\mathbf{x}^T D\mathbf{x} = 2\mathbf{x}^T\mathbf{x}$ and hence

$$\delta = \frac{1}{2}\min_{\mathbf{x}\neq 0}\frac{\mathbf{x}^T A\mathbf{x}}{\mathbf{x}^T\mathbf{x}} = \frac{1}{2}\lambda_{\min} = 2\sin^2(\pi h/2) = O(h^2).$$

For γ we note that elementary computations show that $\tilde{L} := LD^{-1}R - \frac{1}{4}D$ has only one non-zero entry, which is $\mathbf{e}_1^T\tilde{L}\mathbf{e}_1 = -1/2$, which shows

$$\gamma = \max_{\mathbf{x}\neq 0}\frac{\mathbf{x}^T\tilde{L}\mathbf{x}}{\mathbf{x}^T A\mathbf{x}} = -\frac{1}{2}\max_{\mathbf{x}\neq 0}\frac{x_1^2}{\mathbf{x}^T A\mathbf{x}} \le 0,$$

as A is positive definite. Moreover, for each $\mathbf{x} \in \mathbb{R}^d \setminus \{\mathbf{0}\}$ it is easy to see that

$$\mathbf{x}^T A \mathbf{x} = 2 \sum_{j=1}^{n} x_j^2 - 2 \sum_{j=1}^{n-1} x_j x_{j+1} \le 2 \sum_{j=1}^{n} x_j^2 - \sum_{j=1}^{n-1} \left(x_j^2 + x_{j+1}^2 \right)$$
$$= x_1^2 - x_n^2 \ge x_1^2.$$

This gives the lower bound

$$\gamma = -\frac{1}{2} \max_{\mathbf{x} \ne 0} \frac{x_1^2}{\mathbf{x}^T A \mathbf{x}} \ge -\frac{1}{2},$$

which is independent of h. Hence, the lowest eigenvalue of $P(\omega^*)A$ can be bounded by

$$f(\omega^*) = O(\delta^{-1/2}) = O(h),$$

which is significantly better then the behaviour of $O(h^2)$ of the smallest eigenvalue of the original matrix A.

The above example makes heavy use of the specific structure of the matrix. Though this can be generalised to a certain extent, the application of Theorem 8.6 is only of limited use for other matrices.

8.2 Incomplete Splittings

In Section 3.3, we saw that Gaussian elimination without pivoting is equivalent to computing a factorisation $A = LU$ of a matrix $A \in \mathbb{R}^{n \times n}$ into the product of a normalised lower triangular matrix L and an upper triangular matrix U. Though in some special cases (see for example Theorem 3.16) the LU factorisation of a sparse matrix A yields also sparse factors L and U, this is in general not the case. Usually, the matrices L and U are denser than the original matrix A.

To avoid this *fill-in*, one might try to create an approximate LU factorisation of the form

$$A = \tilde{L}\tilde{U} + E,$$

where $\tilde{L}$ and $\tilde{U}$ have a prescribed sparsity pattern, ideally that of the original matrix A, and the error E should be sufficiently small.

To give a precise definition of an incomplete LU factorisation we need to describe the pattern of zeros or, alternatively, the pattern of non-zeros.

Definition 8.8 A *non-zero pattern* $\mathcal{M}$ is a subset of $\{(i, j) : 1 \le i, j \le n\}$.

The non-zero pattern associated with a matrix $A \in \mathbb{R}^{n \times n}$, also called the *matrix pattern*, is defined to be

$$M_A := \{(i, j) : a_{ij} \neq 0, 1 \leq i, j \leq n\}.$$

Ideally, we would like to have an approximate LU factorisation where $\tilde{L}$ is a normalised lower triangular matrix and $\tilde{U}$ is an upper triangular matrix, where the non-zero parts have the same matrix pattern as the original matrix, meaning that $\tilde{L}$ and $\tilde{U}$ have together the same space requirement as the original matrix A.

Definition 8.9 Let $M \subseteq \{(i, j) : 1 \leq i, j \leq n\}$. The matrix $A \in \mathbb{R}^{n \times n}$ has an *incomplete LU factorisation* with respect to the non-zero pattern M if there exists a decomposition

$$A = LU + E, \tag{8.5}$$

where the normalised lower triangular matrix $L = (\ell_{ij}) \in \mathbb{R}^{n \times n}$, the regular upper triangular matrix $U = (u_{ij}) \in \mathbb{R}^{n \times n}$ and the remainder E also satisfy

$$\begin{aligned}
\ell_{ij} &= 0 && \text{for } (i, j) \notin M, \\
u_{ij} &= 0 && \text{for } (i, j) \notin M, \\
e_{ij} &= 0 && \text{for } (i, j) \in M.
\end{aligned}$$

If (8.5) exists, we call $P := (LU)^{-1}$ the *incomplete LU preconditioner*.

Obviously, we have $\ell_{ii} \neq 0$ and $u_{ii} \neq 0$ for all $1 \leq i \leq n$. Hence, in what follows we will assume M contains all pairs (i, i), $1 \leq i \leq n$, or equivalently that the complement M^c of M is contained in $\{(i, j) : i \neq j, 1 \leq i, j \leq n\}$.

There are still three questions at hand. Firstly, we have to pre-determine the set M of indices. As pointed out above, a desirable pattern would be the matrix pattern M_A. Secondly, we have to determine whether an incomplete LU factorisation exists. Finally, we have to compute the incomplete LU factorisation. The latter, however, can in general be achieved by a simple modification of the standard Gaussian elimination process. In Algorithm 44 we state the modified algorithm. The output is once again overwriting the input and is more precisely given by $L = (\ell_{ij})$ and $U = (u_{ij})$ with

$$\ell_{ij} = \begin{cases} \delta_{ij} & \text{for } i \leq j, \\ a_{ij} & \text{for } i > j, (i, j) \in M, \\ 0 & \text{for } i > j, (i, j) \notin M, \end{cases} \quad u_{ij} = \begin{cases} a_{ij} & \text{for } i \leq j, (i, j) \in M, \\ 0 & \text{for } i \leq j, (i, j) \notin M, \\ 0 & \text{for } i > j. \end{cases} \tag{8.6}$$

As in the case of the standard Gaussian elimination, there is in general no guarantee that the process does not terminate prematurely because of one of

---

Algorithm 44: Incomplete LU factorisation

Input : $A \in \mathbb{R}^{n \times n}$, non-zero pattern $\mathcal{M}$.

Output: L normalised lower triangular, U upper triangular.

1 **for** $k = 1$ to $n - 1$ **do**
2   **for** $i = k + 1$ to n **do**
3   **if** $(i, k) \in \mathcal{M}$ **then**
4       $a_{ik} := a_{ik}/a_{kk}$
5   **for** $j = k + 1$ to n **do**
6   **if** $(i, j) \in \mathcal{M}$ **then** $a_{ij} := a_{ij} - a_{ik}a_{kj}$

---

the u_{jj} becoming zero. Hence, an implementation of Algorithm 44 has to make sure that $a_{kk} \neq 0$ before executing line 4. Nonetheless, we have the following result, which is a generalisation of Theorem 3.10.

Theorem 8.10 *Let $A \in \mathbb{R}^{n \times n}$ be a strictly row diagonally dominant matrix. Let $\mathcal{M} \subseteq \{(i, j) : 1 \leq i, j \leq n\}$ contain all the diagonal pairs (i, i), $1 \leq i \leq n$. Then, there exists a normalised lower triangular matrix L, an upper triangular matrix U and a matrix R with*

$$\ell_{ij} = 0 \qquad\qquad \text{for } (i, j) \notin \mathcal{M},$$
$$u_{ij} = 0 \qquad\qquad \text{for } (i, j) \notin \mathcal{M},$$
$$r_{ij} = 0 \qquad\qquad \text{for } (i, j) \in \mathcal{M},$$

such that

$$A = LU - R.$$

Proof The proof essentially mimics the Gaussian elimination process, making sure that each step of the process is allowed even after dropping elements with indices not in the non-zero pattern.

By assumption, we have for the complement $\mathcal{M}^c \subseteq \{(i, j) : i \neq j, 1 \leq i, j \leq n\}$. We start by setting those entries in the first column and first row of A to zero which have indices in $\mathcal{M}^c$. Formally, we achieve this by writing

$$A =: A^{(1)} = \tilde{A}^{(1)} - R^{(1)},$$

where $\tilde{a}_{1j}^{(1)} = 0$ and $\tilde{a}_{i1}^{(1)} = 0$ if $(1, j) \in \mathcal{M}^c$ or $(i, 1) \in \mathcal{M}^c$. All other entries of $\tilde{A}^{(1)}$ are simply those entries of $A^{(1)}$. This also defines the matrix $R^{(1)}$ which has only non-zero entries in the first row and first column, if at all. Note that the diagonal element of $R^{(1)}$ is zero since $(1, 1) \in \mathcal{M}$.

By construction, the new matrix $\tilde{A}^{(1)}$ is certainly also strictly row diagonally dominant, since we have only dropped off-diagonal elements in the first row and column. Thus, as in the proof of Theorem 3.10, we can perform the first step of Gaussian elimination on $\tilde{A}^{(1)}$, i.e. we can form a matrix $A^{(2)} = L^{(1)}\tilde{A}^{(1)}$, which is also strictly row diagonally dominant.

Moreover, since the elementary lower triangular matrix is of the form $L^{(1)} = I - \mathbf{m}_1 \mathbf{e}_1^T$ with $\mathbf{m}_1 = (0, \tilde{a}_{21}^{(1)}/a_{11}, \ldots, \tilde{a}_{n1}^{(1)}/a_{11})^T$, we see that the matrix $L^{(1)}$ has zeros wherever the pattern $\mathcal{M}^c$ requires it. Now, we can drop those entries from $A^{(2)}$ in the second row and column which have indices in $\mathcal{M}^c$, i.e. we write $A^{(2)} = \tilde{A}^{(2)} - R^{(2)}$, where the matrix $R^{(2)}$ has only non-zero entries in row and column 2. But if for example $(1, 2) \in \mathcal{M}^c$ then we would have removed the corresponding entry already in the first step. This means that $R^{(2)}$ has only entries in the second row and second column beyond the diagonal element.

Proceeding in this manner, we can generate sequences of matrices $A^{(k)}$, $\tilde{A}^{(k)}$, $R^{(k)}$ and $L^{(k)}$ which satisfy

$$A^{(k+1)} = L^{(k)}\tilde{A}^{(k)}, \quad \tilde{A}^{(k)} = A^{(k)} + R^{(k)}, \qquad 1 \le k \le n - 1.$$

Moreover, the matrix $L^{(k)}$ has zeros wherever the pattern $\mathcal{M}^c$ requires it; the same is true for the first $k - 1$ rows of $A^{(k)}$. The matrix $R^{(k)}$ has at most non-zero entries at $r_{kj}^{(k)}$ for $k + 1 \le j \le n$ and at $r_{ik}^{(k)}$ for $k + 1 \le i \le n$ with zero entries if $(k, j) \in \mathcal{M}$ or $(i, k) \in \mathcal{M}$.

This gives iteratively the representation

$$\begin{aligned}
A^{(n)} &= L^{(n-1)}\tilde{A}^{(n-1)} = L^{(n-1)}A^{(n-1)} + L^{(n-1)}R^{(n-1)} \\
&= L^{(n-1)}L^{(n-2)}A^{(n-2)} + L^{(n-1)}L^{(n-2)}R^{(n-2)} + L^{(n-1)}R^{(n-1)} \\
&= \cdots \\
&= L^{(n-1)}L^{(n-2)} \cdots L^{(1)}A^{(1)} + L^{(n-1)}L^{(n-2)} \cdots L^{(1)}R^{(1)} \\
&\quad + L^{(n-1)}L^{(n-2)} \cdots L^{(2)}R^{(2)} + \cdots + L^{(n-1)}L^{(n-2)}R^{(n-2)} + L^{(n-1)}R^{(n-1)}.
\end{aligned}$$

Since the matrix $R^{(k)}$ has only zero entries in its first $k - 1$ rows and since the matrix $L^{(m)}$ leaves the first m rows of the matrix it is applied to unchanged and changes the jth row for $m + 1 \le j \le n$ by subtracting a multiple of the mth row (see Lemma 3.4), we have $L^{(m)}R^{(k)} = R^{(k)}$ for $m \le k - 1$. In other words, we have

$$L^{(k-1)}L^{(k-2)} \cdots L^{(1)}R^{(k)} = R^{(k)}$$

and hence

$$L^{(n-1)}L^{(n-2)} \cdots L^{(k)}R^{(k)} = L^{(n-1)}L^{(n-2)} \cdots L^{(1)}R^{(k)},$$

which allows us to rewrite the representation of $A^{(n)}$ as

$$A^{(n)} = L^{(n-1)} L^{(n-2)} \cdots L^{(1)} \left[A + R^{(1)} + R^{(2)} + \cdots + R^{(n-1)} \right].$$

Thus, if we define $L := [L^{(n-1)} \cdots L^{(1)}]^{-1}$, $U := A^{(n)}$ and $R := R^{(1)} + \cdots + R^{(n-1)}$, then we have the desired representation $LU = A + R$. Furthermore, by construction, $R = (r_{ij})$ satisfies $r_{ij} = 0$ for $(i, j) \in \mathcal{M}$. The upper triangular matrix $U = (u_{ij})$ also has the property $u_{ij} = 0$ for $(i, j) \notin \mathcal{M}$ and because of Lemma 3.4 the same is true for L.   □

Note that the matrix (4.9) of our standard example from Section 1.1.2 is not strictly row diagonally dominant but still has a sparse LU factorisation even with $R = 0$ according to Example 3.17.

The above theorem holds for more general matrices. Suppose the matrix A has positive diagonal elements $a_{ii} > 0$ and non-positive off-diagonal elements $a_{ij} \leq 0$ for $i \neq j$ and has an inverse A^{-1} with non-negative entries. Such a matrix is called an *M-matrix* and for such a matrix we can also find an incomplete factorisation $A = LU - R$, which is *regular* in the sense that both R^{-1} and $(LU)^{-1}$ have non-negative entries. Furthermore, though in general the matrices L and U are not uniquely determined, they are in this specific situation. For details, see for example Meijerink and van der Vorst [94].

Obviously, we want the matrix LU in the factorisation $A = LU + E$ to be close to A such that E is close to the zero matrix. From this, it seems to follow that $P = (LU)^{-1}$ is a good preconditioner. While this is indeed often the case, there might be exceptions. According to Lemma 8.1, the matrix $(LU)^{-1}A$ has the same eigenvalues as

$$L^{-1} A U^{-1} = I + L^{-1} E U^{-1}$$

and badly conditioned factors L and U can make the preconditioned system worse than the original system even if E is small.

The remaining question we still have to answer is how to choose the nonzero pattern $\mathcal{M}$. As pointed out above, a natural choice would be the matrix pattern given by the original matrix, i.e.

$$\mathcal{M}_A = \{(i, j) : a_{ij} \neq 0\}. \tag{8.7}$$

This obviously means that both L and U can only have non-zero entries where A has non-zero entries, which is for this reason also called *zero fill-in*.

Unfortunately, even if an incomplete LU factorisation for the non-zero pattern $\mathcal{M}_A$ exists, it does not have to be a good approximation to A. One reason for this is that even though L and U have the same zero pattern as A, their product LU might have additional non-zero entries.

Hence, in such a situation it is desirable to allow more non-zero entries in L and U. Here, various possibilities are at hand. We only want to describe a level-based fill-in concept and a thresholding strategy.

We start with describing the idea of a level-based approach by looking at the update formula

$$a_{ij} := a_{ij} - a_{ik}a_{kj} \tag{8.8}$$

of Gaussian elimination, i.e. Algorithm 3 or Algorithm 44. Assume that in each step of the algorithm we assign a *fill level* lev_{ij} to the element a_{ij} and assume that we can somehow express the size of the element a_{ij} by $\epsilon^{\text{lev}_{ij}}$ with a fixed $\epsilon \in (0, 1)$. Then, the update formula (8.8) yields that the newly computed a_{ij} has a size

$$\epsilon^{\text{lev}_{ij}} - \epsilon^{\text{lev}_{ik}}\epsilon^{\text{lev}_{kj}} = \epsilon^{\text{lev}_{ij}} - \epsilon^{\text{lev}_{ik} + \text{lev}_{kj}}$$
$$= O\left(\epsilon^{\min\{\text{lev}_{ij}, \; \text{lev}_{ik} + \text{lev}_{kj}\}}\right),$$

which defines the new level of the newly computed a_{ij}. It is usual to shift the level by one, i.e. to define a level function by $\text{level}(i, j) := \text{lev}_{ij} - 1$. This gives the following definition

Definition 8.11 The initial fill level of a matrix entry a_{ij} is defined by

$$\text{level}^{(0)}(i, j) := \begin{cases} 0 & \text{if } a_{ij} \neq 0 \text{ or } i = j, \\ \infty & \text{otherwise.} \end{cases} \tag{8.9}$$

For $\ell = 1, 2, \ldots$, the fill level of a_{ij} in iteration ℓ is defined by

$$\text{level}^{(\ell)}(i, j) := \min\left\{\text{level}^{(\ell-1)}(i, j), \text{level}^{(\ell-1)}(i, k) + \text{level}^{(\ell-1)}(k, j) + 1\right\}.$$

Obviously, the level of an element is non-increasing, meaning that once an element a_{ij} has a certain level $\text{level}^{(\ell)}(i, j) = p$, it will have no higher level for all following iterations.

The initialisation step can obviously also be based on different non-zero pattern $\mathcal{M}$.

From the derivation of the level function it seems natural to apply the level update while going through the Gaussian elimination process. This, however, means that different elements a_{ij} of the matrix will have level values from different iterations. Consequently, the non-zero pattern that is used depends on the implementation of the Gaussian elimination process, in particular on the ordering of the three significant loops. In practice, usually the so-called "*ikj*" version of the elimination process is used in the context of incomplete LU factorisations of level $p > 0$, which essentially switches the two outer loops of Algorithm 44. This has the advantage that the ith rows of both L and U are generated at the same time and only entries of the first $i - 1$ rows are required in order to achieve this.

Hence, we can describe the *incomplete LU factorisation of level p*, ILU(p), as follows. We perform the Gaussian elimination as before but restrict ourselves to elements which have a level smaller than or equal to p. We update the fill level each time with the update formula from Definition 8.11. After row i has benn updated, we drop all elements of row i which have level greater than p. Details of this are given in Algorithm 45.

Algorithm 45: $ILU(p)$ factorisation

Input : $A \in \mathbb{R}^{n \times n}$, level p.
Output: L normalised lower triangular, U upper triangular.

1 **for** *all* (i, j) **do**
2 $\quad$ **if** $a_{ij} \neq 0$ **then** level$(i, j) = 0$
3 $\quad$ **else** level$(i, j) = \infty$

4 **for** $i = 2$ **to** n **do**
5 $\quad$ **for** $k = 1$ **to** $i - 1$ **do**
6 $\quad\quad$ **if** level$(i, k) \leq p$ **then**
7 $\quad\quad\quad$ $a_{ik} := a_{ik}/a_{kk}$
8 $\quad\quad\quad$ **for** $j = k + 1$ **to** n **do**
9 $\quad\quad\quad\quad$ $a_{ij} := a_{ij} - a_{ik}a_{kj}$
10 $\quad\quad\quad\quad$ level$(i, j) = \min \{$level$(i, j),$ level$(i, k) +$ level$(k, j) + 1\}$

11 $\quad$ **for** $j = 1$ **to** n **do**
12 $\quad\quad$ **if** level$(i, j) > p$ **then** $a_{ij} = 0$

As in the case of the ILU algorithm, the entries of the matrices L and U are over-writing the entries of the original matrix. The entries of L and U are given by (8.6), if the non-zero set $\mathcal{M}$ is defined by

$$\mathcal{M} := \{(i, j) : \text{level}(i, j) \leq p\}.$$

Since we need to store the information on the level, we have direct access to these entries.

The ILU(p) algorithm can also be split into two phases. The determination of the fill levels can be computed without even knowing the actual matrix entries a_{ij}. It suffices to know the non-zero pattern. Hence, one can distinguish between a *symbolic factorisation*, in which the levels will be computed, and an *actual factorisation*, which then carries out the computation of the entries of L

and U. This is advantageous if more than one matrix with the same non-zero pattern must be dealt with.

While the ILU(p) method can also stop prematurely, it often works well, particularly for smaller p. Nonetheless, there are some drawbacks to this method. The amount of fill-in and the computational cost are not predictable. Also, for some matrices, the fill level might not be a good indicator for the actual size of the matrix elements.

The latter problem can be handled by a thresholding-based approach, which we want to introduce now. To this end, we need a *dropping rule*, which is mathematically a Boolean function

$$\text{drop} : \mathbb{R} \to \{\text{true}, \text{false}\},$$

which determines which elements are set to zero during the elimination process. Given a dropping rule, a generic incomplete LU factorisation algorithm is given in Algorithm 46.

Algorithm 46: ILUT factorisation

Input : $A \in \mathbb{R}^{n \times n}$, dropping rule.
Output: L normalised lower triangular, U upper triangular.

1 **for** $i = 2$ **to** n **do**
2   **for** $k = 1$ **to** $i - 1$ **do**
3        $a_{ik} := a_{ik}/a_{kk}$
4   **if not** drop(a_{ik}) **then**
5   **for** $j = k + 1$ **to** n **do**
6              $a_{ij} := a_{ij} - a_{ik}a_{kj}$
7   **for** $j = 1$ **to** n **do**
8   **if** drop(a_{ij}) **then** $a_{ij} := 0$

The matrix entries of the lower and upper triangular matrices L and U are once again stored in the original matrix A. Again, they are given by (8.6) if we define

$$\mathcal{M} := \{(i, j) : \text{drop}(a_{ij}) = \text{false}\}.$$

However, since the function drop is applied to the entries a_{ij} which are dynamically created during the elimination process, a realisation of Algorithm 46 requires that this information is stored separately.

As one can easily see, Algorithm 46 is a generalisation of Algorithm 45.

Hence, ILU(p) can be interpreted as a thresholding algorithm, simply by defining the dropping function by

$$\text{drop}(a_{ij}) := \begin{cases} \text{true} & \text{if } \text{level}(i, j) > p, \\ \text{false} & \text{if } \text{level}(i, j) \leq p. \end{cases}$$

However, as mentioned above, the idea of the ILUT algorithm is to use thresholding strategies for dropping matrix entries. One possibility is to drop a_{ij} in line 8 of Algorithm 46 if

$$|a_{ij}| \leq c|a_{ii}a_{jj}|^{1/2},$$

where $0 < c < 1$. Another possibility, which is referred to as ILUT(p, τ), actually employs two dropping strategies. In line 4 an element is "dropped" if it is less than τ times the norm of the original ith row of A. In line 8, the same rule is applied but after that only the p largest elements in the L part and the p largest elements in the U part of that row are kept. Details can be found in Saad [104] and Axelsson [6].

There are other incomplete factorisations available. Most importantly, if A is symmetric and positive definite, we know that A has a Cholesky factorisation. Hence, in this situation one usually looks for an *incomplete Cholesky factorisation* $A = LL^{\mathrm{T}} + E$ satisfying $\ell_{ij} = 0$ for $(i, j) \notin \mathcal{M}$ and $e_{ij} = 0$ for $(i, j) \in \mathcal{M}$, rather than for an incomplete LU factorisation. A possible implementation is given in Algorithm 47, which corresponds to an IC(0) method, as we can clearly use the ideas outlined above to also define an IC(p) method or an ICT method corresponding to the ILU(p) method and the ILUT method, respectively.

There are further variants of ILU and IC factorisations, for example, the *modified incomplete LU factorisation (MILU)*, the *incomplete LU factorisation with thresholding and pivoting (ILUTP)*, and the *incomplete Crout LU factorisation (ILUC)*. Details can again be found in the above-mentioned books.

8.3 Polynomial and Approximate Inverse Preconditioners

Another class of preconditioners is given by *polynomial preconditioners*. In Section 8.1 we discussed preconditioners based upon a splitting scheme for iterative methods. Such a splitting is based upon rewriting the matrix A as $A = A + B - B$ with an invertible matrix B. This can also be written as

$$A = B + A - B = B[I - B^{-1}(B - A)] =: B(I - C), \qquad C := B^{-1}(B - A),$$

Algorithm 47: Incomplete Cholesky factorisation

Input : $A = A^T \in \mathbb{R}^{n \times n}$, non-zero pattern $\mathcal{M}$.
Output: L lower triangular.

1 **for** $k = 1$ **to** n **do**
2      $\ell_{kk} = a_{kk}$
3   **for** $j = 1$ **to** $k - 1$ **do**
4   **if** $(k, j) \in \mathcal{M}$ **then**
5              $\ell_{kk} := \ell_{kk} - \ell_{kj}^2$
6      $\ell_{kk} := \sqrt{\ell_{kk}}$
7   **for** $i = k + 1$ **to** n *with* $(i, k) \in \mathcal{M}$ **do**
8          $\ell_{ik} := a_{ik}$
9   **if** $(i, j) \in \mathcal{M}$ **and** $(k, j) \in \mathcal{M}$ **then** $\ell_{ik} := \ell_{ik} - \ell_{ij}\ell_{kj}$
10          $\ell_{ik} := \ell_{ik}/\ell_{kk}$

---

where C is the iteration matrix of the iteration associated with the splitting. Hence, if $I - C$ is invertible than we can express the inverse of A as

$$A^{-1} = (I - C)^{-1}B^{-1}.$$

The crucial point for building our first polynomial preconditioners is then the following result.

Theorem 8.12 (von Neumann) *Let $C \in \mathbb{R}^{n \times n}$ be a matrix with spectral radius $\rho(C) < 1$. Then, $I - C$ is invertible with inverse*

$$(I - C)^{-1} = \sum_{j=0}^{\infty} C^j, \qquad m \in \mathbb{N}_0.$$

Here, the infinite sum on the right-hand side is defined as the limit of the matrix-valued sequence (C_m) with

$$C_m := \sum_{j=0}^{m} C^j.$$

Proof Since $\rho(C) < 1$, we can choose an $\epsilon > 0$ such that $\eta := \rho(C) + \epsilon < 1$. From Theorem 4.5 we know that there is a compatible matrix norm $\| \cdot \|$ with $\|C\| \leq \rho(C) + \epsilon = \eta < 1$. As a compatible matrix norm, the norm is multiplicative so that in this norm the matrix C_m has the bound

$$\|C_m\| \leq \sum_{j=0}^{m} \|C\|^j \leq \sum_{j=0}^{m} \eta^j \leq \frac{1}{1 - \eta}$$

and since this bound is independent of m the sequence (C_m) converges. It converges in any norm since all matrix norms are equivalent. Let us denote the limit by

$$F := \sum_{j=0}^{\infty} C^j.$$

We have the identities

$$(I - C)C_m = (I - C) \sum_{j=0}^{m} C^j = \sum_{j=0}^{m}(C^j - C^{j+1}) = I - C^{m+1}.$$

The term on the left-hand side converges to $(I - C)F$, while the term on the right-hand side converges to I since $\|C\| < 1$. This shows that F is indeed the inverse of $I - C$. $\quad\square$

This general approach allows us to define a polynomial preconditioner associated with such a splitting.

Definition 8.13 Let $A = B(I - C)$ be a consistent splitting with $B \in \mathbb{R}^{n \times n}$ invertible and $C \in \mathbb{R}^{n \times n}$ satisfying $\rho(C) < 1$. Then, for each $m \in \mathbb{N}_0$ a *polynomial preconditioner* associated with this splitting is defined as

$$P_m := \sum_{j=0}^{m} C^j B^{-1}. \tag{8.10}$$

From the above considerations we can immediately conclude that P_m converges to $(I - C)^{-1}B = A^{-1}$. In the special case of choosing $B = I$ and hence $C = I - A$, under the assumption of $\rho(I - A) < 1$, we have in particular

$$P_m := \sum_{j=0}^{m}(I - A)^j \rightarrow A^{-1}, \qquad m \rightarrow \infty.$$

Obviously, the quality of a polynomial preconditioner (8.10) depends on the number $\rho = \rho(C)$, since we have in any multiplicative norm

$$\|A^{-1} - P_m\| \leq \|B^{-1}\| \sum_{j=m+1}^{\infty} \|C\|^j \leq \|B^{-1}\| \frac{\rho^{m+1}}{1 - \rho}. \tag{8.11}$$

As we have seen before, the condition $\rho(C) < 1$ is sometimes difficult to verify. However, we know from Theorem 4.9 that the iteration matrix $C = I - D^{-1}A$ of the Jacobi method with $D = \text{diag}(a_{11}, \ldots, a_{nn})$ satisfies $\rho(C) < 1$ if $A \in \mathbb{R}^{n \times n}$ is strictly row diagonally dominant. Hence, we have the following result.

Theorem 8.14 *Assume that $A \in \mathbb{R}^{n \times n}$ is strictly row diagonally dominant. Let $B = D = \text{diag}(a_{11}, \ldots, a_{dd})$. Then, we have $\rho(I - D^{-1}A) < 1$ and hence*

$$A^{-1} = \left[\sum_{j=0}^{\infty} (I - D^{-1}A)^j \right] D^{-1}.$$

Thus, the sequence P_m of preconditioners defined by

$$P_m := \left[\sum_{j=0}^{m} (I - D^{-1}A)^j \right] D^{-1} \tag{8.12}$$

converges to A^{-1} with an error, which can be bounded by (8.11).

Obviously, we can use all the other results on the convergence of iterative schemes from Chapter 4 to derive more sophisticated results.

Here, however, we want to change the approach slightly. To this end, let us assume that the matrix A is normalised in such a way that all diagonal elements satisfy $a_{ii} = 1$, $1 \le i \le n$. Then, the Jacobi polynomial preconditioner (8.12) can be written as

$$P_m = \sum_{j=0}^{m} (I - A)^j = \sum_{j=0}^{m} \gamma_j A^j \tag{8.13}$$

with certain well-known constant factors $\gamma_j \in \mathbb{R}$. The same is true, as we have observed above, if we choose $B = I$ under the assumption of $\rho(I - A) < 1$.

The idea now is to consider all possible coefficients γ_j to build a preconditioner, i.e. we are now allowing arbitrary polynomials to form our preconditioner:

$$P_m := \sum_{j=0}^{m} \gamma_j A^j =: p_m(A), \qquad p_m \in \pi_m. \tag{8.14}$$

Another motivation of this approach comes from the following theoretical observation.

Lemma 8.15 *Let $A \in \mathbb{R}^{n \times n}$ be invertible. Then, there is a polynomial $p \in \pi_{n-1}$ such that $A^{-1} = p(A)$.*

Proof Define the polynomial $\varphi \in \pi_n$ by $\varphi(t) := \det(A - tI)$. This polynomial can be written in the monomial base as

$$\varphi(t) = \sum_{j=0}^{n} \gamma_j t^j$$

with certain constants $\gamma_j \in \mathbb{R}$. Since A is invertible we have that $\gamma_0 = \varphi(0) =$

$\det(A) \neq 0$. Now, the Cayley–Hamilton theorem states that $\varphi(A) = 0$. Thus, if we rewrite $\varphi(A)$ in the form

$$0 = \varphi(A) = \gamma_0 \left[I + A \sum_{j=1}^{n} \frac{\gamma_j}{\gamma_0} A^{j-1} \right]$$

we see that $A^{-1} = p(A)$ with

$$p(t) = -\sum_{j=0}^{n-1} \frac{\gamma_{j+1}}{\gamma_0} t^j. \qquad \qquad \square$$

It remains to discuss how to choose the polynomial $p_m \in \pi_m$ for our preconditioner $P_m = p_m(A)$. From now on, we will restrict ourselves to symmetric matrices, noticing that with $A \in \mathbb{R}^{n \times n}$ symmetric also the matrices $P_m = p_m(A)$ and $P_m A$ are symmetric. Moreover, if $\lambda_1 \leq \cdots \leq \lambda_n$ are the eigenvalues of A then $p_m(\lambda_j)$ and $p_m(\lambda_j)\lambda_j$ for $1 \leq j \leq n$ are the eigenvalues of P_m and $P_m A$. We want P_m to be a good approximation to A^{-1} or, in other words, $P_m A$ should be a good approximation to the identity matrix I. We can try to achieve this by solving

$$\min_{p \in \pi_m} \| I - p(A)A \|$$

in a given, specific norm. For the Euclidean norm, the above considerations together with Corollary 2.21 show that this boils down to the discrete Chebyshev approximation problem

$$\min_{p \in \pi_m} \| I - p(A)A \|_2 = \min_{p \in \pi} \max_{1 \leq j \leq n} |1 - p(\lambda_j)\lambda_j|.$$

We now define $q(t) = 1 - p(t)t$, which is a polynomial satisfying $q \in \pi_{m+1}$ with $q(0) = 1$ and note that any polynomial $q \in \pi_{m+1}$ with $q(0) = 1$ must necessarily have this form, i.e. that there is a one-to-one mapping between p and q. With this, we can transform the above discrete Chebyshev approximation problem into a continuous Chebyshev approximation problem that we have encountered before:

$$\min_{\substack{q \in \pi_{m+1} \\ q(0)=1}} \max_{1 \leq j \leq n} |q(\lambda_j)| \leq \min_{\substack{q \in \pi_{m+1} \\ q(0)=1}} \max_{\lambda \in [\lambda_1, \lambda_n]} |q(\lambda_j)|. \qquad (8.15)$$

As mentioned above, we have discussed these Chebyshev approximation problems before, namely in the case of the CG method and the MINRES method. In the case of a positive definite matrix all eigenvalues are positive and we can use Theorem 6.18 to solve (8.15). Recall that T_m denotes the Chebyshev polynomial of degree m, defined by $T_m(t) = \cos(m \arccos(t))$, $t \in [-1, 1]$. As in the proof of Theorem 6.19, the properties of the Chebyshev polynomials stated in Lemma 6.17 yield the following result.

Theorem 8.16 *Let $A \in \mathbb{R}^{n \times n}$ be symmetric and positive definite with minimum eigenvalue λ_1 and maximum eigenvalue λ_n. Let $m \in \mathbb{N}_0$ be given. Then, the Chebyshev preconditioner $P_m := p_m(A)$ defined by $p_m(t) = (1 - q_{m+1}(t))/t$ with*

$$q_{m+1}(t) = T_{m+1}\left(\frac{\lambda_n + \lambda_1 - 2t}{\lambda_n - \lambda_1}\right) \bigg/ T_{m+1}\left(\frac{\lambda_n + \lambda_1}{\lambda_n - \lambda_1}\right), \qquad t \in [\lambda_1, \lambda_n],$$

satisfies the error bound

$$\|I - p_m(A)A\|_2 \leq 2\left(\frac{\sqrt{\kappa_2(A)} - 1}{\sqrt{\kappa_2(A)} + 1}\right)^{m+1}. \tag{8.16}$$

Consequently, if we denote the expression on the right-hand side of (8.16) by ϵ_m, then we have $|1 - p(\lambda_j)\lambda_j| \leq \epsilon_m$ for all $1 \leq j \leq n$. Hence, the condition number of the preconditioned matrix $P_m A = p(A)A$ can be bounded by

$$\kappa_2(p(A)A) \leq \frac{1 + \epsilon_m}{1 - \epsilon_m},$$

provided that $\epsilon_m < 1$. While this shows that the condition number can become arbitrarily close to 1, it also shows the imminent problem of this type of pre-conditioner. We need a large m if the condition number of A is too large, which renders this preconditioner inpractical in those cases where we actually need to precondition.

In the case of a symmetric but indefinite matrix, the situation is even worse. However, we can proceed as in the case of proving convergence of MINRES, see Theorem 6.26.

Theorem 8.17 *Let A be symmetric and invertible. Let the eigenvalues of A be contained in $[a, b] \cup [c, d]$ with $a < b < 0 < c < d$ and equal length $b - a = d - c$. Then, the polynomial $p_m \in \pi_m$ defined as*

$$p_m(t) = \frac{1}{t}\left(1 - \frac{T_{\lfloor (m+1)/2 \rfloor}(q(t))}{T_{\lfloor (m+1)/2 \rfloor}(q(0))}\right)$$

with

$$q(t) = 1 + 2\frac{(t - b)(t - c)}{ad - bc}, \qquad t \in [a, b] \cup [c, d],$$

defines a polynomial preconditioner $P_m := p_m(A)$ which satisfies the error bound

$$\|I - p_m(A)A\|_2 \leq 2\left(\frac{\sqrt{|ad|} - \sqrt{|bc|}}{\sqrt{|ad|} + \sqrt{|bc|}}\right)^{\lfloor (m+1)/2 \rfloor}.$$

For a general polynomial preconditioner $p_m(A) \in \mathbb{R}^{n \times n}$ of the form (8.14) and a vector $\mathbf{x} \in \mathbb{R}^n$ we can compute the product $p_m(A)\mathbf{x}$ using the *Horner scheme* for evaluating polynomials (see Algorithm 48). In the situation of a Chebyshev preconditioner we can alternatively use the update formula (6.13) to compute $p(A)\mathbf{x}$.

Algorithm 48: Horner scheme

Input : $p_m(A) \in \mathbb{R}^{n \times n}$ from (8.14) via $\gamma_0, \dots, \gamma_m$, $\mathbf{x} \in \mathbb{R}^n$.
Output: $p_m(A)\mathbf{x}$.

1 $\mathbf{y} := \gamma_m \mathbf{x}$
2 **for** $j = m - 1$ **downto** 0 **do**
3 $\quad\lfloor\ \mathbf{y} := \gamma_j \mathbf{x} + A\mathbf{y}$

So far, we have tried to find a polynomial $p \in \pi_m$ such that $\|I - p(A)A\|_2$ is close to zero and hence $p(A)$ is a good left preconditioner to A. We can, of course, use different norms and look, more generally, for invertible matrices $P \in \mathbb{R}^{n \times n}$ such that $\|I - PA\|$ is close to zero. In this context, P would be called an *approximate inverse preconditioner*. We will now have a closer look at this concept with the following two modifications. First, we will employ the Frobenius norm, which is usually used in this context. Second, we will look at right preconditioners, i.e. we will try to find a $P \in \mathbb{R}^{n \times n}$ such that $\|I - AP\|_F$ becomes small. This is no real restriction since we have

$$\|I - PA\|_F = \|I - A^{\mathrm{T}} P^{\mathrm{T}}\|_F,$$

i.e. computing a left preconditioner to A is equivalent to computing a right preconditioner to A^{T}. As we would like the preconditioner to be sparse, it seems natural to include the following in our considerations.

Definition 8.18 Let $A \in \mathbb{R}^{n \times n}$ be invertible and let $\mathcal{M}$ be a non-zero pattern. Then, an invertible matrix $P = (p_{ij}) \in \mathbb{R}^{n \times n}$ is called a *sparse approximate (SPAI, AINV) preconditioner* if it solves

$$\min \left\{ \|I - AP\|_F : P \in \mathbb{R}^{n \times n} \text{ invertible with } p_{ij} = 0 \text{ for } (i, j) \notin \mathcal{M} \right\}. \quad (8.17)$$

Note that P might have additional zero entries with indices in $\mathcal{M}$. This is usually not a problem, but, alternatively, we could also try to solve

$$\min \left\{ \|I - AP\|_F : P = (p_{ij}) \in \mathbb{R}^{n \times n} \text{ invertible with } \mathcal{M}_P = \mathcal{M} \right\}$$

instead. However, this might not have a solution, see Exercise 8.3.
Since the Frobenius norm of a matrix can be computed by summing the squares of the Euclidean norms of its columns, we have

$$\|I - AP\|_F^2 = \sum_{j=1}^{n} \|\mathbf{e}_j - A\mathbf{p}_j\|_2^2$$

if $\mathbf{p}_j = P\mathbf{e}_j$ denotes the jth column of P. Hence, instead of minimising the matrix expression $\|I - AP\|_F$ we can simply minimise the n vector expressions $\|\mathbf{e}_j - A\mathbf{p}_j\|_2$ under the given sparsity constraints. Obviously, a significant advantage of the latter is that it can easily be done in parallel.

To incorporate the sparsity pattern into the problem of minimising $\|\mathbf{e}_j - A\mathbf{p}_j\|_2$ let us define the *non-zero column pattern*

$$\mathcal{M}_j := \{i \in \{1, \ldots, n\} : (i, j) \in \mathcal{M}\}$$

associated with a given non-zero pattern $\mathcal{M}$. Let us further denote the number of indices in $\mathcal{M}_j$ by n_j and let us denote the $n \times n_j$ sub-matrix of A consisting of the columns of A with index in $\mathcal{M}_j$ by $A_{\mathcal{M}_j}$. In the same way $\mathbf{p}_{M_j} \in \mathbb{R}^{n_j}$ should contain only those entries of $\mathbf{p} \in \mathbb{R}^n$ with index in $\mathcal{M}_j$, i.e. $\mathbf{p}_{M_j} = (p_i)_{i \in \mathcal{M}_j}$. Then, for any $\mathbf{p} = (p_i) \in \mathbb{R}^n$ with $p_i = 0$ for $i \notin \mathcal{M}_j$ we have

$$Ap = \sum_{k=1}^{n} \mathbf{a}_k p_k = \sum_{k \in \mathcal{M}_j} \mathbf{a}_k p_k = A_{\mathcal{M}_j} \mathbf{p}_{\mathcal{M}_j},$$

if $\mathbf{a}_k = A\mathbf{e}_k$ denotes the kth column of A. In the case of a sparse matrix A, it often can happen that the reduced matrix $A_{\mathcal{M}_j} \in \mathbb{R}^{n \times n_j}$ has several zero rows. These rows obviously do not contribute to the norm of the product $Ap = A_{\mathcal{M}_j} \mathbf{p}_{\mathcal{M}_j}$ and hence we can remove them from $A_{\mathcal{M}_j}$ giving a smaller matrix $\hat{A}_{\mathcal{M}_j} \in \mathbb{R}^{m_j \times n_j}$ with m_j being the number of rows in $A_{\mathcal{M}_j}$ not identically zero. Thus if we denote by $\hat{\mathbf{e}}_j \in \mathbb{R}^{m_j}$ the corresponding reduced unit vector then we have converted the constrained minimisation problem (8.17) into n smaller unconstrained problems.

Proposition 8.19 *Let $A \in \mathbb{R}^{n \times n}$ be invertible and let $\mathcal{M}$ be a non-zero pattern. Then, the minimisation problem (8.17) can be solved by solving the n unconstrained minimisation problems*

$$\min\left\{\|\hat{\mathbf{e}}_j - \hat{A}_{\mathcal{M}_j} \mathbf{p}_{M_j}\|_2 : \mathbf{p}_{M_j} \in \mathbb{R}^{n_j}\right\}, \qquad 1 \le j \le n. \qquad (8.18)$$

The matrix P assembled from these $\mathbf{p}_j$ is invertible, provided that $\|I - AP\| < 1$ for any compatible matrix norm.

Proof It only remains to show that P is invertible under the stated condition. However, since $AP = I - (I - AP)$ and $\|I - AP\| < 1$, this follows directly from the proof of Theorem 8.12. □

The unconstrained least-squares problems (8.18) can be solved by means from Section 3.8. In particular, we can use a QR factorisation as outlined in Proposition 3.42.

This approach once again requires a pre-determined non-zero pattern $\mathcal{M}$. A natural choice would once again be $M = M_A$. However, there is no guarantee that this does indeed lead to a good preconditioner such that $\|I - AP\|_F$ is small. But the above approach allows us to develop a dynamical, adaptive method. In each step, after computing the least-squares solution of (8.18) we can expand the pattern for column j if the error $\|\mathbf{e}_j - A\mathbf{p}_j\|_2$ is larger than a certain threshold. This has also the consequence that we can ensure the invertibility of P. If, for example, we require $\|\mathbf{e}_j - A\mathbf{p}_j\|_2 \le \epsilon_j$, $1 \le j \le n$, then we will have

$$\|I - AP\|_F \le \left(\sum_{j=1}^{n} \epsilon_j^2 \right)^{1/2}$$

and, once the term on the right-hand side is smaller than 1, our matrix P is invertible. If the condition $\|\mathbf{e}_j - A\mathbf{p}_j\|_2 \le \epsilon_j$ is not satisfied then we can try to add a new index $k \notin M_j$ to M_j, giving a bigger non-zero pattern $M_j^+ = M_j \cup \{k\}$. The new index should be chosen such that the new matrix $A_{M_j^+}$ still has full rank $n_j + 1$ and such that the residual $\|\mathbf{e}_j - A_{M_j^+}\mathbf{p}\|_2$ decreases if $\mathbf{p} \in \mathbb{R}^{n_j+1}$ is chosen as its minimiser. However, since this means we have to test several such new indices, we can try to simplify the decision process as follows. Since

$$\mathbf{e}_j - A_{M_j^+}\mathbf{p} = \mathbf{e}_j - A_{M_j}\tilde{\mathbf{p}} - \mathbf{a}_k p_k$$

with $\mathbf{a}_k = A\mathbf{e}_k$ and with $\tilde{\mathbf{p}} \in \mathbb{R}^{n_j}$ constructed from $\mathbf{p} \in \mathbb{R}^{n_j+1}$ by dropping p_k, we could, instead of minimising over all $\mathbf{p} \in \mathbb{R}^{n_j+1}$, replace $\tilde{\mathbf{p}}$ by $\mathbf{p}_{M_j}$ and then minimise only over $p_k \in \mathbb{R}$. Noting that $\mathbf{r}_j := \mathbf{e}_j - A\mathbf{p}_j = \mathbf{e}_j - A_{M_j}\mathbf{p}_{M_j}$, this means we want to solve

$$\min \left\{ \|\mathbf{r}_j - \mu \mathbf{a}_k\|_2 : \mu \in \mathbb{R} \right\}.$$

The solution is given by

$$\mu_j^{(k)} = \frac{\langle \mathbf{r}_j, \mathbf{a}_k \rangle_2}{\langle \mathbf{a}_k, \mathbf{a}_k \rangle_2}$$

and the actual new residual can be approximated by

$$[\rho_j^{(k)}]^2 := \|\mathbf{r}_j - \mu_j^{(k)} \mathbf{a}_k\|_2^2 = \|\mathbf{r}_j\|_2^2 - \frac{\langle \mathbf{r}_j, \mathbf{a}_k \rangle_2^2}{\|\mathbf{a}_k\|_2^2}.$$

Taking these considerations into account, we have a possible version of computing a sparse approximate inverse as outlined in Algorithm 49.

Instead of the thresholding strategy in line 10, one can also simply add those indices corresponding to, say, the ℓ_j largest $|\rho_j^{(k)}|$, which was originally suggested by Grote and Huckle in [72]. Also, the computation of the next approximation $\mathbf{p}_j^{(i+1)}$ can benefit from the previously computed approximation $\mathbf{p}_j^{(i)}$ or, to be

---

Algorithm 49: Sparse approximate inverse (SPAI)

Input : $A \in \mathbb{R}^{n \times n}$, initial non-zero pattern $\mathcal{M}$.

Output: Approximate inverse P.

1   **for** $j = 1$ **to** n **do**

2   **repeat**

3   Determine the non-zero rows of $A_{\mathcal{M}_j}$ to form $\hat{A}_{\mathcal{M}_j}$

4   Compute $\mathbf{p}_j$ via $\mathbf{p}_{M_j} = \arg\min\{\|\hat{\mathbf{e}}_j - \hat{A}_{\mathcal{M}_j}\mathbf{p}\|_2 : \mathbf{p} \in \mathbb{R}^{n_j}\}$

5       $\mathbf{r}_j := \mathbf{e}_j - A\mathbf{p}_j$

6       $\mathcal{L} := \{\ell : \mathbf{e}_\ell^T \mathbf{r}_j \neq 0\}$

7       $\tilde{\mathcal{M}}_j := \mathcal{L} \setminus \mathcal{M}_j$

8   **for** $k \in \tilde{\mathcal{M}}_j$ **do**

9         $\rho_j^{(k)} := \left(\|\mathbf{r}_j\|_2^2 - \langle \mathbf{r}_j, A\mathbf{e}_k \rangle_2^2 / \|A\mathbf{e}_k\|_2^2 \right)^{1/2}$

10       $\mathcal{M}_j := \mathcal{M}_j \cup \{k \in \tilde{\mathcal{M}}_j : |\rho_j^{(k)}| \geq \eta_j\}$

11   **until** $\|\mathbf{r}_j\|_2 \leq \epsilon$

---

more precise, from its QR factorisation, using an update strategy to compute the new QR factorisation instead of computing it from scratch.

Finally, in some situations, the estimate $|\rho_j^{(k)}|$ is not a good indicator for the actual residual $\|\mathbf{e}_j - A_{\mathcal{M}_j}\mathbf{p}_{\mathcal{M}_j}\|_2$. It was pointed out by Gould and Scott in [68] that it is possible to use an update strategy to compute the real residual $\|\mathbf{e}_j - A_{\mathcal{M}_j}\mathbf{p}_{\mathcal{M}_j}\|_2$ with only a modest overhead in computational time.

Yet another approach is to minimise the expression $\|\mathbf{e}_j - A\mathbf{p}_j\|_2$ using a finite number of steps of an iterative method. One such method, which is often used in this context, is based on minimising the residual and proceeds as follows. Let $\mathbf{p}_j^{(i)}$ denote the current approximation to $\mathbf{p}_j$ and let $\mathbf{r}_j^{(i)} = \mathbf{e}_j - A\mathbf{p}_j^{(i)}$ be the current residual. Then, the next iteration $\mathbf{p}_j^{(i+1)}$ is searched in the direction of $\mathbf{r}_j^{(i)}$, i.e. it is of the form

$$\mathbf{p}_j^{(i+1)} = \mathbf{p}_j^{(i)} + \alpha^{(i)}\mathbf{r}_j^{(i)},$$

and the coefficient $\alpha^{(i)}$ is determined by minimising the function

$$f(\alpha) := \|\mathbf{e}_j - A\mathbf{p}_j^{(i+1)}\|_2^2 = \|\mathbf{e}_j - A\mathbf{p}_j^{(i)} - \alpha A\mathbf{r}_j^{(i)}\|_2^2 = \|\mathbf{r}_j^{(i)} - \alpha A\mathbf{r}_j^{(i)}\|_2^2.$$

The solution is easily seen to be

$$\alpha_j^{(i)} = \frac{\langle \mathbf{r}_j^{(i)}, A\mathbf{r}_j^{(i)} \rangle_2}{\langle A\mathbf{r}_j^{(i)}, A\mathbf{r}_j^{(i)} \rangle_2}.$$

Sparsity is achieved by setting to zero all entries of $\mathbf{p}_j^{(i)}$, which are not in the non-zero pattern $\mathcal{M}_j$ for row j. Dropping the index i again, and assuming that we know the number of steps k_j of the iterative method we want to use to approximately compute $\mathbf{p}_j$, yields the algorithm given in Algorithm 50.

Algorithm 50: Approximate inverse with residual minimisation (AINV-MR)

Input : $A \in \mathbb{R}^{n \times n}$, non-zero pattern $\mathcal{M}$.
Output: Approximate inverse P.

1   Choose an initial guess $P = (\mathbf{p}_1, \ldots, \mathbf{p}_m)$
2   **for** $j = 1$ **to** n **do**
3   **for** $i = 1$ **to** k_j **do**
4       $\mathbf{r}_j := \mathbf{e}_j - A\mathbf{p}_j$
5       $\alpha_j := \langle \mathbf{r}_j, A\mathbf{r}_j \rangle_2 / \langle A\mathbf{r}_j, A\mathbf{r}_j \rangle_2$
6       $\mathbf{p}_j := \mathbf{p}_j + \alpha_j \mathbf{r}_j$
7   **if** $(i, j) \notin \mathcal{M}$ **then** $(\mathbf{p}_j)_i = 0$

The initial guess in Algorithm 50 is often chosen as $P = \beta G$ with $G = I$ or $G = A^T$. The coefficient β is usually determined by minimising $g(\beta) = \|I - AP\|_F^2 = \|I - \beta AG\|_F^2$. Since the Frobenius norm is defined by the inner product

$$\langle A, B \rangle_F := \sum_{i,j=1}^{n} a_{ij} b_{ij},$$

we see that we can proceed as usual to determine $g'(\beta)$ and find that

$$\beta = \frac{\langle I, AG \rangle_F}{\|AG\|_F^2} = \frac{\text{tr}(AG)}{\|AG\|_F^2}$$

minimises g. There is an improvement of this algorithm if the matrix P is used to precondition the process on the fly. This self-preconditioning process has been described and analysed by Chow and Saad in [36], see also Saad [104].

Finally, for a symmetric matrix $A \in \mathbb{R}^{n \times n}$ the preconditioner P derived from minimising $\|I - AP\|_F$ is usually not symmetric. However, symmetry can be enforced by computing P in the form $P = LL^T$, where L is a sparse and lower triangular matrix. Details can be found in Kolotilina and Yeremin [87], but also in Benzi *et al.* [19, 18], where a method for deriving a preconditioner of the form LDL^T was suggested and analysed.

Before discussing the application and implementation of preconditioners in the context of Krylov subspace methods, let us finish this part of the chapter, which was concerned with the construction of preconditioners, with some additional remarks.

When solving partial differential equations with finite elements, preconditioners based upon domain decomposition methods or multigrid methods are also very popular, see for example Brenner and Scott [25] and the literature therein. This can also be done in other more general situations. As a matter of fact, we have already encountered such a preconditioner based upon a domain decomposition method. Let us recall the situation that led us to the block Jacobi method as described in Algorithm 42. Here, we decomposed the set $\{1, \ldots, n\}$ into disjoint sets $J_1, \ldots, J_p$. These sets have defined subspaces $V_j = \text{span}\{e_k : k \in J_j\}$ of dimension n_j and projections $P_j : \mathbb{R}^n \to V_j$ defined by (7.42) as

$$P_j = E_j (E_j^T A E_j)^{-1} E_j^T A$$

where $E_j \in \mathbb{R}^{n \times n_j}$ is the extension matrix from V_j to $\mathbb{R}^n$ and $A_{J_j, J_j} := E_j^T A E_j \in \mathbb{R}^{n_j \times n_j}$ is the sub-matrix of A with entries defined by J_j. If we now define the operators

$$\tilde{P}_j := E_j A_{J_j, J_j}^{-1} E_j^T, \qquad 1 \le j \le p,$$
$$\tilde{P} := \tilde{P}_1 + \cdots + \tilde{P}_p$$

then we have $P_j = \tilde{P}_j A$ and $P := P_1 + \cdots + P_p = \tilde{P} A$ and we see that solving $Ax = b$ is equivalent to solving $\tilde{P} A x = \tilde{P} b$ so that $\tilde{P}$ serves as an example of a *block preconditioner*.

8.4 Preconditioning Krylov Subspace Methods

In this part of the chapter, we want to discuss possible applications and possible ways of implementing methods for solving a preconditioned system which go beyond the simple idea of just applying the previous algorithms to the preconditioned matrix. We will do this only for Krylov subspace methods and concentrate on the most important examples: CG, MINRES, GMRES and BiCGSTAB.

If the matrix $A \in \mathbb{R}^{n \times n}$ is symmetric and positive definite, we can solve the linear system $Ax = b$ using the conjugate gradient method from Section 6.1. From Theorem 6.19 we know that the convergence of the CG method depends on the condition number, which means we are exactly in the situation that we need to reduce the condition number for improving the speed of convergence. Since we are dealing with a symmetric and positive definite matrix, we will choose a symmetric and positive definite preconditioner of the form $P = SS^T$, i.e. we will solve the problem

$$S^TASx = S^Tb. \tag{8.19}$$

Introducing the notation $\hat{A} = S^TAS$, $\hat{b} = S^Tb$ and denoting the solution to (8.19) by $\hat{x}^*$, we know that the original system $Ax = b$ has the solution $x^* = S\hat{x}^*$. Moreover, Algorithm 22 tells us that the relevant quantities we have to compute after the initialisation with $\hat{r}_0 = \hat{p}_0 = \hat{b} - \hat{A}\hat{x}_0 = S^T(b - AS\hat{x}_0)$ are given by

$$\hat{\alpha}_j = \frac{\langle \hat{r}_j, \hat{r}_j \rangle_2}{\langle S^TAS\hat{p}_j, \hat{p}_j \rangle_2}, \tag{8.20}$$

$$\hat{x}_{j+1} = \hat{x}_j + \hat{\alpha}_j\hat{p}_j, \tag{8.21}$$

$$\hat{r}_{j+1} = \hat{r}_j - \hat{\alpha}_jS^TAS\hat{p}_j, \tag{8.22}$$

$$\hat{\beta}_{j+1} = \frac{\langle \hat{r}_{j+1}, \hat{r}_{j+1} \rangle_2}{\langle \hat{r}_j, \hat{r}_j \rangle_2}, \tag{8.23}$$

$$\hat{p}_{j+1} = \hat{r}_{j+1} + \hat{\beta}_{j+1}\hat{p}_j, \tag{8.24}$$

from which an algorithm can easily be derived. Note that we still only have to compute one matrix–vector product but this time with the preconditioned matrix $\hat{A} = S^TAS$, which, in this setting, first has to be computed, which might not be desirable. Later on, we will see that this split preconditioner is equivalent to a left preconditioner with $P = SS^T$.

However, let us first shortly analyse the convergence behaviour. Since A is symmetric and positive definite, so is S^TAS. Hence, Theorem 6.19 gives for the iterations of the preconditioned CG method, defined by (8.20) to (8.24), the bound

$$\|\hat{x}^* - \hat{x}_i\|_{S^TAS} \le 2\|\hat{x}^* - \hat{x}_0\|_{S^TAS} \left(\frac{\sqrt{\kappa_2(S^TAS)} - 1}{\sqrt{\kappa_2(S^TAS)} + 1} \right)^i. \tag{8.25}$$

This estimate is only of limited use because it gives a bound for the iterations $\hat{x}_i$ which converge to the solution $\hat{x}^*$ of $S^TASx = S^Tb$ and it gives this bound in the norm induced by the matrix S^TAS instead of the norm induced by the matrix A. However, if $\hat{x}_i$ solves the problem $S^TASx = S^Tb$ then $S\hat{x}_i =: x_i$ solves the original problem $Ax = b$. Hence, it is more important to look at the convergence of the sequence of vectors defined by $x_i := S\hat{x}_i$. Here, we have the following result.

Theorem 8.20 *Let $\{\hat{x}_i\}$ be the sequence generated by the preconditioned CG* *method to solve* $S^T A S \mathbf{x} = S^T \mathbf{b}$. *Let* $\mathbf{x}_i := S \hat{\mathbf{x}}_i$ *and* $\mathbf{x}^* = S \hat{\mathbf{x}}^*$. *Then,*

$$\|\mathbf{x}^* - \mathbf{x}_i\|_A \leq 2\|\mathbf{x}^* - \mathbf{x}_0\|_A \left(\frac{\sqrt{\kappa_2(S^T A S)} - 1}{\sqrt{\kappa_2(S^T A S)} + 1} \right)^i.$$

Proof We have $\mathbf{x}^* - \mathbf{x}_i = S(\hat{\mathbf{x}}^* - \hat{\mathbf{x}}_i)$ and hence

$$\|\mathbf{x}^* - \mathbf{x}_i\|_A^2 = \langle A(\mathbf{x}^* - \mathbf{x}_i), \mathbf{x}^* - \mathbf{x}_i \rangle_2 = \langle AS(\hat{\mathbf{x}}_i - \hat{\mathbf{x}}^*), S(\hat{\mathbf{x}}^* - \hat{\mathbf{x}}_i) \rangle_2$$

$$= \langle S^T A S(\hat{\mathbf{x}}_i - \hat{\mathbf{x}}^*), \hat{\mathbf{x}}_i - \hat{\mathbf{x}}^* \rangle_2$$

$$= \|\hat{\mathbf{x}}_i - \hat{\mathbf{x}}^*\|_{S^T A S}^2.$$

The result then follows from the above bound (8.25) from Theorem 6.19. □

To understand this theorem better, it is useful to also look at the Krylov spaces. According to Theorem 6.12, the iteration $\hat{\mathbf{x}}_j$ is the best approximation to $\hat{\mathbf{x}}^*$ in the $\| \cdot \|_{S^T A S}$-norm from the shifted Krylov space $\hat{\mathbf{x}}_0 + \mathcal{K}_i(S^T A S, \hat{\mathbf{r}}_0)$ with

$$\mathcal{K}_i(S^T A S, \hat{\mathbf{r}}_0) = \text{span} \left\{ \hat{\mathbf{r}}_0, (S^T A S) \hat{\mathbf{r}}_0, (S^T A S)^2 \hat{\mathbf{r}}_0, \ldots, (S^T A S)^{i-1} \hat{\mathbf{r}}_0 \right\}.$$

If we now set $\mathbf{x}_0 := S \hat{\mathbf{x}}_0$, $\mathbf{z}_0 := S \hat{\mathbf{r}}_0$ and use that

$$S(S^T A S)^i \hat{\mathbf{r}}_0 = (S S^T A)^i S \hat{\mathbf{r}}_0 = (PA)^i \mathbf{z}_0$$

with $P = S S^T$ holds for all $i \in \mathbb{N}_0$ then we see that $\mathbf{x}_i$ comes from the shifted Krylov space

$$\mathbf{x}_0 + \mathcal{K}_i(PA, \mathbf{z}_0),$$

and, because of the above-observed norm equality, represents the best approximation from this space to $\mathbf{x}^*$ in the $\| \cdot \|_A$-norm.

Corollary 8.21 *If* $\{\hat{\mathbf{x}}_i\}$ *denote the iterations of the preconditioned conjugate gradient method and if* $\mathbf{x}_i := S \hat{\mathbf{x}}_i$ *then* $\mathbf{x}_i$ *is the best approximation to the solution* $\mathbf{x}^*$ *of* $A\mathbf{x} = \mathbf{b}$ *from* $\mathbf{x}_0 + \mathcal{K}_i(PA, \mathbf{z}_0)$ *with* $\mathbf{z}_0 := S \hat{\mathbf{r}}_0$.

Since we are more interested in the transformed iteration $\mathbf{x}_j = S \hat{\mathbf{x}}_j$ instead of the iteration $\hat{\mathbf{x}}_j$ produced by the above-described algorithm, we are now reformulating the algorithm as follows. Let us introduce the new vectors $\mathbf{p}_j := S \hat{\mathbf{p}}_j$, $\mathbf{x}_j := S \hat{\mathbf{x}}_j$, $\mathbf{z}_j := S \hat{\mathbf{r}}_j$ and $\mathbf{r}_j := (S^T)^{-1} \hat{\mathbf{r}}_j$. Then, we have

$$\mathbf{r}_j = (S^T)^{-1} \hat{\mathbf{r}}_j = (S^T)^{-1} S^{-1} \mathbf{z}_j = (S S^T)^{-1} \mathbf{z}_j = P^{-1} \mathbf{z}_j.$$

Moreover, we can express the inner products in the definition of $\hat{\alpha}_j$ and $\hat{\beta}_j$ as

$$\langle \hat{\mathbf{r}}_j, \hat{\mathbf{r}}_j \rangle_2 = \langle S^T \mathbf{r}_j, S^{-1} \mathbf{z}_j \rangle_2 = \langle \mathbf{r}_j, S S^{-1} \mathbf{z}_j \rangle_2 = \langle \mathbf{r}_j, \mathbf{z}_j \rangle_2,$$

$$\langle S^T A S \hat{\mathbf{p}}_j, \hat{\mathbf{p}}_j \rangle_2 = \langle AS \hat{\mathbf{p}}_j, S \hat{\mathbf{p}}_j \rangle_2 = \langle A\mathbf{p}_j, \mathbf{p}_j \rangle_2.$$

Hence, if we rewrite $\hat{\alpha}_j$ and $\hat{\beta}_j$ using these two equalities and if we multiply

(8.21) and (8.24) by S and (8.22) by $(S^T)^{-1}$ then we have the preconditioned conjugate gradient algorithm stated in Algorithm 51, where we also had to introduce a new step to update the vector $\mathbf{z}_j$ to $\mathbf{z}_{j+1} = P\mathbf{r}_{j+1}$.

Algorithm 51: Preconditioned CG method

Input : $A, P \in \mathbb{R}^{n \times n}$ symmetric and positive definite, $\mathbf{b} \in \mathbb{R}^n$.

Output: Approximate solution of $A\mathbf{x} = \mathbf{b}$.

1 Choose $\mathbf{x}_0 \in \mathbb{R}^n$.

2 Set $\mathbf{r}_0 := \mathbf{b} - A\mathbf{x}_0, \quad \mathbf{p}_0 := \mathbf{z}_0 := P\mathbf{r}_0, \quad j := 0$.

3 **while** $\|\mathbf{r}_j\|_2 > \epsilon$ **do**

4 $\quad$ $\mathbf{t}_j := A\mathbf{p}_j$

5 $\quad$ $\hat{\alpha}_j := \langle \mathbf{r}_j, \mathbf{z}_j \rangle_2 / \langle \mathbf{t}_j, \mathbf{p}_j \rangle_2$

6 $\quad$ $\mathbf{x}_{j+1} := \mathbf{x}_j + \hat{\alpha}_j \mathbf{p}_j$

7 $\quad$ $\mathbf{r}_{j+1} := \mathbf{r}_j - \hat{\alpha}_j \mathbf{t}_j$

8 $\quad$ $\hat{\beta}_{j+1} := \langle \mathbf{r}_{j+1}, \mathbf{z}_{j+1} \rangle_2 / \langle \mathbf{r}_j, \mathbf{z}_j \rangle_2$

9 $\quad$ $\mathbf{z}_{j+1} := P\mathbf{r}_{j+1}$

10 $\quad$ $\mathbf{p}_{j+1} := \mathbf{z}_{j+1} + \hat{\beta}_{j+1} \mathbf{p}_j$

11 $\quad$ $j := j + 1$

Besides the original matrix–vector product $A\mathbf{p}_j$ we now have one additional matrix–vector product $P\mathbf{r}_{j+1}$, which shows that it is desirable to have a sparse matrix P to reduce the computational cost here.

There is an alternative way of deriving Algorithm 51 from the original conjugate gradient algorithm for the system $PA\mathbf{x} = P\mathbf{b}$. The idea is based on the observation that the matrix PA is self-adjoint with respect to the inner product $\langle \mathbf{x}, \mathbf{y} \rangle_{P^{-1}} = \langle P^{-1}\mathbf{x}, \mathbf{y} \rangle_2$, as long as P is symmetric:

$$\langle PA\mathbf{x}, \mathbf{y} \rangle_{P^{-1}} = \langle A\mathbf{x}, \mathbf{y} \rangle_2 = \langle \mathbf{x}, A\mathbf{y} \rangle_2 = \langle \mathbf{x}, P^{-1}PA\mathbf{y} \rangle_2 = \langle \mathbf{x}, PA\mathbf{y} \rangle_{P^{-1}}.$$

Thus, if in Algorithm 22 we replace all standard inner products $\langle \cdot, \cdot \rangle_2$ by $\langle \cdot, \cdot \rangle_{P^{-1}}$ and use the residual vectors for the preconditioned system given by $\mathbf{z}_j := P\mathbf{r}_j = P(\mathbf{b} - A\mathbf{x}_j)$ then we will derive exactly Algorithm 51 if we take also

$$\langle \mathbf{z}_j, \mathbf{z}_j \rangle_{P^{-1}} = \langle \mathbf{r}_j, \mathbf{z}_j \rangle_2, \qquad \langle PA\mathbf{p}_j, \mathbf{p}_j \rangle_{P^{-1}} = \langle A\mathbf{p}_j, \mathbf{p}_j \rangle_2$$

into account.

In the same way it is possible to modify the conjugate gradient method to solve the right preconditioned system, i.e. $AP\mathbf{x} = \mathbf{b}$, using the inner product $\langle \cdot, \cdot \rangle_P$. However, similar considerations to those just made show that the right preconditioned CG method built upon the $\langle \cdot, \cdot \rangle_P$ inner product leads to the same algorithm as the left preconditioned CG method built upon the inner product $\langle \cdot, \cdot \rangle_{P^{-1}}$, which is exactly Algorithm 51.

We will now discuss the process of preconditioning the GMRES and MINRES methods. Recall that in both cases the residual $\|\mathbf{b} - A\mathbf{x}\|_2$ is minimised over the Krylov space $\mathbf{x}_0 + \mathcal{K}_j(A, \mathbf{r}_0)$ to compute the jth iteration $\mathbf{x}_j$.

Let us start with MINRES, i.e. in the situation that A is symmetric but indefinite. In this case, it seems prudent to choose again a preconditioner of the form $P = SS^T$ with an invertible S and to discuss the system $S^TAS\mathbf{x} = S^T\mathbf{b}$. The preconditioned MINRES method then solves for each j the minimisation problem

$$\hat{\mathbf{x}}_j = \arg\min\left\{\|S^TAS\hat{\mathbf{x}} - S^T\mathbf{b}\|_2 : \hat{\mathbf{x}} \in \hat{\mathbf{x}}_0 + \mathcal{K}_j(S^TAS, \hat{\mathbf{r}}_0)\right\}. \tag{8.26}$$

As in the case of the preconditioned CG method, we have a one-to-one relation between the shifted Krylov spaces $\hat{\mathbf{x}}_0 + \mathcal{K}_j(S^TAS, \hat{\mathbf{r}}_0)$ and $\mathbf{x}_0 + \mathcal{K}_j(PA, \mathbf{z}_0)$ given by the mapping

$$\hat{\mathbf{x}}_0 + \mathcal{K}_j(S^TAS, \hat{\mathbf{r}}_0) \to \mathbf{x}_0 + \mathcal{K}_j(PA, \mathbf{z}_0), \qquad \hat{\mathbf{x}} \mapsto \mathbf{x} := S\hat{\mathbf{x}},$$

provided that $\mathbf{x}_0 := S\hat{\mathbf{x}}_0$ and $\mathbf{z}_0 := S\hat{\mathbf{r}}_0$. This time, however, we are minimising the ℓ_2-norm of the residual of the preconditioned system. The norm identities

$$\|S^TAS\hat{\mathbf{x}} - S^T\mathbf{b}\|_2^2 = \langle S^T(A\mathbf{x} - \mathbf{b}), S^T(A\mathbf{x} - \mathbf{b})\rangle_2 = \langle SS^T(A\mathbf{x} - \mathbf{b}), A\mathbf{x} - \mathbf{b}\rangle_2$$
$$= \|A\mathbf{x} - \mathbf{b}\|_P^2$$

show that (8.26) is equivalent to

$$\mathbf{x}_j = \arg\min\left\{\|A\mathbf{x} - \mathbf{b}\|_P : \mathbf{x} \in \mathbf{x}_0 + \mathcal{K}_j(PA, \mathbf{z}_0)\right\}$$

and allow us to derive the following error estimate, using Proposition 6.25.

Proposition 8.22 *Let $A \in \mathbb{R}^{n \times n}$ be symmetric and invertible and let $P = SS^T$ with invertible S. Denote the eigenvalues of S^TAS by $\lambda_1 \leq \cdots \leq \lambda_n$. Let $\mathbf{x}^*, \hat{\mathbf{x}}^* \in \mathbb{R}^n$ denote the solutions of $A\mathbf{x} = \mathbf{b}$ and $S^TAS\hat{\mathbf{x}} = S^T\mathbf{b}$, respectively. Let $\{\hat{\mathbf{x}}_j\}$ denote the iterations from MINRES applied to the system $S^TAS\hat{\mathbf{x}} = S^T\mathbf{b}$ and let $\mathbf{x}_j = S\hat{\mathbf{x}}_j$. Then the residuals $\mathbf{r}_j := \mathbf{b} - A\mathbf{x}_j$ satisfy*

$$\|\mathbf{r}_j\|_P \leq \min_{\substack{p \in \pi_j \\ p(0)=1}} \max_{1 \leq k \leq n} |p(\lambda_k)| \|\mathbf{r}_0\|_P. \tag{8.27}$$

Obviously, we can now proceed as in the case of the unpreconditioned MINRES method to bound the right-hand side of (8.27) under certain assumptions on the distribution of the eigenvalues of S^TAS, or of PA, see Lemma 8.1. By Sylvester's theorem of inertia, Theorem 5.6, we know at least that PA has the same number of negative and positive eigenvalues as A. Hence, a goal of the preconditioning process could be to transform A so that the eigenvalues of PA satisfy the conditions of Theorem 6.26.

However, the result of Proposition 8.22 might be misleading as the residual is now measured in the $\| \cdot \|_P$-norm instead of the ℓ_2-norm. This can become problematic as pointed out by Wathen [130, 131].

To derive the algorithmic description of the preconditioned MINRES, and eventually also the GMRES method, we first have a look at how to precondition the Lanczos method for computing an orthonormal basis of $\mathcal{K}_j(A, \mathbf{r}_0)$. Hence, we rewrite Algorithm 27 for the system $S^T A S \mathbf{x} = S^T \mathbf{b}$, i.e. we start with an initial vector $\hat{\mathbf{r}}_0$ and set $\hat{\mathbf{v}}_0 = \mathbf{0}$, $\hat{\mathbf{v}}_1 = \hat{\mathbf{r}}_0 / \|\hat{\mathbf{r}}_0\|_2$ and $\hat{\beta}_0 = 0$. Then, for $1 \le k \le j$ we have to compute

$$\hat{\mathbf{w}}_k := S^T A S \hat{\mathbf{v}}_k - \hat{\beta}_{k-1} \hat{\mathbf{v}}_{k-1}, \tag{8.28}$$

$$\hat{\alpha}_k := \langle \hat{\mathbf{w}}_k, \hat{\mathbf{v}}_k \rangle_2, \tag{8.29}$$

$$\hat{\mathbf{w}}_k := \hat{\mathbf{w}}_k - \hat{\alpha}_k \hat{\mathbf{v}}_k, \tag{8.30}$$

$$\hat{\beta}_k := \langle \hat{\mathbf{w}}_k, \hat{\mathbf{w}}_k \rangle_2^{1/2}, \tag{8.31}$$

$$\hat{\mathbf{v}}_{k+1} = \hat{\mathbf{w}}_k / \hat{\beta}_k, \tag{8.32}$$

where we understand (8.30) in the sense that the new $\hat{\mathbf{w}}_k$ is replaced by the right-hand side $\hat{\mathbf{w}}_k - \hat{\alpha}_k \hat{\mathbf{v}}_k$.

We now proceed much as in the case of the preconditioned CG method and introduce new quantities $\mathbf{v}_k := S^{-T} \hat{\mathbf{v}}_k$, $\mathbf{w}_k := S^{-T} \hat{\mathbf{w}}_k$ and $\mathbf{z}_k := P \mathbf{v}_k$ with $P = S S^T$. Noting that we have in particular

$$\mathbf{w}_k = S^{-T} \hat{\mathbf{w}}_k = A S S^T S^{-T} \hat{\mathbf{v}}_k - \hat{\beta}_{k-1} S^{-T} \hat{\mathbf{v}}_{k-1}$$
$$= A P \mathbf{v}_k - \hat{\beta}_{k-1} \mathbf{v}_{k-1} = A \mathbf{z}_k - \hat{\beta}_{k-1} \mathbf{v}_{k-1},$$
$$\hat{\alpha}_k = \langle S^T \mathbf{w}_k, S^T \mathbf{v}_k \rangle_2 = \langle \mathbf{w}_k, P \mathbf{v}_k \rangle_2 = \langle \mathbf{w}_k, \mathbf{z}_k \rangle_2,$$
$$\hat{\beta}_k = \langle S^T \mathbf{w}_k, S^T \mathbf{w}_k \rangle_2^{1/2} = \langle \mathbf{w}_k, P \mathbf{w}_k \rangle_2^{1/2},$$

and reformulating (8.30) and (8.32) in the new variables by multiplying both equations by S^{-T} from the left results in the preconditioned Lanczos method given in Algorithm 52, which also requires an update step for the new vector $\mathbf{z}_k := P \mathbf{v}_k = S \hat{\mathbf{v}}_k$, which we realise by $\mathbf{z}_{k+1} = P \mathbf{v}_{k+1} = P \mathbf{w}_k / \hat{\beta}_k$ so that we need only compute one additional matrix–vector product with the matrix P.

As we already know, the mapping $\hat{\mathbf{x}} \mapsto \mathbf{z} := S \hat{\mathbf{x}}$ maps the Krylov space $\mathcal{K}_j(S^T A S, \hat{\mathbf{r}}_0)$ bijectively onto the Krylov space $\mathcal{K}_j(PA, S \hat{\mathbf{r}}_0)$ because of the relation $S (S^T A S)^k = (S S^T A)^k S$. Similarly, the obvious relation $S^{-T} (S^T A S)^k = (A S S^T)^k S^{-T}$ shows that the mapping $\hat{\mathbf{x}} \mapsto \mathbf{x} := S^{-T} \hat{\mathbf{x}}$ maps the Krylov space $\mathcal{K}_j(S^T A S, \hat{\mathbf{r}}_0)$ bijectively to the Krylov space $\mathcal{K}_j(AP, S^{-T} \hat{\mathbf{r}}_0)$. This allows us to prove the following result.

Lemma 8.23 *Assume that the preconditioned Lanczos method from Algorithm 52 does not stop prematurely. Then, the vectors $z_1, \ldots, z_j$, form a P^{-1}-orthonormal basis of $\mathcal{K}_j(PA, S\hat{r}_0)$ and $v_1, \ldots, v_j$ form a P-orthonormal basis of $\mathcal{K}_j(AP, S^{-T}\hat{r}_0)$.*

Proof The orthonormality follows from the two relations

$$\delta_{k\ell} = \langle \hat{v}_k, \hat{v}_\ell \rangle_2 = \langle S^T v_k, S^T v_\ell \rangle_2 = \langle SS^T v_k, v_\ell \rangle_2 = \langle v_k, v_\ell \rangle_P,$$

$$\delta_{k\ell} = \langle \hat{v}_k, \hat{v}_\ell \rangle_2 = \langle S^{-1} z_k, S^{-1} z_\ell \rangle_2 = \langle (SS^T)^{-1} z_k, z_\ell \rangle = \langle z_k, z_\ell \rangle_{P^{-1}}. \qquad \square$$

Algorithm 52: The preconditioned Lanczos method

Input : $A = A^T, P = SS^T \in \mathbb{R}^{n \times n}$, S invertible, $\hat{r}_0 \in \mathbb{R}^n \setminus \{0\}$.
Output: Orthonormal bases of $\mathcal{K}_j(PA, S\hat{r}_0)$ and $\mathcal{K}_j(AP, S^{-T}\hat{r}_0)$.

1   $v_0 := 0$, $v_1 := S^{-T}\hat{r}_0/\|\hat{r}_0\|_2$, $z_1 := Pv_1$, $\hat{\beta}_0 := 0$
2   **for** $k = 1, 2, \ldots, j-1$ **do**
3      $w_k := Az_k - \hat{\beta}_{k-1}v_{k-1}$
4      $\hat{\alpha}_k := \langle w_k, z_k \rangle_2$
5      $w_k := w_k - \hat{\alpha}_k v_k$
6      $\tilde{w}_k := Pw_k$
7      $\hat{\beta}_k := \langle w_k, \tilde{w}_k \rangle_2^{1/2}$
8   **if** $\hat{\beta}_k = 0$ **then break**
9   **else**
10         $v_{k+1} := w_k/\hat{\beta}_k$
11         $z_{k+1} := \tilde{w}_k/\hat{\beta}_k$

Note that our initial value $\hat{r}_0$ will be of the form $\hat{r}_0 = S^T(b - AS\hat{x}_0) = S^T(b - Ax_0) = S^T r_0$ if we set $x_0 := S\hat{x}_0$ and $r_0 := b - Ax_0$, which means that the initialisation in Algorithm 52 simplifies to

$$v_1 = \frac{r_0}{\|S^T r_0\|_2}, \qquad z_1 = Pv_1.$$

We could also change the normalisation in the definition of v_1 to $v_1 = r_0/\|r_0\|_2$, which would only change the normalisation of the vectors in Lemma 8.23, so that, for example, $z_1, \ldots, z_j$ form a P^{-1}-orthogonal basis for $\mathcal{K}_j(PA, Pr_0)$. In this situation, we have completely eliminated S from the algorithm and hence can use Algorithm 52 also for general, non-singular left preconditioners P.

Having an algorithm for the preconditioned Lanczos method, it is now easy to derive an algorithm for the preconditioned MINRES method. Essentially, except for some notational changes we only have to translate the iterations

$\hat{\mathbf{x}}_k$ and directions $\hat{\mathbf{p}}_k$ which MINRES creates when applied to $S^TASx = S^T\mathbf{b}$ satisfying

$$\hat{\mathbf{p}}_k = [\hat{\mathbf{v}}_k - r_{k-1,k}\hat{\mathbf{p}}_{k-1} - r_{k-2,k}\hat{\mathbf{p}}_{k-2}]/r_{kk}, \qquad (8.33)$$

$$\hat{\mathbf{x}}_k = \hat{\mathbf{x}}_{k-1} + \beta q_k \hat{\mathbf{p}}_k, \qquad (8.34)$$

see (6.29) and (6.30). We can do this either by going over to the Krylov space $\mathcal{K}_j(PA, S\hat{\mathbf{r}}_0)$, i.e. by replacing $\hat{\mathbf{v}}_k$ by $\mathbf{z}_k$ or by going over to the space $\mathcal{K}_j(AP, S^{-T}\hat{\mathbf{r}}_0)$, i.e. by replacing $\hat{\mathbf{v}}_k$ by $\mathbf{v}_k$. We will follow our usual strategy and go with the left preconditioner. Hence, we define $\mathbf{x}_k := S\hat{\mathbf{x}}_k$ and $\mathbf{p}_k := S\hat{\mathbf{p}}_k$, which transforms (8.33) and (8.34) into

$$\mathbf{p}_k = [\mathbf{z}_k - r_{k-1,k}\mathbf{p}_{k-1} - r_{k-2,k}\mathbf{p}_{k-2}]/r_{kk},$$

$$\mathbf{x}_k = \mathbf{x}_{k-1} + \beta q_k \mathbf{p}_k.$$

Then, as outlined in Section 6.2 we can simplify the formulas by noting that we do not have to save $r_{k-2,k}$, $r_{k-1,k}$ and r_{kk} since they are not required in the next iteration. The same is true for the vector $\mathbf{q}_k$. The complete algorithm for the preconditioned MINRES method is given in Algorithm 53.

Finally, let us look at the preconditioning of GMRES. Since GMRES is used for unsymmetric matrices $A \in \mathbb{R}^{n \times n}$ it is unusual to use a symmetric preconditioner. Hence, we have mainly the two options of using a left preconditioner, i.e. solving the system $PAx = P\mathbf{b}$, or using a right preconditioner, i.e. solving $APy = \mathbf{b}$ with $\mathbf{x} = Py$. In both cases we mainly have to precondition the Arnoldi process, i.e. Algorithm 23. For left preconditioning this means that we have to compute an orthonormal basis for the Krylov space $\mathcal{K}_j(PA, \mathbf{z}_0)$ with $\mathbf{z}_0 := P(\mathbf{b} - A\mathbf{x}_0) = P\mathbf{r}_0$. This basis is given by vectors $\mathbf{v}_1, \ldots, \mathbf{v}_j \in \mathbb{R}^n$ constructed during the process. After that, we have to solve a least-squares problem involving the Hessenberg matrix $H = (h_{\ell k}) \in \mathbb{R}^{(j+1) \times j}$ defined by the Arnoldi process, this time as

$$PA\mathbf{v}_k = \sum_{\ell=1}^{k+1} h_{\ell k}\mathbf{v}_\ell, \qquad 1 \le k \le j.$$

Details can be found in Section 6.2 for the unpreconditioned system. The final algorithm is Algorithm 54 for the system $PAx = P\mathbf{b}$.

Algorithm 54 represents the GMRES(j) method. As described in Section 6.2 it might still be necessary to restart the procedure, though the hope is, of course, that a small j will suffice if the system is well enough preconditioned.

In the same way, we can use the Arnoldi process to compute an orthonormal

---

Algorithm 53: Preconditioned MINRES

Input : $A = A^T, P = SS^T \in \mathbb{R}^{n \times n}$, S invertible, $\mathbf{b} \in \mathbb{R}^n$, $\mathbf{x}_0 \in \mathbb{R}^n$.
Output: Approximate solution of $A\mathbf{x} = \mathbf{b}$.

1   $\beta_0 := 0, \quad s_{-1} = s_0 = 0, \quad c_{-1} = c_0 = 1, \quad \mathbf{p}_{-1} := \mathbf{p}_0 := \mathbf{v}_0 = \mathbf{0}$
2   $\mathbf{r}_0 := \mathbf{b} - A\mathbf{x}_0, \quad \delta := \|\mathbf{r}_0\|_2, \quad \mathbf{v}_1 := \mathbf{r}_0/\delta, \quad \mathbf{z}_1 := P\mathbf{v}_1$
3   **for** $k = 1, 2, \ldots,$ **do**
4      $\mathbf{w}_k := A\mathbf{v}_k - \beta_{k-1}\mathbf{v}_{k-1}$
5      $\alpha_k := \langle \mathbf{w}_k, \mathbf{z}_k \rangle_2$
6      $\mathbf{w}_k := \mathbf{w}_k - \alpha_k \mathbf{v}_k$
7      $\tilde{\mathbf{w}}_k := P\mathbf{w}_k$
8      $\beta_k := \langle \mathbf{w}_k, \tilde{\mathbf{w}}_k \rangle_2^{1/2}$
9   **if** $\beta_k = 0$ **then** stop
10     $\gamma_0 := c_{k-1}\alpha_k - s_{k-1}c_{k-2}\beta_{k-1}$
11     $\gamma_1 := \sqrt{\gamma_0^2 + \beta_k^2}$
12     $\gamma_2 := s_{k-1}\alpha_k + c_{k-1}c_{k-2}\beta_{k-1}$
13     $\gamma_3 := s_{k-2}\beta_{k-1}$
14     $c_k := \gamma_0/\gamma_1 \quad s_k := \beta_k/\gamma_1$
15     $\mathbf{p}_k := [\mathbf{z}_k - \gamma_2\mathbf{p}_{k-1} - \gamma_3\mathbf{p}_{k-2}]/\gamma_1$
16     $\mathbf{x}_k := \mathbf{x}_{k-1} + c_k\delta\mathbf{p}_k$
17     $\delta := -s_k\delta$
18     $\mathbf{v}_{k+1} := \mathbf{w}_k/\beta_k$
19     $\mathbf{z}_{k+1} := \tilde{\mathbf{w}}_k/\beta_k$

---

basis of the Krylov space $\mathcal{K}_j(AP, \mathbf{r}_0)$ to solve the right preconditioned system $AP\mathbf{y} = \mathbf{b}$. The GMRES($j$) algorithm for this system is given in Algorithm 55. As we would expect from our discussion about the convergence of the preconditioned MINRES method, there is also a difference in the norm that is minimised in the preconditioned GMRES method. The differences are summarised in the following proposition. Nonetheless, recall that by virtue of Lemma 8.1 the matrices AP and PA have the same eigenvalues.

Proposition 8.24 *Let* $\{\mathbf{x}_j\}$ *the the approximate solution computed by the preconditioned GMRES method.*

1. In the case of left preconditioning $\mathbf{x}_j$ *is the solution of*

$$\min\left\{\|P(\mathbf{b} - A\mathbf{x})\|_2 : \mathbf{x} \in \mathbf{x}_0 + \mathcal{K}_j(PA, \mathbf{z}_0)\right\}.$$

Algorithm 54: GMRES with left preconditioning

Input : $A, P \in \mathbb{R}^{n \times n}$ invertible, $\mathbf{b} \in \mathbb{R}^n$, $\mathbf{x}_0 \in \mathbb{R}^n$, $j \in \{1, \ldots, n\}$.

Output: Approximate solution of $A\mathbf{x} = \mathbf{b}$.

1   $\mathbf{z}_0 := P(\mathbf{b} - A\mathbf{x}_0)$, $\beta := \|\mathbf{z}_0\|_2$, $\mathbf{v}_1 := \mathbf{z}_0/\beta$

2   **for** $k = 1, 2, \ldots, j$ **do**

3      $\mathbf{w}_k := PA\mathbf{v}_k$

4   **for** $\ell = 1$ **to** k **do**

5         $h_{\ell k} := \langle \mathbf{w}_k, \mathbf{v}_\ell \rangle_2$

6         $\mathbf{w}_k := \mathbf{w}_k - h_{\ell k}\mathbf{v}_\ell$

7      $h_{k+1,k} := \|\mathbf{w}_k\|_2$

8   **if** $h_{k+1,k} = 0$ **then break**

9   **else** $\mathbf{v}_{k+1} := \mathbf{w}_k/h_{k+1,k}$

10 Compute $\mathbf{y}_j$ as the solution of $\|\beta \mathbf{e}_1 - H_j \mathbf{y}\|_2$

11 $\mathbf{x}_j = \mathbf{x}_0 + V_j \mathbf{y}_j$

---

2. *In the case of right preconditioning* $\mathbf{x}_j$ *is the solution of*

$$\min\left\{\|\mathbf{b} - A\mathbf{x}\|_2 : \mathbf{x} \in \mathbf{x}_0 + P\mathcal{K}_j(AP, \mathbf{r}_0)\right\}$$

with the notation $\mathbf{r}_0 := \mathbf{b} - A\mathbf{x}_0$ *and* $\mathbf{z}_0 := P\mathbf{r}_0$. *In both cases* $\mathbf{x}_j$ *has a representation of the form*

$$\mathbf{x}_j = \mathbf{x}_0 + p_{j-1}(PA)\mathbf{z}_0 = \mathbf{x}_0 + p_{j-1}(PA)P\mathbf{r}_0 = \mathbf{x}_0 + Pp_{j-1}(AP)\mathbf{r}_0 \qquad (8.35)$$

with a polynomial $p_{j-1} \in \pi_{j-1}$, *though the polynomials for the left and right preconditioners might differ.*

Proof   The first statement about left preconditioning is obvious by definition. Also, since $\mathbf{x}_j \in \mathbf{x}_0 + \mathcal{K}_j(PA, \mathbf{z}_0)$ there is a polynomial $p_{j-1} \in \pi_{j-1}$ such that $\mathbf{x}_j = \mathbf{x}_0 + p_{j-1}(PA)\mathbf{z}_0$. The second representation in (8.35) follows from $\mathbf{z}_0 = P\mathbf{r}_0$ and the third from $(PA)^i P = P(AP)^i$ for all $0 \le i \le j$.

In the situation of right preconditioning, we have $\mathbf{x}_j = P\hat{\mathbf{x}}_j$, where $\hat{\mathbf{x}}_j$ solves the minimisation problem

$$\min\left\{\|\mathbf{b} - AP\hat{\mathbf{x}}\|_2 : \hat{\mathbf{x}} \in \hat{\mathbf{x}}_0 + \mathcal{K}_j(AP, \mathbf{r}_0)\right\}$$

with $\mathbf{x}_0 := P\hat{\mathbf{x}}_0$ and $\mathbf{r}_0 := \mathbf{b} - A\mathbf{x}_0$. The change of variable $\mathbf{x} := P\hat{\mathbf{x}}$ then gives the second statement. The polynomial identities (8.35) then follow much as in the first case.   □

Again, the error analysis of Section 6.2 applies. However, as we have seen

---

Algorithm 55: GMRES with right preconditioning

Input : $A, P \in \mathbb{R}^{n \times n}$ invertible, $\mathbf{b} \in \mathbb{R}^n$, $\mathbf{x}_0 \in \mathbb{R}^n$, $j \in \{1, \ldots, n\}$.

Output: Approximate solution of $A\mathbf{x} = \mathbf{b}$.

1   $\mathbf{r}_0 := \mathbf{b} - A\mathbf{x}_0, \quad \beta := \|\mathbf{r}_0\|_2, \quad \mathbf{v}_1 := \mathbf{r}_0/\beta$

2   **for** $k = 1, 2, \ldots, j$ **do**

3     $\mathbf{w}_k := AP\mathbf{v}_k$

4   **for** $\ell = 1$ **to** k **do**

5       $h_{\ell k} := \langle \mathbf{w}_k, \mathbf{v}_\ell \rangle_2$

6       $\mathbf{w}_k := \mathbf{w}_k - h_{\ell k} \mathbf{v}_\ell$

7     $h_{k+1,k} := \|\mathbf{w}_k\|_2$

8   **if** $h_{k+1,k} = 0$ **then break**

9   **else** $\mathbf{v}_{k+1} := \mathbf{w}_k/h_{k+1,k}$

10   Compute $\mathbf{y}_j$ as the solution of $\|\beta \mathbf{e}_1 - H_j \mathbf{y}\|_2$

11   $\mathbf{x}_j = \mathbf{x}_0 + PV_j \mathbf{y}_j$

---

in the unpreconditioned situation, things are more difficult than in the case of symmetric matrices. In particular, it might not suffice to choose the preconditioner with the goal of reducing the condition number of the matrix since we also have to take the effect of the transformation matrix into account, see Corollary 6.27.

We finally also want to address the preconditioning of biorthogonalisation methods. Here, we will choose the BiCGSTAB method as our example. All other methods can be treated in a similar way. We will immediately concentrate on split preconditioners, i.e. we want to derive the BiCGSTAB method for a system of the form

$$P_L AP_R \mathbf{x} = P_L \mathbf{b}$$

without, of course, actually computing the matrix $P_L AP_R$. As the right preconditioner P_R is easily absorbed into the iteratives, we will only discuss the changes to Algorithm 33 coming from the left preconditioner and assume, for the time being, that $P_R = I$. For simplicity and for the sake of notation, we will also assume that we have chosen $\hat{\mathbf{r}}_0 := \mathbf{r}_0$ in Algorithm 33. Then, we can use the hat notation to denote all iteratives of the BiCGSTAB algorithm when applied to $P_L A\mathbf{x} = P_L\mathbf{b}$. In particular, we have $\hat{\mathbf{r}}_0 = \hat{\mathbf{p}}_0 = P_L(\mathbf{b} - A\mathbf{x}_0)$ and then while $\|\hat{\mathbf{r}}_j\|_2 \geq \epsilon$ we compute

$$\hat{\mathbf{v}}_j := P_L A\hat{\mathbf{p}}_j, \tag{8.36}$$

$$\hat{\alpha}_j := \langle \hat{\mathbf{r}}_j, \hat{\mathbf{r}}_0 \rangle_2 / \langle \hat{\mathbf{v}}_j, \hat{\mathbf{r}}_0 \rangle_2,$$

$$\hat{\mathbf{s}}_{j+1} := \hat{\mathbf{r}}_j - \hat{\alpha}_j \hat{\mathbf{v}}_j, \tag{8.37}$$

$$\hat{\mathbf{t}}_{j+1} := P_L A \hat{\mathbf{s}}_{j+1},$$

$$\hat{\omega}_{j+1} := \langle \hat{\mathbf{s}}_{j+1}, \hat{\mathbf{t}}_{j+1} \rangle_2 / \langle \hat{\mathbf{t}}_{j+1}, \hat{\mathbf{t}}_{j+1} \rangle_2,$$

$$\hat{\mathbf{x}}_{j+1} := \hat{\mathbf{x}}_j + \hat{\alpha}_j \hat{\mathbf{p}}_j + \hat{\omega}_{j+1} \hat{\mathbf{s}}_{j+1},$$

$$\hat{\mathbf{r}}_{j+1} := \hat{\mathbf{s}}_{j+1} - \hat{\omega}_{j+1} \hat{\mathbf{t}}_{j+1}, \tag{8.38}$$

$$\hat{\beta}_{j+1} := (\hat{\alpha}_j / \hat{\omega}_{j+1}) \times (\langle \hat{\mathbf{r}}_{j+1}, \hat{\mathbf{r}}_0 \rangle_2 / \langle \hat{\mathbf{r}}_j, \hat{\mathbf{r}}_0 \rangle_2),$$

$$\hat{\mathbf{p}}_{j+1} := \hat{\mathbf{r}}_{j+1} + \hat{\beta}_{j+1} (\hat{\mathbf{p}}_j - \hat{\omega}_{j+1} \hat{\mathbf{v}}_j).$$

As expected, only the two matrix–vector products in the definition of $\hat{\mathbf{v}}_j$ and $\hat{\mathbf{t}}_{j+1}$ actually change. However, our stopping criterion is now based upon the preconditioned residual $\hat{\mathbf{r}}_j = P_L \mathbf{r}_j$, which can become problematic if the preconditioner P_L is badly conditioned since then a small $\hat{\mathbf{r}}_j$ does not automatically mean a small $\mathbf{r}_j$. It is, however, possible to retrieve the actual residual with only three additional matrix–vector products with P_L. To this end, we introduce the vector $\mathbf{v}_j := A \hat{\mathbf{p}}_j$ at the beginning of the loop. Then, we can change (8.36) to $\hat{\mathbf{v}}_j := P_L \mathbf{v}_j$. Moreover, with $\hat{\mathbf{r}}_j = P_L \mathbf{r}_j$ we have

$$\hat{\mathbf{s}}_{j+1} = \hat{\mathbf{r}}_j - \hat{\alpha}_j \hat{\mathbf{v}}_j = P_L (\mathbf{r}_j - \hat{\alpha}_j \mathbf{v}_j).$$

Hence, if we introduce $\mathbf{s}_{j+1} := \mathbf{r}_j - \hat{\alpha}_j \mathbf{v}_j$ right after the definition of $\hat{\alpha}_j$ then we can replace (8.37) by $\hat{\mathbf{s}}_{j+1} = P_L \mathbf{s}_{j+1}$. Finally, we see that the additional definition $\mathbf{t}_{j+1} := A \hat{\mathbf{s}}_{j+1}$ leads to the update $\hat{\mathbf{t}}_{j+1} := P_L \mathbf{t}_{j+1}$ and from (8.38) we see that

$$\hat{\mathbf{r}}_{j+1} = \hat{\mathbf{s}}_{j+1} - \hat{\omega}_{j+1} \hat{\mathbf{t}}_{j+1} = P_L (\mathbf{s}_{j+1} - \hat{\omega}_{j+1} \mathbf{t}_{j+1}),$$

from which we can conclude that the new residual of the unpreconditioned system is given by

$$\mathbf{r}_{j+1} = \mathbf{s}_{j+1} - \hat{\omega}_{j+1} \mathbf{t}_{j+1}.$$

Hence, we can retrieve the original residual by introducing three new vectors into the system. Taking all this into account and introducing also the possibility of an additional right preconditioner P_R yields finally Algorithm 56, where we compute the approximate solution $\mathbf{x}_j$ only at the end just before termination. We could, however, with the additional cost of a matrix–vector multiplication, compute it in each iteration.

Exercises

8.1   Let $A, P \in \mathbb{R}^{n \times n}$ be symmetric and positive definite. Show that the matrix AP is self-adjoint with respect to the inner product defined by $\langle \mathbf{x}, \mathbf{y} \rangle_P :=$

Algorithm 56: Preconditioned BiCGSTAB

Input : $A, P_L, P_R \in \mathbb{R}^{n \times n}$ invertible, $\mathbf{b} \in \mathbb{R}^n$, $\mathbf{x}_0 \in \mathbb{R}^n$.

Output: Approximate solution of $A\mathbf{x} = \mathbf{b}$.

1 $\mathbf{r}_0 := \mathbf{p}_0 := \mathbf{b} - A\mathbf{x}_0$, $\hat{\mathbf{r}}_0 := \hat{\mathbf{p}}_0 := P_L\mathbf{r}_0$, $\hat{\rho}_0 = \langle \hat{\mathbf{r}}_0, \hat{\mathbf{r}}_0 \rangle_2$, $j := 0$

2 **while** $\|\mathbf{r}_j\|_2 \geq \epsilon$ **do**

3 $\quad$ $\mathbf{v}_j := AP_R\hat{\mathbf{p}}_j$

4 $\quad$ $\hat{\mathbf{v}}_j := P_L\mathbf{v}_j$

5 $\quad$ $\hat{\alpha}_j := \hat{\rho}_j/\langle \hat{\mathbf{v}}_j, \hat{\mathbf{r}}_0 \rangle_2$

6 $\quad$ $\mathbf{s}_{j+1} := \mathbf{r}_j - \hat{\alpha}_j\mathbf{v}_j$

7 $\quad$ $\hat{\mathbf{s}}_{j+1} := P_L\mathbf{s}_{j+1}$

8 $\quad$ $\mathbf{t}_{j+1} := AP_R\hat{\mathbf{s}}_{j+1}$

9 $\quad$ $\hat{\mathbf{t}}_{j+1} = P_L\mathbf{t}_{j+1}$

10 $\quad$ $\hat{\omega}_{j+1} := \langle \hat{\mathbf{s}}_{j+1}, \hat{\mathbf{t}}_{j+1} \rangle_2/\langle \hat{\mathbf{t}}_{j+1}, \hat{\mathbf{t}}_{j+1} \rangle_2$

11 $\quad$ $\hat{\mathbf{x}}_{j+1} := \hat{\mathbf{x}}_j + \hat{\alpha}_j\hat{\mathbf{p}}_j + \hat{\omega}_{j+1}\hat{\mathbf{s}}_{j+1}$

12 $\quad$ $\mathbf{r}_{j+1} := \mathbf{s}_{j+1} - \hat{\omega}_{j+1}\mathbf{t}_{j+1}$

13 $\quad$ $\hat{\mathbf{r}}_{j+1} := \hat{\mathbf{s}}_{j+1} - \hat{\omega}_{j+1}\hat{\mathbf{t}}_{j+1}$

14 $\quad$ $\hat{\rho}_{j+1} := \langle \hat{\mathbf{r}}_{j+1}, \hat{\mathbf{r}}_0 \rangle_2$

15 $\quad$ $\hat{\beta}_{j+1} := (\hat{\alpha}_j/\hat{\omega}_{j+1}) \times (\rho_{j+1}/\rho_j)$

16 $\quad$ $\hat{\mathbf{p}}_{j+1} := \hat{\mathbf{r}}_{j+1} + \hat{\beta}_{j+1}(\hat{\mathbf{p}}_j - \hat{\omega}_{j+1}\hat{\mathbf{v}}_j)$

17 $\quad$ $j := j + 1$

18 $\mathbf{x}_j := P_R\hat{\mathbf{x}}_j$

$\langle P\mathbf{x}, \mathbf{y} \rangle_2$, $\mathbf{x}, \mathbf{y} \in \mathbb{R}^n$. Use this to derive a CG method for the right preconditioned system $AP\mathbf{x} = \mathbf{b}$ and show that it coincides with Algorithm 51.

8.2 Let $A, P \in \mathbb{R}^{n \times n}$ be symmetric and positive definite. Show that the matrix PA is self-adjoint and positive definite with respect to the inner product defined by $\langle \mathbf{x}, \mathbf{y} \rangle_A := \langle A\mathbf{x}, \mathbf{y} \rangle_2$, $\mathbf{x}, \mathbf{y} \in \mathbb{R}^n$. Use this to derive a CG method for the preconditioned system $PA\mathbf{x} = P\mathbf{b}$ which needs only one matrix–vector multiplication per step.

8.3 Let $A = (\mathbf{e}_3, \mathbf{e}_1, \mathbf{e}_2) \in \mathbb{R}^{3 \times 3}$. Determine the non-zero column pattern $\mathcal{M}_1$ and show that the problem

$$\min\{\|\mathbf{e}_1 - A\mathbf{p}\|_2 : \mathbf{p} \in \mathbb{R}^3 \text{ with non-zero pattern } \mathcal{M}_1\}$$

has no solution.

9

Compressed Sensing

9.1 Sparse Solutions

So far we have dealt with the problem of solving systems of the form $A\mathbf{x} = \mathbf{b}$ with given $A \in \mathbb{R}^{m \times n}$ and $\mathbf{b} \in \mathbb{R}^m$ in the following two situations.

The first case was that we were looking at the problem with $m = n$ and assumed that we had a unique solution $\mathbf{x} \in \mathbb{R}^n$, i.e. we assumed that the matrix was a square matrix and invertible. The second case was that we assumed that we had an over-determined system, i.e that $m \geq n$ and we were looking at the solution in a least-squares sense, knowing that the solution will not satisfy all equations exactly.

We now want to shift our focus to the remaining case. We still want to find a solution vector $\mathbf{x} \in \mathbb{R}^n$ from linear observations of the form

$$A\mathbf{x} = \mathbf{b}. \tag{9.1}$$

But, in contrast to the previous situation, we now assume $n > m$, i.e. we have more variables than equations. Without restriction, we will assume throughout this chapter that the given linear equations are linearly independent, or, that the matrix $A \in \mathbb{R}^{m \times n}$ has full rank m. This ensures that we always have a solution $\mathbf{x}^*$ solving (9.1). However, as we now have $n > m$, this solution will not be unique.

In signal processing $\mathbf{x}$ is often a discrete version of a signal and (9.1) can be considered as a *dimension reduction*. The matrix $A \in \mathbb{R}^{m \times n}$ reduces the high-dimensional *signal* $\mathbf{x} \in \mathbb{R}^n$ to some low-dimensional information $\mathbf{b} \in \mathbb{R}^m$.

The following questions arise naturally.

1. Can we compute a particularly sparse solution $\mathbf{x} \in \mathbb{R}^n$ of $A\mathbf{x} = \mathbf{b}$? Sparse shall mean that as many entries of $\mathbf{x}$ as possible are zero.
2. Is such a sparse solution unique and how many equations, i.e. rows, of $A\mathbf{x} = \mathbf{b}$ do we actually need to reconstruct this "sparse" solution uniquely?

3. What would good observations be, i.e. how should we choose the coefficients a_{ij} such that we need as few equations as possible to uniquely determine $\mathbf{x}$?
4. If we had an algorithm to reconstruct sparse solutions, then what does this algorithm produce if applied to a problem with a non-sparse solution?

To answer the first question, we have to further discuss the concept of sparsity. The answer to the second question will depend on the structure of the matrix and maybe of the right-hand side. An appropriate answer to the third question can only be given if the underlying problem is known. We will not address this in detail here. The final question will only have a satisfactory answer if the solution of the non-sparse problem can be well approximated by sparse vectors, which brings us back to the first question and the need to discuss sparsity in the first place.

Hence, we start by defining sparse vectors. The definition is motivated by the fact that particularly in discretisations coming from problems in signal processing, the solution vector $\mathbf{x}$ is often sparse.

Definition 9.1 A vector $\mathbf{x} \in \mathbb{R}^n$ is called *s-sparse* if it has at most $s \leq n$ non-zero entries. We will denote the number of non-zero entries in a vector $\mathbf{x} \in \mathbb{R}^n$ by $\|\mathbf{x}\|_0$. The *support* of a vector is the set $\mathrm{supp}(\mathbf{x}) = \{j \in \{1, \ldots, n\} : x_j \neq 0\}$.

Unfortunately, in contrast to our notation, $\| \cdot \|_0$ is obviously not a norm. If we use, as we have done before, $|S|$ to denote the cardinality of the set $S \subseteq \{1, \ldots, n\}$ then we have in particular the identity

$$|\mathrm{supp}(\mathbf{x})| = \|\mathbf{x}\|_0.$$

Moreover, for a set $S = \{j_1, \ldots, j_s\}$ we will denote by $\mathbf{x}_S$ either the vector from $\mathbb{R}^s$ containing the non-zero components of $\mathbf{x}$ or its extension to a vector from $\mathbb{R}^n$ with zero entries for indices not from S. It will be clear from the context which vector is meant. Finally, for a matrix $A \in \mathbb{R}^{m \times n}$ we denote the columns by $\mathbf{a}_j \in \mathbb{R}^m$ for $1 \leq j \leq n$ and denote by $A_S \in \mathbb{R}^{m \times s}$ the matrix consisting of the columns of A with index in S, i.e. $A_S = (\mathbf{a}_{j_1}, \ldots, \mathbf{a}_{j_s}) \in \mathbb{R}^{n \times s}$.

After having introduced these notations, we can now specify our first goal more precisely.

Definition 9.2 Let $A \in \mathbb{R}^{m \times n}$ with $n > m$ and $\mathbf{b} \in \mathbb{R}^m$ be given. A vector $x^* \in \mathbb{R}^n$ is called a *sparse solution* of $A\mathbf{x} = \mathbf{b}$ if it solves

$$\min \{\|\mathbf{x}\|_0 : \mathbf{x} \in \mathbb{R}^n \text{ with } A\mathbf{x} = \mathbf{b}\}. \tag{9.2}$$

Unfortunately, this problem is known to be NP-hard, which follows from the fact that we have to check all subsets S of $\{1, \ldots, n\}$, i.e. we must check each set in the power set of $\{1, \ldots, n\}$ which has exponential cardinality 2^n. Hence, we will have to find approximate ways of finding such a sparse solution.

9.2 Basis Pursuit and Null Space Property

We will see that it often suffices to solve the following ℓ_1-minimisation problem instead. This problem is numerically easier to solve as the ℓ_1-norm involved is convex and represents a continuous function.

Definition 9.3 Let $A \in \mathbb{R}^{m \times n}$ with $n > m$ and $\mathbf{b} \in \mathbb{R}^m$ be given. The problem of *basis pursuit* is to find a solution $\mathbf{x}^* \in \mathbb{R}^n$ of

$$\min \{\|\mathbf{x}\|_1 : \mathbf{x} \in \mathbb{R}^n \text{ with } A\mathbf{x} = \mathbf{b}\}. \tag{9.3}$$

As mentioned above, we can without restriction assume that our matrix A has full rank. Then, it is easy to see that the basis pursuit problem is well-defined and always has a solution.

Lemma 9.4 *Let $A \in \mathbb{R}^{m \times n}$ with $n > m = \mathrm{rank}(A)$ and $\mathbf{b} \in \mathbb{R}^n$ be given. Then, the basis pursuit problem has a solution.*

Proof As A has full rank, there is a vector $\mathbf{x}_0 \in \mathbb{R}^n$ with $A\mathbf{x}_0 = \mathbf{b}$. Hence, the set $K := \{\mathbf{x} \in \mathbb{R}^n : A\mathbf{x} = \mathbf{b}, \|\mathbf{x}\|_1 \leq \|\mathbf{x}_0\|_1\}$ is non-empty and must contain the solution of (9.3). As an obviously closed and bounded subset of $\mathbb{R}^n$, K is compact. Thus, the continous function $\mathbf{x} \mapsto \|\mathbf{x}\|_1$ attains its minimum in K, which then solves (9.3). $\qquad\qquad\qquad\qquad\qquad\qquad\qquad\qquad\qquad\qquad\qquad\square$

The above proof shows that (9.3) has a solution even if A does not have full rank, as long as the data $\mathbf{b}$ is in the range of A.

After establishing existence we want to discuss when and in which way the solution of the basis pursuit problem is unique. We start by showing that if the solution is unique then it necessarily must be sparse in the following sense.

Theorem 9.5 *Let $A \in \mathbb{R}^{m \times n}$ with $n > m = \mathrm{rank}(A)$ and $\mathbf{b} \in \mathbb{R}^m$. Assume that the basis pursuit problem (9.3) has a unique solution $\mathbf{x}^* \in \mathbb{R}^n$. Then, the columns $\mathbf{a}_j$ of A with $j \in \mathrm{supp}(\mathbf{x}^*)$ are linearly independent. In particular, the solution $\mathbf{x}^*$ is sparse with $\|\mathbf{x}^*\|_0 \leq m$.*

Proof Let us assume that the columns $\mathbf{a}_j$ with $j \in S := \mathrm{supp}(\mathbf{x}^*)$ are linearly dependent. Then, there is a vector $\mathbf{v} \in \mathbb{R}^n \setminus \{\mathbf{0}\}$ with $\mathrm{supp}(\mathbf{v}) \subseteq S$ and $A\mathbf{v} = \mathbf{0}$. This means that each vector $\mathbf{x}_t := \mathbf{x}^* + t\mathbf{v}$ with $t \in \mathbb{R}$ satisfies $A\mathbf{x}_t = \mathbf{b}$ and hence

$$\|\mathbf{x}^*\|_1 < \|\mathbf{x}_t\|_1 = \|\mathbf{x}^* + t\mathbf{v}\|_1 = \sum_{j \in S} |x_j^* + tv_j| = \sum_{j \in S} \mathrm{sign}(x_j^* + tv_j)(x_j^* + tv_j).$$

Since all the x_j^* with $j \in S$ are non-zero, we can choose $t \neq 0$ with $|t|$ so small that $\text{sign}(x_j^* + t v_j) = \text{sign}(x_j^*)$ for all $j \in S$. Hence, we can continue

$$\|\mathbf{x}^*\|_1 < \sum_{j \in S} \text{sign}(x_j^*) x_j^* + t \sum_{j \in S} \text{sign}(x_j^*) v_j$$
$$= \|\mathbf{x}^*\|_1 + t \sum_{j \in S} \text{sign}(x_j^*) v_j.$$

Obviously, we can now choose t such that the second term becomes negative and hence we arrive at the contradiction $\|\mathbf{x}^*\|_1 < \|\mathbf{x}^*\|_1$.

Since the number of independent columns of A is bounded by $m < n$, we also see that $\|\mathbf{x}^*\|_0 \leq m$. $\qquad\square$

While many results of this chapter remain true in the situation of complex matrices and vectors, the previous result does not, see, for example, Foucart and Rauhut [54].

We will now shift our attention slightly. Let us assume that our observation $\mathbf{b} \in \mathbb{R}^m$ is indeed generated by a matrix $A \in \mathbb{R}^{m \times n}$ with $n > m$ from an s-sparse vector $\mathbf{x}^* \in \mathbb{R}^n$. Is this vector the unique solution of the basis pursuit problem? The answer is positive if the matrix A satisfies a certain condition. To formulate this condition and the result, we recall the following notation. For a set $S \subseteq \{1, \ldots, n\}$, the complement S^c is given by $S^c := \{1, \ldots, n\} \setminus S$.

Definition 9.6 A matrix $A \in \mathbb{R}^{m \times n}$ satisfies the *null space property* with respect to a set $S \subseteq \{1, \ldots, n\}$ if

$$\|\mathbf{v}_S\|_1 < \|\mathbf{v}_{S^c}\|_1, \qquad \mathbf{v} \in \ker(A) \setminus \{\mathbf{0}\}. \tag{9.4}$$

The matrix A satisfies the *null space property of order s*, if it satisfies the null space property with respect to each $S \subseteq \{1, \ldots, n\}$ with $|S| \leq s$.

Since we can add $\|\mathbf{v}_S\|_1$ to both sides of the inequality in (9.4), we can immediately conclude that (9.4) is equivalent to

$$\|\mathbf{v}_S\|_1 < \frac{1}{2} \|\mathbf{v}\|_1, \qquad \mathbf{v} \in \ker(A) \setminus \{\mathbf{0}\}. \tag{9.5}$$

With this, we can derive the following answer to the question of whether and when an s-sparse vector $\mathbf{x}^*$ can be recovered from its observation $\mathbf{b} = A\mathbf{x}^*$ using basis pursuit.

Theorem 9.7 *Let $A \in \mathbb{R}^{m \times n}$ with $n > m$ and $S \subseteq \{1, \ldots, n\}$. Then, the following two statements are equivalent.*

1. *For every $\mathbf{x} \in \mathbb{R}^n$ with $\text{supp}(\mathbf{x}) \subseteq S$ the basis pursuit problem (9.3) with data $\mathbf{b} := A\mathbf{x}$ has the unique solution $\mathbf{x}$.*

2. *The matrix A satisfies the null space property with respect to S.*

Proof Let us first assume that the basis pursuit problem has a unique solution in the stated sense. Then, for each $\mathbf{x} \in \ker(A) \setminus \{\mathbf{0}\}$ the vector $\mathbf{x}_S \in \mathbb{R}^n$ is the unique solution of minimising $\|\mathbf{z}\|_1$ subject to $A\mathbf{z} = A\mathbf{x}_S$. From $\mathbf{0} = A\mathbf{x} = A\mathbf{x}_S + A\mathbf{x}_{S^c}$ we can conclude that $-\mathbf{x}_{S^c}$ satisfies $A(-\mathbf{x}_{S^c}) = A\mathbf{x}_S$. Since $\mathbf{x}_S$ is the minimiser amongst all such vectors, we have $\|\mathbf{x}_S\|_1 < \|\mathbf{x}_{S^c}\|_1$, i.e. the null space property.

Let us now assume that the null space property is satisfied and let $\mathbf{x} \in \mathbb{R}^n$ with $\operatorname{supp}(\mathbf{x}) \subseteq S$ be given. Assume that $\mathbf{z} \in \mathbb{R}^n$ is another vector with $A\mathbf{x} = A\mathbf{z}$ and $\mathbf{z} \neq \mathbf{x}$. Then, the vector $\mathbf{v} = \mathbf{x} - \mathbf{z}$ belongs to $\ker(A) \setminus \{\mathbf{0}\}$. Since $\mathbf{x}_{S^c} = \mathbf{0}$ and because of the null space property we can derive

$$
\begin{aligned}
\|\mathbf{x}\|_1 &\leq \|\mathbf{x} - \mathbf{z}_S\|_1 + \|\mathbf{z}_S\|_1 = \|\mathbf{v}_S\|_1 + \|\mathbf{z}_S\|_1 \\
&< \|\mathbf{v}_{S^c}\|_1 + \|\mathbf{z}_S\|_1 = \|\mathbf{z}_{S^c}\|_1 + \|\mathbf{z}_S\|_1 \\
&= \|\mathbf{z}\|_1,
\end{aligned}
$$

showing that $\mathbf{x}$ is indeed the unique minimiser. $\qquad\square$

Obviously, this result extends immediately to the problem of recovering any s-sparse vector uniquely.

Corollary 9.8 *Let $A \in \mathbb{R}^{m \times n}$ with $n > m$ be given. Every s-sparse vector $\mathbf{x} \in \mathbb{R}^n$ is the unique solution of the basis pursuit problem (9.3) with $\mathbf{b} := A\mathbf{x}$ if and only if A satisfies the null space property of order s.*

Another important consequence is that in this situation the solution of the basis pursuit problem also solves the ℓ_0-minimisation problem (9.2).

Theorem 9.9 *Let $A \in \mathbb{R}^{m \times n}$ with $n > m$ satisfy the null space property of order s. Let $\mathbf{x} \in \mathbb{R}^n$ be an s-sparse vector and let $\mathbf{b} := A\mathbf{x}$. Then, the solution of the ℓ_0-minimisation problem*

$$
\min\{\|\mathbf{z}\|_0 : \mathbf{z} \in \mathbb{R}^n \text{ with } A\mathbf{z} = \mathbf{b}\}
$$

is given by $\mathbf{x}$. Moreover, $\mathbf{x}$ is the solution of the basis pursuit problem.

Proof Assume that there is a vector $\mathbf{z} \in \mathbb{R}^n$ with $A\mathbf{z} = \mathbf{b} = A\mathbf{x}$ and $\|\mathbf{z}\|_0 \leq \|\mathbf{x}\|_0$. Then, $\mathbf{z}$ is also s-sparse and since, by Corollary 9.8, every s-sparse vector is the unique solution to the corresponding basis pursuit problem, we must have $\mathbf{z} = \mathbf{x}$. $\qquad\square$

In other words, if the matrix A satisfies the null space property of order s and if the right-hand side $\mathbf{b}$ is generated by an s-sparse vector $\mathbf{x}$ then we can find the solution of the ℓ_0-minimisation problem, which is indeed this $\mathbf{x}$, by any numerical scheme which solves the basis pursuit problem.

Next, let us generalise the ideas so far to situations where the right-hand side $\mathbf{b} = A\mathbf{x}$ is not generated by an s-sparse vector $\mathbf{x} \in \mathbb{R}^n$. Obviously, we would only expect good approximations from solving the basis pursuit problem if $\mathbf{x}$ can be well approximated by s-sparse vectors. This can best be expressed using the following quantity.

Definition 9.10 Let $\mathbf{x} \in \mathbb{R}^n$ and $1 \leq s \leq n$. Then, the best approximation error of $\mathbf{x}$ from the set of all s-sparse vectors is denoted by

$$\sigma_s(\mathbf{x}) := \min\{\|\mathbf{x} - \mathbf{z}\|_1 : \mathbf{z} \in \mathbb{R}^n \text{ is } s\text{-sparse}\}.$$

With this, we will call a vector $\mathbf{x} \in \mathbb{R}^n$ *compressible* if $\sigma_s(\mathbf{x})$ decays rapidly for growing s.

Note that the minimum in the definition of $\sigma_s(\mathbf{x})$ is attained by the vector $\mathbf{z} \in \mathbb{R}^n$ which has exactly the s largest absolute entries of $\mathbf{x}$.

To achieve a quantitative estimate on how well the solution of basis pursuit approximates a data-generating vector $\mathbf{x}$ which is not necessarily sparse, we need to strengthen the definition of the null space property.

Definition 9.11 A matrix $A \in \mathbb{R}^{m \times n}$ with $n > m$ satisfies the *stable null space property* with constant $0 < \rho < 1$ with respect to a set $S \subseteq \{1, \ldots, n\}$ if

$$\|\mathbf{v}_S\|_1 \leq \rho\|\mathbf{v}_{S^c}\|_1, \qquad \mathbf{v} \in \ker(A). \tag{9.6}$$

The matrix A satisfies the *stable null space property* with constant $0 < \rho < 1$ of order s if it satisfies the stable null space property with constant ρ with respect to all $S \subseteq \{1, \ldots, n\}$ with $|S| \leq s$.

With this stronger requirement we are able to prove the following error estimate. Note that the solution of the basis pursuit problem is not unique anymore but any solution enjoys the stated inequality.

Theorem 9.12 *Assume that $A \in \mathbb{R}^{m \times n}$ with $n > m$ satisfies the stable null space property with constant $\rho \in (0, 1)$ of order s. Let $\mathbf{x} \in \mathbb{R}^n$ and $\mathbf{b} := A\mathbf{x} \in \mathbb{R}^m$. Then, any solution $\mathbf{x}^*$ of the basis pursuit problem satisfies the error bound*

$$\|\mathbf{x} - \mathbf{x}^*\|_1 \leq 2\frac{1+\rho}{1-\rho}\sigma_s(\mathbf{x}).$$

Proof Let $\mathbf{z} \in \mathbb{R}^n$ be another vector satisfying $A\mathbf{z} = \mathbf{b} = A\mathbf{x}$. Then, the vector $\mathbf{v} := \mathbf{z} - \mathbf{x}$ belongs to $\ker(A)$ and hence satisfies the stable null space property

$$\|\mathbf{v}_S\|_1 \leq \rho\|\mathbf{v}_{S^c}\|_1$$

for any set $S \subseteq \{1, \ldots, n\}$ of cardinality s.

Furthermore, we have the simple estimates $\|v_{S^c}\|_1 \leq \|x_{S^c}\|_1 + \|z_{S^c}\|_1$ and

$$\|x\|_1 = \|x_{S^c}\|_1 + \|x_S\|_1 \leq \|x_{S^c}\| + \|v_S\|_1 + \|z_S\|_1.$$

Adding the two estimates yields

$$\|x\|_1 + \|v_{S^c}\|_1 \leq 2\|x_{S^c}\|_1 + \|v_S\|_1 + \|z\|_1,$$

which, together with the stable null space property, gives

$$\|v_{S^c}\|_1 \leq \|z\|_1 - \|x\|_1 + \|v_S\|_1 + 2\|x_{S^c}\|_1 \qquad (9.7)$$
$$\leq \|z\|_1 - \|x\|_1 + \rho\|v_{S^c}\|_1 + 2\|x_{S^c}\|_1.$$

Since $0 < \rho < 1$, we can reformulate this as

$$\|v_{S^c}\|_1 \leq \frac{1}{1-\rho}\left(\|z\|_1 - \|x\|_1 + 2\|x_{S^c}\|_1\right).$$

Using the stable null space property once again, we can finally derive the bound

$$\|v\|_1 = \|v_S\|_1 + \|v_{S^c}\|_1 \leq (1+\rho)\|v_{S^c}\|_1 \leq \frac{1+\rho}{1-\rho}\left(\|z\|_1 - \|x\|_1 + 2\|x_{S^c}\|_1\right).$$

Let us now pick S as the set of s indices corresponding to the s largest entries of x, i.e. $\|x_{S^c}\|_1 = \sigma_s(x)$. Moreover, let $z = x^*$ be a solution of the basis pursuit problem. Then we obviously have $Ax^* = Ax$ and the bound $\|x^*\|_1 \leq \|x\|_1$, i.e. $\|z\|_1 - \|x\|_1 \leq 0$, which gives the stated result.   □

Finally, let us make one more modification. We know by now that in many situations it does not make sense to work with exact data. Hence, we can change the basis pursuit problem to the following more robust problem.

Definition 9.13 Let $A \in \mathbb{R}^{m \times n}$ with $n > m$ and $b \in \mathbb{R}^m$ be given. For a given $\eta > 0$, the *robust basis pursuit* problem consists of finding a solution $x^* \in \mathbb{R}^n$ of

$$\min\{\|z\|_1 : z \in \mathbb{R}^n \text{ with } \|Az - b\| \leq \eta\}. \qquad (9.8)$$

Note that we have not specified the norm for the robustness constraint. The actual norm is not important right now. It will eventually depend on the problem and on the numerical scheme chosen to solve the minimisation problem.

If A has full rank or, more generally, if the set $\{z \in \mathbb{R}^n : \|Az - b\| \leq \eta\}$ is non-empty then we can easily prove that (9.8) alwyas has a solution, using the same ideas as in the proof of Lemma 9.4.

If we extend the definition of the stable null space property in the following sense then we will see that the robust basis pursuit problem is also stable.

Definition 9.14 A matrix $A \in \mathbb{R}^{m \times n}$ with $n > m$ satisfies the *robust null space property with constants* $0 < \rho < 1$ *and* $\tau > 0$ with respect to a set $S \subseteq \{1, \ldots, n\}$ if

$$\|v_S\|_1 \leq \rho \|v_{S^c}\|_1 + \tau \|Av\|, \qquad v \in \mathbb{R}^n. \tag{9.9}$$

The matrix A satisfies the robust null space property of order s with constants $0 < \rho < 1$ and $\tau > 0$ if it satisfies the robust null space property with constants ρ and τ for all S with $|S| \leq s$.

Note that for a $v \in \ker(A)$ the robust null space property (9.9) reduces to the stable null space property (9.6). The next theorem generalises the results of Theorem 9.12.

Theorem 9.15 *Let $A \in \mathbb{R}^{m \times n}$ with $n > m$ satisfy the robust null space property of order s with constants $0 < \rho < 1$ and $\tau > 0$. For $x \in \mathbb{R}^n$ let $b = Ax + e$ with $\|e\| \leq \eta$. Then, any solution x^* of the robust basis pursuit problem (9.8) satisfies the error bound*

$$\|x - x^*\|_1 \leq 2 \frac{1 + \rho}{1 - \rho} \sigma_s(x) + \frac{4\tau}{1 - \rho} \eta.$$

Proof The proof is very similar to the proof of Theorem 9.12. Using the same notation, we can employ the robust null space property $\|v_S\|_1 \leq \rho \|v_{S^c}\|_1 + \tau \|Av\|$ together with (9.7) to derive

$$\|v_{S^c}\|_1 \leq \frac{1}{1 - \rho} \left(\|z\|_1 - \|x\|_1 + 2\|x_{S^c}\|_1 + \tau \|Av\| \right).$$

As before, we can use the robust null space property again and find, this time, the bound

$$\|v\|_1 = \|v_S\|_1 + \|v_{S^c}\|_1 \leq (1 + \rho) \|v_{S^c}\| + \tau \|Av\|$$
$$\leq \frac{1 + \rho}{1 - \rho} \left(\|z\|_1 - \|x\|_1 + 2\|x_{S^c}\|_1 \right) + \frac{2\tau}{1 - \rho} \|Av\|.$$

Choosing S now again as in the proof of Theorem 9.12, i.e. such that $\|x_{S^c}\|_1 = \sigma_s(x)$, and letting $z = x^*$ be a solution of the robust pursuit problem gives

$$\|Av\| = \|Ax^* - Ax\| \leq \|Ax^* - b\| + \|b - Ax\| \leq 2\eta$$

and hence the stated error bound. □

Note that in the situation of $\eta = 0$, the result of this theorem reduces to the result of Theorem 9.12.

9.3 Restricted Isometry Property

In the last section, we have seen that the null space property of a matrix A is a good condition to determine whether a sparse signal can be recovered uniquely, using, for example, the basis pursuit idea.

We will now introduce yet another property, which will prove useful particularly in the case of noisy data. This property is based upon weakening the idea of isometric mappings, i.e. mappings $A : \mathbb{R}^n \to \mathbb{R}^m$ which satisfy $\|Ax\| = \|x\|$. In the case of the ℓ_2-norm, these would be orthogonal matrices.

Definition 9.16 A matrix $A \in \mathbb{R}^{m \times n}$ satisfies the *restricted isometry property (RIP)* of order s if there is a $\delta \in (0, 1)$ such that

$$(1 - \delta)\|\mathbf{x}\|_2^2 \le \|A\mathbf{x}\|_2^2 \le (1 + \delta)\|\mathbf{x}\|_2^2 \tag{9.10}$$

is satisfied for all s-sparse vectors $\mathbf{x} \in \mathbb{R}^n$. The smallest $\delta \in (0, 1)$ with this property is denoted by δ_s and called the *restricted isometry constant*.

Obviously, (9.10) is equivalent to $\left| \|A\mathbf{x}\|_2^2 - \|\mathbf{x}\|_2^2 \right| \le \delta$ for all s-sparse vectors $\mathbf{x}$, which means that A "misses" being an isometry on s-sparse vectors by δ.

To understand the importance of this condition in this context, we first note that a matrix satisfying the restricted isometry property of order $2s$ allows us, in principle, to uniquely recover an s-sparse signal.

Lemma 9.17 *Suppose that $s \in \mathbb{N}$ and that $A \in \mathbb{R}^{m \times n}$ with $n \ge m$ satisfies the restricted isometry property of order $2s$ with constant $\delta_{2s} < 1$. If $\mathbf{x} \in \mathbb{R}^n$ is an s-sparse vector, then $\mathbf{x}$ is uniquely determined by its observation $\mathbf{b} := A\mathbf{x}$.*

Proof Let $S := \operatorname{supp}(\mathbf{x})$. Then we have $|S| \le s$ and it suffices to show that there is no other vector $\mathbf{y} \in \mathbb{R}^n$ with $\|\mathbf{y}\|_0 \le s$ and $A\mathbf{y} = \mathbf{b}$. To this end, assume that we have another solution $\mathbf{y} \in \mathbb{R}^n$ with $A\mathbf{y} = \mathbf{b}$ and $\tilde{S} := \operatorname{supp}(\mathbf{y})$ satisfying $|\tilde{S}| \le s$. Then, the vector $\mathbf{z} = \mathbf{x} - \mathbf{y} \in \mathbb{R}^n$ has at most $2s$ non-zero entries with indices in $S \cup \tilde{S}$ and satisfies $A\mathbf{z} = \mathbf{0}$. Thus, (9.10) yields

$$(1 - \delta_{2s})\|\mathbf{z}\|_2^2 \le \|A\mathbf{z}\|_2^2 = 0$$

and, since δ_{2s} is supposed to be less than one, we can conclude that $\mathbf{z} = \mathbf{0}$. $\quad\square$

However, since the problem of recovering a sparse signal via ℓ_0-minimisation is NP-hard, this result is of limited use. It only tells us that we can, in principle, recover the sparse signal uniquely. In the following, we will discuss when the restricted isometry property leads to the null space property and hence allows us to reconstruct the sparse signal constructively using, for example, basis pursuit.

Note that in our situation of having $n > m$, i.e. of having more columns than rows, the matrix $A^T A \in \mathbb{R}^{n \times n}$ is only positive semi-definite since its rank is at most m. This means that the estimate

$$\lambda_{\min}(A^T A)\|\mathbf{x}\|_2 \le \|A\mathbf{x}\|_2^2 = \mathbf{x}^T A^T A \mathbf{x} \le \lambda_{\max}(A^T A)\|\mathbf{x}\|_2^2$$

which holds for all $\mathbf{x} \in \mathbb{R}^n$ is in general not helpful to determine the constant δ_s. We have, however, the following characterisation.

Lemma 9.18 *If the matrix $A \in \mathbb{R}^{m \times n}$ satisfies the restricted isometry property of order s then the restricted isometry constant is given by*

$$\delta_s = \max \left\{ \|A_S^T A_S - I\|_2 : S \subseteq \{1, \ldots, n\} \text{ with } |S| \le s \right\}. \tag{9.11}$$

Proof Let $S \subseteq \{1, \ldots, n\}$ with $|S| \le s$ be given. Since the matrix $A_S^T A_S - I$ is symmetric, we can use Proposition 2.22 to compute its norm:

$$\begin{aligned}
\|A_S^T A_S - I\|_2 &= \max_{\|\mathbf{x}\|_2 = 1} |\langle (A_S^T A_S - I)\mathbf{x}, \mathbf{x} \rangle_2| \\
&= \max_{\|\mathbf{x}\|_2 = 1} \left| \|A_S \mathbf{x}\|_2^2 - \|\mathbf{x}\|_2^2 \right|.
\end{aligned}$$

Thus, A satisfies the restricted isometry property of order s if and only if $\|A_S^T A_S - I\|_2 < 1$ for all $S \subseteq \{1, \ldots, n\}$ with $|S| \le s$ and the restricted isometry constant is therefore given by

$$\delta_s = \max \left\{ \|A_S^T A_S - I\|_2 : S \subseteq \{1, \ldots, n\} \text{ with } |S| \le s \right\}. \qquad \square$$

Note that (9.11) is always well-defined. If a matrix A does not satisfy the restricted isometry property, this number δ_s is simply larger than one.

There are several results available which show that the restricted isometry property implies the null space property. They mainly differ in terms of the assumptions on the restricted isometry constant and the proof techniques. We will now give one such result, which is particularly easy to prove. Before we can prove it, we need the following auxiliary result.

Proposition 9.19 *Let $A \in \mathbb{R}^{m \times n}$ be given. Let $\mathbf{x}, \mathbf{y} \in \mathbb{R}^n$ with $\|\mathbf{x}\|_0 \le s$ and $\|\mathbf{y}\|_0 \le t$. If the supports of $\mathbf{x}$ and $\mathbf{y}$ are disjoint then*

$$|\langle A\mathbf{x}, A\mathbf{y} \rangle_2| \le \delta_{s+t}\|\mathbf{x}\|_2\|\mathbf{y}\|_2.$$

Proof Let S be the union of the supports of $\mathbf{x}$ and $\mathbf{y}$, then we have $|S| = s + t$. Since $\mathbf{x}$ and $\mathbf{y}$ have disjoint support, their inner product and hence also the inner product between $\mathbf{x}_S$ and $\mathbf{y}_S$ is zero. Thus, we have

$$\begin{aligned}
|\langle A\mathbf{x}, A\mathbf{y} \rangle_2| &= |\langle A_S \mathbf{x}_S, A_S \mathbf{y}_S \rangle_2 - \langle \mathbf{x}_S, \mathbf{y}_S \rangle_2| \\
&= \left| \langle (A_S^T A_S - I)\mathbf{x}_S, \mathbf{y}_S \rangle_2 \right| \\
&\le \|A_S^T A_S - I\|_2 \|\mathbf{x}_S\|_2 \|\mathbf{y}_S\|_2
\end{aligned}$$

and the result follows from Lemma 9.18.   □

With this, it is now easy to prove a result on the null space property.

Theorem 9.20 *Let $A \in \mathbb{R}^{m \times n}$ be given. Suppose that its restricted isometry constant δ_{2s} of order $2s$ satisfies $\delta_{2s} < 1/3$. Then, A satisfies the null space property of order s. Consequently, any s-sparse signal $\mathbf{x} \in \mathbb{R}^n$ is the unique solution of the basis pursuit problem (9.3) with right-hand side $\mathbf{b} := A\mathbf{x}$.*

Proof   We have to show that (9.5) is satisfied, i.e. that we have

$$\|\mathbf{x}_S\|_1 < \frac{1}{2}\|\mathbf{x}\|_1$$

for all $\mathbf{x} \in \ker(A) \setminus \{\mathbf{0}\}$. Obviously, if such an $\mathbf{x} \in \mathbb{R}^n$ is given, it suffices to show this for the set $S = S_0$, which contains the indices of the s largest absolute entries of $\mathbf{x}$. Next, let S_1 denote the indices of the s largest absolute entries of S^c. Then, let S_2 denote the indices of the s largest absolute entries of $(S_0 \cup S_1)^c$ and so on. Since $\mathbf{x} \in \ker(A)$, we have

$$A\mathbf{x}_{S_0} = A(-\mathbf{x}_{S_1} - \mathbf{x}_{S_2} - \cdots) = -\sum_{k \geq 1} A\mathbf{x}_{S_k}.$$

Viewing $\mathbf{x}_{S_0}$ as a $2s$-sparse vector, this, together with (9.10) and Proposition 9.19, yields

$$\|\mathbf{x}_{S_0}\|_2^2 \leq \frac{1}{1 - \delta_{2s}}\|A\mathbf{x}_{S_0}\|_2^2 = \frac{1}{1 - \delta_{2s}}\left\langle A\mathbf{x}_{S_0}, -\sum_{k \geq 1} A\mathbf{x}_{S_k}\right\rangle_2$$

$$\leq \frac{1}{1 - \delta_{2s}}\sum_{k \geq 1}|\langle A\mathbf{x}_{S_0}, A\mathbf{x}_{S_k}\rangle_2|$$

$$\leq \frac{\delta_{2s}}{1 - \delta_{2s}}\|\mathbf{x}_{S_0}\|_2 \sum_{k \geq 1}\|\mathbf{x}_{S_k}\|_2,$$

i.e.

$$\|\mathbf{x}_{S_0}\|_2 \leq \frac{\delta_{2s}}{1 - \delta_{2s}}\sum_{k \geq 1}\|\mathbf{x}_{S_k}\|_2. \qquad (9.12)$$

Now, the specific sorting of our index sets S_k allows us to bound

$$\|\mathbf{x}_{S_k}\|_2 = \left(\sum_{j \in S_k}|x_j|^2\right)^{1/2} \leq \sqrt{s}\max_{j \in S_k}|x_j| \leq \sqrt{s}\min_{j \in S_{k-1}}|x_j|$$

$$\leq \sqrt{s}\frac{1}{s}\sum_{j \in S_{k-1}}|x_j| = \frac{1}{\sqrt{s}}\|\mathbf{x}_{S_{k-1}}\|_1.$$

Inserting this into (9.12) yields

$$\|\mathbf{x}_{S_0}\|_2 \leq \frac{\delta_{2s}}{1 - \delta_{2s}} \frac{1}{\sqrt{s}} \sum_{k \geq 1} \|\mathbf{x}_{S_{k-1}}\|_1 = \frac{\delta_{2s}}{1 - \delta_{2s}} \frac{1}{\sqrt{s}} \|\mathbf{x}\|_1$$

and hence

$$\|\mathbf{x}_{S_0}\|_1 \leq \sqrt{s}\|\mathbf{x}_{S_0}\|_2 \leq \frac{\delta_{2s}}{1 - \delta_{2s}} \|\mathbf{x}\|_1.$$

The result now follows from the fact that $\delta_{2s}/(1 - \delta_{2s}) < 1/2$ is equivalent to $\delta_{2s} < 1/3$. □

Obviously, the condition $\delta_{2s} < 1/3$ restricts the possible candidates and it is desirable to generalise this result in such a way that also larger δ in the restricted isometry property lead to the null space property. Furthermore, taking also measurement errors into account, it seems reasonable to verify the robust null space property instead. One possible result of this form is the following one, which is proven using ideas similar to those employed in the proof of Theorem 9.20. Details can be found in [54].

Theorem 9.21 *Let $A \in \mathbb{R}^{m \times n}$ satisfy the restricted isometry property of order $2s$ with $\delta_{2s} < 4/\sqrt{41}$. Then, A satisfies the robust null space property with certain $\rho \in (0, 1)$ and $\tau > 0$, depending only on δ_{2s}. In particular, if $\mathbf{x} \in \mathbb{R}^n$ satisfies $\|A\mathbf{x} - \mathbf{b}\|_2 \leq \eta$ and if $\mathbf{x}^*$ is the solution of the robust basis pursuit problem (9.8) then*

$$\|\mathbf{x} - \mathbf{x}^*\|_1 \leq C_1 \sigma_s(\mathbf{x}) + C_2 \sqrt{s}\eta$$

with certain constants $C_1, C_2 > 0$ depending only on δ_{2s}.

We now want to further discuss the restricted isometry property. To this end, we can use (9.11), the fact that $A_S^T A_S - I$ is a symmetric matrix and hence that the norm $\|A_S^T A_S - I\|_2$ is given by the largest eigenvalue of $A_S^T A_S - I$. If $S = \{k_1, \ldots, k_s\}$ with $s = |S|$, then the entries of $A_S^T A_S - I$ are given by

$$(A_S^T A_S - I)_{ij} = \langle \mathbf{a}_{k_i}, \mathbf{a}_{k_j} \rangle_2 - \delta_{ij}, \qquad 1 \leq i, j \leq s.$$

Here, $\mathbf{a}_j \in \mathbb{R}^n$ denotes as usual the jth column of $A \in \mathbb{R}^{m \times n}$. Hence, from now on and without restriction, we will assume that the columns of A are normalised, i.e. that we have $\|\mathbf{a}_j\|_2 = 1$, so that all the diagonal elements of $A_S^T A_S - I$ are zero. Furthermore, the following notion naturally arises.

Definition 9.22 *Let $A \in \mathbb{R}^{m \times n}$ be a matrix with normalised columns $\mathbf{a}_j \in \mathbb{R}^m$, $1 \leq j \leq n$. The coherence $\mu = \mu(A)$ of A is defined as*

$$\mu := \max\{|\langle \mathbf{a}_i, \mathbf{a}_j \rangle_2| : i, j \in \{1, \ldots, n\}, i \neq j\}.$$

This definition ensures that each off-diagonal entry of $A_S^T A_S$ has absolute value less than μ. Thus, Gershgorin's theorem (Theorem 5.1) yields for the maximum (actually for any) eigenvalue λ_{max} of $A_S^T A_S - I$ an index i such that the bound

$$\|A_S^T A_S - I\|_2 = |\lambda_{max}| = |\lambda_{max} - 0| \leq \sum_{\substack{j=1 \\ j \neq i}}^{s} |\langle \mathbf{a}_{k_i}, \mathbf{a}_{k_j} \rangle_2| \leq (s-1)\mu$$

holds. This means that we have $\delta_s \leq (s-1)\mu$ and such a bound is useful if $(s-1)\mu < 1$. In view of Lemma 9.17, we have the following consequence.

Corollary 9.23 *Let $A \in \mathbb{R}^{m \times n}$, $n > m$, have normalised columns and a coherence μ satisfying $\mu < 1/(2s-1)$, then each s-sparse vector $\mathbf{x} \in \mathbb{R}^n$ is uniquely determined by its observation $\mathbf{b} := A\mathbf{x}$.*

To see what we can actually expect from this bound, we need to know how small μ can actually be.

Theorem 9.24 (Welsh bound) *The coherence of a matrix $A \in \mathbb{R}^{m \times n}$ with $n > m$ satisfies*

$$\mu \geq \sqrt{\frac{n-m}{m(n-1)}}.$$

Proof Let us consider the matrices $B := A^T A \in \mathbb{R}^{n \times n}$ and $C := AA^T \in \mathbb{R}^{m \times m}$. Then, the matrix B has entries $B_{ij} = \langle \mathbf{a}_i, \mathbf{a}_j \rangle_2$. Since both matrices have the same trace, we particularly have

$$\text{tr}(C) = \text{tr}(B) = \sum_{j=1}^{n} \|\mathbf{a}_j\|_2^2 = n.$$

However, we can also use the Frobenius norm (see Definition 2.30), which is defined by the inner product

$$\langle G, H \rangle_F := \text{tr}(GH^T) = \sum_{i,j=1}^{m} G_{ij} H_{ij}, \qquad G, H \in \mathbb{R}^{m \times m},$$

to derive

$$n = \text{tr}(C) = \langle C, I \rangle_F \leq \|C\|_F \|I\|_F = \sqrt{m} \sqrt{\text{tr}(CC^T)}.$$

Observing that

$$\text{tr}(CC^T) = \text{tr}(AA^T AA^T) = \text{tr}(A^T AA^T A) = \text{tr}(BB^T) = \sum_{i,j=1}^{n} |\langle \mathbf{a}_i, \mathbf{a}_j \rangle_2|^2$$

$$= n + \sum_{i \neq j} |\langle \mathbf{a}_i, \mathbf{a}_j \rangle_2|^2 \leq n + n(n-1)\mu^2$$

yields

$$n^2 \le m\left(n + n(n-1)\mu^2\right),$$

from which we can cancel out an n and rearrange it to find the stated inequality for μ. □

In the situation we are particularly interested in, namely in the case of n much larger than m, we see that this lower bound behaves roughly like $1/\sqrt{m}$. Hence, our analysis above only holds for such s being much smaller than $\sqrt{m}$.

Finally, it is interesting to see in what situations the Welsh bound is sharp. Inspecting the proof of the last theorem shows that this is exactly the case if the two inequalities in the proof are actually equalities. This means that, on the one hand, we need

$$\langle C, I \rangle_F = \|C\|_F \sqrt{m},$$

i.e. we must have equality in the Cauchy–Schwarz inequality. This is exactly the case if C and I are linearly dependent, which means here that there is a constant $\lambda \ne 0$ such that $C = AA^{\mathrm{T}} = \lambda I$, i.e. the rows of A are orthogonal and have equal length.

On the other hand, we need

$$\sum_{i \ne j} |\langle \mathbf{a}_i, \mathbf{a}_j \rangle_2|^2 = n(n-1)\mu^2.$$

Since each summand is non-negative and satisfies $|\langle \mathbf{a}_i, \mathbf{a}_j \rangle_2| \le \mu$, this is possible only if all entries satisfy $|\langle \mathbf{a}_i, \mathbf{a}_j \rangle_2| = \mu$.

Definition 9.25 A system of normalised vectors $\mathbf{a}_j \in \mathbb{R}^m$, $1 \le i \le n$, is called *equiangular* if there is a number $\mu > 0$ such that

$$|\langle \mathbf{a}_i, \mathbf{a}_j \rangle_2| = \mu, \qquad 1 \le i \ne j \le n.$$

An equiangular system of vectors $\mathbf{a}_1, \ldots, \mathbf{a}_n \in \mathbb{R}^m$ is called an *equiangular tight frame* if the rows of the matrix $A = (\mathbf{a}_1, \ldots, \mathbf{a}_n) \in \mathbb{R}^{m \times n}$ are orthogonal with equal norm.

With this definition, we see that equiangular tight frames are exactly those families for which we have equality in the Welsh bound.

Corollary 9.26 *The coherence μ of a matrix $A \in \mathbb{R}^{m \times n}$ is given by*

$$\mu = \sqrt{\frac{n-m}{m(n-1)}}$$

if and only if the columns of A form an equiangular tight frame.

The construction of good *sensing* matrices $A \in \mathbb{R}^{m \times n}$, i.e. matrices which satisfy the null space property or the restricted isometry property, is a difficult and to a large extent still open research problem. The situation improves dramatically if the matrices are generated randomly.

Example 9.27 Assume that the entries of $A \in \mathbb{R}^{m \times n}$, $n > m$, are independently sampled from the normal distribution with mean zero and variance $\sigma = 1/m$. Then, if $s \leq Cm/\log(n/m)$, the matrix A satisfies the restricted isometry property and allows the reconstruction of an s-sparse vector $\mathbf{x} \in \mathbb{R}^n$ from its observation $\mathbf{b} := A\mathbf{x}$ with probability $1 - O(\exp(-\gamma n))$ for some $\gamma > 0$.

A proof of this example was first given by Candès and Tao in [31] and was based on certain concentration results about the singular values of Gaussian matrices. See also Baraniuk *et al.* [10] and Candès [29]. The latter survey also contains information about other randomly generated matrices such as matrices from binary, Fourier and incoherent measurements.

The construction of deterministic sampling matrices is a different matter. So far, there is only the construction by DeVore [45] on finite fields and the general discussion [9] by Bandeira *et al.*

9.4 Numerical Algorithms

As pointed out before, the original problem

$$\min\{\|\mathbf{x}\|_0 : \mathbf{x} \in \mathbb{R}^n \text{ with } A\mathbf{x} = \mathbf{b}\} \tag{9.13}$$

is NP-hard simply because any deterministic algorithm must eventually check all possible subsets of the index set $\{1, \ldots, n\}$ and has hence an exponential computational complexity. Thus, approximate algorithms are necessary. Here, we have essentially two possibilities. We can try to define an approximate algorithm which tackles the ℓ_0-minimisation problem directly. Alternatively, the results of Theorem 9.9 and the subsequent discussion show that, under certain assumptions, algorithms for the basis pursuit problem

$$\min\{\|\mathbf{x}\|_1 : \mathbf{x} \in \mathbb{R}^n \text{ with } A\mathbf{x} = \mathbf{b}\} \tag{9.14}$$

will also work. The latter is particularly appealing as we can recast the basis pursuit problem as a linear program. To see this, let us introduce *slack variables* $\mathbf{x}_+ = (x_j^+)$, $\mathbf{x}_- = (x_j^-) \in \mathbb{R}^n$ by setting

$$x_j^+ = \begin{cases} x_j & \text{if } x_j > 0, \\ 0 & \text{if } x_j \leq 0, \end{cases} \qquad x_j^- = \begin{cases} 0 & \text{if } x_j > 0, \\ -x_j & \text{if } x_j \leq 0. \end{cases} \tag{9.15}$$

Then, using the notation $\mathbf{z} := (\mathbf{x}_+^T, \mathbf{x}_-^T)^T \in \mathbb{R}^{2n}$, (9.14) can equivalently be formulated as

$$\min\left\{\sum_{j=1}^{2n} z_j : \mathbf{z} \in \mathbb{R}^{2n} \text{ with } (A, -A)\mathbf{z} = \mathbf{b}, \mathbf{z} \geq \mathbf{0}\right\}, \qquad (9.16)$$

where $\mathbf{z} \geq \mathbf{0}$ is meant component-wise. Indeed, we have the following result.

Remark 9.28 If $\mathbf{x} \in \mathbb{R}^n$ solves (9.14), then obviously $\mathbf{z} := (\mathbf{x}_+^T, \mathbf{x}_-^T)^T$ with $\mathbf{x}^+, \mathbf{x}^-$ defined by (9.15) solves (9.16). If, however, $\mathbf{z} = (\mathbf{x}_+^T, \mathbf{x}_-^T)^T \in \mathbb{R}^{2n}$ with $\mathbf{x}_+, \mathbf{x}_- \in \mathbb{R}^n$ solves (9.16) then $\mathbf{x} := \mathbf{x}^+ - \mathbf{x}^-$ solves our original basis pursuit problem (9.14).

This remark means that essentially all algorithms from linear programming are available to us, including the simplex method as well as more sophisticated methods like interior point algorithms. Moreover, the robust basis pursuit problem (9.8) can, in a similar way, be recast as a convex program with a conic constraint. To describe such algorithms is beyond the scope of this book and the reader is referred to the literature on linear programming and convex optimisation. However, as these methods are more general purpose methods, they were clearly not designed for compressed sensing problems. Because of this, specific ℓ_1-minimisation algorithms have been applied to compressed sensing problems, which rather solve the unconstrained problem

$$\min\left\{\frac{1}{2}\|A\mathbf{x} - \mathbf{b}\|_2^2 + \lambda\|\mathbf{x}\|_1 : \mathbf{x} \in \mathbb{R}^n\right\} \qquad (9.17)$$

with a given regularisation parameter $\lambda > 0$. Here (9.17) is equivalent to the LASSO (least absolute shrinkage and selection operator) problem, first introduced by Tibshirani in [122],

$$\min\left\{\|A\mathbf{x} - \mathbf{b}\|_2 : \mathbf{x} \in \mathbb{R}^n \text{ with } \|\mathbf{x}\|_1 \leq \tau\right\}, \qquad (9.18)$$

given appropriate constants λ and τ. Hence, numerical schemes for solving the LASSO problem can be employed for solving the unconstrained problem (9.17) and vice versa. A seemingly simple example of how (9.17) can be used for solving the basis pursuit problem (9.14) is by *Bregman iterations* as introduced by Yin *et al.* in [138] and as described in Algorithm 57.

Again, it is possible that the unconstrained optimisation problem (9.17) has more than one solution. Nonetheless, we have the following result.

Theorem 9.29 *Let $A \in \mathbb{R}^{m \times n}$ and $\mathbf{b} \in \mathbb{R}^n$ be given. Let $\{\mathbf{x}_k\}$ denote the sequence generated by Algorithm 57.*

Algorithm 57: Bregman iteration

Input : $A \in \mathbb{R}^{m \times n}$, $\mathbf{b} \in \mathbb{R}^m$, $\lambda > 0$.
Output: Sparse representation $\mathbf{x} \in \mathbb{R}^n$.

1 $\mathbf{x}_0 := \mathbf{0}$, $\quad \mathbf{b}_0 := \mathbf{0}$
2 **for** $k = 0, 1, 2, \ldots$ **do**
3 $\quad \mathbf{b}_{k+1} := \mathbf{b} + (\mathbf{b}_k - A\mathbf{x}_k)$
4 $\quad \mathbf{x}_{k+1} := \arg\min \left\{ \frac{1}{2}\|A\mathbf{x} - \mathbf{b}_{k+1}\|_2^2 + \lambda\|\mathbf{x}\|_1 : \mathbf{x} \in \mathbb{R}^n \right\}$

---

1. *If there is a $k \in \mathbb{N}$ such that $\mathbf{x}_k$ satisfies $A\mathbf{x}_k = \mathbf{b}$ then $\mathbf{x}_k$ is a solution of the basis pursuit problem (9.14).*
2. *There is an index $k_0 \in \mathbb{N}$ such that each $\mathbf{x}_k$ for $k \geq k_0$ is a solution of (9.14).*

Proof We will only prove the first part of this theorem. A proof of the second part can be found in Yin *et al.* [138]. Let us introduce the notation $J(\mathbf{x}) := \lambda\|\mathbf{x}\|_1$ and $K_k(\mathbf{x}) := \frac{1}{2}\|A\mathbf{x} - \mathbf{b}_k\|_2^2$, $\mathbf{x} \in \mathbb{R}^n$. Then we already know that K_k is differentiable with gradient gradient $\nabla K_k(\mathbf{x}) = A^{\mathrm{T}}(A\mathbf{x} - \mathbf{b}_k)$. Even if J is not differentiable, we have that $\mathbf{x}_k$ satisfies the first-order optimality condition for minimising $J(\mathbf{x}) + K_k(\mathbf{x})$, which is

$$\mathbf{0} \in \partial J(\mathbf{x}_k) + \nabla K_k(\mathbf{x}_k) = \partial J(\mathbf{x}_k) + A^{\mathrm{T}}(A\mathbf{x}_k - \mathbf{b}_k).$$

This means that the direction $A^{\mathrm{T}}(A\mathbf{x}_k - \mathbf{b}_k)$ belongs to the subdifferential $\partial J(\mathbf{x}_k)$ of J at $\mathbf{x}_k$ and therefore we have for the *Bregman distance*

$$J(\mathbf{x}) - J(\mathbf{x}_k) - \langle A^{\mathrm{T}}(\mathbf{b}_k - A\mathbf{x}_k), \mathbf{x} - \mathbf{x}_k \rangle_2 \geq 0, \qquad \mathbf{x} \in \mathbb{R}^n.$$

This then yields

$$\begin{aligned}
J(\mathbf{x}) &\geq J(\mathbf{x}_k) + \langle A^{\mathrm{T}}(A\mathbf{x}_k - \mathbf{b}_k), \mathbf{x} - \mathbf{x}_k \rangle_2 \\
&= J(\mathbf{x}_k) + \langle A\mathbf{x}_k - \mathbf{b}_k, A\mathbf{x} - A\mathbf{x}_k \rangle_2 \\
&= J(\mathbf{x}_k) + \langle \mathbf{b} - \mathbf{b}_k, A\mathbf{x} - \mathbf{b} \rangle_2,
\end{aligned}$$

which shows that $J(\mathbf{x}) \geq J(\mathbf{x}_k)$ for all $\mathbf{x} \in \mathbb{R}^n$ with $A\mathbf{x} = \mathbf{b}$, i.e. $\mathbf{x}_k$ is indeed a solution of the basis pursuit problem. $\qquad \square$

The rest of this section is devoted to discussing some of those algorithms which tackle the original problem (9.13) more directly.

We start our discussion of such algorithms with *Orthogonal Matching Pursuit (OMP)*, see Algorithm 58. The algorithm is an example of a simple greedy algorithm, which extends the set of indices in the following way. It starts by finding the index of the column of A which correlates best with the measurements.

It then repeats this step by correlating the columns with the residual. To formulate the algorithm, it is helpful to introduce the so-called hard-thresholding operator.

Definition 9.30 Let $1 \leq s \leq n$ and $\mathbf{x} \in \mathbb{R}^n$ be given. The *hard-thresholding operator* H_s maps $\mathbf{x}$ to $H_s(\mathbf{x}) \in \mathbb{R}^n$ by setting all entries of $\mathbf{x}$ to zero except for the s largest absolute entries.

In other words, $H_s(\mathbf{x})$ is the best approximation to $\mathbf{x}$ from all s-sparse vectors in $\mathbb{R}^n$. This implies particularly

$$\sigma_s(\mathbf{x}) = \|\mathbf{x} - H_s(\mathbf{x})\|_1.$$

Moreover, the index of the largest absolute entry of $\mathbf{x}$ is simply given by $\mathrm{supp}(H_1(\mathbf{x}))$. With this definition, we can describe the algorithm as follows. In the first step, we look at the correlation of each of the columns $A\mathbf{e}_j$, $1 \leq j \leq n$, and $\mathbf{b}$ which is given by the inner product $\langle A\mathbf{e}_j, \mathbf{b} \rangle_2$. Hence, the column with the largest correlation has index $\mathrm{supp}(H_1(A^\mathrm{T}\mathbf{b}))$. Later on, we look at the largest correlation of the columns of A with the current residual. Again, we can express the corresponding new index j_{k+1} by using $j_{k+1} = \mathrm{supp}(H_1(A^\mathrm{T}\mathbf{r}_k))$ for the kth iteration. It remains to explain how OMP determines the next iteration after having determined the index. This is described in step 6 of Algorithm 58. The main part of the new iteration is computed as $\mathbf{x}_{S_{k+1}} := A^+_{S_{k+1}} \mathbf{b}$ employing the pseudo-inverse of $A_{S_{k+1}}$. To understand this better, let us set $S := S_{k+1}$ and $\mathbf{y}^+ := \mathbf{x}_{S_{k+1}} \in \mathbb{R}^s$. According to Corollary 3.44 this means that $\mathbf{y}^+ \in \mathbb{R}^s$ is the norm-minimal solution of the least-squares problem

$$\min\{\|A_S\mathbf{y} - \mathbf{b}\|_2 : \mathbf{y} \in \mathbb{R}^s\}$$

which we can also solve by first solving

$$\min\{\|\mathbf{w} - \mathbf{b}\|_2 : \mathbf{w} \in \mathrm{range}(A_S)\} \tag{9.19}$$

and then finding the norm-minimal $\mathbf{y}$ with $A_S\mathbf{y} = \mathbf{w}$. Problem (9.19) has a unique solution $\mathbf{w}^* \in \mathrm{range}(A_S)$, which is uniquely determined by the orthogonality conditions

$$0 = \langle \mathbf{b} - \mathbf{w}^*, \mathbf{w} \rangle_2, \qquad \mathbf{w} \in \mathrm{range}(A_S),$$

which we can now recast as

$$0 = \langle \mathbf{b} - A_S\mathbf{y}^+, A_S\mathbf{y} \rangle_2 = \langle A_S^\mathrm{T}(\mathbf{b} - A_S\mathbf{y}^+), \mathbf{y} \rangle_2, \qquad \mathbf{y} \in \mathbb{R}^s. \tag{9.20}$$

Defining now the residual $\mathbf{r} := \mathbf{b} - A_S\mathbf{y}^+$ and setting $\mathbf{y}$ alternatively to the unit vectors of $\mathbb{R}^s$, we see that the residual is orthogonal to the columns of A_S, i.e.

we have $\mathbf{a}_j^T\mathbf{r} = 0$ for all $j \in S$. This explains the *orthogonal* in the name of the algorithm and will us also allow to derive the subsequent convergence result.

Algorithm 58: Orthogonal matching pursuit (OMP)

Input : $A \in \mathbb{R}^{m \times n}$, $\mathbf{b} \in \mathbb{R}^m$.

Output: Sparse representation $\mathbf{x} \in \mathbb{R}^n$.

1 $\mathbf{x}_0 := \mathbf{0}, \quad \mathbf{r}_0 := \mathbf{b}, \quad S_0 := \emptyset, \quad k := 0$
2 **while** *stopping criterion is not met* **do**
3 $\quad \mathbf{g}_k := A^T\mathbf{r}_k$
4 $\quad j_{k+1} := \operatorname{supp}(H_1(\mathbf{g}_k))$
5 $\quad S_{k+1} := S_k \cup \{j_{k+1}\}$
6 $\quad (\mathbf{x}_{k+1})_{S_{k+1}} := A_{S_{k+1}}^+\mathbf{b}, \quad (\mathbf{x}_{k+1})_{S_{k+1}^c} := \mathbf{0}$
7 $\quad \mathbf{r}_{k+1} := \mathbf{b} - A\mathbf{x}_{k+1}$
8 $\quad k := k + 1$

According to Lemma 9.17, the restricted isometry property of order $2s$ is sufficient for reconstructing s-sparse vectors. Moreover, by Corollary 9.23 this is satisfied if the coherence of the matrix A satisfies $\mu < 1/(2s - 1)$. The next theorem shows that in the latter case OMP also recovers the signal after at most s steps.

Theorem 9.31 *Let $A \in \mathbb{R}^{m \times n}$, $m > n$, have normalised columns. If the coherence μ of A satisfies*

$$\mu < \frac{1}{2s - 1}$$

then every s-sparse vector $\mathbf{x}$ is exactly recovered by OMP from its data $\mathbf{b} := A\mathbf{x}$ after at most s steps.

Proof Let $S \subseteq \{1, \ldots, n\}$ be an arbitrary set with $|S| \leq s$. Then, the matrix $A_S^T A_S$ is positive definite. This follows from the general considerations about the coherence and Gershgorin's theorem. To be more precise, $A_S^T A_S$ is obviously positive semi-definite and hence each eigenvalue λ of $A_S^T A_S$ is non-negative. Moreover, such an eigenvalue must also satisfy

$$|\lambda - 1| \leq \max_{k \in S} \sum_{\substack{j \in S \\ j \neq k}} |\langle \mathbf{a}_j, \mathbf{a}_k \rangle_2| \leq (s - 1)\mu < \frac{s - 1}{2s - 1} < 1,$$

i.e. $\lambda > 0$. Consequently, the matrix A_S is injective.

Next, we want to establish the relation

$$\max_{j \in S} |\langle \mathbf{a}_j, \mathbf{r} \rangle_2| > \max_{\ell \in S^c} |\langle \mathbf{a}_\ell, \mathbf{r} \rangle_2|, \qquad \mathbf{r} \in \text{range}(A_S) \setminus \{\mathbf{0}\}. \tag{9.21}$$

To see this, let us write $\mathbf{r} \in \text{range}(A_S)$ as $\mathbf{r} = \sum_{j \in S} r_j \mathbf{a}_j$. Moreover, let $k \in S$ be an index with $|r_k| = \max_{i \in S} |r_i| > 0$. Then, on the one hand we have for each $\ell \in S^c$

$$|\langle \mathbf{r}, \mathbf{a}_\ell \rangle_2| \le \sum_{i \in S} |r_i| |\langle \mathbf{a}_i, \mathbf{a}_\ell \rangle_2| \le |r_k| s \mu.$$

On the other hand, we have

$$|\langle \mathbf{r}, \mathbf{a}_k \rangle_2| = \left| \sum_{i \in S} r_i \langle \mathbf{a}_i, \mathbf{a}_k \rangle_2 \right| \ge |r_k| - \sum_{\substack{i \in S \\ i \ne k}} |r_i| |\langle \mathbf{a}_i, \mathbf{a}_k \rangle_2| \ge |r_k|(1 - (s-1)\mu).$$

Both together yield

$$\max_{j \in S} |\langle \mathbf{r}, \mathbf{a}_j \rangle_2| \ge |\langle \mathbf{r}, \mathbf{a}_k \rangle_2| \ge |r_k|(1 - (s-1)\mu) \ge \frac{1 - (s-1)\mu}{s\mu} |\langle \mathbf{r}, \mathbf{a}_\ell \rangle_2| > |\langle \mathbf{r}, \mathbf{a}_\ell \rangle_2|$$

for all $\ell \in S^c$.

After these preparatory steps, we will now show by induction that OMP needs at most s steps to recover the s-sparse signal $\mathbf{x}$. We will do this by showing that $S_k \subseteq S := \text{supp}(\mathbf{x})$ with $|S_k| = k$ for $0 \le k \le s$. From this it follows in particular that $S_s = S$ and, since $A_S \in \mathbb{R}^{m \times s}$ has full rank s, the least-squares problem $\min \|A_S \mathbf{w} - \mathbf{b}\|_2$ has, according to Theorem 3.40, a unique solution, which means that $\mathbf{x}_s = \mathbf{x}$.

We obviously have $S_0 = \emptyset \subseteq S$ and $|S_0| = 0$. Assuming that the statement is correct for $0 \le k \le s - 1$, we might also assume that $A\mathbf{x}_1 \ne \mathbf{b}, \ldots, A\mathbf{x}_k \ne \mathbf{b}$ because otherwise we would have stopped with the solution prematurely. Since $S_k \subseteq S$, we see that $\mathbf{r}_k = \mathbf{b} - A\mathbf{x}_k = A(\mathbf{x} - \mathbf{x}_k) = A_S(\mathbf{x} - \mathbf{x}_k)_S$ belongs to $\text{range}(A_S) \setminus \{\mathbf{0}\}$. Hence, (9.21) yields

$$\max_{j \in S} |\langle \mathbf{a}_j, \mathbf{r}_k \rangle_2| > \max_{\ell \in S^c} |\langle \mathbf{a}_\ell, \mathbf{r} \rangle_2|, \tag{9.22}$$

which means that the new index

$$j_{k+1} := \text{supp}(H_1(A^{\mathrm{T}} \mathbf{r}_k)) = \arg\max \left\{ |\langle \mathbf{a}_j, \mathbf{r}_k \rangle_2| : j \in \{1, \ldots, n\} \right\}$$

must belong to S. Thus, we have $S_{k+1} \subseteq S$. We are done with our induction step once we have shown that $j_{k+1} \notin S_k$. However, we have for each index $j \in S_k$ that $\langle \mathbf{a}_j, \mathbf{r}_k \rangle_2 = 0$ by the consideration proceeding this theorem. Thus, $j_{k+1} \in S_k$ would contradict (9.22). $\qquad \square$

Remark 9.32   A close inspection of the proof shows that we actually have shown that we can recover any s-sparse vector $\mathbf{x} \in \mathbb{R}^n$ from its observation $\mathbf{b} = A\mathbf{x} \in \mathbb{R}^m$ if the matrix A satisfies (9.21) for each $S \subseteq \{1, \ldots, n\}$ with $|S| \leq s$ and if for each such S the restricted matrix A_S is injective. It can also be shown that these two conditions are not only sufficient for the reconstruction of any s-sparse signal but also necessary.

If the sparsity of the signal is known or can be estimated, Theorem 9.31 gives a possible stopping criterion for OMP. One could simply stop after s steps. Alternatively, one could stop if the norm of the residual $\mathbf{r}_{k+1}$ falls below a certain threshold.

Orthogonal matching pursuit is a typical greedy algorithm. However, it lacks one concept of greedy algorithms. A previously selected index will always remain within the set of active indices. Typically, greedy algorithms also evaluate previously selected indices and discard them if necessary.

Algorithm 59: Compressive sampling matching pursuit (CoSaMP)

Input : $A \in \mathbb{R}^{m \times n}$, $\mathbf{b} \in \mathbb{R}^m$, sparsity level s.
Output: Sparse approximation $\mathbf{x} \in \mathbb{R}^n$.

1 $\mathbf{x}_0 := \mathbf{0}, \quad k = 0$
2 **while** *stopping criterion is not met* **do**
3 $\quad$ $S_{k+1} := \operatorname{supp}(\mathbf{x}_k) \cup \operatorname{supp}(H_{2s}(A^{\mathrm{T}}(\mathbf{b} - A\mathbf{x}_k)))$
4 $\quad$ $\mathbf{y}_{k+1} := A_{S_{k+1}}^+ \mathbf{b}$
5 $\quad$ $\mathbf{x}_{k+1} := H_s(\mathbf{y}_{k+1})$
6 $\quad$ $k := k + 1$

It is possible to speedup the process by considering more than one index per iteration. This gives the so-called *Compressive Sampling Matching Pursuit* and is outlined in detail in Algorithm 59. The idea here is not only to simply add the index of the largest correlation between the columns of A and the current resdidual to define the current set of indices but to use the indices of the $2s$ largest correlations in addition to the support of the current iteration to define S_{k+1}. Then, as before, the least-squares problem is solved, yielding a vector $\mathbf{y}_{k+1}$ which now might have more than s non-zero entries. This is remedied by defining the next iteration as $\mathbf{x}_{k+1} = H_s(\mathbf{y}_{k+1})$ using the hard-thresholding operator again. Obviously, this comes at the price of solving larger-sized least-squares problems than in OMP.

Other greedy algorithms for solving the ℓ_0-minimisation problem are so-called *thresholding algorithms*. We will now discuss one such algorithm, which is essentially based on the idea of steepest descent, see Algorithm 20. The result is the hard-thresholding algorithm described in Algorithm 60, using once again the hard-thresholding operator H_s.

Since we will need to argue with the components of the iteratives created in this method, we will, as we have done before in such a situation, use upper indices to denote the vector iterations.

Algorithm 60: Hard-thresholding pursuit

Input : $A \in \mathbb{R}^{m \times n}$, $\mathbf{b} \in \mathbb{R}^m$, sparsity level s.
Output: Sparse approximation $\mathbf{x} \in \mathbb{R}^n$.

1 $\mathbf{x}^{(0)} := \mathbf{0}, \quad S_0 = \emptyset, \quad k = 0$
2 **while** *stopping criterion is not met* **do**
3 $\quad \mathbf{z}^{(k+1)} := \mathbf{x}^{(k)} + A^{\mathrm{T}}(\mathbf{b} - A\mathbf{x}^{(k)})$
4 $\quad S_{k+1} := \mathrm{supp}\, H_s(\mathbf{z}^{(k+1)})$
5 $\quad \mathbf{x}_{S_{k+1}}^{(k+1)} := A_{S_{k+1}}^+ \mathbf{b}, \quad \mathbf{x}_{S_{k+1}^c}^{(k+1)} := \mathbf{0}$
6 $\quad k := k + 1$

As in the case of OMP, we will analyse this algorithm using the coherence of the matrix A. The proof of the following theorem does not require that the initial guess $\mathbf{x}^{(0)}$ is $\mathbf{x}^{(0)} = \mathbf{0}$ but works for an arbitrary starting value.

Theorem 9.33 *Suppose $A \in \mathbb{R}^{m \times n}$ has normalised columns. If the coherence μ of A satisfies $\mu < 1/(3s - 1)$ with $s \in \mathbb{N}$ then each s-sparse vector $\mathbf{x} \in \mathbb{R}^n$ can be recovered from its observation $\mathbf{b} := A\mathbf{x}$ using at most s iterations of hard-thresholding pursuit.*

Proof Let $S = \mathrm{supp}(\mathbf{x}) = \{j_1, \ldots, j_s\}$ be ordered such that $|x_{j_1}| \geq |x_{j_2}| \geq \cdots \geq |x_{j_s}|$. We want to show that the components of $\mathbf{z}^{(k+1)}$ defined in the algorithm satisfy

$$\min_{1 \leq i \leq k+1} |z_{j_i}^{(k+1)}| > \max_{\ell \in S^c} |z_\ell^{(k+1)}| \tag{9.23}$$

for $0 \leq k \leq s - 1$. By its definition, the set S_{k+1}, contains those $k + 1$ indices corresponding to the $k + 1$ largest absolute components of $\mathbf{z}^{(k+1)}$ and hence (9.23) shows that $\{j_1, \ldots, j_{k+1}\} \subseteq S_{k+1}$ for all such k. In particular, we have $S = \{j_1, \ldots, j_s\} = S_s$ since each set S_k has cardinality s. But then the solution $\mathbf{x}_{S_s}^{(s)} = A_{S_s}^+ \mathbf{b} = A_S^+ \mathbf{b}$ is unique and hence $\mathbf{x}^{(s)} = \mathbf{x}$.

To see (9.23) we first note that the definition of $\mathbf{z}^{(k+1)} = \mathbf{x}^{(k)} + A^{\mathrm{T}} A(\mathbf{x} - \mathbf{x}^{(k)})$ can be written component-wise as

$$z_j^{(k+1)} = x_j^{(k)} + \sum_{i=1}^{n}(x_i - x_i^{(k)})\langle \mathbf{a}_i, \mathbf{a}_j \rangle_2 = x_j + \sum_{i \neq j}(x_i - x_i^{(k)})\langle \mathbf{a}_i, \mathbf{a}_j \rangle_2,$$

which gives the bound

$$|z_j^{(k+1)} - x_j| \leq \sum_{\substack{i \in S_k \\ i \neq j}} |x_i - x_i^{(k)}||\langle \mathbf{a}_i, \mathbf{a}_j \rangle_2| + \sum_{\substack{i \in S \setminus S_k \\ i \neq j}} |x_i||\langle \mathbf{a}_i, \mathbf{a}_j \rangle_2|. \tag{9.24}$$

Since each sum contains at most s terms, we can bound this using the coherence μ by

$$|z_j^{(k+1)} - x_j| \leq s\mu \left[\|(\mathbf{x} - \mathbf{x}^{(k)})_{S_k}\|_\infty + \|\mathbf{x}_{S \setminus S_k}\|_\infty \right].$$

From this we can conclude that for $1 \leq i \leq k + 1$ we have in particular

$$|z_{j_i}^{(k+1)}| \geq |x_{j_i}| - s\mu \left[\|(\mathbf{x} - \mathbf{x}^{(k)})_{S_k}\|_\infty + \|\mathbf{x}_{S \setminus S_k}\|_\infty \right]. \tag{9.25}$$

Moreover, for $\ell \in S^c$ we have $x_\ell = 0$ and hence

$$|z_\ell^{(k+1)}| \leq s\mu \left[\|(\mathbf{x} - \mathbf{x}^{(k)})_{S_k}\|_\infty + \|\mathbf{x}_{S \setminus S_k}\|_\infty \right]. \tag{9.26}$$

With this, it is easy to see that (9.23) is satisfied for $k = 1$. Indeed, in this situation we have $S_0 = \emptyset$ and hence $\|(\mathbf{x} - \mathbf{x}^{(0)})_{S_0}\|_\infty = 0$. Thus, from (9.25) and (9.26) we can conclude that

$$|z_{j_1}^{(1)}| \geq |x_{j_1}| - s\mu\|\mathbf{x}_S\|_\infty = (1 - s\mu)\|\mathbf{x}\|_\infty > s\mu\|\mathbf{x}\|_\infty \geq |z_\ell^{(1)}|$$

for all $\ell \in S^c$, where we have used that $\mu < 1/(3s - 1) \leq 1/(2s)$ implies $1 - s\mu > s\mu$.

Next, let us assume that $s \geq 2$ and that (9.23) is true for $k - 1$, i.e. we have in particular $\{j_1, \ldots, j_k\} \subseteq S_k$. The definition of the iteration $\mathbf{x}^{(k)}$ together with (9.20) yields

$$\langle A_{S_k}^{\mathrm{T}} A_{S_k}(\mathbf{x} - \mathbf{x}^{(k)})_{S_k}, \mathbf{y} \rangle_2 = 0, \qquad \mathbf{y} \in \mathbb{R}^s,$$

and hence $A_{S_k}^{\mathrm{T}} A_{S_k}(\mathbf{x} - \mathbf{x}^{(k)})_{S_k} = \mathbf{0}$, i.e.

$$(A^{\mathrm{T}} A(\mathbf{x} - \mathbf{x}^{(k)}))_{S_k} = \mathbf{0}.$$

For $j \in S_k$ this means $z_j^{(k+1)} = x_j^{(k)}$ and (9.24) yields for such a $j \in S_k$ the better bound

$$|x_j^{(k)} - x_j| \leq (s - 1)\mu \left[\|(\mathbf{x} - \mathbf{x}^{(k)})_{S_k}\|_\infty + \|\mathbf{x}_{S \setminus S_k}\|_\infty \right].$$

Taking the maximum over all $j \in S_k$ and rearranging the terms then gives

$$\|(\mathbf{x} - \mathbf{x}^{(k)})_{S_k}\|_\infty \leq \frac{(s - 1)\mu}{1 - (s - 1)\mu}\|\mathbf{x}_{S \setminus S_k}\|_\infty. \tag{9.27}$$

Inserting this into (9.26) and using $\|\mathbf{x}_{S \setminus S_k}\|_\infty = |x_{j_{k+1}}|$ shows

$$
\begin{aligned}
|z_\ell^{(k+1)}| &\leq s\mu \left[\|(\mathbf{x} - \mathbf{x}^{(k)})_{S_k}\|_\infty + \|\mathbf{x}_{S \setminus S_k}\|_\infty \right] \\
&\leq s\mu \left[\frac{(s-1)\mu}{1-(s-1)\mu} + 1 \right] |x_{j_{k+1}}| \\
&= \frac{s\mu}{1-(s-1)\mu} |x_{j_{k+1}}|
\end{aligned}
$$

for all $\ell \in S^c$. Similarly, inserting (9.27) into (9.25) and using the last estimate finally gives

$$
\begin{aligned}
|z_{j_i}^{(k+1)}| &\geq |x_{j_i}| - s\mu \left[\|(\mathbf{x} - \mathbf{x}^{(k)})_{S_k}\|_\infty + \|\mathbf{x}_{S \setminus S_k}\|_\infty \right] \\
&\geq |x_{j_{k+1}}| - \frac{s\mu}{1-(s-1)\mu} |x_{j_{k+1}}| \\
&\geq \left[1 - \frac{s\mu}{1-(s-1)\mu} \right] \frac{1-(s-1)\mu}{s\mu} |z_\ell^{k+1}| \\
&= \left[\frac{1-(s-1)\mu}{s\mu} - 1 \right] |z_\ell^{(k+1)}| > |z_\ell^{(k+1)}|,
\end{aligned}
$$

for all $1 \leq i \leq k+1$ and $\ell \in S^c$, using $\mu < 1/(3s-1)$ in the last step. Hence, we have shown that (9.23) holds also for $k+1$, which finishes the proof. □

Exercises

9.1 A system of vectors $\mathbf{a}_1, \ldots, \mathbf{a}_n \in \mathbb{R}^m$ is called a *tight frame* if there is a constant $A > 0$ such that

$$
\|\mathbf{x}\|_2^2 = A \sum_{j=1}^n |\langle \mathbf{x}, \mathbf{a}_j \rangle_2|^2, \qquad \mathbf{x} \in \mathbb{R}^m. \tag{9.28}
$$

Show that this is equivalent to

$$
\mathbf{x} = A \sum_{j=1}^n \langle \mathbf{x}, \mathbf{a}_j \rangle_2 \mathbf{a}_j, \qquad \mathbf{x} \in \mathbb{R}^m,
$$

and also to $AA^{\mathrm{T}} = \frac{1}{A}I$ if $A = (\mathbf{a}_1, \ldots, \mathbf{a}_n) \in \mathbb{R}^{m \times n}$.

9.2 Show that the $m + 1$ vertices of a regular simplex in $\mathbb{R}^m$ centred at the origin form an equiangular tight frame.

9.3 Let $A \in \mathbb{R}^{m \times n}$ have normalised columns $\mathbf{a}_1, \ldots, \mathbf{a}_n$. The ℓ_1-coherence function μ_1 is defined for $1 \leq s \leq n-1$ as

$$
\mu_1(s) := \max_{1 \leq i \leq n} \max \left\{ \sum_{j \in S} |\langle \mathbf{a}_i, \mathbf{a}_j \rangle_2| : S \subseteq \{1, \ldots, n\}, |S| = s, i \notin S \right\}.
$$

- Show $\mu \leq \mu_1(s) \leq s\mu$ for $1 \leq s \leq n-1$, where μ is the coherence of A.
- Show $\max\{\mu_1(s), \mu_1(t)\} \leq \mu_1(s+t) \leq \mu_1(s)+\mu_1(t)$ for all $1 \leq s, t \leq n-1$ with $s + t \leq n - 1$.
- Show that if $\mu_1(s) + \mu_1(1 - s) < 1$ then every s-sparse vector $\mathbf{x} \in \mathbb{R}^n$ is exactly recovered from its observations $\mathbf{b} := A\mathbf{x}$ after at most s iterations of OMP.
- Show that $\mu_1(s)$ can alternatively be expressed as

$$\mu_1(s) = \max_{|S| \leq s+1} \|A_S^T A_S - I\|_1 = \max_{|S| \leq s+1} \|A_S^T A_S - I\|_\infty.$$

9.4 Suppose $A \in \mathbb{R}^{m \times n}$ satisfies the restricted isometry property of order s with constant $\delta_s < 1$. Show for any $S \subseteq \{1, \ldots, n\}$ with $|S| \leq s$ the estimates

$$\frac{1}{1 + \delta_s} \leq \|(A_S^T A_S)^{-1}\|_2 \leq \frac{1}{1 - \delta_s} \quad \text{and} \quad \frac{1}{\sqrt{1 + \delta_s}} \leq \|A_S^+\|_2 \leq \frac{1}{\sqrt{1 - \delta_s}}.$$

9.5 Consider the matrix

$$A = \begin{pmatrix} 1 & 0 & c & 1 & 0 & -c \\ c & 1 & 0 & -c & 1 & 0 \\ 0 & c & 1 & 0 & -c & 1 \end{pmatrix}.$$

Determine $c \in \mathbb{R}$ such that the columns of A form an equiangular system of six vectors in $\mathbb{R}^3$.

9.6 Let A be given as

$$A = \begin{pmatrix} 1 & -1/2 & -1/2 \\ 0 & \sqrt{3}/2 & -\sqrt{3}/2 \\ 1 & 3 & 3 \end{pmatrix}.$$

Show that the 1-sparse vector $\mathbf{x} = \mathbf{e}_1$ cannot be recovered via OMP. What changes if instead of A the matrix B is considered, if B is A without its last row?

Bibliography

[1] Allaire, G., and Kaber, S. M. 2008. *Numerical linear algebra*. New York: Springer. Translated from the 2002 French original by Karim Trabelsi.

[2] Arnoldi, W. E. 1951. The principle of minimized iteration in the solution of the matrix eigenvalue problem. *Quart. Appl. Math.*, **9**, 17–29.

[3] Arya, S., and Mount, D. M. 1993. Approximate nearest neighbor searching. Pages 271–280 of: *Proceedings of the 4th Annual ACM-SIAM Symposium on Discrete Algorithms*. New York: ACM Press.

[4] Arya, S., and Mount, D. M. 1995. Approximate range searching. Pages 172–181 of: *Proceedings of the 11th Annual ACM Symposium on Computational Geometry*. New York: ACM Press.

[5] Axelsson, O. 1985. A survey of preconditioned iterative methods for linear systems of algebraic equations. *BIT*, **25**(1), 166–187.

[6] Axelsson, O. 1994. *Iterative solution methods*. Cambridge: Cambridge University Press.

[7] Axelsson, O., and Barker, V. A. 1984. *Finite element solution of boundary value problems*. Orlando, FL: Academic Press.

[8] Axelsson, O., and Lindskog, G. 1986. On the rate of convergence of the preconditioned conjugate gradient method. *Numer. Math.*, **48**(5), 499–523.

[9] Bandeira, A. S., Fickus, M., Mixon, D. G., and Wong, P. 2013. The road to deterministic matrices with the restricted isometry property. *J. Fourier Anal. Appl.*, **19**(6), 1123–1149.

[10] Baraniuk, R., Davenport, M., DeVore, R., and Wakin, M. 2008. A simple proof of the restricted isometry property for random matrices. *Constr. Approx.*, **28**(3), 253–263.

[11] Beatson, R. K., and Greengard, L. 1997. A short course on fast multipole methods. Pages 1–37 of: Ainsworth, M., Levesley, J., Light, W., and Marletta, M. (eds.), *Wavelets, multilevel methods and elliptic PDEs. 7th EPSRC numerical analysis summer school, University of Leicester, Leicester, GB, July 8–19, 1996.* Oxford: Clarendon Press.

[12] Bebendorf, M. 2000. Approximation of boundary element matrices. *Numer. Math.*, **86**(4), 565–589.

[13] Bebendorf, M. 2008. *Hierarchical matrices – A means to efficiently solve elliptic boundary value problems*. Berlin: Springer.

[14] Bebendorf, M. 2011. Adaptive cross approximation of multivariate functions. *Constr. Approx.*, **34**(2), 149–179.

[15] Bebendorf, M., Maday, Y., and Stamm, B. 2014. Comparison of some reduced representation approximations. Pages 67–100 of: *Reduced order methods for modeling and computational reduction.* Cham: Springer.

[16] Benzi, M. 2002. Preconditioning techniques for large linear systems: a survey. *J. Comput. Phys.*, **182**(2), 418–477.

[17] Benzi, M., and Tůma, M. 1999. A comparative study of sparse approximate inverse preconditioners. *Appl. Numer. Math.*, **30**(2–3), 305–340.

[18] Benzi, M., Cullum, J. K., and Tůma, M. 2000. Robust approximate inverse preconditioning for the conjugate gradient method. *SIAM J. Sci. Comput.*, **22**(4), 1318–1332.

[19] Benzi, M., Meyer, C. D., and Tůma, M. 1996. A sparse approximate inverse preconditioner for the conjugate gradient method. *SIAM J. Sci. Comput.*, **17**(5), 1135–1149.

[20] Björck, Å. 1996. *Numerical methods for least squares problems.* Philadelphia, PA: Society for Industrial and Applied Mathematics (SIAM).

[21] Björck, Å. 2015. *Numerical methods in matrix computations.* Cham: Springer.

[22] Boyd, S., and Vandenberghe, L. 2004. *Convex optimization.* Cambridge: Cambridge University Press.

[23] Brandt, A. 1977. Multi-level adaptive solutions to boundary-value problems. *Math. Comp.*, **31**(138), 333–390.

[24] Brandt, A., McCormick, S., and Ruge, J. 1985. Algebraic multigrid (AMG) for sparse matrix equations. Pages 257–284 of: *Sparsity and its applications (Loughborough, 1983).* Cambridge: Cambridge University Press.

[25] Brenner, S., and Scott, L. 1994. *The Mathematical Theory of Finite Element Methods.* 3rd edn. New York: Springer.

[26] Briggs, W., and McCormick, S. 1987. Introduction. Pages 1–30 of: *Multigrid methods.* Philadelphia, PA: Society for Industrial and Applied Mathematics (SIAM).

[27] Briggs, W. L., Henson, V. E., and McCormick, S. F. 2000. *A multigrid tutorial.* 2nd edn. Philadelphia, PA: Society for Industrial and Applied Mathematics (SIAM).

[28] Bruaset, A. M. 1995. *A survey of preconditioned iterative methods.* Harlow: Longman Scientific & Technical.

[29] Candès, E. J. 2006. Compressive sampling. Pages 1433–1452 of: *International Congress of Mathematicians. Vol. III.* Zürich: European Mathematical Society.

[30] Candès, E. J. 2008. The restricted isometry property and its implications for compressed sensing. *C. R. Math. Acad. Sci. Paris*, **346**(9–10), 589–592.

[31] Candès, E. J., and Tao, T. 2005. Decoding by linear programming. *IEEE Trans. Inform. Theory*, **51**(12), 4203–4215.

[32] Candès, E. J., and Wakin, M. B. 2008. An introduction to compressive sampling. *IEEE Signal Processing Magazine*, **25**(2), 21–30.

[33] Candès, E. J., Romberg, J. K., and Tao, T. 2006. Stable signal recovery from incomplete and inaccurate measurements. *Comm. Pure Appl. Math.*, **59**(8), 1207–1223.

[34] Chan, T. F., Gallopoulos, E., Simoncini, V., Szeto, T., and Tong, C. H. 1994. A quasi-minimal residual variant of the Bi-CGSTAB algorithm for nonsymmetric systems. *SIAM J. Sci. Comput.*, **15**(2), 338–347.

[35] Cherrie, J. B., Beatson, R. K., and Newsam, G. N. 2002. Fast evaluation of radial basis functions: Methods for generalised multiquadrics in $\mathbb{R}^n$. *SIAM J. Sci. Comput.*, **23**, 1272–1310.

[36] Chow, E., and Saad, Y. 1998. Approximate inverse preconditioners via sparse–sparse iterations. *SIAM J. Sci. Comput.*, **19**(3), 995–1023.

[37] Coppersmith, D., and Winograd, S. 1990. Matrix multiplication via arithmetic progressions. *J. Symbolic Comput.*, **9**(3), 251–280.

[38] Cosgrove, J. D. F., Díaz, J. C., and Griewank, A. 1992. Approximate inverse preconditionings for sparse linear systems. *International Journal of Computer Mathematics*, **44**(1–4), 91–110.

[39] Cosgrove, J. D. F., Díaz, J. C., and Macedo, Jr., C. G. 1991. Approximate inverse preconditioning for nonsymmetric sparse systems. Pages 101–111 of: *Advances in numerical partial differential equations and optimization (Mérida, 1989)*. Philadelphia, PA: Society for Industrial and Applied Mathematics (SIAM).

[40] Cullum, J. 1996. Iterative methods for solving $Ax = b$, GMRES/FOM versus QMR/BiCG. *Adv. Comput. Math.*, **6**(1), 1–24.

[41] Datta, B. N. 2010. *Numerical linear algebra and applications*. 2nd edn. Philadelphia, PA: Society for Industrial and Applied Mathematics (SIAM).

[42] Davenport, M. A., Duarte, M. F., Eldar, Y. C., and Kutyniok, G. 2012. Introduction to compressed sensing. Pages 1–64 of: *Compressed sensing*. Cambridge: Cambridge University Press.

[43] de Berg, M., van Kreveld, M., Overmars, M., and Schwarzkopf, O. 1997. *Computational Geometry*. Berlin: Springer.

[44] Demmel, J. W. 1997. *Applied numerical linear algebra*. Philadelphia, PA: Society for Industrial and Applied Mathematics (SIAM).

[45] DeVore, R. A. 2007. Deterministic constructions of compressed sensing matrices. *J. Complexity*, **23**(4–6), 918–925.

[46] Donoho, D. L. 2006. Compressed sensing. *IEEE Trans. Inform. Theory*, **52**(4), 1289–1306.

[47] Elman, H. C., Silvester, D. J., and Wathen, A. J. 2014. *Finite elements and fast iterative solvers: with applications in incompressible fluid dynamics*. 2nd edn. Oxford: Oxford University Press.

[48] Escalante, R., and Raydan, M. 2011. *Alternating projection methods*. Philadelphia, PA: Society for Industrial and Applied Mathematics (SIAM).

[49] Faber, V., and Manteuffel, T. 1984. Necessary and sufficient conditions for the existence of a conjugate gradient method. *SIAM J. Numer. Anal.*, **21**(2), 352–362.

[50] Fischer, B. 2011. *Polynomial based iteration methods for symmetric linear systems*. Philadelphia, PA: Society for Industrial and Applied Mathematics (SIAM). Reprint of the 1996 original.

[51] Fletcher, R. 1976. Conjugate gradient methods for indefinite systems. Pages 73–89 of: *Numerical analysis (Proceedings of the 6th Biennial Dundee Conference, University of Dundee, Dundee, 1975)*. Berlin: Springer.

[52] Ford, W. 2015. *Numerical linear algebra with applications*. Amsterdam: Elsevier/Academic Press.

[53] Fornasier, M., and Rauhut, H. 2011. Compressive sensing. Pages 187–228 of: Scherzer, O. (ed.), *Handbook of Mathematical Methods in Imaging*. New York: Springer.

[54] Foucart, S., and Rauhut, H. 2013. *A mathematical introduction to compressive sensing*. New York: Birkhäuser/Springer.

[55] Fox, L. 1964. *An introduction to numerical linear algebra*. Oxford: Clarendon Press.

[56] Francis, J. G. F. 1961/1962a. The QR transformation: a unitary analogue to the LR transformation. I. *Comput. J.*, **4**, 265–271.

[57] Francis, J. G. F. 1961/1962b. The QR transformation. II. *Comput. J.*, **4**, 332–345.

[58] Freund, R. W. 1992. Conjugate gradient-type methods for linear systems with complex symmetric coefficient matrices. *SIAM J. Sci. Statist. Comput.*, **13**(1), 425–448.

[59] Freund, R. W. 1993. A transpose-free quasi-minimal residual algorithm for non-Hermitian linear systems. *SIAM J. Sci. Comput.*, **14**(2), 470–482.

[60] Freund, R. W., and Nachtigal, N. M. 1991. QMR: a quasi-minimal residual method for non-Hermitian linear systems. *Numer. Math.*, **60**(3), 315–339.

[61] Freund, R. W., Gutknecht, M. H., and Nachtigal, N. M. 1993. An implementation of the look-ahead Lanczos algorithm for non-Hermitian matrices. *SIAM J. Sci. Comput.*, **14**(1), 137–158.

[62] Gasch, J., and Maligranda, L. 1994. On vector-valued inequalities of the Marcinkiewicz–Zygmund, Herz and Krivine type. *Math. Nachr.*, **167**, 95–129.

[63] Goldberg, M., and Tadmor, E. 1982. On the numerical radius and its applications. *Linear Algebra Appl.*, **42**, 263–284.

[64] Golub, G., and Kahan, W. 1965. Calculating the singular values and pseudo-inverse of a matrix. *J. Soc. Indust. Appl. Math. Ser. B Numer. Anal.*, **2**, 205–224.

[65] Golub, G. H., and Reinsch, C. 1970. Singular value decomposition and least squares solutions. *Numer. Math.*, **14**(5), 403–420.

[66] Golub, G. H., and Van Loan, C. F. 2013. *Matrix computations*. 4th edn. Baltimore, MD: Johns Hopkins University Press.

[67] Golub, G. H., Heath, M., and Wahba, G. 1979. Generalized cross-validation as a method for choosing a good ridge parameter. *Technometrics*, **21**(2), 215–223.

[68] Gould, N. I. M., and Scott, J. A. 1998. Sparse approximate-inverse preconditioners using norm-minimization techniques. *SIAM J. Sci. Comput.*, **19**(2), 605–625.

[69] Greenbaum, A. 1997. *Iterative methods for solving linear systems*. Philadelphia, PA: Society for Industrial and Applied Mathematics (SIAM).

[70] Griebel, M. 1994. *Multilevelmethoden als Iterationsverfahren über Erzeugendensystemen*. Stuttgart: B. G. Teubner.

[71] Griebel, M., and Oswald, P. 1995. On the abstract theory of additive and multiplicative Schwarz algorithms. *Numer. Math.*, **70**(2), 163–180.

[72] Grote, M. J., and Huckle, T. 1997. Parallel preconditioning with sparse approximate inverses. *SIAM J. Sci. Comput.*, **18**(3), 838–853.

[73] Gutknecht, M. H. 2007. A brief introduction to Krylov space methods for solving linear systems. Pages 53–62 of: Kaneda, Y., Kawamura, H., and Sasai, M. (eds.), *Frontiers of Computational Science*. Berlin: Springer.

[74] Hackbusch, W. 1985. *Multi-grid methods and applications*. Berlin: Springer.

[75] Hackbusch, W. 1994. *Iterative solution of large sparse systems of equations.* New York: Springer. Translated and revised from the 1991 German original.

[76] Hackbusch, W. 1999. A sparse matrix arithmetic based on $\mathcal{H}$-matrices. I. Introduction to $\mathcal{H}$-matrices. *Computing*, **62**(2), 89–108.

[77] Hackbusch, W. 2015. *Hierarchical matrices: algorithms and analysis.* Heidelberg: Springer.

[78] Hackbusch, W., and Börm, S. 2002. Data-sparse approximation by adaptive $\mathcal{H}^2$-matrices. *Computing*, **69**(1), 1–35.

[79] Hackbusch, W., Grasedyck, L., and Börm, S. 2002. An introduction to hierarchical matrices. *Mathematica Bohemica*, **127**(2), 229–241.

[80] Hackbusch, W., Khoromskij, B., and Sauter, S. A. 2000. On $\mathcal{H}^2$-matrices. Pages 9–29 of: *Lectures on applied mathematics (Munich, 1999).* Berlin: Springer.

[81] Hansen, P. C. 1992. Analysis of discrete ill-posed problems by means of the L-curve. *SIAM Rev.*, **34**(4), 561–580.

[82] Henrici, P. 1958. On the speed of convergence of cyclic and quasicyclic Jacobi methods for computing eigenvalues of Hermitian matrices. *J. Soc. Indust. Appl. Math.*, **6**, 144–162.

[83] Hestenes, M. R., and Stiefel, E. 1952. Methods of conjugate gradients for solving linear systems. *J. Research Nat. Bur. Standards*, **49**, 409–436 (1953).

[84] Higham, N. J. 1990. Exploiting fast matrix multiplication within the level 3 BLAS. *ACM Trans. Math. Software*, **16**(4), 352–368.

[85] Higham, N. J. 2002. *Accuracy and stability of numerical algorithms.* 2nd edn. Philadelphia, PA: Society for Industrial and Applied Mathematics (SIAM).

[86] Householder, A. S. 1958. Unitary triangularization of a nonsymmetric matrix. *J. Assoc. Comput. Mach.*, **5**, 339–342.

[87] Kolotilina, L. Y., and Yeremin, A. Y. 1993. Factorized sparse approximate inverse preconditionings. I. Theory. *SIAM J. Matrix Anal. Appl.*, **14**(1), 45–58.

[88] Krasny, R., and Wang, L. 2011. Fast evaluation of multiquadric RBF sums by a Cartesian treecode. *SIAM J. Sci. Comput.*, **33**(5), 2341–2355.

[89] Lanczos, C. 1950. An iteration method for the solution of the eigenvalue problem of linear differential and integral operators. *J. Research Nat. Bur. Standards*, **45**, 255–282.

[90] Lanczos, C. 1952. Solution of systems of linear equations by minimized-iterations. *J. Research Nat. Bur. Standards*, **49**, 33–53.

[91] Le Gia, Q. T., and Tran, T. 2010. An overlapping additive Schwarz preconditioner for interpolation on the unit sphere with spherical basis functions. *Journal of Complexity*, **26**, 552–573.

[92] Liesen, J., and Strakoš, Z. 2013. *Krylov subspace methods – Principles and analysis.* Oxford: Oxford University Press.

[93] Maligranda, L. 1997. On the norms of operators in the real and the complex case. Pages 67–71 of: *Proceedings of the Second Seminar on Banach Spaces and Related Topics.* Kitakyushu: Kyushu Institute of Technology.

[94] Meijerink, J. A., and van der Vorst, H. A. 1977. An iterative solution method for linear systems of which the coefficient matrix is a symmetric M-matrix. *Math. Comp.*, **31**(137), 148–162.

[95] Meister, A. 1999. *Numerik linearer Gleichungssysteme – Eine Einführung in moderne Verfahren.* Braunschweig: Friedrich Vieweg & Sohn.

[96] Meister, A., and Vömel, C. 2001. Efficient preconditioning of linear systems arising from the discretization of hyperbolic conservation laws. *Adv. Comput. Math.*, **14**(1), 49–73.

[97] Morozov, V. A. 1984. *Methods for solving incorrectly posed problems.* New York: Springer. Translated from the Russian by A. B. Aries, Translation edited by Z. Nashed.

[98] Ostrowski, A. M. 1959. A quantitative formulation of Sylvester's law of inertia. *Proc. Nat. Acad. Sci. U.S.A.*, **45**, 740–744.

[99] Paige, C. C., and Saunders, M. A. 1975. Solutions of sparse indefinite systems of linear equations. *SIAM J. Numer. Anal.*, **12**(4), 617–629.

[100] Parlett, B. N. 1998. *The symmetric eigenvalue problem.* Philadelphia, PA: Society for Industrial and Applied Mathematics (SIAM). Corrected reprint of the 1980 original.

[101] Pearcy, C. 1966. An elementary proof of the power inequality for the numerical radius. *Michigan Math. J.*, **13**, 289–291.

[102] Quarteroni, A., and Valli, A. 1999. *Domain decomposition methods for partial differential equations.* New York: Clarendon Press.

[103] Saad, Y. 1994. Highly parallel preconditioners for general sparse matrices. Pages 165–199 of: *Recent advances in iterative methods.* New York: Springer.

[104] Saad, Y. 2003. *Iterative methods for sparse linear systems.* 2nd edn. Philadelphia, PA: Society for Industrial and Applied Mathematics (SIAM).

[105] Saad, Y., and Schultz, M. H. 1986. GMRES: a generalized minimal residual algorithm for solving nonsymmetric linear systems. *SIAM J. Sci. Statist. Comput.*, **7**(3), 856–869.

[106] Saad, Y., and van der Vorst, H. A. 2000. Iterative solution of linear systems in the 20th century. *J. Comput. Appl. Math.*, **123**(1-2), 1–33.

[107] Schaback, R., and Wendland, H. 2005. *Numerische Mathematik.* 5th edn. Berlin: Springer.

[108] Schatzman, M. 2002. *Numerical Analysis: A Mathematical Introduction.* Oxford: Oxford University Press.

[109] Simoncini, V., and Szyld, D. B. 2002. Flexible inner–outer Krylov subspace methods. *SIAM J. Numer. Anal.*, **40**(6), 2219–2239.

[110] Simoncini, V., and Szyld, D. B. 2005. On the occurrence of superlinear convergence of exact and inexact Krylov subspace methods. *SIAM Rev.*, **47**(2), 247–272.

[111] Simoncini, V., and Szyld, D. B. 2007. Recent computational developments in Krylov subspace methods for linear systems. *Numer. Linear Algebra Appl.*, **14**(1), 1–59.

[112] Sleijpen, G. L. G., and Fokkema, D. R. 1993. BiCGstab(*l*) for linear equations involving unsymmetric matrices with complex spectrum. *Electron. Trans. Numer. Anal.*, **1**(Sept.), 11–32 (electronic only).

[113] Smith, K. T., Solmon, D. C., and Wagner, S. L. 1977. Practical and mathematical aspects of the problem of reconstructing objects from radiographs. *Bull. Amer. Math. Soc.*, **83**, 1227–1270.

[114] Sonneveld, P. 1989. CGS, a fast Lanczos-type solver for nonsymmetric linear systems. *SIAM J. Sci. Statist. Comput.*, **10**(1), 36–52.

[115] Sonneveld, P., and van Gijzen, M. B. 2008/09. IDR(s): a family of simple and fast algorithms for solving large nonsymmetric systems of linear equations. *SIAM J. Sci. Comput.*, **31**(2), 1035–1062.

[116] Steinbach, O. 2005. *Lösungsverfahren für lineare Gleichungssysteme.* Wiesbaden: Teubner.

[117] Stewart, G. W. 1998. *Matrix algorithms. Volume I: Basic decompositions.* Philadelphia, PA: Society for Industrial and Applied Mathematics (SIAM).

[118] Stewart, G. W. 2001. *Matrix algorithms. Volume II: Eigensystems.* Philadelphia, PA: Society for Industrial and Applied Mathematics (SIAM).

[119] Stewart, G. W., and Sun, J. G. 1990. *Matrix perturbation theory.* Boston, MA: Academic Press.

[120] Strassen, V. 1969. Gaussian elimination is not optimal. *Numer. Math.*, **13**, 354–356.

[121] Süli, E., and Mayers, D. F. 2003. *An introduction to numerical analysis.* Cambridge: Cambridge University Press.

[122] Tibshirani, R. 1996. Regression shrinkage and selection via the lasso. *J. Roy. Statist. Soc. Ser. B*, **58**(1), 267–288.

[123] Toselli, A., and Widlund, O. 2005. *Domain decomposition methods – algorithms and theory.* Berlin: Springer.

[124] Trefethen, L. N., and Bau, III, D. 1997. *Numerical linear algebra.* Philadelphia, PA: Society for Industrial and Applied Mathematics (SIAM).

[125] Trottenberg, U., Oosterlee, C. W., and Schüller, A. 2001. *Multigrid.* San Diego, CA: Academic Press. With contributions by A. Brandt, P. Oswald and K. Stüben.

[126] Van de Velde, E. F. 1994. *Concurrent scientific computing.* New York: Springer.

[127] van der Vorst, H. A. 1992. Bi-CGSTAB: a fast and smoothly converging variant of Bi-CG for the solution of nonsymmetric linear systems. *SIAM J. Sci. Statist. Comput.*, **13**(2), 631–644.

[128] van der Vorst, H. A. 2009. *Iterative Krylov methods for large linear systems.* Cambridge: Cambridge University Press. Reprint of the 2003 original.

[129] Varga, R. S. 2000. *Matrix iterative analysis.* Expanded edn. Berlin: Springer.

[130] Wathen, A. 2007. Preconditioning and convergence in the right norm. *Int. J. Comput. Math.*, **84**(8), 1199–1209.

[131] Wathen, A. J. 2015. Preconditioning. *Acta Numer.*, **24**, 329–376.

[132] Watkins, D. S. 2010. *Fundamentals of matrix computations.* 3rd edn. Hoboken, NJ: John Wiley & Sons.

[133] Wendland, H. 2005. *Scattered data approximation.* Cambridge: Cambridge University Press.

[134] Werner, J. 1992a. *Numerische Mathematik. Band 1: Lineare und nichtlineare Gleichungssysteme, Interpolation, numerische Integration.* Braunschweig: Friedrich Vieweg & Sohn.

[135] Werner, J. 1992b. *Numerische Mathematik. Band 2: Eigenwertaufgaben, lineare Optimierungsaufgaben, unrestringierte Optimierungsaufgaben.* Braunschweig: Friedrich Vieweg & Sohn.

[136] Wimmer, H. K. 1983. On Ostrowski's generalization of Sylvester's law of inertia. *Linear Algebra Appl.*, **52/53**, 739–741.

[137] Xu, J. 1992. Iterative methods by space decomposition and subspace correction. *SIAM Rev.*, **34**(4), 581–613.

[138] Yin, W., Osher, S., Goldfarb, D., and Darbon, J. 2008. Bregman iterative algorithms for l_1-minimization with applications to compressed sensing. *SIAM J. Imaging Sci.*, **1**(1), 143–168.

[139] Young, D. M. 1970. Convergence properties of the symmetric and unsymmetric successive overrelaxation methods and related methods. *Math. Comp.*, **24**, 793–807.

[140] Young, D. M. 1971. *Iterative Solution of Large Linear Systems*. New York: Academic Press.

Index

403